Community Psychology

Community Psychology

Guiding Principles and Orienting Concepts

Jennifer Kofkin Rudkin

Upper Saddle River, New Jersey 07458

Library of Congress Cataloging-in-Publication Data

Rudkin, Jennifer Kofkin.
    Community psychology / Jennifer Kofkin Rudkin.
       p. cm.
    Includes bibliographical references and index.
    ISBN 0-13-089903-8
    1. Community psychology. I. Title.

RA790.55 .R83 2003
362.2'0425—dc21   2002030782

Editor-in-Chief: *Leah Jewell*
Acquisitions Editor/Project Manager: *Stephanie Johnson*
Managing Editor: *Joanne Riker*
Production Liaison: *Joanne Hakim*
Project Manager: *Jennifer Murtoff/Lithokraft II*
Prepress and Manufacturing Buyer: *Tricia Kenny*
Cover Art Director: *Jayne Conte*
Cover Designer: *Bruce Kenselaar*
Cover Art: Daryl Elaine Wells, "Untitled", 16' × 25' acrylic mural, SPARC Great Walls Unlimited:
      Neighborhood Pride 1993, www.sparcmurals.org
Permission Specialists: *Murray Kofkin and Marlene Gassler*
Director, Image Resource Center: *Melinda Reo*
Manager, Rights and Permissions: *Zina Arabia*
Interior Image Specialist: *Beth Boyd-Brenzel*
Cover Image Specialist: *Karen Sanatar*
Image Permission Coordinator: *Debbie Latronica*
Artist: *Steve Shiplett*
Marketing Manager: *Sheryl Adams*

This book was set in 10/12 Berkeley Book by Lithokraft II and
was printed and bound by R. R. Donnelley and Sons Company.
The cover was printed by Phoenix Color Corp.

Prentice Hall © 2003 by Pearson Education, Inc.
Upper Saddle River, New Jersey 07458

Printed in the United States of America

10 9 8 7 6

ISBN 0-13-089903-8

Pearson Education Ltd., London
Pearson Education Australia PTY. Limited, Sydney
Pearson Education Singapore, Pte. Ltd
Pearson Education North Asia Ltd, Hong Kong
Pearson Education Canada, Ltd., Toronto
Pearson Educación de Mexico, S.A. de C.V.
Pearson Education—Japan, Tokyo
Pearson Education Malaysia, Pte. Ltd
Pearson Education, Upper Saddle River, New Jersey

Contents

Foreword

In psychology as in other disciplines, textbooks are essential to the development and subsequent well being of the field. Many are written, but only a few have major impact. Such books either help to establish an area of study, e.g., Gordon Allport's (1937) *Personality: A Psychological Interpretation* provided the framework for the field of personality research, and Robert White's (1948) *The Abnormal Personality* established the field of abnormal psychology. Others breathe new life into the field, e.g., Brendan Maher's (1966) *Principles of Psychopathology: An Experimental Approach* did this for abnormal psychology. For Community Psychology, Julian Rappaport's (1977) passionately written *Community Psychology: Values, Research, and Action* was instrumental in providing a framework and structure for this newly developing field and influenced several generations of students. However, even a classic must be updated to keep abreast of new developments and new societal circumstances. Although several good community textbooks have been written over the past twenty-five years, none have provided a new integration and framework. I believe that Jennifer Rudkin's book fills the void for such an innovative overview while being comprehensive in its coverage of past and present issues, research advances, and, perhaps most importantly, the evolving values of the field.

Rudkin's book is accessible and exciting. It will spark true interest in undergraduates who are being introduced to community psychology for the first time and in graduate students who have entered the field but need a boost of adrenalin. Over the past several years, while Rudkin was drafting this text, I had the good fortune to be able to expose graduate students at the University of Virginia to drafts of the chapters in my seminar on "Community Psychology and Prevention Science." For the first time in more than a decade (since I stopped using Rappaport's book), a true sense of adventure was created. Seminar discussions were buoyant, uplifting, and intense. The students were stimulated by the examples, the theoretical positions, and the use of research findings to develop innovative interventions and public policies. I felt invigorated and could feel the old enthusiasm and passion returning as I read these chapters and engaged with the students in animated discussions.

I taught my first course in community psychology as co-instructor with Seymour B. Sarason at Yale in the fall of 1968. At the time, I knew very little about this budding field but was intrigued because of its emphasis on context as well as individual behavior, and its willingness to confront the dilemma of values. I had recently obtained my Ph.D. in Clinical Psychology in the Department of Social Relations at Harvard University and had been exposed to the traditional research and theories of the time, all of which were individually focused with little notion of the person in context. The exceptions to this rule were obtained in courses taught by two sociologists, Talcott Parsons and Alex Inkeles, which fulfilled interdisciplinary requirements, but weren't viewed as essential to the study of human behavior by psychologists. It wasn't until I arrived at Yale that I realized how much these perspectives had influenced my perceptions regarding the need to understand human development and behavior in context. However, with Sarason as mentor, I clearly developed a community/societal/historical perspective and an appreciation for the ecological perspective that community psychology endorses. Moreover, the need for systematic research in natural settings that takes into account person–environment interaction became crystal clear.

When I relocated to the University of Virginia in 1976 to become director of its newly developing clinical psychology program, I also negotiated for a small but separate community psychology program so that we could attract high quality students who cared about the worlds of action and research, but did not want to go through a clinical program. Over the past twenty-five years, we have educated a small but talented group of these individuals who have moved into faculty, research, and policy positions. Jennifer Rudkin is one of these students. From the beginning, her diverse interests were noted and appreciated. She was multitalented, e.g., she illustrated children's books in her spare time; she was an exceptionally fine conceptualizer and writer; and she was always concerned about the "underdog." Her comprehensive exam paper focused on risk and protective factors and the concept of resilience, and it provided new insights that are further developed in this book. Her dissertation examined the concept of stressful life events, and many of the issues are clearly developed in the chapter on stress and coping. A post-doctoral fellowship with Susan Harter at the University of Denver enhanced her knowledge of the social development of children. Subsequent experiences have included conducting evaluation projects on risk and resilience in gay, lesbian, and bisexual youth; how children develop concepts of race and gender; partnerships between the educational psychology division at the University of Colorado and school-based teacher preparation programs; facilitating youth academic engagement through art, video, computer, and bicycle clubs; and building social capital in a low income neighborhood through youth photography. These experiences, along with teaching courses on social change and community studies at Evergreen State College and other universities, have deepened her understanding and appreciation of social action, prevention, and empowerment interventions and expanded her comprehension of the complexity of social problems and the central importance of diversity.

Now a decade after receiving her Ph.D., Rudkin has produced a book that takes seriously the idea of answering the questions of what is community psychology, who are the community psychologists, and what values underlie their work. Her division of the field into five guiding principles and four orienting concepts that summarize critical areas of research and theory is masterful. She has managed to incorporate these principles and concepts in an integrated, insightful and creative manner to provide a broad overview of the field as it exists today. Each chapter concludes with class exercises that are

exceptionally useful to instructors and students. They frequently entail experiential learning to illustrate the issues discussed and often result in significant personal impact. The judicious use of cartoons and examples throughout the book to demonstrate concepts, principles, and behavior are right on target. Each chapter suggests paths that could and should be pursued, and it is clear that the field is ever expanding and taking on new and meaningful challenges. The last chapter provides a look to the future and whole new areas in which community psychology may flourish. It challenges students to move aggressively into the field, developing and applying systematic scientific knowledge in complex community settings and to use this knowledge to derive effective interventions. The book is a testament to the acceptance of the traditional academic value of seeking knowledge for the sake of understanding but combines this with the co-equal value of using that knowledge for the sake of action.

This is an important textbook. It instills the field with new life and excitement. I am in awe of Rudkin's accomplishment and proud that she is a graduate of our program. I am also a bit intimidated knowing that as a community psychologist working primarily in the field, she wrote this book without the usual help of research assistants and graduate students, or even faculty colleagues whom she could use as sounding boards. The book is a remarkable achievement. I fully expect it to play a major role in attracting the next generation of students to become community psychologists. Read it and enjoy it!

N. Dickon Reppucci, Ph.D.
Professor of Psychology
Director of the Community Psychology Program
University of Virginia
January, 2002

Allport, G. W. (1937) *Personality: A psychological interpretation*. New York: Holt.

Maher, B. A. (1966) *Principles of psychopathology: An experimental approach*. New York: McGraw-Hill.

Rappaport, J. (1977) *Community psychology: Values, research and action*. New York: Holt, Rinehart & Winston.

White, R. A. (1948) *The Abnormal Personality*. New York: The Ronald Press Company.

Writing a textbook in community psychology requires the resolution of two challenges. First, community psychology consists of a way of thinking more than a set of accumulated facts. Second, the field's values inform action as much as basic research and theory. Textbooks traditionally focus on received knowledge—the stable, time-tested, agreed-upon "facts" of a field. This cannot be done for community psychology, at least not in the same way. A hallmark of community psychology is the view of understanding as contextual. Knowledge develops within a sociocultural and historical setting, and science is not pure, objective, and value-free. Moreover, the goal of community psychology is not solely to increase understanding but to use our knowledge to create a more just and humane society. Community psychology's existence as a way of thinking and acting rather than a body of facts helps explain why there have been a dearth of textbooks, but it also makes the field immensely exciting.

Guiding Principles and Orienting Concepts as the Organizational Schemes

The organizing scheme of this textbook makes clear community psychology's unique approach. The book is divided into two main sections: *guiding principles*, which anchor community psychologists to a coherent set of fundamental values, and *orienting concepts*, that allow us to remain open to paradigm-shaking perspectives.

Throughout the years, community psychologists have delineated a set of principles that define our way of thinking. These principles differentiate community psychology from other areas of psychology. They give the field its singular character, instill a sense of identity and pride in its practitioners and permit the field to exist as a stable and circumscribed entity.

Two introductory chapters ground the inquiry into community psychology. The first describes where community psychology came from and what it is. The second describes who community psychologists are and what we do. The next section consists of five chapters, each of which examines one of community psychology's guiding principle. The five principles are:

- A view of knowledge as fluid and value based;
- The belief that one cannot understand an individual without also understanding the many-leveled social contexts in which that individual lives;
- Attention to the voices of diverse (and often disenfranchised) groups;
- A commitment to improving the lives of individuals through intervention and social change;
- An emphasis on a strengths model rather than deficit model of mental health.

While the guiding principles are the stable foundation on which the practice and research of community psychology build, orienting concepts allow the field to remain relevant in a changing world. Orienting concepts are frameworks that summarize past research and theory, give meaning to current knowledge, and guide future research and action. They put the guiding principles into action. Orienting concepts, unlike fundamental principles, are *supposed* to change. As our knowledge grows and Zeitgeists shift, so too do our orienting concepts. The field needs new orienting concepts to inspire new insights, bring new energy, and shake us out of our collective intellectual complacency. Without new orienting concepts, community psychology's research and practice would become "one-sided" (Rappaport, 1981, p. 21).

The third section of this book describes the field's orienting concepts. Four chapters examine each orienting concept, thereby providing a review and application of the guiding principles, and a chronological overview of the development of the field. The orienting concepts are:

Stress and coping
Prevention
Empowerment
Resilience

In keeping with community psychology's emphasis on the *context* of knowledge, each chapter begins with a description of the surrounding culture from which the chapter's ideas emerged and ends with a forward-looking section entitled *The Promise of Community Psychology*. In this section I examine an idea from the chapter that has captured my own imagination and may have implications for future inquiry. The book also concludes with a final chapter dedicated to an exploration of the future of community psychology. Thus, I have tried to attend to the past, present, and future of community psychology, balancing reviews of classic work, descriptions of the current state of the field, and emerging perspectives.

Textbooks frequently present information as definitive, objective summaries of a field. My goal, however, is not to line up silent and obedient facts that students can march into examination booklets. I hope readers feel invited into a dialogue about community psychology that continues after the last word of this text is read. Toward this goal, I have provided numerous references as resources for future inquiries.

Community psychology recognizes that researchers and practitioners are not disengaged observers of life, but active participants whose own beliefs and experiences influence their work. One goal of the field has been to resist the temptation to present scientific endeavors as value-free and to be candid instead about the viewpoints that inform our own understanding. In keeping with this perspective, I have adopted a personal approach to the material and relate how my experiences have influenced my thinking about community psychology. At the same time, I realize the limitations of one person's perspective (limitations that I expect will be even more apparent to readers), but I hope that my perspective provides a helpful window to the material and encourages readers to bring themselves and their varied experiences to the table as well. This book is not intended as a definitive attempt to cover the field, but as an invitation to students to discover the field and make it their own.

Action Orientation

Community psychology views knowledge as constructed and therefore focuses on ways of thinking rather than facts per se. Learning to think like a community psychologist is *not,* however, an end goal. Community psychology succeeds as a field only to the extent that its unique ways of thinking promote useful ways of acting in the world. The study of community psychology should result in a raised consciousness about the sorts of problems that require intervention and an increased awareness of how to intervene effectively.

Community psychology's emphasis on the practical application of knowledge is at odds with the traditional view of academia. Webster's Dictionary offers the following among its definitions of *academic:* "theoretical without having an immediate or practical bearing... having no practical or useful significance." This view is not compatible with community psychology. Kurt Lewin, a forefather of the field, held that generating a knowledge base and effecting social change were two equally important and highly compatible goals of community research. Similarly, teaching in community psychology can and should be socially useful as well as theoretically meaningful. Thus, the textbook encourages informed student involvement in their communities.

Students interested in community psychology have likely been attracted to the field because they have a good dose of inspiration to start with, believe that change is possible, and want to make a difference. This book succeeds if it fuels rather than stifles student creativity and activism. Photographs, cartoons, and other pedagogical devices are included to further engage the imagination. The dual interest in academics and action is also reinforced through the inclusion of *Classic Research* and *Community Intervention* boxes. The *Classic Research* boxes describe influential studies relevant to the chapter topic, sometimes in areas other than community psychology. The *Community Intervention* boxes show how the field's principles have been put into action by community psychologists and by others. (Admittedly, in a field that combines research and action, the distinction between research and intervention sometimes blurs.)

Encouragement of student action permeates the text and becomes explicit at the end of each chapter in a section entitled *Action Agenda*. The activities in this section allow students to use information from the chapter as a basis for: (1) seeing themselves and their communities with new eyes; (2) generating ideas for needed changes; and (3) taking initial steps toward change. Certainly not all of these activities can be completed in the span of a semester, but hopefully they present some provocative ideas for living out community psychology in the process of studying it. Attention in this section to the dynamics of the classroom and the use of cooperative learning also allows students to explore ways of creating a community in the classroom as a microcosm of the larger society.

In summary, this textbook explores the past, present, and future of community psychology. The guiding principles and orienting concepts of the field constitute the main organizing structure. Readers are encouraged to think about the field, learn about themselves, and apply their knowledge to the world around them.

A Few Words of Thanks

There are numerous people who contributed to this book from near and from afar. Reviewers of this manuscript, many of whom were unknown to me provided invaluable insights. They include Jennifer Woolard (University of Florida), Beverly

Palmer (California State University), Heidi Wayment (University of Northern Arizona), Mojisola Tiamiyu (University of Toledo), Kelly Hazel (University of Alaska-Fairbanks), Jim Emshoff (Georgia State University), and Mark Aber (University of Illinois). Among the people closest to me, let me single out a few.

I have always wondered about dedications to spouses. Obviously one's partner is a companion on life's biggest journeys, including the writing of a book. Why thank them for that? I now see that spouses are also the people who have the most opportunity and cause to ask, "When is that dang book going to be finished already?" Some of us are lucky enough to have spouses who never ask. My thanks to Dani. I also thank Dick Reppucci for agreeing to write the forward, and for mentoring me directly in how to become a community psychologist and indirectly in how to be a mensch.[1] Thank you to my parents, Murray and Joy Kofkin, for their support, both tangible and intangible, and to my sons, Asher and Zev, who remind me of the magic of life and strengthen my resolve to leave this world a little better.

A Final Note

Textbooks take a long time to write and publish. Thus, it is important that they not become too dated too quickly. Yet, they are products of their particular historical contexts.

I was putting the final touches on this manuscript when hijackers crashed two planes into the World Trade Center and a third into the Pentagon, while a fourth plummeted to the ground in rural Pennsylvania. News reports in the weeks that followed took me back to New York, the city in which

---

[1] In his book *How to Talk Jewish*, (New York: St. Martin's Press) Jackie Mason (1990) defined *mensch* as "a human being with class, with feeling, and with a sense of humanity" (p. 85). A mensch looks out for the well-being of others and acts in ways that express her or his caring. To call someone a *mensch* is to pay "the ultimate compliment" (p. 86).

I was born and lived for twenty-two years and where most of my family lives today. I looked at the gaping hole in the Manhattan skyline and felt that a failure to address September 11 would be a hole in this book as well.

I considered briefly the possibility of a rewrite, if not of the whole book, at least of the sections that highlighted the void most plainly, such as the section on community disasters in Chapter Eight. The task of rewriting was quite impossible given the publishing timetable and the recency of the event. The cloud of darkness that swept through the streets of downtown Manhattan when the twin towers collapsed continues to swirl in my own head and heart. I could not rewrite the text from a new vantage point since the view from there had not yet cleared.

It is too early to know how this event will reverberate in the weeks, months, and years to come. We are still very much in the middle of making sense of and reacting to it as individuals, as cities, as countries, and as a world community. My hesitancy to speak too much too soon has been reinforced by the varied and sometimes surprising responses of those closest to me. The barrage of conflicting postings on the community psychology electronic mailing list following the event attested further to the incredible diversity of initial responses, even within a group that is in many ways quite homogeneous.

When the question of whether to rebuild the towers or some other large-scale memorial to the tragedy emerged, some proposed that the gaping absence in the New York City skyline spoke more loudly than any new building ever could. I hope that the absence of references to September 11 in this text speaks to the reader as well.

Jennifer Kofkin Rudkin

Community Psychology

Chapter 1

Community Psychology:
Where It Came From and What It Is

⌘ Introduction

Historical events do not take shape in isolation and appear out of nowhere. They result from the interplay of many existing factors. Seymour Sarason, a prolific theoretician and parent of community psychology whose ideas we will encounter throughout this text, coined the term **before the beginning** to indicate that any phenomenon emerges from and is shaped by preexisting forces (Sarason, 1972). This is true of all events, and it is true of community psychology. In order to understand how the field came to be, we need to look at the events that preceded and coincided with its birth in 1965.

To understand a phenomenon, we need to look into the past. But how far back? And across how many domains? We may assign the birth date of July 4, 1776, to the United States of America, but the signing of the Declaration of Independence and the "birth of our nation" resulted from many earlier "before-the-beginning" events. Doesn't U.S. history include the voyage of the Mayflower, and to understand that voyage don't we also need to consider the persecution in England that led the Pilgrims to set sail in the first place? What about the American Indians who lived on this continent long before the

1

arrival of English settlers, or should we say English *invaders?* Shouldn't we try to understand how the cultures and experiences of indigenous people also shaped the United States?

Explanations of the origins of a phenomenon can adopt a wide or narrow lens. Some chroniclers of community psychology have adopted wide lenses. Seymour Sarason (1974) traced the field's origins to societal events that took place decades earlier and in different countries: World War II in the 1930s; the publishing of B. F. Skinner's book *Walden Two* in 1948; the Russian launching of Sputnik in 1957. A second important thinker in community psychology, Julian Rappaport, used an even wider lens to capture the history of the field in his classic text *Community Psychology: Values, Research, and Action* (Rappaport, 1977). He began his historical review in 377 B.C., with Hippocrates' attempt to understand deviance.

Sarason and Rappaport were two different historians and presented two different histories.

History is not a chronology of facts that proceeds linearly from year A to year B. Rather, it is a living social construction that depends on human minds for its substance and vitality. Our understanding of history depends as much on the mindset of our historians as on the actual events of the past. For example, contrary to the "facts" that many of us learned in elementary school, most of us no longer hold that the United States was discovered in 1492 when Columbus sailed the ocean blue. American Indians lived on this continent long before Columbus' voyage. European immigrants stole this land, attempted to obliterate native culture, and killed many Indians in the process. Interestingly, one of the first steps many oppressed groups take in their pursuit of liberation is to reclaim the histories denied to them by mainstream historians. For example, an important part of Black liberation was the recognition that during the 1800s slaves were not

The one duty we owe history is to rewrite it.

—Oscar Wilde

sitting around patiently waiting for a lanky Caucasian savior with a scraggly beard and stovepipe hat to free them. African Americans orchestrated their own liberation. The efforts of Harriet Tubman, Frederick Douglass, and countless other known and unknown heroines and heroes led to the eventual downfall of slavery. Efforts to rewrite history continue today, and community psychologists may even find professional roles in helping members of oppressed groups reconstruct existing narratives. Natalie Contos (2000) worked with indigenous people in Western Australia to relabel the deadly ambush of Aboriginal people in 1834 as a "massacre" rather than a historical "battle" and to create a memorial on the massacre site.

This chapter explores some of the forces that predate the birth of community psychology and then seeks to define and delineate the field, although the lens is not as wide as those of Sarason or Rappaport. I begin with a discussion of the **Zeitgeist** into which community psychology was born, that is to say the intellectual, moral, and cultural climate of the 1960s (Merriam-Webster, 2000). This Zeitgeist gave shape to the field as we know it and contains the seeds from which community psychology can continue to grow. As Sarason (1986) wrote, "Community psychology arose as a reaction to all those forces that gave rise to the sizzling sixties, and therein [lies] its promise to enlarge the social horizons of psychology" (p. 405).

⌘ The Sixties

What comes to mind when you think of the 1960s? *Fire.* Burning bras, burning draft cards, burning cities beset by protesters, and napalm charred villages in Vietnam. *Speeches.* Martin Luther King reporting from the mountaintop and John F. Kennedy asking us to ask ourselves what we can do for our country. *Protests.* Two hundred fifty thousand African Americans and their supporters marching on Washington and college students refusing to study war no more. *Optimism.* Neil Armstrong taking a giant step for humankind and Peace Corps volunteers packing their bags for journeys to poverty-stricken communities across the globe. *Music.* Long-haired men with British accents proclaiming "I Want to Hold Your Hand" and young people in flowers, beads, and little else swaying to the rhythms of peace and love at Woodstock. *Death.* Social and political leaders assassinated in their prime and rock stars overdosing before the untrustworthy age of 30.

Now let's zoom in on one particular year: 1965. Radios tune into "My Generation" by the Who, and "The Times They Are A Changin'" by Bob Dylan. Feelings about the Vietnam War divide the country and police arrest an antiwar protester for the first time. United States troops take the offensive in South Vietnam and Martin Luther King, who had received the Nobel Peace Prize one year earlier, calls for an end to the war. Despite the passage of the Civil Rights Bill, discrimination continues and marchers in Selma, Alabama, face attack from segregationists. Malcolm X is assassinated, and 18,000 national guards arrive at the Watts housing projects in Los Angeles to end three days of rioting that resulted in 74 deaths, 900 injuries, and 4,000 arrests (Jennings & Brewster, 1998).

Another event of 1965 that did not have a social impact on the same scale serves nevertheless as a touchstone for readers of this book. In 1965 a group of forty psychologists convened in a suburb of Boston and established a new approach to psychology that they called "community psychology." The fires, speeches, protests, and music of the 1960s all embodied challenges to the status quo. Voices of silenced people began to rise up in rebellion. In psychology, too, the usual order of business was questioned, and the social upheavals more generally helped pave the way for the emergence of a new field in psychology. In order to set the stage for the birth of community psychology, let's look more closely at the freedom struggles that defined the decade.

FREEDOM STRUGGLES

In many ways, the freedom struggles of the 1960s were a reaction to the conformity of the previous

decade. During the 1950s, a rabid fear of communism swept the U.S., resulting in antiliberal and antiforeigner sentiments that culminated in the McCarthy hearings. Wisconsin Senator Joseph McCarthy relentlessly persecuted artists and other forward-thinking "subversives," ruining their careers and reputations with groundless accusations of conspiracies against the country. At the same time, a new invention, television, promulgated images of the ideal family. Shows such as *Ozzie and Harriet* and *Father Knows Best* depicted American families as White, suburban, and financially secure. The father went to work, the mother stayed home, and everyone delighted in such an arrangement. In her book, *The Way We Never Were: American Families and the Nostalgia Trap*, Stephanie Coontz (1992) traced the ways in which popular images of the family in the 1950s became a standard that never actually existed, but to which many people later hoped to "return."

One reason for this nostalgia is that in the 1950s, many of society's ills had not yet been formulated as social problems warranting attention. Citizens did not often discuss rape, discrimination, and hate crimes. When women, African Americans, and other marginalized groups began to speak out, the country was forced to come to terms with problems of prejudice, discrimination, and oppression that it had previously ignored.

FREEDOM MOVEMENTS

The Black civil rights movement began to gather momentum in the 1950's, aided in no small part by the 1954 Supreme Court decision that "separate but equal" facilities were inherently unconstitutional. Interestingly, the Supreme Court supported this decision with reference to studies conducted by two psychologists, Kenneth and Mamie Clark (see Classic Research box). Thus, the landmark *Brown v. Board of Education* case suggested a role for research and psychology in the social debates of the time.

The Black civil rights movement was the most visible freedom struggle of the era and provided a valuable model for other disenfranchised citizens who spoke out for their rights in the 1960s. In the

📑 CLASSIC RESEARCH

Kenneth and Mamie Clark
Contexts of Interpretation

The research of Kenneth and Mamie Clark provides a heartening example of the power of psychological research to effect major social reform. Their work on race and child development was cited in the *Brown v. Board of Education* Supreme Court decision, the decision that ended segregation in the public schools. Although the Clarks' simple study might not be publishable using today's scientific criteria, it continues to influence research and thinking about the importance of race in child development

In their research, Clark and Clark asked African American children ranging in age from three to seven years to choose either a White doll or a Black doll in response to a variety of requests. The experimenters asked, for example: "Give me the doll you would like to play with;" "Give me the doll that is a nice doll;" or "Give me the doll that looks bad" (Clark & Clark, 1939; Clark & Clark, 1947). The Clarks found that children viewed White dolls as embodying positive characteristics, and Black dolls as embodying negative ones. Moreover, children who were relaxed and playful during the earlier questions became tearful and agitated when asked, "Give me the doll that looks like you." Two children responded by running from the test room, in tears and unable to be soothed. The Clark's contended that African American children's assessments of the relative goodness of Black versus White dolls was based in societal views of Blackness as inferior, and had important implications for child development.

The influential studies of Clark and Clark generated a great deal of subsequent research and theorizing. Doll studies have been criticized on many levels. One early criticism was that neither Black nor White children had much experience with Black dolls, and so the children might really be demonstrating a preference for familiar toys. Today dolls of different races are more readily available. Have such changes brought us closer to realizing the idyllic vision of girls and boys of different races happily playing together, judging each other not by the color of their skin but by the content of their character? Do more recent doll studies find that Black children's preferences for White dolls has lessened?

The results are mixed. Studies of European American children find a consistent preference for White dolls, but the preferences of Black children are less clear. Some recent studies contradict the findings of the Clarks and document a same-race preference among African American children (Finkelstein & Haskins, 1983; Newman, Liss, & Sherman, 1983). A number of other studies, however, continue to demonstrate a White preference in African American children when choosing dolls and when selecting prospective playmates from photographs (Jaffe, 1988; Kofkin, Katz, & Downey, 1995; Porter, 1991).

Social progress can be difficult to assess. Doll studies do not provide clear evidence of social change. What *has* changed, however, is the context in which our interpretations of findings occur. The Supreme Court accepted the interpretation of White preferences in Black children as evidence of their rejection of Blackness and lack of self-esteem. This interpretation resulted, in large part, from the assumption that because White children—the standard against which other children were judged—chose same race dolls and Black children did not, there must be something different (i.e. deficient) with regard to the Black children, a poor sense of self-esteem, for example. In more recent years, researchers have become less likely to define observed differences between majority group and minority group members as evidence of the minority group's inferiority. White preferences in doll or playmate choices is no longer assumed to indicate problems with the Black children's sense of themselves (e.g., Cross, 1985; Spencer, 1984).

How might our interpretation of findings such as those of Clark and Clark change if we used Black children's behavior as a standard from which to judge all children? James Jones (1993) suggested that European Americans are deviant in that they suffer from elevated self-esteem (e.g., feelings of superiority and entitlement). This would suggest that White children's consistent preference for White dolls and playmates indicates not healthy self-acceptance but rather cross-race rejection. Black children may be demonstrating a valuable trait: a willingness to make play choices across the bounds of their own race. If we are to reach the ideal of children of all colors happily playing together, won't it be necessary for children to value differences and to display a desire to interact with children who are *not* of the same race?

This reinterpretation does not account for the Clarks' finding that Black children resisted identifying with the less-preferred Black dolls. Nevertheless, a re-examination of their research from a modern vantage point does cast old findings in a new light. Perhaps both old and new interpretations have elements of truth in them. It can be difficult for African American children growing up in the U.S. to feel good about their racial identity *and* White children demonstrate an unwillingness to play with children of other races that works against cross-cultural understanding and better race relations. Even if the findings of doll studies such as those conducted by Clark and Clark do not show clear changes over time, the social progress made since *Brown vs. Board of Education* may be evident in our willingness and ability to consider alternative interpretations of those findings.

1960s, the modern women's movement also came of age. Women became more aware of how "the personal is political." They met in **consciousness-raising groups** to talk about their lives. Small groups of four to ten women convened in living rooms and kitchens across the nation to commiserate about the ways in which they were treated unfairly in society, in the workplace, and in their homes. Together they realized that their intimate relationships reflected the subordinate status they held in the larger world and began to appreciate the social causes of their most personal difficulties. The activism nurtured locally in these small groups both resulted from and led to larger societal changes. Women entered the work force in increasing numbers and concerns about affordable childcare and equal pay became pressing. The availability of birth control pills allowed women greater choice in their personal lives and career paths. Large organizations, such as the National Organization for Women (NOW), furthered local campaigns for justice and help set a national agenda for change.

The women's movement questioned the rigid social mores and prescribed gender roles of the 1950s. This questioning also gave strength to the incipient movement for gay liberation. In the 1960s, gay, lesbian, bisexual, and transgendered (GLBT) people were viewed as deviant. At the time, both the American Psychological Association and the American Psychiatric Association classified homosexuality as a mental illness. In the 1960s, this view was challenged, and GLBT people began to organize as an oppressed group deserving of civil rights. One event in history symbolizes this shift in perspective.

The Stonewall Inn was a dimly lit bar in New York City's Greenwich Village that catered to a GLBT clientele. Police raids on such establishments occurred frequently, but for some reason in the early morning hours of June 28, 1969, bar patrons determined that they had had enough. Instead of quietly disappearing into the night, they launched a counterattack. The outermost fringe of this marginalized group—drag queens and kings, many of whom were African American and Latino—led the charge. The resistance of bar patrons caught the small group of policemen by surprise. They summoned reinforcements. Word of the uprising spread across the city. The confrontation lasted for three days and became a defining moment in GLBT history (Marcus, 1992a).

An important year for such defining events was 1969. In that year, American Indian students from Bay Area colleges occupied Alcatraz Island in San Francisco in an attempt to reclaim this abandoned federal property for Native Americans. They declared that an 1868 treaty had given the island to American Indians and demanded a transfer of title in order to establish an educational center for Indians on Alcatraz (DeLoria, 1997). A growing national organization, the American Indian Movement (AIM) added its voice to the protest and attempted to focus attention on a variety of Indian plights, such as deplorable living conditions for urban and reservation Indians and civil rights violations perpetrated against Indians by police. Although the specific demands of the Indians occupying Alcatraz may not always have been precisely articulated, the message that Indians would control their own destiny rang clear (DeLoria, 1997; Smith & Warrior, 1996).

The Chicano movement also gained momentum during the 1960s and reached a pinnacle in 1969. This movement had coalesced around a number of causes. Cesar Chavez spearheaded an effort to unionize farm workers in California and Texas. Barrio residents attempted to increase the availability of health care and to involve residents in the political process. In perhaps the most widespread movement, student activists across the nation called for increased representation of Chicano perspectives in school curricula and a better quality of education (Marin, 1991). Toward this goal, students established several organizations, such as the Mexican

American Youth Organization and United Mexican American Students. In April of 1969, hundreds of Chicano students convened at the University of California at Santa Barbara for a three-day conference. Student organizations changed their name to MEChA (El Movimiento Estudiantil Chicano de Aztlán) and drafted a plan of action that focused on Chicano cultural nationalism, self-determination, and the education of Chicano youth (Rosales, 1996). Student groups took the lead in a growing Chicano movement, and activism flourished through the creative efforts of its members. Information on liberation activities spread through newspapers and magazines, as well as powerful posters and murals that brought the message of change to a wide base of people who would not have been reached through mainstream media.

The decision of Indian college students to take over Alcatraz and the formation of MEChA exemplify the activism of young people in the 1960s. Young adults filled the ranks of most civil rights organizations at the time. In part, this reflected demographic changes in the U.S. population. In the years following World War II, the number of young people had grown at twice the rate of the general population, and in 1965 more people than ever entered college—6.5 million as compared to 1.7 million in 1946 (Chalmers, 1996). In the 1960s, a youth generation emerged for the first time as a powerful force

American Indians play ball outside the prison wall on Alcatraz Island in this November 26, 1969, photo. The sign reading "INDIANS WELCOME" is one of the few physical reminders of the nineteen-month occupation that captured the attention of the world and ignited a passion for civil rights. *AP/WIDE WORLD PHOTOS.*

for social change. Young adults warned each other not to trust anyone over the age of thirty, and confronted the established political system with tactics inspired by youthful irreverence. The Youth International Party (Yippies), established by Abbie Hoffman and Jerry Rubin, attended the 1968 Democratic Convention in Chicago to promote their candidate for president—a hog named Pigasus. Their platform, which included seducing delegates' wives and seizing the Nabisco factory in order to distribute free cookies, incited a major disturbance. In the uproar surrounding the convention, 10,000 protesters took to the streets and were met by 23,000 members of the police force and National Guard. Several activists were arrested, including a group that came to be known as the Chicago Seven, which included Hoffman, Rubin, and Bobby Seale, cofounder of the Black Panthers (Jennings & Brewster, 1998; Rector and Visitors of the University of Virginia, 1998; Chalmers, 1996).

Despite the insolent overtones of some youthful change efforts, the need for social reform was increasingly clear to many lay people and to more staid professionals. The moral authority of young adults and others who were willing to question existing authorities and social conventions had far-reaching ramifications. No institution remained untouched by the fervor of the 1960s; certainly the mental health system would never be the same.

FREEDOM-FIGHTING PSYCHOLOGISTS

In the 1960s, activists generally viewed the mental health system as part of the problem. As we will see in the next section, the mental health profession tended to support the status quo. Before leaving this section on freedom fighters, however, let's look at a few progressive researchers and practitioners who helped fuel the freedom struggles of the era.

A psychiatrist named Thomas Szasz launched one of the most profound attacks on the mental health system. Szasz (1961) characterized psychiatric diagnoses as grossly unreliable and contended that under the guise of "medical treatment," individuals were incarcerated in mental hospitals for doing nothing more than annoying others with their unusual behavior. Szasz delineated his theory of the **myth of mental illness,** stating that psychological illness was a meaningless construct designed to remove from the larger society those "deviants" who made upstanding citizens uncomfortable. The Scottish psychiatrist Ronald Laing echoed several of Szasz' claims (e.g., Laing & Esterson, 1970). Laing held that schizophrenia was nothing more than the coping response of perceptive individuals trying to function in a society that relied on deception and denial.

While some mental health professionals questioned established facts through theoretical arguments, others used scientific research to highlight injustices in society. Perhaps most notable was the research of Kenneth and Mamie Clark described in the Classic Research box. Another lesser-known psychological study of that era was conducted by Evelyn Hooker (1957; Marcus, 1992b). Hooker challenged the view of homosexuality as a mental illness. She had a panel of national and international experts attempt to distinguish mentally healthy heterosexual men from homosexual men based on their responses to accepted tests. Much to the surprise of these experts and to the mental health establishment, the experts could not differentiate healthy heterosexual respondents from homosexual respondents.

A study by Inge Broverman and colleagues (1970) exposed gender biases in clinicians' definitions of mental health and illness. They had three sets of clinically trained psychotherapists complete checklists of the qualities of either healthy people, healthy men, or healthy women. The researchers found that clinicians who rated healthy people endorsed the same qualities as the clinician who rated healthy men. The clinicians who rated healthy women, on the other hand, did not endorse the same qualities as clinicians who rated healthy people. So, for example, healthy people are seen as self confident, but self confidence was seen as a quality of healthy men but not healthy women. In her book *Women and Madness*, originally published in 1972, Phyllis Chesler also examined how diagnoses of mental illness allowed the mental health establishment to support gender oppression.

All of these scholars questioned the ability of mental health "experts" to define mental illness and showed the ways personal and professional biases perpetuated oppression. Let's turn now to the context of mental health practice in the 1960s and consider how this context also contributed to the founding of community psychology.

THE COMMUNITY MENTAL HEALTH MOVEMENT

The practice of psychology came under scrutiny in the 1960s for a variety of reasons, not the least of which was that "[i]n a political climate in which human rights were being advanced for minority groups in many sectors of American life, those of the mental patient also became a focus of concern" (Maher, 1988, p. 162). This concern culminated in a movement to remove mental patients from hospitals and serve people with mental difficulties within their communities.

THE CONDITION OF MENTAL HOSPITALS

The first mental hospital had been established in the 1830s with the hope that curing mentally ill people would reduce their dependence on welfare. Asylums for the mentally ill began to appear across the United States. These institutions were generally supportive and well-ordered sanctuaries for people who were seen as not functioning well in the outside world. By the turn of the century, however, hospitals had become overcrowded. Promises of a cure were not delivered, and the high cost of long-term institutionalization meant that only the most deviant people entered the mental health system. In the middle of the twentieth century, several exposés documented abuses in mental hospitals, and even when abuse did not occur, the overcrowded and under-staffed state hospitals provided little more than custodial care to residents, many of whom were severely disturbed (Price & Smith, 1983). Increasing costs, loss of public support, and the inefficacy of intervention led state hospitals to abandon their treatment orientation and adopt a business administration orientation (Rappaport, 1977; Torrey,

1997). Hospitals focused on cost and management rather than quality of care. Many inpatients did not receive any therapeutic intervention at all, and evidence accumulated that the routine and control of hospital environments actually made patients *less* able to function outside the confines of the institution (Goffman, 1961; see also Goldstein, 1979).

As hospitals began to come under scrutiny, new therapies emerged that changed the face of mental health treatment. Major tranquilizers and antipsychotic medications became available, the use of electroconvulsive therapy (ECT) gained popularity, and psychosurgery came into vogue. By the 1960s, the widespread use of somatic treatments came to be seen as social control rather than therapeutic treatment. Social commentators raised moral objections to the management of mental illness though biochemical and surgical intervention and also criticized the use of involuntary commitment as a violation of mental patients' civil rights. Ken Kesey's (1962) book *One Flew over the Cuckoo's Nest* (which was made into a movie in 1975) popularized concerns about the mental health system.

The civil rights struggles of disenfranchised groups also brought the mental health system into examination. Studies demonstrated that while low-income African American populations suffered from high rates of emotional problems, they most often received custodial or somatic care, if they received any care at all. At the same time, dissatisfaction with state hospitals led to the development of private facilities catering to middle and upper class (and largely White) populations. The most preferred treatment of the era—intensive and personalized psychotherapy by experienced professionals—was reserved for wealthy clients (Hollingshead & Redlich, 1958; Myers & Schaffer, 1954), which is not to say that the wealthiest clients received *effective* treatment. In the 1960s, the ability of mental health professionals to improve the health status of mentally ill clients using even the most prestigious, costly, and time-consuming techniques was cast into doubt (e.g., Eysenck, 1961).

In the 1960s, questions abounded as to whether the established way of doing things was the best way. Activists exposed the overcrowding and abuses of state hospitals, objected to the overuse of drugs and surgery in treating inpatients, highlighted the discriminatory nature of service delivery, and questioned the ability of psychiatrists and psychologists to cure mental illness even under the most favorable conditions. The belief that the mental health system must change became widespread. John F. Kennedy expressed this sentiment clearly in his 1963 address to Congress.

Kennedy's address is sometimes cited as the single event that led most directly to the founding of community psychology. It certainly inspired a widespread movement to rely less on state hospitals for mental health treatment. Kennedy's address, too, has a before-the-beginning. Let's start setting the stage for the address when John F. Kennedy was just a baby.

KENNEDY'S SISTER

When John F. Kennedy was one year old, his sister Rosemary was born. She was a pretty baby whom her mother described as "sweet and peaceful" (Goodwin, 1987) Within a few years, however, it became clear that Rosemary's development lagged behind that of her siblings. She was slower to crawl, walk, talk, feed herself, and reach various developmental milestones. She also acted erratically. The Kennedy parents took Rosemary to numerous doctors who provided little hope and recommended that their daughter be placed in an institution. The Kennedys rejected this expert advice. While the other Kennedy children grew up and found their places in the larger world, Rosemary remained at home under the care of her parents (Goodwin, 1987).

In the early 1940's, elite doctors hailed psychosurgery as a miracle cure for troubled individuals. Rosemary's father decided to try this promising technique on his daughter. During the surgery, something went terribly wrong and Rosemary emerged less able to care for herself (Goodwin, 1987). Although the surgery ended her mood swings and outbursts, it also substantially altered her personality. Eventually, Rosemary's parents sent her to a nursing home in Wisconsin where she had her own apartment, a personal attendant, and access to a chauffeured car. Rosemary became plump

and disoriented, and her ties to the family diminished. The Kennedys told those who asked that Rosemary had turned out to be quite shy and withdrawn and had joined a religious order dedicated to working with retarded children (Collier & Horowitz, 1984).

Rosemary's trials most likely contributed to John F. Kennedy's appreciation for the plight of people in the U.S. with mental challenges. The Kennedy family's attempts to foster Rosemary's development and help her to live a rewarding life revealed the lack of options available for people with mental difficulties. Kennedy's 1963 address to Congress can be traced to a number of societal trends—the interest in reform that characterized the era, the nation's growing awareness of overcrowding and abuse in state hospitals, and research on the ineffectiveness of treatment. It was also informed by the experiences of a brother who watched his sister struggle to find a place in the world.

THE JOINT COMMISSION AND KENNEDY'S CONGRESSIONAL ADDRESS

In trying to understand the before-the-beginning of Kennedy's address, we have looked at the Zeitgeist of the 1960s, the conditions of state mental hospitals, and his family's efforts to find a place for his sister, Rosemary. A more direct impetus for Kennedy's address was a report from the Joint Commission on Mental Illness and Health.

In 1955, Congress created the Joint Commission in order to assess the current state of mental health care in the U.S. and to make recommendations for federal action. The Joint Commission on Mental Illness and Health issued its report in 1961, as John F. Kennedy began his presidency. The report recognized that the current overburdened hospital system left many people untreated and that existing mental health practices did not always help the small percentage of people who did receive services. Among the reforms they suggested were increased financial support for mental health research, additional training for and utilization of nonprofessional mental health practitioners, the establishment of more services outside of hospital settings, and public education about mental illness

(Joint Commission on Mental Illness and Health, 1961). Kennedy responded to that report in his 1963 Congressional address, in which he proposed reforms even more sweeping than those advocated by the Commission.

Kennedy's address had a profound impact on the understanding and treatment of mental illness. In their book *The Social History of Helping Services*. Murray and Adeline Levine (1970) identified Kennedy's address as one of three major revolutions in mental health, the other two being Pinel's insistence on the moral treatment of mental patients in France and Freud's development of his psychodynamic theory in Vienna.

What was so revolutionary about Kennedy's address? First, it called for a reintegration of mental patients into the community. At the time, responsibility for mentally ill and retarded citizens fell to the state hospital system. Kennedy proposed that large numbers of these patients be released from mental hospitals and served instead within their communities.

Second, Kennedy advocated a preventive approach to mental illness, which included attention to positive mental health. He suggested that the elimination of illness should not be the sole objective of our mental health system. Rather, people should achieve a state of well-being that allowed them to realize their full potential.

Third, Kennedy's bold new approach called attention to the social factors that affected the adjustment of individuals. Kennedy recognized that poverty, crime, alcoholism, unemployment, and racial discrimination seriously undermined mental health. Thus, the role of the mental health practitioner was no longer confined to physician and healer, but also encompassed roles as educator, social critic, reformer, and social planner (Levine & Levine, 1970).

Finally, mental health practitioners could no longer cater to a small segment of society. Under the existing patterns of service delivery, only a small number of people in need of help received services. Given the extent of the need, it would be virtually impossible to train enough professionals to meet the need (Albee, 1959). Thus, Kennedy called for an overhaul in mental health service delivery systems, which might include the training of paraprofessionals

so that the psychological needs of all citizens could be met.

Shortly after Kennedy's address, the Community Mental Health Centers Act became law. This act mandated the transfer of resources from public institutions to the community. It became the basis for the **community mental health movement**, an effort to provide services for mentally ill people within local communities, thereby reducing the need for long-term hospitalization.

DEINSTITUTIONALIZATION AND ITS RAMIFICATIONS

In 1955, large numbers of mentally ill people left state hospitals and took up residence in community settings. The advent of effective antipsychotic medications that enabled people with serious mental illnesses to live without constant supervision is widely seen as an impetus for the movement know as **deinstitutionalization** (for an alternative perspective, see Albee, 1980). The community mental health movement further hastened the removal of patients from mental hospitals. Furthermore, legal challenges made it increasingly difficult to hospitalize people against their will (Bok, 1992; Levine, 1981; Price & Smith, 1983).

The magnitude of the change that occurred in a short period of time is astounding. Deinstitutionalization is one of the largest social experiments in American history (Torrey, 1997). The population of mentally ill and mentally retarded people residing in hospitals today is a small fraction of what it was half a century ago (see Figure 1.1).

Although the worthy goal of humanizing mental health services propelled the deinsitutionalization movement, it was not an unmitigated success. This movement exemplifies how today's solutions can become tomorrow's problems. The emptying of hospitals occurred without the establishment of alternative community supports. Indeed, the vast majority of state mental health budgets continued to fund inpatient services despite the fact that hospitals came to serve a smaller and smaller number of mental health consumers. Without funding for community supports, many people who would previously have been hospitalized were not "returned to the community" at

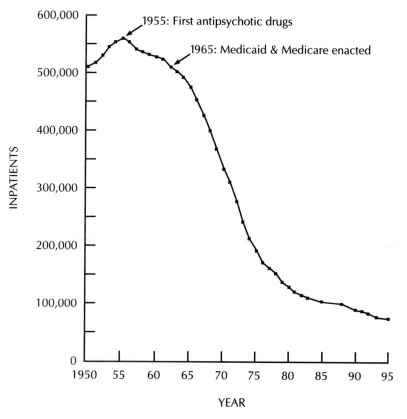

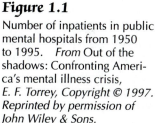

Figure 1.1

Number of inpatients in public mental hospitals from 1950 to 1995.   *From* Out of the shadows: Confronting America's mental illness crisis, *E. F. Torrey, Copyright © 1997. Reprinted by permission of John Wiley & Sons.*

all (Roesch 1995). They ended up instead in other marginal settings. One such setting was jail. A 1999 report of the U.S. Bureau of Justice identified 16% of the prison and jail population (283,000 inmates) as mentally ill (Ditton, 1999). Mentally ill people also took up residence on city streets or in homeless shelters. The rise in the homeless population is due, in part (though only in part), to deinstitutionalization. Research finds that about one quarter of homeless people (22% to 24%) had previously received treatment in psychiatric hospitals, and this number is even higher—as high as 75%—when looking specifically at homeless people in large cities (Jencks, 1994; Torrey, 1997). Nursing homes are another setting where elderly people with mental illness often end up, and in many of these homes, the care received is substandard (Price & Smith, 1983).

Criticisms of deinstitutionalization should not suggest the need for a "reinstitutionalization" movement.

Community-based care is indeed preferable to hospitalization. A review of ten studies in which psychiatric patients were randomly assigned to either inpatient care or alternative care outside hospital settings found that in no case was hospitalization associated with more positive outcomes (Kiesler, 1982). Patients placed in alternative care were more likely to find employment, live independently, and receive formal education. In addition, most psychiatric patients reported being happier outside hospitals than inside them, especially if they were released into well-staffed and structured community settings (Okin, Borus, Baer, & Jones, 1995). These consistent results have not led to a reallocation of resources to community settings, however, and community psychologists and others have continued to explore ways of promoting the integration of people with mental illness and mental retardation into their communities.

THE FATE OF THE COMMUNITY MENTAL HEALTH MOVEMENT

Kennedy was assassinated not long after his landmark address to Congress, but Kennedy's vice president, Lyndon Johnson, continued along the path set by his predecessor, developing several federal initiatives to support social reform. Johnson pushed for the passage of the 1964 Civil Rights Act and the 1965 Voting Rights Act. He established a domestic version of the Peace Corps (called Volunteers in Service to America, or VISTA), and created Medicare. He also launched the War on Poverty, an innovative attempt to establish comprehensive new programs that were planned, in part, by the poor people they targeted. The most famous of these programs was Head Start (Jennings & Brewster, 1998). which is described in the Community Intervention box.

The community mental health movement became associated with the progressive politics of Kennedy and Johnson. The movement lost its footing under the Republican administrations of Richard Nixon and Gerald Ford. The Democratic administration of Jimmy Carter tried to revive interest in the mental health needs of U.S. citizens, inspired in large part by First Lady Rosalyn Carter. When the Republicans regained control of the presidency in 1980, however, they decided not to recast the mental health movement according to conservative principles, but to find a cause more in keeping with their philosophy (Humphreys & Rappaport, 1993). A view of mental illness as a biomedical rather than a social problem was repopularized, and community mental health centers lost both political support and federal funding. Substance abuse was presented as *the* pressing social problem that merited national attention. Historically, approaches to treating substance abuse—from the days of prohibition to the widespread establishment of Alcoholics Anonymous meetings—have been more consistent with the conservative focus on individual responsibility and moral character. Between 1981 and 1991, federal spending on drug programs increased 679%, and the drinking age was raised to 21 in many states. In addition, the Anti-Drug Abuse Acts of 1986 and 1988 were passed, and Nancy Reagan launched her "Just Say No" campaign.

After analyzing the shift in national priorities in the 1980s and 1990s, Keith Humphreys and Julian Rappaport (1993) concluded that the days of federally sponsored community mental health programs are over. The changes in administrations altered the landscape for community providers, but the news is not *all* bad. The new environment has inspired adaptations that would not have occurred otherwise. The lack of government sponsorship paved the way for a community revolution of sorts (see Riger, 2001). Local agencies, underfunded though they may be, have become the hub for community services (Riger, 2001), and previously isolated settings have begun to band together to solve problems in coalition (Wolff, 2001). This Zeitgeist, while different from the Zeitgeist of the 1960s into which community psychology was born, presents both new challenges and unprecedented opportunities for practitioners of community psychology.

⌘ Community Psychology

Freedom struggles and the community mental health movement set the stage for community psychology, but the field actually has a specific birth date. On May 5, 1965, a group of forty clinical psychologists convened for a conference in Swampscott, Massachusetts, a suburb of Boston, to discuss new directions for the profession.

THE SWAMPSCOTT CONFERENCE AND BEYOND

The clinical psychologists at the **Swampscott Conference** recognized a variety of problems in their discipline and called for a novel approach to mental health that emphasized prevention over treatment, targeted the social systems in which individuals lived, and participated in social change efforts. Although the meeting was entitled *Boston Conference on the Education of Psychologists for Community Mental Health,* participants chose not to identify with the community mental health movement. The mission of community psychology was defined as

COMMUNITY INTERVENTION:

Head Start: Child Development or Community Development?

Head Start was conceived in 1964, shortly after Lyndon Johnson launched his War on Poverty. This new program had far-reaching and impressive goals. It adopted a holistic approach to improving low-income communities that involved health care for children, family social services, early childhood education, community participation in program governance, in-service training for staff, and a structure for the advancement of Head Start workers, many of whom were parents of the children served (Bok, 1992; Zigler & Muenchow, 1992). The program was designed not simply to teach young children, but to provide training and leadership opportunities for adult members of the community.

Head Start was a popular program from the beginning. In the first summer, it enrolled 561,359 low-income preschoolers—five times as many as initially anticipated (Bok, 1992). Two years later, it served 733,000 children and had an operating budget of almost 200 million dollars. By 1985, the budget passed the billion dollar mark, and continued to grow, approaching 4 billion dollars in 1997. Interestingly, the number of children served has not increased proportionally. In 1997, only 793,809 children were served—a fraction of those eligible based on income guidelines (Department of Health and Human Services, 1999).

In the 1960s, the country buzzed with enthusiasm about the role of the federal government in solving social problems. This helps explain the early support for and exponential growth of Head Start. By the 1980s, however, the Zeitgeist had changed decidedly. Big government was disparaged, antipoverty campaigns abandoned, and funding for most social programs eliminated or drastically cut. But Head Start was spared. It remained a popular, federally funded program despite the fact that serious questions about its effectiveness had been raised. Head Start is one of the most researched social programs with over a thousand studies completed by 1979 (Ellsworth & Ames, 1998a), but these studies do not unanimously attest to the efficacy of the program. A review of twelve years of evaluation research concluded that Head Start does have an immediate effect on children's performance. Program graduates enter

primary schools near or at national norms on measures of school readiness. By second or third grade, however, this effect usually disappears. Children who attended Head Start did not show any advantages over nongraduates in their performance (e.g., Datta, 1979).

Some argue that Head Start has not realized its potential because its most important early goals were abandoned. It was supposed to afford low-income families an opportunity to restructure their social institutions as they saw fit (Ellsworth & Ames, 1998b). This has not happened. As the program became less a community action program and more an early education program, the emphasis on community control and parent empowerment (which, not insignificantly, meant *women's* empowerment—see Kuntz, 1998) diminished. Parent empowerment became parent involvement—mothers helped with day-to-day classroom chores but generally did not design curriculum. Critics of the child-focused Head Start that has emerged since the 1960s have argued that the possibility of ending poverty "never existed in merely teaching poor children colors and numbers before they got to kindergarten" (Ellsworth & Ames, 1998b, p. 336).

After more than a quarter of a century, it appears that well-funded, well-run early education programs can help children avoid many of the problems associated with poverty, such as welfare dependence, teenage childbearing, and incarceration (Barnett, 2000). They cannot, however, guarantee future success amidst the continued challenges children face in their stressed families, under-funded schools, and low-income neighborhoods. This has led some scholars to argue that the empowerment of low-income families and communities ultimately matters more than early childhood education (see Halpern, 2000)

Jeanne Ellsworth and her colleagues (Ellsworth, 1998; Ellsworth & Ames, 1998b) proposed that Head Start continues to receive support in the face of disappointing research results because it does indeed serve its function, "which is not necessarily to raise test scores and certainly not to end poverty" (p. 339). These authors contended that Head Start succeeds in *appearing* to address intractable problems without actually challenging the power structures in society that systematically work against the advancement of poor people (Ellsworth & Ames, 1998b). This raises the question of whether Head Start would continue to receive support if it inspired the fundamental structural and societal changes necessary to eradicate poverty.

much broader (Newbrough, 1970). Participants believed that the time had come to expand psychology's areas of inquiry and action. Community psychology would embrace a comprehensive agenda that included such activities as antipoverty campaigns and educational reform (Bennett, Anderson, Cooper, Hassol, Klein, & Rosenblum, 1966).

Shortly after the Swampscott Conference, community psychology became established as a unique field in psychology. In 1967 the **American Psychological Association (APA)** officially approved **Division 27** as the division dedicated to community psychology. Within a few years, the field had its own journal. In 1973 the *American Journal of Community Psychology* began publishing articles. The *Journal of Community Psychology* also emerged as a vehicle for disseminating contributions to the field, and the Division 27 newsletter, *The Community Psychologist,* provided a more informal forum for the exchange of ideas and information. Ten years after Swampscott, the Austin Conference at the University of Texas was organized to discuss training in the field (see Iscoe, Bloom, & Spielberger, 1977). Community psychology programs were established across the country.[1] In 1987 Division 27 underwent a name change and became the **Society for Community Research in Action (SCRA)**, a name that better conveyed the field's applied and interdisciplinary nature.[2] Since 1987, the SCRA has held the **Biennial Conference on Community Research and Action.**

The field continues to grow. In the 1990s, community psychology listservs became another way for community psychologists to exchange information.[3] In the summer of 2001, SCRA revised its mission statement (which appears in the box on p. 15), in order to emphasize its commitment to diversity and recognize community psychology as an international discipline. Community psychology exists not only in the U.S., but around the world. Indeed one Canadian argued that the term was used in Canada as early as 1951 and so "like basketball, community psychology is a Canadian invention" (Walsh-Bowers, 1998, p. 280). Australia, Canada, Italy, New Zealand (Wingenfeld & Newbrough, 2000), and many other parts of the world practice community psychology in some form, including Canada (see Walsh, 1988; Walsh-Bowers, 1998), Latin America (Freitas, 2000; Montero, 1996; Serrano- Garcia & Lopez-Sanchez, 1991; Wiesenfeld, 1998), Italy (Prezza & Constantini, 1998), Hong Kong (Lam & Ho, 1989), Japan (Nobuo, 1989), India (Omprakash, 1989), Thailand (Tapanya, 1989), Australia (Fisher, 1992), and South Africa (Lazarus & Prinsloo, 1995; Edwards, 1998). Although the field takes a somewhat different form in each of these countries, an international perspective also reveals striking parallels in the development of the field across the globe. For example, a community mental health movement of the 1960s ushered in the field of community psychology not only in the U.S., but also in Hong Kong (Lam & Ho, 1989) and Thailand (Tapanya, 1989).

---

[1]For a list and description of programs, see *http://www.msu.edu/user/lounsbul/cpdcra.html.*
[2]The Division 27/SCRA website can be found at *http://www.apa.org/divisions/div27/.*

[3]To subscribe, send e-mail to *LISTSERV@lists.apa.org.* In the body of your e-mail type: SUBSCRIBE SCRA-L <yourfirstname> <yourlastname>. Leave the subject line blank. Information on subscribing to other listservs, including the student listserv, is available at the Division website.

DEFINITIONS OF COMMUNITY PSYCHOLOGY

Although attendants of the Swampscott Conference agreed on the need for a new field called community psychology, the definition of the field continued to evolve over many years. Indeed, a questioning of who we are and what we do continues to be an integral part of community psychology.

SOME EXISTING DEFINITIONS

Over the years, a number of definitions of community psychology have been proposed to help ground and direct the field. The pioneering psychologists of Swampscott offered the earliest definition.

> Community psychology... is devoted to the study of general psychological processes that link social systems with individual behavior in complex interactions... such linkages were seen as providing the basis for action programs directed toward improving individual, group, and social system functioning. (Bennett et al., 1966, p. 7)

This first definition holds up quite well several decades later. It posits that individuals are inextricably linked to their social contexts and points to the need for social action.

In 1974 Seymour Sarason published one of the first influential texts on the field entitled *Psychological Sense of Community: Prospects for a Community Psychology*. Sarason wrote that community psychology entails a

> . . . shift from an emphasis on intrapsychic factors to understanding and changing larger social contexts; adapting such a focus would require new conceptualizations and tactics; amid the major criterion by which these new efforts would be judged was the degree to which they led to a greater psychological sense of community. (p. 155)

This definition also recognizes the importance of context, implies a need for social action, and introduces

---

SCRA Mission Statement
Sept. 26, 2001

The Society for Community Research and Action (SCRA), Division 27 of the American Psychological Association, is an international organization devoted to advancing theory, research, and social action. Its members are committed to promoting health and empowerment and to preventing problems in communities, groups, and individuals. Four broad principles guide SCRA:

1. Community research and action requires explicit attention to and respect for diversity among peoples and settings;
2. Human competencies and problems are best understood by viewing people within their social, cultural, economic, geographic, and historical contexts;
3. Community research and action is an active collaboration among researchers, practitioners, and community members that uses multiple methodologies;
4. Change strategies are needed at multiple levels in order to foster settings that promote competence and well-being.

We welcome all who share these values.

the concept of a sense of community. This concept, which we will examine more closely in chapters four and twelve, has received some but perhaps not enough attention in the field.

In the classic textbook of the field, Julian Rappaport (1977) proposed the following definition:

> Community psychology is, in part, an attempt to find other alternatives for dealing with deviance from societal-based norms. What is sought is an approach that avoids labeling differences as necessarily negative or as requiring social control. Community psychology viewed in this way is an attempt to support every person's right to be different without risk of suffering material and psychological sanctions. (p. 1)

This definition adds to the others an emphasis on social disenfranchisement and diversity. It is difficult to capture all of community psychology in a sentence or two. A set of defining features, or guiding principles, better captures the important dimensions of community psychology.

GUIDING PRINCIPLES AND ORIENTING CONCEPTS

Several authors have sought to identify recurring themes in the field (e.g., Elias, 1994, p. 300; Sarason, 1977, pp. 39–40; Trickett, 1990, p. 210). A number of themes consistently emerge as characteristic of community psychology. These common themes have been distilled into five **guiding principles** that capture the essence of the field and give community psychology its unique character (see Table 1.1). Each principle will be examined in its own chapter, but we will briefly consider them here.

Rappaport highlighted the importance of the first principle by featuring the word "values" in the title of his classic textbook, *Community Psychology: Values, Research, and Action* and in his statement. "The hallmark of community psychology is a self-consciousness about its values (Rappaport, 1984a,

p. 210). Sarason (1977) astutely observed that community psychologists "are not neutral about values, if for no other reason than that nobody is" (p. 39).

The second principle, the importance of social context, is perhaps the most frequently cited tenet. It appears in the previously cited definitions and is viewed by important scholars in the field as the theme that unifies all of community psychology (e.g., Sarason, 1986; Trickett, 1990).

The second principle leads to the third principle in that attention to context requires a consideration of culture, broadly defined. As Rappaport (1984b) wrote, "the defining values of the community psychology movement have been cultural relativity, diversity, and an ecological perspective" (pp. 19–20; see also Rappaport, 1977, p. 2).

The fourth principle is an emphasis on social change. Although not all community psychology agendas are radical, Irma Serrano-García (1994) asserted that the "main goal of community psychology is to promote social change" (p. 2) and Edward Seidman (1988) argued that community psychologists must put ambivalence about social activism "behind us once and for all, or we will fail to bring to fruition our own distinct and mature identity." (p. 5; see also Albee, 1981; Elias, 1994; Sarason, 1974; Trickett, 1990). Finally, community psychology requires an emphasis on people's strengths. As Maurice Elias (1994) wrote, this field is "oriented toward wellness, competence, and prevention rather than remediation" (p. 300; see also Albee, 1981; Cowen, 2000; Cowen & Work, 1988; Rappaport, 1977).

The guiding principles of community psychology define the field. Research studies and interventions do not necessarily address each of these principles explicitly. One intervention might emphasize social change and a particular study might focus on diversity (see Figure 1.2). Nevertheless, community psychology endeavors should be conceptually consistent with all of the guidelines. A project emphasizing social change would not fall under the rubric of community psychology if it sought to label some cultures as deficient when compared to others. Although the five guiding principles of community psychology are pulled

Table 1.1   The Five Guiding Principles of Community Psychology

1. Research, theory, and practice develop within a value system.
2. One cannot understand an individual without also understanding the many-leveled social context in which that individual lives.
3. The perspectives of diverse groups, especially disenfranchised groups, must be honored.
4. The meaningful improvement of people's lives often requires social change.
5. Research, theory, and practice are best advanced through a strengths model rather than a deficit model.

apart and examined separately in this book, it is important to remember that they operate in concert.

This text draws an important distinction between guiding principles and orienting concepts. The guiding principles do not depend on a specific Zeitgeist. They are enduring tenets of the field. **Orienting concepts**, on the other hand, change as the field develops. They are focal concepts from which the field germinates and around which it coalesces (Cowen & Work, 1988; Seidman, 1988).

Orienting concepts put the guiding principles into action. They both inspire and organize our research and action at any point in time. For the field to grow, orienting concepts must change (Rappaport, 1981). After examining each guiding principle, this textbook examines the four major orienting concepts that have emerged in community psychology: stress and coping, prevention, empowerment, and resilience.

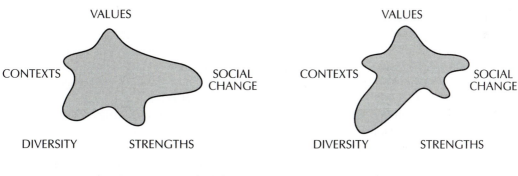

Project 1: Focus on Social Change   Project 2: Focus on Diversity

Figure 1.2

Research studies and intervention efforts emphasize different values.

DELINEATING THE FIELD

Establishing a new field requires "carving out an exclusive domain of expertise" (Trickett & Lustman, 1977, p. 192). We need to know what it is and how it differs from other areas of expertise. A review of the similarities and differences between community psychology and related fields may help delineate what we mean when we talk about community psychology.

COMMUNITY PSYCHOLOGY AND COMMUNITY MENTAL HEALTH

In the 1960s, the community mental health movement emerged in response to a new national policy toward people with mental challenges. The same social context that gave rise to this movement also inspired community psychology. Nevertheless, the Swampscott Conference participants called for a separation between community psychology and community mental health (Bennett, et al., 1966; see also Goodstein & Sandler, 1978; Rappaport, 1977). These psychologists identified problems with the community mental health movement, which was linked to a bureaucratic federal government. Although Kennedy had advocated prevention and the promotion of positive mental health in his Congressional address, the community mental health movement, in practice, concentrated on rehabilitation and the restoration of functioning. It sought to achieve the more easily measured goal of providing better mental health services. Swampscott Conference participants maintained that community psychology would indeed emphasize prevention and health promotion.

Leonard Goodstein and Irwin Sandler (1978) distinguished community mental health from community psychology in several additional ways. The community mental health movement targeted *catchment areas*—localities designated by geographic boundaries for which each community mental health center was responsible. Community psychology targeted contexts in a more holistic way, unconstrained by arbitrary physical borders. In addition, the community mental health movement fo-cused on the concerns of people with mental illness and developmental disabilities, while community psychology adopted a much broader interest in problems of living. Finally, community mental health sought to improve services for individuals, while community psychology emphasized systemic change and intervention in social settings.

CLINICAL PSYCHOLOGY AND COMMUNITY PSYCHOLOGY

Although the community mental health movement paved the way for community psychology, it had stronger disciplinary ties to clinical psychology. The founders of community psychology at Swampscott were all trained in clinical psychology and practicing clinicians. When Division 27 of APA was established a year later, the majority of charter members were clinical psychologists (Iscoe & Spielberger, 1977).

Certainly these pioneer clinicians were dissatisfied with clinical psychology, so dissatisfied that they established a new field. Nevertheless, their approach to problems had already been formed by their socialization as clinical psychologists. In the report of the Austin Conference on training in community psychology, Charles Spielberger and Ira Iscoe (1977) noted that although conference attendees embraced the philosophy of community psychology, they continued to deliver traditional clinical services. Seymour Sarason (1986) voiced similar concerns a decade later. He stated that the most important threat to community psychology was that all of its founders were traditionally trained clinical psychologists who, despite their desire to go beyond clinical psychology's focus on intrapsychic experience and personal deficits, could not free themselves from their training.

A tension has existed between clinical and community psychology; indeed, several of the guiding principles of community psychology are a reaction against traditional clinical psychology. Historically clinical psychology has focused on the individual in isolation, has sought to improve people's lives through individual adaptation, and has relied on a medical model that views clients as deficient and in need of help from experts. In contrast, community psychology considers the person in social context, advocates social change, and seeks to collaborate with citizens in order to enhance their competencies.

Questions of how clinical psychology and community psychology could best coexist first emerged at Swampscott and debate continued for many years. As Spielberger and Iscoe (1977) put it, "While many feel that divorce from clinical psychology is inevitable, others recommended marital counseling" (p. 324). Since that time there may have been a few trial separations but no divorce decree. Ties between the two fields remain strong. The Council of Program Directors in Community Research and Action surveyed US graduate programs offering a Ph.D. in community psychology in 1999 (Lounsbury, Skourtes, & Cantillon, 1999). They found eleven free-standing community psychology programs and eleven combined community–clinical programs. Ten programs combined community psychology with another discipline.

Certainly the 1960s changed the field of clinical psychology and distinctions between clinical and community psychology are not as sharp as they once were. For example, in 1964, a group of psychologists that included Carl Rogers and Abraham Maslow launched a new school of thought called **humanistic psychology,** which focused on human potential. Dominant themes were the exaltation of freedom and the belief in each person's ability to overcome external constraints (Kendler, 1987; Murray, 1988). These themes echo the call for freedom that permeated the broader society in the 1960s and coincide with the strength-based perspective of community psychology. As another example, feminist clinical psychology has developed since the 1960s and overlaps with community psychology. Laura Brown (1994) described the therapeutic relationship in feminist therapy as a "subversive dialogue" in which therapists help clients to uncover and resist patterns of behavior that result from injustices at different levels of the social environment.

Clinical psychology and community psychology remain distinct fields, however. Community psychology shares with clinical psychology a concern for an individual well-being and family relationships but generally attends more to the larger social context, especially in devising interventions. Clinical psychologists focus on the diagnosis and treatment of mental illness, while community psychologists more often consider problems of living more broadly —housing, employment, recreation, crime, poverty. Clinical psychology, unlike community psychology, retains ties to the medical model. It seems unlikely that community psychologists would ever, for example, lobby for the privilege of prescribing drugs.

SOCIAL PSYCHOLOGY AND COMMUNITY PSYCHOLOGY

Modern social psychology began at the turn of the twentieth century and gained momentum in the 1920s when the first influential textbook appeared. Social psychological research burgeoned in response to problems of the time, particularly the influx of immigrants from Eastern Europe. In the first half of the twentieth century, research and theory on applied issues predominated. Social psychologists studied such topics as relations among ethnic groups, the Great Depression, and leadership. After World War II, a shift to the laboratory occurred and by 1965, an experimental approach predominated (Pancer 1997). Social psychologists resisted perceptions of the field as "sloppy and softheaded" and reinvented itself in the model of the hard sciences (Berscheid, 1992). As aresult, social psychology flourished. Fewer than 600 studies in social psychology were published before 1954. During the 1960s, the number of published studies more than tripled. The explosion in research has been attributed to the field's adoption of an experimental approach (Zimbardo, 1988).

Community psychology and social psychology agree that most of us underestimate the power of social influences. In seeking to understand these influences, however, community psychology attends to forces in the outside world. Social psychology focuses on individual interpretations of the environment. Despite the qualifier of *social,* social psychology has been largely concerned with the intrapsychic life of individuals. This includes individuals' perceptions, thoughts, and feelings about the social world. Eliot Aronson and his colleagues (1997) began their influential *Social Psychology* textbook with the statement, "Social psychology is about what goes on in the hearts and minds of human beings" (p. 5). Community psychology, is on the other hand, more interested in the multilevel contexts that impact our hearts and minds.

In the tradition of experimental science, social psychology has tried "to identify universal properties of human nature that make everyone—regardless of social class or culture—susceptible to social influence" (Aronson, et al., 1997, p. 10). Community psychology maintains a greater interest in the particularities of social position and context, and values social action as much as theoretical understanding. The methods of the two fields reflect this different emphasis. Social psychologists are more inclined to observe volunteer research participants in a controlled laboratory setting. Community psychologists more often study people in real-world contexts.

Some social psychologists do study people in natural settings, and many use their findings as a basis for social interventions. The branch of social psychology called **applied social psychology** has much in common with community psychology, and the work of some applied social psychologists may be indistinguishable from the work of many community psychologists. Indeed Kurt Lewin, an important father of applied social psychology, is viewed by many community psychologists as an intellectual founder of that field as well (see Chapter Four). Nevertheless, the different historical backgrounds and resulting foci distinguish the two fields when viewed in their totality.

SOCIAL WORK AND COMMUNITY PSYCHOLOGY

The profession of social work emerged in the late nineteenth century. At the time, numerous social welfare agencies tried to address the prevalent ills, particularly poverty. Charity Organization Societies (COS) developed to deliver social services through private charities. Paid agents directed volunteer visitors who met with aid applicants and tried to locate resources within families before dispensing aid. As academic institutions became increasingly interested in social sciences, casework methods evolved, and volunteer charity workers were replaced with professional social workers who provided one-to-one services to people in need. Caseworkers were most often women who had pursued higher education and sought suitable niches after completing their studies. Social work became increasingly professionalized. It should be noted that welfare organizations of the nineteenth and early twentieth centuries were engaged in community organizing activities. The settlement house movement (see the Community Intervention box in Chapter Four) exemplified how social services and social advocacy could be combined. Nevertheless, social work grew primarily from the COS response to individual needs (Austin, 2000; Dubois & Krogsrud, 1996) and maintained a conviction that poverty could best be alleviated by promoting personal changes among poor people (Schorr, 1997).

Social work and community psychology have much in common. Both acknowledge the importance of values, focus on the interface of the individual and society, attend to societal forces, advocate for social justice, seek to enhance people's strengths, and pay special attention to marginalized people, including the poor and mentally ill (Dubois & Krogsrud, 1996; Rein, 1983). Social workers tend to intervene in the lives of individuals and families rather than at the organizational or community level, however. In addition, social work as a field is predominantly applied. Community psychology is more oriented toward research and theory. Social work is often characterized as a profession, whereas community psychology is a discipline. Although community psychologists also work in the field, practitioners are more likely to identify as community organizers, community developers, or consultants, rather than caseworkers. Community psychology is practiced, but community psychologists do not *have* practices.

ENVIRONMENTAL PSYCHOLOGY AND COMMUNITY PSYCHOLOGY

Environmental psychology is a smaller, less well-known field of study, but it overlaps with community psychology in many ways (e.g., Saegert & Winkel, 1990). Environmental psychology and community psychology both focus on settings with the goal of improving the quality of people's lives. Community psychology is more concerned, however, with the socially constructed environment and social problems. Popular areas of study include AIDS, homelessness, and community violence. The discipline's roots in clinical psychology orient it toward those aspects of the environment that are most often seen as affecting mental health. Environmental psychology, on the other hand, is more concerned with the physical environment—both the built and, to some extent, the natural environment. Areas of focus in environmental psychology include crowding, noise pollution, and resource conservation. Its roots in social psychology also result in a somewhat greater emphasis on experimental methods.

Both community psychology and environmental psychology value interdisciplinary approaches to research and practice. The different foci of the two fields lead practitioners to seek out different collaborators, however. Community psychologists often partner with other mental health practitioners, social service providers, educators, policymakers, and community activists. Environmental psychologists more often work with resource managers, community planners, and architects (Stokols & Altman, 1987). Certainly collaborations between community psychologists and environmental psychologists would also yield fruitful insights. A greater focus on the role of the physical environment in mental health could enhance community psychology's theories and strengthen our interventions.

THE ONGOING ISSUE OF DEFINITION

Although we can now delineate guiding principles and differentiate community psychology from other fields, its development has been marked by the struggle to define itself. New endeavors often generate a burst of activity without the conceptual clarity and supporting structures necessary to shape and direct that energy (Cowen 1973). The unbridled enthusiasm that accompanied the birth of community psychology was heightened by the optimism and excitement of the times and the sense that funding existed to support the new social programs and alternative settings community psychologists might design.

While questions of how best to define community psychology would be expected in the early formative years, such questions have lingered. Ten years after its birth, community psychology was still "under construction," as evidenced by the title of the Austin Conference report, *Community Psychology in Transition* (Iscoe, Bloom, & Spielberger, 1977). One chronicler of that anniversary conference was even more blunt. He described community psychology as "a 10-year-old creature who doesn't know where its mouth is, who can't comprehend what its eyes see, who spends its time working with skills acquired before it was born, and who on anniversary occasions looks down at its navel trying to decide to what species it belongs" (Reiff, 1977, p. 46). Twenty years after the birth of the field, calls for "the emergence of a conceptual center" continued (Sarason, 1986), and a review of community psychology in the 1990s described the tenets of the field as "still hazy after all these years" (Trickett, Watts, and Birman, 1993).

As a graduate student in community psychology in the late 1980s, I remember the angst my fellow students and I shared around how to explain our nebulous field to friends and relatives. When it became our university's turn to host the regional eco-community conference, we decided to stage a contest for the best concise definition of community psychology. We eagerly awaited entries, excited that we would finally have a clear and pithy definition to present to skeptical relatives at family reunions and college friends visiting from the well-structured worlds of law school and corporate America. But our contest did not have a clear winner. Worse than that, we didn't have a single entry. It seemed no one wanted to venture a definition of this elusive field.

One might argue that no field of study could capture its total essence in a sentence or two. It may be equally difficult to develop a concise and universally agreed-upon definition of social psychology, clinical psychology, or developmental psychology. These other fields, however, do not seem to dwell on the question of definition to the extent that community psychology has.

Perhaps the questioning of identity actually constitutes a core part of community psychology's identity. To some degree, community psychology is a metapsychology. It grew from self-scrutiny and self-consciousness. It depends on our willingness to undergo uncomfortable self-examination in the hopes of creating something new, something better. Several of the guiding principles require that we, as community psychologists, spy on ourselves. What are the unconscious values and assumptions that guide our work? How do biases in our thinking about disenfranchised groups affect our theory, research, and practice? Have we adequately guarded against the tendency to conceptualize phenomena in individual terms? Do our planned interventions promote social change or actually serve the status quo, a status quo that may benefit us professionally or financially?

Julian Rappaport (1984) proposed that the "raison d'etre for the field [of community psychology] has been, at least since Swampscott, a confrontation with accepted social and professional values" (p. 209). Community psychology's development was largely reactive—it was a rejection of the social conditions of the time and of the current practice of clinical psychology (see Reiff, 1977). Nevertheless, the search for more just, more humane, and more empowering social relationships requires a proactive stance. Community psychology needs visionaries. The ability to formulate new visions depends on our ability to question ourselves and our discipline. Community psychology is, may always be, and perhaps *should* be a field in flux. A number of years ago, Julian Rappaport (1981) proposed Rappaport's rule: "When most people agree with you, worry" (p. 3). A discipline comprised of people abiding by such a rule cannot help but challenge assumptions and keep questions about who we are and where we are going open for debate.

⌘ The Promise of Community Psychology: Look Both Ways— Historical and Future Perspectives

When I look back at the 1960s, I see a time of optimism—an exciting era of unbounded possibility. As a college graduate searching for a field of advanced study in 1984, community psychology drew me in because of its 1960s idealism, its belief in the goodness of people and the possibility of realizing greater human potential through social revolution. In their book, *A Social History of the Helping Professions*, Murray and Adeline Levine (1970) observed that "when the predominant ethos favors social change, people will be viewed as essentially good and the cause of problems seen in their living conditions" (p. 279). In the 1960s, we believed in the power of the people and looked to solve problems by changing the social environment. Social ills such as poverty and discrimination were seen as causes of mental distress and during the Kennedy and Johnson eras, citizens believed that a national commitment to eradicating such ills would lead to a more equitable and healthy society.

To paraphrase Bob Dylan, the times they have a changed. In the 1960s, there was growth in social awareness, an increase in the perceived importance of equality, and a decrease in concerns about a comfortable life and personal accomplishment. After 1971, however, a reversal occurred. Americans became increasingly preoccupied with the self and individual advancement (Rokeach & Ball-Rokeach, 1989). In the 1980s, excitement about federal initiatives waned. "Big Government" was construed as the problem, not the solution. Intrapsychic and biological explanations of societal ills returned to favor (e.g., Humphreys & Rappaport, 1993; Linney, 1990), and citizens became less and less likely to galvanize around social concerns (e.g., Putnam, 2000).

In the late 1970s and 1980s, some veterans of the sixties abandoned their ideals and were co-opted by models of individual success (and excess). Ex-yippee Jerry Rubin became the successful owner of the elite and trendy New York City disco Studio 54 where the beautiful people converged to see, be seen, and dance the night away. Other survivors of the 1960s looked back at that era with the impassive cynicism of disappointed dreamers who no longer believe in people's ability to change the world.

In 1990, Jean Ann Linney observed that community psychology had also become more complacent.

"The ardor, zeal, optimism, and commitment that once characterized the field has faded" (pp. 1–2). A change in Zeitgeist may be one explanation for this change, but Linney suggested a second possible reason: the life stage of the field. Community psychology entered its adulthood in the 1980s, and Linney posited that fields, like people, become more conservative with age.

No matter the cause, complacency and community psychology cannot walk hand in hand. In the words of Julian Rappaport (1981), those of us working toward change must "burn with fervor for some higher purpose. . . The most important contributions from community psychology have been fueled with a sense of urgency. To give up such urgency is to live with mediocrity" (p. 8).

The pull toward conservativism Mike Thompson/Copley News Service

This chapter argues for the importance of a historical perspective as one way of maintaining a sense of urgency. The demoralizing feeling that "the more things change, the more they stay the same" is exacerbated by the failure to learn from the past. Every phenomenon, including the social problems of interest to community psychologists (and community psychology itself) has a before-the-beginning. An understanding of past efforts can help us avoid past mistakes.

At the same time community psychology must embrace the future. Ours is a forward-looking field and the field's future lies with the next generation of scholars. College students fueled the freedom struggles of the 1960s; similarly, the enthusiasm, questioning attitudes, and vision of today's students can counteract tendencies toward cynicism, rigidity, and complacency. Research and theory in community psychology and other fields suggest the importance of student vision and activism as a vaccine against the increased conservatism and loss of innovation associated with socialization into professional life (Mcleod & Meyer, 1967; Sarason, 1974; Zeichner, 1983). Such urgency, enthusiasm, and idealism, though associated with youth, may also burn within older students returning to school in order to realize their deferred dreams or better accomplish their life goals.

Community psychologists have wisely established many structures to support student involvement. Students will find columns dedicated to student issues in *The Community Psychologist,* a listserv for student exchanges; roles for student editors in the *American Journal of Community Psychology;* annual dissertation awards; and scholarships to support student travel to Society for Community Research and Action conferences. By taking advantage of these and other opportunities for involvement, members of the next generation of community psychologists enhance their professional development while simultaneously enriching the field for us all.

Action Agenda

Preventing Burnout: Examining Expectations

Community psychology emphasizes the importance of prevention—we can eliminate or mitigate the effects of problems by intervening early. Thus, the first action agenda item calls upon us to anticipate a problem that may await future community psychologists. Many of us come to the field with dreams of changing the world. While excitement and vision are necessary, enthusiastic idealism can lead to problems that might best be addressed preventively.

In a book about the helping professions, Jerry Edelwich and Archie Brodsky (1980) proposed that a discrepancy between high expectations and actual accomplishments leads to **burnout**. Burnout is a sense of inefficacy that is accompanied by apathy, a loss of creativity, and resistance to change (Cherniss, 1980). Edelwich and Brodsky listed numerous expectations that pave the way for burnout in the helping professions. In reflection papers or small groups, discuss the five expectations listed below that are relevant to both novice helpers and novice activists. Which expectations are most likely to interfere with your own work? You might also talk about these expectations with practicing community psychologists and other experienced helpers/activists, or you could organize a panel discussion on this topic. What strategies counter the disappointments that stem from unfulfilled expectations?

- *Expectations for Improvement:* Novice helpers often expect that our work will decisively alter the course of people's lives. *Questions for reflection: Are we, as helpers, in control of the change process? If not us, who is? How can we keep our desire to make change in proper perspective? Might the desire to cause change come from our own needs, such as the need to feel useful or powerful? Might a focus on the need for other people to change lead us to avoid our own challenges? How would we know?*
- *Expectations of Simple Solutions:* Change is difficult and takes time. Although all of us can make important contributions, we will not discover some secret formula for ending intractable social problem such as homelessness or poverty. *Questions for reflection: Why is social change so difficult? If ending intractable social problems is unrealistic, what are our goals? How do we know that we are making progress?*
- *Expectations of Immediate Success:* Novice helpers often expect immediate and clear results from their efforts. We would like to see that a specific action we undertook led to a specific positive result, but this rarely occurs. *Questions for reflection: What does it mean to say that problems are multiply determined? Given the lack of immediate success, how do we get feedback about our effectiveness?*
- *Expectations of Client Motivation:* Novice helpers may devise plans for helping others and be disillusioned to find that the targets of our intervention do not always fit neatly into our plans. Not everyone wants to be helped or to be helped in the way that we want to help them. *Questions for reflection: Why might clients/client populations seem to lack motivation? What might you do in these situations?*
- *Expectations of Appreciation:* Many of us would like to feel that the people we seek to help are grateful for our efforts, but this is not always the case. *Questions for reflection: Why might client populations not feel or express appreciation? Is it possible that our helping efforts, even if well intentioned, are not beneficial? Why is a lack of appreciation so disappointing (or an expression of appreciation so welcome)?*

Although we can anticipate and limit the power of unfulfilled expectations, most helpers and activists sometimes feel overwhelmed and unable to make a difference. In their 1985 book *How Can I Help?*, Ram Dass and Paul Gorman (1985) remind us that:

> [B]urnout need not always be an enemy. If not a best friend, it can at least be a catalyst, even a guide, for the inner work, the work on ourselves, that is the foundation of all true service, and the only way, finally, to maintain energy and inspiration. If we can view the places where we encounter fatigue and guilt as clues and signposts of that inner work, our journey will not only go more lightly but go further, deeper. We will not simply survive. We will grow. (p. 211)

Before the Beginning

It may seem counterintuitive to think that our understanding of a phenomenon deepens when we examine events that happened *before* the phenomenon occurred. This exercise is designed show how an historical approach can enrich our understanding of individuals and groups.

Think about yourself: your personality traits, your interests, your beliefs about the world, your goals in life. Now consider how your family history may have shaped these characteristics. What features of your immediate family and more distant family have helped make you who you are? Have you ever been compared to a relative from another generation? What might account for intergenerational similarities? What important events in your parents' lives that occurred before you were born may have helped shape how they treated you and how you developed? Can you think of ways in which events in your grandparents' lives might continue to affect you? Now look beyond the family level to society more broadly. What was happening in the world *before* you were born that helped determine who you are today? How might you be different if important historical events had not occurred?

Now think about a group to which you belong: your workplace, a social club, the college you attend. Think about the characteristics of this group—how would you describe it to someone unfamiliar with it? What is this setting's personality? How do you think the group came to have its characteristics? What events happened *before* the group's current members joined that affect how the group operates today? Think about important individuals in the history of the group and the dynamics at play when the group was first founded. What aspects of the before-the-beginning context continue to reverberate in the group's structure, mission, membership, etc.?

Learning from the Past: Today's Solutions, Tomorrow's Problems

Humanitarian concern for people with mental illnesses led to the building of public psychiatric hospitals. When these hospitals were resoundingly denounced in the 1960s, little attention was paid to the fact that these institutions had originally grown from a desire to provide better care for mentally ill people. Many humanitarians of the 1960s advocated deinstitutionalization, and a large number of mentally ill people who left the hospitals took up residence in jails and city streets. Deinstitutionalization was blamed for subsequent social ills, notably the rise in homelessness.

As we marshal support against a particular social situation, our thinking can become one-sided. We fail to see how today's problems result from yesterday's solutions. Nor do we anticipate how today's solutions will usher in tomorrow's problems. The following exercise is designed to point out the unintended consequences that may result from our attempts to address important social problems ahistorically.

Think of a social problem of concern to you. What previous attempts at solving this problem have been tried? Why does the problem persist nonetheless? Are there any benefits (to individual, families, communities, the country) of *maintaining* the status quo with regard to the problem? In what ways might we *need* this problem? What new problems might arise from "solving" this problem? For example, although most would agree that we should end school drop out, the ramifications are not purely positive. Keeping students in school who do not wish to be there disrupts the learning of other students and diverts resources from them as school personnel attend to pressing behavior problems. At a more distal level, where would this country be without a large pool of unskilled labor?

Given the insights gleaned from your exploration of past efforts and future consequences, which of your solutions seem most promising and why? What would be a first step toward that solution? Is this a step you might take individually or as a class?

Key Terms

American Psychological Association (APA)

applied social psychology

before the beginning

Biennial Conference on Community Research and Action

burnout

community mental health movement

consciousness-raising groups

deinstitutionalization

Division 27

guiding principles

humanistic psychology

myth of mental illness

orienting concepts

Society for Community Research and Action (SCRA)

Swampscott Conference

Zeitgeist

Chapter 2

Community Psychologists: Who We Are and What We Do

⌘ **Introduction**

Chapter One described the field of community psychology: where it came from and what it is. Now let's look at the people in the field—who we are and what we do. Community psychologists assume a plethora of different roles. We are organizers, consultants, teachers, program directors, politicians, educators, co-learners, service deliverers, writers, evaluators, activists, mediators, analysts, fundraisers, facilitators, administrators, managers, planners, documenters/historians, workshop leaders, researchers, advocates, policymakers, technical assistants, ambassadors, problem solvers, healers, visionaries, and troublemakers. Community psychologists perform these roles in a wide variety of settings. We work in and with schools, hospitals, correctional facilities, mental health centers, research institutes, businesses, colleges and universities, non-profit agencies, grassroots organizations, neighborhood associations, advocacy groups, and governmental offices at the local, state, and federal level. Despite this vast array of job descriptions and environments, there are commonalities that unite us all.

⌘ Who Are Community Psychologists?

Community psychologists are united by our shared belief in the tenets of the field. Our guiding principles attract people with certain qualities, and our training and experiences strengthen these qualities. Several community psychologists have specified the characteristics necessary for work in our field, most notably, James Kelly.

KELLY'S QUALITIES FOR THE COMMUNITY PSYCHOLOGIST

In 1971, when community psychology was a young and burgeoning field, James Kelly outlined seven important qualities for the community psychologist. Since that time, others have constructed lists of their own (e.g., Iscoe, 1997; Wolff, 1987). Kelly's original seven qualities and one additional quality are described below.

CLEARLY IDENTIFIED COMPETENCE

Kelly argued that in order to solve pressing problems, a community psychologist must have a recognizable area of competence. He saw this as the key attribute, the quality on which all other qualities built. Although some area of competence is necessary, the exact nature of the competence can vary. In 1971 Kelly's list of possible competencies included the abilities to be therapeutic with individuals, to organize a community service, to study a complex social problem, or to create a sense of community. A list of competencies for community psychologists compiled today might differ from this original list. Therapy with individuals appears less often in the

———————— ◎ ————————

In the arena of human life the honors and rewards fall to those who show their good qualities in action.

—Aristotle

job descriptions of community psychologists, while the analytical competence of a researcher has gained importance.

Most people trained as community psychologists conduct research as part of their postgraduate work (Nemec, Hungerford, Hutchings, & Huygens, 2000; O'Donnell & Ferrari, 2000). One study followed graduates from three types of academic programs: community-clinical psychology; applied social psychology; and community psychology (Feis, Mavis, Weth, & Davidson, 1990). The clinical psychology programs focused on imparting human service skills, and program graduates found jobs in which they provided direct services to clients. Applied social psychology programs centered on developing administrative and organizational skills, and graduates tended to find consulting jobs. Graduates of community psychology programs most often obtained jobs in which they conducted research.

The most obvious components of research competence are knowledge about methodology and statistics. All researchers need to know how to design studies, collect data, and analyze information. Equally important to community psychologists, however, is an understanding of the *context* of research. In reviewing lessons learned as researchers in the field, Geoffrey Nelson (1998) and his colleagues observed that their "notions of what it means to be a good researcher have changed from an emphasis on expertise in research design and measurement to more of an emphasis on the interpersonal and political dynamics of the research process" (p. 894).

Research is not the only competency important to community psychologists today. A recent study of community psychology program graduates cited the importance of written and oral skills, since many jobs required reports and presentations (Nemec, et al., 2000). Program graduates also reported using their organizing and consultation skills. Perhaps most importantly, the unique perspective of community psychology was viewed as a competence in and of itself (see also O'Donnell & Ferrari, 2000). The principles of the field allowed community psychologists to approach problems from multilevel, interdisciplinary, and strengths-based perspectives, a skill valued by numerous employers.

CREATING AN ECO-IDENTITY

Kelly believed that community psychologists must identify with the communities in which they work. This means creating an **eco-identity** by stepping out of one's professional role and becoming emotionally involved in the social setting. The community psychologist Julia Green Brody recognized the importance of an eco-identity in her work for Texas Agriculture Commissioner Jim Hightower. When she began her work, the U.S. Department of Energy was deciding which of nine sites to choose as the locale for a nuclear waste depository. Two sites in Texas were among the final nine. Brody's job was to ensure that the dump would not be located in either of the two Texas panhandle counties that produced 10 billion bushels of wheat and a half billion head of cattle each year.

In her work, Brody (1986) came into frequent contact with farmers whose livelihood depended on beef. She recounted the story of a representative from the U.S. Department of Energy who declared his vegetarianism to an audience of ranchers. She wrote:

> I am a vegetarian, too. But when I go to Tulia, I eat at K-Bob's Steakhouse. . . You do not have to be a community psychologist to know that it is unsafe to tell a roomful of cattleman that you are a vegetarian. But it does help to have a conscious sense that learning about the community where you work is more than a common courtesy: It's part of doing your job well. (p. 142)

Brody, like other community psychologists, followed the sage advice of her teacher, Ira Iscoe: "If you want to be invited in, be prepared to share the food" (Brody, 1986, p. 142).

According to Kelly, creating an eco-identity involves caring enough about the community to explore all its sectors: the interrelationships among subcommunities, the politics of the area, the needs and resources of different physical localities.

Community psychologists need "to sense the range of behavior, styles of life, and conflicts, without becoming immune to the diversity and seeing only chaos" (Kelly, 1971, p. 900). The ability to recognize and appreciate the community's diversity constitutes Kelly's third key quality.

TOLERANCE/APPRECIATION OF DIVERSITY

In 1971 Kelly cited the importance of honoring a community's diversity, although in today's language the term *appreciation* would replace his word *tolerance*. For community psychologists, appreciating diversity means recognizing and responding to various **stakeholders** in the community—the legislators, politicians, community leaders, citizens, and others who have an investment in the issue at hand. These stakeholders often have conflicting perspectives that stem not only from social roles (e.g., agency director versus service recipient) but also from **social position.** Social position refers to those salient aspects of identity, such as race, gender, and socioeconomic status, along which a given society is stratified (e.g. García Coll, Lamberty, Jenkins, McAdoo, Crnic, Wasik, & Vásquez García, 1996). These two sources of diversity, social role and social position, are confounded. The targets of social programs often occupy subordinate social positions (e.g. poor, ethnic minority), while the people with the most decision-making power tend occupy dominant social positions (e.g. White, financially secure, male).

Kelly (1971) asserted that appreciating diversity means not only acknowledging a community's heterogeneity, but also searching out what these differences mean. This exploration should be guided by the maxim "There is something valid in each example, yet something incomplete in all of them" (p. 900). Differences among people easily lead to misunderstandings, breakdowns in communication, and entrenchment in opposing camps. Too often the potential for diverse perspectives to expand our understanding of an issue remains unrealized.

Consider, for example, the struggle for women to overcome gender-based oppression. Historically, many women have been left out of the women's movement. In 1851 attendees of a women's convention in Akron, Ohio, tried to keep the ex-slave Sojourner Truth from speaking for fear that the women's movement would lose credibility if confused with the abolition movement. Truth spoke all the same and changed the terms of the debate on women's rights when she proclaimed, "Nobody ever helps me into carriages, or over mud-puddles, or gives me any best place! And ain't I a woman? I could work as much and eat as much as a man—when I could get it—and bear the lash as well! Ain't I a woman?" (Schneir, 1972, p. 94–95). Similarly, leaders of the women's movement in the 1960s silenced and disavowed lesbians at the movement's vanguard for fear that alignment with gay rights would impede the progress of the women's movement (Marotta, 1981). Poor women have also remained on the fringes of the modern women's movement.

Nevertheless, the perspectives of diverse women add to the arsenal of those battling for women's equality. Gender oppression hurts *everyone*. As Sojourner Truth proclaimed, equal rights for women are about much more than chivalrous behavior. The concerns highlighted by Black women's experiences also merit consideration (see also Lorde, 1984), and lesbian activists know that rigid gender roles contribute to both women's oppression and gay oppression (Pharr, 1988). Johnnie Tillmon, an early leader of the welfare rights movement declared, "Welfare is a women's issue," since many "women are one man away from welfare" (West, 1990, p. 149). More recent research on the disproportionate number of female-headed households living in poverty and the declines in income following divorce gives credibility to Tillmon's assertion (e.g., Sherman, Amey, Duffield, Ebb, & Weinstein, 1998).

The perspective of any one group is limited, and consideration of multiple viewpoints allows insights that would not be possible otherwise. Indeed, men have recently recognized the ways their own development has been compromised by social constructions of gender (Garbarino, 1999; Levant & Pollack, 1997; Pollack, 1998; Silverstein, & Rashbaum, 1994). The social problems of interest to community psychologists are complex and multifaceted. The

more community psychologists honor diverse voices, the more complete our understanding.

COPING EFFECTIVELY WITH VARIED RESOURCES

A diversity of people means a diversity of resources. One job of the community psychologist is to assess and mobilize the resources available to tackle problems of interest. By searching out the skills and talents of community members and organizations and pointing out the relevance of these resources to the challenges at hand, the community psychologist promotes innovative ways of addressing entrenched problems.

Interventions have traditionally focused on deficits rather than strengths. They have sought to correct what went wrong rather than build on what went right. Community psychologists take a different tack. We seek to enhance capacities by identifying and supporting individual and community assets. All communities have untapped resources. For example, community psychologists might develop new opportunities for involvement that utilize senior citizens, youth, artists, people with disabilities, and members of other marginalized groups whose capacity to contribute to the social good is underappreciated (Kretzmann & McKnight, 1993). In addition, to creating new roles, existing roles might be reinforced. Emory Cowen (1982) tried to enhance community resources by improving the helping capabilities of "informal" or "natural" helpers such as bartenders and hairdressers (see Classic Research box on p. 33).

In addition to people, local organizations and institutions (e.g. religious groups, libraries, schools) may also constitute untapped resources. For example, in the era of megabookstores and the internet, public libraries across the country have become more essential to neighborhoods by shifting away from strictly scholarly pursuits toward functions once associated with community centers and community colleges. Some libraries now offer meeting places, lectures, and a variety of classes, from aerobics for older adults to English classes for immigrants (Murphy, 2001). As another example, Edward Zigler,

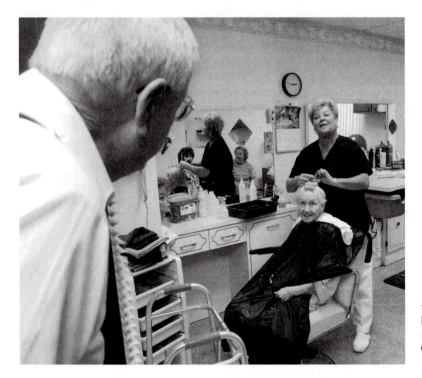

"Natural helpers," such as hairdressers, often play important roles in the lives of their clients. *Kevin Seifert/ Durham Herald Sun.*

a principal architect of Head Start, proposed the concept of *21st Century Schools*. He suggested that school buildings could serve as hubs for comprehensive and affordable family support services, such as preschool child care, before- and after-school care for older children, information and referral services for families, and support and training for child care providers (Zigler & Finn-Stevenson, 1999; see also New York City's Beacon schools reported in Schorr, 1997).

COMMITMENT TO RISK-TAKING

Community psychologists seek to create change. Change entails risk. First and foremost is the risk of failure. Kelly advised that a high probability of "failure" should not act as a deterrent because "losing" often allows for invaluable learning opportunities. N. Dickon Reppucci and four colleagues demonstrated the truth of this notion in a chapter entitled

We Bombed in Mountville: Lessons Learned in Consultation to a Correctional Facility for Adolescent Offenders (1973). This "failed" intervention resulted in much new learning. It offered the authors numerous insights into the dynamics of community consultation (some of which will be examined later in this chapter). It also led four of the five clinically trained consultants to pursue careers in a new field: community psychology.

Not only do challenges to change efforts often fail, success brings new risks as counterforces seek to resist changes in the status quo. The applied community psychologist Thomas Wolff found this out when he taught a course on planned organizational change strategies to university students. The training program enjoyed considerable success, and one year a number of campus activists enrolled, each with a goal she or he hoped to achieve. The president of Student Government wanted to turn that organization into a union. The leader of the

📄 CLASSIC RESEARCH

Emory Cowen
Helping Helpers to Help

As the 1950s gave way to the 1960s, three insights about the nature of mental health service delivery led to new ways of thinking about how to help. First, there was a growing awareness that professional helpers could not be trained in numbers sufficient to meet the demands for help (e.g. Albee, 1959). Second, only a small percentage of people in need of mental health services ever sought help from mental health professionals (Joint Commission on Mental Illness and Health, 1961). Finally, doubt existed as to whether trained professionals were even capable of helping people. The efficacy of the most prestigious techniques of the time remained unproven (Eysenck, 1961), and some treatments, particularly hospitalization, seemed to make clients *less* able to function in society (Goffman, 1961).

Community psychologists elaborated on these early findings. Some warned that professional helping relationships exacerbated problems by fostering the help-seekers' dependence on expert helpers (e.g. Tyler, Pargament, & Gatz, 1983). Some conducted research to show that informal helpers may be as effective, perhaps even more effective, than professional helpers (e.g. Durlak, 1979. See Christensen & Jacobson, 1994 for a more recent review, and Halpern, 2000 for a dissenting view). One of the leaders in community psychology, Emory Cowen, conducted a classic study entitled, *Help Is Where You Find It* (1982), to explore the nature and extent of nonprofessional helping channels. He studied four informal help-givers: hairdressers, bartenders, divorce lawyers, and industrial supervisors.

As one might expect, the nature of the assistance given by these informal helpers differed in systematic ways. The numbers of people helped varied substantially across categories of helpers. On average, divorce lawyers assisted 20 clients each year, while hairdressers saw 55 customers per week, and bartenders served an impressive 104 patrons in a day. The types of problems raised by clients also varied. Hairdressers most often heard about clients' difficulties with their children. Bartenders and supervisors most often heard about job problems. Divorce lawyers heard about problems with spouses. In addition, the help-givers responded in different ways. Hairdressers and bartenders listened, offered support and sympathy, or tried to be light-hearted. Lawyers asked questions, gave advice, and pointed out the consequences of bad ideas.

Cowen found that helpers from these four groups enjoyed giving assistance, felt reasonably competent in the help-giving role, and saw help-giving as part of their job. Nevertheless, they wanted to improve their ability to help. Thus, Cowen and his colleagues organized ten workshops on such topics as listening and attending skills, and referral resources and mechanisms.

Cowen attempted to use his professional competencies to build community strengths. Although he found that his workshops changed the ways in which the helpers offered assistance, the larger question of whether they became more or less helpful remained unanswered. When Cowen conducted his groundbreaking study, community psychologists were less aware of the potential for interventions to have unintended negative consequences. Today, community psychologists would likely evaluate the effectiveness of such an intervention.

Black Studies Action Office hoped to double the Office's budget. The head of the Women's Center sought to effect several campus-wide changes. The university administration unexpectedly canceled Wolff's course. Upon hearing the news, Wolff reported regaining perspective by rereading Kelly's article on the qualities of the community psychologist (Wolff, 1987). A commitment to risk-taking means expecting some measure of opposition—indeed it can be a testament to one's effectiveness.

METABOLIC BALANCE OF PATIENCE AND ZEAL

Community psychologists are concerned about pressing social problems. As described in Chapter One, a sense of urgency fuels many of our activities. At the same time, entrenched problems are not easily solved and perhaps can never be solved once and for all (Sarason, 1978). The status quo is perpetuated by ingrained ways of thinking and behaving at all levels of society, including individual minds, institutional practices, and cultural worldviews.

Thus, the importance of both patience and zeal. Leonard Jason reported sitting on the Chicago Lung Association's Smoking and Health Committee for three years, waiting patiently for the right opportunity to launch a media-based smoking cessation project (Jason, 1998). Balancing patience and zeal means attending to timing, persevering in the face of obstacles, and maintaining a realistic sense of how much time and energy is required to make a difference. Community psychologists need to remember long-term goals while working to achieve short-term objectives Although not a community psychologist per se, Wallace Lambert (1992) exemplifies a researcher balancing patience and zeal, as the following example shows.

In the late 1950s, French speakers comprised 80% of the population of Quebec, but English speakers owned most of the businesses. Thus, a condition of "one-way bilingualism" existed. Success required that French speakers know English, but English speakers did not need to know French. While riding on a bus in the winter of 1958 Lambert overheard a conversation between two anglophones in which they disparaged the francophones who were laughing behind them. Lambert hypothesized that the English speakers feared that the francophones, whom they could not understand, were laughing at them. This hypothesis led to a thirty-year research program geared toward social change.

In his initial studies, Lambert found that when unseen bilinguals spoke English, they were rated as taller, better looking, more intelligent, more dependable, kinder, and more ambitious than when these same bilinguals spoke French. Interestingly, French Canadians evaluated the French speakers even *more* negatively than the English Canadians did (see the section in Chapter Six entitled *Awakening to Injustice* for a discussion of internalized oppression). Lambert challenged the widespread assumptions of inferiority by demonstrating that bilingualism actually corresponded with an increased proficiency in one's first language, higher school achievement, and greater facility in concept formation.

Lambert and his colleagues used this information to launch a social experiment. In collaboration with a group of English Canadian parents who wanted their children to gain the academic edge bilingualism offered, they instituted an immersion language program led by teachers who spoke only French. During the next twenty-five years, Lambert and his colleagues demonstrated the efficacy of these programs. Not only did the English Canadian students learn a second language, they demonstrated an increase in IQ scores, more proficiency on measures of divergent thinking, and greater competence in their first language (English, in this case). Perhaps most importantly, immersion students developed a deeper appreciation and affection for French Canadians. They had learned about French Canadian culture from their teachers, and their ability to speak French afforded them the opportunity to interact with francophones. If they overheard French speakers laughing on a bus, they did not need to hypothesize about the reasons for laughter. These English Canadian students could understand what the francophones were saying and could join them in conversation.

GIVING AWAY THE BYLINE

Kelly asserted that the hallmark of a community psychologist is her or his satisfaction in realizing the six qualities outlined above. He contended that our main goal should be to foster the development of the people and communities with whom we work. Visibility and congratulations for our accomplishments should not be motivators. Indeed, they are counter-productive to the nonhierarchical, collaborative relationships needed for the tasks at hand. Kelly stated that if one's professional vanity required recognition and appreciation, short-term pseudo-solutions would be attractive and real change impossible. The reward of community psychology is the improvement of the community, not the gratitude of community members (Kelly, 1971; see also Iscoe, 1974).

One challenge for community psychologists is how to develop community resources without fostering dependence. We have a competence to bring but do not want to be solely responsible for community change. The notion of **planned obsolescence** offers a solution. In the business world, planned obsolescence means sustaining a market for one's products by ensuring that they do not last too long—designing cars to break down upon reaching the 100,000 mile mark, for example, even when technology exists to build engines that last much longer. In community psychology, the goal of planned obsolescence is just the opposite—we plan our *own* obsolescence. We find ways of ensuring that the competence we bring to (or bring out of) any community can eventually be realized by that community alone. And then we move on.

Kelly recognized that an orientation toward giving away the byline runs counter to the reward systems of the universities and colleges where many community psychologists work. Indeed, several of the qualities outlined by Kelly do not fit into academic merit systems. Community efforts require time as settings must be entered carefully, eco-identities forged slowly, and work conducted in a collaborative, and therefore time-consuming fashion. This is inconsistent with university requirements for individual achievement in the form of multiple publications in academic journals, large research grants, and national reputations.

Since Kelly's article, the need to remodel the ivory tower has been recognized by many. As one example, the Society for the Teaching of Psychology's Task Force on Defining Scholarship in Psychology (1998) recommended a definition of scholarship that extends beyond the production of original research. They noted the importance of integrating knowledge into a larger body of concepts and facts, and translating knowledge for legal, popular, and community audiences (see also Boyer, 1990; Gray, Froh, & Diamond, 1992). Community psychologists, led by Kelly, recognized the need for a redefinition of scholarship years ago. Kelly wrote that the community should be the final judge of what is 'good,' and that effective community workers are rewarded by being "invited to work on still tougher problems" (Kelly, 1971, p. 903).

AN ADDITIONAL QUALITY: TOLERANCE FOR AMBIGUITY

One additional characteristic has frequently appeared as a quality for community psychologists since Kelly constructed his list in 1971. I first heard about this quality in 1986. As a first year graduate student, I was overcome with confusion. I wasn't sure how best to become a community psychologist. There seemed to be an overabundance of possible research topics for my master's thesis, a myriad of community concerns to tackle in my fieldwork, and countless courses in related disciplines that would enrich my education. Which would be the best path, and how would I know? During a particularly angst-filled meeting, my mentor, N. Dickon Reppucci, conveyed this memorable piece of advice: "Jennifer, if you want to be a community psychologist, you have to have a tolerance for ambiguity" (see also Bond, 1999; Iscoe, 1997).

My appreciation for the wisdom of these words increased in the years that followed. As Dick forewarned, I have conducted numerous job searches and have never once come across an employer looking for community psychologist. Only a handful of colleagues have even heard of the field.

Many other community psychologists echo this experience. After using community psychology principles in a mental health agency for over a decade, John Morgan (2000) reported that "few of my colleagues in the agency or the community know that I am a 'community psychologist'; fewer still would know what one was" (p. 745). Similarly, Judith Meyers (2000) observed that "Nowhere, neither in my job description nor in my everyday work in various policy positions from 1986 through 1989, have I been identified as a community psychologist" (p. 761).

Community psychologists redefine themselves in accordance with the demands of each new position. And there may be many. One study of 38 community psychology program graduates found that only 7 people had worked in a single job, and 6 of these had graduated just one year prior. Most study respondents spent only one to three years in each position, and several juggled multiple part-time jobs or contracts at the same time (Nemec, et al., 2000). Community psychologists, especially those affiliated primarily with applied settings, spend their careers "carving out jobs, incomes, and support systems in order to follow a belief in the value of applied community psychology" (Wolff, 2000, p. 772). When we tolerate ambiguity we can (in our more reflective moments) see the lack of prescribed roles as an opportunity to affirm the value of community psychology in unlimited ways.

The routes to becoming a community psychologist are varied. After graduation, we rarely encounter employers looking specifically for community psychologists. In addition, throughout our careers we will likely walk the line between academia and practice, science and values. Perhaps most importantly, the community problems on which we work are often entrenched and multifaceted. The process of change is unpredictable, and change efforts do not always lead in a direct way to observable results. For all of these reasons, tolerance for ambiguity is a key characteristic of community psychologists.

⌘ What Do Community Psychologists Do?

So now we have some sense of who community psychologists are—key qualities that help us to do our work. Next, let's look at what this work consists of.

The work of community psychologists bridges the domains of scientific research (conducted primarily in academic settings) and applied practice (conducted primarily in the field). Academia and practice have traditionally been construed as different, even diametrically opposed, domains. Indeed one definition of *academic* is "having no practical or useful significance" (Merriam-Webster, 2000). This dichotomy, like all dichotomies, is false. Science is not removed from the "real world." The questions, methods, and findings of research are all shaped by the surrounding context, and the research process is itself an intervention, regardless of whether or not the researcher intends to effect changes (Swift, 1990). Similarly, practitioners continually gather evidence about whether or not their actions led to the desired results and elaborate their theories of why things happen as they gather evidence.

For community psychologists, research and practice are inextricably linked (e.g. Galano, 1996). Early in community psychology's history, Richard Price and Cary Cherniss (1977) delineated four characteristics of community research, each of which emphasizes the link between research and practice. They posited that community research should 1) be stimulated by community needs, 2) drive action, 3) result in products that are useful to the community—a new program or training manual rather than publication in an esoteric journal or a new line on the researcher's vitae, and 4) be evaluated to ensure that good intentions did indeed lead to positive effects. Several years later, Irma Serrano-García (1984, 1990) proposed an Intervention within research model that viewed the processes of research and intervention as simultaneous and interdependent, though also distinguishable. This model recognizes participants as integral to the research process and views the researcher/intervener as needing competencies not only in research, but also in community organizing and political analysis.

Although community psychology brings academia and practice together, tensions remain. One tension for academic community psychologists is the often-lamented inverse relationship between rigor and social relevance—as one increases, the other decreases (e.g., Fawcett, 1991; Lounsbury, Leader, Meares, & Cook, 1980; Novaco & Monahan, 1980). Robert Reiff proposed that the only distinction between community psychologists and citizens seeking change is that the "professionals" attempt to bring greater order into change efforts (1977; see also Kelly, 1970). This order can be burdensome as community researchers struggle to balance a commitment to the scientific methods with a desire to effect change. Attempts to study phenomena rigorously may lead academic psychologists to ask small questions, focus on methodological details, and delay action.

A challenge for community practitioners, on the other hand, is to maintain ties with a profession that seems oriented toward science and research. A review of the published literature on community psychology would likely lead to the conclusion that the field is primarily an academic one. Applied community psychologists do not always see themselves and their concerns reflected in the field's formal institutions and publications (Wolff, 2000). In a study designed to elucidate the differences between academic and nonacademic community psychologists, Maurice Elias and his colleagues identified "exemplary" community psychologists whose work embodied significant elements of the field's paradigm. These "exemplars" were nearly all affiliated primarily with academic settings (Elias et al., 1984).

One reason for the imbalance in representations of academic and applied perspectives may relate to time. For academics, reflection and writing are part of the scholarship required in research settings, while practitioners may be too busy *doing* community psychology to write about it. Regardless of the reasons, the "promise of community psychology is half filled without defined practices" (Chavis, 1993, p. 179). Academic community psychologists who lead the field's institutions have tried to right this imbalance, but it is difficult to transcend one's own perspective. Before the 2001 SCRA Biennial Conference, several postings on the community psychology listserv promoted sessions focusing on nonacademic perspectives. Gloria Levin caused a stir when she objected to the very use of the term "NONacademic" to describe community psychology practitioners. How would academics feel, she asked, if they were always referred to as "NONpractitioners" (Levin, June 6, 2001)?

Although academic psychologists work to improve communities and practitioners conduct research and develop theory, researchers and practitioners have different priorities, face different challenges, and receive different rewards. In the next section we will look at the work of community psychology through the lens afforded by an academic perspective and then turn to a more explicit examination of practice. The academic perspective is better documented in the community psychology literature on which this textbook is based. Thus, I will outline issues that flow from the five guiding principles that will frame the discussion of research that occurs in subsequent chapters. I will also review two forums through which academic researchers often engage in practice. The practice section will examine three important roles for applied community psychologists.

THE ACADEMIC SIDE OF COMMUNITY PSYCHOLOGY

Psychology, like other sciences, rests on the tradition of **logical positivism**. This tradition views knowledge as grounded in objective, incontrovertible facts that accumulate through scientifically rigorous study. In these studies, hypotheses about how the world works are generated, tested, and either retained or rejected based on their ability to survive experimental tests. The logical positivist tradition presents challenges to each of the five guiding principles of community psychology.

RESEARCH AND THE GUIDING PRINCIPLES

Table 2.1 summarizes characteristics of community research that flow from the guiding principles. Each principle has important implications for academic psychology, which inherits notions of scientific integrity from a logical positivist tradition.

Research and the Importance of Values. The logical positivist tradition attempts to eliminate biases, which are construed as "highly personal and unreasoned distortions of judgment" (Merriam-Webster, 2000). In psychology, an agreed-upon set

Table 2.1   How Community Psychology's Guiding Principles Affect Research

Guiding Principle	Challenge to Traditional Research
VALUES: Knowledge develops within a value system.	Research is not objective and value free.
CONTEXT: Individuals are embedded in a many-leveled social context.	Research should capture processes that occur beyond the level of the individual.
DIVERSITY: The voices of diverse groups must be honored.	Researchers should be culturally sensitive.
SOCIAL CHANGE: People's lives should be improved through social change efforts.	Research should not simply add to the body of scientific knowledge, but be socially useful.
PEOPLE'S STRENGTHS: The strengths of those we seek to help should be emphasized rather than their deficits.	Respect for people's competence should be reflected in what we study and how we study it.

of scientific procedures has developed to remove personal biases from the process of inquiry. For example, scientists try to establish **reliability**, which means that findings from one study can and should be replicated in other studies that different researchers conduct at different times with different people.

The objective scientific observer who removes himself or herself from the fact-finding process has long been an ideal in science. In the modern era, however, even the "hard" science of physics has found that the observer inevitably affects the process of inquiry (as described in Heisenberg's uncertainty principle). Few contemporary philosophers of science believe that scientific endeavors can exist untouched by value-laden personal, political, and social forces (e.g., Kane, 1998). Indeed, researcher bias has become a topic of study in and of itself (e.g., MacCoun, 1998).

Some scholars suggest that the impartial observer is not only impossible, but undesirable as well. Research is, after all, a human endeavor. Does our humanity weaken our science? Is our ability to understand reality necessarily enhanced by a stance that is impersonal, reasoned, dispassionate, and

distant? Parker J. Palmer (1998) warned that the effort to be objective prevents us from truly relating to the world around us. "When we distance ourselves from something, it becomes an object; when it becomes an object, it no longer has life; when it is lifeless, it cannot touch or transform us. . ." (pp. 51–52).

Despite advances in the philosophy of science, positivism remains in many ways the unspoken gold standard for good science. Ironically, even though logical positivism rejects the importance of values, its elevation to the purest and best way of knowing is itself a value that can be questioned... and rejected. Often, this questioning does not occur. The "influence [of logical positivism] is so pervasive as to be unrecognized by those enmeshed in its web of meaning" (Moke & Bohan, 1992, p. 7). Community psychologists, too, get caught in the web of logical positivism, and despite our guiding principles, most of our research studies have embodied this approach (Speer, Dey, Griggs, Gbson, Lubin, & Hughey, 1992; Tolan, Chertok, Keys, & Jason, 1990; Walsh, 1987).

At the same time, Ana Marie Cauce (1990) warned against "logical positivism bashing," which results in the summary dismissal of everything associated with this tradition (p. 205). Under the rubric of community psychology there is room to for many research approaches, including logical positivism (see also Dokecki, 1992). Nevertheless, researchers in this tradition must still recognize that values determine what is studied, how it is studied, and how results are interpreted.

David Chavis and his colleagues (1983) suggested that one mechanism for remaining aware of and accountable for our values is to collaborate with the community members who are consumers of our research. The myth of neutral objectivity is quickly dispelled as researchers "clarify their expectations, values, and priorities with the nonscientific community. Conflicts may arise, but they are conflicts not between science and nonscience but between alternative values, priorities, and ways of problem solving" (1983, p. 425).

Research and the Context Beyond the Individual. The logical positivist tradition views science as value free. It also assumes that context does not matter (Moke & Bohan, 1992). The goal of science is to isolate single causes with universal effects. If *A* then *B*. Always. Everywhere. With everyone. To community psychologists, however, the context is all important. We do not believe that we can understand individuals independent of their multilevel environments.

In order to isolate single causes with universal effects, the positivist tradition depends on experimental control. The scientist seeks to demonstrate that the manipulation of one variable of interest (the **independent variable**) causes the predicted effects on another variable of interest (the **dependent variable**). All extraneous factors are **confounding variables** that must be nullified through experimental design or statistical analysis. Attempts to gain control have led many researchers into the laboratory to conduct elegantly designed studies.

The developmental psychologist Urie Bronfenbrenner, who has had a large impact on community psychology (see Chapter Four section entitled *Bronfenbrenner's Ecological Model*) warned against the scientific practice of putting research subjects in unfamiliar and artificial situations for exceedingly short periods of times in order to elicit unusual behaviors. He questioned whether results obtained under such controlled and contrived conditions could be generalized to people in normal environments. He coined the term **ecological validity** to indicate the extent to which the research environment contained properties relevant to the real-world settings that the experimenter hoped to elucidate (Bronfenbrenner, 1977). The philosopher, educator, and psychologist John Dewey (1899) recognized the tradeoff between control and applicability a century ago.

> The great advantage of the psychological laboratory is paid for by certain obvious defects. The completer the control of conditions, with resulting greater accuracy of determination, demands an isolation, a ruling out of the usual media of thought and action, which leads to remoteness, and easily to a certain artificiality. (p. 145)

The "media of thought and action" are not the source of confounds, but the all-important context of behavior of interest to community psychologists.

To further complicate the task for community researchers, this context is multileveled. Our thoughts and actions are affected by dynamic processes that occur within our hearts and minds, in interaction with the people around us, and also at higher levels of analysis that are more difficult to study. A researcher interested in child abuse, for example, might consider the abuser's mental health status, the interaction patterns in families where abuse occurs, the existence of neighborhood support systems, the contributing stress of poverty or unemployment, and the role of cultural norms with regard to violence (Belsky 1980; Phillips 2000).

Research and the Appreciation of Diversity. In the logical positivist tradition, lack of attention to real-world environments has led to a de-emphasis of the cultural context of research (Gergen, Gulerce, Lock, & Misra, 1996; Sue, 1999). In the search for universals researchers assumed that scientific findings applied to all people. As a result, the unique experiences of minority group members went unstudied, a situation aptly captured in the book entitled *Even the Rats Were White* (Guthrie, 1998; see also Bohan, 1995). Many researchers have hesitated to consider social position in a conscious and critical way. Analyses of the impact of race, ethnicity, gender, and other dimensions of difference have often occurred either as an afterthought (Scarr, 1988) or as an attempt to control for "nuisance" variables (Spencer, 1990). Community psychology attempts to "overcome this tradition and replaces it with the intention to understand different groups and individuals on their own terms," (Rappaport, 1984c, p. 360). This intention brings many challenges. Let's consider a few of them.

The Difficulty of Obtaining Samples. When we no longer assume universal effects we can no longer rely on samples of convenience. Undergraduate psychology students who receive course credit for participation in research may be readily available, but not necessarily representative of diverse voices (Sears, 1986). Reliance on convenient samples has led to theories of human behavior based primarily on White and middle class people (Graham, 1992; see also Reid, 1994; Rogler, 1999; Segall, Lonner, & Berry, 1998). To rectify this situation, more research is needed on the life experiences of members of disenfranchised groups. Such samples are more difficult to obtain for a variety of reasons, however. Researchers have less access to and credibility with people of different social positions, and members of marginalized groups may have less time and energy to devote to activities from which they do not directly benefit. Disenfranchised people may not see research as advancing their own causes, a perception that has too often been accurate.

Our Ability to Interpret the Thoughts and Behaviors of Others Must Be Questioned. Marginalized groups have historically been studied in comparison to mainstream groups and observed differences explained in terms of minority group deficits (e.g., Betancourt & Lopez, 1993; McHugh, Koeske, & Frieze, 1986; Moghaddam & Studer, 1997; Vega, 1992). Majority group behavior has served as the norm—the "gold standard" for understanding the behavior of all other groups (Vega, 1992, p. 381; see also Katz & Kofkin, 1997). These standards are often inappropriate as different groups live in different contexts. For example, keeping a 12-year-old under constant supervision may seem over-restrictive (i.e. negative parenting) in low-crime areas. In high crime areas, however, it may constitute responsible and necessary (i.e. positive) parenting (Hughes, Seidman, & Williams, 1993).

Appropriate Measures and Methodologies May Not Exist. Measurement issues pose additional challenges (e.g., Caldwell, Jackson, Tucker, & Bowman, 1999; Cauce, Coronado, & Watson, 1998). Many standard measures have been developed and tested on samples of convenience and do not reflect the experiences of people who are not White and middle class (e.g., Manson, Shore, & Bloom, 1985; Prelow, Tein, Roosa, & Wood, 2000; Rogler, 1999). This is true not only in terms of scale content (e.g., what behaviors constitute positive parenting), but also in terms of scale usage. When completing rating scales, African American and Hispanic respondents endorse more extreme response categories as compared to Euro-American respondents (Bachman & O'Malley, 1984; Hui & Triandis, 1989; Marín, Gamba, & Marín, 1992).

While some culturally sensitive researchers seek to adapt existing measures and methodologies for use with under-represented groups (see Caldwell, et al., 1999), others call for new epistemologies—new ways of seeking knowledge. For example, William Vega advocated the **emic approach** used by anthropologists. In the emic approach, research methods allow the systems of meaning inherent in the group under study to guide the research process (Vega 1992; see also Berry & Kim, 1993; Kim & Berry, 1993; see Belenky, Clinchy, Goldberger, & Tarule, 1986, for a woman-centered approach). This contrasts with the **etic approach**, which assumes universality in human experience, therefore disregarding ethnicity and culture. In this approach, structures for understanding the experiences of the people under study are predetermined by researchers (who often belong to dominant social groups) and imposed from the outside.

Attention to Broad Categories Is Only the Tip of the Diversity Iceberg. Cultural insensitivity is also reflected in researchers' willingness to reduce complex groups into single categories based on superficial similarities (e.g., Bernal & Enchautegui-de-Jesus, 1994; Helms, 1994; Hughes et al., 1993; Vega, 1992). This has been most evident with regard to ethnic background. All people from Spanish-speaking countries (Mexico, Puerto Rico, Cuba) are considered Hispanic, and people from such diverse countries as Japan, China, Korea, Cambodia, Vietnam, and India are grouped together as Asian. These groupings may facilitate statistical analyses that require a minimum number of people in each group examined, but they fail to account for differences among subgroups along socially and theoretically meaningful variables, such as socioeconomic status and level of acculturation (e.g., Linville, Fischer, & Salovey, 1989). Multiethnic people add further to the challenge of categorization (see Root, 1996; Kerwin & Ponterotto, 1995; Williams, 1999). In recognition of biracial and multiethnic people, the 2000 U.S. census allowed respondents to check *all* ethnic categories to which they belonged, an option chosen by 7 million people, or 2.5% of the population (U.S. Bureau of the Census, 2001). This change makes quantitative analysis of the census data much more complex.

The challenges of accounting for diversity are significant. The perspectives of women, people of color, individuals with disabilities, and others have been under-represented not only in mainstream scientific publications, but in community psychology journals as well (e.g., Angelique & Culley, 2000; Serrano-Garcia & Bond, 1994; Loo, Fong, & Iwamasa, 1988). Community psychologists have proposed guidelines to facilitate research with disenfranchised populations, such as involving diverse stakeholders in the research process from beginning to end, attending to the meaning behind group categorization, and choosing from (and developing) a wide variety of methods (Hughes et al., 1993; Vega, 1992).

Research and Social Change. Community psychology's emphasis on social change also puts researchers at odds with a strict positivist view of science. In the words of Seymour Sarason (1986), "because community psychology reflected and required, in part at least, an activist stance, it would not be viewed by academic psychology as fitting in with psychology's picture of the neutral, objective, fact-finding, theory-building researcher" (p. 405).

Community psychologists generally do not conduct **basic research,** which is designed to test hypotheses and add to the body of scientific knowledge. Some favor **applied research,** which has clear and purposeful implications for social intervention. Others advocate more radical approaches. In his presidential address to Division 27, Ed Seidman (1988) held that community psychologists should conduct **action research** that, unlike either applied or basic research, challenges the status quo and promotes social change.

The term *action research* is often traced to the influential work of social psychologist Kurt Lewin (Lewin, 1948; Lewin, 1951; see also Argyris, Putnam, & Smith, 1985; Dewey, 1946). Lewin posited that researchers do not learn best by objectively studying the world from a distance. Rather, we gain insight by rolling up our sleeves, trying to make a difference in the world, and documenting the change process as it unfolds. Knowledge accumulates through continuous cycles of planning, acting, observing the effects of one's actions, and using the observed results to plan anew (see Figure 2.1). Lewin's research model challenged prevailing perspectives that pitted science against practice. Lewin saw the two as complementary.

Research and a Strengths-Based Approach. "Action research" has become an exceedingly popular term to describe a variety of applied research projects. These projects do not necessarily challenge the status quo and may even proceed from traditional paradigms that objectify the people who provide data. In the logical positivist tradition, the individuals studied are not seen as unique and competent contributors to the research process. They are, instead, a necessary means to the data, and the data are what *really* matter. Research subjects are anonymous, interchangeable, silent, and subservient to the experimenters (Fawcett, 1991; Madigan, Johnson, & Linton, 1995). Such a view is

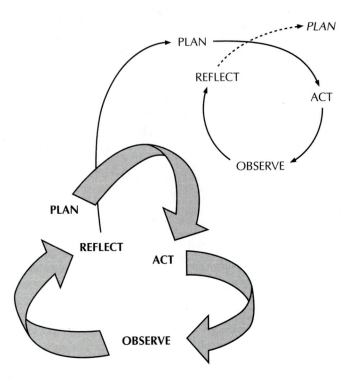

Figure 2.1

The cycle of research and action: plan, act, observe, reflect, then plan again.

inconsistent with the fifth guiding principle of community psychology—a focus on the strengths and capabilities of the people we seek to understand and assist.

In psychology, the term *research participant*[1] has replaced the term *subject*. (American Psychological Association, 1994). The new term suggests that people in studies are active contributors—*participants* in the research process. Those who take this notion most to heart advocate **participatory research**. Participatory research has been defined as more radical than action research (Brown & Tandon, 1983). The approach emerged in the 1970s from work with oppressed people in developing countries and was greatly influenced by the writings of

South American philosopher and educator Paulo Freire (Smith, 1997; Yeich, 1996). It was designed to enhance the psychological and political power of oppressed people by providing a forum for members of dominated or subordinated populations to articulate their own points of view (Hall, 1993). Participatory research entails a democratization of information. Knowledge is no longer under the purview of learned professors in white lab coats and other members of the educated elite, but belongs to everyone—stay-at-home mothers concerned about the potability of their drinking water or youth in high-crime neighborhoods determined to make their streets safer (Gaventa, 1993; Park, 1993).

Participatory research overlaps conceptually with *empowerment research* (e.g., Rappaport, 1990; Fetterman, Kaftarian, & Wandersman, 1996) and *feminist research* (e.g., Bond, Hill, Mulvey, & Terenzio, 2000). All of these types of research appeal to community psychologists in that they reject the myth of scientific objectivity, appreciate the complexity of social reality, advocate social action, attend to the voices of

[1]The term *research participant* is also used in this text, but it is not an ideal term. It refers only to the people of interest to researchers and not to the researchers themselves, who are co-participants in the research process. Distance between the examined and the examiner is therefore retained.

Calvin and Hobbes   by Bill Watterson

Unlike traditional academic researchers, participatory researchers do not exclude community members through esoteric jargon. CALVIN AND HOBBES © Watterson. Reprinted with permission of UNIVERSAL PRESS SYNDICATE. All rights reserved.

disenfranchised people, and foster community ownership of the research process (e.g., Yeich, 1996).

In participatory research, the disenfranchised people of concern to researchers do not simply supply the data or comment on questionnaires. They set the research agenda, define the research questions, interpret the findings, and disseminate results (Gaventa, 1993). This requires a shift in perspective for everyone involved. The research participants, who have been imbued with traditional ideas about science as a professional activity, may hesitate to take ownership of the research process (Serrano-Garcia, 1990). Meanwhile, the researcher must learn to relinquish control and the expert role. Geoffrey Nelson and his colleagues suggested numerous mechanisms for promoting participatory research, including:

- Establish research steering committees that include those affected by the research.
- Hire those affected by the research to conduct the studies.
- Locate and collaborate with group(s) who can use the research findings for education and advocacy.
- Encourage the development of authentic and supportive relationships among all participants. (Nelson et al., 1998)

General Implications of the Guiding Principles. The guiding principles affect how community psychologists conduct research. We recognize the need for methods that embrace subjectivity, honor the voices of diverse participants, consider ecology at multiple levels, have the potential to build individual and community strengths, and encourage more just social relationships. Although methodologies based in the logical positivist tradition have their place, new methodologies or ways of studying issues of interest are of paramount importance (Denzin & Lincoln, 2000; Speer et al., 1992; Tolan et al., 1990; Walsh, 1987).

Many community psychologists have come to rely on qualitative research techniques (see Guba & Lincoln, 1994; Miller & Banyard, 1998). **Qualitative research** attempts to capture the richness and complexity of people's lived experience (Gilbert, 2001; Miles & Huberman, 1984; Patton, 1987). This contrasts with logical positivism's emphasis on **quantitative research,** which reduces complex phenomenon to numerical values that are statistically analyzed in order to support or refute predetermined hypotheses. Quantitative techniques are preferable when all the cases studied "fall in line," a requirement that is often not met in community research where the particularities of context and social position are integral to our questions of interest (Rapkin & Luke, 1993). Another way of distinguishing qualitative and quantitative research is that quantitative research is about counting while qualitative research is about conversing (Stewart, 2000). Many alternative methodologies employed by community psychologists, such as ethnographies (Fetterman, 1998), oral histories (Kelly, 2001), narratives (Rappaport, 1990, 1995), and dialogic methods (e.g., Keiffer, 1984; Bond, Belenky, & Weinstock, 2000) rely on conversation and story telling (see also the *Promise of Community Psychology* section in Chapter Ten).

WHERE SCIENCE MEETS ACTION

The preceding discussion highlights the challenges community psychology's guiding principles present to the science of psychology. Academically based community psychologists not only put the guiding principles into effect by pursuing science in a new way, but they also have one foot firmly planted in the world of action. There are many forums for academic psychologists to engage in community practice. Two common applied activities are developing and evaluating community programs and using social science research to inform legal and policy decisions.

Program Development and Evaluation A common applied activity for many academically oriented community psychologists is program development and evaluation (e.g., O'Donnell & Ferrari, 2000). Community psychologists have implemented and assessed countless research-based intervention programs. Several books examine effective interventions in detail, such as *14 Ounces of Prevention: A Casebook for Practitioners* (Price, Cowen, Lorion, & Ramos-McKay, 1988) and *Primary Prevention Works* (Albee & Gullotta, 1997). Many programs summarized in these books are described throughout this textbook. In Chapter Nine, for example, I describe the STEP program, which organized school structures to facilitate students' transition to high school, and the ICPS program to teach interpersonal problem-solving skills to preschoolers. The Community Intervention boxes that appear in each chapter also describe innovative programs, many of

which have been developed and/or evaluated by community psychologists (in this chapter, for example, I describe the development and evaluation of George Fairweather's program for people with mental illness).

Program evaluation is conventionally seen as falling into two categories (e.g., Scheirer, 1994; Wholey, Hatry, & Newcomer, 1994). **Process evaluations** (also called *formative evaluations*) monitor and measure the delivery of the program during implementation. **Outcome evaluations** (also called *summative evaluations*) occur at the end of a program cycle and assess the program's success in meeting its goals. Program evaluations may also include a **cost-benefit analysis**, which determines whether the planned intervention was a fiscally sound one. Do the benefits of the program in comparison to other possible interventions justify its costs?

Evaluations hold the program accountable to funders and to the larger community (Brown, 1995). They can also build a setting's capacity. Dialogues among researchers, setting members, and community stakeholders that occur during the course of a program evaluation can help staff gain insight about how to intervene effectively. Setting capacity is also increased when the staff learns to conduct its own evaluation research.

Program evaluation also adds to the larger body of knowledge about community change. A strong research base generated from a multitude of evaluations has allowed scholars to draw conclusions about what makes an intervention effective. Successful programs offer a broad spectrum of services, transcend traditional professional boundaries, remove bureaucratic barriers to service delivery, consider the contexts in which individuals live, provide comprehensive and easy-to-use services, are run by skilled staff members who truly care about and respect the people served, and have a clear mission and long-term goals (Schorr, 1988, 1997).

Because community evaluations serve several functions, evaluators cannot rely on research skills alone. Effective program evaluators need to have several competencies. They must have pedagogical skills so that they can teach setting members to become their own evaluators. Political skills help community researchers assess and address the multiple and potentially conflicting interests of various stake-holders. Interpersonal skills are needed to gain the stakeholders' trust and sustain their commitment to the program development and evaluation process (Brown 1995).

Research with Policy Implications. Many community psychologists who work in academic settings (as well as applied community psychologists in various settings) become involved in policymaking (e.g., Melton, 1995, 2000; Perkins, 1988; Phillips, 2000; Solarz, 2000; Wilcox, 2000; Wursten & Sales, 1988). Often, this means conducting research with legal and policy implications. For example, Deborah Phillips and her colleagues (1992) assessed how the stringency of state childcare regulations and compliance with these regulations affected the quality of caregiving environments. Leonard Jason and colleagues (1999) studied how the enforcement of laws prohibiting youth access to tobacco affects the prevalence of smoking. Psychologists who conduct policy-relevant research may have opportunities to offer expert testimony in Congress or in the courtroom, as Jason did (Jason, 1999; see also Greenberger, 1983).[2] Community psychologists involved in policy arenas may not only conduct original research but also summarize the legal and policy implications of other people's research. The Public Policy Office of the American Psychological Association (APA),[3] for example, prepares policy-relevant briefs on a wide variety of issues—mental and physical health, education, and poverty to name a few. For example, Allison Rosenberg and her colleagues summarized a policy agenda to combat homelessness (e.g., Rosenberg, Solarz, and Bailey, 1991).

Psychologists interested in influencing policy must translate research into a form usable by public officials (e.g., Fiske, Bersoff, Borgida, Deaux, and

Heilman, 1991). First, we must learn to be brief. Academic audiences want to know about sample composition, methodology, confounding variables, and other factors that could affect results. Policy audiences do not. Meticulous and verbose professional reports are not read by public officials who have only minutes—even seconds—to review briefs or hear testimony (e.g., Lawrence, Phillips, & Rundquist, 1993). In addition, social science research is based on probabilities and is bound by its reliance on particular samples, methods, and theories. Thus, psychologists are trained to present both sides of issues and not to take stands (i.e. to be "objective"). Public decision-makers, however, need to make decision and want to hear what the research suggests they do (Perkins, 1988).

In order to bridge the gap between research and action, psychologists in policy and legal worlds need to make brief, engaging, and memorable research presentations with the major points clearly identified and recommended actions specified (Wursten & Sales, 1988). They must also realize that one-shot briefings are unlikely to be effective. "Ideas must percolate in the policy process before they obtain enough support from relevant interest groups and key decision makers to result in action" (Melton, 1995, p. 769; see also Lindblom and Cohen, 1979). Social policy is a diffuse, imprecise, and largely unpredictable process (Loftus, 1991; Seekins, Maynard-Moody, & Fawcett, 1987; Vincent, 1990). Deborah Phillips (2000) described it as a human drama with the requisite unfolding plot and diverse cast of characters.

Social science research can affect legislative decisions, however. As described in Chapter One, the research of Kenneth and Mamie Clark played a prominent role in the Supreme Court's 1954 ruling that segregation in the schools was unconstitutional. This decision signaled the potential role of psychological research in legal decisions (e.g., Haney, 1993; Perkins, 1988). Since the 1960s, conservative and liberal judges alike have recognized the importance of social science data (Melton, 2000).

Some community psychologists engage in the policy process in order to broaden the impact of their research. They believe that intervening at higher levels is more effective because "working strictly

[2]Some community psychologists leave academia to spend time on Capitol Hill, often through the APA Congressional Fellowship Program. On the Hill, academic psychologists assess and summarize research that bears on policy decisions and work to get desired legislation passed (e.g., Wilcox, 2000).
[3]The website of APA's Public Policy Office is *http://www.apa.org/ppo/*.

within the confines of a community may ultimately limit the scope of an intervention" (Wursten & Sales, 1988, p. 488). The notion that top-down policy interventions inspire more wide-ranging changes is arguable (e.g., Fox, 1993; Haney, 1993) as is the assumption that policy does indeed operate in a top-down fashion. Phillips (2000) noted that policies around domestic violence, for example, occur at all levels, from court-mandated treatment of individual offenders to income support legislation and public education campaigns.

Social problems are multiply determined. Thus, effective interventions can address the problem at a variety of levels. One can, for example, volunteer to help a battered woman obtain her GED, fundraise for the local shelter, and/ or lobby for anti-violence legislation. Top-down and bottom-up approaches are by no means mutually exclusive. Michael Fullan (1999) noted that

> you can't mandate local commitment and capacity, but mandates do matter. They put needed pressure on local reform, and they provide opportunities for legitimizing the efforts of local change agents working against the grain. . . Top-down mandates and bottom-up energies need each other. (p. 19)

All levels of the social context affect behavior, and community psychologists in courtrooms and hearing rooms open up new opportunities for social change.

THE APPLIED SIDE OF COMMUNITY PSYCHOLOGY

Although the published literature of community psychology emphasizes the academic side of the discipline, it is our work in the field that makes us community psychologists. In receiving a Division 27 award for his applied work, David Chavis (1993) observed that, "If we are a profession, then we must define our place of action" (p. 179). He advised that our values, theories, and research do not house families, provide teenage mothers with daycare and jobs, or prevent young men of color from crowding the jails. "Only a practice of community psychology can show the difference our field can make" (1993, p. 179). Although academically based community psychologists engage in applied activities as part of their professional work, community psychology practitioners are based in applied settings and focus on the practice side of community psychology.

There are almost as many job descriptions for applied community psychologists as there are applied community psychologists. In this section, we explore three commonly identified roles for community psychologists in applied settings: consultant, creator of new settings, and community organizer/ coalition builder. Although academic community psychologists may assume these roles as part of their professional work, these three roles provide opportunities for employment outside of academia.

The three roles are both overarching and overlapping. For example, in 1971, Ira Goldenberg wrote a classic book on his efforts to establish a Residential Youth Center (RYC) for low-income adolescents. RYC was an innovative center that employed a nonprofessional staff and utilized a horizontal, nonhierarchical organizational structure. It promoted close relationships among youth, families, and staff, and emphasized the development of community resources. Initially, Goldenberg worked as a creator of this setting but later operated as a consultant.

CONSULTATION

In 1970 Gerald Caplan distinguished four models of consultation (see also Mannino & Shore, 1972). *Client-centered* consultations help individuals better meet the needs of other individuals. A client-centered consultant might help a teacher design a learning program for a student with reading difficulties, for example, or help a clinical psychologist work more effectively with a client in an abusive relationship. Consultee-centered consultations help an individual meet the needs of an entire group of similar clients. A *consultee-centered* consultant might help a teacher identify and plan for learning-disabled students in general or sensitize clinical psychologists to the issues of women living with domestic violence. The remaining types of consultation, program-centered administrative consultation and consultee-centered administrative consultation,[4] fall under the rubric of **community consultation.** Community consultation is of central interest to community psychologists. In this type of consultation, the "client" is not an individual (e.g., teacher or psychologist), but an entire program, group, staff, or agency.

A community consultant is sought out and hired by a setting because she or he has some expertise that the setting needs in order to achieve its goals. Community consultants have a variety of competencies. They may be skilled in diagnosing organizational problems and promoting organizational functioning (O'Neill & Trickett, 1982). This might entail, for example, altering the decision-making processes or restructuring organizational charts. Community consultants may have expertise in reducing conflict among subgroups, perhaps helping agencies address racial and other tensions. As one of many examples, the Public Conversations Project in Watertown Massachusetts is a nonprofit organization that uses consultation as a way of facilitating conversations across people's differences (Madsen, 2001; see also ***http://www.publicconversations.org***).

Regardless of the problem of focus, community consultants strive to create change by contributing to the efficacy of an existing setting. Thus, they provide indirect support rather than direct services to clients (Trickett, Barone, & Watts, 2000). Community psychologists consult to a variety of settings: schools, police departments, mental health centers, neighborhood associations. The possibilities are vast. Edward Lichtenstein and his colleagues (1996) described a tobacco control consultation to Northwest Indian tribes. Stephanie Reinharz (1983) described a community consultation to an alternative bakery whose collectivist values of fairness, cooperation, and tolerance interfered with the goal of operating a profitable business.

---

[4]The main difference between these two types of consultation is that former attempts to address problems around a program or organization while the latter focuses on the professional functioning of the staff.

Characteristics of Community Consultation. The most important feature of community consultation is its system orientation. A community consultant must be sensitive to group processes and networks of relationships within the setting and across settings. The awareness of multilevel contexts promoted by community psychology can serve community consultants well. For example, Edison Trickett and his colleagues (Trickett & Birman, 1989; Trickett et al., 2000) described a consultation with a public school focusing on problems associated with its many foreign-born students. As teachers become more aware of the challenges the students faced, they became more compassionate. Sleeping in class and incomplete homework assignments were no longer attributed to laziness, but to the exhaustion of students who worked long hours after school and on weekends to support themselves and their families. Teachers also became more cognizant of their own pressures, such as the national movement for excellence and accountability in teaching. These pressures augmented the teachers' investment in test scores and reduced their willingness to tolerate poor performance. As a result of community consultation, teachers became more interested in individual students, classroom dynamics, school-wide challenges, and also district policies that impinged on them. Thus, the effects of a community consultation can radiate throughout interrelated systems (Trickett et al., 2000).

On the other hand, the larger ecology of the consultation can also limit effectiveness. Based on their "failed" consultation to a program for adolescent offenders, Dick Reppucci and his colleagues (1973) recommended viewing the target system in broad terms. The small Mountville Camp for offending adolescents, the setting with which the consultants contracted, actually had little authority to enact recommended changes. In retrospect, the consultants believed that they would have achieved more success if the central governing office of the Corrections Department had been involved in the consultation from the beginning.

A second important characteristic of community consultation is that the setting is in charge. Consultants do not issue orders, they dispense advice.

all levels of operation (Campbell et al., 2000). Factors that affect the likelihood that settings remain antibureaucratic may include a view of the setting as transitory, a definition of the setting as opposing the status quo, a sense of belonging to a larger social movement, and established opportunities for reflection and criticism (Rothschild-Whitt, 1979).

COMMUNITY ORGANIZING AND COALITION BUILDING

To paraphrase Bill Berkowitz, **community organizing** consists of intentional activities to bring community residents together in joint action designed to improve the context of their lives both locally and in the broader society (Berkowitz, 2000a). This has traditionally involved confronting external powers, though it has come to entail strengthening existing resources or developing new community structures (Rothman, 1995).

Bill Berkowitz (2000a) argued that community organizing, as a process for enhancing community life and establishing more equitable social relations in the larger world, ought to spark the interest of community psychologists. It is, however, neither dominant nor even prominent in the field's research, theory, training, or practice. Saul Alinsky's classic primer *Rules for Radicals* (1971) is required reading in many community psychology classes, but community organizing is rarely discussed as a career option in today's world.

Saul Alinsky helped existing community settings (e.g., churches, labor unions) trace the injustices they experienced to a visible enemy and organize confrontational encounters that compelled the enemy to behave more equitably. For example, a store that only hired Blacks for menial jobs was targeted in one of Alinsky's efforts. Alinsky threatened to have three thousand Black people enter the main floor of the store, occupy the attention of all the salespeople, order merchandise COD, and ultimately refuse delivery. The department store responded to this threat by requesting a meeting to discuss personnel changes (for more on Alinsky, see the Community Intervention box in Chapter Six).

Community organizing traditionally seeks to redistribute social power through confrontation with individuals and social systems that wield control (Speer & Hughey, 1995). In recent decades this approach has changed (e.g., McKnight, 1995). Rates of participation in existing community settings have decreased (e.g., Putnam, 2000), and so they less often serve as a hub for organizing activities. In addition, enemies are less visible and tangible in this era of globalization (e.g., Gamson, 1989). Community organizing around resistance to a common enemy has given way to collaborative efforts that augment neighborhood and community capacity (McKnight, 1995; Gittell & Vidal, 1998). Traditional community organizing has given way to building **community coalition building.** This currently popular community-level change activity brings together groups of diverse community members, organizations, and constituencies to resolve local problems and meet resident needs (Feighery & Rogers, 1989; Wolff, 2001a).

As an early example of community coalition building, Michael Morris and Linda Frisman (1987) described their efforts to establish networks among community groups in Connecticut in order to facilitate the reintegration of youth into the community after the federal government mandated deinstitutionalization of juvenile status offenders. Morris and Frisman held meetings for individuals representing a variety of agencies affected by the new legislation. The meetings were facilitated by a networker who could respond to questions about the legislation, steer the group away from unproductive "gripe sessions," and encourage the exchange of information. These meetings also provided a forum for the recognition of connections that already existed among participants (e.g., "You did a good job with that family I referred to you last month," or "It's nice to match a face with a voice on the phone" [p. 32]).

Morris and Frisman identified several obstacles to the commitment, communication, mutual awareness, and collaborative spirit necessary for community coalitions to function competently. First, individuals within an agency or organization often pursued their own agency's mission with dedication but lacked a broader imperative that would sensitize them to community-wide concerns and the perspectives of other agencies. The lack of identification with the local community and focus only the agenda of one's own agency disrupted the flow of information within the community. For example, a community educator was more likely to discuss the new legislation with a fellow educator who lived in another part of the country rather than with a police officer in her own town. In addition, agencies often saw themselves as competing with other agencies for scarce resources, which further reduced the community's ability to work together as a whole.

The inherently controversial and political nature of community organizing may help explain its neglect as a topic of study in community psychology, but coalition building is not inherently controversial, and this change strategy also remains an understudied example of community psychology practice. Bill Berkowitz (2000a, 2001) proposed that these practices are understudied because they involve complex and multilevel processes that are exceedingly difficult to document. As a result, most of what we currently know about community organizing comes from homemade manuals, booklets, tip sheets, anecdotal accounts, and the popular press (Berkowitz, 2000a; Wolff, 2001b).

It is also true that in these necessarily community-based endeavors, tensions between academia and practice become evident. Alinsky (1971) asserted that professional training makes community organizers less radical; "they organize to get rid of four-legged rats and stop there; we organize to get rid of four-legged rats so that we can get on to removing two-legged rats" (p. 68). Recently, the tension between academia and practice emerged in a special issue of the *American Journal of Community Psychology* dedicated to the Block Boosters Project (see also the Classic Research box in Chapter Ten). In addition to articles by the researchers involved in this project, practitioners were invited to present their observations. A block association president wrote of his frustrations over the researchers' emphasis on data collection (Burgess, 1990). A grassroots community organizer noted that tensions, feuds, and issues of 'turf' arose often (Kaye, 1990). In commenting on this special issue, Richard Price (1990) wrote: "One cannot read these articles without a breathtaking sense of how wide the gulf is between the culture of social science and the culture of community organizing and block leadership" (p. 165).

For community psychologists, however, the gulf between science and practice constitutes a worthy challenge, not an insurmountable stumbling block. Community organizing and coalition building remain largely unexplored, but potentially powerful professional activities for applied—and academic—community psychologists.

⌘ The Promise of Community Psychology: Putting the "Work" into Network

Early in this chapter I discussed the various competencies useful for the work of community psychology. Not explicitly mentioned in that list was an acute interest and investment in human relationships. The desire to spend time with, talk to, learn about, and learn from different people facilitates all that we do as community psychologists.

This is true for academic community psychologists and practitioners alike. Community research, unlike traditional research, requires close relationships between the researcher and the researched. Meg Bond (1990) described community research as a pooling of resources between researcher and participant. These resources are not equivalent, however. The researcher's most important resource is scientific knowledge. The participants' major contribution is their lived experience. Scientific knowledge is viewed by society as more valuable. It is also less personal. The more intimate information contributed by the participants results in a vulnerability that can reinforce the unequal power relationship between researcher and participant (Bond, 1990).

Thus, the community researcher must work to deconstruct the barriers that separate the examiner and the examined (Nelson et al., 1998). More equal and intimate research relationships present new challenges (Perkins & Wandersman 1990; Wicker & Sommer, 1993; Stewart, 2000), but the rewards are immense. Our data are more accurate and more complete, and our research is better valued and utilized. In addition, reciprocal relationships with research participants are often personally rewarding and help us to integrate our personal, professional, and political selves (Nelson et al., 1998).

Community psychology practitioners, too, recognize the importance of deconstructing professional boundaries. Dick Reppucci (1973) and his colleagues advised community consultants to disclaim "the magical aura professionals often either intentionally or unintentionally carry with them" (p. 149). Lisbeth Schorr (1997) noted that "[i]nterventions that are successful with high-risk populations all seem to have staffs with the time and skill to establish relationships based on mutual respect and trust" (p. xxii). In addition, psychologists involved in advocacy activities repeatedly find that networking and personal connections shape the course of a bill or the ruling of a judge (e.g., Greenberger, 1983).

For community psychologists, the boundaries between professional and personal life blur, and the most effective way of entering a community setting may not be a formal display of scholarly knowledge through written or oral presentations. It might be preferable to find ways to let community members get to know the "outsider" a bit and develop a basis for personal relationships *before* focusing on the tasks at hand (Gibbs, 1980).

Effective community psychologists need to develop professional competencies. We also need to take advantage of invaluable opportunities to catch a bite to eat, go for a walk, carpool, or simply tell a joke. Eco-identities may be forged over dinner (e.g., Brody, 1986) and working alliances developed on a fishing trip (Jeffrey & Reeves, 1978; cited in Trickett et al., 2000). As Thomas Wolff (2001b) advised, "post-meeting 'schmoozing' is as critical as the meeting itself" (p. 187), and the community psychologist Kurt Ribisl (2000) resolved, "when I attend conferences, I am committed to always attending the happy hour" (p. 99).

Action Agenda

Qualities Inventory

Review the eight qualities for a community psychologist described in this chapter. Which ones come easiest to you? Which ones present challenges? What ideas do you have about how best to capitalize on your strengths? What ideas do you have about how best to compensate for or eliminate your weaknesses? What can you do personally? What can you do in your collaborations with others? Think about the sorts of community psychology jobs that appeal to you. How do your areas of strengths and challenges match the demands of potential jobs?

What Kind of Job?

People who study community psychology are often asked, "What kind of a job would you get?" The job title "community psychologist" rarely appears in classified advertisements. Jobs do exist, of course, but community psychologists need to think creatively about where our skills and interests can best be utilized.

Conduct a mock job search to identify the range of jobs appropriate for someone trained in community psychology. This exercise might take place across the semester. Clip and copy classified advertisements and position announcements from various sources. What sorts of titles and settings would you look for? How would you locate job openings (newspapers, on-line directories, personal networking)? What experiences would you stress on a job application for each of the potential jobs you find? What additional educational experiences do you think would strengthen your application to those jobs that most appeal to you?

Here are a few job descriptions that I have clipped:

> COMMUNITY SERVICES REPRESENTATIVE: This highly visible and challenging position acts as a liaison between the State Hospital and the local community. . .

> COUNSELOR: A non-profit agency seeks energetic individual to co-facilitate drop out prevention/leadership program for high school females. . .

> PARENT INVOLVEMENT COORDINATOR: Parent involvement coordinator wanted to implement the parent involvement component of a Head Start program. . .

> EXECUTIVE DIRECTOR: Needed for developing Children's Advocacy Center to provide services relating to child abuse including outreach and family support services, volunteer management, team leadership, and grant writing. . .

Students in community psychology who are conducting or are about to conduct real job searches might read the article *Practicing What We Preach: Integrating Community Psychology into the Job Search Process* (Campbell, Angelique, BootsMiller, & Davidson, 2000). This chapter describes a job club formed to support community psychologists in their search for employment after graduation.

Shadow a Practitioner

Identify someone whom you believe embodies the characteristics of a community psychologist and/or does the kind of work community psychologists do. Arrange to follow that person throughout the day. You might want to call on the networks of classmates, friends, and teachers in identifying and approaching possible candidates to shadow. If possible, arrange to observe this person at work and also interview him or her with regard to the issues raised in this chapter: What personal characteristics help the person to succeed at work? Are there any key experiences that made him or her want to do this job (such as Lambert's overheard conversation on the bus, [see section on *Metabolic Balance Between Patience and Zeal*])? How does the person's current job fit into his or her career path (educational background, job history, future goals)? Which, if any, of the five principles of community psychology guide this person's work? Do you think you could (or would want to) do what this person does? Why or why not?

Key Terms

action research

applied research

basic research

community coalition building

community consultation

community organizing

confounding variables

cost-benefit analysis

dependent variable

eco-identity

ecological validity

emic approach

etic approach

independent variable

lodge societies

logical positivism

outcome evaluation

participatory research

planned obsolescence

process evaluation

qualitative research

quantitative research

reliability

social position

stakeholders

Chapter 3

The Importance of Values

....

⌘ Introduction

Allow me to describe for you two worlds. The first is the world of objectivity. This world is filled with empirical observations. It is predictable and controllable. Reality exists outside of us, and its universal truths and natural laws can be discovered through scientific methods. The contents of this world can be analyzed—broken into smaller pieces. Isolated objective facts then accumulate into an increasingly complete picture of the world that is value free. Rationalism, realism, determinism, and reductionism constitute this world's core assumptions. This world may seem orderly and comprehensible, but also sterile, mechanistic, and cold. The second world is the world of subjectivity. It is filled with feelings and beliefs. These feelings and beliefs define what we care about and give life its meaning. Knowledge is not absolute and universal, but relative and particularistic. Reality is not discovered but constructed, and values shape these constructions. This world is founded on assumptions of multiple realities, uncertainty, interrelatedness, and holism. It may seem not only messy and inexact, but also mysterious and wonder-filled.

For the most part, psychology in the modern era has tried to live in the first world while the second world has continuously pressed upon us. In the previous chapter we saw how community psychology

57

bridges the ivory tower of academia, which belongs to the objective world, and the subjective world of practice and action. This chapter examines another schism: the gap between facts and values. The implications of psychological "facts" for moral values have been explored since psychology's earliest days (see Gorsuch, 1988), yet no bridge exists between science and morality. The world of facts and the world of values continue to stand a world apart.

As described in Chapter Two, much of the published literature in community psychology depicts an academic, research-based field in which attempts to gain knowledge rely on established scientific practices. At the same time, it holds that values are of paramount importance; they shape our research and practice and drive our efforts to build a more just world. Thus, we begin this chapter with community psychologists once again straddling a vast divide.

This is, of course, a precarious position. Julian Rappaport (1984a) asserted that the "call for a clear statement of values is so much a part of the community movement that it is virtually impossible to understand it without such values explication" (p. 210). Nevertheless, few community psychologists have expounded on precisely how values shape our work. One exception is Isaac Prilleltensky (1998). When he attempted to articulate a value system for psychology he "discovered that talking about values and assumptions is dangerous" (p. 326). His writings generated heated debates and led one colleague to advise Prilleltensky to leave the field altogether. And so it is with considerable trepidation that I commence this chapter on values.

⌘ What are Values?

Let's begin by looking at what we mean when we talk about **values.** In this section, I first ground the discussion in definition then explore some of the values that social scientists have found to be important. We will then look at how values influence the work of psychologists, especially community psychologists.

DEFINITIONAL ISSUES

Half a century ago, Clyde Kluckhorn (1951) offered the following definition:

> A value is a conception, explicit or implicit, distinctive of an individual or characteristic of a group, of the desirable which influences the selection from available modes, means, and ends of action. (p. 395)

This definition has much to recommend it. First, it notes that values exert their influence whether or not they are acknowledged. Values can be explicit, or they can be implicit and difficult to see. This definition also recognizes that values operate at different levels—on an individual basis and at broader group levels. In addition, the definition highlights the importance of choice. We continuously make choices from among various available options, and the choices we make reflect our values. The definition also presents values as the means and ends of action. That is, they define what our goals are and how we achieve them. Finally, this definition asserts that values concern the desirable.

Values are not the same as preferences, however (e.g., Williams, 1979; Kilby, 1993). Eliot Turiel has distinguished three categories of social rules corresponding to their broadness and the seriousness of transgression (Turiel, 1998; Turiel, Killen, & Helwig, 1987; see also Nucci, 1996). When we talk of values, we generally refer to the most abstract level. These general rules, which Turiel called *moral rules,* reflect principles of justice and welfare that exist in all societies. Many believe moral rules result from a divine imperative. The Ten Commandments, for example, delineate moral rules for Judeo-Christian cultures. The next category of rules, *social conventions,* provide a framework for orderly social relationship. Social conventions vary across societies. Examples in the U.S. include the expectations that people wear shoes to work each day and that men don't cry. The most local category of rules are *personal rules,* which are individually determined codes of behavior, such as responding to gifts with thank you notes or bathing every night.

Calvin and Hobbes

by Bill Watterson

Shalom Schwartz has offered an alternative to Kluckhorn's definition of values that highlights some additional aspects of importance. Schwartz (1994) described values as "desirable, transsituational goals, varying in importance, that serve as guiding principles in the life of a person or other social entity" (p. 21). This concise definition adds two important elements. In defining values as transsituational, Schwartz recognized that values exhibit some stability—they are consistent across time and contexts. They are core beliefs (or *guiding principles*) that can change but are not capricious. Research suggests that values do remain stable over time, especially when considered at the group level (e.g., Inglehart, 1985; Rokeach & Ball-Rokeach, 1989). Second, by defining of values in the plural and referring to their varying importance, Schwartz implied that values occur in groups or sets that can be ordered and prioritized. Research suggests that a relatively small set of distinct values guide human behavior; it is their differential weights that account for seemingly endless variations in individual, interpersonal, institutional, and cultural value orientations (Rokeach & Ball-Rokeach, 1989). One study demonstrated that fascist, capitalist, socialist, and communist ideologies could be distinguished by their relative rankings of only two values: freedom and equality (Rokeach, 1973).[1] Such findings suggest that even if

[1]Countries vary not only in the importance they place on different values as a country, but also on the amount of consensus that exists within the country. In countries such as the U.S. there exists considerable heterogeneity in value assessments (Schwartz & Sagie, 2000).

people could agree on a universal set of values, we would never agree on how to weight each one in a given situation.

Taken together, the above definitions elucidate a number of important characteristics of values. Values

- are sometimes elusive
- operate at different levels
- involve choice
- pertain to the desirable (and the moral)
- refer to goals
- motivate action
- exist in ordered sets.

These characteristics of values will be examined in more detail throughout this chapter.

EXAMPLES OF VALUE SETS

Several researchers have attempted to specify the human values that guide our actions. Perhaps the most ambitious of these research projects was conducted by Shalom Schwartz (1992, 1994). Between 1988 and 1993, Schwartz confirmed the existence of ten values by surveying 25,863 people in 97 samples drawn from 44 countries that represented every continent in the world. These ten values comprise two overarching dimensions (see Table 3.1). The two higher-order dimensions (conservation/openness to change and self-transcendence/self-enhancement) appear to be nearly universal.

Schwartz briefly surveyed as many different people as possible in order to identify universal

📄 Table 3.1   Ten Values Underlying Two Dimensions

Conservation (1,2,3) vs. Openness to Change (4,5,6)	Self-Transcendence (7,8) vs. Self-Enhancement (6,9,10)
1. **Conformity:** Restraint of actions, inclinations, and impulses likely to upset or harm others and violate social expectations and norms.	7. **Universalism:** Understanding, appreciation, tolerance, and protection for the welfare of all people and for nature.
2. **Tradition:** Respect, commitment, and acceptance of the customs and ideas that traditional cultures and religions provide.	8. **Benevolence:** Preservation and enhancement of the welfare of people with whom one is in frequent personal contact.
3. **Security:** Safety, harmony, and stability of society, of relationships, and of self.	9. **Power:** Social status and prestige, control or dominance over other people or resources.
4. **Self-direction:** Independence of thought and choice of actions, creativity, exploration.	10. **Achievement:** Personal success through demonstrating competence according to social standards.
5. **Stimulation:** Excitement, novelty, and challenge in life.	
6. **Hedonism:** Pleasure and sensuous gratification for oneself.	6. **Hedonism:** Pleasure and sensuous gratification for oneself.

Based on Schwartz, S. H. (1994). Are there universal aspects in the structure and content of human values? *Journal of Social Issues, 50,* p. 19–45. Published by Blackwell Publishing, Oxford, U.K.

elements in the content and structure of human values. In his research, values that were not confirmed in all groups were not included. Thus, Schwartz excluded an eleventh value, *spirituality.* He argued that not all cultures recognized this value, which concerns the search for meaning in life and inner harmony, and that it could be derived from the other ten values.

An alternative to Schwartz's approach is to define important values through the intensive study of only one group. Randolph Potts (1999a, drawing on the work of Oliver, 1989) adopted this approach and delineated a set of five values important in the African American communities with which he worked. In his research, *Spirituality* emerged as a crucially important value. The second value, *Sankofa,*

refers to the importance of drawing lessons from history in order to navigate the future successfully. The third, *Kujichagulia,* emphasizes the need for the group to define and speak for itself, rather than be defined by others. Fourth is *Ujamaa,* which requires the equitable and fair distribution of resources within the community. The final value, *Uhuru,* pertains to the quest for social justice that African people have pursued throughout history. Although some overlap exists between the value set identified by Schwartz and the set identified by Potts, there are significant discrepancies as well.

The search for universal principles has considerable appeal. It is comforting to think that a common set of values unites all human societies on every continent of the world. At the same time, the local flavor and richness of distinct cultures is lost in the homogenization required by a search for universality. The different approaches taken by Schwartz and Potts reflect different worldviews, different foci, and different ideas about what is important or interesting to study. One might argue that the preference for a universalistic versus a particularistic study of values may reflect the different value systems of the researchers themselves. In these studies, values not only comprise the content of the research, but also shape the research process.

HOW VALUES INFLUENCE PSYCHOLOGY

Although discourse in values is not widespread, the view of science as purely fact based and verifiable has lost favor. Science may appear to be objective because values are difficult to see. Nevertheless, values affect the pursuit of science every step of the way, from our first decisions about what to study, to our final conclusions about what our findings mean and what we should do with them. Let me provide some illustrations.

Values determine which social problems are studied. This occurs at different levels, from the individual scientist to the highest levels of government. At an individual level example, some researchers may be interested in examining how intellectual abilities vary across racial groups while others view such questions as unimportant or even unethical. Values also determine how problems are studied. Consider two researchers interested in homelessness. One might ask, "How do such factors as substance abuse and mental illness interfere with homeless people's ability to integrate into society?" The second (a community psychologist, maybe) might ask, "How do homeless people survive in a society that fails to meet the needs of all its members?" (Paradis, 2000). The framing of research questions is of paramount importance because **problem definition determines problem solution**. Results gathered by the first researcher would likely indicate the need for individually oriented, deficit-based interventions, such as psychiatric

counseling and substance abuse treatment. The second study might pave the way for strength-based strategies, perhaps even collective action among the homeless to change the status quo.

At higher levels of analysis, the university department in which the researcher works might value and reward studies of particular topics or the use of specific methodologies. Values prevalent in the larger discipline (e.g., community psychology, developmental psychology, cultural anthropology) also influence research decisions since studies that elaborate on popular orienting concepts and utilize favored methodologies are more likely to be published and presented at conferences. At still higher levels, national funding priorities set scientific agendas (e.g., Fawcett, 1991).

We saw in Chapter One that Presidents Kennedy and Johnson sought to reform and revitalize the mental health system through the community mental health movement. Values helped shape this movement's agenda: the belief that mental health consumers have a right to live in their communities; the conviction that governments have responsibility for addressing social problems. During the Kennedy and Johnson administrations, government agencies earmarked funding for research and practice in community mental health. When more conservative administrations took control of the White House, funding for mental health initiatives dwindled. These administrations focused instead on a social problem more in keeping with their philosophy—substance abuse (Humphreys & Rappaport, 1993). The War on Drugs embodied a very different value system. While the community health movement centered on a concern for the welfare of all people (what Shalom Schwartz would call universalism), the War on Drugs emphasized individual achievement—officials should get tough on crime and compel people to take personal responsibility for their actions (Humphreys & Rappaport, 1993).

Different political ideologies and value systems impact the work of psychologists by determining which research agendas and social interventions receive political support and funding. Between 1981 and 1991, federal spending on drug programs increased 679% (Humphrey & Rappaport, 1993). In the 1980s, psychologists who could generate an interest in combating drug abuse had an easier time obtaining federal funds than psychologists committed to community mental health.

In addition to determining what gets studied, values also come into play when it comes time to make sense of our findings. Contrary to popular opinion, facts do not speak for themselves (Howard, 1985). They require human ears to hear them. In Chapter One (see the Classic Research box), we saw how the same results were interpreted in decidedly different ways by different people in different historical eras. In the 1950s, scholars interpreted the finding that African American children preferred White dolls as indicative of African American children's *lack* of self-esteem (e.g., Clark & Clark, 1947). In the 1990s, psychologists entertained the possibility that White children's consistent preference for White dolls reflect their *inflated* self-esteem (Jones, 1993).

Values enter the realm of psychological science in that there is always more possible science than actual science (Rose & Rose, 1980). In a world of limited resources (time, money, and energy), we have to decide what is most important. We must make choices, and our choices are value based. Choice of social problem to address, choice of research question to ask, choice of topics to fund, choice of variables to study, choice of methodology to employ, choice of how to interpret findings, choice of strategies for disseminating results—all of these choices fall at least as much in the realm of values as the realm of science.

⌘ Why Psychology Has Not Embraced Values

Given the ubiquity of values, what accounts for psychology's inattention to this topic? There are at least four compelling reasons why the field has shied away from a discourse on values. First, the conception of psychology as a pure science has served psychology well for many years. Given the progress made using this paradigm, it may seem unwise to abandon well-established logical positivist methods and empirical observations. Second, by embracing values, we risk losing respectability. Our authority rests on the portrayal of psychologists as objective professionals. Third, when one opens the door to values, one cannot control which values enter. A value-laden science can support oppression as well as liberation. Finally, psychologists tend to be left of center in the political spectrum, while the political right has appropriated the discourse on values. Thus, allusions to values may call to mind dogmatic or repressive social agendas. Each of these conditions is examined in more detail below.

FAITH IN SCIENCE

Psychology's current inattention to values has a before-the-beginning. As audacious as it is to review a century of thought in a single paragraph, let's begin our analysis of values in Western psychology in the Age of Enlightenment, also called the Age of Reason. In eighteenth-century Europe, Isaac Newton, Rene Descartes, Francis Bacon, John Locke, and other important thinkers promoted a rational and scientific approach to understanding. Their work supported the belief in natural laws and universal order. Of course, the Age of Reason had a before-the-beginning as well, and we could review the earlier trials of Galileo and the tension between his scientific inquiries and the prevailing religious belief systems upheld by the papal court. But let's focus on the Enlightenment Era. During this time, a secular conception of the world gained favor over a more faith-based view. Not everyone accepted this shift. Romanticism of the eighteenth and nineteenth centuries constituted a philosophical revolt against rationalism. Romanticism emphasized subjective experience, mystery, emotion, and imagination. This revolt did not bring rationalism to a halt, however, and most scholars marched through the end of the nineteenth century and into the twentieth century waving the banner of rationality.

This transition from the premodern to the modern world entailed a shift from religious conviction to a new belief system—faith in science. At first, religion and science coexisted. Scientific inquiry was seen as a tool for revealing the perfectly ordered world of God. By the end of the nineteenth century, however, there was widespread belief that scientific research, not piety and worship, would allow humanity to reach its highest potential. Many important thinkers at the end of the nineteenth century contributed to the displacement of religion. August Comte founded positivism and proposed that phenomena could best be explained through observation, hypothesis testing, and experimentation. Charles Darwin, through careful observation and data collection, developed his theory of evolution. God did not create the world in seven days and form man, the ruler of all nature, in God's own image. Rather, all living beings developed from the same protoplasmic mass. Random and purposeless changes in existing genetic material led to new life forms if those changes increased the organism's ability to survive and pass the changes on to future generations. Even Karl Marx invoked the "inevitable" laws of history in his ideas about economic and social structures, envisioning communism not as a moral crusade but as scientific process.

By the start of the twentieth century, psychology also prescribed to a scientific and rational approach, largely ignoring its more philosophical roots. Two major schools of thought emerged at this time. The first was behaviorism, introduced by John Watson in 1913. Behaviorism attempted to understand all animals, including humans, by documenting observable and measurable responses to stimuli in the laboratory. It presented a seemingly objective and mechanistic view of human behavior. Behavior was simply a response to reinforcements in our environment. There was no need to look beyond the observable world and refer to invisible thoughts, feelings, and beliefs. One of behaviorism's most famous advocates, B. F. Skinner, viewed religion as a form of superstitious thought used by religious organizations as a mechanism of control (Skinner, 1948/1976). The disparagement of religion was one of the few areas of agreement between Skinner and Sigmund Freud, the father of the second major school of thought, psychoanalysis (Hill, 2000).

Psychoanalysis stood in opposition to behaviorism by emphasizing subjective phenomena—unconscious drives and nonobservable psychological entities, such as the id, ego, and superego. Despite this interest in unseen forces, Freud (e.g., 1907/1963) incorporated ideas of natural laws into his theories and dismissed religion as superstition. In his view, religion was a refuge for maladapted individuals who could not come to terms with either the human impulses they deemed unacceptable or the external forces they perceived as uncontrollable. According to Freud, religiosity reflected maladaptive coping mechanisms, such as escapism, denial, avoidance, and passivity (see Pargament & Park, 1995). In short, religion was a crutch for the weak. Although other important psychologists in the early nineteenth century cast religion in a more positive light (e.g., William James, G. Stanley Hall, and Carl Jung), they had far less impact on modern psychology (for a review, see Wulff, 1996).

As premodernism gave way to modernism, the world of science (the first of the two worlds described at the beginning of the chapter) and the world of religion (constituent of the second world) diverged. Indeed, the two worlds came to be seen as completely separate and fundamentally incompatible. Science rested on fact while religion rested on faith. Scientific claims were verifiable or falsifiable while religious claims could not be evaluated objectively. Clear, reason-based criteria existed for choosing between scientific theories, but choosing between religions was subjective and arguable (Barbour, 1974). In addition, science seeks to predict and control while religion stresses human limitation and subordination to God. As recently as 1981, the National Academy of Sciences passed a resolution stating that, "Religion and science are separate and mutually exclusive realms of human thought whose presentation in the same context leads to a misunderstanding of both scientific theory and religious belief" (cited in Jones, 1996, p. 117).

Psychologists who advocate for a separation between facts and values believe that science cannot dictate moral imperatives. Questions of right and wrong may be informed but can never be decided by empirical study. Howard Kendler (1999) exemplifies this perspective. He asked us to consider the possibility that reliable data exist to indicate that bilingual education enhances ethnic identification while slowing academic progress. He asserted that this finding would be value neutral—it does not lead to any particular conclusion about bilingual education. It provides empirical evidence that bears on value decisions about education policies, but according to Kendler, such value decisions belong in the realm of politics, not psychology.

Even proponents of the separation of facts and values concede that the scientific process cannot be removed *entirely* from the influence of values, but that we should try nonetheless. Many community psychologists would agree that important psychological knowledge has been gained through the prevailing logical positivist methods, and so these methods should not be abandoned (see Tolan, Keys, Chertok, & Jason, 1990). We are likely, however, to endorse other ways of knowing, question the degree to which values *can* indeed be removed from the scientific process, and argue against the desirability of keeping the two worlds separate.

THE CLOAK OF RESPECTABILITY

In the modern era, psychology fashioned itself as a natural science. Earlier ties to philosophy and other "soft" sciences were severed in an attempt to gain legitimacy as a "hard" science in the same category as physics and chemistry. Not all scholars supported psychology's movement in this direction. John Dewey (1931) distinguished physical facts from social facts. Physical facts eliminate all human biases. They are the "ultimate residue after human purposes, desires, emotions, and ideas and ideals have been systematically excluded" (p. 64). Dewey warned that while physical facts might help explain the inanimate world, an understanding of human behavior required the consideration of social facts. How can we understand human behavior by eliminating from our studies all that is distinctly human?

Subsequent scholars have echoed Dewey's sentiment. Sigmund Koch (1959) noted forty years ago that one of the main problems with psychology was that its commitment to science outweighed its commitment to humanity. More recently, George Howard (1985) argued that values take on added significance in studying the human world because people are

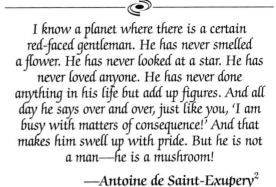

I know a planet where there is a certain red-faced gentleman. He has never smelled a flower. He has never looked at a star. He has never loved anyone. He has never done anything in his life but add up figures. And all day he says over and over, just like you, 'I am busy with matters of consequence!' And that makes him swell up with pride. But he is not a man—he is a mushroom!

—Antoine de Saint-Exupery[2]

reflexive entities. This means that research, while documenting our life, also changes it. Light does not (as far as we know) respond to theories of physics by altering its behavior in any way. Humans, however, not only shape theories, but are shaped by them. We are influenced by how science views us. Thus, scientific theories affect how people think of themselves and risk becoming self-fulfilling prophesies (Miller, 1999; B. Schwartz, 1997).

As one example, consider the possibility that knowledge of the psychological research purporting African Americans' intellectual inferiority actually interferes with African Americans' ability to perform well on standardized tests. The social psychologist Claude Steele (1997) conducted an experiment that provided evidence for this hypothesis. In one testing situation, race was made salient and African American research participants believed that difficult verbal tests were diagnostic of their cognitive ability. In this situation, they underperformed. If the same tests were presented simply as problem-solving tasks unrelated to ability, Black research participants performed as well as White participants. Steele found similar effects for gender. For this study, half of the participants were told before taking a difficult math test that the test generally showed gender differences. The other participants simply took the test. Women who expected the test to show gender differences underperformed. When gender was not made salient, women performed as well as men (see Figure 3.1).

[2]Excerpt from THE LITTLE PRINCE by Antoine de Saint-Exupery, Copyright 1943 and renewed 1971 by Harcourt, Inc., reprinted by permission of the publisher.

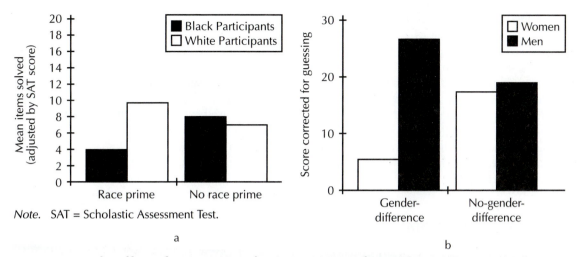

a   b

Figure 3.1 The effect of stereotype salience on test performance.
Figure 3a shows the mean performance of Black and White participants on a difficult verbal test when race was and was not primed. Figure 3b shows mean performance of women and men on a difficult math test when gender was or was not primed. *Steele, C. M. (1997). A threat in the air: How stereotypes shape intellectual identity and performance.* American Psychologist, 52, 613–629. Copyright © 1997 by the American Psychological Association. Reprinted with permission.

In their classic article *On Being Useful: The Nature and Consequences of Psychological Research on Social Problems*, Nathan Caplan and Stephen Nelson (1973) remarked on the reflexivity of research. They wrote, "The repercussions of our research findings—the views of the world they inspire or perpetuate—may seem like epiphenomena to us, but they are often painfully real for those affected by them" (p. 206).

Howard (1985) posited that "the shift in roles for research psychologists from neutral truth seekers to chroniclers and molders of human action, implies a greater acknowledgement of subjectivity and value judgments in science" (p. 263). That acknowledgement, however, has been slow in coming. Although psychologists generally recognize the conflation of science and values, many prefer not to advertise this situation. There exists a widespread fear that "a clearly stated moral vision [would] erode the already tenuous perception of the field as a scientific endeavor" (Nicholson, 1998, p. 322). This fear appears justified as recent studies have linked the growth of the profession to its reputation as an objective science (Nicholson, 1998, with reference to Danziger, 1990). Thus, involvement in

policy making, advocacy, and other action activities may be frowned upon not only due to the doubt that psychological knowledge can bear directly on value-laden political issues, but also for fear that activism will ruin psychology's professional and scientific reputation.

Attempts to advance psychology as a pure science have resulted in what U.S. Court of Appeals Judge David Bazelon (1982) called a *veiling of values*. Psychologists have framed issues purely in scientific terms, even when the fire behind their debate is fueled by moral imperatives. Judge Bazelon argued that the appropriate remedy was not for psychologists to remove themselves from legal and policy arenas, but to unveil their values.

Howard Kendler (1999) would disagree. He warned that if psychologists become actively involved in the political system, then they risk losing credibility, since valid psychological knowledge will be dismissed as politically tainted and so unreliable. Kendler argued that there could be a synergistic, cooperative relationship between natural science methodology and democratic processes. Such a relationship had two requirements, however. Psychologists must "provide relevant empirical evidence that is not first contaminated by political goals" and "avoid interpreting results as directly justifying a particular social policy" (p. 833). He contended that psychologists interested in shaping public policy should stop obscuring their political efforts under the cloak of psychological research and run for public office instead. As you might guess, Kendler is the psychologist who responded to an article on values written by Isaac Prilletlensky by recommending that Prilleltensky best leave the field of psychology altogether (Prilleltensky, 1998).

THE SLIPPERY SLOPE

The third reason why psychologists shy away from a discourse on values is that a bridge between science and values can be crossed by anyone—not only scientists committed to humanism and equality, but also those invested in imperialism and oppression, as well. Some scholars have distinguished the relatively safe domain of **descriptive values** from the more dangerous territory of **prescriptive values** (Shadish, 1990; Kendler, 1987). Descriptive values simply delineate the principles held by a group of people. They do not entail judgments about whether the principles are or are not desirable. The research of Shalom Schwartz (1992, 1994) and Randolph Potts (1999a) mentioned earlier center on descriptive values. Prescriptive values indicate which values people *should* hold. The community psychologist William Shadish (1990) echoed Kendler's concern, stating that, "once the Pandora's box of prescriptive values is opened, it becomes increasingly difficult to justify the choice of one prescription over another" (p. 15). Many community psychologists believe, however, that prescriptive values inevitably influence all human actions, including our research and practice. Even efforts to document descriptive values are affected by prescriptive values in numerous ways—in deciding to adopt a universalistic versus a particularistic approach, for example.

Given the likelihood that prescriptive values enter into our research and practice, how do community psychologists guard against the inherent dangers? Accountability to the communities in which we work can provide a toehold as we negotiate the slippery slope of prescriptive values. By involving community members in the scientific process from beginning to end, researchers are less able to impose their own values in a peremptory way and also benefit from contact with a wide and potentially illuminating universe of alternative value perspectives.

Stephen Fawcett (1991) described strategies for involving community members in all phases of research: setting the research agenda, determining the research methodology, making sense of the findings, and developing action plans based on the results. He used, for example, a Concerns Report process that combined surveys and community forums to encourage both researchers and community members to identify their value priorities and consider alternative perspectives (see also Serrano-García, 1990). Such a strategy does not, however, define a process for deciding among priorities and reaching consensus when disagreements arise (Winett, 1991). Nevertheless, clearly identifying conflicting value perspectives is a first step toward greater understanding and healthier collaborations. Prilleltensky (1998) argued that by admitting the importance of values and proposing a value system, "we can at least agree on what values, assumptions, and practices we disagree on" (p. 325).

Prilleltensky (1999) identified four roles for leaders, including community psychologists, interested in helping settings identify and discuss values. First, the leader can clarify the position of the group with respect to values. In this capacity, community psychologists might help negotiate differences in values among diverse stakeholders. Second, leaders can try to enhance the zone of congruence among collaborators. When value differences threaten to divide groups, the identification of common ground can unify setting participants around a shared mission. For example, stakeholders in an alternative school who disagree about curriculum issues might begin to build a common agenda from their shared conviction that all children have the right to learn. Third, leaders need to promote a state of affairs where personal power and self-interest do not undermine others in the group. Community psychologists can help maintain an environment in which diverse voices are heard and respected. Finally, leaders need to confront people who subvert values of inclusion and/or abuse power. In order for diverse viewpoints to be heard, overbearing or threatening voices need to kept in check.

When community psychologists involve community members as equal participants and support environments where diverse voices can be heard, we situate ourselves in a value system while learning about the value systems of others. Robert Kane (1998) argued that because values are embedded in social inquiry, scientists need to make all efforts to *minimize narrowness*, that is to minimize the limitations and parochialness of one's own point of view.

Since the birth of the field in the 1960s, community psychologists have recognized the liberatory potential of exposing and questioning implicit values. Julian Rappaport (1984a) proposed that "[t]he raison d'etre for the field [of community psychology] has been, at least since Swampscott, a confrontation with accepted social and professional values" (p. 209). Thus, several community psychologists have proposed ways of revealing our own and others' values.

Edward Seidman (1983) observed that unexamined values and assumptions constrain our ability to think creatively about social problems and recommended several strategies to help us break free of these constraints. These strategies involve invoking paradox (see also Rappaport, 1981). For example, we can try to resist the Western tendency to believe in *one* right theory or *one* truth, seek out criticism, and continuously attempt to reframe our questions of interest. Meg Bond (1999) suggested another strategy for invoking paradox. She recommended searching for **countervalues.** In her work with organizations. Bond noted that U.S. culture embraces values of independence, which can work against a sense of mutual responsibility. Thus, "in order to rock a shared complacency that is supported by individualistic values dominant in our society, organizational settings need to actively promote *counter*values and create a community of support for the values of accountability and connection" (p. 347).

RELINQUISHING THE MORAL TERRAIN

A third reason why psychologists may steer clear of discussions of values is fear that the invocation of values encourages dogmatism and discourages critical thinking (Prilleltensky, 1997). To many of us, *moral* connotes *moralistic*, which means "expressive of a narrow and conventional moral attitude" (Merriam-Webster, 1999). In public discourse, the familiar terms, "family values" and "traditional values" are often code words for anti-progressive, anti-feminist, and anti-gay sentiments. The narrow-mindedness and dogmatism associated with some nonscientific and vocal religious groups have likely contributed to psychology's emphasis on science and rationalism. Although religion and values are not synonymous, they are related, and ideas about religion and spirituality often lurk behind our efforts to discuss, or our refusals to discuss, our values (e.g., Sollod, 1998).

Research in the 1930s to the 1970s confirmed that psychologists hold more negative attitudes toward religion than almost any other group (Hill, 2000). Subsequent research also supports this contention. In a 1984 survey of academicians, psychologists ranked among the least religious with 50% reporting no religious preference. In comparison, only 10% of the general population reported no religious preference (see Jones, 1996; Goldman, 1991).[3] A 1990 study found that only 33% of psychologists endorsed the item, "My whole approach to life is based on my religion," as compared to 72% of the lay public (Bergin & Jensen, 1990).

_____

[3]A few studies suggest that psychologists are fairly religious. One study of therapists found that 80% reported a religious preference (vs. 91% of the general public) and 77% tried to live according to their religious beliefs (vs. 84% of the general public) (Bergin and Jensen, 1990).

A lack of interest in, if not an active expulsion of, religion is reflected in the psychology literature, as well. Between 1991 and 1994, fewer than 3% of the quantitative studies appearing in seven major APA journals included a religious or spiritual variable, and this construct was almost always assessed superficially using a single question (Weaver, Kline, Samford, Lucas, Larson, & Gorsuch, 1998).

There is evidence that psychologists' rejection of religion may be, at least in part, a rejection of the dogmatism of organized religion. One recent study allowed respondents to identify as spiritual as opposed to religious. **Religiosity** encompassed institutional beliefs and practices while **spirituality** relied on a more personal view of religion. Mental health workers often self-identified as "spiritual" rather than "religious" (Zinnbauer, Pargament, Cole, Belavich, Hipp, Scott, & Kader, 1997).

Research suggests that religiosity is indeed associated with conformity, authoritarianism, and an emphasis on tradition (e.g., Roccas & S. Schwartz, 1997; Zinnbauer et al., 1997). The association, however, is not absolute (nor necessarily regressive and repressive). Indeed, several community psychologists have challenged the rigid, conformist, and overly simplistic views of religiosity held by many people, including psychologists (e.g., Pargament & Maton, 2000). Some religious traditions are progressive and consistent with community psychology's value. For example, liberation theology, including Black liberation theology and Latin American liberation theology, draw on Biblical injunctions to free oppressed people (Balcazar, 1999; Dokecki, 1982; Potts, 1999b). Other community psychologists have examined the social change implications of Islamic (Abdul-Adil & Jason, 1991) and of feminist and womanist theology (Molock & Douglas, 1999).

It is unfortunate that fear of dogmatism, fanaticism, and authoritarianism may dissuade psychologists from engaging in value discussions. When more liberal-minded people refrain from participation in values discourse, they allow the discourse to be shaped exclusively by more repressive and regressive voices who enter into such discussions loudly and forcefully. In a talk at the University of Colorado entitled *Multicultural Democracy: Beyond Race, Gender, and Class Oppression,* Manning Marable (February 1, 1999) put it this way: "Conservatives do something better than liberals—they ground their action in values. But they have the wrong damn values."

⌘ Why Community Psychology Requires Discourse in Values

The five guiding principles that organize this text may be seen as a statement of community psychology's values. Because values generally occur in holistic sets, the first guiding principle, the importance of values, hinges on the other four. Let's look at how a discourse on values relates to community psychology's other four guiding principles.

VALUES AND THE CONTEXT BEYOND THE INDIVIDUAL

A discourse in values requires a consideration of context. First and foremost, contexts shape values. Families are generally charged with inculcating important values into children, but schools also provide moral socialization, most recently under the label *character education* (e.g., Brooks & Goble, 1997). In addition to families and schools, other settings also subscribe to particular value systems: peer groups, clubs, workplaces, and of course religious organizations and political groups.

The recognition that different contexts support different values suggests that well-being may depend, in part, on the congruence between personal values and the values that prevail in various contexts. One small study found that students who personally valued power and achievement fared better in business schools as compared to psychology programs that supported more universalistic values (Sagiv & S. Schwartz, 2000). As another example, the survival of "captive" people who live in institutions (e.g., mental patients, prison inmates) may depend on their ability to abide by the norms and values of that institution (e.g., Paradis, 2000, with reference to Rosenthal, 1991). Captives may benefit from embracing what Shalom Shwartz (1992, 1994) called Conformity, even if they personally value Self-Direction.

Individuals are affected not only by the values that prevail in their immediate settings, but by values of larger systems, as well. The life of U.S. citizens is very much shaped by U.S. society's emphasis on individual advancement. A variety of policies and practices—business incentives and tax breaks for example, reflect the importance afforded to achievement values. The emphasis on individualism (which falls under Shalom Schwartz's value of self-direction) in the U.S. also means that values are often construed as essentially private—a matter of personal integrity and choice. Indeed, one reason why some people embrace spirituality as opposed to religiosity is that the former involves a personal relationship with God while the latter entails agreed-upon institutional practices (Zinnbauer et al., 1997). Individualism frees people from the dogma and conformity required by most religious, but it also removes us from the richness of spiritual community. Religious involvement in the U.S. has mostly been studied in terms of individual attitudes and behaviors (Pargament & Maton, 2000). The power of religion derives from the combined forces of a personal relationship with God and communion with others. Leonard Jason (1997) noted that one of the most eloquent spokespeople on community life is the Trappist monk Thomas Merton, who lived much of his life in seclusion (see also Claassen, 2000).

VALUES AND THE APPRECIATION OF DIVERSITY

There are two ways in which community psychology's attention to diverse, especially disenfranchised groups leads to a consideration of values. First, an appreciation of diversity forces us to recognize that Western psychologists' attachment to positivist science and rationality reflects only one of many possible worldviews. Other groups value different ways of knowing. (e.g., Walsh-Bowers, 2000). Second, our attention to disenfranchised groups makes clear that psychology's supposedly value-free science has a history of reinforcing the status quo and contributing to the oppression of marginalized groups (Prilleltensky, 1989). Much injustice has been perpetrated under the guise of objective science.

WORLDVIEWS OF DIVERSE GROUPS

In the modern era, psychology's efforts to be a "hard" science and live in the world of objectivity have led us to blot out the world of subjectivity. Not every group similarly worships rationalism and seeks to exorcise subjectivity. For example, Easterners from China, Japan, and Korea, as compared Westerners from the United States, rely more on experience-based knowledge rather than abstract logic, think more holistically, pay greater attention to context and relationship, and show more tolerance for contradiction (Goode, 2000; Ji, Peng, & Nisbett, 2000). Many scholars believe that a similar set of characteristics distinguish the worldviews of women as compared to men (see the Classic Research box). Consequently, the rejection of all things subjective disrespects the worldviews of many people.

Historically, psychologists have tried to live in the world of objectivity. Thus, the finding of psychologists' lack of religiosity is not surprising. The people we serve, however, often *are* religious. As of 1993, there were 500,000 churches in the U.S., which 40% of the population attended weekly and 60% attended monthly (Gallup, 1993). Furthermore, these religious institutions play important roles in addressing human problems. Lisbeth Schorr (1997) observed that healing relationships are easier to establish in faith-based as compared to secular settings. People with mental health diagnoses are more likely to seek assistance from clergy than from psychologists and psychiatrists (Hohmann & Larson, 1993). In addition, clergy receive higher

CLASSIC RESEARCH

Lawrence Kohlberg and Carol Gilligan
Moral Reasoning in Context

Lawrence Kohlberg (1964, 1976) stands out as a psychologist interested in rigorously studying morality. His research addressed the question: How do people learn to distinguish right from wrong?

In order to address this question, Kohlberg asked children and adults to reason out loud about various hypothetical dilemmas. The most famous of these is Heinz' dilemma—should Heinz save his dying wife by stealing an expensive drug from a pharmacist who is overcharging for that drug? Kohlberg found that people of different ages reasoned differently about this dilemma. He posited that people pass through three developmental levels of *moral reasoning.*

The first level is the *preconventional level*: People at this level base moral decisions on the physical consequences of an act, such as punishment. Someone at this level might reason that Heinz should not steal the drug because he will get into trouble. Next is the *conventional level*: People at this level base moral decisions on social rules and the expectations of one's family or other group. Someone at this level might reason that Heinz should not steal the drug because stealing is illegal. Finally comes the *postconventional/autonomous level*: At this level, moral decisions reflect attempts to define overarching values and principles. Someone at this level might reason that if everyone who wanted something just took it, there would be no social order. Note that in Kohlberg's theory, the content of one's moral choice has no bearing on one's level of reasoning. People can also formulate reasons why Heinz *should* steal the drug at each of the three levels.

Kohlberg's influential theory has received considerable empirical support. The stages do appear to occur in the predicted order (e.g., Colby, Kohlberg, Gibbs, & Lieberman, 1983). In addition, there is evidence for the universality of his model across 27 different cultures (Snarey, 1985. For an alternative view, see Shweder, Mahapatra, & Miller, 1987).

Kohlberg does have his critics, however. Most important among them is Carol Gilligan (1982). Gilligan questioned Kohlberg's conception of justice and fairness as the only relevant issue in moral reasoning. She argued that there exist at least two distinct moral orientations: the *justice orientation* proposed by Kohlberg and also a *care orientation*. While the justice orientation concerns the moral requirement for people to treat each other fairly, the care orientation emphasizes the importance of helping those in need. Gilligan suggested that Kohlberg's emphasis on justice resulted from his over-reliance on male research participants and an androcentric (i.e., male-centered) worldview. Gilligan proposed that women's concerns about relationships and social ties lead them to a care orientation, while men's focus on legal issues and abstract rules lead them to a justice orientation.

Although Gilligan's hypothesized sex differences have not been consistently documented (e.g., Walker, de Vries, & Trevethan, 1987; Walker, Pitts, Henning, & Matsuba, 1995; Turiel, 1998), her work has contributed greatly to the literature on morality and the literature on the psychology of women. Research shows that both care and justice orientations are important components of moral reasoning for both men and women (Gilligan & Attanucci, 1988). In addition, her emphasis on relationships has energized a growing body of research on women's development (e.g., Jordan, Kaplan, Miller, Stiver, & Surrey, 1991), and on the ethics of care (e.g., Faver, 2001; Noddings, 1984).

The most influential aspect of Gilligan's work was her proposition that moral reasoning entails a consideration of care as well as justice. A second contribution was her questioning of the use of hypothetical dilemmas to assess moral reasoning. Hypothetical dilemmas provide a degree of experimental control. Because no research participant actually faced Heinz's dilemma, there was some measure of uniformity in the experimental manipulation across all respondents. For her research, Gilligan chose to use a real-life dilemma and studied women's actual decision-making process concerning having an abortion. Because each woman's experience with abortion was unique, the use of this dilemma introduced considerable variability across research participants. On the other hand, assessing reasoning about an actual, salient event may have elicited a depth of responding that hypothetical dilemmas cannot simulate. This illustrates a long-standing concern in science—in the pursuit of understanding, should researchers sacrifice methodological rigor or psychological relevance? In deciding how to resolve this dilemma, each scientist's value system (once again) comes into play. Gilligan's work argued for a consideration of morality not only in abstract, theoretical terms, but in terms that capture the messiness of our lived experience and the richness of our day-to-day lives.

ratings than psychologists and psychiatrists on such skills as warmth, caring, stability, and professionalism (Schindler, Berren, Hannah, Beigel, & Santiago, 1987).

Participation in religious and spiritual practices are important to many U.S. citizens but may be particularly important in the lives of ethnic minority group members (e.g., Pargament, Smith, Koenig, & Perez, 1998; Snowden, Martinez, & Morris, 2000). Roderick Watts (1993a) asserted that spirituality was essential to the programs for young African American men that he studied, and central to the worldview of many Blacks, other people of color, and White ethnic groups. He concluded that community psychology's lack of attention to spirituality impeded its efforts to devise culturally valid and effective interventions. Watts said of the area of spirituality, "Work here is urgently needed" (1993a, p. 355).

Since Watts wrote those words, community psychology has stretched to embrace worldviews that value spirituality. The question remains, however, as to how far community psychology can and should stretch to respect diverse value systems. We have come again to the slippery slope. Do we accept all other value systems? Does the value we place on appreciating diverse views take precedence over our other values, such as the promotion of social justice? Does community psychology's appreciation of diversity mean that we must also accept other cultures' lack of acceptance of diversity or active oppression of others? Can we, as individuals and as a field, take a position on female circumcision or other cultural practices that we find objectionable if not immoral? We find ourselves in a conundrum: The appreciation of diversity is in and of itself a value and one that not

all cultures share. Should we honor the ethnocentric, racist, and misogynistic views of other cultural groups in the name of multiculturalism?

Calls for cultural sensitivity have resulted in the unquestioning celebration of group differences and the depiction of all worldviews as equally valid (Fowers & Richardson, 1996). This is inherently problematic. Community psychology, too, has relied on cultural relativism as a moral posture (Davidson, 1989). Relativism means that we can judge the ethics of behavior only within the context of the specific culture in which the behavior occurs. Absolute judgments cannot be defended. This may help explain why, despite its social change rhetoric, community psychology has often failed to take a stand on controversial social issues (Mulvey, 1988). Ultimately, cultural relativism makes the discussion of ethical issues unnecessary. A view of all values as equally meritorious is merely the flip side to dogmatism.

In their work with Puerto Rican and Dominican women, Blanca Ortiz-Torres, Irma Serrano-García, and Nélida Torres-Burgos (2000) argued for **transculturation**, whereby people retain some values, perspectives, and traditions from their own cultures but also choose to adopt patterns and practices from the dominant culture (and potentially other nondominant cultures). It is a dialectical process—exposure to different cultures changes the individual's worldview, and individual transformation leads to changes in cultural worldviews. Ortiz-Torres and her colleagues argue against the conservative nationalist goal of idealizing, preserving, and transmitting cultures intact to future generations. They advocated for cultural growth and regeneration toward a particular goal. "Culture, we believe, cannot become a haven for oppression, but must instead be a space where respect for diversity and participation in the development of new values leads all of us closer to health, dignity, and freedom" (Ortiz-Torres et al., 2000, p. 877).

Linda Silka and Jahnvibol Tip (1994) provided an example of how contact with another culture can transform the root culture in a way that leads to the reduction of oppression. They noted that after living in the U.S., women from Southeast Asia often question traditional gender hierarchies and speak out against sexual assault and domestic abuse. Some Southeast Asians view women's activism as a destabilizing force that threatens the Southeast Asian family. Silka and Tip proposed reframing the issue. Female empowerment may be construed not as conflicting with Southeast traditions concerning the place of women, but rather as consistent with cultural assumptions about women's responsibility for the next generation. The notion that Southeast Asian women are *obligated* to leave abusive relationships to protect the future of the community remains true to Southeast Asian values, *and* responds to the need to abandon oppressive cultural practices.

Community psychology's appreciation of diverse worldviews has inspired us to challenge some tenets of Western psychology, such as the worship of objectivity and indiscriminate rejection of religion and spirituality. Challenges remain, however, in discriminating aspects of diverse worldviews that are worthy of embrace from those that demand repudiation.

ROLE OF "VALUE-FREE" SCIENCE IN OPPRESSION

Community psychology's appreciation of diversity leads us to honor worldviews that incorporate subjectivity and values. It also forces us to confront the role of supposedly value-free science in perpetuating oppression. With the acute vision of hindsight, we can identify numerous examples in the history of psychology. For example, in the 1950s and 1960s, psychologists labeled women as maladjusted

if they did not fulfill traditional gender roles.[4] Thus, the finding of greater sex-role flexibility in girls as compared to boys was interpreted as evidence of the girls' unresolved Oedipal conflict (e.g., Brown, 1957; see also Chesler, 1972). In the 1970s, androgyny came to be viewed as desirable, and sex-role flexibility came to be viewed as an asset (Bem, 1975). In another reversal, the American Psychological Association, which considered lesbian and gay people to be mentally ill in the 1970s, now spearheads gay rights efforts (see American Psychological Association's *Resources for the Public: What You Need to Know About Gay, Lesbian, and Bisexual Issues*, 2000).

People in the helping professions have a unique moral responsibility to the public. We are charged with the responsibility of defining normalcy. Psychology can easily abuse its power to diagnose and label vulnerable populations. This is a key reason why the American Psychological Association (1992) developed its Ethical Principles of Psychologists and Code of Conduct.[5] Laura Brown (1997) noted, however, that even when psychological research or practice follows the letter of the law with regard to our codes of conduct, it may still violate the spirit of that law. As a recent example, consider the work of Richard Herrnstein and Charles Murray (1994).

In their book, *The Bell Curve*, Herrnstein and Murray documented the intellectual inferiority of African Americans as compared to other racial groups. The studies described in their book appear to obey the letter of the law. The researchers may have, for example, obtained informed consent, honored research participants' confidentiality, and followed established methodological guidelines.[6] Nevertheless, using study results to disparage a

---

[4]Actually, a double bind has existed as women have been seen as maladjusted even if they do fulfill traditional roles, see the research by Broverman and colleagues (1970) described in Chapter One.

[5]As this textbook goes to press, the APA Ethical Principles of 1992 are being revised. The principles can be reviewed at *http://www.apa.org/ethics/code.html*.

[6]This is not to say that the research cited in *The Bell Curve* is indisputably sound methodologically. See Devlin, Fienberg, Resnick, & Roeder, 1997; Fraser, 1995; Kincheloe, Steinberg, & Gresson, A., 1996; Nisbett, 1998.

group of people is not a morally neutral endeavor. Technically ethical research can still breach more general ethics, such as the injunction to avoid harming vulnerable populations (e.g., APA's *Principle D* requires "respect for people's rights and dignity," and *Principle E* mandates a "concern for others' welfare"). The disparagement of African Americans occurs under the aura of scientific respectability. Herrnstein and Jensen perform this sleight of hand by hiding behind the cloak of objectivity. Their work represents a modern day example of purportedly value-free research perpetuating societal injustice.

VALUES AND SOCIAL CHANGE

Values enter into discussions of social change because they both direct and sustain change efforts. Social change requires a vision of how things *should* be (or at least how they should *not* be). In addition, our value-based social convictions enable us to pursue social justice despite risks, opposition, ambiguity, and the awareness of how overwhelming our task really is. As Roderick Watts and his colleagues observed, "a 'higher purpose' produces zeal and a basis for solidarity" (Watts, Griffith, & Abdul-Adil, 1999, p. 260).

Community psychologists and other activists do not always connect their value base, sense of urgency, and solidarity with others to organized religion. Indeed, some see religion as an impediment to social change. Studies have documented an inverse relationship between activism and religiosity (e.g., Hilliard, 1972). Religious faith may discourage earthly commitments and encourage the belief that rewards come in the hereafter, thereby fostering complacency and acceptance of the status quo. Karl Marx contended that religion is the opiate of the masses. In the same passage, however, Marx described religion as "a sigh from the oppressed, the soul of a heartless world, the spirit of spiritless conditions" (cited in Walsh-Bowers, 2000, p. 225).

The relationship between religion and social justice is not simple (see Hunsberger, 1995; Pargament & Park, 1995). Religion has inspired struggles for liberation as well as efforts to oppress. Nevertheless,

the link between religious faith and commitment to social change is undeniable. Many of the most renowned recipients of the Nobel Peace Prize have strong ties to religion, including Martin Luther King Jr., Mother Teresa, the fourteenth Dalai Lama, and Bishop Desmond Tutu. Perhaps the most influential of social change activists in the twentieth century, Mahatma Gandhi, drew his vision and strength from a deep spiritual base. Interestingly, Gandhi counted science without humanity as one of the seven sins. He would not condone the separation of the two worlds described in the opening of this chapter.

VALUES AND A STRENGTHS-BASED PERSPECTIVE

Community psychology rejects the medical model, which focuses on people's deficits. It seeks instead to identify people's strength as a way of promoting positive mental health. This agenda leads to a discourse on values for two reasons. First, in order to enhance mental health we need to know how people *should* behave—what does it mean to be psychologically healthy? Second, values are an important source of strength for many people.

VALUES AND THE DEFINITION MENTAL HEALTH

Throughout its history, psychology has focused more on psychological problems than psychological health. Howard Kendler (1999) argued that psychologists can agree on what constitutes *negative* mental health; dysfunctional behaviors such as "debilitating depression, incapacitating anxiety, and hallucinations" (p. 834). When it comes to *positive* mental health, however, he posited that moral pluralism rules.

Kendler's assertion that psychologists can clearly define poor mental health is debatable. Although we may agree about psychological illness in the extreme (e.g., *debilitating* depression and *incapacitating* anxiety), diagnoses are not always clear cut. We do not all agree, for example, about when sadness crosses over into depression.

Assumptions underlying assessments of mental illness may be more unanimously shared but are value-based and prone to bias nonetheless. There are numerous examples. One study found that psychologists and psychiatrists identified different causes and treatments for pathology when protagonists in vignettes were identified as older adults (i.e., in their sixties or seventies) versus young adults (Caplovitz & Rodin, 1980, reported in Rodin & Langer, 1980). The work of the freedom-fighting psychologists cited in Chapter One highlighted the ways in which society's value-based notions of mental illness contributed to the oppression of women (Broverman, Broverman, Clarkson, Rosenkrantz, & Vogel, 1970) and gay people (Hooker, 1957).

Indeed, biases of psychologists are evident in the assumption that religiosity is a sign of poor mental health. As described earlier, the most influential psychological theorists of the early twentieth century claimed that religiosity indicated maladjustment (e.g., Skinner, 1948/1976, Freud, 1907/1963). More recent evidence suggests that religion is associated with health (Kloos & Moore, 2000a; Kress & Elias, 2000). A review of the literature on religion and mental health found a positive relationship between religiosity and some aspect of well-being (Payne, Bergin, Bielema, & Jenkins, 1991). For example, people who engage in religious practices (e.g., church and synagogue attendance, prayer, Bible study) are less likely to use drugs, alcohol, and tobacco[7] (see Booth & Martin, 1998; Gartner, 1996; Gorsuch, 1995). Research also suggests a relationship between religiosity or spirituality and *recovery* from substance abuse (e.g., Plante & Pardini, 2000). This may explain the popularity of **twelve-step programs**, most of which have a strong spiritual component (see the Community Intervention box).

On the other hand, researchers have documented only a small correlation between religiosity and mental health per se (Levin & Chatters, 1998). The relationship between religion and health is complex

(Ventis, 1995), as religion can be used in both healthy and nonhealthy ways. It can engender self-acceptance or shame. It can lead people to see themselves as made in the image of God or as imperfect beings tainted by original sin. It can bring people together to actualize humanity's greatest potential or foster divisions among people that limit them and make them bitter. Religion can lead to complacency or inspire activism. In addition, the relationship between religion and mental health may differ across groups. Most studies have used predominantly White (and Christian) samples. Research suggests that religion and spirituality may be a particularly important component of mental health for African Americans (Edwards, 1999; Myers, 1999).

The role of religion in mental health may also be increasing. More and more Americans recognize the importance of a value base and spiritual connection to their mental health (e.g., Bellah, Madsen, Sullivan, & Tipton, 1985; Schneider, 1998). A Gallup poll in 1994 found that 58% of Americans reported a need to experience spiritual growth. By 1998, the percentage had risen to 82% (Gallup & Lindsay, 2000).

To say that a strong value base and commitment to spirituality may be associated with mental health is not to say *which* values and *which* spirituality. Few studies bear on such prescriptive assessments. One study of 1261 students from Israel and the former East and West Germany found that people who valued achievement, self-direction, and stimulation evidenced greater affective well-being. Students who valued conformity and security evidenced lower affective well-being (Sagiv & Schwartz, 2000). It seems unlikely, however, that the same values will relate to well-being for all people across all contexts.

VALUES AS A SOURCE OF STRENGTH

Jean Hill (2000) argued that community psychology must consider values and spirituality because they matter to the people with whom we work. She wrote, "in a field that seeks to focus on people's strengths rather than deficits, spirituality and religion are definitely sources of strength for many

---

[7]Although some religious groups, including Jews, Christians, and Muslims, are associated with abstinence from mind-altering substances, some religions their use. For example, peyote is used in spiritual practices by some American Indian groups (Booth & Martin, 1998).

COMMUNITY INTERVENTION:

Twelve-Step Programs:
Spirituality and Community

One of the largest and most influential models of community interventions is the twelve-step program. The first of these programs, Alcoholics Anonymous (AA), has grown enormously since its founding in 1935. As of 1999, there were over 50,000 AA groups in the US, which counted more than one million members (Alcoholics Anonymous, 1999a). As many as 15 million people attend AA meetings each week (Bailey, 1991). AA also serves as a model for programs catering to people with other addictive disorders, such as Narcotics Anonymous, Overeaters Anonymous, and Gamblers Anonymous.

Twelve-step programs have a strong spiritual dimension. Of the twelve steps to recovery on which the programs are based, six mention "God" or "a Power greater than ourselves" and a seventh speaks to a "spiritual awakening" (Alcoholics Anonymous, 1999b). Twelve-step programs generally do not advocate a specific religious orientation, however, and participants need not believe in God or follow a particular teaching.

Is the spiritual component crucial to these programs? The spiritual dimension is controversial among professionals, some of whom see it as detracting rather than contributing to the program's success (Buxton, Smith & Seymour, 1987). Professionals also hesitate to refer nonreligious patients to these programs, even though a study of more than 3,000 substance abuse inpatients found that nonreligious as well as religiously inclined patients benefited from twelve-step programs (Winzelberg & Humphreys, 1999). Members of twelve-step programs do not evidence the same ambivalence about the spiritual component, however. In one study of twelve-step programs, 100% of the members who were successful in their recovery affirmed the importance of Step 2: coming "to believe that a Power greater than ourselves could restore us to sanity" (Brown & Peterson, 1991).

Why might a spiritual component be important in recovery? One appeal of twelve-step programs is that they celebrate the reality of human limitation (Hopson, 1996). Ironically, many members find the strength to overcome their addictions when they recognize that they are powerless over them.

Perhaps more importantly, twelve-step programs honor the necessity of relationships. Personal healing occurs within a community that fosters a sense of connection to oneself, to others, and to the world (Hopson, 1996). The first of the "Twelve Traditions" established by twelve-step programs is: "Our common welfare should come first; personal recovery depends upon AA unity" (Alcoholics Anonymous, 1999c). In these groups, the community orientation and spiritual component are inextricably linked. Both reflect the human desire to join forces with something larger than oneself in the hopes of becoming something more than one is (see *The Promise of Community Psychology* section).

individuals, and for most communities" (p. 143). At both individual and community levels, a sense of what is right can lead people to find inspiring reservoirs of strength, even under conditions of extreme adversity. Belief in a spiritual world that transcends earthly abuse may account for African Americans' ability to emerge from slavery with their humanity intact (Myers, 1999). As another example, consider the story of the small French village of Le Chambon.

During World War II, the rates of Jewish survival in different European countries varied enormously. While 95% of the Jews in Denmark survived, 90% of the Jews in Poland perished. How do we explain this difference? Irving Greenberg (1986) asserted that the difference did not lie in Jewish behavior. Jews who obeyed commands and Jews who took up arms suffered the same fate. Similarly, Nazi behavior could not account for differences in survival rates, since Nazis everywhere were relentless in their killing. "The single critical difference was the behavior of the bystanders. The more bystanders there were who resisted, the greater was the chance that Jews would survive" (Greenberg, 1986, p. 3).

As World War II progressed, gendarmes became handmaidens of the Nazis, and Jews who lived in or had fled to France were not aided by French bystanders in large numbers. The residents of a small farming community on an isolated plateau in southern France, however, refused to collaborate with the Nazi regime. In what has been called a "conspiracy of goodness" (Sauvage, 1990), the villagers of Le Chambon hid Jews in their homes, sometimes for several years. They provided them with forged identification and ration cards and assisted them in crossing the border to safety in Switzerland. They shared their meager provisions and refused to surrender the Jews, even under the threat of death.

Scholars seeking to understand the willingness of the Chambonais to illegally shelter Jews despite risk to their own lives and the lives of their family members have identified several contributing factors (e.g., Hallie, 1979; Sauvage, 1990). Many of these factors pertain to the villagers' grounding in religious values. First, the Chambonais themselves had a history of religious persecution, a history kept alive through story and song. The majority of Chambonais villagers were Huguenots, descendants of the first Protestant sect. The plight of the Jews paralleled their own history of persecution at the hands of Catholics in sixteenth-century France. In addition, the Chambonais honored their religious ties to the Old Testament and viewed Jews not disdainfully as subhuman enemies, but affectionately as "People of the Book." Finally, the village pastor, André Trocmé, and his wife Magda Trocmé, were conscientious objectors who provided unfailing moral leadership.

This intellectual analysis of the villagers' actions disrespects the reality of the Chambonais, however. They insisted that there was nothing remarkable about what they did. They did not consider and debate their responsibility to help. Fleeing Jews appeared on their doorsteps and the decision, often made by the women who opened the doors, was to let them in or not. Over and over again in what Philip Hallie (1979) called "kitchen struggles," the women of the house said, "Come in." In the words of Magda Trocmé (1986); "Sometimes people ask me, 'How did you make the decision?' There was no

decision to make. The issue was: Do you think we are all brothers or not? Do you think it is unjust to turn in the Jews or not? Then let us try to help!" (p. 102). The villagers of Le Chambon did not view their efforts on behalf of the Jews as acts of courage. These acts were instead the inevitable response of people with an unshakable sense of who they were and what they believed.

Deeply religious convictions do not inevitably lead to righteous actions. History is replete with examples of religious crusades that spread death, destruction, and oppression in the name of God. In an early attempt to separate the good and the bad of religion, Gordon Allport and his colleagues (Allport, 1950; Allport & Ross, 1967) distinguished **intrinsic religiosity** and **extrinsic religiosity.** Intrinsically religious people *live* their religion, while extrinsically religious people *use* their religion. Intrinsic religiosity is associated with inner conviction, spiritual experiences, and resistance to social pressures contrary to one's beliefs. Extrinsic religiosity is associated with dogmatism, prejudice, and fear of death. Extrinsically religious individuals depend on religion for emotional support, social approval, and social influence. More recently, Bernard Spilka (1989) made a parallel distinction between functional religious values, which foster human potential and enhance feelings of control over life, and dysfunctional values, which restrict liberty, separate people from each other, and arouse fear and insecurity.

For the people of Le Chambon, religious convictions provided an anchor in dark and tumultuous times. Researchers have found that religion helps people cope with adversities, such as death, chronic illnesses, and accidents (Donahue & Benson, 1995; Maton, 1987, Maton, 1989, Maton & Wells, 1995; McFadden, 1995; Pargament et al., 1990; Pargament et al., 1998). Kenneth Pargament and Crystal Park (1995) identified several ways that religion might facilitate coping (see also Levin, 1994; Levin & Chatters, 1998; McIntosh, Silver, & Wortman, 1993; Pargament et al., 1990; Pargament & Maton, 2000; Smith, Pargament, Brant, & Oliver, 2000; Thorson, 1998). The rituals and beliefs associated with religion unite people and sustain connections among them. Involvement in religious communities decreases loneliness and alienation. Community members are also a source of tangible support during times of economic distress (Maton, 1989) and engage in reciprocal help-giving, which is associated with life satisfaction (Maton, 1987). Religion can also provide a sense of personal rootedness (Kress & Elias, 2000)

Religion and psychology, despite their purported opposition, have strikingly similar goals. Both are responses to the human need to find meaning in experience, to make sense of our lives and of suffering. Both seek to define what behaviors are normal and desirable. Both seek to explain and influence human behavior. Both are concerned with personal development and interpersonal relationships. Both seek to help people deal with life crises and life transitions. Many psychologists who provide direct services, especially clinical psychologists, function in much the same way that clergy do. Both types of helpers emphasize truth and honest self-awareness, both encourage transformation through insight and confession, and both rely on acceptance and forgiveness as mechanisms for healing and growth. Despite their seeming incompatibility, religion and psychology have found some areas of agreement in their efforts to help people survive and thrive in a sometimes harsh world.

GUIDING PRINCIPLES OF COMMUNITY PSYCHOLOGY AND A DISCOURSE ON VALUES

All the guiding principles of community psychology point to the importance of incorporating a value perspective into our research and practice. This process has certainly begun, especially with regard to attending to spirituality. The 1999 and 2001 Biennial Conferences on Community Research and Action featured well-attended sessions on spiritual issues. Both the *Journal of Community Psychology* (Kloos & Moore, 2000b) and *The Community Psychologist* (Harrell & Potts, 1999) recently dedicated special issues to this topic. In addition, a community psychology listserv now exists to discuss issues of spirituality.[8] There remains, however, more work to do in both community psychology research and practice.

Community psychologists, led by Ken Maton and Ken Pargament, have identified the role of religion in coping with stress. Roderick Watts and his colleagues (Watts, 1993a; Watts et al., 1999) recommended that community psychologists study religion not only as a coping strategy, but as an important aspect of daily life (see also Kress & Elias, 2000). We might also pay more attention to religions outside of the Judeo-Christian tradition, and religious organizations other than Christian churches.

The practice of community psychology might benefit from collaborating more with religious settings (e.g., Shinn, 1987). Religious institutions have received very little attention as compared to the attention given to schools, families, workplaces, and hospitals (Kloos & Moore, 2000a). Why work in religious settings? Marybeth Shinn (1987) noted that although people spend less time in religious settings than in schools or the workplace, religious settings inspire more loyalty and hold more influence (see also Coakes & Bishop, 1996). Religious organizations also reach an broad cross-section of the population. About two-thirds of the U.S. population attends religious services, including people in groups that may be absent from other settings. Clergy are frontline mental health workers who reach people most in need of help: poor people; the elderly (over half of whom attend church weekly); women victimized by domestic violence; and individuals experiencing a variety of traumas (Weaver, 1998).

Community psychology's interest in tackling issues at multiple levels of analysis also suggests a role for collaboration with religious institutions. When community psychologists work with schools, we primarily target children. When we intervene in the workplace, we focus mostly on adults. By collaborating with churches, temples, mosques, and other religious settings, community psychologists can

[8]To subscribe, send e-mail to *listserv@email.rutgers.edu* with the subject line blank and "SUBSCRIBE SCRA_Spirit *<Your Name>* as the message.

work at different levels—not only with individuals of different ages, but also with the family as a whole, and with the larger community.

Many religious tenets correspond to community psychology's value perspective. Traditional psychology is individually oriented and applauds self-actualization rather than service to others (Bergin, Payne and Richards, 1996). Community psychology, like many world religions, centers on well-being at a community level and aspires to improve the human condition more generally (Kloos & Moore, 2000a). Both emphasize nurturance and connections with others and reject extreme individualism and materialism (Maton & Wells. 1995). Community psychology and religious institutions both attempt to provide human services and address unmet needs (Shinn, 1987). Many religious institutions share with community psychology an interest in social change; as much as 37% of all volunteer activity in the US is church-related, and congregations contribute more to community causes ($6.6 billion) than do corporations ($6.1 billion—see Maton & Wells, 1995). Community psychology, like many religions, embraces visionary thinking and strives to bring visions of a better future into fruition.

The foregoing discussion should not imply that the worldviews of community psychologists coincide with the views of *all* religious institutions. Much variability exists across religious groups (and across community psychologists, as well). Different religious settings have different theological beliefs, missions, organizational structures, and strategies for influence (Pargament & Maton, 2000). Decisions to join forces with particular settings require a consideration of the value match (Shinn, 1987).

⌘ Values for Psychologists

Thus far, we have discussed what values are, why psychologists have shied away from a discourse on values, and why community psychologists need to incorporate a value orientation into our work. Community psychologists generally agree that our field must not only consider the values of the individuals, groups, communities, and cultures around us, but also explicate our own value system (e.g., Hanley, O'Donohue, & Krasner, 1984; O'Donohue, Hanley, & Krasner, 1984; Prilleltensky, 1989; Rappaport, 1984a). In this section, we will look at the professional values of psychologists in general and community psychologists in particular.

Discussions of professional values most often occur in the context of the discipline's **ethical guidelines**. Ethical guidelines are professional principles established to protect the interests of group members and of the people they serve. After a discussion of ethical guidelines as they pertain to psychology in general and community psychology in particular, we will consider how professional ethics might better serve our field.

PROFESSIONAL ETHICS

Although psychology in the United States is over 100 years old, the American Psychological Association did not institute a code of ethics until 1953. The **APA Ethical Principles and Code of Conduct** was developed in the wake of World War II. Psychologists, shocked by the horrors of fascism and especially the torture conducted in the name of science, sought to limit psychology's ability to abuse power (Brown, 1997). Since 1953, the APA code of ethics has been revised numerous times (American Psychological Association, 1992). In recent years, interest in ethics has grown rapidy. There was, for example, a 900% increase in the number of articles on professional ethics published in psychological journals from 1993 to 1988 (Hoagwood, Jensen, & Fisher, 1996).

Ethical considerations often concern how to balance individual welfare with the advancement of science. For example, one issue discussed in the APA code of ethics is the need to obtain **informed consent** for research. Research participants must be told of the nature of the study, advised of their right to decline to participate or to withdraw at any time, and forewarned about aspects of the study that might affect their willingness to take part, including potential discomfort and emotional distress

(American Psychological Association, 1992). A number of psychology's most influential studies would not be allowed today because they failed to obtain informed consent. For example, Stanley Milgram's (1963, 1974) classic studies of obedience relied on deception and led participants to experience considerable stress.

U.S. culture's valuing of individual responsibility permeates the APA code of ethics. The issues afforded the most attention (e.g., informed consent, confidentiality) pertain to personal autonomy. The code pays less attention to issues arising from work within complex communities. Although no formal code of ethics exists specifically for community psychology, several authors have discussed issues relevant to our research and our practice (e.g., Fawcett, 1991; Heller, 1989; O'Neill, 1989; Pettifor, 1998; Prilleltensky, 1997; Rappaport 1984a; Serrano-Garcia, 1994). This section introduces some of the complexities in research and practice that derive from a community approach.

ETHICS AND RESEARCH

Let's take a closer look at the issue of informed consent to participate in research as it pertains to community psychology research. As we will see, the complexity of ethical issues increases as the scope of our research and practice expands to the level of the community.

In 1999 Leonard Jason initiated a heated discussion about the ethics of **active consent** and **passive consent** on the Society for Community Research and Action listserv (see also Jason, Pokorny, & Katz, 2001). Active consent means that research participants must agree to participate in a study. In passive consent, express agreement is not required. For example, a researcher may want to study students in a school. Active consent would require the parents to agree explicitly that their children can participate in the study, often by signing and returning a consent form. If only passive consent is required, minors can participate in the research without the express consent of their parents. Parents may simply receive a letter informing them of the study, or the school may agree to sponsor the study without notifying the parents at all. Parents can still decline to have their child participate, but this requires considerable initiative on the part of the parent.

One might conclude, based on this brief discussion, that passive consent makes it easier for the researcher to conduct a study, but that respect for individuals and communities requires active consent (see Weithorn, 1987). This is often the case, but in some instances, active consent may make the research less meaningful or impossible to conduct. Active consent is not always the obvious ethical choice. The number of parents who read consent forms, complete them, and return them is often quite low. Thus, active consent means that the sample of students participating in a study will likely be smaller and less representative than the sample of students obtained using passive consent. A smaller and more restricted sample makes conclusions based on findings more tentative. Moreover, the most vulnerable populations may be most underrepresented. Studies requiring active consent are more likely to exclude families who do not have positive and trusting relationships with the school, including many poor and/or ethnic minority families. By not including the perspective of underrepresented groups, we may devise ineffective interventions that are culturally inappropriate for the people most directly impacted.

Community psychologists who advocate for active consent often argue that we need to expend the time and effort necessary to do effective outreach with vulnerable populations. We must explain the research and gain their trust. Such a position would seem to occupy higher moral ground, but are the real-world constraints of time and money completely irrelevant? And is active consent always the better choice? What if we want to study gay and lesbian youth? Must we obtain active consent from parents even if this entails "outing" their children (revealing their sexual orientation), which could put the young people at risk for rejection, abuse, or homelessness? How do we balance the requirements of science, the real-world constraints of the researcher, the rights of the research participants, and, in the case of minors, the rights of the parents or guardians? Do answers to these question depend on the expected worth of the study?

Some community psychologists argue that the potential benefit to society of the research should outweigh the need for active consent. But who decides on a research project's worth? The pressures to obtain funding, publish research, and obtain tenure may mean that an investigator is not the best judge of her or his own study's worth. This is one reason for the establishment of **institutional review boards (IRBs).** IRBs are comprised of people who are familiar with research methods and procedures and who can assess the risks and benefits of a given study. They decide whether and under what conditions proposed studies should proceed and may determine whether passive or active consent should be required. Some researchers must submit proposals to multiple IRBs. Academically based community psychologists must have proposals approved by the university IRBs. If the research involves another setting or settings (e.g., schools, hospitals, mental health centers, homeless shelters), those settings will likely have review boards as well. The various review boards each respond to different governing bodies, each with its own system of accountability, susceptibility to lawsuits, faith in science, and so on.

For many researchers, approval by IRBs constitutes permission to conduct the study. Another important ethical consideration for community psychologists is whether IRBs or other administrators can provide consent, or if we must also request permission from the people who will actually participate—the children, inpatients, inmates, or clients (Paradis, 2000). Should a representative of a setting make decisions for the populations served? The failure to obtain consent from the actual research participants (or program recipients) may exemplify how existing and unquestioned professional practices perpetuate the power imbalances we may purport to renounce. And the complexities of the issue don't stop there. Even if the setting members consent to participate, a coercive relationship between setting administrators and the people served may mean that the consent was not given freely. Payment for participation raises another ethical complication when working with vulnerable populations. A token honorarium for participation is standard practice.

Researchers, in an attempt to compensate disenfranchised participants fairly may offer a payment comparable to what a graduate research assistant would receive. Twenty or thirty dollars may not be a token sum for poor populations, however. Honoraria large enough to actually induce people to participate may be deemed unethical (Paradis, 2000).

The discussion of informed consent demonstrates the complexity of community accountability. Furthermore, informed consent is only one of many considerations. Additional ethical questions arise at all stages of the research process. Who owns the data? Whose interpretation of the results counts? Who has veto power over research decisions? What are our post-data collection obligations to the communities with which we work? (O'Neill, 1989). While a community psychologist may have a professional commitment to testing hypotheses and building theory, community members may be more concerned with action (Heller, Price, Reinharz, Riger, Wandersman, & D'Aunno, 1984).

In addition to ethical dilemmas already identified in the community psychology literature, new questions arise as the field begins to embrace diverse methodologies. APA's ethical codes for research assume that investigators conduct large-scale, quantitative studies in the positivist tradition. For example, the APA code emphasizes the importance of preserving participants' anonymity. Although this presents few problems in large-scale quantitative studies where researchers can simply assign research numbers to participants, anonymity can be difficult to maintain in small-scale ethnographic research. In these studies, identifying characteristics of the participants, such as their personal histories and roles in the setting under study, may be necessary in order to understand the results. Moreover, in some instances, where the goal of research is to give voice to silenced groups, anonymity may be counterproductive (Paradis, 2000).

ETHICS AND PRACTICE

In terms of practice, APA's code of conduct focuses on the issues involved in clinical psychology.

Psychological interventions with communities rather than individuals present new dilemmas (e.g., O'Neill, 1989). Clinical psychology traditionally takes place within the therapist's office where only the therapist and the client are present. Community psychologists, however, work in community settings where a number of people and groups may have a vested interest in our work (O'Neill, 1989).

Isaac Prilleltensky proposed five areas where the values and assumptions of community psychologists are manifested in practice: problem definition, role of the client, role of the helper, type of intervention, and time of intervention. Let me illustrate the importance of each of these areas with an example from my own experiences. I once worked as part of a consultation team hired by a community action agency to establish a residential program for homeless families. We entered the consultation believing that the common goal of helping families to leave homelessness united team members and agency personnel. A few months later, value differences became apparent across all five of the dimensions outlined by Prilleltensky.

First, consultation team members and agency personnel defined the problem of homelessness in decidedly different ways. We believed that a variety of factors at different levels contributed to homelessness, while agency personnel adhered to an individual, deficit-oriented explanation. From this differing perspective on the problem flowed different ideas about the clients' roles. Team members viewed future program participants as collaborators who could help agency personnel shape the program, while the agency sought to provide training and therapy to clients whom they saw as in need of professional help. In terms of the consultants' role, we saw our task as facilitating the development of an effective program. The agency wanted us to provide the clients with motivation so that they would attend and benefit from money management classes and job training programs the agency planned to offer. The agency viewed the intervention to consist primarily of skill development, while team members preferred a more proactive approach that

sought to identify and address the root causes of homelessness. With regard to time of intervention, we saw our involvement as crucial in the early stages of program development and less important in the future. The agency thought we could be most helpful in providing direct services after the residence opened.

The consultation team facilitated a series of brainstorming sessions to help the agency shape the program. Each session focused on a component, such as the admissions process, content of on-site classes, and graduation criteria. Agency members usually attended the session but did not participate actively. The only meeting that generated sustained and energetic exchanges was the session on the rules and regulations of the residence. Agency personnel had a long list of expectations for client behavior, and during the planning session the list grew and grew. It soon included standards of behavior that few of us in the room would likely meet. The homeless families would be expected to know CPR, adhere to strict nutritional guidelines, and ensure that their children never left the shelter without hats on winter days.

This consultation effort consisted largely of helping the agency articulate its vision of the residential program while offering an alternative vision more in keeping with the values of the consultation team members. Some ethicists have argued that consultants should not proceed with consultations in which their value system differs from that of the host agency. A. Michael Dougherty (1990) warned that consultants who impose their values on consultees "are on very shaky ethical ground" as they "deprive [the consultees] of their due freedom" (p. 137). Similarly, Edison Trickett and his colleagues (2000) posited that consultants who fail to consider and respect the belief systems and modes of operation of the consultees are guilty of "consultative imperialism." In the extreme, this is certainly true. On the other hand, consultants can offer insights and innovative suggestions only if differences do exist between their point of view and the point of view of the setting. In addition, community consultants are accountable to more than one stakeholder.

In our case, team members felt a responsibility to the homeless families who would participate in the residential program and tried to nudge the agency toward a value perspective we believed would better serve the future clients. This desire was in keeping with the ethical guideline that when the interests of different stakeholders conflict, ethical priority should be given to the most vulnerable persons or groups (e.g., O'Neill, 1989; Pettifor, 1998).

David Snow and his colleagues (2000) offered another example of how accountability to various stakeholders affects community psychologists. The principal of a local school approached a community psychologist based in a mental health facility. The school had begun a sex education program for older elementary school children. Parents objected to this curriculum, but the principal saw a desperate need for it and feared that parent opposition would ultimately deprive students of potentially life-saving information and assistance. Providing sex education was consistent with the prevention-oriented mission of the mental health center where the community psychologist worked. To whom was the community psychologist responsible? To the mental health center that employed her and sought to promote prevention programming? To the principal who approached her and feared for the children's well-being? To the parents who objected to the curriculum and asserted their right to shape their children's education? Did she have obligations to the other constituencies, such as the teachers and the school board? And what about the voices of the children? In this example, the community psychologist would likely find that acting on one belief (e.g., a belief that prevention ultimately reduces harm) required compromising another (e.g., a belief that parents should have a say in their children's education).

HOW DO WE USE ETHICAL CODES?

Despite the pervasiveness of ethical dilemmas in psychology, ethical discussions often occur as an afterthought (Brown, 1997). We generally refer to ethical codes of conduct when we encounter problematic situations and need assistance in deciding what to do (Dokecki, 1996). People look to rules of conduct for concrete and easy-to-understand guidelines that allow them to resolve a specific dilemma (Pettifor, 1998).

Nevertheless, universal guidelines cannot speak directly to specific situations. Take, for example, a dominant issue in the APA code of ethics: sexual contact between therapists and clients. Consensus exists that sexual contact should not occur in the context of a professional relationship. The intimacy of the therapist–client relationship, and the unequal power balance in that relationship, make sexual contact unethical. The ethics of sexual contact with ex-clients is more equivocal. For two different approaches to this ethical dilemma, compare the American Psychological Association and Canadian Psychological Association guidelines (Pettifor, 1998). The Canadian Psychological Association holds that sexual intimacy should not occur until the power imbalance that characterized the therapeutic relationship can no longer be reasonably expected to influence the client's personal decision making. The American Psychological Association holds that two years must pass. The Canadian guideline clearly gets to the heart of the issue in a way that the American guideline does not. The Canadian guideline is, however, a judgment call. A psychotherapist who finds his or her client sexually attractive may not be in the best position to make such a judgment. The American guideline is specific—no judgment is required. It does, however, suggest a uniformity in experience that does not exist. Two years post-therapy may not be long enough for some clients to free themselves from the therapist's influence, while some may free themselves of this influence much sooner.

Although ethical codes are designed to guide the behavior of professionals in difficult situations, they cannot prescribe one-size-fits-all solutions. One reason for establishing IRBs is to provide an opportunity for members of the community to perform case-by-case examinations. Abstract codes cannot be applied universally and mechanically. On the other hand, a purely local application of ethics without a guiding framework opens the door to abuse even wider. We cannot become overly attached to our own moral stances, but must work with others to map a universe of morally acceptable solutions.

As Kenneth Heller (1989a) astutely observed,

> We cannot expect ethics codes to answer our dilemmas because they were never intended to remove value decisions from professional encounters. . . In this sense, ethical dilemmas in community intervention often do not have 'correct' solutions, because they are intertwined with a process that requires ongoing value decisions. (p. 377)

Given the subjective nature of value decisions, community psychologists must be accountable to the communities with which we work. This means explicating our own value system while remaining open to its re-evaluation in light of insights from community members. If we fall in love with our own moral pronouncements, we are less able to work collaboratively with others to identify an ethically permissible range of options (DeRenzo, 1996). Input from a wide array of moral perspectives and thoughtful deliberation of competing values enhances our ability to make ethical decisions.

LIBERATORY ETHICS

Laura Brown (1997) described APA's ethical guidelines, as "lowest-common-denominator values." Although they serve the public by promoting ethical practices, their primary function is to protect the interests of professionals. Thus, they offer a narrow, legalistic interpretation of ethics (Prilleltensky, 1997; see also Fawcett, 1991; Serrano-Garcia, 1994). Brown described the current APA code of ethics as heavy on the "thou shalt nots," but weak on the "thou shalts." She wondered if psychologists could create ethical standards that did not simply protect the public from the worst of our excesses and ourselves from complaints, but actively promoted a more just society. Such **liberatory ethics** would pay attention not only to overtly unethical

behavior, but also to sins of omission and collusion. It would specify what we as psychologists *should* do. For example, the current code of ethics establishes parameters so that hierarchical psychologist–client relationships do not lead to the abuse of power. Liberatory ethics might focus not on preventing the abuse of power, but on establishing more balanced and collaborative relationships (Brown, 1997).

Isaac Prilleltensky (1997) noted that a discrepancy exists between psychology's awareness that values play an important role and our limited resolve to discuss what these values should be. He is one of the few psychologists to offer a liberatory code of ethics. Prilleltensky's set of values appear in Table 3.2, along with the questions each value poses to psychologists.

The specification of a liberatory code of ethics is only a first step. The question of how to weight each value remains. For example, even among people who agree with Prilleltensky's set of values, a strong concern for distributive justice may lead some to advocate for affirmative action programs while a stalwart belief in self-determination may lead others to reject such programs. Meg Bond's (1999) notion of countervalues suggests one way to weight values. Community psychologists might privilege those values that currently receive the least emphasis in a given setting. For example, William Ryan (1994) identified two value systems. "Fair Play" values concern self-reliance, independence, and reliability, while "Fair Share" values emphasize loyalty, respect, sharing, cooperation and fidelity. Ryan identified a role for community psychologists in equalizing the impact of the relatively neglected Fair Share values.

A liberatory code of ethics may enhance community psychology's ability to put its guiding principles into action. It also holds the potential to enrich the community of community psychologists. "It is easier to be an ethical person if one belongs to an ethical community of professionals who share values and goals and who strive in particular ways to improve the human condition" (Frankel, 1994; cited in Pettifor, 1998, p. 236). A liberatory code might allow community psychologists to better serve the people and communities around us while enhancing our own well-being.

Table 3.2 Prilleltensky's Values for Psychology

Value	Question
Caring and Compassion	Does the psychological approach promote the expression of care, empathy, and concern for the physical and social well-being of other human beings?
Self-Determination	Does the psychological approach promote the ability of individuals to pursue their chosen goals without excessive frustration and in consideration of other people's needs?
Human Diversity	Does the psychological approach promote respect and appreciation for diverse social identities?
Collaboration and Participation	Does the psychological approach promote the peaceful, respectful, democratic process whereby citizens have meaningful input into decisions affecting their lives?
Distributive Justice	Does psychological approach promote the fair and equitable allocation of bargaining powers, resources, and obligations in society?

Adapted from Prilleltensky, I. (1997). Values, assumptions, and practices: Assessing the moral implications of psychological discourse and action. *American Psychologist, 52*, 520. Copyright © 1997 by the American Psychological Association. Adapted with permission.

⌘ The Promise of Community Psychology: Transcendence in Community

Community psychology values self-reflection. As noted in Chapter One, the growth of our field depends on our willingness to engage in critical self-examination in the hope of creating something new and better. As community psychologists, we struggle to hold ourselves accountable to high ideals. The community psychologist who embodies all the desirable qualities described in Chapter Two and lives out all of the guiding principles that delineate this field may not exist, but we try.

A carefully articulated value system may provide the foundation necessary to do the difficult work of community psychology. We must make decisions all

the time. Our ability to make good decisions may be served by a commitment to considering the moral dimensions of our choices and the ways in which our decisions correspond, or do not correspond, to what we believe we *should* do. Seymour Sarason (1978) noted that in attempting to tackle entrenched social problems, the community psychologists' "internal conflict will be not in the form of 'Do I have the right answer?' but rather 'Am I being consistent with what I believe?' " (p. 379).

If we fail to ask such question, there eventually may come a price to pay. Bill Berkowitz (1996) observed that community psychologists over the age of 55 are relatively uninvolved in the field. He suggested that this is because "the community work being done does not meet the needs of the soul, and never has, and that in maturity the demands of the soul can no longer be ignored" (p. 445). He recommended that community psychologists, in deciding what to study, stop focusing on such questions as whether the variables can be easily manipulated or whether the study will yield publishable results. He advised that we ask ourselves instead, "How does this work serve my soul?" (p. 446).

The needs of the soul. We do not often in academic psychology refer to the soul. One definition of *soul* offered by Merriam-Webster (1999) is "The immaterial essence, animating principle, or actuating cause of an individual's life." A second definition is "a person's total self."

How do we practice community psychology as soul work? The question of how to be true to our total selves, in our life and in our profession, is crucial for us as people and as psychologists. How do we stay connected to our total selves in an effort help those with whom we work realize their total selves? The psychologist and student of consciousness Ram Dass and his co-writer Paul Gorman

(1985) held that the roles we adopt (e.g., teacher/student, parent/child, therapist/patient, researcher/subject) keep us from interacting with each other as full human beings. They allow us to make real only a part of ourselves and require that others enact only a part of themselves. "Caught in the models of the separate self, we end up diminishing one another" (Dass & Gorman, 1985, p. 28). In the words of Hassidic philosopher Martin Buber (1958), we no longer have I–Thou relationships, but rather I–It relationships.

The roles in which we cloak ourselves offer security; they provide prescriptions for how we should behave and how others should respond. In his book *Courage to Teach*, Parker J. Palmer (1998) proposed that fear prevents us from interacting as total selves. He stated that by following a spiritual path we could overcome this fear and become more whole. " 'How

"Too bad about old Ainsworth. Published and published, but perished all the same."

Ultimately, the needs of the soul are what matter. © The New Yorker Collection 1982 Tobey from cartoonbank.com. All Rights Reserved.

can we move beyond the fear that destroys connectedness?' I am saying, 'By reclaiming the connectedness that takes away fear" (p. 58).

Connectedness. Seymour Sarason (1993) posited that the human desire to connect with others, that is to form community, is inextricably linked to the need to connect to something bigger than ourselves, which he called **transcendence.** Jean Hill (2000) elaborated on this notion of transcendence. She identified three components: 1) connection to the natural world; 2) connection to humankind, past, present, and future; and 3) a sense that some things are beyond our comprehension. Hill (2000) quoted Albert Einstein, who did not believe in a personal God but did appreciate this aspect of transcendence. Einstein claimed that if we cannot marvel, then we cannot see and need not live. He wrote that the impenetrable beauty of mystery lies at the heart of true art and also true science.

Perhaps a fourth aspect of transcendence is that it entails a sense of oneself as whole and authentic. All of one's thoughts, feelings, ideas, bodily experiences, hopes, and fears belong and somehow, in their totality, make sense. Wholeness constitutes a common theme in the work of psychological theorists who discussed spirituality such as William James (1902/1961), Carl Jung (1933, 1938) and Abraham Maslow (1970). All of them focused on how people realize wholeness:

> wholeness achieved through succumbing to the will of God: a wholeness through discovery of a greater mission in life; a wholeness through the letting go of an unhealthy lifestyle, habit, or relationship in our lives; and a wholeness through full integration of every face in our personhood, bright and dark. (Mack, 1994, p. 24)

It seems that community psychologists' dedication to the pursuit of both objective and subjective knowledge can help us to be both rational and emotional, scientists and activists, researchers and practitioners. Perhaps community psychology can offer a small spiritual space where the two worlds are one.

Action Agenda

Personal Values

Below are several exercises to help you articulate the values you deem important.

1. **Personal Mission Statement.** In *The Seven Habits of Highly Effective People*, Stephen Covey (1989) recommended writing a personal mission statement that delineated what one hopes to be (i.e., character), and what one hopes to do (i.e., contributions). This mission statement should serves as a basis for making decisions. It is a constitution based in personal beliefs that are informed by family creeds and by religious and cultural traditions. It should be able to stand the test of time, although amendments might be added as one grows and changes (see examples in Covey, 1989, pp. 106–107).

2. **Lessons for the Next Generation.** What if your high school (or elementary school) asked you to give a graduation speech. What words of wisdom would you pass on to those younger than you? Or, write a letter for your child (or grandchild or great grandchild) to read when she or he is on the threshold of adulthood. What important life lessons would you want to pass on? Two books that might be helpful preparing for this writing, are

- *The Measure of Our Success: A Letter to My Children and Yours* (1992), written by Marian Wright Edelman's who is the head of Children's Defense Fund; and
- *Hindsights: The Wisdom and Breakthroughs of Remarkable People* (1994), by Guy Kawasaki and his colleagues, which includes messages of hope for the next generation written by 33 influential people.

3. **I Believe...** Finish the sentence, "I believe..." in as many ways as you can. You might want to free associate at first and then refine your ideas afterwards. To get you going, you could listen to Kevin Costner's "I Believe" speech in the 1988 movie *Bull Durham.*

Classroom Values/Classroom Codes

In addition to a personal mission statement, your class, as a group, might want to devise a list of values to help guide the classroom culture. This can be done in several ways.

- Discuss a vision of the kind of class you would like this one to be (e.g., everyone feels free to talk openly, there is a sense of community). What codes of conduct will help you to get there? You might reflect (individually or in small groups) on examples of "successful" classroom communities to which you have belonged in the past. What made these communities successful?
- Choose a set of values from one of the lists in this chapter (e.g., S. Schwartz, 1992, 1994; Prilleltensky, 1997; Potts, 1999a). As a class, discuss these values. Which ones are most important and which matter less? Then discuss the implications of the value sets for your classroom. What codes of conduct do these values suggest?

Your discussion might address questions such as:

◇ Should students always feel comfortable? Why or why not? Can we distinguish between productive and unproductive discomfort?
◇ How do we divide the resources of the class, such as "air time"?
◇ Is it important that all people contribute? Is active listening a contribution, or must people speak?
◇ Are there cultural or other differences that affect our ideas about classroom values (e.g., the amount of authority the teacher should have, our willingness to interrupt or be interrupted)? How do we deal with these differences?
◇ How do we work with classroom power differentials based on social roles (e.g., teacher/student) and social position (e.g., race, gender, age)?
◇ How do we resolve differences of opinion when decisions are required, including differences about the content of the classroom codes? Consensus? Majority rule? Other?

You might want to revisit and revise these codes during the semester or if a problem arises.

Moral Courage

Community psychologists working for social change will likely face resistance, criticism, and perhaps attack by forces that seek to maintain the status quo. A consideration of moral courage might help prepare us for these occasions.

1. **Individual Events.** Can you think of instances in your own life when you exhibited moral courage? This can be a difficult question to answer, since the term "moral courage" seems so big. Think small. Was there a time when you felt compelled to stand up for something you believed in? Try to come up with an example before reading the rest of this exercise. If you can't think of an example of your own actions, can you remember witnessing an act you would consider morally courageous? You might share stories with others in small groups.

   In some informal research on this at the University of Denver, my colleague Patricia Waters and I found that when we asked for stories of moral courage, many people recounted interrupting jokes that were racist, sexist, or otherwise offensive. One woman told of her decision to give a Valentine's Day card to the class scapegoat. Another recounted her spirited participation in the Centennial Day parade. The parade was a town tradition that allowed only bearded participants, and so only men could take part. At the age of eleven, this woman committed her first public feminist act by marching in the parade with her male goat as her proxy.

   What characteristics or recurring themes appear in these stories and those you recalled? Based on our research, we found that morally courageous acts often.
   - are based in convictions;
   - are not a conscious choice (i.e., they appear spontaneously or come from feeling compelled to act);
   - involve going against the grain;
   - entail risk (e.g., fear of attack, threat to existing relationships);
   - are self-relevant (e.g., an act of self-definition at the time and a reminder of one's own integrity in the future);
   - have an emotional charge (emotions include inner strength/pride, anger, and sometimes surprise).

2. **Group-Level Events.** In general, Westerners think of moral courage as occurring at an individual level. The examples gathered in the informal research reported above all entailed an individual acting alone against the crowd (see also President Kennedy's book *Profiles in Courage*, 1956). There are also examples of moral courage at a community level.

   The inspiring story of Le Chambon (see the section entitled *Values as a Source of Strength*) is recounted in the video *Weapons of the Spirit*, a 90-minute PBS Bill Moyers special, written and directed by Pierre Sauvage.[9] Another film on this topic, *Not in Our Town* (60 minutes) documents the responses of residents of

---

[9]A 35-minute classroom version is also available. Films distributed by Chambon Foundation at 8033 Sunset Boulevard #784, Los Angeles, CA 90046. Phone (323) 650–1774. Fax: (323) 654–4689. Email: *sales@chambon.org.* For more information, see ***http://www.chambon.org/weapons.htm.***

Billings, Montana, to anti-Semitic incidents in that town. When a Jewish cemetery was desecrated and a brick thrown into the window of a six-year old boy who displayed a menorah for Hanukkah, non-Jewish townspeople took action. Ten thousand homes and businesses subsequently displayed menorahs in their own windows. Follow-up documentaries (*Not in Our Town II* and *III*) examined responses to hate incidents in other small towns and cities across the U.S.[10]

Watch these remarkable films in class. What are the characteristics of the communities that enable residents to take a stand together? Would you like to see any of these characteristics fostered in your own communities? Why or why not? If you would, what small actions might you undertake to move your classroom, school, family, or neighborhood in that direction? What would be a small sign of success?

[10]Videos can be purchased with study guides from The Working Group, P.O. Box 10326, Oakland, CA 94610–0326. Phone: 510–268–9675, ext. 301. Fax: 510–268–3606 For more information, see ***http://www.pbs.org/niot/***.

# Key Terms

active consent	liberatory ethics
APA Ethical Principles and Code of Conduct	passive consent
countervalues	prescriptive values
descriptive values	problem definition determines problem solution
ethical guidelines	spirituality
extrinsic religiosity	transcendence
informed consent	transculturation
institutional review board (IRB)	twelve-step programs
instrinsic religiosity	values

Chapter 4

Beyond the Individual Level

··

⌘ Introduction

Perhaps the most basic tenet of community psychology is that in order to understand an individual, we must also understand his or her social context. This sounds simple. People do not live and grow in isolation. We can point to familiar sayings that capture this point. "No man is an island unto himself." "It takes a village to raise a child." But why are these sayings so familiar? Perhaps they are familiar, perhaps we hear them and say them so often, because we need to remind each other. Many of us find it difficult to see ourselves as truly interrelated and embedded in social relationships. And this difficulty arises for several reasons. After briefly outlining some of these reasons, I will examine the ways in which community psychology has helped us to understand the social world that exists beyond the individual.

◈

Human beings are a lot like crabgrass.
Each blade of crabgrass sticks up in the air,
appearing to be a plant all by itself. But
when you pull it up, you discover that all
the blades of crabgrass in a particular piece
of lawn share the same roots and the
same nourishment system.

—Fran Peavey (1986, p. 1)

HUMANS AS SOCIAL ANIMALS— AT LEAST INITIALLY

Those of us who watch nature channels have witnessed the amazing birth scenes of gazelles and other hoofed animals. Within minutes of entering this world they hobble to a standing position and before long, bound after their mothers and the rest of the herd in graceful arcs. Even infant monkeys cling tenaciously to mother's belly as she cuts wide swaths through the jungle canopy. The contrasting scenes of wailing human infants with helplessly flailing arms and legs can make a person wonder which is truly the evolved species.

Human helplessness, however, is not an accident of nature. It serves a purpose no less remarkable than the infant deer's ability to flee predators. The helplessness of infants fosters the social bonds necessary for our growth.

The terrible stories of babies deprived of human contact remind us of the depth of our social needs. In the 1940's, René Spitz found that even when babies in foundling homes received appropriate physical care, they failed to thrive and often died if they lacked close contact with caregivers (Spitz, 1945, 1946). One of the most influential theories in developmental psychology, *attachment theory*, grew largely from John Bowlby's (1969) observations of children who lacked nurturing caretakers and who suffered severely from this lack. More recently, the media recounted shocking stories of social deprivation in Romanian orphanages. Children were left alone in their beds for hours, fed from propped

bottles, and never spoken to or called by name. The consequences for these children were often quite severe, as many adoptive parents in the Western world can attest. In one study, 84% of children adopted from Romania showed delays in fine motor abilities, 91% were delayed in gross motor development, 96% had deficits in social interactions, 100% of the children evidenced language delays, and 78% had delays in all four of these domains (Morison, Ames, & Chisholm, 1995).

Compelling evidence of children's need for close contact with others has led many psychologists working with infants and young children to highlight the importance of social bonds. A review of psychological theory and research over the past 100 years, however, would not lead one to suspect that humans are indeed social animals—at least not after the first few years of life. Our *early* dependence on others has long been accepted among psychologists. The notion of an *adult's* dependence is, however, more equivocal.

WHY AN INDIVIDUALISTIC VIEW PREVAILS

For clues as to why adult social interconnectedness has not received much attention, we might look to U.S. culture in general and the culture of psychology in particular (Guisinger & Blatt, 1994; Markus & Kitayama, 1991; E. Sampson, 2000). Western industrialized cultures stress the importance of individuality, autonomy, independence, personal achievement, and self-assertion. An emphasis on individualism is particularly strong in the U.S.[1] This is, after all, the land of opportunity. In the U.S., any Horatio Alger hero can pull himself up by his bootstraps and journey from rags to riches. Ours is a country of rugged individualism.

---

[1]The prototypical view of U.S. citizens described in this chapter does not describe *all* citizens. It may best characterize White middle class men from Western European backgrounds. All citizens of this country, however, likely absorb some of the prevailing individualistic ethos.

A core belief in the U.S. is that any person can, through wit and ingenuity, rise above his (and, more recently, her) humble beginnings. As a country, we celebrate conquering heroes and self-made men. Surroundings are generally seen as the source of challenges that must be overcome on the ascent to the top, rather than the context that enables and gives meaning to our worldly pursuits.

In the United States, freedom is equated with the right to live without the burden of obligation to others (e.g., Bellah, Madsen, Sullivan, Swidler & Tipton, 1991). Marriage is the only social contract where social obligations are embraced. Family historian Stephanie Coontz (1992) observed that as the individualistic ethic developed in the U.S., love relationships became "the repositories for interpersonal dependencies, emotional needs, mutual assistance, and informal reciprocities that were being ejected from economic contracts and political transactions" (p. 56). Apart from marriage, social contracts are seen as infringements of individual rights and downright un-American.[2] This notion is for me epitomized in an exchange I witnessed on the local news between a reporter and a woman exiting a supermarket. The workers at that supermarket were striking for better wages and health care. The reporter asked the woman why she did not shop at a comparable supermarket across the street during the strike. The woman proclaimed with angry indignation her absolute *right* to shop at any store she pleased.

The discipline of psychology echoes and reinforces the individualistic view of human behavior. Traditionally in psychology, as in U.S. culture more generally, the ultimate goals in life have related to individual achievement: *self*-sufficiency; *self*-fulfillment; *self*-realization; *self*-actualization. The current panacea for a host of social problems is the boosting of *self*-esteem.

This emphasis on the self appears in many subdisciplines. Clinical psychology traditionally adopts an individual-focused view of human behavior that attributes adjustment problems to personal deficits and views enmeshment in relationships as problematic. Developmental psychology extols independence as the hallmark of adulthood, as seen in the work of the most renowned theorists: Freud, Piaget, Kohlberg. Even in Erikson's (1950/1963) influential theory of life-span development, trust is the goal of the first stage of development, but each subsequent stage until adulthood entails separation from others and/or development of the individual self (Miller, 1991). Despite its name, *social* psychology also assumes an individual focus, and had been largely concerned with intrapsychic life—perceptions, thoughts, feelings. For example, one of the field's most important theories, **social exchange theory**, holds that social behavior—everything from helping strangers to entering love relationships—results from a cost-benefit analysis in which an individual seek to maximize rewards while minimizing risks (e.g., Blau, 1964; Thibaut & Kelly, 1959). This coincides with the view of most people in the U.S. Unlike people from other cultures, U.S. citizens tend *not* to think of helping as a social responsibility grounded in the moral code, but as a matter of personal choice and product of individual decision-making (Miller, Bersoff, & Harwood, 1990).

Community psychology has questioned the view of people as independent entities relying only on themselves as they traverse life's challenges (van Uchelen, 2000). Before exploring the ways in which this field has sought to understand people within contexts, let me first highlight some other areas of psychology that have departed from the more traditional view.

CHALLENGES FROM THE MARGINS

Psychology's view of independence as the ultimate goal of development and indicator of adult mental health has received some challenges in psychology, often by researchers studying people in marginalized groups. In the past two decades, research on the psychology of women has helped fuel the

---

[2] On occasion, the contract of marriage may also be viewed as an infringement on the rights of men; men maintain their independence (and manhood) by battling against the social obligations nagging wives insist on.

challenge. In her groundbreaking book, *The New Psychology of Women*, Jean Baker Miller (1976) noted that a woman's sense of self is in large part organized around her ability to establish and maintain relationships with others. The psychologists of the Stone Center extended Miller's work and suggested that women's development occurs through increasingly complex but consistently strong interpersonal connections (Jordan, Kaplan, Miller, Stiver, & Surrey, 1991). The social embeddedness of women is also a cornerstone of Carol Gilligan's (1982) well-known work on moral reasoning (see the Classic Research box in Chapter Three).

A deep concern for others tends to be associated with the female gender role and therefore is devalued in the Western World. Nevertheless, a willingness to enter into mutually interdependent relationships may lay the foundation for more equitable societies in which all community members assume responsibility for broad social goals and community life. Stephanie Coontz (1992) argued that women's relegation to the role of emotional caretaker and arbiter of interpersonal relationships allows men to compete in the workplace without regard for others. She found that in the U.S. "female domesticity and male individualism developed together as an alternative to more widely dispersed social bonds, emotional ties, and material interdependencies" (p. 44). For those of us committed to fostering the health of our communities, the ramifications of assigning responsibility for social ties to only one sex warrant examination.

Researchers studying women's lives are not alone in voicing challenges to psychology's focus on people as independent actors. Challenges have also come from researchers of ethnic minority groups. The view of dependence on others as a shameful sign of weakness (and femininity) is somewhat unique among cultures, most of which view interdependence as essential to community survival (Coontz, 1992, Kâgitçibasi, 1996; Kim & Berry, 1993). In the U.S., researchers studying ethnic minority populations have documented the crucial role of social ties. For example, citizens from ethnic minority groups often have extended family networks, pool economic resources within their social groups, and express their social commitments in an

active religious life (e.g., Billingsley, 1968; Delgado & Humme-Delgado, 1992; Harrison, Wilson, Pine, Chan, & Buriel, 1990; Keefe, 1984; McAdoo, 1988; Stack, 1974; Taylor, 1986; Taylor & Roberts, 1995; Vega & Kolody, 1985; Wilson, 1986). A recent study of social support among African American and Caucasian youth in times of stress (i.e., adolescent pregnancy or the first year of college) found that spiritual support and family support were important to African American but not Caucasian youth (Maton, Teti, Corns, & Vieira-Baker, 1996). Given the notion that in mainstream U.S. culture, social connections are confined to spousal relationships, it is interesting to note that, in this study, partner support emerged as important for Caucasian but not African American youth.

One might argue that a view of people as interrelated versus independent results not from gender-based or culture-based worldviews, but from minority status itself. A lack of power, especially economic power, may encourage members of oppressed groups to unite. Survival may depend on mutual concern, shared resources, and collective action (Freire, 1970/1992; Miller, 1976; Stack, 1974). It seems, however, that subordinate status alone does not explain more collectivist worldviews. A conception of people as interrelated constitutes the *dominant* ethos in many non-Western countries (see Triandis, 1995). Asian, African, Latin American, and southern European cultures stress the importance of interdependence, harmony with others, and fitting in (Markus & Kitayama, 1991). Indeed, about 70% of the world population subscribes to a collectivist as opposed to individualist belief system (Triandis, 1989).

In contrast to the exaltation of independence in the U.S., collectivist cultures view self-assertion as a sign of immaturity, while giving in to others indicates flexibility, self-control, and maturity. A study conducted in Turkey found that individual advancement and group loyalties combined to form a "social achievement motivation" (Kâgitçibasi, 1987). This contrasts sharply with the Western view of personal responsibility for success. A social achievement motivation has also been documented among Indians (Misra & Agarwal, 1985) and Chinese (Yang, 1986), as well as Chicanos in the U.S. (Madsen, 1969). Interestingly, there is also evidence of a more social achievement motivation among females in the U.S. Some research in education suggests that girls may be at a disadvantage in learning environments that require autonomous learning behaviors (Fennema & Peterson, 1985) and tend to thrive in schools characterized by positive social relationships and a sense of community (Bank & Hall, 1997).

In recent years, recognition of an essential interdependence that does not end in childhood has begun to emerge in more mainstream psychological research. For example, several clinical and developmental researchers have proposed that the main challenge of adolescence is not simply to assert independence from one's parents, but to assert independence *while* maintaining a sense of connection (Allen, Hauser, Bell, & O'Connor, 1994; Collins, 1991; Grotevant & Cooper, 1985; Hill & Holmbeck, 1986). A growing body of research suggests that although conflicts with parents increase during adolescence, parents remain a major source of support (e.g., Furman & Buhrmester, 1992; Steinberg, 1990). Perhaps recognizing the importance of connections to others beyond childhood and into adolescence represents a step toward better appreciating the social embeddedness of people throughout the life span.

So, what role might community psychology play in the context of psychology and in the still larger context of the U.S.? Many community psychologists have sought to expand our understanding of factors and processes beyond the level of the individual that shape human behavior. By directing attention to the these neglected extra-individual factors we can develop more complete theories of human behavior, devise more effective interventions, and help to create a richer community life from which everyone might benefit.

⌘ Thinking about the Environment

Varied terms exist to describe the area beyond the individual to which community psychology directs attention. One often-used term is *environment*. To community psychologists, this term generally does not signify trees and rivers and the air we breathe, but rather our *social* environment—parents, spouses, teachers, friends, employers, and other people of significance to us. Social environment may also refer to objects, most notably our *cultural tools* (to borrow a term from the Russian psychologist Lev Vygotsky, 1978). Cultural tools are objects through which cultural values are transmitted, such as toys, books, and computers. The term social environment also consists of intangible social influences, such as parenting styles and cultural mores. The exact content and nature of the social environment (or *social context* or *social milieu*) often remains vague, and this fuzziness hampers the development of theory and the clarity of research. Some scholars have engaged in empirical and theoretical work designed to elucidate that which exists beyond the individual.

Although the mainstream of psychology has flowed in the direction of individualism, there have been some notable tributaries throughout its history. In 1938, Henry Murray coined the term **environmental press** to refer to the contextual demands that operate in concert with individual needs in order to determine behavior. A decade later Kurt Lewin (1948, 1951) also emphasized the role of the environment. Two major theoretical tenets of community psychology may be traced to Lewin. First, Lewin advanced the notion of *action research* described in Chapter Two (see section on *Research and the Guiding Principles*). Lewin's second great contribution to the field was his proposal that human behavior is a function of both the person and the environment, summed up in his now famous equation: $B = f (P, E)$.

As a classic illustration of Lewin's equation, James Kelly and his colleagues (1979) showed that the behavior of high school boys was a function of both student characteristics and school characteristics. In 1968, eighth-grade boys were selected for participation in a study based on their preferences for exploring the social environment of the high school. Boys were classified as high, medium, or low in exploration. The researchers then examined the experiences of these boys after entering one of two high schools, Wayne or Thurston. Wayne provided students with a well-structured and responsive environment, whereas boys at Thurston were socialized to become more solitary actors in a loosely structured setting. Kelly and his associates found that behavior was indeed a function of individual dispositions *and* environmental experiences. For example, boys in the two schools interacted differently when placed in small groups. In small groups, high-exploring Wayne boys were more interactive, whereas among Thurston students, low-exploring boys were most active. Perhaps high-exploring boys at Wayne had learned to interact with each other as a means of navigating the school. High exploring boys trying to navigate at Wayne had realized, on the other hand, the benefits of going it alone.

The notion that human behavior results from characteristics of both individuals and environments lies at the heart of the work done by researchers and theoreticians interested in looking beyond the level of the individual. Let's consider some of this work in more detail.

BARKER'S BEHAVIOR SETTINGS

Few researchers have taken as methodical and comprehensive an approach to quantifying the environment as Roger Barker (Barker, 1964, 1965, 1968; Barker & Schoggen, 1973). The inspiration for Barker's impressive body of work came as he looked through a train window at children playing and wondered what he might discover by studying them in their natural environment rather than in the laboratory. Barker began his research program with a study of 16 children, each of whom was assigned a team of 9 researchers to follow them throughout the day and record everything that they did (Burnette, 1997).

BASIC CONCEPTS

Barker noted that human behaviors are not sporadic and distinct episodes randomly occurring in space and time. Instead, behaviors occur in discrete patterns of interaction among people and with objects. Barker coined the term **behavior settings** to refer to naturally occurring small social systems in which prescribed behaviors unfold over time, such as a baseball game or a restaurant. Barker used the term

genotype to refer to settings of a particular category within a given community. Steak houses, diners, and bistros all belong to the genotype of restaurant.

One important feature of behavior settings is that their existence does not depend on particular individuals or locales. Baseball games are clearly identifiable as such whether they occur on sandlots or in stadiums and regardless of which players line up on a given day. Similarly, a restaurant is clearly a restaurant no matter who owns it, what type of cuisine it serves, or how the décor is arranged.

Each genotype is characterized by predictable patterns of behavior, called **setting programs**, which enable the setting to function. The notion of setting program overlaps with the better-known concept of **scripts** (e.g., Nelson, 1981; Schanks, 1982). Scripts are culturally specific customs and routines that structure and regulate daily experiences from eating a meal to taking a bath. At restaurants, for example, people usually arrive around mealtime, are seated at one of many tables, receive menus from which they choose something to eat, tell a server what they wish to order, and so on. Setting programs and scripts require people to assume certain environmental roles (e.g., patron, waiter, and cook, pitcher; batter and outfielder). Furthermore, norms exist that discourage deviant behaviors. Restaurant goers who do not wear shirts and shoes will not be served, and athletes that fail to obey the rules of the game will be penalized, fined, or expelled. Thus, settings generate the forces necessary for their maintenance and survival.

UNDERPOPULATION

Barker's work, which occurred before the birth of community psychology, was of great interest to the field. One particularly influential aspect of his theory is the notion of **undermanning**, more recently referred to by the nonsexist term **underpopulation**. Although the maintenance of settings does not require *specific* people, they do require some critical number of people to fill the necessary roles. If you want to play baseball, you need a pitcher, batter, and so on. In some cases, there are many people available to fill each setting role, and in some cases there are only a few.

Settings are underpopulated if there are many roles relative to the number of people available to fill them. Numerous researchers have explored the consequences of underpopulation.

In an early study, Barker (1964) compared small, underpopulated high schools with large, overpopulated ones and found some important differences. Students in the underpopulated schools participated in a greater number and variety of activities. They also felt a stronger commitment to their school. This makes sense. In an underpopulated school, students with a modicum of talent and interest in a given area might easily find a niche for themselves—performers in the school musical need not sing like angels and football players need not outweigh army tanks. On the other hand, in overpopulated settings competition may be fierce and only the most talented few can partake in the school's behavior settings. Recent research suggests that underpopulation can enhance a setting's ability to attract new members and fosters member development (Luke, Rappaport, & Seidman, 1991; Zimmerman, Reischl, Seidman, Rappaport, Toro, & Salem, 1991). It can also tax the reserves of setting members (Norris-Baker, 1999; Wicker, 1979).

Certainly satisfaction within a setting is not as simple as the ratio between the number of roles and the number of people available to fill them. Underpopulation does not always improve outcomes for setting members. In contrast to the findings reported by Barker (1964), some researchers have found that settings in smaller communities are *less* psychologically satisfying as compared to similar settings in large cities (e.g., Whyte, 1980). The advantages of underpopulation may depend, in part, on the nature of the setting and the nature of the roles. Some settings thrive when certain roles are filled by a large number of people. A community theater performance in which almost everyone had a part would play to an empty hall. And you can never have enough people marching on Washington, at least in the eyes of rally organizers.

BEHAVIOR SETTINGS AND SOCIAL GROUPS

In Barker's theory, no setting depends on a particular individual. Any number of people might fill the required roles. This is not to say, however, that every person has an equal chance of participation. Exclusion from settings might be due to a person's shortcomings—the inability to sing even remotely on key or to withstand the force of a toddler's tackle may eliminate students from school musicals and football teams even in the most underpopulated school.

Calvin and Hobbes   by Bill Watterson

Behavior settings just don't work without enough people to fill the requisite roles. CALVIN AND HOBBES © Watterson.
Reprinted with permission of UNIVERSAL PRESS SYNDICATE. All rights reserved.

More importantly to community psychologists, exclusion may also result from prejudice. Roger Barker and Phil Schoggen (1973) used the term **habitant-inhabitant bias** to refer to the uneven distribution of people from different social groups across behavior settings. They observed, for example, that women were underrepresented in the worlds of business and government. Habitant-inhabitant biases may be less pronounced in underpopulated settings, which must include people who might have been excluded had other candidates been available. Rosie the Riveter might have remained Rosie the Housewife had the men in her community not gone off to war.

In assessing social group participation, it is important to note that not all behavior settings are readily observable. Barker's emphasis on public spaces excluded consideration of nonpublic settings such as kitchen tables, backyards, and clubhouses. "Unofficial" settings matter in the lives of everyone but may play a particularly important role in the lives of people in marginalized social groups. Barker and his colleagues were only able to account for approximately 80% of waking life overall, but for some groups they accounted for a much smaller proportion of behavior. For example, African Americans of all ages and preschoolers of all races were not very involved in the community settings Barker's methods assessed.

Nevertheless, an analysis of social group participation in behavior settings can be useful to community psychologists in a number of ways. A survey of the settings available to particular subgroups within a community, such as adolescents or senior citizens, allows us to assess whether opportunities do or do not coincide with the needs of that group. Is there a demand for more youth recreational activities? Are older people who seek employment integrated into the work force?

EXTENSIONS OF BARKER'S WORK

Subsequent researchers have extended Barker's work in two main ways. First, they have elaborated on the role of time in behavior settings, and second, they have explored the functions as well as the forms of behavior settings.

The Role of Time in Behavior Settings. In Barker's descriptions of community life, he viewed behavior settings as stable entities. Subsequent researchers have noted the importance of incorporating a time perspective into the analysis of a community's settings. There are several ways in which time comes into play.

First, the experiences of members change over time. In a classic study, Alan Wicker (1979) found that Yosemite National Park rangers initially responded to the heavy work challenges of peak season with feelings of excitement and usefulness. As the summer wore on, however, heavy work days were met more often with feelings of exhaustion. Thus, participation in a significantly underpopulated setting may eventually leave members emotionally and physically fatigued.

The settings themselves also change over time. In his 1972 book *The Creation of Settings and the Future Societies*, Seymour Sarason described the life cycle of new settings. Energy and idealism allow settings to take shape, visionary leadership helps them take root, pragmatic directorship may enable them to survive, and so on. Attention to the life-cycle stages of settings might inform community interventions. For example, a study of mutual help groups showed that the amount of time the behavior setting had been in operation related positively to the setting's success in helping members (Luke, et al., 1991). Thus, new settings might benefit from additional support, perhaps from more established settings.

Finally, the larger social context in which behavior settings exist also evolves. Social changes lead to the elimination of some settings, alterations in other settings, and the formation of new settings. Robert Putnam (2000) entitled his book on the breakdown of community since the 1960s *Bowling Alone* to signify the demise of bowling leagues. In the 1980s and 1990s, numerous voluntary associations ceased to exist. As an example of a setting that has changed in response to larger social trends, the armed forces have expanded to include women. This results both from challenges to sex biases in the workplace and also the changed nature of military operations—in this technological age, soldiers fulfill numerous roles other than physical combat. As an example of a new setting developing in response to societal changes, summer camps came into existence after the U.S. became industrialized. School calendars were based on the needs of an agrarian society that required all family members to help bring in the harvest. When families moved to the cities and suburbs, children were left with unstructured free time in the summer months.

Function as well as Form in Behavior Settings.
The second important extension of work in behavior settings is the exploration of setting *functions*, as well as the *forms* that Barker so painstakingly catalogued. Attention only to the form of settings, that is to say their observable, defining features, limits one's understanding of them. Two apparently different settings can actually serve similar purposes. David Perkins and his colleagues (1988) exemplified this point with reference to Emory Cowen's (1982) classic study on helping. Cowen showed that counselors in a mental health clinic and hairdressers in a beauty salon actually performed similar functions—they offer support and guidance to clients in times of need.

Conversely, two settings that appear similar may actually be decidedly different in practice. Douglas Luke and his colleagues (1991) described important differences that distinguished a single category of setting (or genotype)—mutual help groups. They collected data on behavioral interactions that occurred in 512 meetings of 13 different mutual help groups and found four different **phenotypes** (or expressions of the genotype): *impersonal* groups, *personal* groups, *small talk* groups, and *advising* groups. More importantly, some phenotypes helped group members more than others. Participants in the *personal* groups, in which members asked personal questions and disclosed personal information, improved more than members in the *impersonal* groups, which focused on impersonal questions and information exchange. Thus,

seemingly similar behavior settings can actually function in qualitatively different ways.

BARKER'S WORK IN PERSPECTIVE

Barker's contribution to community psychology is great. Most notably, he studied people in their natural environments rather than in laboratory settings. In addition, he chose a unit of analysis larger than the individual (i.e., the behavior setting). Several aspects of his work have inspired subsequent research, notably his notion of underpopulation. Nevertheless, relatively few scholars have pursued the line of inquiry he laid out. There are several possible reasons for this. First, Barker focused on identifying and describing all behavior settings within a community and his approach was nothing if not exhaustive. His initial research required a team of nine scientists to document the daily behaviors of a single child. Barker's efforts to catalog all the behavior settings in the small town of Oskaloosa, Kansas, resulted in a list of more than 800 settings, each of which required 13 pages to describe (Wicker, 1979). Few researchers are in a position to commit that much time and money for uncertain payoffs. Barker's surveys were descriptive, but did not directly elaborate any theoretical perspective or suggest particular interventions.

Another limitation in Barker's empirical work is that while attending to the too-often-neglected social environment, he lost sight of the individual. Indeed, this was purposeful. Barker claimed that "blotting out" the individual enabled him to focus on the settings (Barker, 1968). Although community psychologists believe that increased attention to the social environment is warranted, most believe that to understand human behavior we must keep the individual in the picture.

MOOS' SOCIAL CLIMATE SCALES

Rudolph Moos (1973a, 1974a, 1976, 1979) studied the environment from a person perspective. He devised ways of assessing what social settings mean to individuals and used that information as a starting point for intervention.

BASIC CONCEPTS

Moos believed that settings have personalities just as people do. He also believed that the personality of a setting, which he called its **social climate**, could be assessed using inventories similar to those used to assess people's personalities. Moos developed assessment scales for several categories of environments, including classrooms, families, and university residence halls. All of these scales tapped the same three dimensions, which he believed characterized all settings: relationship orientation, personal development orientation, and system maintenance/change orientation.

The relationship orientation concerns the nature and intensity of interpersonal connections within the setting: Are members mutually supportive? Do they express themselves openly and freely? The second dimension, the personal-development orientation, assesses the setting's view of individual growth. Are members encouraged to become self-sufficient? Do opportunities exist to gain new skills? Finally, the system maintenance/change orientation reflects the extent to which settings are clear about expectations, maintain control, and respond to change. Do members know what to expect each day? Who has the final say when disagreements occur? A valuable feature of Moos' social climate scales is their ease of administration. The scales consist of 90 to 100 true–false items and take about 15 minutes to complete.

Moos' scales have been used in different ways. Some researchers have sought to identify outcomes associated with different climates. These studies find that members of settings that are high in the relationship dimension tend to report greater satisfaction with the setting, heightened self-esteem, and lower irritability (see Moos, 1976). In settings that stress personal development, members tend to acquire new skills (Trickett & Moos, 1974). There is also a body of research examining differences in perceived social climate based on status within the group. As shown in Figure 4.1, differences have been documented between staff and client perceptions of ward atmosphere in psychiatric hospitals (e.g., Archer & Amuso, 1980; BootsMiller, Davidson, Luke, Mowbray, Ribisl, & Herman, 1997; Moos, 1973b).

REAL AND IDEAL CLIMATES

A creative twist on the administration of Moos' scales is to have individuals within a setting report on both the perceived social climate and their view of the setting as it would exist in the ideal. The calculation of real–ideal discrepancies can help determine the degree of **person-environment fit**, that is to say the degree to which there exists a match between an individual's characteristics and the demands and rewards of the surrounding environment. A family characterized by high control might affect siblings in different ways. One child may believe in the importance of following rules and feel safer in a structured environment. Another child may feel that the rules compromise her individuality and creativity. The family environment suits the first child, whose ideal family environment corresponds to the actual family environment. For the second child, the person-environment fit is poor.

Assessments of real and ideal environments also have implications for interventions. At the individual level, knowledge of ideal environments can inform choices about intervention alternatives. For example, a client struggling with substance abuse might be served by professional-led group therapy or by mutual help groups. Mutual help groups are usually more structured, cohesive, and task-oriented, while group therapy tends to allow more expression of anger and other emotions (Toro, Rappaport & Seidman, 1987). Knowledge of the client's preferred setting type and the actual characteristics of various intervention settings allows for appropriate placements.

Real–ideal discrepancies can also guide interventions at the organizational level. Moos (1979) reported an intervention in which clients and staff at a residential center for adolescents completed the real and ideal versions of the Community-Oriented Program Environment Scale (COPES). Although neither residents nor staff wanted to change the center's

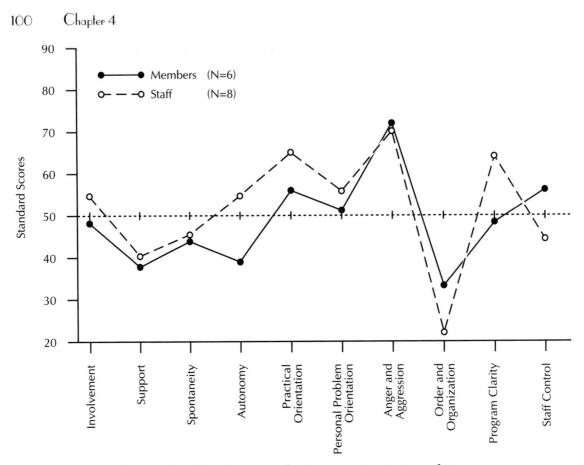

Figure 4.1 Member and staff ratings on the Community Oriented Programs Environments Scale.

Staff perceive more program clarity and autonomy, while members perceive more staff control and order. *Reproduced by special permission of the Distributor, MIND GARDEN, Inc., 1690 Woodside Road #202, Redwood City, CA 94061 USA www.mindgarden.com from the **Community Oriented Programs Environment Scale** by Rudolf H. Moos. Copyright © 1974, 1988, 1996 Rudolf H. Moos. All rights reserved. Further reproduction is prohibited without the Distributor's written consent.*

emphasis on addressing personal problems, both groups wished for increased involvement and a clearer organizational structure. These findings suggested several changes. New positions were established to better delineate responsibility for aspects of the program. Residents took over the orientation of new clients and participated in the assessment of group members' progress. Six months later, residents and staff completed the COPES once again. In the second testing, they viewed the center as closer to their ideals.

MOOS' WORK IN PERSPECTIVE

Rudolph Moos highlighted the importance of *experienced* environments. Certainly subjective assessments enhance our understanding of our surroundings. Not all of the important characteristics of environments can be captured in this way; however. Jean Ann Linney (2000) found that the social climate ratings of a setting made by observers differed substantially from ratings made by setting members and suggested that Moos' scales do not assess characteristics of environments that exist separate and distinct from the personal experiences of setting members. Moos (1973a, 1974a) recognized a role for more objective descriptors of settings, including physical environment (e.g., architecture), member demographics (e.g., socioeconomic class), organizational structure (e.g., decision-making processes), and other features that exist beyond the individual viewpoint. Moos' innovative contribution and focus was, however, the subjective assessment captured by his social climate scales.

Like Barker, Moos formulated an impressive research program and developed some key ideas that subsequent investigators have studied, notably the possibility of assessing organizational character through simple scales. Moos' work did not, however, inspire substantial theorizing and research either. In his case, a limiting factor may be an overly strong reliance on personal perspective.

PSYCHOLOGICAL SENSE OF COMMUNITY

Most of the research conducted using Moos' social climate scales has focused on the relationship dimension. The relationship dimension assesses the degree to which the participants are involved in the setting and support each other (Moos, 1974a). It bears a strong resemblance to another concept that emerged at the time Moos was developing his scales—the **psychological sense of community (PSC)**.

BASIC CONCEPTS

According to Seymour Sarason (1974), an early proponent of PSC, a psychological sense of community includes the feeling that one belongs to a readily available, mutually supportive network of relationships upon which one can depend. A sense of community requires acknowledging one's interdependence and maintaining this interdependence by providing help to others and accepting help from them. This leads to a sense of belonging—the feeling that one is part of a larger, ongoing structure.

Like national patriotism or a sense of homeland, PSC links people to each other and to a symbol system. PSC occurs on a more local level, however, as communities are less distant and abstract than national territories and all community members can come together in relationships (García, Giuliani, & Wiesenfeld, 1999). Indeed, the likelihood that members can interact may affect the level of PSC in a community. Research suggests that PSC is a more meaningful construct in towns and small cities as compared to larger, more impersonal cities (Prezza & Constantini, 1998).

Twelve years after Sarason's initial musings on the psychological sense of community, the concept gained new life with a theoretical reformulation by David McMillan and David Chavis (1986). After reviewing the available literature on the topic, they identified four components of a sense of community. Their conception, which McMillan subsequently refined and elaborated (McMillan, 1996; McMillan, 2001), has stimulated some provocative empirical and theoretical work and helped establish the sense of community as a touchstone concept for community psychology, even though the concept never caught fire in the literature (see Chapter Twelve).

The first component of a sense of community identified by McMillan and Chavis was the feeling of *group membership*. This includes a sense of emotional safety, belonging, involvement, and a shared symbol system. A sense of membership also depends on boundaries that demarcate the group. McMillan (1996) later advocated replacing the notion of "membership" with the idea of "community spirit," to emphasize the energizing aspect of belonging to a community. The second component in a sense of community requires mutual *influence*. The community affects the lives of its members as the members help shape the community. Community members are willing to contribute and conform to community requirements in order to belong. The third component, *integration and need fulfillment*, means that members value and care for each other. Incentives exist for community members to engage with each other in trade (reciprocal exchanges of resources such as information, time, and tenderness). Community members must balance fulfillment of their own needs with the needs of the community. Finally, members of the community have a shared *emotional connection*. This includes a sense of pride in the community, and knowledge of the community's history. Emotional connections both inspire and result from community members' efforts to share stories about the community, celebrate traditions, and come together to laugh.

RESEARCH ON SENSE OF COMMUNITY

Researchers have studied the psychological sense of community in a variety of settings, as well as in different geographic locales, including Latin America (García et al., 1999) and Italy (Prezza & Constantini, 1998). Thomas Glynn (1981) measured of sense of community in a Maryland neighborhood and in an Israeli kibbutz. Unlike members of the Maryland communities, kibbutz members were united by a common religious and cultural heritage and shared a commitment to communal living. As predicted, kibbutz members evidenced higher levels of sense of community. Predictors of a sense of community included the community members' expected length of residency in the community, satisfaction with the community, and the number of neighbors that could be identified by name. Interestingly, Glynn had participants complete an ideal version of his measure and found that members of the Maryland community and members of the kibbutz agreed on the characteristics of their ideal community.

A psychological sense of community is believed to be important for two main reasons. First, it relates to personal well-being—people who are connected to their communities feel better about themselves and their lives and are less lonely (Davidson & Cotter, 1991; Pretty, Andrews, & Collett, 1994; Prezza & Constantini, 1998). Second, the concept relates to involvement in social change. People with a strong sense of community are more likely to participate in block associations, vote, communicate with government officials, and work to solve public problems (Chavis & Wandersman, 1990; Davidson & Cotter, 1989, 1993; Florin & Wandersman, 1984).

Given the potential for PSC to promote well-being and social change, some community psychologists have tried to foster a sense of community in various settings. One intervention attempted to create a sense of community in schools (Solomon, Watson, Battistich, Schaps, & Delucchi, 1996). Toward this goal, the classroom was redesigned to allow for more cooperative learning. Students worked in groups to achieve learning goals, and efforts were made to allow children more involvement in classroom decisions. The intervention succeeded in increasing the children's sense of community within the school, which was in turn associated with other positive student outcomes.

Attempts to foster a sense of community have occurred not only within specific settings, but in entire communities as well. Community planning efforts can incorporate a sense of community into their agenda (e.g., Plas & Lewis, 1996). A classic study by Leon Festinger and his colleagues (1950) showed that the physical arrangement of married student houses, in particular the accessibility of paths and stairways, determined friendship patterns. More recently, the "new urbanism" movement has attempted to create a sense of community through attention to aspects of urban design such as architecture that promotes interaction (e.g., front porches), pedestrian-friendly streets, public spaces where residents can congregate, and mixed land uses that combine homes and shops. A review of the available research suggests that neighborhood form may not link directly to a sense of community but may affect other aspects of community life, such as the level of resident interaction (Talen, 1996).

RELATED CONCEPTS

Although neighborhood form may not promote PSC directly, it can foster **neighboring** (Talen, 1996; see also Katz, 1994). Neighborhood and psychological sense of community are two distinct but overlapping aspects of community connection. Psychological sense of community primarily concerns the qualitative, functional aspects of community life, such as the feelings of belonging. Neighboring refers to more quantifiable, structural indices of community, such as the density of social networks and the frequency with which neighbors exchange help, goods, and greetings (e.g., Skjaeveland, Garling, & Maeland, 1996; Talen, 1996; Unger & Wandersman, 1982, 1985). Donald Unger and Abraham Wandersman (1985) encouraged researchers to integrate these two components. They argued that research on neighboring should expand to include the cognitive and affective components captured in PSC.

A related concept that helps integrate neighboring and PSC is the more recently popular construct of **social capital**. Social capital consists of those aspects of social organization that facilitate mutually beneficial cooperation and action, such as networks, norms, and trust (Coleman, 1988, 1990; Midgeley & Livermore, 1998; Putnam, 1993). Social capital relies on **generalized reciprocity**—the willingness to help someone without the promise of immediate reward, but with confidence that the person helped, or someone else, will return the favor in the future (Putnam, 2000). Social capital refers to personal connections and participation in social groups, but has important implications for the larger social structure, including political, economic, and educational systems. Social capital has mostly been studied by political scientists, sociologists, and economists, but community psychologist have begun to embrace this concept. Numerous scholars presented on the topic at the 2001 Biennial Conference on Research and Action.

While PSC is generally viewed as positive, scholars of neighboring and social capital point out that social interactions have negative dimensions as well. A recent study of neighboring identified positive aspects, such as supportive acts, and also negative aspects, such as neighbor annoyance (Skjaeveland et al., 1996). Similarly, Robert Putnam (2000) wrote:

> Sometimes 'social capital,' like its conceptual cousin 'community,' sounds warm and cuddly. Urban sociologist Xavier de Souza Briggs, however, properly warns us to beware of a treacly sweet 'kumbaya' interpretation of social capital. Networks and the associated norms of reciprocity are generally good for those inside the group, but the

external effects of social capital are by no means always positive. (p. 21)

As one example, the "good old boy network" is generally helpful only to the good old boys.

PSYCHOLOGICAL SENSE OF COMMUNITY IN PERSPECTIVE

Sense of community is an important, though neglected topic in the community psychology literature (Sarason, 1986). Still, we need to go beyond the intraspychic psychological conception of community. The *sense* of community that exists in our heads has important implications, but we also need to explore community life as it is *lived*, not just as it is *perceived*. The criticism of overliance on the phenomenological that has been leveled against Moos' concept of social climates can be leveled against PSC as well. Perhaps if related concepts, such as social capital gain favor, community researchers will find innovative ways of looking beyond the level of the individual to consider larger social forces that impact individual behavior and well-being.

⌘ Ecological Systems

As the discussion of behavior settings, social climates, and the psychological sense of community suggests, it can be difficult to focus simultaneously on both the individual and the environment. By way of illustration, look at the following Necker cube.

If you stare at this picture, you will likely see it flip from a cube with its front face sloping downward and to the left, to a cube with its front face sloping upward and to the right. With practice, you may be able to get the square to flip quickly, yet it is difficult to stop the flipping and see both views simultaneously. The twelve lines that constitute this cube

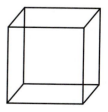

do not determine a particular view, however the human mind organizes the lines according to either one orientation or the other—not both. Similarly, human behavior cannot be traced to the environment or the individual alone; it is a function of both. We have trouble, however, keeping both perspectives in view at the same time.

In a system, all the component parts are interrelated and integral to the functioning of the whole. Indeed, they are inseparable from it. Furthermore, system interactions occur on an ongoing basis. The term **transaction** is more appropriate than *interaction*, since systems change over time and the flow of influence is bidirectional. Settings affect people as people affect settings, and all system components are continuously altered by these interactions.

In community psychology, our understanding of complex social systems is often informed by an analogy to ecological systems. Just as the term "environment" has a particular meaning in psychology, so too has the term "ecology." It does not refer to natural resources such as water, flora, and fauna. It borrows from the more general term a concern with the interrelationships of organisms and their environment. Although Barker referred to ecologies in his work on behavior settings, the term is most often associated with James Kelly.

KELLY'S ECOLOGICAL ANALOGY

James Kelly (1966, 1968) developed an **ecological analogy** to help plan community interventions. He delineated four important ecological principles that have become guideposts in the work of many community psychologists.

INTERDEPENDENCE

The first principle is **interdependence**. The actions of one component in an ecological system have implications for all the others as they operate in concert. Thus, if one shifts, the others must also shift. By way of illustration, consider the workplace as a system. If your employer supervises you closely and constantly criticizes your efforts, this will affect how you feel about your job and the kind of work you

do. Perhaps you will feel less motivated to complete tasks, which may then lead your employer to step up her efforts to monitor your work. Your behavior and the behavior of your employer is influenced by the ongoing interactions between you. However, the workplace system is more complex than that. Let's add a co-worker. The co-worker, unlike you, finds the attention and feedback from the boss helpful and responds by working harder in order to please the boss. This may worsen your situation. When your employer compares your attitude and performance with that of your co-worker, she may feel a need to keep even closer tabs on you. All members of the workplace system are connected in an intricate and evolving web of behavior. If, for example, you take an assertiveness training class and decide to confront your boss about her behavior, this will likely change your relationship with the boss, as well as the other office relationships. If the boss responds well, she may become more accessible to you and your co-workers. If the she does not, she may attempt to turn other employees against you.

A real-world example of interdependence is the deinstitutionalization of mentally ill people that began in the 1960's. Emptying the psychiatric hospitals of its chronically mentally ill patients did not simply change the dynamics of the hospitals. Large numbers of patients were released into the community and this profoundly affected a variety of systems. The previously hospitalized individuals had to look elsewhere to fill their daytime hours, find housing, obtain psychological support, and meet other needs no longer fulfilled by the hospital system.

A more recent example of interrelatedness may be seen in the welfare reform movement that occurred at the close of the twentieth century. In 1996, the Personal Responsibility and Work Opportunity Reconciliation Act required most welfare recipients to find work. Aid to Families with Dependent Children (AFDC) was replaced by Temporary Assistance to Needy Families (TANF), which required states to decrease welfare caseloads dramatically. Such extreme changes in one system have rippling effects through many others. For example, the increased numbers of working poor resulted in a greater needs for transportation and childcare. Only a small percentage of low-income workers have cars, and public transportation routes often do not serve the suburban areas where there is the most job growth. Similarly, working parents needed to obtain care for their children during working hours (Sherman, Amey, Duffield, Ebb, & Weinstein, 1998). In 1999, only 12% of families eligible for federal childcare subsidies received such aid (Administration for Children and Families, 2000).

National shortages in childcare hit former welfare recipients particularly hard. These families did not have the economic resources to take advantage of the childcare opportunities that existed. To further complicate the situation, the need for more childcare placements (an issue of *quantity*) was at odds with the desire for childcare to foster child development, a goal viewed as particularly important for disadvantaged populations (an issue of *quality*). Lax childcare regulations means more available, low-cost placements for working parents, but also the custodial warehousing of children. Strict regulations, on the other hand can improve childcare environments and potentially the life chances of low-income children but prices the poor out of the childcare market (Scarr, 1998).

ADAPTATION

The second principle in Kelly's ecological analogy is **adaptation**. In order for an organism to survive, it must be able to respond to the demands of its context. Survival over time requires effective responses to the shifting character of the environment, including its norms, values, priorities and goals.

Let's return to the workplace example. Management has decided that it can better meet its goals by computerizing the workplace. This means that employees must learn new ways of accounting, disseminating information, and so on. If you welcome these changes and adjust easily, you may also become more valuable to the system by facilitating the adjustment of others.

As an actual example, "old old" people (people over the age of 75) are the fastest growing segment of the population, but we do not yet have a clear understanding of their needs *or* their possible contributions (Longino, 1988). Rabbi Zalman Schacter-Shalomi, a key figure in the Jewish Renewal Movement, proposed that in the grand scheme of life, there must be a reason why so many people are living longer. He contended that individuals must need more time in which to acquire wisdom and then pass it on to the next generation in the process that he called *eldering* (Schachter-Shalomi, 1994). Rabbi Schacter-Shalomi conducts eldering workshops across the country to help seniors find meaningful ways of "downloading" their wisdom for the benefit of the family, community, nation, and planet. These workshops help displaced elders adapt to and find roles in modern society.

CYCLING OF RESOURCES

The third principle Kelly described is the **cycling of resources**. The food chain provides an obvious example. Plants live and grow by converting energy from the sun, vegetarian or omnivorous animals live and grow by consuming the plants, and these animals, in turn, feed carnivorous predators. In the workplace example above, technological skills may be seen as a resource that cycles through the work system. In human social environments, there are many relevant resources, including the talents and skills of community members and community characteristics, such as shared values that foster mutual care.

Economic resources are particularly powerful shapers of community life. In the 1980's, some politicians and economists suggested that money cycles through systems in a free-flowing manner. Thus, wealth released into one segment of the American economy should eventually disperse across the country. This was the foundation of the "trickle down" theory of economics associated with Ronald Reagan. Benefits afforded to the wealthy, it was argued, would eventually flow down to the poor. It appears, however, that the opposite is true (Fields, 1980). Without concerted effort, economic resources flow out of the pockets of working and middle class people and into the portfolios of the wealthy elite. During the Reagan years when trickle down economics was in vogue, the wealthiest 20% of the U.S. population accumulated 99% of the total gain in marketable wealth, while the poorest 80% received only 1% (Wolfe, 1996).

Attention to how financial resources get cycled and where dollars "naturally" flow has led some communities to institute local currencies parallel to the federal one. In Ithaca, New York, this alternative currency, which the residents call "HOURS," can be spent only in that city—they are worthless anywhere else in the country. Thus, HOURS are continually cycled within Ithaca. Since 1991, Ithaca has issued over $60,000 of their own local money to over 1,200 people. As the originator of Ithaca HOURS, Paul Glover put it, "Federal dollars come to town, shake a few hands, then leave to buy rainforest lumber and fight wars" (Glover, No Date, 2). He contended that "dollars make us increasingly dependent on multinational corporations and bankers, HOURS reinforce community trading and expand commerce which is more accountable to our concerns for ecology and social justice" (No Date, 2).

So as not to end this section with the notion that money is the only resource that merits discussion, let me point to a different sort of resource cycling. A few years ago, Oprah Winfrey broadcasted a show on "random acts of kindness" in which she performed small good deeds for strangers—paying for the car behind her at a tollbooth, for example. The idea behind this generosity was that doing good deeds not only makes the deed doer feel better, it also inspires others to do good deeds and this altruism cycles through the community. Social psychological research supports this notion. In one study, researchers left money in the coin return slots of pay phones in a shopping mall. Unsuspecting telephone users collected the coins, and then encountered a clumsy stranger who was actually part of the experiment. The stranger dropped a manila folder at the telephone users' feet. Researchers then assessed whether people who had just found coins would offer assistance more often than people who had not found coins. The results were dramatic. While only 4% of the people who had not found coins helped the stranger gather the fallen papers, 84% of those who had found coins offered assistance (Isen &

Levin, 1972). Good fortune and good will may also cycle through communities (see also George & Brief, 1992).

SUCCESSION

The fourth and final principle in Kelly's ecological analogy is **succession**. According to this principle, systems are not static but in a constant state of flux. Many of the changes that occur within systems are predictable. In the workplace example, promotion and retirement are two common mechanisms of succession.

An actual example of succession familiar to many of us is that of gentrification. Some neighborhoods without financial resources are rich in resident creativity and initiative. The inhabitants of these neighborhoods, who often are artists, establish unique shops and restaurants, create beautiful living spaces, and revitalize deteriorating communities. This creative spirit attracts others, and the demand for housing in the area increases. Eventually, local shops may be forced out of business as superstores and franchises establish themselves in these vibrant neighborhoods. Large businesses are able to pay high rents and drive up property prices. At the same time, by moving large volumes of inventory (inventory that may have been obtained at a bargain price from third world countries) they can offer goods at low prices. Eventually, the visionary individuals who renovated the area and the small businesses that gave it character may be priced out of the local real estate market.

Community psychologists today continue to draw on Kelly's ecological analogy. His model encourages us to consider how people and systems are interrelated and change over time. An important addition to the ecological analogy in more recent years is attention to the existence of systems at different levels. This elaboration is often attributed to Urie Bronfenbrenner (1977, 1979). Interestingly, around the time Bronfenbrenner was developing his model, Alan Wicker recognized the need for a model like Bronfenbrenner's in his attempts to extend Barker's work. Wicker (1979) wrote,

> According to the ecological viewpoint, behavior settings are components of larger,

more complex systems such as communities and institutions. But the various ways in which behavior settings are linked to one another and to such supersystems remains largely unexplored (p. 758).

Bronfenbrenner presented a framework and language that has facilitated the exploration of the various levels of and linkages between settings.

BRONFENBRENNER'S ECOLOGICAL MODEL

In the late 1970's, Urie Bronfenbrenner (1977, 1979) proposed a model of the social environment that helped revolutionize many disciplines. Although Bronfenbrenner is most closely aligned with developmental psychology, his work has had a great impact on community psychology as well.

BASIC CONCEPTS

Bronfenbrenner's **ecological model** (see Figure 4.2) posited that individuals live and develop within nested social systems. The person exists within in a family, and the family lives in a town and these towns are part of a country, and so on. He identified four main levels of social settings. These levels are described briefly here and are used throughout the text.

Microsystem. In Bronfenbrenner's model, **microsystems** are the settings that actually contain the person, such as a family, classroom, or workplace. The microsystem is the most frequently studied level of the social environments. It parallels Barker's notion of genotypes and comprises the settings in which Moos assessed social climate. The transactions among setting members are reciprocal and bidirectional. As an example, Bronfenbrenner

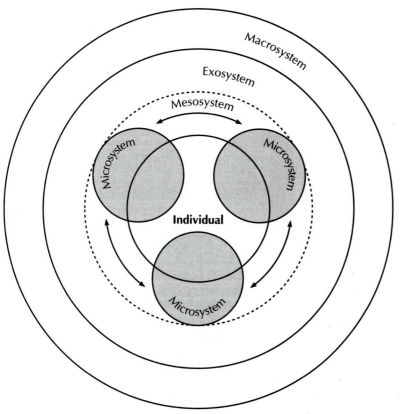

Figure 4.2
Ecological Model

observed that good-natured parents elicit smiles from babies, but smiley babies also increase the parents' joy. The parents' delight in the child increases the child's well-being, which makes the child smile more, which gives the parent more joy, and so on.

Most research on the microsystem focuses on the family, but other settings are important as well. Judith Harris (1998) caused a big stir in the psychological community with the publication of her book *The Nurture Assumption: Why Children Turn Out the Way They Do*, in which she argued that peers have a larger impact than parents. Many community psychologists work in the classrooms and the schools that contain them (Bond & Compas, 1989; Durlak, 1995; Oxley, 2000; Reynolds, Walberg, & Weissberg, 1999).

When psychologists study people within microsystems, they usually attempt to explain how microsystem processes affect an individual-level phenomenon. They might ask, for example, what parenting styles best enable a child to achieve academically or what characteristics of the classroom lead to a sense of community. An alternative approach is to study phenomena at the system level. For example, the mutuality of caregivers and infants has led some developmentalists to suggest that it makes no sense to talk of either competent infants or competent parents. Rather competence is embedded in the caregiving interaction (e.g., Ainsworth & Bell, 1974). Some scientists who study ants, naked mole rats, and other creatures that live in colonies have proposed that colony members are not really individual animals but are comparable to cells, and the colony itself is the organism. Are there ways in which people, too, act as cells within larger systems? Thinking this way requires a shift in perspective that goes against the individualistic conceptions that prevail in society.

Mesosytem. The second level Bronfenbrenner described is the **mesosystem**. The mesosystem consists of the interactions between microsystems. One mesosystem of particular interest to social scientists is the family–school mesosystem. For some children, this mesosystem is strong. The child's parents care about what happens in the classroom, exchange information with teachers, encourage the child to do homework, and attend school functions. For other children, such family–school linkages do not exist.

A commonly cited cause of weak family–school mesosystems is cultural differences between the two microsystems. Cultural differences come into play in a variety of ways. School staff and family members may perceive each other in ways that foster distance. Ethnic minority parents may see teachers and school personnel as powerful, condescending, and uninterested in communicating across language barriers. School personnel may view culturally different families as disinterested in their child's academic achievement or unwilling to cooperate with the teachers' educational agenda. Contrasting socialization goals also weaken the family–school mesosystem for ethnic minority children. When the two settings have different teaching strategies and socialization goals, the children's experiences are disjunctive and family–school transitions are more difficult (Laosa, 1977). For example, researchers have found that immigrant parents from Cambodia, Mexico, the Philippines, and Vietnam encourage conformity in their children; however, conformity is associated with poorer school performance in the U.S. (Okagaki & Sternberg, 1993). American-born parents, in contrast, believe in the importance of their children's autonomy rather than conformity, which is in keeping with the orientation necessary for success in school, and in later life in the U.S.

Although the family–school mesosystem is most often studied, other mesosystems are important as well. The family–workplace mesosystem also has important effects on people's lives. Consider clashes between traditional family structures and the need for all members of low-income immigrant families to contribute economically. While traditional Puerto Rican gender roles may reinforce the subservience and dependence of women, many wives in the U.S. must work outside the home in order to help support the family. These women often find that success in the U.S. workplace requires assertiveness, while husbands at home still expect submissiveness (e.g., García-Preto, 1982).

Exosystem. Bronfenbrenner defined **exosystems** as formal and informal social structures that do not actually contain the individuals of interest but impinge on them nevertheless. For example, parents' social networks affect family life and child development, even if the children never interact with the network members directly. Researchers have found, for example, that support networks reduce poor parents' emotional strain and decrease their punitive treatment of children (McLoyd, 1990, 1998). Conversely, settings that increase the strains experienced by parents may increase the risks for their children. Stresses in the exosystem of the parents' workplace, for example, can reverberate in the children's lives. One study found that the transition to junior high school proved more challenging for students whose parents were simultaneously dealing with changes in their work status (Flanagan and Eccles, 1993).

Macrosystem. The **macrosystem** is the overarching patterns of the culture or subculture. The macrosystem includes political, legal, economic, and other social systems that exert their influences through the micro-, exo-, and mesosystems. The macrosystem provides the "blueprints" from which settings and institutions are constructed. Macrosystems are not specific contexts, but rather prototypes in a culture or subculture. The earlier section of this chapter on how U.S. culture contributes to an individualistic view of people could have been subtitled, "A View from the Macrosystem."

EXTENSIONS OF BRONFENBRENNER'S WORK

A strength of Bronfenbrenner's model is its usefulness in helping us to consider the multiple **levels of analysis** relevant to human behavior: from the individual to the macrosystem and all levels in between. Although inquiries labeled ecological often stop at the level of the microsystem, Bronfenbrenner's model reminds us to consider mesosystems, exosystems, and macrosystems as well. The parent–child relationship, for example, is affected not only

by characteristics of parent (e.g., joy in parenting) and child (e.g., good-naturedness), but by other factors at different levels. The presence and behavior of other caretakers such as fathers, siblings, and grandparents matter, as do neighborhood factors, such as safety and cleanliness. More distal environmental factors also come into play, such as the availability of affordable childcare and healthcare, and overarching social frameworks, including cultural worldviews about how children should behave.

As an illustration, Jay Belsky (1980) used the ecological model to shed light on the child maltreatment. Child maltreatment is affected by individual child and parent characteristics, such as the child's temperament, and the parent's own history of abuse. Higher levels of analysis also come into play. An exosystem factor in child maltreatment is neighborhood support for the family. Social isolation increases the likelihood of child abuse. In addition, paternal joblessness has been found to be an important precursor of child maltreatment. At the level of the macrosystem, relevant factors include cultural acceptance of violence and a lingering view of children as the property of parents.

Even though Bronfenbrenner's model encourages thinking about ever-broader systems, it keeps the individual at the center. So, for example, Belsky began his analysis examining the experiences of individuals involved and then worked his way out to larger and seemingly more remote levels of analysis (see also Cicchetti and Toth's, 1998 analysis of childhood depression). John Ogbu (1981) turned Bronfenbrenner's model inside out by suggesting that we can better understand human behavior if we *begin* our analyses at the level of the macrosystem. He also proposed a **cultural–ecological perspective** to help understand how variations in cultures account for observed differences in individual behavior.

Ogbu argued that in the U.S., psychologists seeking to understand ethnic minority populations consider the level of the individual and perhaps move to the level of the family, but analyses stop there. For example, researchers may find that Black ghetto children as compared to White middle-class children

---

CLASSIC RESEARCH

Glen Elder
Societal Forces in Individual Lives

The sociologist Glen Elder showed the effects of a societal-level event—the Great Depression—on the microsystem of the families and on individual development (Elder, 1974, 1998; Elder, Liker, & Cross, 1984). Elder compared families who had lost more than 35% of their pre-Depression income to families who did not suffer such economic declines. He studied two cohorts of children. The first cohort (the Oakland cohort) was born in 1920 or 1921, and so these children had already entered adolescence when the Great Depression occurred. Children in the second cohort (the Berkeley cohort) were born in 1928 or 1929, and so were just beginning school at the time.

Elder found that financial stress depleted the emotional resources of parents. This had an adverse effect on children in the Berkeley cohort. Parents in that cohort who suffered economic losses were less able to provide nurturing and warm family environments. They had less time and energy to attend to their children's emotional demands, and both mothers and fathers used harsher child-rearing practices

While economic hardship had a negative impact on the younger children, it had a positive impact on the children in the Oakland cohort. These children, who were teenagers during the worst of the Depression, were less dependent on parents for their emotional well-being and could assist their families in meeting the challenges of economic hardship. They worked when they could find odd jobs and assumed responsibility for helping the family survive. They felt needed and useful at a time when they were beginning to explore adult roles. Elder has followed these children into late adulthood and has found that the effects of the Depression reverberated across the life span. As adults, members of the Oakland cohort had a strong work ethic and commitment to family. The Berkeley children ended up completing fewer years of schooling and were less successful.

Despite these general trends, specific life choices mediated the long-term effects of economic hardship. Joining the military, for example, improved the long-term outcomes for stressed children, while marrying early and bearing children at a young age worsened their situations. Elder (1998) concluded that although people make choices about family, education, and work, these choices do not occur in a vacuum—the choices depend on the opportunities and constraints present in the multilevel systems that surround them.

---

perform more poorly in school and that the parents' differing child-rearing practices affect the child's academic performance. Middle-class strategies are presumed to be better since White children are more successful than ghetto children. Ogbu encouraged researchers to look further and consider why different parenting styles arise in the first place. What processes at higher levels of analysis influence the development of particular child rearing strategies?

Ogbu posited that cultures that survive necessarily instill the skills needed for survival in the next generation. Thus, child-rearing strategies develop in order to transmit the cultural competencies necessary for social, economic, and political success in adulthood. These cultural competencies are not individual-level or even microsystem-level phenomena. They are cultural blueprints that exist independent of and prior to particular people or families, but they determine how parents raise their children all the same.

Ogbu argued that in ghetto culture, success rarely occurs by way of conventional jobs, and

COMMUNITY INTERVENTION:

The Settlement House Movement
Expanding Circles of Concern

The idea for settlement houses emerged in nineteenth-century England (Davis, 1994; Trolander, 1987). University students took up residence in poor neighborhoods where they could work to improve local conditions while pursuing their education. Settlement workers hoped that by living side by side with the people they hoped to help, an attitude of neighborliness would replace the air of superiority that characterized charity work in earlier eras.

As rapid industrialization and the influx of immigrants magnified economic disparities in the U.S. in the late nineteenth century, the settlement house movement spread to this country. Settlement houses were established in immigrant neighborhoods to help those arriving from other countries adjust and prosper in their new homeland. This movement exemplified nonprofessionals working within communities to foster positive adjustment in at-risk populations (Rappaport, 1977). In the U.S., the movement reached the pinnacle of its influence and prestige during the Progressive Era of the early twentieth century. About 400 houses existed at that time (Trolander, 1987), the most famous of which was Hull House, founded in 1889 by Jane Addams and Ellen Gates Starr.

Settlement workers generally fit a particular description. The settlement house movement had early roots in religious institutions and a 1905 poll of 339 settlement workers found that 88% were active church members, and nearly all cited religion as an important influence in their lives (Davis, 1994). In addition to being religious, settlement workers were primarily young, usually in their 20s. Jane Addams was 29 when she helped found Hull House (Davis, 1994). Workers were also well educated—90% had attended college, and 50% had completed some graduate study. Finally, many settlement workers were women. Settlement houses offered career options to educated women who enjoyed the opportunity to take part in community life at a time when they still could not vote. The influence of women in the movement helps account for the multitude of settlement activities that centered around chidren, as well as the home-based approach to intervention and their consensus-based mode of operation (Trolander, 1987).

Settlement houses had strong ties to colleges and universities, and the neighborhood offered practical testing ground for theories workers had learned in the classroom (Davis, 1994). Settlement houses operated as action research centers. Many workers learned to collect and analyze data, and despite the focus on residents' pressing, concrete needs, settlement houses sought to develop theories. The opportunity to test out theories, especially education theories, appealed to one of the early formulators of action science, John Dewey (see Chapter Two), who was a member of first board of trustees at Hull House (Davis, 1994).

Settlement houses addressed neighborhood problems in a holistic way. Unlike social welfare agencies, which provided specific services to "needy" individuals, settlement houses sought to improve entire neighborhoods. Common activities included establishing kindergartens and day care centers; setting up community centers and clubs; finding new homes for people displaced by urban renewal; developing special projects to meet the needs of the elderly, the mentally ill, and juvenile delinquents; and developing the residents' marketable skills. A settlement house located near textile factories, for example, might teach unemployed residents how to operate sewing machines.

Settlement workers initially focused on problems within their neighborhoods. As they became increasingly aware of the larger context in which these local problems occurred, their circle of concern broadened. When neighborhood children refused the candy offered by Hull House residents at Christmas, the settlement workers were perplexed until they learned that the children worked six days each week in a candy factory and could not stand the sight of candy (Davis, 1994). Local interest in working conditions expanded to a broader concern about child labor. Workers who initially focused on providing direct services became increasingly involved in influencing elections and legislation, especially on such topics as worker's rights, affordable housing, and education. As action researchers, many settlement workers knew how to collect and analyze data. Their use of statistics in combination with firsthand knowledge of slum life made them powerful advocates in their lobbying efforts (Davis, 1994; Trolander, 1987).

Reform efforts first moved beyond neighborhoods to the level of cities. Jane Addams founded the Chicago Federation of Settlements in 1894. Efforts then moved to the state, national and even international level. The National Federation of Settlements was founded in 1911, and when the U.S. became embroiled in the first World War a few years later, many settlement workers set aside their concerns for housing and welfare and focused instead on the larger problem of war. Jane Addams became a peace advocate during World War I and was awarded the Nobel Peace Prize in 1931.

Interestingly, as Jane Addams and other leaders of the movement broadened their concerns, there occurred a simultaneous drift in the opposite direction.

The settlement house movement gave rise to the field of social work, which focused increasingly on the individual level (see Chapter One section on *Social Work and Community Psychology*). The establishment of social work as a field coincided with a growing emphasis on professionalism. The distance between workers and clients increased as the notion of professional helpers living with clients in dilapidated neighborhoods lost its appeal (Trolander, 1987). When workers were removed from the daily living conditions of their clients, they began to focus more on personal problems and less on social ills. It seems that without an intimate knowledge of the residents' daily lives, helpers can lose sight of how the rippling effects of larger social forces shape and give texture to everyday experiences.

economic advancement more often results from involvement in subcultural systems such as hustling or pimping. Child-rearing techniques that foster the skills necessary for success in these roles include inconsistent demands for obedience, verbal rebuffs, and physical punishment. These techniques are frowned upon by members of the White middle class without adequate consideration of the cultural context of the ghetto. True, if White middle-class families adopted the ghetto parents' child-rearing techniques their children would probably not develop the skills needed for success. In White middle-class culture, success occurs through conventional avenues that remain closed to ghetto children. The ghetto parents' child-rearing techniques are, however, precisely the techniques that maximize the chances for success within the subculture of the ghetto.

Ogbu's insights should not suggest that researchers and practitioners should just leave people in the ghetto alone because parents are doing a fine job instilling the competencies their children need. Problems, such as school failure, still exist. His macrosystemic analysis suggests that intervention is required *at a different level*. Ghetto families do not need parenting workshops, and their children do not need compensatory education. The families need

increased economic opportunities that will lead, *over time* to changes in child-rearing techniques. When success results from different cultural competencies, new child-rearing techniques will evolve to promote the development of those competencies.

An understanding of the macrosystemic causes of a problem (such as school failure) suggests that interventions implemented at lower levels of analysis cannot solve the problem. An **error of logical typing** occurs when one attempts a solution at the wrong level (Rappaport, 1977; see also Watzlawick, Weakland, & Fisch, 1974). If a child fails because she or he lacks academic skills (an individual-level explanation), then tutoring, remedial classes, or another individual-level solution is warranted. If children fail because of family-level problems, such as poor child-rearing practices or family stress, then family-level interventions are necessary, such as parenting workshops or parent support groups. But if failure ultimately results from the lack of opportunity structures, a higher-level intervention is warranted. The very analysis of the problem of interest prescribes a particular range of solutions. When we fail to consider problem causes at higher levels of analyses, our attempts at intervention remain mired at the individual or microsystem level of analysis, and the necessary social changes do not occur.

"I'll tell you what it is. It's two hundred thousand peasants from permissive peasant homes, that's what it is."

Conceptualizing a problem at the wrong level of analysis © The New Yorker Collection 1972 Eldon Dedini from cartoonbank.com. All Rights Reserved.

⌘ The Promise of Community Psychology: From the Microscopic to the Macroscopic

In an attempt to understand human behavior more fully, community psychologists have directed attention to the world *beyond* the individual, including the far-reaching macrosystemic forces that we can see only in their effects. Can our understanding also be enhanced by journeying *within* the individual, to microscopic forces that are similarly invisible to the naked eye but evident in our behavior? Perhaps the journey from the microscopic level of human genes to the macroscopic level of society and culture really isn't as great as it seems.

While the twentieth century was the age of technology, the twenty-first century may usher in the

We do not yet know how to act on our knowledge of genetics. Joe Heller/ Green Bay Press-Gazette

age of the gene. The thousands of genes that make up the human DNA have now been mapped, and the body of evidence in support of the role genes play in shaping human behavior has become overwhelming. Genes shape general cognitive abilities (e.g., intelligence) and specific abilities (e.g., spatial ability). They influence temperament and personality. They also affect the development of problem behaviors of interest to community psychologists, such as alcoholism, schizophrenia, and criminality (Plomin & Rende, 1991; Plomin, Rende, & Rutter, 1991). Researchers have found a genetic component to virtually every human behavior studied, and this component generally accounts for about 20% to 60% of the variance in behavior (Rutter, 1997). The fact of genetic influences seems clear, although the implications of this fact are not yet known.

Despite the evidence for their importance, community psychologists have not embraced the study of genes. An emphasis on genetics seems opposed to the core values and guiding principles of the field. As we have seen throughout this chapter, community psychology has sought to understand behavior at higher levels of analysis. Research on genes seems once again to place the locus of human

behavior within the individual. In addition, genetic research in psychology, such as attempts to document the genetic intellectual inferiority of some racial groups (e.g., Jensen, 1969; Herrnstein & Murray, 1994), has historically advanced oppressive agendas. A third reason why a genetic perspective may seem antithetical to community psychology relates to the field's attention to social change. A genetic view of human behavior would seem to suggest that an individual's fate is sealed at birth. The only role for intervention would then be in the controversial realm of genetic engineering.

The social and ethical implications of a genetic perspective may reflect the terms on which this research has been done, but not necessarily the potential of this research to contribute to our understanding, as community psychologists, of the relationship between people and the larger social environment. If this argument does not reassure community psychologists of the safety of dipping our toes into the seemingly hostile waters of genetics, perhaps we will be heartened to see our old friend Urie Bronfenbrenner comfortably swimming ahead. In recent years, Bronfenbrenner has helped develop a **bioecological model** of human development that incorporates an appreciation of genetic factors into his earlier work on ecological systems (e.g., Bronfenbrenner & Ceci, 1994).

Perhaps the most important aspect of Bronfenbrenner's bioecological model for community psychologists is its distinction between actualized and nonactualized genetic potential. Early in this century, researchers recognized that any given *genotype*[3] might give rise to a variety of different observable expressions (or *phenotypes*). Thus, knowing a baby's genetic makeup does not tell us precisely how that baby will look or behave as an adult. A lifetime of exposure to different environments affects the realization of genetic potentials. The variety of potential expressions defined by genetics is a **reaction range**, and an individual's life experience determines which possibilities within that range are actually realized. Bronfenbrenner argued that a serious limitation in our current methodologies for assessing the extent of genetic versus environmental contributions to behavior is our complete inability to assess the genetic *potential* of any individual. We cannot know where along a reaction range an individual might have fallen under different conditions.

In order for genetic potential to be realized, there must exist opportunity structures within the environment that scaffold the expression of that potential. A chess prodigy cannot make herself known if no one shows her the rules of the game. Similarly, the chances for stunning legal minds to emerge from urban ghettos are severely compromised by limited educational opportunities, lack of models of conventional success, and constant threats to safety. Behavior geneticists who subscribe to repressive social agendas have argued that poor achievement among minority group members results from genetic risk, and so environmental resources should be directed to gifted people who can make better use of them. Bronfenbrenner's analysis leads to the opposite conclusion: minority group members have the least opportunity to realize their genetic potential and so may benefit *most* from the influx of environmental resources (see Rutter, 1997).

The perception of genetic effects as fixed is erroneous. If any driving force, including genetics, prescribed a specific, stereotyped response to the environment, then the flexibility that allows people to survive would be compromised (Cairns, Gariepy, & Hood, 1990). We would be unable to adapt to environmental change. Indeed, the ability to respond flexibly, to learn from experience, may be what is inherited, rather than any way of responding per se.

Thus, a consideration of genetics brings us to evolutionary theory; the attempt to understand how opportunities and constraints in our environment affect, over time, who we become as individuals. Some scholars associated with community psychology have drawn on theories of evolution. Kelly referred to evolutionary theory in outlining the ecological principle of adaptation. Jay Belsky (1995), who examined child maltreatment using Bronfenbrenner's ecological model, suggested that a circle representing evolutionary influences on human development be added to the model's nested spheres. Nevertheless, evolutionary theory, like behavior genetics, has not figured prominently in the thinking of community psychologists, and the reasons for resistance are similar. Both of these areas of study have advanced oppressive rather than liberating social agendas by focusing on individual-level fitness rather than social change and by embracing determinism.

Darwin's theory of natural selection has traditionally been conceived as an individualistic theory. It views animals and people as motivated by self-interest —to survive and pass on genetic material. Evidence of biological bases for empathy, altruism, and helping behaviors have challenged this view (e.g., Gould, 1992; Hoffman, 1981). Shan Guisinger and Sidney Blatt (1994) suggested that natural selection actually proceeds along two lines, one encouraging individual advancement, and the other promoting interrelatedness among species members. This coincides with a central thesis of this chapter: while much of the Western world focuses on individual advancement

[3]Note that the term genotype is used here as biologists use it, to refer to the inherited genetic make-up of a person. This differs from Barker's use of the term to indicate categories of behavior settings.

and self-interest, we are also social animals with strong relational bonds. Indeed, human interdependence is likely encoded in our genes.

Although we are only beginning to understand how individual and environmental forces work together to make us who we are, it is clear that both matter. Blotting out potentially important perspectives will not enrich our understanding in the long run. Negative association to behavior genetics, evolutionary psychology, or any other theoretical perspective should not preclude a consideration of what such theories have to offer. Community psychology is a field that values multidisciplinary approaches. Sometimes, the further we have to stretch to accommodate a differing viewpoint, the more we grow as a result. Our ability to conceive of and enact new social arrangements and ways of living depends on our willingness to think in new ways.

Bronfenbrenner's notion of nonactualized potential helps us to remember that what has been is not what needs to be. He observed that *Homo sapiens* is uniquely able to adapt to, and create the ecologies in which we live and grow. This has led to enormous variation in human ecologies across history and cultures. "[T]his diversity suggests the possibility of ecologies as yet untried that hold a potential for human natures as yet unseen, perhaps possessed by a wiser blend of power and compassion than has thus far been manifested" (Bronfenbrenner, 1979, p. xiii; Bronfenbrenner & Ceci, 1994, p. 584).

Action Agenda

Ecological View of Social Problems . . . and Solutions

Jay Belsky (1980) demonstrated how Bronfenbrenner's ecological model expands our thinking about child maltreatment. Similar ecological analyses can inform our understanding of other problems as well. Work together as a class or in small groups to assess the causes and solutions at different levels for a social problem of interest, such as homelessness, substance abuse, poverty. What factors contribute to this problem at the level of the individual, the microsystem, the mesosystem, the exosystem, and the macrosystem? List the potential causes of the problem at each level on one side of the chalkboard or paper. Next, think about what sorts of solutions are suggested by the causes at different levels.

For example, one might examine the social problem of school drop out. Possible causes at different levels include: student learning disabilities (individual), competitive learning environments (microsystem of classroom); poor familial support for education or school support for familial culture (family–school mesosystem); parents' workplace schedules that preclude monitoring homework or attending school conferences (exosystem); and a cultural view of education as a private family matter (macrosystem). Each of these possible causes suggests very different solutions: individual tutoring; teacher training; increased communication between school and parents; reform of workplace policies; and public education campaigns.

After conducting an ecological analysis of the problem of interest, investigate the efforts currently underway to address the problem in your community. On which of Bronfenbrenner's levels do most efforts occur? Do the levels at which solutions are attempted match the hypothesized causes of the problem? Are there levels that you believe to be important that are not being addressed? To whom might you talk about your insights? When can they meet with you?

Who's Missing?

Habitant–inhabitant biases often go unnoticed. In a workshop on diversity, the activist Suzanne Pharr reported that whenever she enters a room full of people, she asks herself, "Who is not here and why not?" Although it can be difficult to attune oneself to what is missing rather than what is present, this question has proven invaluable to me in my work as a community psychologist.

For some period of time, perhaps a week, ask yourself "Who is missing?" each time you walk into a setting that is full of people. Do this when you enter parties, dining halls, restaurants, buses, classrooms, grocery stores, concerts, etc. Are there equal numbers of men and women? Which ethnic groups appear to be represented, and do the proportions reflect actual proportions in your community? What are the age ranges of the people present? Are there people with visible disabilities? Can you tell anything about the socioeconomic status of the people?

For a few settings where you notice exclusions, think about why certain groups might be missing. Is their absence a problem? Why or why not? Do you think efforts should be made to address any observed absences? If so, what might you do? Keep in mind that sometimes the homogeneity of groups serves a purpose. For example, the members of my Jewish women's book group are intentionally all female and Jewish. The limited age range (30's and 40's) was not planned, however. After noticing the lack of age diversity, we sought to recruit young and old group members, recognizing that our exclusion of diverse ages critically undermined our understanding of Jewish women's experience, the explicit goal of the book group.

Buying Power

In our capitalistic country, it is said that money talks. After reading the section on cycling resources, what strategies can you devise to help your money become more articulate? Here are some thoughts to get you started.

Identify the business practices you believe are important (e.g., "fair" wages, nondiscrimination policies, minimal environmental impact). Then, keep track of where you spend your money for a month. Analyze the businesses you support (restaurants, stores, movie theaters, etc.) and the companies that produce the products you buy (cosmetics, clothing, cleaning supplies, foods, etc.). Do they meet your standards? You might look at some books that rate businesses based on socially conscious considerations. One example is *The Feminist Dollar: The Wise Woman's Buying Guide* by Phyllis and Margaret Katz, (1997). You might also contact the Council on Economic Priorities (30 Irving Place, NY, NY 10003; phone: 212-420-1133). See also http://www.procott.org.

If the businesses you support do not operate in ways you deem important, how might you work to hold them accountable? Are there other businesses that you might patronize instead? Are there ways of encouraging superstores to keep resources within your community?

If you have trouble locating the information you think is important to assess business practices in your community, you might consider working as a class or in small groups to develop a survey that you could administer to businesses in your area. For example, which of the local pizzerias that cater to college students have the best employment policies? These findings might make an interesting article in the school newspaper—perhaps even a monthly column. Each month, you might review nearby businesses competing for student customers—pizzeria policies one month, ice cream parlor practices the next, then CD stores, clothing retailers, pubs, and so on.

Key Terms

adaptation

B=f(P,E)

behavior settings

bioecological model

cultural-ecological perspective

cycling of resources

ecological analogy

ecological model

environmental press

error of logical typing

exosystem

generalized reciprocity

genotype

habitant-inhabitant bias

interdependence

levels of analysis

macrosystem

mesosystem

microsystem

neighboring

person-environment fit

phenotype *(two meanings)*

psychological sense of community (PSC)

reaction range

scripts

setting programs

social capital

social climate

social exchange theory

succession

transaction

undermanning

underpopulation

Chapter 5

Appreciating Diversity

⌘ Introduction

During the 1960s, a number of disenfranchised groups joined the struggle for recognition and respect launched by African Americans in the civil rights battles a decade earlier. Women, gays and lesbians, Chicanos, and American Indians spoke out against the discrimination they faced. Other groups, notably people with disabilities, soon added their voices to the call for justice. To some degree, mainstream America responded. Attention to issues of diversity grew, and as the twentieth century drew to a close, countless schools, businesses, human service agencies, and government offices sought to become more inclusive of diverse groups.

The outward face of the United States has changed. One sign of change is the visibility of marginalized groups in the media. An African American friend shared with me the childhood memory of his family's excitement when a fast food chain first featured African American customers in its television commercials. Today, images of people from different groups pervade the media. Movies, books, magazines, and newspapers focusing on diverse groups are readily available. All of the most popular prime-time television shows about lawyers and doctors feature women and people of color in positions of leadership. Gay and lesbian protagonists star in situation comedies, and one, *Will and Grace*, won the Emmy for best comedy of 2000.

Unfortunately, success on television stands in stark contrast to the painful injustices that remain in the real world. According to the Bureau of Labor Statistics, women still earn less than 77 cents to a man's dollar (Barakat, 2000). The lower earning potential of women adds to the challenges faced by single mothers. The poverty rate in the U.S. is 7% among all families with children under 18, but 39% for female-headed households (U.S. Bureau of the Census, 1998). The economic outlook is bleak for people of color as well. For example, one in six children in the U.S. is poor, but one in three African American and Hispanic children fall below the poverty line (Children's Defense Fund, 2000).

Economics are not the only arena where dire statistics abound. Black youths are more than twice as likely as White youths to be held in a detention facility for similar offenses (U.S. Department of Justice, 1999). People in ethnic minority groups receive needed mental health services less often and receive poorer quality services (U.S. Surgeon General, 2001). And members of all disenfranchised groups are targeted for hate crimes, a problem that led to the enactment of the Hate Crime Statistics Act in 1990. This act required the Justice Department to acquire data on crimes that "manifest prejudice based on race, religion, sexual orientation, or ethnicity"[1] from law enforcement agencies across the country and to publish an annual summary of the findings.

Although issues of diversity have received unprecedented attention, attempts at inclusiveness often entail superficial adjustments rather than fundamental changes in attitudes, behaviors, and social relationships. Even when good intentions exist, progress can be slow. This chapter examines some of the barriers to a more inclusive society and some ideas about how we might overcome those barriers.

[1]In 1994, the Act was extended to include crimes based on disability status.

⌘ The Importance of Appreciating Diversity

In this section, we will consider why an appreciation of diversity matters and how well psychologists in general and community psychologists in particular have represented the voices of diverse groups.

WHY CONSIDER DIVERSITY?

Discussions of diversity raise difficult questions. Should we treat all people the same, or do the differences among us warrant scrutiny? If differences are important, which ones matter? Do all differences merit respect and if not, how do we decide? Let's begin this chapter with perhaps the most basic question: why is it important to appreciate diversity?

DEMOGRAPHIC ARGUMENTS

Why should we become culturally aware and appreciative of diversity? Many respond to this question with reference to the changing demographics of the United States. (e.g., Betancourt & Lopez, 1993; Sue, Bingham, Porche-Burke, & Vasquez, 1999). The U.S. has become an increasingly diverse place to live (see Table 5.1). According to the U.S. Bureau of the Census, the rate of increase in the majority White population has been less than 10% over each of the past two decades, while the rates of increase for other racial and ethnic groups have consistently topped 10% and in some instances topped 100%. The way we think about race and ethnicity has also changed. In the 2000 census, respondents could identify as multiracial for the first time. This recategorization altered the portrait of diversity in the U.S. dramatically. For example, the number of people who identified as American Indian or Alaskan Native was just under 2 million in 1990, and almost 2.5 million in 2000, an increase of 26%. If multiracial people were included in the count, however, over 4 million people identified as being either wholly or part American Indian in 2000—an increase of 110% over the 1990 figure (U.S. Bureau of the Census, 2001).

Table 5.1   Growth in Sub-Populations 1980–2000

Group	Growth Rate			
	1980–1990	**1990–2000**		
		Exclusive category		*Including multiracial respondents*
White	6%		6%	9%
African American	13%		16%	22%
American Indian	38%		26%	110%
Asian American and Pacific Islander	108%	Asian:	48%	72%
		Hawaiian/Pacific Islander:	1%	140%
Hispanic American (any race)	53%		58%	—

Based on U.S. Bureau of the Census, 1992, 2001

As this country becomes increasingly more diverse, the likelihood of encountering people from cultures other than our own increases. Proponents of cultural sensitivity argue that interactions with members of other groups will be more productive and satisfying for everyone involved if they flow from a base of understanding and respect rather than ignorance and fear. Scholars concerned about the implications of cultural diversity for the practice of psychology implore psychologists to respond to the changing demographics so that the profession does not become irrelevant or even harmful to increasing numbers of people (e.g., Hall, 1997).

COMMUNITY PSYCHOLOGY'S CONVICTION

Although the changing demographics of U.S. society underscores the importance of cultural awareness, community psychology's call to appreciate diversity does not hinge on the number of non-White people in U.S. society. Even if the tide somehow reversed and people of color left the country in large numbers, community psychologists would still attend to issues of diversity. This is because community psychology views culture as an important determinant of human behavior. It sees *all* people as embedded in multilevel social systems, including cultural systems, and so a full understanding of *any* person requires an accounting of her or his cultural context. Community psychologists also believe that much can be learned from different worldviews (see *The Promise of Community Psychology* section).

Community psychology's emphasis on social justice also necessitates a consideration of diversity. As described in Chapter One, community psychology arose, in part, out of the awareness that people in marginalized groups suffered disproportionately from social ills that negatively impact mental (and physical) health. The disadvantages that accrue from minority group membership stem from processes of **oppression**. Oppression refers to asymmetric power relations in which dominating persons or groups exert their greater power by restricting access to resources and instilling fear and a sense of inferiority in the subordinated person or groups (Prilleltensky & Gonick, 1996). The link between oppression and poor health is clear (e.g., Clark, Anderson, Clark, & Williams, 1999; Liebkind & Jasinskaja-Lahti, 2000), and poverty and discrimination have emerged as key mechanisms that account for this link (e.g., García Coll, Lamberty, Jenkins, McAdoo, Crnic, Wasik, & Vásquez García, 1996; Snowden, Martinez, & Morris, 2000). As Edison Trickett (1990) put it, "opportunities are not randomly distributed across race and gender [and] social structures are not equally supportive for minorities, women, gays and lesbians, and those with disabilities" (pp. 213–214). Respect for the fundamental rights, dignity, and worth of all people compels community psychologists to attend to issues of diversity. Thus, the field's commitment to diversity derives from both practical and value-based sources.

REPRESENTATION OF DISENFRANCHISED GROUPS

Regardless of the motivation, psychology in general and community psychology in particular recognizes the importance of appreciating human diversity. To what extent have we succeeded?

Psychology has not historically included the voices of marginalized groups in its research, theory, and practice (e.g., Bohan, 1995; Guthrie, 1998). Studies conducted in 1992 found that fewer than 4% of the articles published in APA journals reported on African American participants, (Graham, 1992), and only 1% of the articles published in six major counseling journals addressed lesbian and gay issues (Buhrke, Ben-Ezra, Hurley, & Ruprecht, 1992). As recently as 1999, Derald Sue and his colleagues (1999) described the curriculum of psychology as "woefully inadequate in its coverage of ethnic minorities, women, sexual minorities, and the disabled" (p. 1066).

Reviews of community psychology journals in the late 1980s and 1990s showed that our field, too,

has underrepresented the perspectives of women, people of color, people with disabilities, and gay, lesbian, bisexual and transgender people (e.g., Garnets & D'Augelli, 1994; Loo, Fong, & Iwamasa, 1988; Serrano-Garcia & Bond, 1994). A gap has existed between community psychology's rhetoric and its practice (e.g., Cauce, 1990; Hughes, Seidman, & Williams, 1993; Trickett, 1990). A 1994 survey of 86 community and clinical-community psychology programs found that 72% of the program directors believed in the importance of teaching students about ethnic and cultural issues, but only 48% of the programs required a course on this topic (Suarez-Balcazar, Durlak, Smith, 1994; see also Alcade & Walsh-Bowers, 1996).

In 1994, Rhona Weinstein stated that community psychologists needed to change not only what we study, but how we study it. In Chapter Two (see section on *Research and the Guiding Principles*) I identified some of the ways in which research fails to account for diversity (e.g., using methodologies and measures developed with and normed on dominant groups, and reducing complex groups to single, broad categories). Our efforts to change *what* we study and *how* we study it might be enhanced if we also change *who* does the studying.

Community psychologists have not been a very diverse group. All of the 39 attendees of the Swampscott conference that launched the field were White. By 1994, only half of all community psychology programs had *any* minority faculty members (and most of these had only one) and one third had only one or two students of color (Suarez-Balcazar et al., 1994; see also Mulvey, 1988). A more recent study of community psychology programs conducted by the Council of Program Directors in Community Research and Action (Lounsbury, Skourtes, & Cantillon, 1999) also found that most community psychology faculty members and students identified as non-Hispanic White.

Community psychology has historically been male dominated, as well (e.g., Swift, Bond, & Serrano-García, 2000). Only one Swampscott attendee was female. In a 1984 study of community psychologists whose work embodied significant elements of the field's paradigms, nearly all "exemplars" were male (Dalton, Elias, & Howe, 1985; Elias, Dalton,

Franco, & Howe, 1984). Between 1974 and 2000, women received the Award for Distinguished Contributions to Theory and Research in Community Psychology only four times, and on two of those occasions, the female recipient shared the award with a male.

Community psychology's ability to broaden its understanding of human behavior depends in large part on its success in attracting people of different cultural backgrounds to the field (Rappaport, 1986; see also Hall, 1997). Fundamental changes in observations, insights and research relationships require diverse perspectives (Cauce, 1990). Since 1990, Division 27/SCRA has attempted to improve its representation of minority group members. Initiatives that have been explored or implemented include pairing graduate programs as "partners" and "external critics" to enhance each others' focus on diversity; dedicating special journal issues and conferences to issues of diversity and privilege; directing outreach efforts to other minority professional groups; and mentoring undergraduates from diverse backgrounds who might become community psychology graduate students (Maton, 1999). These and other efforts have led to some progress. Compared to other APA divisions, a relatively high percentage of Division 27 members identify as ethnic minority, 12% as compared to 7% for developmental psychology, 7% for personality and social psychology, and 6% for clinical psychology (American Psychological Association Research Office, 1999). Women in community psychology programs now outnumber men, and women comprise half of the Division 27/SCRA executive committee.

Despite progress, more work remains to be done. For example, almost three times as many feminist articles were published in community psychology journals after 1990 as compared to the years before, but the actual number remained low—fewer than 5 articles per year on average (Angelique & Culley, 2000). Despite large numbers of female community psychologists women's perspectives are not well represented. After a period of self-study, members of one community psychology program concluded that given "insufficient feminist content in the curriculum, and the lack of feminist process in the culture of training, the relationships in the program cannot help but reproduce the larger patriarchal order" (Alcade & Walsh-Bowers, 1996; p. 405). There can be no quick fixes to patterns of thought and behavior that are deeply embedded in U.S. culture and history. In the remainder of this chapter, we explore some of the ways in which entrenched social patterns prevent us from making changes that many U.S. citizens, and most community psychologists, recognize as needed.

A focus on diversity highlights the intricate ties between our social realities and the language used to describe and shape those realities. Language both constitutes and is constituted by social practice. It spans the conceptual divide between individual and culture, private and public (Stewart, 2000). A discussion of the power and limits of language will illustrate some of the ways in which efforts to honor diversity can be thwarted—or promoted.

⌘ Language

Stephanie Reinharz (1994) proposed that *voice* is an important metaphor for power. Voice encompasses not only to the ability to express oneself, but also the means and the right to do so. In our society, not everyone has a voice. Children, for example, are often silenced—we have all heard the saying, "Children should be seen and not heard." Children are not the only people prevented from speaking. In mixed-sex settings, especially public settings, men often overpower the voices of women and monopolize speaking time (Stewart, Cooper, Stewart, & Friedley, 1998). During President Clinton's Administration, it became legal for gay soldiers to serve in the armed forces provided they did not let anyone know that they were gay (the *Don't Ask, Don't Tell* policy). The "ideal" of a colorblind society renders race invisible, and so it may even be considered rude to notice differences at all. An outspoken child who breaks social taboos by asking, "Why is that person chocolate-colored (or vanilla-colored)?" or "Why does that person have only one leg?" may be chastised for their impertinence. The first barrier to overcome in discussing the differences among us is to find the words to talk about it.

TERMINOLOGY

Read these terms slowly, pausing after each, and notice what comes to mind.

minority groups	*marginalized* groups
diverse groups	*underrepresented* groups
oppressed groups	

Although these terms are used interchangeably, each conjures somewhat different thoughts and feelings. The term *minority groups* probably calls to mind African Americans and perhaps other people of color. It may also evoke a sense of powerlessness. The term implies that people are vulnerable in that they are outnumbered. In actuality, not all groups who suffer injustice are numerical minorities. Women in the United States outnumber men but do not have the lion's share of societal power. Blacks in South Africa outnumbered Whites, but were still persecuted and relegated to an inferior social position under apartheid.

In the 1980s, the term *minority* lost favor and we spoke more of *diversity*. The latter term encompasses a broader domain of concern (Trickett, Watts, & Birman, 1993). When we speak of diversity, we generally refer not only to minority racial and ethnic groups, but to others dimension of difference as well: age, sex, socioeconomic class, sexual orientation, ability status. The term *diversity* also extends beyond a concern about discrimination, and reflects an interest in different cultures more generally, (Trickett et al., 1993; Trickett, Watts, & Birman, 1994). It shifts our focus from the psychological toll of oppression to the possible contributions of various cultures, a shift that is in keeping with community psychology's mandate to focus on people's strengths. Human *diversity* suggests a positive regard for human differences. A final advantage of the term *diversity* is that it avoids problematic dualisms in which one exists as either a member of the majority or the minority, oppressor or oppressed. The term includes all of us—men as well as women, Whites as well as people of color.

One shortcoming of the term *diverse groups*, however, is that it does not explicitly recognize the crucial issue of power. It implies a kind of harmony and good feeling that deflects attention from historic and ongoing inequities based on group membership (see also Bond & Pyle, 1998). The term *diversity* like its cousin term *multicultural*, has a veneer of goodwill that reinforces a **tourist approach** to human differences in which attempts to understand various groups are reduced to a discussion of ethnic foods, exotic costumes, and quaint customs (e.g., Derman-Sparks, 1989; Ahlquist 1992). Issues of social justice can be conveniently ignored.

The next term on the list, *oppressed groups*, recognizes inequities in the existing social order. It acknowledges that group differences correspond to differences in power, such that some groups are constricted and constrained in systematic ways. It is, however, an inflammatory term and has been overused to the point of meaninglessness. The all-important *system* of oppression is trivialized when individual members of dominant groups claim to be oppressed. Unlike the term *oppressed groups*, the terms *marginalized groups* or *disenfranchised groups* or *underrepresented groups* are less common and carry less emotional baggage. They encompass a variety of socially marginalized groups, and recognize the existence of power imbalances. The terms do, however, promote dualistic thinking (one is either marginalized or not, underrepresented or not) and they do not emphasize the positive contributions of different groups.

No ideal term captures all the important dimensions of difference. New terms will likely develop as overlooked dimensions become salient. Language evolves along with our understanding. Changes in terminology reflect evolving perspectives, not only of dimensions of difference in general, but also of specific groups.

POWER OF NAMING

A source of frustration for people in dominant groups can be the ever-changing labels underrepresented groups prefer in referring to themselves. We need to remember which terms are currently in favor—Black, Afro-American, or African American? Girl, lady, or woman? Hispanic, Chicano, or

Mexican American? Handicapped, disabled, or physically challenged? Homosexual, gay, or queer? Native American, American Indian, or Indian? The emotionally laden nature of group labels can lead to the sense that one cannot say *anything* without offending someone. Nevertheless, dismissing concerns about terminology as political correctness trivializes the psychological significance of self-definition for people who have been, and continue to be, silenced and defined by others.

One of the powers enjoyed by dominant groups in society is the power to name. The African names of slaves were lost as slavemasters assumed the privilege of assigning new names to those they viewed as their property. At Ellis Island, immigration officers "Americanized" the difficult-to-pronounce names of newly arrived foreigners. In patrilineal societies surnames retain the lineage of forefathers only, and the identity of maternal ancestors is lost.

Socially powerful people enjoy the power to name individuals and the groups to which less powerful people belong. As many of us learned in school, Christopher Columbus did not set sail with the intention of "discovering" a new country, but to find an alternate trade route to India. Thus, the lost explorer called the indigenous people of America *Indians*. The term *negro*, meaning "black" in Spanish, originated in the fifteenth century when Portuguese and Spanish people entered the slave trade.

Language and naming are reflections of power. Given the close tie between our names and our sense of identity, it is not surprising that an important part of ridding oneself of domination lies in asserting the right to name oneself. This occurs at different levels. As an individual-level example, Malcolm X was born Malcolm Little but chose to honor the African family name he could never know with the designation "X." Many women who marry men now decide to retain their "maiden" names. Group-level struggles against domination also center on the right to name. Social change activities of oppressed groups usually include attempts to modify the speech of their oppressors. Members of marginalized groups may, for example, demand respect in public address by coining the term *Ms.* or

objecting to the practice of referring to grown African American men as "boys."

It is in the context of the power of naming that we need to consider the efforts of oppressed people to establish what labels should be used to refer to their social group. In the 1960s, many activists objected to the terms *negro* and *colored*, and proclaimed themselves to be *Black*. They associated this new term with strength and pride. Slogans announced the arrival of "Black power," and Black citizens were encouraged to "Say it loud, I'm Black and I'm proud." The new term helped unite Black people under a political ideology that stressed self-respect and self-determination.

Adopting a new group name can help people from marginalized groups enhance their sense of a positive collective identity. New group names also redefine the groups' place in society. They send messages to members of the dominant group, as well. In the 1930s, social psychologists first studied how a group's name can invoke mental images that intensify prejudices (e.g., Katz & Braly, 1935). This has also been found in more recent decades. Research in the 1980s found that White university undergraduates had more negative associations to the term *Chicano* than to either *Hispanic* or *Mexican American* (Fairchild & Cozens, 1981), and that students believed teachers who preferred the title *Ms.* taught more interesting courses than teachers who used either *Mrs.* or *Miss* (Rubin, 1986; cited in Stewart et al., 1998).

As our concepts continually evolve, so too do our associations with particular terms. While *Negroes* were at one time evaluated more positively than *Blacks*, this difference diminished for Whites in the 1970s and reversed for Blacks (see Longshore, 1979 for a review). As the term *Black* gained favor over *Negro*, yet another term emerged. Since the 1960s, many Black leaders have voiced a preference for the term *African American*. This term reflects a dual heritage in both Africa and America. *African American* also escapes the negative connotations of the color black, which is associated with dirt, evil, and sadness. Moreoever, the term reinforces the group's unique identity. African Americans are not simply the opposite of White.

WORDS THAT DICHOTOMIZE

When we dichotomize people into two opposing groups, we may inadvertently reinforce antagonistic relationships between those groups. Too often, *black* and *white* are defined and conceptualized as mutually exclusive and opposites. "Reason and logic would suggest that race relations are impeded by a constant emphasis on differences in self definition instead of a conceptual focus on commonalities and similarities" (Ghee, 1990, p. 78). Many of the terms used in discussions of oppression and diversity divide people into opposite camps. A person is either minority or majority, oppressed or oppressor, dominant or subordinate. Black is the opposite of White, and men and women are of the "opposite" sex.

Although Westerners tend to think dualistically (Maruyama, 1983), reality is not so simple. People who fall under the category of "oppressed" do not feel oppressed all the time. In some contexts they may feel satisfied or powerful (Reinharz, 1994). In some contexts they may even be oppressors.

MULTIPLE IDENTITIES

Here is a simple exercise. The social identity grid depicted in Table 5.2 lists social categories that have been the basis for consistent and systematic discrimination. For each social category listed below, circle whether you identify as a member of the **agent group** (i.e., dominant group) or **target group** (i.e., subordinate group).

Many people completing this grid circle only agent identities (the proverbial "White male"), but virtually no one belongs solely to target groups. Chances are that no one in your class is a non-Christian disabled lesbian working class senior citizen or child prodigy of color.

Oppression is one of the great evils of society, and most socially conscious people prefer to see ourselves as victims rather than tyrants. In discussions of oppression and diversity, people with membership in *any* oppressed group may call upon that group identity, while White, Christian, able-bodied, heterosexual men are cast in the role of the enemy. Although many of us have target identities, *all* of us

📄 Table 5.2   Social Identity Grid

Social Category	Agent Identity	Target Identity
Sex	Male	Female
Race	White	Racial or ethnic
Ethnicity	Euro-American	Minority
Religion	Christian	Non-Christian (Jewish, Muslim, Hindu, etc.)
Sexual Orientation	Heterosexual	Lesbian or gay
Ability Status	Currently able-bodied	Disabled
Socioeconomic Background	Middle or upper class	Working class
Age	Young adult to middle age	Child or old adult

Adapted from DiversityWorks training materials; Amherst, MA. 1994.

have agent identities. Exclusive focus on target identities frees us from acknowledging the ways in which we also act as agents. We all carry within us the ability to exercise the unjust power of the oppressor.

The Invisibility of Agent Status. A lack of focus on the agent perspective is reflected in the psychological literature as well. Studies of racism, sexism, and other "isms" focus almost exclusively on the experiences of the victims of discrimination rather than perpetrators (Sue et al., 1999. For an exception, see Frankenberg, 1993). As researchers, practitioners, and citizens, we need to recognize and understand the other, less visible side of this dynamic—the dynamics of agent status.

I once had an officemate who ran violence prevention programs with youth. One day he spoke with me about a concern. A sex difference was interfering with the effectiveness of his program. The young men in his workshops were much more outspoken than the young women, and some of the girls remained silent for entire sessions. He wondered if he should hold assertiveness training classes to teach the young women to speak up *before* trying to implement his antiviolence curriculum. I wondered aloud why he did not propose a prerequisite class for the young men—maybe they needed to learn how to keep quiet and listen to what the women had to say.

From our agents statuses we tend to conceptualizae problems in ways that hold marginalized people accountable. It is easy to assume that victims, who are often silenced and stereotyped, are to blame (this is discussed in detail in Chapter Seven). William Ryan (1971) recommended that when thinking about social problems we ask:

> To whom are social problems a problem?" And usually, if truth be told, we would have to admit that we mean they are a problem to those of us who are outside the boundaries of what we have defined as the problem. Negroes are a problem to racist whites, welfare is a problem to stingy taxpayers, delinquency is a problem to nervous property owners. (p. 12)

Nathan Caplan and Stephen Nelson (1973) posed some similar questions for research psychologists. "Why do we study nonachievement among minority group members as undesirable behavior, but do not study exaggerated profit motive among 'successful' businessmen as a form of deviance?" "Why do we study the poor rather than the nonpoor in order to understand the origins of poverty?" (p. 207).

Robert Coles wrote an award-winning book series called *Children of Crisis*. The series grew from Coles' admiration for the resolve of Black children at the forefront of the battle for school desegregation whom he saw walking past angry White people each day on their way to formerly all-White schools (Coles, 1977). Coles decided to try to better understand their youthful heroism. From the beginning, research participants questioned Coles' focus. Black parents advised him to "go talk with those mobs who were coming forth with such hate and rage. 'They really do need a psychiatrist!' " (Coles, 1977, p. ix). Over the years, the Black parents continued to urge Coles to go talk to the powerful White people—"The rich folks are the ones who decide how the poor folks live" (p. x). Coles followed his first book in the *Children of Crisis* series with three subsequent volumes looking at children of migrant laborers, Eskimos, Chicanos, and Indians. Finally, Coles heeded the sage advice he had received over the years and wrote his fifth, final and perhaps most important volume of the series: *Privileged Ones: The Well-Off and the Rich in America.*

Although those of with target identities may be painfully aware of the ways in which we are silenced and discriminated against, we may remain oblivious to the silencing we perpetuate in our agent statuses (e.g., Mulvey, Terenzio, Hill, Bond, Huygens, Hamerton, & Cahill, 2000). An individual may

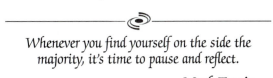

Whenever you find yourself on the side the majority, it's time to pause and reflect.

—Mark Twain

We often remain oblivious to the ways in which entitlement flows from our agent identities. From FEIFFER: JULES FEIFFER'S AMERICA FROM EISENHOWER TO REAGAN by Jules Feiffer. Edited by Steven Heller, copyright © 1982 by Jules Feiffer. Used by permission of Alfred A. Knopf, a division of Random House, Inc.

experience discrimination based on one aspect of social identity (e.g., race), while enjoying benefits from another aspect (e.g., sex). Martin Luther King and Malcolm X fought to eradicate racism without recognizing their own sexist attitudes (Cone, 1991). (For more on multiple identities, see Frable, 1997; Gibbs & Fuery, 1994; Pittinsky, Shih, & Ambady, 1999; Wilson, 1997).

Multiple Identities and the Complexity of Social Interaction. Given the complexity of our multiple social identities, it can be difficult to ascertain which aspect of our selves is relevant to a given situation. Let me provide an example. In 1993, my colleague Arthur Jones and I decided to develop a class entitled *Psychology and Social Change*. We were both committed to this topic, looked forward to the opportunity to work together, and believed that the course would be enriched by our social identities, which complement each other along almost every dimension on the social identity grid. Indeed, our dimensions of difference go beyond those captured on the grid—my coteacher was trained as a clinical psychologist while I am a community psychologist! We campaigned with students to put this course on the books, began preparing our syllabus a year in advance, and started the class with great enthusiasm.

After a few short weeks, I was surprised and dismayed to find that I had begun to disengage from the class. Arthur and I were on great terms, we had wonderful, dedicated students, and I felt passionately about the topic. Why was I having such a hard time staying present? I soon realized that students had begun to look to Arthur as the authority. They made eye contact with him when they spoke and directed questions to him. I had begun to feel unheard and had consequently begun to speak less. Silencing myself was only making the situation worse—it reinforced Arthur's position as the authority. As soon as I identified the dynamic, I talked to Arthur. He had not noticed that anything was wrong but said he would watch for the dynamic during the next class, after which he quickly confirmed that my perception had indeed been accurate.

We then tried to figure out why this was happening. Arthur thought it was likely due to gender, as he had experienced similar situations coleading workshops with his wife. I wondered if being African American gave him a legitimacy to talk about oppression and social change that I lacked. We also thought that age might be a factor—he was older and more established at the university than I was. In addition to the contributions of our social identities, we also considered the roles our personalities might contribute to the dynamic. I tend to be soft-spoken while he is a performer as well as a teacher and feels at home on center stage. Because Arthur and I are close friends who know each other well, I also felt comfortable confessing my fears that the responsibility lay not in *our* social identities or *our* teaching styles, but in *my* personal inadequacies. I was simply less interesting, less informed, less intelligent, less knowledgeable—less, less, less. He helped me resist the temptation to personalize the situation (which would have allowed him to personalize his "success" in the classroom).

After discussing the topic between ourselves, we brought it to the class. The students were appalled to recognize that this dynamic had been operating. Class members had different ideas about why it occurred, resulting in part from their own position on the social identity grid. For example, an Asian-American man reported feeling intimidated by the intensity of my gaze, and a gay man admitted a need to connect with my co-teacher, a heterosexual male. Although members of the social change class could not agree about why the dynamic occurred, we each made a commitment to recognizing it, acknowledging our own part in it, and working against it.

THE INADEQUACY OF DUALISMS

Although the social identity grid helps us to recognize membership in multiple social categories, social identities are far more complex than even the grid depicts. One aspect of complexity not captured on the grid is the ways in which various social categories interact. For example, the loss of social power associated with aging may be more dramatic for women as compared to men. One particularly important between-category link is the close connection between socioeconomic status and race or ethnicity (e.g., Dumas, Rollock, Prinz, Hops, & Blechman, 1999).

A second shortfall of the social identity grid is that it assumes homogeneity within each category. The variability within categories also has important implications. Not all working class people are poverty stricken, and the life circumstances of the wealthy elite differ dramatically from those in the middle class. As another example, different disabilities entail different functional challenges (e.g., blindness versus mental retardation) and even within a category of disability, important differences occur (e.g., mild versus profound retardation).

Furthermore, the boundaries between agent and target status also blur. Most people complete the social grid without pause, but some find themselves wondering on which side of the divide they fall. Even social categories that appear dichotomous are not really discrete. Biracial people may see themselves as having *both* agent and target racial identities, or *neither*. Bisexual people may hesitate to identify as either gay or straight. Even the social category that we most often see as clearly dichotomous, sex, may not be as clear cut as many of us think.

Although some social categories, such as race, religion, and income level, may be taboo topics, gender distinctions are apparent everywhere. (e.g., Kofkin, Katz, & Downey, 1995). In a baby's first introduction to the world we proclaim; "It's a boy!" or "It's a girl!" Pink and blue outfits convey the child's gender to anyone who failed to receive a birth announcement. Ambiguity about gender makes people uncomfortable. Some of you may remember the character Pat from Saturday Night Live. Pat was not identifiable as either male or female, and humor resulted from the audience's mounting frustration in not being able to assign a sex to Pat. The comedy sketches teased us into believing that we would finally find out if Pat was a man or a woman—for example when we learned that we were about to meet Pat's "significant other." But we never found out what Pat was. The significant other was an equally androgynous character named Chris.

We as a society are only beginning to recognize the ways in which our assumption of dichotomous sexes silences those among us whose identity is ambiguous. Until recently, doctors whisked newborns with the physical characteristics of both sexes (hermaphrodites) to operating rooms and assigned a sex surgically. The medical profession believed that if the social environment treated the baby as belonging to a particular sex beginning at birth, the child would develop a consistent gender identity without problems. Recent books indicate that is not the case and suggest that the surgical assignment of sex constitutes genital mutilation (Colapinto, 2000; Feinberg, 1998). Transgender people, who appear physically to be of one sex, but feel themselves to belong the *other* sex (I am purposely refraining from using the term *opposite* sex) also challenge our notions of sex as a dichotomous category. Sex may not be a dichotomous biological classification after all (e.g., Devor, 1989).

As members of an oppressed group, people of ambiguous gender experience language as limiting. Advocates of women's rights have highlighted some ways in which language is sexist (e.g., Stewart et al., 1998). In recent years, the terms police officer, letter carrier, and firefighter have replaced policeman, postman, and fireman. People who are not decidedly male or female point to another problematic aspect of our language: singular pronouns cannot be used with our reference to sex. While the plural "they" can be used for any sex, the singular form requires us to classify people as either a "he" or a "she." It is exceedingly difficult to converse without using pronouns, so how do we converse about a person of ambiguous gender? The activist and transgender warrior Leslie Feinberg (1998) proposed that we replace "she" and "he" with the new pronoun *sie* (pronounced "see"), and use *hir* (pronounced "here") in place of "him" and "her". As an added benefit for us all, such new terms would also eliminate the need to refer to a general "other" only in the plural ("they" or "their") in order to avoid using "he," as was the convention in earlier times.

DUALISMS AND HIERARCHIES

Dualistic social categories position people in opposing relationships, oversimplify reality, and render some people invisible. They also serve as a basis for hierarchies. The tendency to assign hierarchies to even meaningless group distinctions has been well documented in the social psychology literature. Countless distinctions exist that serve as a basis for asserting one group's superiority over another, and if a group distinction is not readily available, we easily invent new ones. In their classic **Robber's Cave** experiment, Muzafer and Carolyn Sherif and their colleagues (1953, 1961) demonstrated that when boys are arbitrarily divided into groups and placed into competition, group identities quickly solidify and boys favor their own group while demeaning the other group (see the Classic Research box).

Jane Elliot (1970; Jones, 1997) also found it easy to establish group identities and favoritism. She conducted an informal classroom experiment in her elementary school class in Riceville, Iowa, during the 1960s. Upon learning that Martin Luther King had been assassinated, one of the children in her class asked, "Why did they kill a king?" Elliot realized that these third graders did not appreciate the significance of the civil rights battles being waged in the U.S., and so she developed an exercise to help the children in her all-White class appreciate the motivation of these freedom fighters.

One day, Elliot told the children they were really not all alike even though they were all White and came from the same town. In reality, blue-eyed children were better, nicer, and smarter than brown-eyed children. The superior blue-eyed children would therefore be allowed to enjoy privileges at school—longer play time at recess, second helpings in the cafeteria, more praise in the classroom. Brown-eyed children were ordered to wear cloth collars so that their inferior status could be more quickly recognized by all.

Over the course of the day, the classroom became a prejudiced society. Blue-eyed children refused to play with their brown-eyed classmates, taunted them, and quickly tattled for the smallest transgression. The "superior" children were invested in maintaining the social structure, suggesting, for example, that the cafeteria staff be alerted to the rule prohibiting second helpings for the inferior children. They even devised new restrictions and punishments. The

CLASSIC RESEARCH

Muzafer Sherif
Transforming Conflict into Cooperation

In their classic experiments, Muzafer and Carolyn Sherif and their colleagues (1953, 1961) studied the ways in which intergroup conflicts arise in a natural setting. Eleven- and twelve-year-old boys were placed in a camp setting in Robber's Cave State Park in Oklahoma. Each boy was assigned to one of two groups, either "Rattlers" or "Eagles." Most boys in each group had not previously established friendships, and so the group identity as Rattler or Eagle was based almost entirely on interactions that occurred *after* the group was formed.

The researchers first tried to establish feelings of cohesiveness within each group. The Rattlers and Eagles stayed in different cabins, which were some distance apart, and used the camp facilities according to a staggered schedule (e.g., different meal times). During this phase, the boys engaged in fun group activities that avoided competition—hiking, swimming, building projects. After each group established a sense of cohesiveness, the boys were allowed to discover that there were actually two groups in camp.

During the next phase of the study, researchers engaged the two groups in competitive activities—baseball, football, tug-of-war, treasure hunts, and tent-pitching competitions. Trophies and valued prizes were prominently displayed to heighten competitive feelings, and staff manipulated events to keep the tension and frustration levels high. By the second day of competition, the good sportsmanship that had been exhibited initially was no longer in evidence. Tournaments and sporting games between the Rattlers and the Eagles quickly deteriorated into mean-spirited competitions. Biases favoring one's own group developed and members of the other group were demeaned and devalued. Name-calling became common, (e.g., "stinkers" and "sissies") and distaste for the other group was clearly demonstrated (e.g., holding noses when in the vicinity of members of the other group). By the time the competitions ended on the fourth day, neither group wanted anything to do with the other, objecting even to eating in the mess hall at the same time.

The researchers had documented the emergence of intergroup conflict and in the final stage of the experiment sought to restore harmony between the two groups. First, they did away with competitive events and engaged the boys in communal social activities. They found that eliminating competition did not suffice. When the boys ate meals together, they exchanged insults and resorted to throwing leftovers at each other. Even watching movies became a forum for hostile interactions. Intergroup hostility did not abate until the children needed to work together to achieve common goals. For example, a broken truck required the boys to join forces in a collective tug-of-war in order to pull the vehicle up a steep hill. Collective efforts were also required to restore drinking water to the camp and to secure popular movies. After repeatedly working together in such cooperative situations, stereotyping decreased, and boys became less likely to assign favorable traits to their own group and unfavorable traits to the other group. As cooperation increased, more and more boys reported that their closest friend was a member of the other group.

This research showed that even among similar boys with a short history of contact, intergroup hostility can develop quickly and become quite rancorous. A context of mutual interdependence and collaborative work towards a common goal was necessary to reverse negative intergroup attitudes and interactions.

brown-eyed children became demoralized and performed poorly on reading tests administered that day.

The next day, Elliot informed the children that she had made a mistake. Brown-eyed children were actually better. She had the brown-eyed children place the dreaded collars around the necks of their blue-eyed classmates. The tables turned, and now the brown-eyed children taunted and rejected their inferior classmates. On this day, blue-eyed children became demoralized and performed poorly on reading tests.

On the third day, Elliot explained to the children that they had been learning about prejudice, discrimination, and racism. The children discussed their experiences over the past two days in relation to what it meant to be Black in U.S. society. The children took the lesson to heart. Many years later, Elliot met with these students again, at a reunion when the children were in their midtwenties. They recalled the experiment in detail, reported that it had had a profound effect on them, and believed that they were less prejudiced because of this two-day exercise. By experiencing discrimination firsthand, the children became more sensitive to the subtle (and not-so-subtle) ways in which agent group members treat people from target groups unfairly.

Henri Tajfel (1969) extended the findings of the Sherifs and Jane Elliot by demonstrating that intergroup conflict does not require competitive or conflictual interactions. He coined the term **minimal groups** to capture this phenomenon (Tajfel, 1969). Even the most trivial, insignificant differences can inspire feelings of group identity and superiority. In one experiment, strangers were assigned to groups based on their preference for artists they had never heard of—either Paul Klee or Wassily Kandinsky. The research participants were strangers before the study and did not interact with each other during the course of the experiment. Nevertheless, they rated members of their own group as more pleasant and more competent than members of the other group. Moreover, they preferred reward allocations that favored their own group even if that diminished the rewards they received. They preferred giving themselves only $2 and members of the other group $1 rather than giving members of the other group $4 while receiving $3 for themselves (Brewer, 1979).

Differences between groups easily lead to self-serving biases in favor of one's own group (the **in-group**) and against the other group (the **out-group**).

Attachment to one's own group does not inevitably coincide with dislike of the outgroup, however. Cross-cultural and experimental research suggests that negative attitudes toward outgroups are more likely in particular contexts, such as when one group receives preferential treatment (Brewer, 1999).

Group distinctions do not necessarily coincide with ill will. One might argue that the tendency to categorize people into groups reflects an inevitable and useful human cognitive process. The world around us is complex and ever changing. In order to function we need to find mental shortcuts that allow us to focus only on relevant information, and these mental shortcuts are the basis of stereotypes (Allport, 1954). Gordon Allport (1954) called these mental shortcuts the "law of least effort," and they are the basis of stereotypes. Stereotyping simplifies our complex world. **Stereotypes** are generalizations about groups in which virtually all members are seen as having similar characteristics regardless of the actual variation within the group.

Although stereotyping is a cognitive process, our stereotypes often lead us to view people different from us in an unfavorable light. When we fail to appreciate people's unique qualities, we can more easily deny them their humanity. **Prejudice** is the term commonly used for negative attitudes about people based solely on their group membership. Interestingly, recent research suggests that prejudices are not necessarily negative. Some outgroups, such as people with disabilities, migrant workers, and housewives, may be perceived as warm but incompetent, thereby eliciting a seemingly benevolent attitude. Susan Fiske and colleagues (1999) labeled this *paternalistic prejudice*. Other groups, such as feminists, Jews and gay men, are seen as competent but not warm, which elicits what the researchers called *envious prejudice*.

Although the tendency to categorize and stereotype is widespread, it does not necessarily result in prejudice, and prejudice does not inevitably lead to **discrimination** (e.g., Devine, 1989). When discrimination does occur, however, the effects can be devastating. Discrimination consists of harmful actions toward people based solely on their membership in particular groups. Although acts of discrimination can occur at individual and small group levels (e. g., a person who harasses an African-American neighbor or a real estate office that will not show African-American clients houses in White neighborhoods), these acts exist within a larger system of oppression.

In systems of oppression, members of the op*pressed* groups experience some sort of *press*. Presses are used to mold, squeeze, or flatten; they restrain and restrict (Frye, 1983). Oppression reduces a person's options and often places her or him in a double bind situation where all choices entail censure. For example, young, single women who choose to be sexually active are "sluts," while those who remain celibate are "prudish" and "frigid." Oppressive systems simultaneously punish people who do not conform to required social roles and reward those who do. Glick and Fiske (2001) found that just as prejudices come in different forms, so too do oppressive actions. They distinguished *benevolent sexism*, which is a chivalrous ideology that benefits women who accept conventional roles and subordinate status from *hostile sexism* that punishes women seen as usurping male privilege.

Cultural worldviews may influence our tendencies to establish dualisms and hierarchies. While some cultures (e.g., Chinese) try to deal with seeming contradictions by retaining basic elements of both perspectives, Euro-Americans polarize contradictory perspectives so that one can clearly emerge as better (Peng & Nisbett, 1999). Magoroh Maruyama (1983) observed that Westerners often adopt a **zero-sum perspective** in which one person's gain is automatically viewed as another person's loss. Adherence to a zero-sum orientation may increase the likelihood that differences serve as a basis for hierarchies. It can lead, for example, to the notion that sanctioning lesbian and gay unions threatens heterosexual couples. When adhering to a zero-sum perspective, one can forget that some commodities such as love, commitment, honor, and respect (what philosopher Albert O. Hirschman called "moral resources," see Putnam, 1993) are not limited. Quite the contrary: they increase rather than decrease through use. Loving and honorable behavior on the part of one person generally inspires the same in others.

Members of oppressed groups often find themselves in double-bind situations. TOLES © 2000. The Buffalo News. Reprinted with permission of UNIVERSAL PRESS SYNDICATE. All rights reserved.

" WELL, IF THE ECONOMIC BOOM BENEFITS EVERYONE, WHAT GOOD IS IT ?!"

Economics as a zero-sum game. Reprinted with special Permission of King Features Syndicate.

Not every interaction is a zero-sum game. There can be win–win situations in which everyone benefits. And there can be lose–lose situations. Interestingly, one of the hierarchies that often arises in discussions of diversity and oppression is who is *more* oppressed. Conversations get stalled in efforts to prove which was worse, slavery or the holocaust, or who is more discriminated against, people of color or gays and lesbians. In such competitions everyone loses. One person's injustice does not negate the injustice experienced by another. Oppression, too, can be self-perpetuating.

BEYOND DUALISMS: "OUR SIMILARITIES ARE DIFFERENT"

James Jones (1994) highlighted one of the challenges faced by those of us interested in diversity and willing to look beyond false dichotomies. He began a chapter on diversity with the following quote by Dale Berra about his father Yogi: "I am a lot like him, only our similarities are different!" (Jones, p. 27). Jones observed that this seemingly nonrational statement conveys an important insight. We are all of us, as individuals and members of various groups, both the same and different.

People are generally comfortable with the extremes of sameness and differentness. We easily affirm the notion that we are all the same under our skin, all part of the universal human family. We can also embrace the notion that each of us is a completely unique individual—no two the same, like snowflakes. These two seemingly opposed positions actually function in similar ways—they absolve us of the need to come to terms with group differences. The notion that everyone is a minority of one suggests that all differences are equal and downplays the fact that some group differences are associated with a lack of power and limited access to resources (Bond & Pyle, 1998). Similarly, the notion that everyone is really the same suggests that we should not care about—maybe not even notice—group differences. In these extreme views, any observed difference (e.g., in test scores or job success) is attributed to individual talent and natural processes (Bond, 1999).

Roderick Watts observed that social scientific paradigms for understanding cultural groups have struggled with the issue of sameness and differentness. One popular paradigm is *cross-cultural* research (Watts, 1994; see also Betancourt & Lopez, 1993; Moghaddam & Studer, 1997). Most cross-cultural research is *race comparative* (McLoyd & Randolph, 1985). Psychological findings that emerged in studies of dominant groups are examined in other groups, and the main question of interest is how the subordinate group deviates from the dominant group. This paradigm tends to emphasize group differences and adopts a deficit perspective with regard to nondominant groups.

A second paradigm, termed *population-specific psychologies,* focuses on a single group (Watts, 1994). Comparisons with other groups are of minimal interest. Two problems are associated with this paradigm: ignoring differences that exist within the group in an attempt to characterize the population as a whole and adhering to stereotyped and unproved assumptions about the group under study (Ortiz-Torres, Serrano-García, & Torres-Burgos, 2000). Thus, this approach, too, highlights differences between groups.

Groups' similarities *and* differences merit attention. Table 5.3 shows a few dimensions across which various social groups might be compared, dimensions that highlight areas of common ground, as well as uncommon ground. The list is certainly not exhaustive. For example, important dimensions of difference among ethnic-cultural groups that do not appear in the table include English as a first or second language, number of generations in the U.S., conditions under which the immigration occurred (escaping persecution versus seeking opportunity), and degree of assimilation. Nevertheless, Table 5.3 outlines some of the ways in which social groups have points of convergence as well as divergence.

Table 5.3   Some Dimensions of Commonality and Difference among Target Groups[4]

Target Identity	Group culture and strategies for coping with oppression are transmitted intergenerationally	Group membership is lifelong as opposed to acquired	Group membership is apparent	Group membership is a choice
Person of color	Yes	Yes	Yes	No
Female	Yes	Yes	Yes	No
Gay, lesbian or bisexual	No	Debatable	No	Debatable
Disabled	No	Varies	Varies	No
Religious minority	Yes	Yes	No	Varies
Working class background	Yes	Varies	No	No
Very young or very old	No	No	Yes	No

[4]Note that "Yes" and "No" designations depict the usual case. There are numerous exceptions: women and men who change their genders; religious minorities who convert to Christianity; people of color who appear to be White; disabled people who share their ability status with their parents, and so on. Once again we see that dichotomies help us to organize our thinking but simplify and distort reality.

EXAMPLES: INVISIBILITY, COPING, AND IDENTITY DEVELOPMENT

The dynamics of oppression constitute one basis for similarities across disenfranchised groups. Oppression operates in a similar fashion across different social identities. At the same time, different groups experience these dynamics in somewhat different ways. One excellent example is that of invisibility. Virtually all marginalized groups experience invisibility (which coincides with voicelessness), but the exact nature of this phenomenon differs from group to group. Here are some titles of books, chapters, and essays:

- *Invisible Man*
- *Invisible Lives: The Truth About Millions of Women-Loving Women*
- "A Hidden Army for Civil Rights"
- "Invisibility Is an Unnatural Disaster: Reflections of an Asian American Woman"

Let's look at each of these works.

In his classic novel *Invisible Man*, Ralph Ellison (1947) described the ways in which the African American narrator remains unseen by the majority culture, which viewed Black people as less than human and unworthy of recognition. Although his race was immediately apparent to all, it had the effect of rendering him invisible.

Sexual orientation, on the other hand, is generally not an apparent dimension of difference (see Table 5.3). In *Invisible Lives*, Martha Barrett (1990) examined the ways in which society's assumption of heterosexuality prevents gays and lesbians from being seen as such by heterosexuals and by other gays. Some activists have proposed that the struggle for gay civil rights would make enormous strides if all gay, lesbian, and bisexual people turned pink for a day—everyone could see that "we are everywhere"—in the workplace, army, neighborhood, and government.

In "A Hidden Army for Civil Rights," Joseph Shapiro (1993) examined the ways in which physical obstacles, such as curbs and stairs (as well as institutionalization) keep people with disabilities out of sight. In "Invisibility Is an Unnatural Disaster: Reflections of an Asian American Woman," Mitsuye Yamada (1981) expressed how she, as a woman and as an Asian American, was expected to be quiet and subservient. Her opinions and perspectives remained invalidated and unseen.

Four different target groups, four different contexts, but the same effect: invisibility.

As another example, consider coping efforts in response to oppression. Different groups have come upon some common ways of thriving in oppressive contexts (e.g., Serrano-García & Bond, 1994). For example, a lack of support from majority cultures compels members of various marginalized groups to strengthen existing or develop new support networks. Members of many disenfranchised groups rely on extended family, especially when all family members share the target status (e.g., minority racial identity or low economic status). People who are less able to depend on family members because the status is not shared create alternative settings to provide needed services (e.g., rape crisis centers for women, hospices for people with AIDS).

Research on the identity development of target group members points to another way in which the experience of marginalization results in similar dynamics. Members of all disenfranchised groups struggle to develop a positive sense of themselves as members of a group that the larger society fails to celebrate and often disparages. Minority identity development proceeds along similar lines across groups. William Cross' (1971, 1978, 1995) groundbreaking work on stages of Black racial identity development has been extended to numerous other groups, including Asian, Latino, biracial, and gay and lesbian populations (Cross, 1995; D'Augelli, 1994; Walters & Simoni, 1993). Although the specifics of these models vary (e.g., African American people generally do not need to "come out" to others as gay people do), the overall course of development remains the same. In the first stage, the negative definitions of society remain unexamined. Subsequently, individuals move to a period of confrontation with society's stereotypes and immerse themselves in the minority group's own history and culture. In the final stages of development, individuals achieve a secure sense of themselves as members of the marginalized group (Phinney, 1996).

SOURCES OF DIFFERENCE AND SIMILARITY: A MODEL

Oppression and the reactions to oppression are important sources of similarity among target groups. Although oppression is a major player in the life stories of oppressed groups, it is by no means the whole story. We cannot understand diverse groups solely by focusing on oppression. As Roderick Watts (1994) warned, culture must not be confused with the byproducts of oppression. Members of marginalized groups should not be forced to claim as a part of their cultural heritage elements of their behavior or thinking that result from discrimination and oppression. John Ogbu, (1988) used the term **secondary cultural characteristics** to refer to the competencies and socialization patterns that arise to meet the demands of intercultural contact, which is often oppressive (see section on *Extensions of Bronfenbrenner's Work* in Chapter Four). It is easy for agent group members and target group members alike to confuse the two. African American youth's notion that achieving academically is synonymous with "acting White" shows how secondary cultural characteristics may come to be seen as primary (Fordham & Ogbu, 1986).[2]

The African American clinical psychologist Arthur Jones (1985) developed a model (see Figure 5.1) for psychologists working with African American clients that can be applied to other marginalized groups (see also Boykin & Toms, 1985). In this model, behavior can be understood as influenced by the experience of oppression and also by one's root culture. The model identifies two other sources of variation as well. First is the influence of the dominant culture. Members of marginalized

groups are also members of the larger society, and so dominant cultural forces also shape behavior. Individual characteristics also matter. All of us are unique individuals with unique personal histories, as well.

The degree of overlap and the relative size of each circle vary from individual to individual, from group to group, and across time. The overlapping circles indicate the difficulty of separating the influences of these different sources. This model helps us to consider different sets of influences that account for both similarities and differences among social groups and among individuals. Remember, however, that we all have multiple social identities. To account adequately for all our social identities, we would need to multidimensionalize these circles to reflect our multiple target identities.

One advantage of recognizing people's multiple identities and the different sources of influence on behavior is that in-group and out-group distinctions break down. People can recategorize themselves along a variety of dimensions to highlight similarities as well as differences (see Gaertner, Dovidio, Anastasio, Bachman, & Rust, 1993). Chicano and Asian American citizens have different ethnic identities but may have similar experiences as residents of this country, or as women, or as cancer survivors. Our multiple identities increase our opportunities for connection as well as conflict. Indeed, recognition of the common elements of oppression across target groups has the potential to link oppressed people in a common effort to overcome root causes of injustice. Some activists have observed that in the U.S., single-issue approaches to combating racism or sexism have prevented insight into the common bases of oppression, such as broad economic structures (Biklen, 1983; Pharr, 1988).

⌘ Implications for the Work of Community Psychology

The preceding discussion highlights some of the difficulties involved in trying to understand and appreciate diversity: legacies of silence; imprecise and

---

[2]For a fascinating photographic study that depicts this phenomenon, see Wendy Ewald's [2000] project on how Black and White children depict their "Black selves" and their "White selves".

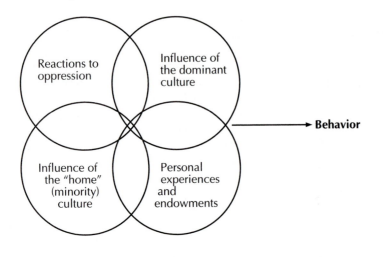

Figure 5.1
Four influences on behavior for minority group members. *Adapted from Jones, A. C. (1985). Psychological functioning in Black Americans: A conceptual guide for use in psychotherapy.* Psychotherapy, 22, 363–369. *Adapted with permission.*

changing terminology; false dualisms; the complexity of similarities and differences that exist within and across groups; multiple influences on behavior. This section examines how an awareness of the difficulties delineated above might impact the work of community psychologists.

DIFFICULT DIALOGUES

Language has the power to oppress. It also has the power to liberate. Talking and being listened to aids empowerment (Rappaport, 1995; Reinharz, 1994; Thomas & Rappaport, 1996).

THE TARGET'S PERSPECTIVE: FACILITATING EXPRESSION

As researchers and practitioners, community psychologists can help people find and express their voices. Italian historian Carlo Ginsburg observed, "the Minority World lives in a culture where we are constantly being offered solutions before we have asked the critical questions" (cited in Dahlberg, Moss, & Pence, 1999). Community researchers can make room for people in underrepresented groups to formulate their critical questions and articulate responses.

A particular promising avenue for such efforts derives from a narrative approach. In research, such an approach allows people from disenfranchised groups to express themselves freely without the constraints of multiple choice surveys or structured interviews imposed by researchers operating from dominant paradigms (e.g., Gergen, Gulerce, Lock, & Misra, 1996; Rappaport, 1995; Stewart, 2000). Practitioners, too, can create contexts for people to express themselves. Mutual help groups are one forum for telling stories and redefining identities. For example, Lynne Bond and her colleagues, (2000) established a support group called "The Listening Partners Program," where rural mothers of young children who felt unheard, isolated, and powerless came together to articulate their experiences and find strength in their voices.

Liberating narratives do not require the spoken word. During slavery, Negro spirituals brought people together, gave them courage, and conveyed secret messages of resistance to slaves attempting to escape (A. Jones, 1993). Almost a century after slavery ended, freedom songs served a similar function in the civil rights movement (Reagon, 1991; see also Crosby & Bender, 2000). The visual arts have used visual narratives to advance social justice. The AIDS quilt puts a human face on the AIDS crisis (Jones, 2000). The murals of Chicano artists instill cultural pride and spread messages of rebellion (Cockcroft & Barnet-Sánchez, 1993). Small tapestries called **arpilleras** express the pain

In this arpillera, made by the late Gala Torres, women are united by their shared grief as they search for their loved ones. *From M. Agosín. (1996) Tapestries of hope, threads of love. Albuquerque: University of New Mexico Press. Used with permission.*

experienced by bereaved mothers and wives during General Pinochet's regime in Chile and drew worldwide attention to the suspicious disappearances of thousands of people (see the Community Intervention box).

THE AGENT'S PERSPECTIVE: LEARNING TO LISTEN

Difficult dialogues require that oppressed people find ways of articulating their experiences. Difficult dialogues also require receptive listeners. Stephanie Reinharz (1994) stated that, "to utilize the concept of voice within diverse groups, we must be willing to hear what others are saying, even when it violates prior expectations or threatens our interests" (p. 195). Those of us who seek to appreciate diversity must listen from our agent statuses, even when the target groups' expression makes us uncomfortable. Agent groups sometimes resist such messages by accusing target group members of being too shrill, too emotional, too angry, too loud, (or, in academic realms, too political or not rigorous enough). The attempt to hold disenfranchised people responsible for their failure to be heard and taken seriously constitutes yet another abuse of power. Three common impediments to attentive listening (as researchers, practitioners, teachers, and citizens) are described below: discomfort with emotion, attachment to the expert role, and a focus on the agent group members' intent rather than impact.

Emotion. Talking about diversity and oppression triggers emotions (see Smith, 1993). By engaging in difficult dialogues, target group members may risk confirming negative stereotypes (e.g., sounding too shrill or too angry) or having the wounds of oppression reopened. The participation of agent group members also brings emotions. Anxiety may result from the fear of appearing racist or sexist or simply ignorant (e.g., Steele, 1990). A sense of complicity in oppression, even unwitting complicity, can inspire guilt, shame, and anger in agent group members (Ahlquist, 1992). Thus, discussions of diversity and oppression often result in a lot of heat. Miscommunications abound and strong emotions may ambush us. Discussants (be they students, research participants, or community members) may end up feeling unheard or misunderstood. Defenses go up. Feelings get hurt. Communication gets stuck.

COMMUNITY INTERVENTION:

Chilean Tapestries
Threads of Despair and Hope

From 1973 to 1989, the people of Chile lived under a military dictatorship run by Augusto Pinochet. During Pinochet's regime, censorship, curfew, exile, arbitrary detention, prison, and torture became commonplace. Many people were taken from their homes by the police, never to be seen again (Agosín, 1996; Sepúlveda, 1996). At least 3,000 disappearances were reported a few weeks after the military coup, and approximately 400 people were arrested each month thereafter. According to Amnesty International, as many as 90,000 people disappeared under military dictatorships in Latin America during a 20 year period (Agosín, 1996).

Under Pinochet's rule, thousands of mothers, wives, and sisters spent countless hours inquiring about their lost loved ones in prisons, police stations, and detention centers. In their searches, they met other women in similar situations. These bereaved family members shared their sorrow and their struggles to survive economically in the absence of the family breadwinners.

The Catholic Church formed a new institution, the Vicariate of Solidarity, to help indigent people survive. Sewing appeared to be one way for women, most of whom had never worked outside the home, to make a little money. The Vicariate organized craft shops throughout the country. In 1974 fourteen women attended a new sewing workshop. The women had previously met and spoken together during their searches for their family members. Now, they convened as a group, united in their grief over loved ones whose fate they did not know and overcome with the pressure of feeding their children who now had no fathers. (Agosín, 1996). The women already knew how to sew and spontaneously made the first arpilleras—small tapestries woven from colored threads and scraps of cloth that expressed their personal and shared stories of pain, grief, loss, anger, fear, love, and hope. Some arpilleristas sewed their first tapestries from scraps torn from their own clothes and the clothes of their disappeared relatives. As one arpillerista explained, "We wanted to tell people, with pieces of our very clothing, about our personal experiences" (Sepúlveda, 1996, p. 49). Additional arpillera workshops were organized in church basements throughout

Chile's shantytowns. The colorful tapestries, sewn by hand, became repositories for powerful emotions. The cloths depicted scenes of disappearance, of searches, of torture. They also captured memories of happier times and hopes for the return of loved ones.

Some of the arpilleristas created a folk music group where they could compose, sing, and dance—notably the *cueca sola,* a solo version of the traditional *cueca,* a partner dance. The rock musician Sting wrote and performed a song called "They Dance Alone" as a tribute to these women. Sting had seen their performances on tour in Chile with his band, the Police. He reported in an interview with *Timeout* magazine,

> The mothers and the wives of 'the disappeared' do this amazing thing; they pin photographs of their loved ones to their clothes and go out in groups and do this folk dance with invisible partners in front of the police station. It's this incredible gesture of grief and protest . . . what can the police do? These women are simply dancing. (*Timeout,* No date, 14)

By incorporating the highly personal and lovingly sewn arpilleristas into their political struggles, the women added dimensions of caring and personal commitment to political protest. Many of the women artists became activists. The traditional role of Chilean women was transformed as they took their protests to the streets, risking arrest and worse. They marched in demonstrations carrying photographs of their missing relatives. They organized hunger strikes and chained themselves to the doors of important buildings, such as the Supreme Court and Pinochet's house.

The arpilleras became a way not only of expressing deeply personal experiences and paying tribute to disappeared relatives, but also of bringing truth to light. As one woman explained, "We are here to denounce what happened to us and to put our anguish into the arpilleras so others will know" (Agosín, 1996, p. 14). Arpilleras became a way of communicating with the outside world. Sympathetic foreigners helped smuggle the arpilleras out of the country to exhibit and sell. The arpilleristas often sewed little pockets in the backs of their tapestries where they would place personal notes to the foreigners who might one day buy the arpillera. One woman recounted that she had made an arpillera of her son "as a little boy running across the sand on the beach, and in a little pocket on the back, I put a message that said, 'When I find my son, I will take him to the sea so he can run barefoot across the sand again' " (Agosín, 1996, p. 17).

The women created a culture of resistance in a country where few dared question authoritarian rule. The arpilleras live on as a testament to what happened in Chile, the human potential for cruelty and domination and also the vibrancy of the human spirit that continues to struggle and hope under the direst of circumstances.

In Western society, many of us in dominant groups are socialized to believe that argument, conflict, debate and disagreement can and should be avoided (e.g., Maruyama, 1983). Euro-American culture also reinforces a view of emotion as detrimental to understanding (e.g., Kochman, 1981). The discomfort surrounding issues of diversity threatens to keep people silent—dialogues are resisted or begun with trepidation (e.g., Tatum, 1992). Nevertheless, continued silence precludes even the possibility of increased understanding. The emotions generated in discussions of diversity and oppression may be better viewed not as an impediment to progress but as an opportunity for and perhaps a necessary precondition of progress. They are a sign that that the topic matters. Emotions signal the personal relevance of the discussion, and it is when people are engaged and involved that real change becomes possible. The community psychologist Rhona Weinstein (1994) observed, "Despite the rage, despite the fear, and despite the silencing, these are healthy engagements" (p. 816). The disequilibrium created by difficult dialogues can allow for insight, innovation, and new connections—emotional, intellectual, and interpersonal.

A preference for rational discussion may be particularly evident in academic environments (Sue et al., 1999). As discussed in Chapter Three, emotion and rationality are seen as diametrically opposed—belonging to two different worlds. Academicians may feel most comfortable in the world of objectivity and detached observations. Thus, academically trained researchers, consultants, workshop facilitators, program directors, and teachers may attempt to keep conversations about diversity on the plane of abstraction in order to avoid emotionality and promote logical analysis. Diversity and oppression are, however, inherently emotional topics.

The emotion that poses the greatest difficulties for people in agent groups may be the anger of target group members. Carol Tavris (1989) called anger the "misunderstood emotion." It is viewed by many as a destructive force, dangerous to ourselves and others, but anger can also be constructive. It clarifies discontentment and brings injustice to light. Anger is a moral emotion in that it involves an element of righteousness (Miller, 1986; Tavris, 1989). People confront injustice only when the situation is recognized as unfair (Frye, 1983). If a person or group does not feel worthy or important, they will not feel slighted or wronged. Anger is also a relational emotion (Frye, 1983, Miller, 1986; Tavris, 1989). It orients one person or group vis-à-vis another. It requires "uptake" from someone else. Social protests often entail a demand for the recognition of an oppressed group's anger (Frye, 1983). Laying claim to anger defines oneself as worthy of respect. Agent group members often refuse to legitimate the anger of target group members, dismissing it as an indication of shortcomings rather than a response injustice. Angry women are shrill, shrewlike, and castrating. Angry Black people are irrational, violent and in need of confinement. Angry gay people are pursuing their "*militant* homosexual agenda" and threatening family values. Refusing to uptake anger is an important social control mechanism.

Anger exchanged between people, regardless of social position, often entails confusion and incomprehension. In one study, the same people provided two autobiographical narratives, one describing a situation where they became angry at someone else and another describing an occasion where someone else became angry at them (Baumeister, Stillwell, & Wotman, 1990). Respondents constructed the two narratives in systematically different ways. People described becoming angry only after a series of earlier provocations in which the anger was stifled. Thus, expressed anger was often accumulated anger. When these same people told stories of being the targets of anger, however, they described the other person's anger as an overreaction to a single incident. Thus, when a person becomes angry, the anger seems justified and sensible. When a person is the recipient of the anger, the anger seems unnecessary and unreasonable.

This situation is exacerbated when the players differ in social position. People in dominant groups enjoy the privilege of remaining blissfully oblivious to injustices experienced by target group members on a regular basis. For example, White people are not routinely followed by store security guards or pulled over on the highway for "driving while Black." Thus, majority group members may not understand what all the fuss is about and accuse marginalized groups of *creating* conflict rather than *exposing* conflict (Miller, 1986). Agent group members may be baffled by the anger of target group members who act from a history of oppression that the agent group member does not (and perhaps does not *want*) to see.

Expertise. Difficult dialogues require us to leave the ordered realm of objective science where the world can be predicted and controlled. It requires that we enter the subjective world of emotions, values, multiple realities, and indeterminacy. The Western belief in one true answer (Maruyama, 1983) is untenable in this world. Teachers, researchers, and practitioners who position themselves as experts will inevitably feel uncomfortable as they shoulder the obligation of shedding the light of truth on topics that are inherently multidimensional and evolving (Ahlquist, 1992; see also Roberts, 2000).

In his article on methodological sources of cultural insensitivity in mental health research, Lloyd Rogler (1999) suggested that researchers learn to think of themselves not as the experts, but as a listeners. The culturally different research participants become the speakers, the "experts" on the proper interpretations of their thoughts and behaviors. Researchers as outsiders need to come into communities as learners and facilitators rather than teachers and overseers (Gutiérrez-Mayka & Contreras-Neira, 1998).

Reluctance to relinquish expert status may help explain why interventionists sometimes pay only superficial attention to issues of diversity. For example, AIDS prevention booklets are translated into Spanish but the appropriateness of the content, developed by experts, is not questioned. Intended audiences may not resonate to intervention materials devised from dominant perspectives, however, even if protagonists in the materials are renamed José and Maria. For example, advising women to request that their male partners wear condoms will be ineffective in cultures where women do not confront men directly (Marín, 1993) and male sexuality is believed to be controlled by passion rather than reason (Marín, Tschann, Gomez, & Gregorich, 1998). Nor will advice to refrain from anal sex be heeded by Latinas who prefer the risk of contracting HIV through anal sex to the risk of rendering themselves unmarriageable by losing their virginity through vaginal sex (Arguello, 1983, reported in Cauce, Coronado, & Watson, 1998). Messages about condom use that frame sexual activity in the context of play (e.g., "Play It Safe") may conflict with religious teachings of ethnic minority communities (Mays & Cochran, 1990).[3]

Cultural competence is not achieved simply by hiring a bilingual researcher or practitioner, or by either sponsoring or attending a workshop in diversity (see Bernard, 1998; Vega, 1992). The expertise about effective ways of gathering or conveying information lies within the communities of interest, and researchers and interventionists must learn to listen to this expertise. Culturally appropriate research and practice require careful consideration of the values, subjective experiences, and behavioral preferences

[3]For guidelines on working with specific groups, see the APA brochure entitled, "Guidelines for Research in Ethnic Minority Communities" available at: *http://www.apa.org/pi/oema/onlinebr.html*.

and expectations of the target group (Marín, 1993). This requires an openness to the influence of participants, and a symmetry in the relationship between professional and consumer (e.g., Dumas et al., 1999). The very tenets of established research and intervention protocols are challenged by a view of knowledge as socioculturally bound and co-constructed by everyone willing to engage in difficult dialogues.

Intent versus Impact. Discomfort with emotion and an unwillingness to relinquish one's role as expert are two impediments to liberating dialogues. To frame this in the positive, difficult dialogues are promoted by making room for emotions and fostering horizontal, collaborative relationship. A third impediment to dialogue is the desire to deny personal bias or to resist recognizing its impact (Tatum, 1992). Agent group members enjoy the privilege of remaining oblivious to benefits that accrue from agent status. Able-bodied diners never have to call restaurants ahead of time to ensure that it is accessible to them. Euro-American parents need not entertain the possibility that their children might not receive school instruction in their home language.

In some instances, when acting in our agent statuses we may think we are being inclusive of diversity while actually alienating members of target groups. Heterosexual couples may believe themselves to be reaching out to gay and lesbian couples by inviting them to their weddings, not realizing that the invitation may be a painful reminder that their own unions are denied legitimacy in this society. Organizers of the office "holiday" party may congratulate themselves for using an inclusive term and for decorating the room with menorahs and dreidels as well as candy canes and reindeer, while failing to recognize that Hanukkah actually occurred in early December that year and is long past.

Cultural sensitivity requires vigilance, effort, and a willingness to stand corrected. It is exceedingly difficult to understand the subjective experience of others without walking in their shoes. For difficult dialogues to flourish, it is incumbent on all of us to realize that in our agent identities, we wittingly and unwittingly perpetuate the exclusion of target group members.

In the U.S. today, such exclusions are usually not overt and are often unintended, but they exist nonetheless. Roberta Ahlquist (1992) suggested that the appropriate question is not how we could possibly act as oppressors, but rather how we could *not* act out oppression in a society where racism, sexism, and classism are embedded in the dominant culture. The blatant racism of lynchings and Jim Crow laws is largely a phenomenon of the past, but that does not mean racism has disappeared. Samuel Gaertner and John Dovidio (1986) coined the term **aversive racism** to describe the conflict between a sincere belief in egalitarian values and the anti-Black feelings that continue to permeate this society (one might similarly hypothesize about "aversive sexism" or "aversive able-ism"). Such subtle, forms of racism have also been called **modern racism** or **symbolic racism** (Kinder & Sears, 1981; McConahay, 1986).

Social psychology researchers have conducted creative experiments to document the existence of aversive racism. In one study, White female college students were asked for help by either Black or White partners (also female) (Frey & Gaertner, 1986). These partners were really confederates of the experiment who behaved according to a predetermined script. Sometimes the partner needed help because of her personal shortcomings (she had not worked at the task very hard) and sometimes help was needed because of circumstances beyond the partner's control (the task was unusually difficult). The researchers found that when the task was hard, the White college students offered help regardless of their partner's race. When the partner had been lazy, however, Blacks received significantly less help than their White counterparts. This finding suggests that although Blacks and Whites are treated similarly when the right thing to do is clear, Blacks are punished disproportionately when an excuse for negative treatment is at hand. It seems unlikely that any of the participants in this experiment acted from an oppressive agenda or realized that aversive racism was at play, but differential and unfair behavior occurred nonetheless.

Difficult dialogues require participants to take responsibility for agent status and the potential to act oppressively from agent identities. A focus on benevolent intentions will not make the world more just. Accountability for one's actions means recognizing the *impact* of actions. As community psychologist Meg Bond (1999) noted, focusing on intent privileges the dominant group because the status quo remains in place. No changes are required as long as dominant group members mean well. "Focusing on impact forces a setting to expand to include the marginalized realities and this confronts the very dynamics that have marginalized those experiences" (p. 347).

WORKING TOGETHER

The preceding sections emphasized the importance of individuals speaking out from target identities and listening in agent identities. The facilitation of difficult dialogues also requires an awareness of the settings in which these dialogues occur. We need to create environments where silenced people feel able to speak and others can listen (Reinharz, 1994). Let's look at some aspects of settings that bear on our efforts to appreciate diversity.

INTERGROUP CONTACT

During the 1950s, there was widespread belief that simply bringing diverse groups into contact with each other would reduce prejudice and discrimination. The **contact hypothesis** held that distortions flourish when people from different groups remain at a distance—unknown, invisible, and unheard (Aronson, Wilson, & Akert, 1997). If diverse people could meet each other and talk together, they would dispel stereotypes and intergroup understanding would result. This hypothesis assumes that prejudice results solely from one group's ignorance of the other, which is not always the case (Hewstone & Brown, 1986).

The belief that contact would reduce prejudice helped fuel school desegregation. Desegregation brought children of different racial groups to the same schools, but not into close relationships (e.g., Gerard & Miller, 1975; Schofield, 1978; Lewin, 2000). During lunch hours across the country, diverse students in integrated schools continue to segregate themselves at different cafeteria tables and intercultural conflicts are commonplace. Simply desegregating schools did not change student attitudes and behaviors. Contact alone does not suffice. As James Jones (1994) observed, "Contact itself may sow the seeds of conflict or compassion" (p. 39).

A few weeks after the schools were desegregated in 1971 in Austin, Texas, White, African American, and Mexican American children could be found fighting with each other in the halls and schoolyards. At the invitation of the school superintendent, the social psychologist Eliot Aronson developed an intervention to create more harmony among the culturally diverse students (Aronson et al., 1997). The intervention was based on the work of Gordon Allport (1954), who recognized two decades earlier that simply bringing diverse groups together did not lessen prejudice. The contact must be of a specific nature (see also Amir, 1969). Perhaps most importantly, the different groups must perceive a common, **superordinate goal** that required joint action and mutual interdependence. This was the condition that ultimately united the Rattlers and Eagles in Robber's Cave (see the Classic Research box).

Traditional classrooms value individual achievement and competition as students vie for the highest grades and class ranking. Aronson believed that intergroup understanding would be fostered in classrooms characterized by cooperation. He developed what became known as **jigsaw classrooms** (e.g., Aronson, 1978; Aronson & Bridgeman, 1979; Aronson & Thibodeau, 1992; see also Johnson & Johnson, 1992). Students learned in groups comprised of six children. The day's lesson was divided into six parts, and each child in a group has responsibility for learning one unique part. Completing the lesson, like completing a jigsaw puzzle, required that all the separate pieces be joined together. Thus, the group's success depended on each child learning his or her (or "hir") section and teaching it to the others.

In addition to common goals and interdependence, Allport (1954), identified several other conditions necessary for intergroup contact to result in a lessening of prejudice. The two groups must have the opportunity to interact in informal settings, and there must be multiple opportunities for contact. Structured and infrequent encounters do not facilitate intergroup harmony. Yet another condition is that the group members must be of equal status. If, for example, in the Robber's Cave experiment the Rattlers or the Eagles consisted of boys who differed in race socioeconomic class, or another dimension that serves as the basis for social hierarchies, good feelings would probably have been more difficult to restore.

Psychological research on intergroup conflict suggests that even meaningless distinctions of a short duration (e.g., designation as Rattlers versus Eagles in a camp setting, preferences for particular painters in an experimental context) can lead to biased perceptions and overt hostility. The implications of these and other findings for entrenched conflicts based on fundamental differences in values remain to be examined (e.g., Cooper & Denner, 1998; Mays, Rubin, Sabourn, & Walker, 1996; Roesch & Carr, 2000). Some social scientists examine the relevance of existing research and theory to global problems of intergroup conflict: the 1994 genocide in Rwanda, in which the Tutsi population was nearly eliminated (Smith, 1998); the longstanding Israeli-Palestinian dispute (Rouhana & Bar-Tal, 1998); conflicts between Protestants and Catholics in Ireland (Cairns & Darby, 1998). A pressing need exists to assess the extent to which social psychological laboratory findings and observations from community practice and research in the U.S. apply to the problems of intergroup conflict in our multiracial, multiethnic, and multinational world.

The final condition of intergroup contact identified by Allport is that it should occur in a context where social norms promote equality (see also Kelly, Azelton, Burzett, & Mock, 1994). In this section we will look at the final condition in more detail.

GROUP NORMS

Group norms affect a setting's willingness and ability to engage in difficult dialogues. The norms of the diverse group (e.g., desegregated classroom, community coalition), and also of the root cultures of the diverse participants (e.g., African American or White) both come into play. Different group identities may create particular challenges for authentic dialogues. For women, an unwillingness to hurt the feelings of others or to usurp the authority of men may inhibit expression. African Americans, especially African American men, might fear fulfilling the stereotype of being angry and dangerous by speaking out about prejudice in an unrestrained fashion. In addition, cultural groups have different norms about how much emotion to display (especially during conflict), how much conflict can be tolerated, how problems should be handled, how important it is for each individual to have a chance to speak, and how respect and friendship are conveyed (e.g., Kochman, 1981; Hernandez, Isaacs, Nesman, & Burns, 1998; Maruyama, 1983; Peng & Nisbett, 1999).

People from different groups may also enter the diverse setting with different ideas about how to establish working relationships. For example, African Americans may prefer personal, non-task-oriented conversations initially and then become more task oriented later on. Thus, personal interactions form a basis of trust on which work relationships can be built. Euro-Americans, on the other hand, have been found to exhibit the opposite pattern. They focus on tasks initially, and personal relationships develop as an outgrowth of the common work (Gibbs, 1980).

When diverse groups come together in classrooms, boardrooms, or elsewhere, the new setting also has its own group norms. In studying workplace environments, Meg Bond (e.g., Bond, 1999; Bond & Pyle, 1998) observed that different settings promote equality in different ways. Some groups believe that equality requires that we not dwell on differences and focus instead on the ways in which we are all the same. These groups may be said to have a *norm for homogeneity*. Other groups may contend that a focus on sameness denies us the opportunity to appreciate the varieties of human experience from which we all can learn. Groups that value the expression of differences may be said to operate from a *norm of heterogeneity*. James Kelly and his colleagues (1994) held that community psychologists need to create social settings where participants value diversity, settings that permit interdependence while honoring individuality and that operate under a norm of heterogeneity.

Valuing heterogeneity does not mean fostering a sense of separateness among group members.

Group cohesion requires recognizing the ways in which various group members are the same as well as different; the common values and superordinate goals that unite diverse group members as well as their unique insights and approaches to problem-solving. Bond (1999) used the term **connected disruption** to capture what is needed in our efforts to become more inclusive of diverse people. We need to disrupt the collective complacency that perpetuates the status quo while also maintaining the human connections that allow us to engage in difficult dialogues and empathize with each other. Bond suggested that marginalized groups need to believe disruption of the status quo is possible in order to risk connection. At the same time, dominant group members need to feel that connections are secure in order to risk disruption. For diverse groups to flourish, people with agent status(es) must be willing to recognize and be accountable for the privileges they enjoy, even when these privileges are largely unseen by them. They must recognize the *impact* of their behavior, regardless of their intentions. Group members with target status(es), on the other hand, need to resist equating impact with intent, and make room for misunderstandings and mistakes.

BOUNDARY SPANNERS

In bringing people from different groups together, several community researchers have cited the importance of **boundary spanners** (see Kelly et al., 1994; Kelly, Ryan, Altman, & Stelzner, 2000). Boundary spanners are people who are trusted by and understand the language and conceptual frameworks of more than one group. They can enhance communication between different groups by presenting the alternative perspective in a way that can be understood and appreciated. Boundary spanners are often people who belong to minority groups and are comfortable in their root culture and the majority culture. Thus, many boundary spanners are **bicultural**. Boundary spanners often serve as **key informants**, people familiar with the population of interest who can help researchers or practitioners think through the appropriateness of their research study or change effort (e.g., Dumas et al., 1999).

Boundary spanners can facilitate the work of community psychologists who are perceived as outsiders (and boundary spanners can make good community psychologists). They can sensitize community psychologists to important community issues while vouching for our legitimacy to community members. It is incumbent on us to recognize, however, that being a bicultural boundary spanner has its costs (e.g., Birman, 1994). The identification and cooperation of boundary spanners does not obviate the need for community psychologists to develop their own understanding of and sensitivity to the diverse groups with which we work.

⌘ Appreciation of Diversity Expanded

In this chapter, I discussed community psychology's valuing of diversity primarily in the context of social position. This is a crucial aspect of diversity for community psychology because race, gender, and other social identities affect people's opportunities in life and impact mental health. In addition, because marginalized people are often silenced, our ability to learn from them requires concerted effort. Social identities are only one dimension across which individuals vary, however. Community psychologists need to be sensitive to other sources of diversity as well. Different stakeholders in a community will have a different perspective and operate from a different set of assumptions that affect the research or intervention. In working with the schools, for example, students, parents, teachers, support staff, principals, and school board members all have differing information, loyalties, and agendas.

A second important source of diversity is disciplinary training. Addressing social problems from the perspective of a single discipline will lead to a sense of powerlessness and a lowering of goals (e.g., Maton, 2000). We can design better interventions when allied disciplines collaborate. Although different disciplines converse in somewhat different languages, use different methodologies, and hold different values, discussions across fields enrich our work. Community psychology's relevance and scope are strengthened by familiarity with other subdisciplines in psychology, and other fields, such as social work, philosophy, political science, anthropology, sociology, criminology, law, public policy, and education.

⌘ Promise of Community Psychology: Affirmative Diversity

To a large degree, calls to consider diversity focus on the negative ramifications of cultural insensitivity. If we do not attend to issues of diversity we will lose a competitive edge in the marketplace, fail to provide relevant services, devise ineffective interventions, face lawsuits, be accused of racism, and so on. Relatively little attention is paid to the benefits that accrue from attending to human diversity. James Jones coined the term **affirmative diversity** to refer to concerted efforts to enhance the performance of individuals and groups by drawing on the diversity of human experience. The time has come to focus on what we all stand to *gain* from appreciating diversity.

Gunilla Dahlberg and colleagues (1989) observed that people absorb their own worldviews and theories so completely that:

> they govern our ideas and actions, although we may not recognize what is going on— even to the extent of confusing theory with truth. As such, theories can become 'taken for granted,' self-evident, unquestioned, and seen as the only right way to think and act, rather than being understood as just one possible way of thinking and acting. (p. 12; see also Fowers & Richardson, 1996)

There are countless "givens" that people in dominant cultures take for granted and accept without question—until challenged by people with different worldviews. Some of these givens may be constraining (albeit comfortable and familiar). Mainstream psychologists might feel uncomfortable and uncertain entering into the realms of religion or emotional connectedness among adults, but our work might be enriched by the effort. People who live on the margins of mainstream society have a unique vision from which dominant groups can learn, citizens and psychologists alike. In the two preceding chapters, we have seen how marginalized groups have helped psychologists recognize the potential role of religion and spirituality in our work and lives and better appreciate the importance of social bonds to growth and development across the life span.

Psychologists have only begun to question (due in part to pressure from Third World countries) the assumptions "(a) that there is a universally acceptable conception of psychological science, and (b) that all cultures should emulate psychology as practiced in North America" (Gergen et al., 1996, p. 496). The resulting expansion in psychology's appreciation of human behavior can greatly enrich the discipline. For example, Indian (Hindu) conceptions of psychological functioning would direct attention to neglected areas, such as continuities in experience across all life forms, the socially constituted nature of people, and the significance of the search for eternity in life (Gergen et al., 1996). The native Hawaiian notion of health suggests that well-being does not depend on the actualization of a delimited self. The person, family, nature, and the spiritual world all connect in a psychic unity (Marsella, Oliveira, Plummer, & Crabbe, 1998).

This chapter offers many examples of how group differences can be educational and lead to transformations in how we think, act, and interact. Alternative worldviews may even contain insights that can help us short-circuit prejudice and discrimination. Magoroh Maruyama (1983) identified several problematic tendencies in Euro-Americans' thinking about differences. First, Euro-Americans see all ways of thinking and acting as falling along a hierarchy. Given two or more alternatives, one is necessarily better (e.g., Hodge, Struckman, & Trost, 1975; Peng & Nisbett, 1999), and when it comes to cultures, the American way is always best. Not all cultures adopt a deficit view to difference. For example, Navajos do not conform to the Western view that children's disabilities make them both different and problematic (Connors, & Donnellan, 1998).

A second problematic tendency in Euro-American thinking is that American culture values homogenization; we tend to view sameness as the basis of peace and diversity as the source of conflict (Maruyama, 1983). The long-popular notion of America as a "melting pot" reflects this value on homogenization. Third, Euro-Americans advocate unanimous consensus in decision making so that disagreements are seen not as inevitable, but as due to errors or ignorance or lack of objectivity. A fourth error described earlier in this chapter is the assumption of a zero-sum game where benefits for one person or group are assumed to require losses on the part of another person or group (Maruyama, 1983).

Non-Western cultures are generally less concerned with assessing which one among several views is correct. The Japanese, Mandenka, and Navajo take for granted that different people have different views on a given issue, and recognize that these differences can enrich everyone's understanding. In Japan, there is no word that means "objectivity." The foreign word "objective" has been translated as *kyakkanteki*, which means "the guest's point of view" while "subjective" has been translated as *shukanteki*, "the host's point of view." In Japan, understanding an issue means incorporating multiple points of view. This contrasts with the Euro-American goal of factoring out all individual perspectives into an "objective" analysis in order to discover the one *true* view (Maruyama, 1983).

Thus, people embedded in the dominant Western culture can learn from other cultures that heated debate may be healthy, that there is not always a single right answer, and that win–win situations can be devised in which more than one group benefits. We can learn to search for ways in which each person and each social group holds some piece of truth that can be added to the complex and multifaceted puzzle of human experience.

In his recent theoretical work on sense of community, David McMillan (1996, 2001) noted the importance of appreciating differences among group members. He argued that shared values are *not* an essential aspect of a sense of community because differences do not preclude intimacy. Homogeneity characterizes only the most immature levels of community, where agreement is a precondition for membership. Mature communities see differences not as sources of contention (or not *only* as sources of contention), but as teaching and learning resources. Trading among community members is not based solely on need fulfillment (I'll make dinner for you if you repair my roof) but also on education (I'll teach you to cook if you teach me carpentry). He called this "transforming trade," as opposed to the "consensual trade" that occurs in immature communities.

Attention to group differences is necessary for a number of reasons. Group differences help make us who we are as people. They also underlie societal inequities that compromise health and well-being. In addition, they embody culturally unique forms of human ecology from which we all can learn. "Ethnocultural diversity is as important for human survival as is biological diversity because it provides social and psychological options in the face of powerful and unpredictable environments" (Marsella, 1998, p. 1288). Cultures need to be stable and pass on knowledge gleaned over generations, but they must also be dynamic enough to respond to modern challenges that ancestors could never have foreseen. Each culture may be viewed as a partial solution to previously encountered human problems (D'Andrade, 1996)—dealing with pain and loss, balancing personal needs with the community good, resolving conflicts between people and groups. When we attend to different worldviews, our horizons expand and our solutions to problems can become more complete. When silenced groups find their voice, they express new perspectives that add to the universe of divergent solutions, a universe that could never be adequately mapped by any one culture.

James Jones (1994) observed the social sciences have not yet "through disciplined inquiry, demonstrated exactly how diversity confers strengths to us as individuals and as a society" (p. 43). Community psychology, with its focus on diversity and emphasis on people's strengths rather than deficits, is in a prime position to advance the notion of affirmative diversity. Much might be gained if, as Meg Bond (1999) suggested, we all "wonder more actively about the perspectives of those who stand on the 'fringe,' and recognize 'outliers' as important sources of information" (p. 352).

Action Agenda

The Importance of Names

Does everybody in your class know everyone else's name? If not, you might take the time now to learn them.

I recently cofacilitated a five-day seminar with 20 participants. In order to help learn each other's names as quickly as possible, my coteacher and I took Polaroids of each person on the first day of class. Participants labeled their pictures with their name and some other relevant information. We then mounted the photographs on poster board for everyone to see and refer to. We thought this was a good way to help seminar participants get to know each other quickly.

The second day of the seminar, a guest speaker, the artist and activist Rebecca Rice, visited the class, and our guest spent almost an hour of her allotted three hours learning the names of each participant in the following way. We all sat in a circle, and one by one, we said out loud the name by which we wanted to be known in the seminar. The first person in our circle said her name, and everyone in the room repeated it. Then the second person said his name. Everyone responded by saying the first person's name, and then the second. Each person added her or his (hir) name in turn, and the chain of repeated names grew longer and longer. Our guest artist guided us through the process, encouraging us not to adopt a sing-song rhythm that took away from our conscious effort to remember each person's name. As we went around the circle, she asked us to look carefully at the faces of those whose names we had trouble remembering. She warned us that after our chant included the name of every person in the circle, we would then scramble our seats and go around the room again.

At the end of this exercise people felt more relaxed and included. Several people had given names that were different than those they had written on their Polaroids and this led to interesting discussions on the meaning of names and naming. Time spent attending to names may be time well spent.

Revisiting Class Guidelines

Think together about how to create a welcoming context in your classroom—how can you establish a setting where the norm of heterogeneity prevails and class members feels safe enough to risk feeling *un*safe? Beverly Tatum (1992) proposed that we create safe classrooms by establishing and upholding clear guidelines for discussion. If you have not yet established classroom guidelines, you might consider doing so now. Establishing guidelines can seem like an elementary task—outlining basic courtesies that should be self-evident. When discussions get heated, however, common courtesies can be quickly forgotten. What other ways can you create a welcoming and safe environment?

Identifying Privilege

The feminist Peggy McIntosh (1989, 1992) reported her frustration with men who did not understand male privilege. One day she realized that although she was in a target group as a woman, she had other identities that conferred agent status. She wondered if she enjoyed unseen privileges in her dominant statuses that frustrated target members as unacknowledged male privileges frustrated her. She determined to identify her White privileges and then her heterosexual privileges.

Choose a social category in which you have an agent identity and list the privileges you have as a member of that group. You might choose to work in small groups with others who share that agent identity. Try to be as specific as possible. After working in small groups, come together as a class and discuss your lists. Working together, can you expand the lists developed in the small groups (perhaps because of the insights from class members of target status with regard to each identity)? McIntosh's (1992) list eventually included 46 White privileges—everything from being able to arrive late for a meeting without the lateness reflecting on her race, to being able to find "flesh" colored Band-Aids that actually correspond to her skin tones.

As a next step, you might try to find common elements among the privileges across social categories. Which privileges relate to visibility or voice? What are some other recurring themes in the privileges different groups enjoy? What are some privileges that appear to be specific to particular groups? Table 5.3 might help you think about some of the possible sources of common and different privileges.

 **Key Terms**

affirmative diversity

agent group

arpilleras

aversive racism

bicultural

boundary spanners

connected disruption

contact hypothesis

discrimination

in-group

jigsaw classrooms

key informants

minimal groups

modern racism

oppression

out-group

prejudice

Robber's Cave

secondary cultural characteristics

stereotypes

superordinate goal

symbolic racism

target group

tourist approach (to multiculturalism)

zero-sum perspective

Chapter 6

Embracing Social Change

••

⌘ Introduction

In the late 1960s, when social reforms were sweeping the nation, George Miller (1969) delivered a presidential address to the American Psychological Association in which he challenged psychologists to use our insights to promote human welfare. He observed that psychology had contributed relatively little of importance to the search for new and better personal and social arrangements.

Miller's address seemed radical and controversial to many, but community psychology, which came of age during this era of reform, agrees unequivocally with the notion that psychologists have a professional responsibility to intervene not only with the individual, but also in the social patterns and structures that adversely affect individual well-being. The field's social change agenda has attracted many of its influential figures, academics and practitioners alike. The action-researcher Leonard Jason (1991) described his attraction to this emerging area of study as a graduate student in 1971.

> Although I was impressed with the new conceptualization of expanding the reach of psychological services, and the more ecological

approach for understanding problems, clearly it was the social action feature of the ideology that captured my imagination. (p. 1)

The community activist Thomas Wolff (2000) wrote, "When I left graduate school, I was attracted to community psychology because I sensed that it would allow me to focus on two issues: social change and community" (p. 771).

A commitment to making a difference in the world distinguishes community psychology from more traditional branches of the discipline. Historically, psychology in the United States has *reacted* to societal change and preserved social stability (e.g., Prilleltensky, 1989). Fathali Moghaddam (1990) attributed this to U.S. psychology's development in response to the vast and rapid social changes associated with industrialization and urbanization. The goal of psychology was to maintain a sense of social order under conditions of extreme change. Moghaddam contrasted psychology in the U.S. which he labeled **modulative psychology**, with a second type labeled **generative psychology**. Generative psychology *initiates* rather than reacts to societal change. While modulative psychology views change as adaptation, generative psychology views change as transformation. For example, modulative psychologists might study how poor people maintain a sense of control in the midst of disruptive life events whereas generative psychologists might research how poor communities can best mobilize for better housing and land reform. Although some U.S. psychologists prefer generative psychology (community psychologists among them), Moghaddam argued that Third World countries *require* it. The devastating toll of widespread hunger and poverty demands fundamental changes in societal structures (Kroeker, 1995; Omprakash, 1989; Sinha & Holtzman, 1984; Wiesenfeld, 1998).

According to Moghaddam, a country's sociocultural context, particularly the perceived need for stability versus innovation, affects psychology's orientation toward change. A second relevant sociocultural factor is the country's worldview. Change is itself a culture-bound concept. Western cultures view persistence, or sameness, as the natural state of things and change as the problem to be explained.

African, Asian, and Native American cultures, on the other hand, see change as natural and normative (Maruyama, 1983; Watzlawick, Weakland, & Fisch, 1974). Western cultures also view change as resulting from individual efforts while most other cultures stress the importance of God, nature, and nonhuman forces (Maruyama, 1983). Thus, U.S. psychology is less likely to see widespread change as either necessary or inevitable.

Our sense of the world as always in flux or essentially constant is largely a matter of focus. Change and stability are twin processes—without stability there can be no change, nor change without stability. Here are two different paragraphs that might open our discussion of change.

Opening One

Life in the United States at the turn of the twenty-first century differs substantially from life in bygone eras. The country of today bears little resemblance to the land into which Columbus sailed in 1492, or to life in the colonial era that followed, or even to the U.S. of the industrial age. Life circumstances change drastically not only across eras, but across the span of a single generation—so much so as to result in the proverbial generation gap.

I remember learning with awe that my mother and father carried ice from a truck to a wooden box in their homes in order to keep food cold and that they actually grew up without television. Surely my parents, like the characters in the Flintstones cartoon I watched in the mornings, lived in Stone Age families. Now, I watch my own son grow and ponder the ways in which he will think of my childhood as Neanderthal. Typewriters instead of computers. Only a handful of channels on TV—and we changed them by getting up off the couch and manually turning a dial on the set. No microwave ovens or cell phones or email. In addition to the vast technological changes of the past 30 years, there have been profound social changes as well, such as the growth of alternative family forms. Some children who flip through cartoon channels as they eat microwaved oatmeal would not have been born thirty years ago, a time when virtually all planned children were born to husband–wife pairs.

Clearly enormous changes occur in the world. How do we explain these changes? Can we influence the direction of change? How can we bring about changes that improve the quality of people's lives? These are some of the questions explored in this chapter.

Opening Two

Change seems to occur at every level. Cells divide and die within our bodies. Babies grow into adults. Families pass through different life stages. Neighborhoods rise and fall. The boundaries around countries and the quality of life within them shift and change as new leaders with new agendas gain and lose control. Even the universe itself is expanding as you read these words. But what of significance really changes? The cells of a human body replace themselves every few years, but the person remains the same. Is there ever really anything new under the sun?

Consider the issues relevant to this text. Are the phenomena of interest to psychologists different today than they were in past decades, or even past centuries? Perhaps not. The insights into human behavior Shakespeare captured in his plays still enlighten audiences 400 years later. The Bible, Qur'an, and other sacred texts continue to provide seemingly timeless lessons in living to those who study them. Today's college courses on philosophy begin with a consideration of Socrates, Plato, Aristotle, and other ancient thinkers who shape modern thought. If life really changed so drastically, would the wisdom of the ages continue to have such profound relevance?

So much of what makes us human remains unchanged through the millennia—the desire to make a home for ourselves where we can feel safe, our struggles with aggression in our close relationships and between groups of people. We continue to contemplate our purpose on earth and the existence of God. We still try to raise healthy children who can thrive in the world of tomorrow. Although the specific components of the proverbial generation gap change every twenty years or so, there always seems to be a generation gap to bridge.

How do we explain the continuity that underlies our perceptions of change? Why is meaningful change so difficult to effect? Is it possible at all? Can we inspire and direct important social transformations? The constancy of human behavior over time gives meaning to the popular saying, "The more things change, the more they remain the same."

This chapter describes some of the ways community psychologists can work to bring about beneficial change, as well as some of the forces that mitigate against it. Let's begin with a key conceptual distinction.

⌘ First- and Second-Order Change

In seeking to elucidate why "the more things change, the more they remain the same," Paul Watzlawick, John Weakland, and Richard Fisch (1974) distinguished between **first-order change** and **second-order change** (see also Bateson, 1972). First-order change involves doing "more of the same." Second-order change sees our customary solutions as part of the problem. Second-order change recognizes the need to change the systems that prescribe role relationships and constrain behavior. Let's look at some examples.

In her popular book *Dance of Anger*, Harriet Lerner (1985) examined first- and second-order change within intimate relationships. She described the classic scenario of the emotional pursuer (often the woman in a heterosexual couple) and the emotional distancer (usually the man). In times of stress, the emotional pursuer reaches out, shares her feelings, and seeks closeness. The distancer yearns instead for a logical approach and attempts to disengage from the emotionality of the pursuer. These opposite ways of responding strain both members of the couple, and each may try to improve the situation. The pursuer may devise new contexts for sharing, perhaps preparing a fancy home-cooked meal. The distancer may assure the pursuer of his feelings with tangible gifts of flowers or jewelry. These, however, are first-order change efforts. The dynamic does not change. The pursuer still tries to engage the distancer emotionally, while the distancer offers reassurance in a way that permits continued emotional disengagement. The more the pursuer pursues, the more the distancer distances, and the conflict escalates. Each sees no option other than more of the same. This constitutes the "dance" of anger.

Dances require that each person move with the other. If one partner takes an entirely new step, the other must find a way to respond, and so the dance will change. Let's say that the pursuer decides to stop pursuing her partner and finds other emotional outlets. She may then come to appreciate her new freedom from the old role of emotional caretaker for the family. The distancer will likely be confronted with the fact that he actually misses some of the closeness that he had been resisting. At this point, there is a danger that the couple will resume the familiar dance pattern with a simple reversal of roles—the distancer now pursuing and the pursuer distancing. However, the opportunity for second-order change also exists. If the distancer recognizes his need for closeness, and the pursuer acknowledges her need for separation, an entirely new dance can emerge.

Let's consider another example at a higher level of analysis. Protests involving large groups of people often escalate to riotous proportions. Any act of violence from one side, either the police or the protesters, elicits more of the same from the other side. In the heat of such battles, it can be exceedingly difficult to ascertain who threw the first rock, and it makes no difference in terms of what happens next. Protesters express their rage in whatever ways they can: launching Molotov cocktails, overturning cars, setting fires. Police put on riot gear and explode tear gas and if that doesn't work, they call in armed reinforcements.

When civil rights protesters first launched their campaigns of nonviolence, police fulfilled their assigned roles, not knowing that the rules of the game had changed. The protesters were no longer dancing the old dance. They did not fight back. The result was confusion on the part of law enforcement, which did not know how to respond. At first, police followed the old rules of engagement, and the public saw images of peaceful Black men, women, and children attacked by thundering billy clubs, exploding fire hoses, and lunging police dogs. The protesters continued their peaceful protests. "Ain't gonna let nobody turn me around," they sang into the storm of brutality. The new rule of nonviolent engagement required that the powers-that-be respond in new ways, and a shift in the national consciousness opened wider the door to transformative change.

cathy®   **by Cathy Guisewite**

An example of first order change: trying to solve the problem of too much stuff by buying more stuff. CATHY ©2000 Cathy Guisewite. Reprinted with permission of UNIVERSAL PRESS SYNDICATE. All rights reserved.

⌘ Social Change: Some Components

When community psychologist talk about **social change** we generally refer to second order change that restructures "the basic ways in which people in a society relate to each other with regard to economics, government, education, religion, family life, recreation, language, and other basic human interaction activities" (Nagel, 1970, p. 8). This restructuring has the goal of reducing oppression by establishing more just social systems (e.g., Goldenberg, 1978). Social change does not refer to unplanned alterations in the social landscape, such as demographic shifts in the size of ethnic minority or old old populations. Nor does it refer to planned efforts to increase repression, as when fundamentalist leaders backed by military regimes seize power. Social change seeks to equalize power relationships in society either directly (e.g., through social change movements or community organizing) or indirectly (e.g., through consultation, the creation of alternative settings, innovative program development, education or participatory action research).

Second order change is difficult. Many social change efforts have no long-lasting effects, and the more ambitious one's goals, the greater the obstacles to success. In this section we look at some factors that promote and prohibit social change. As described in this chapter's opening, persistence and change are twin processes. Thus, this discussion could be cast in terms of factors that promote change or factors that prohibit it (see Table 6.1. See also the section entitled *Behavioral Aspect* in Chapter 10). Consistent with community psychology's fourth guiding principle, the emphasis here is on how to *promote* change. Let's look more closely at the factors delineated in Table 6.1.

ENVISIONING RULE-BREAKING SOLUTIONS

Social change requires new ways of thinking and interacting (Biklen, 1983; Watzlawick et al., 1974). It challenges the unexamined premises that constrain

> *I want to remind you that if you told Gandhi, "But that has never happened before," he would say. "So what? Think of all the things that never happened before they happened."*
>
> —Vincent Harding
> (personal communication)

our attempts to solve problems, which constitute the accepted rules of the game or steps in a dance.

CREATIVE THINKING

Second order change can be exceedingly difficult because we usually fail to see our own habits of thought and our taken-for-granted assumptions. Thinking in fundamentally different ways requires creativity. A puzzle will illustrate this point (also used by Seidman, 1983). Try to join the nine dots by drawing four straight lines and without lifting your pen from the paper. Take a few minutes to attempt this now before reading further and then look at the solution at the end of the chapter.

As the solution demonstrates, people make assumptions that constrain what we do. In seeing nine dots arranged in a square, most of us resist drawing lines that extend beyond the perceived boundaries of that square. This assumption, an *unnecessary* rule for our behavior, prevents us from solving the problem. If we can think "outside the box," we find innovative, seemingly rule-breaking solutions that seem obvious in hindsight. Watzlawick and his colleagues (1974) observed that second-order solutions are often "a-ha" experiences that surprise us with their simplicity. This is not to say that every problem has a single second-order solution. Some readers may have devised solutions that are even further "outside the box" than the one presented at the end of this chapter, solutions that involve folding or cutting the paper, or even traveling around

Table 6.1 Factors that Affect the Social Change Process

Factors that Promote Social Change	Factors that Prohibit Social Change
Creative thinking/challenges to "assumptive worlds" (e.g., through encounters with crises, cross-cultural exchange, interdisciplinary contact, exposure to artistic visions)	Habits of thought/unexamined assumptions (e.g., cultural insulation, disciplinary specialization)
Mindscapes that favor social equality (e.g., political tolerance, democracy)	Mindscapes that favor social inequality (e.g., just world, karma, social Darwinism)
Willingness to undergo disruption of change (e.g., tolerance for anxiety, sense of competence to handle new challenges)	Unwillingness to undergo disruption of change (e.g., fear of the unknown, lack of faith in ability to meet new demands)
Investment in changing reward structures (e.g., commitment to fairness, promise of gains from change)	Investment in maintaining reward structures (e.g., commitment to individual advancement, unwillingness to risk personal losses)
Conscientization/becoming an ally (e.g., appreciation of marginalized people's worthiness, recognition of injustice, awareness of limiting social forces, belief in action)	Internalized oppression/acceptance of oppression (e.g., sense of inferiority in target group member or superiority in agent group members, disbelief of own efficacy)
Common cause with others (e.g., positive view of shared social identity for target group members, shared awareness of and responsibility for privileges for agent group members)	Isolation (e.g., competition/anger towards others in group or other oppressed groups)
Strong value base (e.g., spiritual anchor, hope, commitment to positive change)	Rootlessness (despair, apathy)

the circumference world in a straight line, trailing our pen behind us.

Anything that exposes unexamined assumptions about how things need to be can promote social change. Major events, be they person caused (e.g., a major scientific discovery or an act of terrorism) or naturally occurring (e.g., an earthquake or a flood), can fuel social change efforts. As we will see in Chapter Eight, crises at all levels, from individual life events to community incidents and global crises, entail both danger and opportunity. The danger and opportunity stem, in part, from the challenge

major events pose to our "assumptive worlds" (to borrow a term from C. Murray Parkes, 1971). As an individual-level example, the hauntingly beautiful hymn *Amazing Grace* was written by the captain of a slaveship whose blindness to injustice lifted at the end of a brutal storm at sea that he did not expect to survive. He subsequently assumed a spiritual path and preached against slavery. As a community-level example, school shootings that have occurred throughout the country have forced numerous communities to confront the assumption that "it can't happen here."

EXPOSURE TO ALTERNATIVE VIEWPOINTS

Cultural exchange can also foster social change. Each culture explains and interprets the world for its members, encouraging them to "focus their attention on or ignore certain aspects of their environment, and instructing and forbidding them to act in certain ways." (Cushman, 1990, p. 601, with reference to Heiddeger). When we see our cultural assumptions as neither universal nor necessary, we can envision new social orders.

One anthropological study described this process of social transformation from intercultural contact. For several generations the Waorani people of the Ecuadorian Amazon were a war-based society, as evidenced by a homicide rate of 60%. A marked change occurred after the Waorani came into contact with missionaries. The study authors reasoned that missionaries provided

> a new view of a world in which not all outsiders were implacable enemies and cannibals, an alternative value system that stressed nonviolence and, perhaps most importantly, a glimpse of a world without constant fear of violent death. (Robarchek & Robarchek, 1992, p. 205)

The chance to glimpse other worldviews is a key benefit of encountering people who differ from us in important ways. When individuals, groups, and even societies open themselves to diverse viewpoints through such experiences as contact with minority group members, immigration, travel abroad, or study under foreign teachers, creativity increases (Lambert, Tucker, & D'Anglejan, 1973; Nemeth & Kwan, 1987; Simonton, 1997; Simonton, 2000). Encountering diversity can alert us to untried and more equitable social arrangements that exist elsewhere and help us make the changes necessary to get there.

People have, however, a seemingly natural inclination to seek out the company of similar others who share our fundamental assumptions (Greenwald, 1980). Meaningful change may require that we resist this tendency and instead seek out disagreement. Michael Fullan (1999) remarked that people who embrace meaningful change must make friends with conflict and diversity. Research demonstrates that although people usually prefer to work in homogeneous groups, diverse groups may be more creative than homogeneous groups if they can overcome the difficulty of working together (Bond, 1999; Chemers, Oskamp, & Constanzo, 1995).

Cultural differences challenge our limiting assumptions. Other sources of diversity can also fuel creative thinking about problems. Differing political perspectives embody decidedly different worldviews that can expose our unexamined assumptions. Richard Redding (2001) argued that a lack of sociopolitical diversity in psychology prevents its practitioners from framing questions of interest in broad terms and so limits the repertoire of solutions considered. Interdisciplinary contact can also expand our thinking. Academic disciplines fragment fields of knowledge in the interest of developing expertise (Palmer, 1998). As a result, the "experts" may subscribe to narrow visions of reality that keep us from dealing productively with the important problems of our times (e.g., Capra, 1982; Cowen, 2000a; Maton, 2000). We become like blind people touching different parts of the elephant; some find a rope (the tail), others discover a pole (the tusk), and no one ever succeeds in identifying the beast.

The importance of thinking differently and creatively about social problems places artists at the forefront of social change. The singers of spirituals, freedom songs, and folk songs, the painters of community murals, the performers in guerilla theater, and even irreverent joke tellers help inspire and guide change efforts. Creative expression can bring unseen aspects of the human experience to light, create community, challenge conventions, and incite new visions of how life can be (e.g., Baldwin, 1985; Becker, 1994; Edelman, 1995; Felshin, 1995; Lippard, 1990; McMillan, 1996; Miller, 1986).

MINDSCAPES AND SOCIAL INEQUALITY

In the preceding section we discussed exposure to different worldviews as one process that can lead us to question assumptions that mire us in first-order change efforts. However, even if we expose ourselves (or become exposed) to another culture, its alternative worldview is filtered through our own. Any particular worldview can, in and of itself, either foster or stifle social change. That is to say, some cultural assumptions pertain directly to our openness to encounter with diversity and our willingness to create more equitable social arrangements.

Magoroh Maruyama (1983) used the term **mindscapes** to refer to patterns of reasoning, cognition, conceptualization, decision-making, and planning that differ from culture to culture and within cultures. Mindscapes embody the values and norms that delineate acceptable and desirable attitudes and circumscribe human behavior. George Albee (1986) discussed two assumptions underlying the mindscapes of many North Americans that work against social change efforts (see also Biklen, 1983).

The first is a phenomenon that social psychologists have labeled the **just world hypothesis**. People tend to think that the world is fair and everybody gets what they deserve (Lerner, 1970, 1980). If one believes in a just world, social change is unwarranted. People are hungry, poor, enslaved, diseased, or unhappy through their own fault. Cultural mindscapes also exist outside of North America that reinforce a view of misfortune as ordained. Many East Indians believe that suffering is *karma*—atonement for sins committed in previous lives. The belief in karma can block social change. In one rural Hindu village, residents living in dire poverty resisted efforts to improve their lot in life out of the belief that their suffering existed for a higher purpose (Omprakash, 1989).

Social Darwinism is the second assumption Albee (1986) identified as working against social change in North America. Social Darwinists believe that the evolution of human societies parallels genetic evolution. "Survival of the fittest" ensures that the strongest, smartest, best-equipped people rise to the top of the social ladder. The flow of resources to privileged people simply reflects their greater fitness. Disadvantaged groups huddle at the bottom of the social ladder because of their own inferiority. Social programs that try to lift up disadvantaged (i.e., inferior) groups are wasted efforts that hinder social progress. Social Darwinism was popularized

in the latter half of the nineteenth century with the work of Galton and Spencer (see Albee, 1986).

While some worldviews work against social change, others advance it. As described earlier, non-Western views of change as natural and inevitable may result in a greater tolerance for changes that people in Western cultures would experience as upheaval. As another example, mindscapes that embrace citizen involvement, political tolerance, democratic values, and the support for civil liberties help pave the way for social change (Sullivan & Transue, 1999).

THE REWARDS AND COSTS OF CHANGE

In our examination of factors that promote social change, we have thus far looked at the importance of thinking creatively about societal problems and possible solution and of considering the role of mindscapes that promote or prohibit interest in creating a more equitable society. Let's bring our discussion now to the perspective of the individuals who stand to be affected by changes. A cost-benefit analysis can help us to understand why some oppose a social change effort while others embrace it (Prestby, Wandersman, Florin, Rich, & Chavis, 1990; Ryan, 1993). Simply put, people resist change when they stand to lose more than they gain (see also section entitled *The Behavioral Aspect* in Chapter Ten).

DISRUPTIVENESS OF CHANGE

Change of any kind requires new ways of thinking and acting, and this disrupts routine. Routines offer comfort. Even people who suffer under unjust systems obtain a sense of security from knowing what to expect within existing structures, and have likely adapted to these structures. The status quo offers predictability and a sense of control. Change entails unpredictability and insecurity, and the more "outside the box" change efforts are, the more disruptive they may appear to be (e.g., Rogers, 1995).

Research suggests that even when people are willing to embrace change, confusion about how to proceed can prevent them from embracing change efforts (Gilbert, 1988). Some anxiety in the face of routine-breaking change results from people's sense that they will need new skills or abilities in order to adjust. They may also feel that they do not have enough information to respond adequately (Ryan, 1993). The professionalization of social change that has occurred since the 1960s, not only in the U.S., but also in Western and Central Europe, can exacerbate these concerns (Meyer & Tarrow, 1998). For example, lobbyists are often highly paid specialists, and community organizing has become a science of sorts. Professionalization makes social change efforts more hierarchical and less democratic. Lay people feel ill equipped to enter into debate about issues they perceive as out of their intellectual grasp and are relegated to the role of outsider (see also Biklen, 1983; Gilbert, 1988). Efforts to help people feel more certain about what the change will entail and more competent to handle the challenges involved will more likely facilitate the change process.

Another reason why a change in routine can lead to anxiety is that most people already feel overloaded by the demands of daily living. Additional demands that come from disrupted routines may seem overly burdensome if they are not commensurate with the promise of gain (e.g., Gilbert, 1988; Ryan, 1993). The comfort of routine is certainly not insurmountable. Fran Peavey (1986) suggested that "each of us has within us the will to make the world a better place, as well as a longing for stability. We live in a tension between these two drives" (p. 152). Belief that rewards will come from change can tip the balance in favor of action.

REWARD STRUCTURES

Steven Kerr (1983) used a social learning framework to demonstrate that no matter how compelling the call for change, people will not alter their behavior if existing reward structures remain in place. In his article entitled, *The Folly of Rewarding A While Hoping for B*, he illustrated this point in different domains.

In politics, candidates campaign on high acceptance platforms that are vague and uncontroversial.

Kerr (1983) called these *official goals*. Improve education. Reduce taxes. Get tough on crime. *Operative goals*, on the other hand, are specific but controversial. They delineate how to achieve official goals: Issue school vouchers. Cut social security. Establish mandatory sentences. Politicians know that popular consensus occurs only with official goals; operative goals inevitably incur debate. Citizens may be frustrated by the slick double-talk of politicians, but this mode of campaigning will persist as long as we reward those who espouse only official goals with our votes.

Kerr provided a second example from the realm of higher education. Professors, especially in prestigious universities, are *expected* to take their teaching seriously, but they are *rewarded* for their research. A university may present a handful of teaching awards that come with small amounts of prize money, but the true rewards—promotion and tenure—depend on research publications and grants. The fame of prolific professors enhances the reputation of their universities, which can then attract highly qualified students, which adds further to the university's reputation. Incoming students may be disappointed to find, however, that they rarely encounter prestigious faculty members who devote little time and energy to teaching, especially undergraduate teaching (see also Haberman, 1971).

Changing reward structures is not easy. In addition to costs associated with a disruption of routine, people who benefit from "the game" as currently played do not want the rules to change. They have enjoyed some measure of success within existing systems and change may entail a loss of status or influence (Ryan, 1993). Campaign reform may be popular with the public, but it is resisted by Washington power brokers who profit from the political status quo. Tenured professors resist changes in the university structure that threaten their long sought-after job security. In short those who have a stake in the status quo resist change.

In order to engage in change efforts, people must be willing to disrupt the existing social order. Even people who benefit least from existing reward structures may fear that their situation could go from bad to worse, a fear often fulfilled in backlashes that punish subordinate groups for their insubordinance. Still, people who benefit the least from the status quo are most often willing to break from routine and try to alter existing reward structures.

Paulo Freire observed that when people in power initiate change, they usually offer false charity. Their humanitarian efforts are merely an expression of their generosity, a generosity made possible by their advantaged position. They offer handouts to assuage their guilt without changing reward structures. Christmas baskets for poor employees, but no redistribution of the company's wealth. Freire (1970/1992) asserted that, "True generosity consists precisely in fighting to destroy the causes which nourish false charity" (p. 29).

Freire believed that only oppressed people could fundamentally alter the social order and establish a just system in which false charity could not occur. In such a system, *all* people would be more fully human. One way in which oppression sabotages the humanity of dominant group members is that they lose their humanity in the very act of treating another unfairly (Freire, 1970/1992).

In addition, oppression allows agent group members to project unwelcome parts of ourselves onto target groups. Carl Jung (e.g., 1951/1983) popularized the notion that we all have shadow sides. People who are "other" in terms of race, gender, or other identity may be used as receptacles for the shadow sides of the dominant group members' personalities (Connolly & Noumair, 1997). For example, Chapter Four (see section on *Challenges from the Margins*) described how women have become responsible for emotional connections and social ties, which allows men to express the more valued characteristics of independence and individualism. This role division can prevent both sexes from realizing their full humanity and contributes to the aforementioned dance of anger. As another example, people with disabilities allow able-bodied people to see themselves as independent, powerful, and in control. "Attributing neediness and lack of control to people with disabilities permits those of us who are not disabled to view themselves as having more control and strength in their lives than may be the case" (Fine & Asch,

1988, p. 16; see also Dass & Gorman, 1985; Wortman & Lehman, 1985).

Freire (1970/1992) argued that when people in subordinate positions take away the dominant group's ability to repress, everyone becomes more fully human. For many of our great social change activists, including Martin Luther King, Jr., Mahatama Gandhi, and Desmond Tutu, the highest reward offered by freedom struggles is the promise of humanity for dominant and subordinate groups alike. People who receive tangible benefits from unjust systems, however, may not appreciate the power of this reward.

AWAKENING TO INJUSTICE

People in subordinate groups suffer most acutely from oppression and so are in the best position to overturn unjust systems. They have, however, their own barriers to overcome.

Oppression has both political and psychological dimensions (Prilleltensky & Gonick, 1996). Political oppression involves the creation and maintenance of material, legal, military, economic, and other barriers that limit target group members' self-determination, access to resources, and democratic participation. Psychological oppression involves an internalized view of one's self as inferior and not deserving of resources. Social change requires overcoming both political and psychological barriers (Yeich & Levine, 1994). With regard to politics, subordinate groups face barriers from their lack of leverage in the economic, political, and social systems they seek to change (Goldenberg, 1978). With regard to psychology, powerless people may come to believe the dominant group's view of them as subordinate due to their own inadequacies.

For people in oppressed groups, the restrictions and limitations of everyday life, the social expectations for failure, and the negative images that prevail in the media are often taken to heart (e.g., Frye, 1983, Kroeker, 1995; Pharr, 1988). Through the process of **internalized oppression**, those who suffer discrimination may believe themselves to be worthy of unfair treatment. People from target and agent groups alike blame those who experience injustice for the difficulties they face (Ryan, 1971; see also Chapter Seven).

Social change requires recognizing inequities as such. The South African activist Steven Biko taught that the most potent weapon of the oppressor is the mind of the oppressed (Biko, 1978). Paulo Freire (1970/1992) described the process of freeing one's mind, which he called **conscientization**. Members of oppressed groups must develop a critical consciousness in which the reality of their oppression is recognized (this corresponds to psychological liberation) so that social conditions can be confronted (political liberation) (see also Tarrow, 1992; Trickett, Watts, & Birman, 1994; Watts, Griffith, & Abdul-Adil, 1999). When target group members refuse to be blamed for their lack of achievement or depressed living conditions or other correlate of marginalization, then the social forces at play can be addressed.

Although target group members generally drive social change efforts, agent group members who recognize the legitimacy of these efforts can become collaborators. People in dominant groups who recognize injustice and seek to interrupt oppression are called **allies**. White people advance African American liberation, able-bodied individuals promote justice for physically challenged people, men support the liberation of women, and so on (e.g., Kivel, 1995, Thompson, 1992).

In many ways, community psychologists can be seen as working for change in the role of ally. First, as outlined in Chapter Five, most of us belong to several dominant groups. "Exemplars" of the field are primarily male, White, and middle class. Thus, we often have more power than the people with whom we work based on our positions on the social identity grid. Second, power flows to us from our position as educated professionals.

A number of community psychologists have asserted that in order to be true collaborators in the change process, we must recognize and deconstruct the power differences that exist between us and those we seek to help through our research and practice (e.g., Nelson, Ochocka, Griffin, & Lord, 1998; Bond, 1999). True collaborators, or allies, do not position themselves as saviors with the power to legitimize and direct the struggles of target groups (Ellsworth, 1997). They reject paternalistic attitudes. As allies, community psychologists are informed by and responsible to those we seek to assist and act in a manner consistent with *their* agendas (Biklen, 1983). This may be one justification for community psychologists' involvement in indirect change efforts, such as consulting or conducting participatory action research, rather than direct actions such as leading marches or organizing protests.

The activist Fran Peavey (1992) maintained that effective change cannot occur when one individual or group imposes its ideas onto another. Efforts prove far more effective when building from the "premise that the change ideas appropriate to a situation are imbedded in the culture or group involved, waiting to be uncovered" (Peavey, 1992, p. 152). Paulo Freire (1970/1992) observed that it would be a contradiction in terms for people in power to implement a liberating intervention. As allies, community psychologists can assist in, but not drive, the change process. Our training in research does not mean that we alone can decide what questions need to be asked, how to ask them, how to understand the answers, and how to use the results. Our background in community mental health practices does not give us the authority to determine for communities what interventions need to be implemented and how best to implement them.

CREATING COMMON CAUSE

No matter how creatively people envision rule-breaking solutions to social problems or how acutely people recognize the social injustices around us, no one can create change alone. Social change hinges on a dialectic between the individual and the group. As Freire (1970/1992) observed, "while no one liberates himself by his own efforts alone, neither is he liberated by others" (p. 53). Social change efforts require creating common cause within target groups, and may also benefit from creating common cause between target and agent groups.

COMMON CAUSE WITHIN TARGET GROUPS

Let's look first at the issues involved for target group members creating common cause within their group. Common cause is a necessary precondition to social change, and processes that prevent the development of common cause serve to maintain the status quo.

The Importance of Common Cause. Acceptance of oneself as a member of a marginalized group paves the way for a sense of connection to others in that group. Cornel West (1982) argued that Malcolm X's ultimate goal was not to breed hatred for White people, but to develop love among African Americans. Only when African Americans ceased to view their bodies, minds, and souls through White lenses would they become capable of controlling their own destinies. The starting point for social change movements has often been an attempt to foster a collective self-love.

> "Black is Beautiful."
> "Gay is Good."
> "The Sisterhood is Powerful."

Conscientization leads to meaningful action only if there exists a *collective* awareness of the injustice and a *shared* desire for change. Roderick Watts and his colleagues (1999) noted that many social change interventions, including those designed or facilitated by community psychologists, focus on the individual level. They wrote:

> Conventional interventions on coping, stress management, conflict resolution, and similar personal skill building are necessary but not sufficient. An exclusive focus on individual psychosocial development neglects the skills for building collective consciousness and promoting social justice. (p. 256)

Connections with others are necessary to overcome both psychological and political oppression.

A variety of contexts can foster these necessary connections. Women's liberation in the 1960s and 1970s grew from countless consciousness raising groups, where women gathered together in small, informal groups to talk about their problems and realized the political dimensions of their personal struggles. Black churches were key to the civil rights movement because they fostered a sense of common cause (based in shared values and experiences) and served as a hub for the dissemination of information about the movement and coordination of protest efforts (Billingsley, 1999). More recently, mutual help groups have been studied by community psychologists as a forum for social change (see Reissman & Bay, 1992).

Mutual help groups have proved particularly useful for people with marginalized social identities (e.g., Kingree & Thompson, 2000; Wuthrow, 1994). They help members overcome psychological oppression by serving as "vehicles through which outcast persons can claim and grow toward new identities" (Katz & Bender, 1976, p. 6). This can pave the way for overcoming political oppression. The sharing of personal stories transforms one's sense of self and also one's understanding of the social world (Rappaport, 1993). As self-stigma decreases, recognition of external causes of personal problems increases (Gottlieb, 1983; Kingree & Thompson, 2000). Thus, mutual help groups have beneficial outcomes in three domains. Intraindividual benefits center on transformations in the members' sense of self. Interpersonal benefits stem from connections with others that foster a sense of belonging and common cause. Finally, sociopolitical benefits result from an increasing understanding of and ability to intervene in the outside world (Solomon, Pistrang, & Barker, 2001).

Barriers to Common Cause. Oppression isolates. When a person internalizes self-hatred as a member of a marginalized group, this hatred easily extends to others who share that group identity. It may also extend to other disenfranchised groups. It is safer for members of oppressed groups to battle each other than to confront dominant forces. The extension of internalized oppression to other members of the same group and to other marginalized groups, has been termed **horizontal hostility**. Those who seek to perpetuate oppression often use horizontal hostility[1] to their advantage: the "divide and conquer" strategy. During the battle over Amendment 2 in Colorado, for example, supporters of legislation legalizing discrimination based on sexual orientation featured people of color prominently in advertising campaigns (see also Gates, 1993).

Divide and conquer strategies prevent people from working together for change—either with other subordinate groups, or with people from one's own group. **Tokenism** illustrates how people within a group can become divided. Tokenism involves granting a very small number of minority group members extremely limited access to positions of power. Many organizations, including universities, have experienced pressure to increase the representation of minority group members. In more than one university hiring meeting, faculty have voiced a desire to attract people of color but have shown an unwillingness to conceptualize "scholarship" in anything other than traditional (Western) terms. Hiring efforts focus on attracting those few minority candidates who do research in mainstream ways; they study topics just like everyone else on the faculty, use the same methods everyone else uses present results in the same way. They just don't *look* like everyone else. It can be exceedingly difficult to find such candidates, but only one is needed. All public relations material can then feature photographs of that single new hire to demonstrate how diverse the school (or company, or political party) really is. The new hire sits on every committee pertaining to minority issues and mentors all minority students in the department. Because a small number of minority group members fulfill a wide variety of functions, they experience a type of role overload that has been labeled "token stress" (Jackson, Thoits, & Taylor, 1995). The token hire fulfills multiple responsibilities, thereby freeing all other members of the organization to behave exactly as they had before.

Tokenism also affects minority group members' willingness to create common cause. Stephen Wright, Donald Taylor, and Fathali Moghaddam (1990) performed several laboratory studies to determine when members of disadvantaged groups accept their situation, when they seek redress through individual efforts, and when they engage in collective action. The researchers found that when an explicit policy of tokenism existed (in their research this was operationalized as a 2% quota), research participants preferred to take individual action in the hope of improving their personal position, rather than engage in collective action that could improve conditions for their entire group. Thus, tokenism reduces the motivation for social change both on the part of the powers that be (who claim that they *have* changed) and for members of the disadvantaged group (who now vie for advancement on an individual level).

In their research, Wright and his colleagues predicted that members of a disadvantaged group who were close to obtaining an advantaged position would be most likely to engage in collective action. Contrary to their expectations, a willingness to disrupt the social order occurred only when the advantaged position was perceived as *completely closed*. Those with nothing to lose had the most freedom to challenge the status quo. Indeed, the most marginalized subgroups of marginalized populations have often played key roles in launching social change movements. Ethnic minority drag queens initiated the Stonewall rebellion, which marked the beginning of the gay rights movement (e.g., Marcus, 1992; Marotta, 1981), and dedicated lesbians helped propel the women's movement of the 1960s and 1970 (e.g., Marotta, 1981; Pharr, 1988). In both cases, the "fringe" groups who helped inspire the movements were later denounced as the struggles for equal rights gained power and legitimacy.

Individuals in isolation can transform neither themselves nor their world. Creating common cause can help change agents envision rule-breaking solutions to social problems, recognize injustice, resist divide and conquer strategies, and risk disruption of the status quo.

COMMON CAUSE WITHIN AGENT GROUPS

A neglected topic in the social science literature is the need for *dominant* group members to find others who share their agent status with whom to build common cause. Being an ally can be a very lonely experience. Speaking against the status quo means calling for a change in the reward structures that benefit the agent group. Thus, the willingness of allies to forfeit group advantages may cast them in the role of traitor. People of agent status who know that something is wrong may silence themselves in order to remain a part of the group.

Social pressure to conform to group sentiment can be exceedingly strong. In his classic "line experiments," Solomon Asch (1951, 1956) found that people gave obviously wrong answers to questions if many before them had consistently given the wrong answer (in these studies, the people giving the wrong answers were, unbeknownst to the research participant, part of the experiment). Research participants who heard one person after another say that line B was longer than line A were likely to concur when it came their turn, even if line B was clearly shorter. Similar dynamics have been identified outside the laboratory as well. Fear of social isolation leads those with viewpoints that go against group consensus to keep quiet even in the face of rank injustice, creating a "spiral of silence" (Noelle-Neumann, 1984). This group pressure to conform, which social psychologists have labeled **normative social influence**, is particularly strong if the group is valued by the person who wants to speak out (e.g., Nowak, Szamrej, & Latane, 1990). All change agents, but especially allies, must be willing to withstand the ostracism and social conflict that result when one dissents from popular opinion (Woliver, 1996).

Support from others can help potential allies resist normative social influence. It is difficult to speak against social consensus when one feels alone. The good news is that a single supporter can make an enormous difference. Asch (1955) found that if even *one* person spoke against group consensus (e.g., asserting that line B was indeed the shorter line), the research participants were emboldened to do the same. Allies can support each other and can begin a "spiral of speaking out."

People interested in creating change need others to support that vision. Indeed, it took a *group* of clinical psychologists at Swampscott to articulate a collective criticism of their profession and found the new field of community psychology. Community psychologists, who often work as allies, continue to benefit from the opportunity to connect with like-minded others. Every two years, community psychologists from across the globe, many of whom work in isolation from others trained in the field, come together at the Biennial Conference on Community Research and Action. There we share stories, reinforce our collective identity as community psychologists, and gain the insight and support necessary to pursue our challenging agendas.

COMMON CAUSE BETWEEN TARGETS AND AGENTS

Social change clearly requires that target group members connect with others in their group. Allies in agent groups also benefit from support from other agent group members. The importance of target group members connecting with people outside the disenfranchised group, especially people in dominant groups, is debatable. Theories of minority identity development agree that the first step to a positive identity is confrontation with society's stereotypes and immersion in the minority group's own history and culture (Phinney, 1996; see Chapter Five section entitled *Examples: Invisibility, Coping, and Identify Development*). This stage may or may not be followed by a desire to reconnect with majority group members.

Some change agents maintain firm group borders and assume an us–them dichotomy. Some change agents seek to include as many people and groups as possible under the umbrella of "us." These differing perspectives suggest different social change tactics in an effort to achieve different social change goals. Malcolm X advocated a separation of the races both as a change strategy and as a social change goal. Martin Luther King, on the other hand, saw a place for White people in the civil rights struggle and viewed the unity of all races as the ultimate goal (Cone, 1991). Let's look more closely at the implications of the different approaches.

Conflict-Based and Cooperative Approaches. As discussed in Chapter Two, two important community-level change strategies are community organizing and coalition building. Community organizing has traditionally been viewed as a conflict-based change strategy, while coalition building adopts a cooperative approach.

Saul Alinsky (1971) is often cited as the quintessential community organizer. He advocated separation, disunity, and conflict. In his view, more equitable social arrangements required confrontation with powerful external forces. Alinsky relied on **direct action** as a change tactic. For this tactic, community organizers help disenfranchised groups *directly* confront people identified as responsible for injustice and use controversial means to attain desire ends (see the Community Intervention box). Redress is not sought indirectly through society's intermediary structures such as the courts or Congress.

Since the 1960s and 1970s, coalition building has gained favor over community organizing. Coalitions bring diverse groups of people together to create change. Although the rhetoric of coalition building suggests a harmonious collaboration, consensus for change usually exists against a backdrop of contention. I once worked on anti-death penalty legislation aimed at excluding mentally retarded people from death sentencing. The coalition included Amnesty International volunteers and the leaders of the Catholic Archdiocese. There was common ground on which to walk, but that ground was narrow and our walks proceeded cautiously.

Bernice Johnson Reagon (1992), a civil rights activist and founder of the a cappella group *Sweet Honey in the Rock*, presented a sobering perspective on coalition work. She asserted that technology has eliminated the possibility of staying in small, isolated villages where everyone looks the same and acts the same, and anyone who doesn't fit in can somehow be eliminated from the realm of concern. She acknowledged the importance of recreating that village on a temporary basis—sitting in what she called a "barred room" with others who are like you in order to gain strength and perspective. The "villagers" can share experiences and laugh together. They can recognize social patterns and support conscientization, foster a sense of communal responsibility, battle burnout, and reinforce a shared sense of a higher purpose. In that barred room one can feel safe and nurtured and have a sense of home. A people cannot, however, stay inside that barred room and survive.

Coalition work is not done in the home, it is done in the streets. If you feel comfortable in a coalition, Reagon (1992) admonished, then "you're not really doing no coalescing" (p. 504). She contended that the basic desire to survive motivates coalition work. Each of us must feel that this is *our* world, and the challenge is to make that *our* as big as we can, to include in it everyone we have to include in order to survive. In her indomitable style, Reagon warned that *our* had better include Bernice Johnson Reagon.

Although coalition building is not always a friendly and peaceful process, its *goal* is not to confront or ridicule, but to build a sense of common cause. The movement away from community organizing and toward coalition building may stem from several causes. First, change agents have a growing

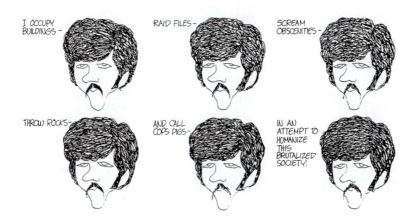

Do the ends justify the means?
From FEIFFER: JULES FEIFFER'S AMERICA FROM EISENHOWER TO REAGAN by Jules Feiffer, edited by Steven Heller, copyright © 1982 by Jules Feiffer. Used by permission of Alfred A. Knopf, a division of Random House, Inc.

COMMUNITY INTERVENTION:

Direct Action
From Saul Alinsky to ACT UP

Saul Alinsky recounted his insights about community organizing in his classic 1971 book *Rules for Radicals*. An example from that book illustrates his direct action approach to social change.

Alinsky was asked by residents of Rochester, New York's, Black ghetto to help fight the city's power structures in order to gain access to the city's resources. In devising a direct action intervention, Alinsky decided to capitalize on Rochester's view of itself as a sophisticated city of culture, with libraries, museums, a university, and a well-known symphony. He publicized his intention to buy 100 seats to a symphony concert. The tickets would then be distributed to his guests, 100 African Americans, who would be treated to a pre-concert dinner of baked beans. Lots of baked beans. Alinsky (1971) predicted that the concert would be over "before the first movement!" (p. 139).

Several of Alinsky''s rules can be identified in this example. First, the situation was outside of the experience of the enemy, who would not know how to respond. Could they forbid eating baked beans? Could they ban anyone from succumbing to natural urges during a concert? Second, the threat was more terrifying than the thing itself. Alinksy asserted that in carefully planned actions, the threat is so powerful that there is no need to follow through with the action. Third, Alinsky posited that a good tactic is one that your people enjoy. Ghetto residents relished the thought of their evening at the symphony. A fourth rule is to recognize that ridicule is the most potent weapon. Any official who railed against the baked bean conspiracy faced derision, not sympathy.

Alinsky was willing to confront, anger, and humiliate external powers in his effort to create change. This stands in opposition to Paulo Freire's (1970/1992) notion that the struggle for liberation has meaning only if the oppressed resist the temptation to regain their humanity at the expense of their oppressors. Can oppressors always be treated with respect? Alinsky argued that the ethics of means and ends cannot be removed from the context in which actions occurs. For example, Gandhi's tactic of passive resistance appealed to the moral conscience of those in power. The tactic worked

in India and in the civil rights struggles of the U.S. Such appeals to conscience would not hold sway against the Nazis or other totalitarian regimes. When powerful regimes lack moral conscience, more unsavory tactics would be necessary and justified.

In his usual irreverent style, Alinsky (1971) delineated several provocative rules pertaining to the ethics of means and ends. For example:

- "concern with the ethics of means and ends increases when more means are available and vice versa" (p. 32).
- "concern with the ethics of means and ends varies inversely with one's personal investment in the issue" (p. 26).
- "any effective means is automatically judged by the opposition as being unethical" (p. 35).

The savvy of this analysis is evident in a consideration one of the most visible direct action groups of the latter half of the twentieth century: AIDS Coalition to Unleash Power (ACT UP). The choice for many AIDS activists in the 1980s was, "Do we play by the rules, court public sympathy, and push steadily and politely for recognition? Or do we make ourselves so unpleasant that yielding to our demands becomes easier than ignoring us?" (Cunningham, 1982, p. 63). While the death toll from AIDS rose rapidly, AIDS-related policies and priorities changed slowly, if at all. Activists founded ACT UP with the following mission statement: "Our job is not to be invited to coffee or to shmooze at a cocktail party. Our job is to make change as quickly as possible and direct action works for that" (ACT UP, No date).

ACT UP conducted a number of actions, or "zaps," which often included thousands of protesters capable of shutting down Wall Street or the Golden Gate Bridge. Often the zaps used ridicule. For example, to protest a hospital's refusal to treat women with AIDS, women activists took over a nearby intersection, laid mattresses on the street, and declared that space the "Cook County Women's AIDS Unit." Two days later, the first women with AIDS were admitted to the hospital (ACT UP,

1990). ACT UP zaps sometimes skirted the borders of good taste and sometimes knocked them down with a vengeance. In 1992 activists questioned the pressure for their grief to remain private and devoid of anger. They decided that the funerals of their friends and lovers who died of AIDS deserved to assume social and political dimensions (Rickkets, 1995). The notion of political funerals was born, and culminated in the *Ashes Action* in Washington, D.C., during which activists threw the cremated remains of dead friends over the White House wall.

The zaps had multiple goals—raising awareness about AIDS, publicizing price-gouging by pharmaceutical companies, and changing the way science was done (e.g., releasing experimental medications before tedious controlled studies verified promising results; see Wachter, 1991). AIDS activists had considerable success in achieving these goals through direct action. One wonders if more people would be dead had they adopted more conciliatory tactics.

awareness that community problems are interrelated and so require holistic, community-wide solutions rather than piecemeal efforts (e.g., Wolff, 2001; Schorr, 1997). Second, it has become increasingly difficult to identify clear enemies in our technological and transnational society (Gamson, 1989; Pilisuk, McAllister, & Rothman, 1996). Saul Alinsky (1971) encouraged activists to "[p]ick the target, freeze it, personalize it, and polarize it" (p. 130). In today's world, local resources are increasingly under the control of transnational power conglomerates. Corporate managers, private financial institutions, and governments are closely linked, and exert their influences through a wide variety of intermediary organizations. Many people are responsible for what happens in local communities, and they often live far away and are difficult to pin down (Pilisuk et al., 1996). The wonderful 1989 movie *Roger and Me* chronicled filmmaker Michael Moore's pursuit of Roger Smith, the president of General Motors, whom Moore held personally responsible for the unemployment that resulted from an automotive plant closing in his home town of Flint, Michigan. Bernice Johnson Reagon suggested a third reason for the movement toward coalition building: in today's technological and international world, our very survival on this planet depends on creating a common cause.

Do Conflict-Based and Cooperative Strategies Conflict or Cooperate? Conflict and cooperation are not mutually exclusive. Although Western notions of "one right way" may cause us to pit different tactics against each other, seemingly competing

approaches may actually work synergistically. Martin Luther King Jr. and Malcolm X are often seen as adversaries—one an advocate for cooperation and the other a proponent of conflict. In actuality, they did have a common goal—to establish respect for African American people. James Cone (1991) argued that in working toward that goal, each spoke a truth about the United States, and so these leaders did not oppose, but rather "complemented and corrected"

Martin Luther King and Malcolm X meet for the only time in March, 1964. *AP/WIDE WORLD PHOTOS.*

each other. The societal changes that occurred during the civil rights era would not have been possible without *both* of their influential voices.

Demonstrations, legal challenges, lobbying efforts, art, entertainment, prayer, education, action research, and a variety of other strategies have all contributed to the change process. In the future, we will need these and also new tactics.

One reason for the success of nonviolent protest during the civil rights era was that people in this country had not seen it before. Police, politicians, and other forces of stability did not know what to do when they found peace where they expected uproar. Saul Alinsky (1971) advised "Whenever possible, go outside of the experience of the enemy" (p. 127). Nonviolence has become a well-known tactic and can no longer take people by surprise. This is true of other social change efforts, as well. *Take Back the Night* marches provided a novel outlet for women's anger and raised awareness about violence against women 20 years ago but have become regularly scheduled mainstays in many communities and no longer have the original effects (Campbell, Baker, & Mazurek, 1998). New tactics are necessary to remain on the edge of change (Schulman, 1994). We cannot foresee the social change strategies of the future, but we can predict that they will take us by surprise, provoke anxiety and controversy, and be breathtakingly creative.

⌘ Social Change from a Systems Perspective

To paraphrase Paulo Freire (1970/1992), no one liberates himself *or* is liberated by others. Social change requires individual insight (e.g., to awaken to injustice, to think creatively about problems and solutions). It also requires creating common cause with others (e.g., to support conscientization, to resist divide and conquer strategies, to foster communal responsibility). Social change is inherently multi-systemic.

Let's look now at individuals and groups organized to create change within a large context.

James Kelly's ecological analogy (see Chapter Four) reminds us that each system component is connected to all other components (interdependence) and change in one part requires adjustments in all other parts (adaptation). In some cases, different system levels cooperate to magnify the impact of change efforts. More often, a change effort in one component causes the rest of the system to conspire to maintain the status quo (see the Classic Research box).

Individuals can work against social change for various reasons—intolerance for the anxiety and ambiguity inspired by change, fear that a bad situation will worsen, unwillingness to forfeit rewards the flow from existing structures. Social institutions also work against change efforts. George Fairweather (1979) observed that, "Organizations are established in order to maintain the status quo" (p. 323). These forces for stability may have admirable beginnings. Parker J. Palmer (1996) noted that organizations adhere to principles of conservation and stability because "[t]hey are the vessel in which a society holds hard-won treasures from the past," (p. 164). Similarly, Lisbeth Schorr (1997) reminded us that "to every rule there is a purpose" (p. 69) and bureaucracies often emerge for good reasons. Nevertheless, these forces for stability must be "tamed" in order for innovations to occur (Schorr, 1988, 1997). Community psychologists dedicated to social change often combat the organizational pull toward stability. This pull can make change difficult to sustain within a setting and hard to disseminate to other settings (Fairweather, 1979; Maton, 2000; Mayer & Davidson, 2000; Schorr, 1997; Rogers, 1995). Without attending to system forces for stability, first order change will occur where second order change was intended

All components of a system are interdependent, and all system levels, from the lone individual to the overarching macrosystem, collaborate to create social change—or to preserve the status quo. Although community psychologists can target any level as an initial point of leverage, an understanding of the multisystem context is essential (e.g., Cohen &

CLASSIC RESEARCH

Juvenile Diversion

The Forces of First Order Change

In 1899 the first juvenile court was established with the goal of diverting young offenders from the adult court system, where they often received harsh punishment. Youth were seen as less culpable due to their immaturity and also more amenable to rehabilitation. The juvenile courts were charged not simply with judging guilt but with investigating cases and prescribing treatments.

By the 1970s, the juvenile justice system had become problematic, and efforts were launched to divert youth from the juvenile courts (which had themselves been established to divert youth from the adult system). Julian Rappaport, Ed Seidman, and William Davidson (1985) developed a local intervention, the Adolescent Diversion Project, for youth about to enter the court system. The project directors specifically ruled out intervening with first time offenders or status offenders (youth who commit crimes that carry no penalty for adults, such as truancy or drinking). This decision was based on the belief that involving low-risk youth in the legal system created more problems than it solved. Most adolescents engage in some illegal activities (Seidman, 1984). A New Zealand study found that 93% of males acknowledged delinquent behavior before the age of 18, and in the U.S., 80% reported contact with police for minor offenses as adolescents (Moffit, 1993). Labeling youth's normative behavior as delinquent may create self-fulfilling prophesies.

Thus, the Adolescent Diversion Project targeted juveniles involved in habitual and serious criminal behavior who were, as a result, on the brink of court involvement. These youth were randomly assigned to either an experimental group or a control group. College students who had been trained in relationship building, child advocacy, and behavioral contracting worked closely with youth in the experimental group. Research showed that program participants as compared to youth in the control group demonstrated a marked decrease in police contacts, committed less serious offenses, and received fewer court referrals. These differences were evident both one and two years after the intervention.

As with most demonstration projects, the researchers developed and evaluated the program then prepared for its takeover by workers in the field. Four years later, few people who had developed the demonstration remained on staff, but the program continued. Some might say it thrived. It operated at full capacity and was supported by county funds. The police cooperated with and took pride in the program. College students waited in line for a chance to work with the youth. The project directors, however, did not see the takeover as successful. The Adolescent Diversion Project was no longer a diversion project! It had come to serve the first-time offenders and status offenders who were purposely excluded from the demonstration project. Meanwhile, adolescents on the verge of involvement with the court system, the adolescents for whom this intervention was designed, no longer received services. Thus an attempt at meaningful diversion was undone by the community systems who adopted the demonstration project.

Would an intervention targeting a higher level of analysis have a better chance of effecting real change? Let's look at another research project studying juvenile diversion efforts. In 1974, the federal government passed the Juvenile Justice and Delinquency Prevention Act, which attempted to limit the number of youth entering the justice system. This Act required states to develop plans to stop placing status offenders in juvenile detention or correctional facilities. In 1977 Virginia implemented a variety of policy changes in order to comply with federal legislation. Edward Mulvey and Ann Hicks (1982) took advantage of this naturally occurring event. They compared outcomes for juveniles before and after the code change.

If youth had indeed been diverted from the justice system as a result of the code change, one would expect an increase in the processing of youth in nonlegal settings and a decrease in court appearances. In actuality, the opposite occurred. *Fewer* were diverted at intake and *more* youth appeared in court after the code change. The investigators saw this paradoxical outcome as evidence of the power of mediating organizations to actively undo policy. Community gatekeepers—the people in charge of admission to the various social settings—altered what they did to keep the existing system in place. For example, an adolescent who slapped his mother might have been labeled by police officers as "incorrigible" before the code change, but as "assaulting" after the change, thereby allowing the juvenile court to retain control over the youth's fate.

Mulvey and Hicks (1982) described a variety of system factors that helped overcome the intent of the juvenile justice policy: the demand for police to maintain social control, the desire to obtain social services for adolescents, the press for organizational stability, and the imprecision of juvenile offense categories. They concluded,

> Without further understanding of these organizational level forces in dictating individual juvenile justice decision-making, the juvenile system will remain a baffling system in which "the more things change, the more they remain the same. (p. 720)

Lavach, 1995; Fullan, 1999; Kelly, Ryan, Altman, & Stelzner, 2000; Maton, 2000). Let's look at how interventions targeting different levels can incorporate a system's perspective.

INDIVIDUAL LEVEL

Everyone is involved in shaping the world in which we live. Countless heroes and heroines drive efforts to create a more equitable society. A few we know. Rosa Parks' refusal to go to the back of the bus helped fuel the civil rights movement. However, most remain unnamed. For example, the power of the women's movement "lay in the myriad events of everyday life in which sexual and gender relationships are constructed and evaluated" (Gusfield, 1981; cited in Woliver, 1996, p.146). The belief that these one-on-one encounters lay the ground work for social change has led promoters of civil rights for sexual minorities to encourage gay, lesbian, and bisexual individuals to "come out" (i.e., reveal their sexual orientation) in their everyday lives.

Indeed, each of us is involved in creating our society. Fran Peavey (1986) ended her book *Heart Politics* with the following words: "I act on the conviction that everyone *is* making a difference. Just by living our lives, consuming space and resources, we are making a difference. Our choice is what kind of a difference to make" (p. 179).

Some community psychologists focus on helping individuals to become more effective in their efforts to make a difference. This may involve helping people overcome psychological oppression. As an example, Craig Brookins (1996; Brookins & Robinson, 1995) described a rites-of-passage program designed to help African American adolescents develop a positive sense of their ethnic identity. This intervention focused on individuals—improving esteem and preparing youth for the challenges they would face as African American adults. At the same time, it fostered conscientization and piqued young people's interest in changing their social environments (see also Watts & Abdul-Adil, 1994).

Alternatively, intervention can enhance the political skills of individuals. We can, for example, help citizens to become more effective leaders of social change efforts who can plan strategically, analyze problems, assess needs and strengths, and identify resources (e.g., Fawcett, Paine-Andrews. Francisco, Schultz, Richter, Lewis, Williams, Harris, Berkley, Fisher, & Lopez, 1995; Seekins, Mathews, & Fawcett, 1984; Wandersman & Florin, 2000).

MICROSYSTEM LEVEL

Some change agents focus on microsystems. As described earlier, the settings that bring change agents into contact with each other, be they consciousness-raising groups, churches, or mutual-help organizations, are crucial to social change efforts. "Although it is individuals who decide whether or not to take up collective action, it is in their face-to-face groups, their social networks, and their institutions that collective action is most often activated and sustained" (Tarrow, 1994, cited in Woliver, 1996, p. 144; see also Berger & Neuhaus, 1977). Margaret Mead is believed to have said, "Never doubt that a small group of thoughtful committed citizens can change the world. Indeed, it's the only thing that ever has" (The Institute for Intercultural Studies, Nov. 11, 2001, 2).

Microsystem-level interventions might involve consulting with existing advocacy organizations to help them foster conscientization among members or combat political oppression more effectively. A second microsystem-level strategy is the creation of new settings for consciousness raising and political action. As one example, Susan Yeich and Ralph Levine (1994) conducted a participatory action research project around the founding of a union for homeless persons. The development of homeless persons' unions is based on the belief that homeless people may themselves be in the best position to take action against homelessness but lack the support structures necessary to do so. The formation of a union provided a context in which homeless people could join forces to develop a sense of efficacy and take collective action to change society (see also Yeich, 1994).

BEYOND THE MICROSYSTEM

Many community psychologists direct their attention to levels of analysis beyond the microsystem. Once again, change efforts at this level entail changes at other levels as well. As an example, consider the Concerns Reports used by Stephen Fawcett and his colleagues (1994).

The Concerns Reports center on community level change. Researchers and local citizens with disabilities worked together to design surveys that captured issues relevant to the local community (e.g., accessibility of public buildings, affordability of health care). Surveys were administered to all people with disabilities in the specified community,

who reported on the importance they accorded to the issue and their satisfaction with how it was being addressed. Thus, the Concerns data identified community strengths (high importance/high satisfaction issues) and needs (high importance/low satisfaction). Researchers summarized the data and people in the disability community organized public meetings to discuss the identified issues and generate suggestions for addressing problems. Researchers assisted in facilitating meetings and building a local agenda.

In the 1980's, nearly 18,000 people with disabilities from over 490 communities in 12 different states completed Concerns Reports. Common concerns included lack of employment opportunities, poor enforcement of handicapped parking ordinances, and potential employers focusing on deficits rather than abilities. Although centered at the community level, the Concerns Report effort has led to change at all levels of analysis. The research process has increased individual citizen's critical consciousness and sense of competence. Community groups have used local concerns data to advocate for change locally—e.g., to increase the enforcement of handicapped parking ordinances. Project participants have also disseminated Concern Reports data to disability rights advocates at state and national levels. Indeed, the data were presented to the United States Congress in support of the Americans with Disabilities Act (ADA) and likely played a role in passing that legislation (Fawcett et al., 1994).

⌘ Social Change for the Long Haul: Short-Circuiting Despair through Paradox

Maurice Elias (1994) observed that community psychologists must work with "the elusive, dynamic process of multifaceted, multisystemic interrelationships that are the essence of change" (p. 302). This elusiveness and complexity can make social change challenging indeed. How do agents of change maintain enthusiasm despite setbacks?

One of the strengths of community psychologists is our willingness and ability to embrace paradox (e.g., Rappaport, 1981). When we recognize the simultaneous truth of two seemingly opposite poles of thought, we gain insight and direction. Below are some words of wisdom, many from notable activists, about the role of paradox in social change efforts.

THE SITUATION IS URGENT, SO TAKE YOUR TIME

There exists a tension between the hopefulness that motivates continued action and the idealism that leads to disappointment and burnout. Julian Rappaport (1981) wrote of the need to maintain a sense of urgency. The work we do is important. It is also never ending. Thus, we must combine a sense of urgency with a long-term commitment—A balance of patience and zeal (Kelly, 1971). As the activist monk Brother David Steindl-Rast noted, "Paradoxically, we have to act as if we had all the time in the world, and as if we had no time at all" (Ingram, 1990, p. 256).

As activists, we must find ways of drawing on the optimistic and even reckless enthusiasm of youth (as described in Chapter One) and also on the more measured wisdom of age. Bernice Johnson Reagon, recognized the importance of youthful energy in *Ella's Song* (1981), praising youth for having courage when adults such as herself feel fear. At the same time, she asked fellow activists to think about being raging radicals fifty years in the future. "What would you be like if you had white hair and had not given up your principles? It might be wise . . . to think about the possibilities of going for fifty years. It calls for some care" (Reagon, 1992, p. 508).

THE OUTCOME IS CRITICAL, SO DON'T WORRY ABOUT IT

The activist Fran Peavey (1986) noted, "It is a paradox that the goals of the change agent, born of high ideals and the noble drive for improvement, can actually interfere with or subvert the change effort" (p. 161). Although the hope for a better world drives one's efforts, attachment to achieving a particular outcome can impede progress.

To some degree, the results of one's work are irrelevant. Israeli peace activist Veronika Cohen stated, "When people ask me, 'Are you an optimist or a pessimist' my answer is 'I'm neither; I'm working'" (Rosenwasser, 1992, p. 83). Karl Weick (1984) made a similar point in his excellent article entitled *Small Wins*: "We justify what we do, not by belief in its efficacy but by an acceptance of its necessity" (p. 48).

David Steindl-Rast observed that the question of whether humankind will ultimately survive is an important question and also one that should *not* be answered. To say we will surely make it means our existence is assured and so no action need be taken to stop destructive social forces. On the other hand, to say we surely will not survive means that all actions are futile. Both answers eliminate the need to work for change. He concluded that we must commit completely to what we are doing "as if whether or not we're going to make it depended upon it. And we must find a way of living in which even if we are not going to make it, in the last second you can say to yourself, 'Well, what I did was worthwhile.'" (Ingram, 1990, p. 264).

THE PROBLEMS ARE HUGE, SO THINK SMALL

Karl Weick (1984) recognized that in attempting to marshal support and compel action, social change agents often cast problems in massive terms. We engage people in the battle against poverty, nuclear buildup, racism, school dropout, homelessness, child abuse, or any other social ill by emphasizing the gargantuan proportions of the problem today, and the likelihood that the problem will only get worse in the future. This approach may be counterproductive in that it overwhelms people's sense of competence to address the problem. When people feel exceedingly aroused, helpless, or frustrated, the quality of thought and action declines and the likelihood of finding creative solutions to problems decreases (Weick, 1984).

Karl Weick (1984) astutely observed that we must break large problems into more manageable pieces—hence the title of his article: *Small Wins*. He argued that we need to think not about catastrophic problems, but about "mere" problems.

When we think of social change we often think about Big Problems such as poverty or racism. Big Problems require Big Solutions: the elimination of capitalism, for example. Our work as community psychologists usually occurs, however, on a less grand scale. Sometimes the work is a lot less grand. Action researcher and social change activist Leonard Jason (1991) once invited a representative of a Chicago alderman to his class. When someone asked what community problem residents complained about most, Jason privately pledged to work on whatever problem the alderman mentioned. The representative cited uncollected dog feces as the most aggravating problem to community residents. And so, Jason and his students could later be found observing the numbers of defecating dogs on a city block for 5 hours each day, and weighing the fecal matter left behind. These researchers assessed the efficacy of two interventions: posting no littering signs (ineffective); and demonstrations to dog owners of how to pick up feces with plastic bags (effective). The alderman later asked Jason to present his data to city officials. Chicago became one of the first cities to pass a "pooper scooper" ordinance and Jason positioned himself as a researcher responsive to official concerns and willing to do what was necessary to make a difference.

Being a social change activist may require a broad view, but a local commitment; a willingness to think globally, but act locally. We may not be able to make the entire world more livable or more beautiful, but we can clean up our own streets and see where that leads.

SOCIAL CHANGE IS COMPLEX, SO KEEP IT SIMPLE

Social change efforts can get lost in complex analyses. A study of why people who opposed nuclear proliferation did *not* become activists found that many citizens felt incompetent to enter the debate (Gilbert, 1988). There were so many technological and political nuances to navigate that the possibility of informed action seemed remote.

Certainly, we can think ourselves into circles and never take action. Academics may be particularly prone to losing the motivation to act in their attempts to be as informed as possible. Most scientists no longer believe in an ordered, precise, rational, and completely knowable world. If action depended on complete knowledge, it would never occur. Still, efforts to understand can lead us on meandering trails that do not end in action. As the folk singer Emily Saliers (1990) of the Indigo Girls put it in one of her songs, sometimes we need to stop thinking ourselves into jail and just get up and get a hammer and nail. We must let the simplicity of our concern shine through the seeming complexity of the situation.

SOCIAL CHANGE IS SERIOUS BUSINESS, SO HAVE FUN

Social change work entails long-term commitment, risk-taking, disappointment, and feelings of discomfort in ambiguous situations where our work leads to uncertain results. Saul Alinsky (1971) pointed out that if we want others to join us in our change efforts, we had better make them fun (see also Wolff, 1987).

Certainly humor can work against social change. We have all heard racist, sexist, anti-Semitic, or otherwise oppressive jokes designed to justify the superior position of the agent group and encourage target group members to participate in their own degradation by laughing along. However, humor can advance social change in many ways.

Oppressed people are often seen as humorless. Feminists never find anything funny (Barreca, 1991; Bunkers, 1997), and the grunting, granite-faced Indian actually seems incapable of cracking a smile (DeLoria, 1992). Perhaps marginalized groups are denied their humor because laughter is inherently subversive (Martineau, 1972; Mindess, 1971). Humor can safely express repressed anger (Boskin, 1997; Bunkers, 1997). Social satirists use what has been termed *protest humor* (Boskin, 1997) to criticize the social order and highlight injustice in a biting but nonthreatening way. "I often counseled people to run for the Bureau of Indian Affairs in case of an earthquake" Vine DeLoria stated, "because nothing could shake the BIA" (DeLoria, 1992, p. 342). Jokes can release tension, bolster morale, redefine group identities, and turn conventional thinking on its head. *Question*: What did one gay man say to the other when a beautiful woman walked by? *Answer*: "Times like these, I wish I were a lesbian."

Humor brings people together. A scholar of feminist humor wrote, "laughter unites us; it awakens our feelings of self-worth; and it confirms our sense of power" (Bunkers, 1997, p. 170). Humor also allows people to maintain perspective. In his essay on Indian humor, Vine Deloria (1992) wrote, "When a

---

A Chance for Community Psychologists to Laugh at Ourselves

A lively exchange on the community psychology listserv occurred in response to a question posted by Jeff Charvat (May 27, 1999):

> In the interest of promoting the value of "not taking ourselves TOO seriously," I wonder if anyone would be willing to help me with the other half of the question: How many community psychologists does it take to replace a light bulb? (I realize I've done the easy part.)

Over the course of several weeks, listserv members posted a multitude of answers. Here is a sampling.

- All depends on how bright the bulb is. . . *(Richard Gist)*
- None. We don't change light bulbs, we prevent them from going out in the first place. *(Keith Humphreys)*
- None, we empower them to change themselves. *(Mary Brydon-Miller)*
- The users of the light should be empowered to change the bulb themselves, or find a new source of light. *(Michaela Parks)*
- If we stop pathologizing the bulb we will see that it changes itself. *(Hiro Yoshikawa)*
- It will take a focused concentration of our resources, as the light bulb should be changed as often as possible. Seeing "reality" through only one filter encourages a monolithic, ethnocentric perspective. Old bulbs tend to become institutionalized in ways that discourage innovation. Every bulb should have its 15 minutes of light, shedding diverse rays upon our world, a condition which cannot be achieved as long as we blindly continue to accept the dominance of a single bulb/light. *(James Emshoff)*
- TRICK QUESTION!!! TRICK QUESTION!!! A community psychologist would *never* replace a light bulb. Rather, he/she would work collaboratively with the bulb to strengthen its damaged filaments. As Emory Cowen is so fond of not [sic] saying, "there's no such thing as a bad bulb." *(Mike Morris)*
- Why are we talking about changing the bulb as opposed to the system that resulted in its breakdown? Sure, we can change one light bulb after another, but isn't this a bit dim? Doesn't this just blame the victim rather than changing the conditions that contributed to its demise? *(Jacob Tebes)*
- IT TAKES FOUR COMMUNITY PSYCHOLOGISTS TO CHANGE A LIGHT BULB: One to do a needs assessment (There may be another community that needs a new light bulb more).
  One to review the relevant social indicators and determine if the domination of white bulbs reflects the disenfranchisement of bulbs of color.
  One to serve as a consultant to a home maintenance self-help collaborative that will select and train a member of the host setting to change the light bulb. The collaborative will then develop indigenous bulb-changers so that when the next one burns out the host setting has the resources to change its own bulb.
  One to evaluate the change process (grant funding permitting). *(Roderick Watts)*

"Don't Be Too Serious" (1999). SCRA Community News. *The Community Psychologist, Summer 1999, Volume 32 (3),* pp. 38–39.

people can laugh at themselves and laugh at others and hold all aspects of life together without letting anybody drive them to extremes, then it seems to me that people can survive" (p. 346).

SOCIAL CHANGE REQUIRES STAYING ON COURSE, SO RELINQUISH CONTROL

Change is difficult. It is emotional, time-consuming, uncertain, complex, and sometimes dangerous. It requires a willingness to stray into the unfamiliar. When entering unknown territory, how does one stay the course?

Social change requires giving up illusions of control. We must recognize instead the myriad chaotic forces operating in society. Effecting change has been compared to white-water rafting—if you over-manage it, you capsize (Fullan, 1999). The Western world holds that change requires a causal agent. We emphasize individual control over events (Hodge, Struckman, & Trost, 1975; Maruyama, 1983). Beginning activists may be dismayed to find that in reality, no one is in charge! We live in nested circles of interrelated systems, and no single person ever deserves all the blame for problems or praise for solutions. Adolph Hitler was not solely responsible for the Holocaust, nor was Martin Luther King Jr. in charge of the civil rights movement.

When one feels tossed and turned like a raft at sea, it can be important to find a stillness and sense of direction, a moral compass, if you will. Many of our most famous social change activists saw their work as deeply rooted in religion, and numerous Nobel Peace Prize recipients have been religious leaders: Martin Luther King Jr., Bishop Desmond Tutu, The Fourteenth Dalai Lama, Mother Teresa. Spirituality can serve as a bulwark against pessimism and disillusionment (Watts, Griffith, & Abdul-Adil, 1999) that anchors us to a higher purpose in the midst of chaos.

People often gauge the amount of hope they should have in a given situation according to the likelihood of a positive outcome. The Czechoslovakian playwright-turned-statesman Vaclav Havel (1980) saw this as a misconception. He wrote that hope is above all:

> a state of the mind, not a state of the world. Either we have hope within us, or we don't; it is a dimension of the soul, and it is not essentially dependent on some particular observation of the world or estimate of the situation . . . It is an orientation of the spirit, an orientation of the heart; it transcends the world that is immediately experienced, and is anchored somewhere beyond its horizons. (p. 181)

⌘ The Promise of Community Psychology: Giving Psychology Away

George Miller, in his 1969 Presidential Address to the American Psychological Association, proposed that psychologists could most effectively promote human welfare if we could "discover how best to give psychology away" (Miller, 1969, p. 1074). Knowledge is power. One way community psychologists can promote a redistribution of social power is by sharing our knowledge.

Unfortunately, insights gained by practitioners are not always communicated beyond the practitioners' immediate circle. Similarly, much of the knowledge generated in academic and research institutions remains completely unknown to people who could use it. Many researchers fail to take the initiative in disseminating results to community groups, legislators, and others whose actions might be informed by the study's findings. Potentially useful information remains unused, languishing in esoteric journals. As Martin Haberman (1971) bitingly observed,

> The growing literature on the effects of field experiences, group change strategies, and processes for learning and instruction are a well-kept secret between the particular

researcher, his funding agent, and the librarian who ultimately catalogues his work. (p. 138)

To rectify this situation, many community psychologists have called for incorporating mechanisms for disseminating information into research plans (and perhaps we should add "practice plans") (Chavis, et al., 1983; Fairweather, 1979; Price & Cherniss, 1977). When community psychologists take on this task, a literature of practice becomes more readily available to practitioners and academics, and the research literature becomes accessible to people who can act on important findings. Some community psychologists might extend their plans beyond their own findings and take on the role of translator more generally, "communicat[ing] the findings of psychology and the behavioral sciences in a language and form that is easily comprehended by the educated public, including policy makers" (Reppucci, 1984, p. 134).

Taking on the role of knowledge disseminator does not mean assuming a didactic stance in which we enlighten others with our expertise. It means taking responsibility for identifying findings from research (and practice) that might prove useful to people and presenting this information in understandable ways.

Attempts to give psychology away require honesty about the limitations of psychological knowledge and of our own perspectives. The limitations are numerous—an ongoing reliance on logical positivist models, a persistent emphasis on individual-level conceptions of problems, lack of attention to marginalized voices, unexamined assumptions about the world. As Kenneth Gergen and his colleagues (1996) observed, "One cannot simply do as George Miller once advocated—give psychology away—when the gift is an imposition, seen as an element in a policing process that denies the validity of a culture [or community] to determine its own ends" (p. 500).

Caution is required, but boldness, too. The possibilities are numerous. Community psychologists can write congressional briefs, publish books in the popular press, appear on television and radio programs, hold community forums, conduct workshops with social action groups. We can share information in our nonprofessional roles, as well: in meetings at our children's schools, when talking with neighbors, over dinner with friends. All of these conversations, both public and private, hold the promise of enriching our own work as well. We can expand our ideas about the important questions to ask, how to ask them, and what to make of the answers we obtain as we contribute to other people's ability to work towards a more just and equitable society.

Action Agenda

Social Change for the Long Haul

How do activists maintain a long-term commitment to social justice work? Talk to the people you know who have worked for social change for many years. Ask them how they maintain their sense of urgency despite disappointments and setbacks. What advice do they have for you? You can also look for inspiration in the stories of other activists. Many insights may be gleaned from the interviews conducted by Penny Rosenwasser in her 1992 book entitled, *Visionary Voices: Women on Power; Conversations with Shamans, Activists, Teachers, Artists, and Healers.* Look also at Christine Ingram's (1990) book, *In the Footsteps of Gandhi: Conversations with Spiritual Social Activists.*

Translating Research

Take on the role of research translator. There are many ways this could be done. Here are a few.

Option 1: Identify a social problem of interest and review the recent research pertaining to that problem. What findings do you think are particularly valuable (in terms of both content and quality of research)? Who might benefit from knowing about these findings? In what form would the information best be conveyed to relevant audiences—a written report, a fact sheet, a telephone conversation, an informal lunch? Devise a dissemination plan to spread the word about the findings. Then take the first step.

After conveying the information, what would be a next step? Might you evaluate how often and under what circumstances your information is used? Might you take responsibility for updating the information in a year?

Option 2: Find a community group who is interested in learning more about recent research in their focus area (e.g., child abuse prevention, community coalition building). How might you be helpful? Would they like you to write a research-based fact sheet? Do they have a particular question that you might research for them (e.g., What child abuse prevention programs are currently being implemented in other cities? What research bears on policy initiatives that may be under consideration in the legislature?). In what form would this information be most useable? Would they like to have a fact-sheet for public dissemination? Might your class to sponsor or cosponsor a community forum on the topic? Again, what would be a first step you could take?

Option 3. Read your local newspaper, particularly the editorials and letters to the editor. Find an issue of interest to you that is in the news—juvenile crime, quality of day care, etc. Identify the ways in which social science research might inform the debate. Write a letter to the editor conveying this information.

Annunciation

There is a tendency for social change activists to focus on what is wrong with the world. We recount all the injustices and tragedies. But equally important is the development of a vision of that for which we are striving. Paulo Freire (1975) called this *annunciation.* Martin Luther King Jr.'s "I Have A Dream" speech drew its vibrancy from the vision he painted of the world as it could be. The activist Deena Metzger advised, "if you keep your eye on what's precious. The fear goes away. It's like if you see your kid running in front of a car, you run out and you get your kid. Because your eye is not on the car. *Your eye is on the kid*" (Rosenwasser, 1992, p. 112).

Individually or in small groups discuss the visions that propel your interest in social change. What would the world look like if your social change goals were achieved? Start small, then expand your vision. For example, people interested in combating violence against women might begin by imagining what it would be like to walk on an unfamiliar street (men might imagine a woman they care about walking down the street) in the middle of the night without any fear of attack. What might you imagine if you pushed this image even further?

Key Terms

allies	mindscapes
conscientization	modulative psychology
direct action	normative social influence
first order change	second order change
generative psychology	social change
horizontal hostility	social Darwinism
internalized oppression	tokenism
just world hypothesis	

Solution to puzzle on p. 155

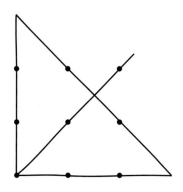

Chapter 7

Strengths Perspective

⌘ Introduction

Think for a moment about the field of mental health. Who do mental health practitioners help? Most mental health practitioners work with individuals who have problems: people who abuse substances, suffer from mental illnesses, or are undergoing severe stress. Mental health researchers study complementary issues such as the etiology of substance abuse problems, the genetic bases of mental illnesses, and the physical and mental toll of stress. The focus is not on mental *health* at all. The "mental *disorder* profession" would be a more appropriate term for much of the work done in the name of psychology, psychiatry, and the other helping professionals.

The editors of one of the earliest books on community psychology challenged this state of affairs. They proposed that community psychology adopt a new fundamental orientation to human and social problems that is "growth oriented" rather than "pathology" oriented (Adelson & Kalis, 1970, p. 2). Throughout the field's history, community psychology's most influential thinkers have echoed this call. Julian Rappaport (1980) urged that community psychologists dedicate themselves to "looking for strengths and assets, competencies and skills, rather than trying to find deficits and weaknesses to categorize" (p. 94). Emory Cowen (1991) encouraged community psychologists to engage in the "pursuit of wellness" rather than the struggle to contain troubles. George Albee (1980) put the choice less equivocally, declaring that the "illness model of mental disturbance is evil" (p. 221).

Psychologists in other professions have begun to add their voices to this call. As one example, in 2000 the *American Psychologist* published a special issue on the topic of *positive psychology*, co-edited by Martin Seligman and Mihaly Csikszentmihalyi. This special issue included articles from several perspectives, including evolutionary bio-cultural, personality, health, and developmental psychology. The editors reminded us that prior to World War II, psychology had three missions: curing the mentally ill, improving the quality of life for everyone, and encouraging the talents of gifted people. They argued that it was time to return to these early roots and shift psychology's focus from a "preoccupation only with the worst things in life to also building positive qualities" (Seligman & Csikszentmihalyi, 2000, p. 5).

The importance of moving towards a strengths-based perspective is also embodied in recent federal, state, and local human service initiatives (e.g., Adams & Nelson, 1995; Foster-Fishman, Salem, Allen, & Fahrbach, 1999). Strengths-based human service delivery views the service recipients as competent collaborators in the change process. This requires a fundamental shift in thinking and behavior. Professionals no longer diagnose problems and devise treatments. Instead, clients are seen as most knowledgeable about what is wrong and what needs to change, and so their voices guide the intervention. Strength-based intervention does not attempt to tackle problems by addressing client deficiencies, but by building on consumer strengths.

As described in Chapter Six, fundamental shifts in thinking and behaving are difficult to achieve (see also Foster-Fishman et al., 1999). Insight into why the deficit model prevails can provide direction for those of us, including community psychologists, who seek to promote a strength-based approach to understanding people and creating change. This chapter first considers the phenomenon of victim blaming as an overarching framework for understanding the deficit perspective and then examines three important psychological theories that elucidate the dynamics of victim blaming: attribution theory, role theory, and labeling theory. Next, we look at the functions served by the deficit perspective and finally delineate why and how community psychology advances a strengths-oriented approach to human behavior.

⌘ A Framework for the Deficit Perspective: Victim Blaming

Psychology's focus on illness rather than health has led to a view of individuals as deficient. People require mental health services because they are sick, weak, or in some way lacking. As researchers and practitioners, psychologists have positioned ourselves as experts seeking to explain and correct the deficits that lie within the people we claim to help. The potential for this expert–patient model of helping to cause harm has been discussed and debated by many, but no one has presented the issues as compellingly as William Ryan.

In 1971, Ryan described the phenomenon of **victim blaming** in a book that revolutionized the thinking of many mental health practitioners. Victim blaming entails seeing people who suffer from a problem as deficient and responsible for that problem even though it results from social conditions.

Part of the genius of Ryan's analysis was his ability to show how well-meaning people harm those we purport to help. When Ryan wrote of victim blamers, he was not referring to uneducated, misguided, or ill-willed oppressors. He was writing about knowledgeable, socially conscious do-gooders. He was writing about you and me.

People who engage in victim blaming are often genuinely concerned for others and do not adopt victim-blaming perspectives out of a conscious desire to downgrade and injure vulnerable people. The negative ramifications of their actions are unintended and unsuspected. "Victim-blaming is cloaked in kindness and concern, and bears all the trappings and statistical furbelows of scientism; it is obscured by a perfumed haze of humanitarianism" (Ryan, 1971, p. 6). This veneer of goodwill and appearance of scientism makes victim blaming exceedingly difficult to combat.

Indeed, it has not been eradicated. Victim blaming is not a phenomenon of the past. Ryan's insights remain relevant more than three decades later. Although some of the terminology and important players have changed, the dynamic endures.

THE CULTURE OF POVERTY

Ryan's book focused on victim blaming in the context of poverty. In 1971, the notion of a **culture of poverty** was in vogue. Believers in the culture of poverty rejected the earlier view of poor people, especially poor Black people, as intellectually inferior, inherently lazy, or lacking in moral fiber. Victim blamers did not directly blame the victims of poverty for their predicament. Rather, they viewed the conditions under which poor people lived as responsible for their inability to get ahead. Fatherless families, uneducated mothers, poor nutrition, and social disorganization resulted in a culture of poverty characterized by defeatism, irresponsible behavior (including sexual promiscuity and poor job skills) and violence. This culture prevented young people from gaining the motivation and skills necessary to succeed.

Although culture-of-poverty explanations have an aura of care and sympathy, they continue to hold poor people responsible for their poverty. Social forces may have caused poverty originally, but the residue of these forces now lies within the individual. The conditions of poverty make poor people irresponsible, pessimistic, and unable to get ahead in this world. Thus, solutions best target poor people themselves: job training, compensatory education (e.g., Head Start), parenting classes, and community mental health services.

Person-centered conceptions of the problem of poverty deflect attention from larger social causes. An alternative problem definition might hold that poor people are poor because they have less money than everyone else. Problem solvers might then look to effect changes at higher levels of analysis, such as the structural barriers, both historical and current, that promote economic inequity. Solutions would *not* entail lecturing poor people about the importance of showing up to work on time or instructing them on how to write snappier resumes. They might not target poor people at all. They might focus instead on eliminating tax cuts, tax shelters, and tax deductions that benefit wealthy people in this nation. They might explore the promise of "caring capitalism" popularized by Ben Cohen and Jerry Greenfield of Ben and Jerry's ice cream, which linked the salary of the highest paid employee to the salary of the lowest paid employee. Success may not always mean tacking zero after zero to the salaries of CEOs while the wages of loading dock workers and receptionists hover around minimum wage (Ben & Jerry's, 2000; Lager, 1994).

By focusing on the shortcomings of people with relatively little social power, the means by which more powerful people gain advantages remain free from scrutiny. Let's look at one of William Ryan's examples (an example that remains relevant today) and a more recent success story.

EXAMPLES OF VICTIM BLAMING

Lead paint is dangerous. Young children who consume flakes of paint containing lead may suffer permanent brain damage or death. Ryan described some efforts to address this problem. A major pharmaceutical manufacturer distributed large posters detailing the dangers of lead paint and warning: "Lead Paint Can Kill!" A health department issued coloring books that urged parents to remain ever vigilant of this danger. These interventions were well intended, but Ryan saw no cause to praise them as "humanitarian" efforts. He recognized the importance of public awareness about the danger of eating lead paint but objected to framing the problem of lead poisoning in children as the result of neglectful mothers. He asked us to consider who really was responsible for the problem. In many slum houses, a succession of resident families experienced the trauma of having a young child seriously injured or killed by lead poisoning. Should we blame each of these families, one after the other, for failing to protect their children, or should we look instead at the problem of neglectful landlords who refused to spend money on necessary repairs and city agencies responsible for enforcing housing codes who turned the other way rather than requiring compliance?

Ryan reminded us that the presence of lead paint is illegal, and it is illegal to permit lead paint to remain exposed in a residence. Thus, we have an instance of victim blaming. The drug company with its poster and the health department with its coloring book displayed genuine concern, but the victims of lead poisoning were held responsible while the system that permitted it remained unchallenged—landlords did not remove the paint and code enforcers did not penalize the landlords. Ryan (1971) held that to ignore these law violations and hold responsible the mothers of sick or dead children is "an egregious distortion of reality. And to do so under the guise of public-spirited and humanitarian service to the community is intolerable" (p. 23).

Lead poisoning remains a common, tragic, and easily prevented disease in the United States. Activists continue to battle the systems that allow this danger to persist. For example, in February, 2001, the New York City Coalition to End Lead Poisoning filed an amicus brief to the New York State Court of Appeals in an attempt to hold a landlord responsible for the poisoning of a young child. They argued that landlords cannot be allowed to hide behind claims of ignorance and have a duty to make reasonable efforts to ascertain whether dangers exist in the houses they rent to others (New York City Coalition to End Lead Poisoning, 2001).

On occasion, efforts to remove the burdens of blame from the backs of individuals do succeed. Consider the tobacco industry. For over four decades, tobacco companies promoted the use of cigarettes. Little was done to stop them. Regulating business was seen as un-American; besides, the tobacco industry was not to blame. Cigarette companies did not force people to smoke. Individuals *chose* to smoke. For more than forty years, cigarette companies won every lawsuit brought against them. The tobacco industry had political clout and hundreds of billions of dollars on hand from the profitable cigarette business to fight attempts to hold them legally accountable for the harm caused by smoking. In the late 1990s, however, two small-town Mississippi lawyers declared war on Big Tobacco and ultimately brought the industry to the negotiating table (Frontline, 1998).

Mississippi's attorney general Mike Moore and his former classmate, attorney Dick Scruggs, gained access to internal documents showing that industry executives knew about the dangers of smoking in the early 1960's but continued to deny them for over thirty years. Perhaps the most damaging documents were those showing that Philip Morris had extensively studied smoking among teenagers. Cigarette companies knew that 90% of all smokers started smoking by the age of 18 and that smokers demonstrated extreme loyalty to their first brand (Coughlin, Janecek, Milberg, Weiss, Bershad, Hynes & Lerach, 1998). If youth could be persuaded that smoking a particular brand of cigarette was cool, they might begin a lifelong addiction that ensured revenue for the tobacco company for years to come.

The cigarette industry's willingness to direct advertising campaigns toward youth contributed to its downfall. Victim blaming holds individuals responsible for their problems, but youth are generally deemed less responsible because they are less mature, less experienced, and less able to make competent decisions. The tobacco industry's lack of concern for vulnerable youth contributed to their image as callous and malevolent, and the tides shifted. The problem of smoking ceased to be attributed to weak, anxious, and insecure individuals who knowingly chose to smoke, but rather to an ill-willed, calculating, and profit-hungry industry that conspired to hide and obscure scientific data that would have informed individual choices. In 1997, the tobacco industry agreed to a historic deal to pay $368 billion in health-related damages, tear down billboards, and retire Joe Camel, the cartoon figure featured in advertising campaigns targeting youth. Against the odds, a powerful industry was held accountable for the suffering previously blamed on individual victims.

HOW VICTIM BLAMING WORKS

Ryan (1971) outlined a four-step process to victim blaming.

> First, identify a social problem. Next, study those affected by the problem and discover in what ways they are different from the rest of us as a consequence of deprivation and injustice. Third, define the difference as the cause of the social problem itself. Finally, of course, assign a government bureaucrat to invent a humanitarian action program to correct the difference. (p. 8)

Let's look at these steps more closely.

In victim blaming, the consequences of a problem are framed as the causes. Marybeth Shinn (1992) provided an excellent example of this distortion in an article on how psychologists should address the problem of homelessness (see also Paradis, 2000). Person-centered studies of homelessness have documented the many ways in which homeless people are deficient. They suffer from psychiatric impairments, histories of unemployment, inadequate social networks, and so on. It's no wonder they are homeless! But do these deficits precede homelessness, or are they a consequence of it? Might mental illness and drinking problems *result* from trying to cope with life on the streets? Does life on the streets, without easy access to clean clothes, bathing facilities, telephones, and transportation, make it difficult to find and maintain a job? Might homeless people actually have extensive social networks that delay, but cannot prevent, homelessness?

In her careful study of homeless families, Shinn found that education history, work history, and social support networks did *not* play a role in causing homelessness. Mental illness and substance abuse increased the *risk* of homelessness but played a minimal role in causing it. Structural factors, such as a tight housing market, were far more important in predicting homelessness. This illustrates Ryan's (1971) notion of **exceptionalistic** and **universalistic viewpoints**. The exceptionalistic viewpoint sees problems as occurring because of an individual's unusual and unique situation. A homeless person becomes homeless because he or she loses a job or has a bout with schizophrenia. Such causes are particular to individuals and unpredictable. The universalistic viewpoint sees problems as occurring because of larger social conditions, such as housing shortages or high unemployment rates. Such conditions have general effects that could be anticipated by people willing to look beyond individual-level, victim-blaming explanations.

Shinn argued that even without data on the causes of homelessness, a historical perspective alone should demonstrate the shortcomings of an exceptionalistic, individual-deficit model of homelessness. She observed that people with substance abuse problems, mental illnesses, and poor employment histories are not a new phenomenon, and yet massive homelessness on the current scale has not existed since the Great Depression. Explanations for homelessness that focus on individual shortcomings cannot account for the dramatic rise in homelessness that began during the 1980s.

And what have we done to solve the problem of homelessness? According to Ryan, in the final step of victim blaming a government bureaucrat invents a humanitarian action program to correct the problem by changing the victim. People who operate from exceptionalistic viewpoints devise interventions that are local and remedial rather than broad based and preventive. Because these programs embody a false view of the victim as responsible for problems over which they actually have little control, such solutions are destined to fail. The failure of these social programs can then also be blamed on the victims, a phenomenon called **second-order victim blaming** (Dressel, Carter, & Balachandran, 1995).

Consider a humanitarian action program that assists its homeless clientele in obtaining low-cost housing. This program might help clients combat their substance abuse problems or other personal barriers to employment, or it might coach them in how to search for housing. It might even offer low-interest loans to cover security deposits. However, if there are no low-cost housing options available, these efforts will come to nothing. If, as is often the case, there are a *few* low-cost housing options, the program might succeed in helping a *few* clients obtain housing. These clients may be held up as examples of the program's success, while the clients who remain homeless (most likely those with more risk factors, such as mental illness or poor education) will experience second-order victim blaming. Other people in the program succeeded. If the unsuccessful clients were more competent/motivated/responsible, they could have succeeded too.

The effectiveness of programs to combat homelessness needs to be assessed at higher level—a documenting programs' impact on the homeless population, not individual success stories. If a shortage of affordable housing exists, helping one person to obtain living quarters simply means that someone else will be left, quite literally, in the cold. Consider the analogy of a game of musical chairs (McChesney, 1990, cited in Shinn, 1992). Individual problems, such as mental illness or substance abuse, do not affect the number of housing units (or, in the analogy, the number of chairs). Individual problems do not *cause* homelessness. They only affect vulnerability to homelessness—they determine who will be left standing when the music stops.

BLAMING AND FIXING

One reason why it is important to understand victim blaming is because of the strong relationship between our willingness to blame and our willingness to help (J. Jones, 1997). When we blame people for their situations, we feel anger at them rather than liking for them and are less willing to provide assistance (especially strength-based assistance).

Philip Brickman and his colleagues (1982) distinguished four models of helping that exist in the minds of both helpers and helpees and in the social institutions that provide help, such as hospitals and mutual help groups. The four models reflect the degree to which individuals are seen as responsible for a problem (who is to blame for past events) versus responsible for the solution (who controls future events) (see Table 7.1).

In the moral model, individuals are seen as responsible for both causing and solving problems. Others are neither obligated nor even able to help. The individual is seen as lazy or weak and helping consists of reminders about personal responsibility and the importance of initiative: "God helps those who help themselves."

In the enlightenment model, individuals are blamed for causing the problem but are not held responsible for the solution. Help consists of encouraging submission to higher powers: "It's in God's hands." The individual is seen as guilty or sinful. The enlightenment model can lead to a core restructuring of one's life that allows for change, but it can also lead to fanaticism.

In the medical model, individuals are responsible for neither the problem nor the solution. People are subject to forces beyond their control and, as a result, become incapacitated or ill. Experts are needed to treat the problem. Exhortations might include, "The doctor knows best." Although the medical model legitimizes helping, it fosters dependency (see also the section entitled *The Helper Role*).

Brickman and his colleagues advocated for a compensatory model in which people are not blamed for the problem but are held responsible for the solution. Helpers attempt to mobilize resources for the affected individuals. The individual is seen as deprived. Exhortations might include, "Life isn't fair," or "You must play the hand you are dealt." This model allows people to direct their energy outward toward problem solving rather than seeking to lay blame.

In distinguishing responsibility for problems versus responsibility for solutions, Brickman and his colleagues highlighted an important point. The way we frame problems influences our willingness to take action, our motivations for doing so, and the approaches we take. The critical shortcoming of all four of these models, however, is that they do not move helping efforts beyond the level of the

📄 Table 7.1   Models of Helping and Coping

Individual Responsibility for Problem	Individual Responsibility for Solution	
	High	*Low*
High	Moral model	Enlightenment model
Low	Compensatory model	Medical model

Based on Brickman, P., Rabinowitz, V. C., Karuza, J., Coates, D., Cohn, E., & Kidder, L. (1982). Models of helping and coping. *American Psychologist, 37*, 368–384.

individual. The compensatory model may foster more respectful and action-oriented helping relationships, but it cannot lead to significant changes if the social problem continues to be located within the individual and the solution is framed solely in terms of individual change.

⌘ Three Elucidating Psychological Theories

Additional insights into victim blaming can be gleaned from three psychological theories: attribution theory, role theory, and labeling theory. Let's look at each.

ATTRIBUTION THEORY

Attribution theory is perhaps the most influential and well-researched theory in social psychology. It seeks to explain how people make sense of human behavior. Social psychologists have found that people's ideas about the causes of behavior, our **attributions,** fall into two categories. **Dispositional attributions** look to personal qualities as the causes of behavior. People who smoke do so because they are anxious and find smoking soothing or because they are insecure and think smoking is cool. **Situational attributions** look to aspects of the environment as causes of behaviors. People smoke because the wealthy tobacco industry aggressively advertises and markets its product to consumers.

Attribution theorists have found that when explaining behavior, most people focus on internal, dispositional traits and underestimate the importance of environmental factors. In other words, we believe that people behave as they do because of who they are rather than the situation in which they find themselves. Lee Ross (1977) coined the term **fundamental attribution error** to refer to this phenomenon. Our preference for intrapersonal explanations increases the likelihood that people will be held personally responsible (i.e., blamed) for events that are actually determined by situational factors.

Many of social psychology's most famous experiments are famous because they demonstrate the unexpected power of the situation. Stanley Milgrams' (1963, 1974) classic studies of obedience surprised us with the finding that large numbers of people were willing to administer dangerous levels of shocks to innocent people. These results shattered predictions that only a handful of research participants, those with pathological and sadistic dispositions, would actually inflict harm willingly (an exceptionalistic viewpoint). Dispositional explanations could not account for finding that the majority of "normal" research participants obeyed the order to shock issued by an experimenter in a white lab coat. Milgram's experiment demonstrated the unexpected power of the situation.

ATTRIBUTIONS FOR OURSELVES VERSUS OTHERS

Interestingly, people do not always rely on dispositional explanations for human behaviors. The fundamental attribution error applies primarily to attempts to understand the behavior of *others*. We are far less likely to rely on dispositional explanations for our own behavior. Actors often see their actions as situationally determined, while observers see the same behavior as dispositionally caused. Social psychologists have termed this the **actor/observer difference** (e.g., E. Jones & Nisbett, 1972).

In part, the actor/observer difference results from our greater access to information about ourselves. If we lash out at an impolite salesperson, we may see this as a legitimate response based on previous difficulties at that store or an overreaction caused by frustrations at work earlier in the day. We do not see our lashing out as reflecting some deficit in our disposition. The next person in line who does not know about our history with the store or our stressful work experiences may simply see us as short tempered.

Greater access to information about ourselves does not completely explain the actor/observer difference, however. Although we generally make more situational attributions for our own behaviors, in some instances we prefer dispositional attributions. Researchers have found that people tend to take personal credit for successes but minimize failures by attributing them to external (situational) factors. Social psychologists refer to this tendency as *self-serving bias*.

ATTRIBUTIONS AND WORLDVIEWS

As described in Chapter Four, Western culture emphasizes autonomy and individual responsibility. Are non-Western cultures less likely to see people as individual actors and attend more to the social context? Is the fundamental attribution error universally pervasive, or do people from other cultures explain behavior as the result of situational factors? Two research studies that bear on these questions (cited in Aronson, Wilson, & Akert, 1997).

In the first study, Hindus living in India and Americans living in the United States were asked to describe behaviors exhibited by their friends and explain why those behaviors occurred (Miller, 1984). As expected, Americans explained their friends'

behaviors with reference to the kinds of people they were (i.e., dispositional attributions), while Hindus saw their friends behaviors as influenced by situational factors. These differences did not appear to be the result of people in the two cultures describing different sorts of behaviors. When American were asked to explain the reasons for the behaviors generated by the Hindu research participants, dispositional explanations again predominated.

A second study involved a comparison between the coverage of two mass murders in two different newspapers, one Chinese-language paper (*World Journal*) and one English-language newspaper (*The New York Times*) (Morris & Peng, 1994). In one case, the murderer was a Chinese graduate student in Iowa, and in the other case, the murderer was a White postal worker in Michigan. In both cases, American reporters focused on the personal attributes of the murderers, describing them as sinister or disturbed. The Chinese reporters emphasized situational factors, highlighting, for example, the murderer's lack of contact with the Chinese community.

Thus, it appears that people in Western cultures are particularly prone to the fundamental attribution error. Although both Westerners and Easterners consider dispositional factors, Westerners simply do not adequately consider situational factors, no matter how salient they are made (Norenzayan, Choi, & Nisbett, 1999; for an alternative view, see Takano & Osaka, 1999).

ROLE THEORY

Attribution theorists have demonstrated that as observers of behaviors, people (especially Westerners) underestimate the power of the situation. When we fail to consider the ways in which situations affect behavior, we risk holding individuals accountable for processes for which they are not responsible, thereby blaming the victim. One aspect of the environment that has a powerful but often invisible influence on behavior is the social roles we assume. Theodore Sarbin (1970) was a key proponent of **role theory**, which holds that in any setting, individuals exist in relation to other individuals. Role theory might be summarized as follows: "Implicit in any model of who *we* think we are is a message to everybody about who *they* are" (Dass & Gorman, 1985, p. 28).

Consider a courtroom. The individuals involved in this setting fulfill such roles as judge, plaintiff, defendant, prosecutor, eyewitness, expert witness, juror, and so on. In order for the setting to function smoothly, each participant must perform according to her or his allotted role. The status afforded to each role is an important determinant of the behaviors allowed to each player. For example, judges can talk whenever they want. Lawyers have prescribed periods of time during which they can talk. Within those time periods, they determine which witnesses get to talk, for how long, and in response to which questions. Lawyers can interrupt witnesses, and judges can interrupt lawyers and witnesses. These courtroom parameters are defined by roles. If a judge goes on trial as a defendant, she or he and can speak only when questioned by the lawyers or the presiding judge.

In explicating the importance of role status, Sarbin (1970) distinguished two types of status. **Ascribed status** flows from biosocial characteristics that cannot easily be changed, such as age, sex, and kinship. **Achieved status** results from one's activities and efforts, notably one's occupation. These two types of statuses are not independent. Ascribed status affects the ease with people can pursue achieved status. For example, the term *glass ceiling* refers to unseen barriers placed on women's professional advancement that prevent them from rising to the top of an organization.

Status is crucially important in society because high-status individuals have more varied and valuable roles available to them, more choice in the roles they perform, and the power to assign social roles to those with less status. People with low status have fewer choices and are subordinate to those of higher status; they have, according to Sarbin, *degraded social identities*. Degradation allows people to be treated unjustly—they are held accountable for (i.e., blamed for) the problems that result from their low social status.

THE POWER OF SOCIAL ROLES

The roles people assume greatly influence behavior. A laboratory study of prison behavior conducted at Stanford University (Haney, Banks, & Zimbardo, 1973) illustrated this well. Based on the flip of a coin, twenty-one psychologically healthy undergraduate men were randomly assigned to the role of either prisoner or guard, "Prisoners" were "arrested" by the local police at their homes and brought to a mock prison in the basement of a university building. There they put on rubber sandals and loose-fitting smocks bearing identification numbers. Stockings were placed over their heads to simulate having their heads shaved, and a locked chain was attached to one ankle to remind them of their captive status. The guards received khaki shirts and pants, a whistle, reflecting sunglasses, and a police nightstick.

The researchers believed that the social role of prisoner or guard would take over the behavior of study participants, but everyone was surprised at how quickly and dramatically this takeover occurred. Prisoners initially rebelled and then became apathetic. Guards became controlling and even sadistic, waking prisoners up in the middle of the night to do sit-ups and devising harsh punishments for small transgressions. The simulation was designed to last for fourteen days but was terminated after only six days. By that time, several prisoners had already experienced breakdowns and left the study. Although the young men knew that they were participating in a study and that they had been randomly assigned to their roles, being cast as prisoner or guard resulted in a startling transformation of behaviors and even personalities. In interviews conducted after the experiment, both prisoners and guards reported that they had not simply acted out their roles but had felt themselves to be prisoners or guards.

The students got so caught up in their roles that they lost sight of who they were and failed to relate to each other as fellow human beings. They were no longer whole individuals—they were simply prisoners or guards. As Ram Dass and Paul Gorman

(1985) observed, our roles (father and daughter, doctor and patient, helper and helped) prevent us from fully relating to each other and so lead us to diminish one another:

> The more you think of yourself as a 'therapist,' the more pressure there is on someone to be a 'patient.' The more you identify as 'philanthropist,' the more compelled someone feels to be a 'supplicant.' The more you see yourself as a 'helper,' the more need for people to play the passive 'helped.' (p. 28)

THE HELPER ROLE

One social role of particular importance to psychologists is that of helper. The most common conception of helping is based in the **medical model**. The medical model views clients as patients. A patient is someone who is sick, passive, powerless, and in need of help from experts. Experts are distant, powerful, prestigious, trained professionals who can assist the patient by applying scientific technologies.

A model of helping in which the power to help resides solely in the helper fosters dependency and can undermine the help recipient's sense of competence and ability to become well. Meanwhile, it reinforces the helpers' sense of themselves as socially useful and socially valued (Gartner & Reissman, 1977; Roberts, Salem, Rappaport, Toro, Luke, & Seidman, 1999). Frank Reissman (1965) called this the **helper therapy principle**. People who provide help reap rewards. Numerous examples exist. Tutoring interventions often find that the academic performance of tutors increases as a result of being cast in the role of helper, even when the person tutored shows no improvements in performance (e.g., Cloward, 1967; Li, 1989). A recent study of mutual help groups found that while group members who offered help to others showed improvements in psychosocial adjustment over time, receiving help was not associated with any mental health benefits (Roberts, et al., 1999).

LABELING THEORY

We have thus far discussed two important theories that elucidate the phenomenon of victim blaming: attribution theory and role theory. As described in role theory, the roles that we choose for ourselves or that others assign to us determine how we act. Proponents of the final psychological theory we will examine, labeling theory, would contend that role pressures occur because roles provide *labels* that define the parameters of interpersonal interactions.

PRIMARY AND SECONDARY DEVIANCE

Labeling theory explains why only some people who violate social norms are labeled deviant (e.g., Becker, 1963; Gove, 1980; Scheff, 1975). Most of us have engaged in illegal acts—drinking underage, driving above the speed limit. Despite these transgressions, we probably did not become "juvenile delinquents" or "criminals." Similarly, most of us have done things that might be considered crazy—talking to ourselves when we're alone in the car or returning to check and recheck that a door is locked or a stove turned off a few more times than necessary. Still, most people are not considered "mentally ill." Why not? Why is it that all of us violate social norms, but only a few of us are labeled as norm violators?

Behavior that violates a social norm may be called **primary deviance.** We all display primary deviance, and this may or may not bring us into contact with systems of social control, such as the legal system or the mental health system. If contact does occur, we may or may not receive the label of deviant. If systems of control do label us as deviant, we often have little choice but to act that role, and **secondary deviance** occurs. Secondary deviance requires systems level reactions to norm-violating acts that sustain these acts of deviance.

Labeling theory holds that two systems have the power to define deviance: the criminal justice system and the mental health system. In her exposé of the prison business, Jessica Mitford (1973) wrote, "When is conduct a crime and when is a crime not a crime? When somebody up There—a monarch, a dictator, a pope, a legislature—so decrees" (p. 71). The same might be said of mental illness. When is conduct a sign of mental illness and when is mental illness not mental illness? When a psychologist, psychiatrist, or someone else up There so decrees (e.g., Szasz, 1961). Psychologists hold enormous social power as labelers of deviance. At the same time, our accuracy in labeling (i.e., diagnosing) psychological disturbance is highly unreliable. This was demonstrated by David Rosenhan (1973) in his classic study entitled *On Being Sane in Insane Places* (see the Classic Research box) and has been reaffirmed by more recent scholars (e.g., Jensen & Hoagwood, 1997; Kirk & Kutchins, 1992).

In order to understand how labeling works, it is instructive to look at the conditions that increase the likelihood of secondary deviance. Thomas Scheff (1975) identified five such factors. First, when rule-breaking behaviors are highly salient due to their severity, frequency, or visibility, labeling is more likely. Someone who occasionally acts a little crazy in the privacy of his own home (getting out of bed a few times a night to confirm that the doors are locked) will likely avoid labeling. Second, if the actor is of low social status then secondary deviance is more likely. Thus, members of disenfranchised groups more often experience social control in response to rule breaking. A man with scraggly hair and tattered clothing wandering around a train station might be arrested for loitering, A clean-shaven man in a business suit lingering around the terminal for the same period of time would likely be ignored or even offered assistance. Social class may constitute the difference between "passing time" and "loitering" or between being labeled "mentally ill" or "eccentric."

The third factor Scheff identified as influencing secondary deviance is the social distance between the rule breaker and agents of social control. Although social power provides an opportunity for people of ill will to exercise social control over subordinate people, even well-intended control agents may misinterpret the behavior of culturally or socially distant people. For example, a Euro-American police officer might interpret a Chinese adolescent's unwillingness to make eye contact as an indication of guilt rather than a sign of deference. A mental health worker may attribute a homeless woman's poor hygiene to an inability to exercise self-care skills rather than a lack of opportunity to bathe or a belief that "unattractiveness" will offer protection from attack while living in the streets (e.g., Stark, 1986).

The fourth factor affecting the occurrence of secondary deviance is the amount of tolerance for deviance within a community. In many metropolitan areas (my home town of New York City comes to mind), there is enormous heterogeneity with regard to residents' dress, styles of speech, behavior, leisure activities, and so on. I remember, for example, a man who roller-skated through the streets of the city in a pink fairy outfit, complete with a magic wand. What is accepted as self-expression in one community might be confronted as deviance in another. The final factor affecting secondary deviance is the availability of alternative roles and interpretations of behavior that can normalize what might otherwise be seen as deviant. In New York City, a roller-skating fairy might be considered a performance artist or even a social critic.

In summary, the response of the community to an individual's primary deviance greatly affects the trajectory of that individual's life course. It determines whether she or he is imprisoned for disturbing the peace, committed to a hospital for the insane, or proudly pointed to as an example of "local color."

SELF-FULFILLING PROPHESIES

Labeling theory clearly demonstrates that social expectations influence future behavior. In an early paper on the relevance of labeling theory to community psychology, Julian Rappaport (1980) explained that, "calling a child retarded, mentally ill, delinquent and so on, may, because of the reactions it creates in the child and in others, narrow the number and kinds of behaviors available for problem solving" (p. 76).

Even if initially inaccurate, social expectations in the form of labels can create self-fulfilling prophesies

CLASSIC RESEARCH

David Rosenhan
On Being Sane in Insane Places

In 1973 David Rosenhan sought to determine if the people charged with caring for mentally ill people could actually distinguish them from mentally healthy people. He recruited three psychologists, one psychiatrist, a graduate student, a painter, and a homemaker to join him in posing as "pseudopatients." The eight pseudopatients made appointments at mental hospitals and upon arrival, complained of hearing voices that said "thud," "hollow," and "empty." This was the sole symptom they presented (and it was chosen because it did not typify any particular mental illness). After admission to the hospital, pseudopatients told the truth about their lives and acted as normally as possible. Indeed, they were motivated to behave normally as their release from the hospitals depended on their ability to convince the clinicians in charge that they were fit to return to the community.

The most important finding from Rosenhan's study is that not one of these pseudopatients was determined to be normal by any of the mental health professionals with whom they came into contact. The pseudopatients' hospital stays ranged from 7 days to 52 days, with an average of 19 days. Their treatments included extensive drug therapy. The eight pseudopatients were given a total of over 2000 pills (which they did not swallow).

One criticism of Rosenhan's study was that admission to the hospitals was based on the self-report of a behavior that was decidedly not normal—the complaint of hearing voices. If someone entered an emergency room with complaints of intestinal pains, she or he would likely be admitted and treated, even if the initial complaint was untrue. (e.g., Spitzer, 1976). Another less known study conducted during the same era did not rely on false symptom reports. Maurice Temerlin (1968) filmed an interview with a healthy individual, which he showed to graduate students in psychology, practicing clinical psychologists, and psychiatrists. Before viewing the film, some of the research participants heard an influential figure remark that the film was of particular interest because the man being interviewed "looks neurotic, but is actually quite psychotic." People in the control group heard no such remark. After viewing the film, research participants were asked to diagnose the man in the film and received a list of thirty possible diagnoses, including "healthy," from which to choose. Not a single person in the control group ever made a diagnosis of psychosis, however 60% of the psychiatrists, 28% of the psychologists, and 11% of the graduate students who overheard the remark diagnosed the man as psychotic.

Temerlin, like Rosenhan, found that the label of mentally ill provided a lens through which all of the labeled person's behavior was viewed. Rosenhan referred to this phenomenon as "the stickiness of diagnostic labels" (1973, p. 131) For example, clinicians interpreted the pseudopatients' normal family histories as pathological. As another example, pseudopatients first attempted to hide their efforts to record their experiences for the study so as not to arouse suspicion. They soon realized this precaution was unnecessary. The staff viewed the note taking as yet another sign of psychopathology.

It should be noted that although hospital staff did not identify the pseudopatients as imposters, the patients at the hospital were not so easily fooled. They often suspected that the pseudopatients were not mentally ill at all. Some of the patients inferred from the note taking that the pseudopatients were actually reporters investigating the conditions of the hospital.

One reason why staff did not identify the pseudopatients as normal while patients did is that staff had minimal contact with patients, and much of the contact that did occur was superficial. Indeed, patients often felt invisible to staff. Psychiatrists habitually ignored the pseudopatients' questions about possible release dates or eligibility for ground privileges, sometimes responding to their queries with absent-minded and disconnected comments, such as, "Good morning, how are you?" One nurse adjusted her bra in full view of the patients, not to seduce, but out of a lack of awareness that seeing eyes were watching her.

This groundbreaking study called into question a key assumption of psychology—that psychologists can indeed distinguish mentally healthy and mentally ill individuals. In addition, Rosenhan argued that hospitalized people take on the role of mental patient because of the way they are treated, not because of their supposed illnesses. Perhaps one reason why mental patients act crazy is that they are simply fulfilling the expectations of those around them.

by constraining the ways in which we interact with the labeled person. When we expect another to behave a certain way—as a criminal, for example, or as a crazy person—we find subtle ways of eliciting the very behaviors we expect. Even rodents are subject to the subtle force of people's expectations. In one study, one group of psychology students was told that their laboratory rats had been bred to be bright, and another group was told that their rats had been bred for dullness. After a training period, the rats believed to be bright actually ran mazes better than the rats labeled dull, even though all the rats actually came from the same strain (reported in Rosenthal & Jacobsen, 1968).

A classic study by Robert Rosenthal and Lenore Jacobson (1968) exemplifies the way in which expectations shape human behavior. Rosenthal and Jacobson objected to the willingness of school personnel to hold children from disadvantaged groups responsible for poor academic performance. Such individual-level explanations failed to consider environmental factors that contributed to the child's failure, such as teacher attitudes. They hypothesized that teachers' low expectations for disadvantaged children created self-fulfilling prophesies, and they devised an elegant experiment to test this idea.

In 1964, teachers at Oak School in South San Francisco (which primarily served low-income families) were asked to help validate a new test. They were told that the test had been developed at Harvard University to predict children's academic "blooming" (i.e., large intellectual gains). The test was actually an intelligence test used to assess the children's initial level of achievement. After taking the test, approximately five children in each classroom were designated as academic spurters, supposedly based on the results of the test. In actuality, the names of the "spurters" had been chosen randomly. The identity of "spurters" was casually conveyed to the teachers during the first staff meeting of the school year: " 'By the way, in case you're interested in who did what in those tests we're doing for Harvard . . .' " (Rosenthal & Jacobson, 1968, p. 6).

The experimental manipulation consisted of nothing more than casually informing teachers of which children they should expect to make large academic gains in the coming year. The children were retested at the end of the year. As Rosenthal and Jacobsen predicted, the children identified as spurters showed greater gains in intelligence than children who were not so identified. This was particularly evident among children in the primary grades (see

Our expectations create self-fulfilling prophesies. © Tribune Media Services, Inc. All Rights Reserved. Reprinted with permission.

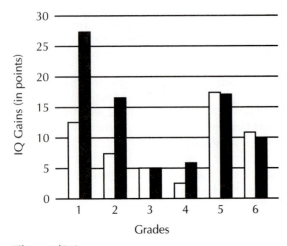

Figure 7.1

Gains in intelligence for spurters (black bars) and non-spurters (white bars). *From Rosenthal, R., & Jacobson, L.F. (1968). Teacher expectations for the disadvantaged.* Scientific American, 218 (4), 22. Copyright by Joan Starwood. Reprinted with permission.

Figure 7.1). Not only did the spurters perform better academically, they also received more favorable reports from their teachers. When asked to describe the children at the end of the year, teachers reported that the spurters as compared to the other children were happier, more curious, and more likely to succeed in later life.

Some children who had not been designated as spurters also showed large gains in achievement during the school year. How were these children perceived? Children who showed unexpected improvements were evaluated *un*favorably by the teachers. The more they gained, the less favorably the teachers rated them. This was particularly true for children in low-ability classrooms. "Slow-track" children in general were rated less positively, but more so when they failed to fulfill the teachers' expectations for failure. When "slow-track" children who were not expected to achieve improved academically, they were rated even more unfavorably than those who did not improve.

LABELING AND MARGINALIZATION

As Scheff (1975) observed, social distance facilitates secondary deviance. It also promotes victim

blaming. In one study research participants heard a story of the sexual assault of another student. In some cases the assaulted student had attitudes and beliefs that corresponded to those of the research participants, and in some cases the victim was dissimilar. If the victim was perceived as different, research participants were more likely to describe her as unintelligent and irresponsible and to blame her for the assault (Thornton, 1984).

One reason why low-status people are targets of victim blaming is that marginalization places them *apart* from mainstream society. Research suggests that people are more willing to assign blame to others who are socially distant and different. This perpetuates a vicious cycle because assignations of blame also justify social distance. For example, one study found that research participants who reported knowing an incest survivor disagreed significantly more with victim-blaming statements as compared to those who did not know an incest survivor (Staley & Lapidus, 1997). Another study found that research participants' desire for social distance from gay men and lesbians was directly related to their tendency to blame victims of AIDS for their illness (Lee, Campbell, & Mulford, 1999).

Stereotyping reinforces the social distance between groups of people. They keep us from coming into close contact with the targets, and they permit us to see targets as less than human. They provide convenient labels that facilitate dispositional, victim-blaming explanations for the problems they face. Black people are lazy. Jews are stingy. Women are hysterical. People with disabilities are incompetent.

As described in Chapter Six, stereotypes are generalizations about groups in which virtually all members are seen as having similar characteristics regardless of the actual variation within the group. Stereotyping may be seen as the application of the fundamental attribution error to an entire group of people. Behaviors that are distorted, if not caused, by marginalization, come to be seen as representative of the kind of people who compose that group. Thomas Pettigrew (1979) called the tendency to assign dispositional attributions to an entire group of people the *ultimate attribution error* (for evidence against the ultimate attribution error, see Hewstone, 1990). It appears that dominant group members not only hold people in outgroups personally responsible for misfortune, they attribute good fortune to situational characteristics (J. Jones, 1997). If a Black person loses a job, it's because he is incompetent, but if he gets a promotion, it's because of the organization's affirmative action policies. This is precisely the opposite of the self-serving bias.

Stereotypes, like other labels, create self-fulfilling prophesies. We stereotype someone in terms of appearance or label them based on their actual or expected behavior. This early impression shapes the way we act toward that person and consequently the way that person behaves towards us. An unwillingness to assign meaningful work to Black people may make them feel unvalued and uncommitted to the menial task at hand, thus they appear "lazy" or "incapable." Biting comments about Jews' tightness with money may disincline them to share anything, making them seem "stingy." Patronizing attitudes about women's emotionality may make them frustrated and angry, which then justifies the label "hysterical" or "overly emotional." Our unsolicited help of disabled people may prevent them from exhibiting competent behaviors, confirming our views of them as "weak" and "helpless."

Stereotypes, which Claude Steele (1997) called "threats in the air" shape not only how dominant group members view target group members, but also how target group members view themselves. Through the process of internalized oppression (see Chapter Six section entitled *Awakening to Injustice*), victims as well as labelers come to accept deficit views. They too believe the stereotypes and negative images that prevail in society and so become convinced of their own inferiority and unworthiness. They may come to see themselves as deserving of blame.

⌘ Functions of the Deficit Perspective

The deficit perspective is a powerful force, a force that many mental health professionals, including community psychologists, strive to counter. I have delineated three important psychological theories that bear on the deficit perspective in the belief that

an awareness of why the deficit perspective prevails can suggest ways of opposing it. Let's now consider the multiple functions served by the deficit perspective at both the individual and systems level. For each of these functions I have delineated general dynamics and then examined specific implications for the mental health profession.

THE NEED TO FEEL SECURE

In general, people devise causal attributions in an effort to render the world more meaningful and stable (e.g., Strickland & Janoff-Bulman, 1980). When we encounter someone who has experienced hardship, we try to understand why that happened and prefer explanations that help us to feel secure.

THE HUMAN NEED FOR SAFETY

In his work on the *just world hypothesis*, Melvin Lerner (1970, 1980) found that people want, even need, to believe that what happens in the world happens for a reason. Thus, we deal with the fact that misfortune and injustice occur by searching out weaknesses in the victims that justify their suffering. If we can hold individuals responsible for falling victim to crime, illness, or accident, then the world is not random. More importantly, *we* need not live in fear of becoming victims ourselves. Bad things only happen to bad people, and so we, by being good, can be spared (see also Walster, 1966; Coates, Wortman, & Abbey, 1979).

The need for safety does appear to play a role in victim blaming. One study found that people who were more fearful of becoming infected with AIDS were more likely to blame gay men for contracting the disease (Anderson, 1992). There is even a social psychological term for explanations of other people's behavior that keep us from feeling vulnerable ourselves: **defensive attributions** (e.g., Burger, 1981; Shaver, 1970).

When we encounter someone who has experienced injustice or misfortune, we may look for a difference between ourselves and the unfortunate victim that explains why they *deserved* the misfortune while we do *not*. Marginalized social identities increase the chances that a person will experience a variety of misfortunes (e.g., poverty, physical and mental illness). At the same time, they provide for agent group members a convenient and salient difference that can explain for why that misfortune occurred (e.g., Fiske & Taylor, 1984; McArthur, 1981). This may be one reason why a society *needs* people who are socially marginalized—to help dominant group members feel safe.

Interestingly, the need to feel safe may also lead people experiencing misfortune to blame themselves. If misfortunes occur through our own fault, the world makes sense and we can avert future traumas by behaving differently. Ronnie Janoff-Bulman (1979) distinguished two types of self-blame. *Behavioral self-blame* leads people to feel more in control by attributing misfortune to behavior, which is modifiable. Rape survivors might, for example, learn self-defense techniques or resolve to travel in risky areas only in the company of others. *Characterological self-blame* involves attributions to a less modifiable source—one's character. Rape survivors may attribute rape to their personal deficiencies, seeing themselves as weak, unworthy, and some how deserving of rape. Although behavioral self-blame may allow individuals to respond more positively to rape, both types of self-blame locate the problem and the solution (if any) within individuals, thereby deflecting attention from the societal factors that perpetuate the problem.

THE DYNAMICS OF DIAGNOSIS

Victim blaming allows people who do not experience trauma, misfortune, or injustice to distance themselves from the victims and feel safer as a result. People in the helping professions have an additional distancing tool at their disposal. Mental health professionals can use diagnostic labels to create a safe distance between themselves and victims of misfortune.

People in helping professions are not immune to the feelings of vulnerability that come from encountering victims of misfortune. Not only do these encounters remind professionals that we too can fall victim to harm, additional feelings of helplessness result if we find ourselves unable to help. Camille

Wortman and her colleagues (1995) observed that one of the most frustrating aspects of dealing with people experiencing extreme suffering is that one can say and do little to improve their situation. When one person is put (or puts herself or himself) in the position of providing help to another, feelings of helplessness result when the need for help exceeds the helper's ability to provide help (e.g., Wortman & Lehman, 1985).

Diagnosis is a distancing technique that can protect professionals from becoming overwhelmed by the reality of another's suffering and the feelings of helplessness that come from an inability to end the pain to which the professional is privy. Ram Dass and Paul Gorman (1985) described the process:

> We put some idea between ourselves and the suffering. In comes Mary Jones, hurting real bad. As she sits across the desk she suddenly becomes Mary Jones, 'schizophrenic.' With a flick of the mind we've turned a person into a problem. (p. 60).

FEELING BETTER ABOUT OURSELVES THROUGH SOCIAL COMPARISON

Seeing others as deficient can allow us to feel secure. It can also help us to feel good about ourselves. People assess their own abilities by comparing themselves to others (Festinger, 1954). Thus, another possible explanation for the tenacity of deficit perspectives is that evaluating someone else unfavorably serves to enhance one's own sense of self (Taylor, 1983; Wills, 1981).

MAINTAINING SELF ESTEEM

Victim blaming in the form of stereotyping and prejudice can help people feel better about themselves. Thus, people may be particularly prone to stereotyping when their sense of self is threatened. Research shows that people with low self-esteem tend to perceive members of outgroups more negatively (e.g., Thompson & Crocker, 1990). In one series of studies, researchers bolstered the self-images of some research participants by engaging them in self-affirmation and threatened the self-image of other participants by providing negative feedback. People with a bolstered self-image were less likely to evaluate others negatively, while people whose self-images had been threatened were more likely to engage in stereotyping and also derogated the stereotyped targets in an effort to increase their own self-esteem (Fein & Spencer, 1997).

A strong sense of self can reduce the need to engage in victim blaming. Another series of studies showed that people who feel that they are liked by others because of who they are (as opposed to what they have achieved) are less likely to try to boost their own sense of self at the expense of others. They also have less need to distance themselves from people who are portrayed negatively (Schimel, Arndt, Pyszczynski, & Greenberg, 2001).

WOUNDED HEALERS

The tendency to feel better about ourselves by viewing others as deficient is particularly dangerous for those of us in the helping professions. Helping is a complex phenomenon that does not always flow from purely altruistic intentions. Helping also fulfills the helper's personal needs for self-esteem, status, power, and intimacy. The notion of the **wounded healer** helps explain why some people are drawn to the helping professions. As discussed in the examination of role theory, to cast one person in the role of helper (strong, expert, needed) is to cast another in the complementary role of helpee (weak, incompetent, needy). Thus, helping professionals may dedicate themselves to helping others as a means of avoiding their own personal shortcomings and weaknesses.

> The therapist who is ill at ease with himself, feeling lonely and lost and without power, finds an almost wholly satisfying refuge in the profession of psychotherapy, where he is admired and seemingly loved and can enjoy intimacy without the risks of involvement, where he learns techniques to deflect criticism and justify himself, and where he is engaged in an unquestionably valuable profession. (Maeder, 1989, p. 257)

Woundedness does not necessarily interfere with one's ability to help. Carl Jung held that, "Only the wounded doctor can heal" (cited in Miller & Baldwin, 2000, p. 246). The experience of being wounded allows the empathy, perspective-taking, and sense of connection necessary to help others. It can also lead to disconnection and a focus on the other's deficiencies.

RECONCILING SELF-INTEREST AND HUMANITARIANISM

Victim blaming allows us to locate problems within individuals. As a result, we need not consider the larger social forces at play. People who benefit from the status quo may promote conceptions of problems that allow existing social forces to remain unexamined.

APOLITICAL PROBLEMS

If poverty can be blamed on poor people's lack of motivation, we need not consider the role of society's opportunity structures, structures that provide some people with social influence and economic security. Many people who benefit from the status quo do not, however, want to believe that benefits occur at a cost to others.

Ryan (1971) saw victim blaming as the resolution of a conflict experienced by well-meaning, liberal, middle-class individuals. These people intend no harm and may find racism, poverty, and oppression personally appalling. At the same time, they stand to lose a lot of power and economic advantage should a massive reorganization of society and a redistribution of wealth occur. Ryan (1971) described victim blaming as a brilliant reconciliation of humanitarianism and self-interest. The victim blamer

> can, all at the same time, concentrate his charitable interest on the defects of the victim, condemn the vague social and environmental stresses that produced the defect (some time ago), and ignore the continuing effect of victimizing forces (right now). (p. 7).

Given the adaptive nature of culture, it would follow that intervention efforts are more effective when they work *with* rather than against cultural forces. When mental health professionals abandon the deficit perspective, interventions with diverse people become life-enhancing, respectful of people's subjective experience, and ultimately more successful. Gerardo Marín (1993) argued that culturally appropriate interventions must reflect the values and subjective experiences of group members. As a result, we find new avenues of influence (see also Ortiz-Torres, Serrano-García, & Torres-Burgos, 2000). For example, Hispanics who smoke cigarettes are particularly concerned with the example they provide to their children. These concerns suggest new approaches to intervention, approaches that could be influential with a variety of populations.

An appreciation of diversity allows us not only to expand our ideas about problems and devise interventions that are more helpful to individuals, it can also change the way we think about communities and community health. Marginalized people suffer from a lack of opportunity. Theodore Sarbin (1970) asserted that one role for community psychologists is to expand opportunities for people with "degraded" social identities, thereby allowing them to assume socially valued roles. This coincides with the notion that building community assets requires a commitment to recognizing and utilizing the gifts of every community member. Kretzmann and McKnight (1993; Kretzmann, 1995) argued that this is particularly important with regard to people who have previously been defined solely in terms of the deficiencies—too young, too old, too disabled, or too poor to make any real contributions. People in socially marginalized groups often constitute an untapped community resource.

Supporting valued social roles for marginalized people may entail creating new social roles or supporting people in the roles they value. A recent study of one marginalized group, senior citizens, highlighted the importance of valued roles to well-being (Krause & Shaw, 2000). The researchers asked a nationwide sample of 884 elderly individuals to identify the social roles that were most important to

them (e.g., parent, grandparent, voluntary worker, church member). Study participants then rated the amount of control they had over this role. The researchers found this sense of control predicted mortality, even after controlling for other factors that affect longevity. Older people actually lived longer if they maintained a sense of control over the social role that they defined as most important to them.

As described above, scholarship on positive mental health at the individual and community level is still in beginning stages. We have much to learn, especially through increased attention to non-Western cultures. For example, scholars of African Americans' health have highlighted the importance of resistance to oppressive environments and the power of spirituality (e.g., Edwards, 1999; García Coll, Lamberty, Jenkins, McAdoo, Crnic, Wasik, & Vásquez García, 1996). Although different social groups may highlight different components of individual and community strengths, these components likely have implications for all of us. If cultures are indeed partial solutions to previously encountered human problems (D'Andrade, 1996; see the *Promise of Community Psychology* section in Chapter Five), then there should be some agreement on what constitutes healthy adjustment to the extent that human problems exist in similar forms across the globe. The basic components of health (and illness) may be fairly constant across cultures and historical eras, although the particularities in the manifestation (and interpretation) of health may vary (e.g., Edwards, 1999). A more complete picture of individual and community health and strengths will emerge from an awareness of the qualities helpful to different groups living under a variety of human conditions.

EMBRACING SOCIAL CHANGE

Deficit perspectives encourage us to locate social problems within individuals, thereby eliminating the need for social change. Because psychologists are charged with labeling deviance, we can perpetuate an unjust status quo with our diagnostic labels. For example, African American slaves who fled servitude were diagnosed with "drapetomania" an illness said to affect Black people and cats (Guthrie, 1998).

Not all deviations from behavioral norms are seen as indicating pathology, only those deviations deemed *undesirable*, and undesirable is often in the eyes of the beholder. Thomas Szasz (1961) warned that the label "mentally ill" is easily applied to people who do little more than make us uncomfortable. People who threaten our sense of security by disrupting the social order risk being labeled deviant.

Health consists of having the same diseases as one's neighbors.

Quentin Crisp

In a 1968 address to psychologists, Martin Luther King Jr. recognized the potential for mental health practitioners to preserve the status quo with labels and diagnoses. He noted psychologists' fondness for the word "maladjusted" and suggested that we consider the possibility for **creative maladjustment**. Sometimes maladjustment is desirable, he argued. "We must never adjust ourselves to racial discrimination and racial segregation. We must never adjust ourselves to religious bigotry. We must never adjust ourselves to economic conditions that take necessities from many to give luxuries to the few . . ." (King, 1968, p. 10).

Lillian Rubin (1976) adopted an extreme notion of creative maladjustment in her vivid description of life in working class families where frustrations and pain were part of everyday life. She suggested that the chronically unemployed and alcoholic inhabitants of working class worlds, the "hardlivers," who would not generally be characterized as healthy or competent may, however, be deserving of respect. These individuals are the ones who resist dehumanizing social conditions. She explained:

> The hard-livers are, in some fundamental way, the nonconformists—those who cannot or will not accept their allotted social status. They are the women and men who rebel against the grinding routine of life; the dulling, numbing experience of going to the

same mindless job everyday; of struggling with the same problems of how to feed, clothe, and tend the children without adequate resources; of fighting an endless and losing battle with roaches, rats, sore throats, and infected ears. (p. 34)

The people viewed as most deficient, most pathological, and most blameworthy may be the people whose voices have the most power to offer us the insights necessary for social change—if we truly listen.

⌘ The Promise of Community Psychology: Secondary Competence

Social expectations are often fulfilled, regardless of the merits of their foundation. As our analysis of the deficit perspective showed, people often respond to perceived deficits in ways that actualize and exacerbate them. Deficit views create vicious circles in which people's ability to demonstrate strengths become less and less likely. We have deviance, and then we have secondary deviance. We have victim blaming, and then we have second-order victim blaming. We have victimization, and then we have secondary victimization.

If we can support belief cycles that perpetuate pathology, can we also promote ways of thinking that maximize health? Can we help set into motion spirals of wellness? Perhaps we can. If psychology students think a rat is bright, it actually comes to run mazes better. If teachers expect children to show significant academic gains, they often do. This suggests an area of promise for community psychologists: the pursuit of what I will call **secondary competence**.

Community psychologists might seek to create self-fulfilling prophesies that bring out the best in individuals, families, schools, and communities. By focusing on the positive potential of people, we can create positive feedback loops that support health, wellness, strength, and competence. I once worked with a community agency to establish a residential program for homeless families. The agency devoted enormous time and energy to the search for a building. A promising, appropriately zoned house was finally found. As soon as the agency's plans became known, residents mobilized against the program, a phenomenon so common it has a name: **NIMBY** (Not In My Back Yard).

The confrontation between neighborhood residents and agency staff culminated in a tense and well-attended city council meeting. At this meeting, a neighborhood organizer presented a petition that he had circulated. It seemed that dozens of other residents agreed that a shelter catering to an unstable and potentially substance abusing, violent clientele should be kept out of this family-oriented neighborhood. He presented his signature sheets to the Council and returned to his seat. The director of the action agency testified next and in a dramatic moment, presented a petition of his own. He too had dozens of signatures from neighborhood residents who affirmed their willingness to have, in their community, a home where families who had fallen on hard times could receive the assistance they needed to help their children grow up to become contributing citizens. The final revelation: the two petitions contained the same signatures! If we can see people as strong, worthy, and motivated to reach their potential, we are more willing to help and more able to help in ways that support this potential.

Community psychologists and other change agents need to remain optimistic about the possibility that things can get better. In his analysis of social change through community organizing, Douglas Biklen (1983) identified several desirable qualities for community organizers: curiosity, a sense of humor, and the ability and desire to listen and analyze. He observed that we can work effectively "even if we lack one or several useful qualities, but one of these is clearly indispensable. Organizers must possess optimism" (p. 89).

At the same time, the problems on which we focus are long-standing, intractable, widespread, and perhaps have no once-and-for-all solution (Sarason, 1978). In doing the work of community psychology, our successes are generally modest and the setbacks inevitable. One might propose that chronic hope in the face of overwhelming odds is foolhardy. Indeed, psychological research suggests that optimism is an illusion. Numerous studies have shown that depressed people see reality clearly, while the more cheerful among us rely on some measure of distortion (e.g., Alloy & Abramson, 1979; Lewinsohn, Mischel, Chaplin, & Barton, 1980). How do we reconcile this with the widespread belief that mentally healthy people perceive their worlds without distortion (e.g., Jahoda, 1958)?

It appears that well-being requires illusions. Physical and mental health benefits accrue from a sense that we are in control over life events (even though our control may be limited), an emphasis on positive personal qualities (even though we have negative qualities as well), and the conviction that we will avoid misfortune and enjoy good fortune (even if we can't know this for sure) (e.g., Taylor & Brown, 1988).

Can we best promote secondary competence by encouraging distortions that have long been the hallmark of negative, not positive, mental health? Sandra Schneider (2001) found a way out of this conundrum through a new construct that she termed **realistic optimism**. She contended that realistic optimists maintain the brightest possible outlook within the constraints of reason. Realistic optimists do not seek to protect illusions by denying the world as it exists and convincing themselves that things are different than they are. Rather, they actively try to learn as much as possible about reality but cast what they learn in the best possible light.

As we have seen repeatedly in this book, there are many worldviews from which to glimpse reality. Although there may be some objective facts, what we make of these facts varies enormously. The amount of water in a glass may be indisputable, but we can choose to see the glass as half empty or half full. In a world of multiple realities, we can opt for perspectives that are both truthful and favorable.

More importantly, when we give ourselves and others the benefit of the doubt, we increase the chances of a positive outcome. Shelley Taylor and her colleagues (e.g., Taylor, Kemeny, Reed, Bower, & Gruenwald, 2000) showed that extremely optimistic beliefs not only help us to feel better about ourselves and our lives, they can actually help us to live longer. As Schneider (2001) put it, "realistically, having a good attitude is likely to pay off" (p. 260).

Social psychologists have coined the term *self-serving bias* to describe people's tendency to take personal credit for successes but attribute failures to external factors. The term suggests that people distort reality, but in all likelihood, people do bear *some* personal responsibility for success and environments do merit *some* blame for failures. Perhaps there is nothing pathological about giving ourselves the benefit of the doubt (unless there is clear evidence to suggest that we are refusing to confront some aspects of reality). The challenge posed by attribution theory is not how to correct self-serving biases, but how to give *other people* the benefit of the doubt as well. If we can find ways to do this, we may well bring out competence and success not only in ourselves, but in the people around us as well.

Pessimism and its cousin cynicism may help us to glimpse the *negative* parameters of indeterminate reality, but pessimism also promotes inertia, poor physical health, defeatism, and unhappiness (e.g., Seligman, 1990). As Leonard Duhl (1995), initiator of the healthy community movement put it, "A human race that believes it is drifting fatally and inevitably toward destruction of life will destroy life. The challenge is to retain some hope while not looking away from human cruelty, ignorance, and greed" (p. 8).

The realism afforded by a pessimistic desire to see the world as it is must be tempered by the optimistic desire to see the world as it could be. Optimism sustains action, promotes health, and also makes a more fulfilling world possible. Psychologists who are charged with helping people can best do their jobs by focusing on strengths and expecting the best. Schneider (2001) recommended that psychologists "take a lenient perspective in understanding human mistakes and frailties, cultivate an appreciation of human strengths and achievements, and actively create opportunities for improving people's life experiences" (p. 260).

Action Agenda

Person Blame in the Media?

In their classic article, *On Being Useful: The Nature and Consequences of Psychological Research on Social Problems*, Nathan Caplan and Stephen Nelson (1973) highlighted psychology's tendency toward victim blaming. They examined entries in *Psychological Abstracts* during the first six months of 1970 and found that 82% of the research concerning African Americans interpreted their problems as due to personal shortcomings. Other studies of newspaper coverage show that the tendency to conceptualize problems at individual levels is not confined to psychologists (e.g., Morris & Peng, 1994).

For a specified period of time (perhaps six months), collect articles from a variety of publications about a social problem of interest, preferably one in which marginalized identities play a role. You might, for example, collect articles about poverty among White people and among people of color or delinquency in poor and non-poor adolescents. You will best be able to collect a large number of articles if you work in groups. After you have accumulated a large number of articles, assess the attributions (situational and dispositional) the authors make about the people who "have" the problem. You might have to spend some time deciding how to assess attributions and establishing inter-rater reliability (i.e., everyone who makes these assessments uses the same criteria and comes up with the same classifications).

Which type of attributions predominate? Do you find different attributions for people in agent versus target groups? Do some newspapers favor more situational attributions (e.g., college newspapers, liberal publications, newspapers geared toward the marginalized group in question)? How do you think these attributions affect the readership?

If you obtain any interesting findings, might you write an article or letter to the editors of these papers describing your results and the implications?

Mapping Community Resources

All communities have strengths that can be built upon. Map your community's assets. There are many ways to do this. Here are a few ideas to get you started.

Consider the parameters of the community in which your college or university is located. Colleges in towns or small cities would likely consider that town or city itself as the community. Colleges in larger cities might define community in terms of a local neighborhood. After your class has agreed on the parameters, start getting ideas about assets from maps (e.g., parks, schools, libraries) or from the phone book (neighborhood associations, historical societies, recreational facilities). Ask residents what they like about the community. You might consider walking your community or parts of your community in small groups and noting assets that don't appear on maps (e.g., popular coffee shops, community gardens; see *http://www.communityyouthmapping.org.*). There are a variety of ways you might use these data. Here are a few suggestions:

▶ Obtain or create a large map of your community and plot the resources on the map. Do they appear in similar areas? Does this suggest interventions that might be targeted to particular areas?

▶ Consider what assets are available to different age groups or ethnic groups. You might want to talk to people in different groups to see what assets they appreciate. Do all people in the groups of interest know about and use the resources? Are there additional resources that need to be developed for particular groups?

▶ Think about the domains in which communities should be competent. For what needs should competent communities provide (e.g., spiritual, economic, educational, social, recreational)? How might you assess these domains of community competence? In what domains do you believe your community is competent? In what domains is it less competent? Think of a small step you might take, as an individual or as a class, to contribute to your community's competence in a particular domain.

▶ What do these assets say about your community? Think of a community problem of interest. How might these strengths be useful in tackling the problem? To whom might your information about community assets be useful? How best can you convey this information?

Community Competence Questionnaire

Using the parameters of your community defined above, complete the community competence survey (see Figure 7.3 on pp. 210–11) developed by Jean Goeppinger and A. J. Baglioni (1985), based on the work of Leonard Cottrell (1964, 1976). After completing this survey, discuss its strengths and weaknesses. Consider such questions as:

- What aspects of community competence does this survey capture well? Does it fail to capture aspects of community competence that you think are important?
- What might you assess differently? Think about the content of the questions and also the way the questions are asked. How does the information obtained from surveys differ from information that could be tapped using other methodologies (e.g., interviews, observations)?
- Do you think the survey would better capture community competence for some communities as compared to others? How so?
- What did you learn about the relationship of college students to communities? What are the ramifications of this relationship for students and for communities?
- Did you learn anything about yourself and your relationship to your community?

 **Key Terms**

actor/observer difference	medical model
achieved status	NIMBY
ascribed status	primary deviance
attribution theory	role theory
competent community	secondary competence
creative maladjustment	secondary deviance
culture of poverty	secondary victimization
defensive attributions	second-order victim blaming
dispositional attribution	situational attribution
exceptionalistic viewpoint	universalistic viewpoint
fundamental attribution error	victim blaming
handicapping environments	wellness
helper therapy principle	wounded healer
labeling theory	

Figure 7.3   Community Competence Survey

Adapted from Goeppinger, J., & Baglioni, A. J. (1985). Community competence: A positive approach to needs assessment. American Journal of Community Psychology, 13, *507–523.*

Community Competence Survey

        (C) = Commitment

        (P) = Participation

        (CC) = Conflict containment and accommodation

        (M) = Machinery for facilitating participant interaction and decision making

        (R) = Management of relations with the larger society

        (A) = Self–other awareness and clarity of situational definitions

(This survey does not directly assess Articulateness and Communication)

1. How long have you lived around this community?

2. About what part of your total family reside within this community? (C)

    a. A quarter or fewer   c. About three quarters

    b. About half   d. Nearly all

3. A. When you go to the bank, how often do you use a bank located in this community? (C)

    a. Always   b. Frequently   c. Sometimes   d. Never

   B. How often do you do your shopping in this community? (C)

    a. Always   b. Frequently   c. Sometimes   d. Never

   C. If you attend church/synagogue, how often do you attend in this community? (C)

    a. Always   b. Frequently   c. Sometimes   d. Never

   D. How often do you use recreation areas within this community? (C)

    a. Always   b. Frequently   c. Sometimes   d. Never

   E. When you need medical care, how often do you use doctors within this community? (C)

    a. Always   b. Frequently   c. Sometimes   d. Never

4. A. Do you belong to any local or service clubs? (P)

   B. Do you belong to any local patriotic or fraternal organization? (P)

   C. Do you belong to any organizations sponsored by local church/synagogue? (P)

   D. Do you belong to any local advisory boards, planning commissions, the town board or town council? (P)

   E. Do you belong to any other local groups or organizations? Specify _____ (P)

5. A. You probably know that people in a community have some different opinion about things. How much do the people in this community speak out about these differences? Would you say the people speak out always, frequently, sometimes, or never? (CC)

   B. How about working together to settle their differences? Would you say people work together always, frequently, sometimes, or never? (CC)

6. A. "People living in this community try to influence what goes on in the County." Do you: strongly agree, mildly agree, mildly disagree, or strongly disagree? (R)

   B. Would you say this influence is mostly phone calls or personal contacts or is it mostly membership on boards and advisory councils? (R)

7. A. How about the statement, "People living in this community try to influence what goes on in it." Do you strongly agree, mildly agree, mildly disagree, or strongly disagree? (M)

   B. Would you say this influence is mostly phone calls or personal contacts or is it mostly membership on boards and advisory councils? (M)

8. How do you feel about this statement: "The town council gets very little done here." Do you strongly agree, mildly agree, mildly disagree, or strongly disagree? (M)

9. What about this statement: "A few people have this town's politics pretty well sewn up." Do you strongly agree, mildly agree, mildly disagree, or strongly disagree? (M)

10. How do you feel about this statement: "My representatives to the county government do a good job presenting my views on most subjects." Do you strongly agree, mildly agree, mildly disagree, or strongly disagree? (R)

11. People in some towns are concerned with the issue of crime. How do you feel about this statement: "Crimes against persons or property are a problem in this community." Do you strongly agree, mildly agree, mildly disagree, or strongly disagree? (CC)

12. How about the statement: "Juvenile crimes are a problem in this community." Do you strongly agree, mildly agree, mildly disagree, or strongly disagree? (CC)

13. In many towns, there are a variety of services provided, such as parks and libraries, and places where people may get help for their physical or mental health problems. How do you feel about the statement: "The kinds of services located within this community are enough to take care of most people's needs." Do you strongly agree, mildly agree, mildly disagree, or strongly disagree? (A)

14. How do you feel about this statement: "Power to make community decisions is shared among leaders and the people living in this community." Do you strongly agree, mildly agree, mildly disagree, or strongly disagree? (M)

15. How do you feel about this statement: "Not many people around here seem to care much how the community looks." Do you strongly agree, mildly agree, mildly disagree, or strongly disagree? (C)

16. How about this statement: "All the residents of this community feel they can join clubs or organizations if they want to." Do you strongly agree, mildly agree, mildly disagree, or strongly disagree? (P)

17. On a little more personal level, in the past month, about how often did you get together with other folks who live in this community, that is, outside of work? Would you say you did this frequently, sometimes, rarely, never? (C)

18. Also in the part month, how often did you exchange favors, such as lending goods or helping with chores with others living in this community. Did you do this frequently, sometimes, rarely, never? (C)

19. Now, suppose for some reason or another you had to move from this community. Assuming your money situation would not suffer from the move, how would you feel about moving from this community? Would you be very sad, somewhat sad, somewhat happy, or very happy? (C)

Chapter 8

Stress and Coping

· ·

⌘ Introduction

Community psychology is a rich and diverse area of study. Thus, numerous theoreticians have sought ways of unifying the multitude of activities and viewpoints that fall under its rubric. Some have argued that community psychology is what community psychologists *do* (e.g., Spielberger & Iscoe, 1977). This tautological definition does not adequately capture the unique perspective and mission of the field.

In the preceding five chapters, I have described what community psychology *is* by identifying and examining each of its guiding principles. These principles are the foundation for the field's practice and research. They are stable, generally agreed-upon precepts that give the field its identity.[1] The next four chapters center on orienting concepts. Orienting concepts both reflect and influence what community psychology *does* (Novaco & Vaux, 1985). They are frameworks that summarize extant research, theory, and practice; give meaning to current efforts; and guide new inquiries. They bridge past knowledge, present practice, and future accomplishments.

As our knowledge base evolves and the context of inquiry changes, so do our orienting concepts.

[1]To be exact, the guiding principles do not describe what the field *is* but what the field *strives to be.* They embody the ideals of practice and research toward which we aim.

Indeed, orienting concepts, unlike fundamental principles, are *supposed* to change. We need new concepts to inspire novel insights, renew our energy, and shake us out of our collective intellectual complacency.

We begin our exploration of orienting concepts shortly after community psychology's birth. Five years after Swampscott, Betty Kalis (1970) noted that the concept of stress had begun to appear with increasing frequency in the community psychology literature. She proposed that crisis theory serve as an orienting concept to help shape and direct community psychology, arguing that it provided a user-friendly and open-ended conceptual model that suggested new and diverse directions of investigation.

In presenting her preferred orienting concept, Kalis (1970) recognized that a variety of other concepts might and should emerge. She observed, "As the field of community psychology develops, a number of conceptual models are appropriately being invoked in understanding and guiding research and practice" (p. 69). She reasoned that a field with such a complexity of concerns required a variety of theoretical approaches to meet the formidable challenge of synthesizing information.

As Kalis predicted, crisis theory and the closely related stress-and-coping framework did become a major orienting concept for community research and practice beginning in the 1970s and extending into the 1980s. Although Kalis laid the groundwork, the establishment of stress and coping as an orienting concept for the field is most often linked to another community psychologist, Barbara S. Dohrenwend. In 1978, Dohrenwend was elected president of Division 27 along with her husband Bruce P. Dohrenwend. In her presidential address, Barbara Dohrenwend proposed a model of stress and coping that could "provide a framework within which the apparently disparate activities of community psychologists takes on a satisfying coherence and directedness" (Dohrenwend, 1978, p. 2). We will examine Dohrenwend's framework in more detail later in this chapter.

Although the bulk of research and theory using a stress and coping paradigm occurred in the 1970s and into the 1980s, Barbara Dohrenwend was not the last to advocate for this orienting concept. In 1985, Raymond Novaco and Alan Vaux again lamented the lack of coherence in the field and echoed the previous calls by Kalis and Dohrenwend to use a stress-and-coping framework to organize the work of community psychology. More recently, in their 1997 community psychology textbook *Principles of Community Psychology: Perspectives and Applications*, Murray Levine and David Perkins affirmed the utility of stress and coping as an orienting concept. They described this concept in an early chapter entitled "A Conceptual Road Map of Community Psychology." While other orienting concepts have gained favor in the past few decades and have, to some degree, displaced the stress-and-coping framework, this early orienting concept remains a useful map for those of us navigating our way through the vast and complex landscape that is community psychology.

⌘ The Concept of Stress

One reason for the appeal of the concept of stress is that it is a familiar concept to which most of us can relate. The trials of Job described in the Bible are but one example of an ancient accounting of stress (Hobfoll, 1998). Through no fault of his own Job experienced a variety of stressful life events—his oxen, donkeys, and camels were carried off, his sheep and servants burned in a fire, his brother's house collapsed on his children, and his body became covered with boils. Job lost his family, his wealth, and his health. As he tried to make sense of his misfortune, he received support from three friends who came to comfort him.

All compelling heroes in literature and mythology, from Hercules to Harry Potter, confront major challenges that change the protagonist in fundamental ways. This is true in most people's life stories. Challenging events become defining moments in life as turmoil opens the door for insights and untried ways of behaving that would never have occurred otherwise. With the wisdom of hindsight, events that seemed threatening, harmful, or even tragic when they occurred (e.g., break up with first love, death of close family member) actually come to be seen as the experiences that made us who we are, sometimes changing our lives for the better.

Stress is broad concept. Many events and circumstances qualify as stresses—extraordinary events such as Hercules' attack from a many-headed serpent or Harry Potter's encounter with an escaped prisoner of Azkaban. More mundane events, such as the loss of one's first love, also qualify as stressful events. The breadth of the concept has both advantages and disadvantages. When a concept refers to such a wide variety of events and situations, it is difficult to know if all stress researchers are actually studying the same phenomenon. Attempts to draw conclusions across studies must therefore proceed tentatively. At the same time, the advancement of knowledge does not require unanimous agreement on precise definitions. Indeed, advancement may depend on generality as well as precision. Although each study requires an explicit definition of how the researchers define and measure key concepts (that is, their **operationalization**), a more complete understanding of the concept emerges when a multitude of researchers each approaches their studies from a somewhat different perspective. All of psychology's important constructs (stress, aggression, and intelligence, to name a few) have differing definitions that capture layers of meaning.

Still, our understanding depends on some agreement about what it is we are studying. **Stress** is a disturbance in the homeostatic balance of a person's life. It is induced by environmental demands that exceed the individual's (or system's) coping resources. Thus, stress is taxing and has adverse cognitive, behavioral, and physiological effects. The nature of these effects varies, however, because stress results from a transaction between the person and the environment. Its effects are mediated by individual and social factors. As we track the development of stress-and-coping frameworks, the relevance of these characteristics should become increasingly clear.

EARLY STRESS RESEARCHERS

Modern research on stress is often traced to the work of Erich Lindemann. In 1942, a tragic fire at the Coconut Grove nightclub killed 500 people. Lindemann (1944) studied how relatives of those who perished adjusted to the deaths of their loved ones. He found that family members needed to do "grief work," which entailed letting go of the relationship with the deceased person, accepting life without that person, and forming new attachments. If people did not grieve adequately, they suffered psychological impairment. If, however, they succeeded with their grief work, they could become psychologically stronger than they had been before the trauma. Interestingly, Lindemann predated many community psychologists in warning that psychiatrists and other mental health professionals could never assume responsibility for ensuring that grief work occurred due to the vast number of people who experienced loss. He recommended training other service providers (e.g., social workers, ministers) to help people deal with losses.

Lindemann's groundbreaking work focused on the psychological effects of a stressful event. A decade later, another early stress researcher named Hans Selye (1956) focused on physiological responses to the experience of stress. In order to elucidate the mind–body link, Selye studied a variety of different stresses, including overcrowding and everyday hassles. He found that diverse events triggered similar defensive reactions, which he called the **general adaptation syndrome (GAS)**. The GAS consists of three stages. First is the *alarm* stage, during which the experience of stress activates the sympathetic nervous system. This stage is characterized by a short-lived physiological reaction, as indicated by an increase in heart and respiration rates. In the second stage, the *resistance* stage, the body attempts to defend against the chemical changes triggered during the alarm stage. If the stress persists, the third stage, *exhaustion*, occurs. This stage is characterized by physical depletion and can ultimately result in death. When multiple stresses occur, they take a cumulative toll on already-taxed individuals. Selye asserted that by helping people manage their responses to stress, psychological and physiological impairment could be avoided.

This early work inspired a colleague of Lindemann's, Gerald Caplan (1961, 1964; see also Golan, 1978), to delineate the dynamics of **crisis theory** (McGee, 1980). Caplan's theory drew on several of Selye's premises. Caplan believed that different types of crises resulted in similar responses. He also agreed that the experience of stress led to an initial, short-term response that paved the way for long-term adjustment. Caplan drew on Lindemann's work, as well. Caplan saw crises as events that disrupt a person's equilibrium and require some sort of effort to restore homeostasis. And like Lindemann, he believed that the crisis could result in either new vulnerabilities *or* new strengths. The word *crisis* comes from the Greek word meaning "to decide" and suggests a choice point—a situation that might be resolved in more than one way. Depending on how the crisis is resolved, people can grow as a result of their experience, or their functioning can be compromised. Crises entail both danger and possibility.

Developmental psychologists have long understood the role crises play in inspiring growth. Erik Erikson's stage model holds that crises at different ages lead to growth or problems in development. Jean Piaget highlighted the role of disequilibrium in motivating development. "Every classical theory of development has held—whether implicitly or explicitly stated, whether empirically or intuitively derived—that challenge and disequilibrium are harbingers of growth" (Gist, Lubin, and Redburn, 1999, p. 16). The growth potential of stress outlined by Caplan was largely forgotten, however, in the wave of research that followed.

⊙

What does not destroy me, makes me stronger.

—Friedrich Nietzsche

In the 1970s, interest in stress burgeoned. Provocative theories and research brought the concept to the attention of many, but the development of a simple user-friendly research tool revolutionized the field. A decade after Selye's work, Thomas Holmes and Richard Rahe (1967) constructed a list of major life events called the **Schedule of Recent Events (SRE)** and a companion list of event weights, the Social Readjustment Rating Scale (SRRS). The list of events resulted from the examination of the medical records of 5,000 patients. The forty-three events included on the SRE were the ones that frequently occurred in the months preceding the onset of illness (Brown, 1986). The SRE requires respondents to check any listed events that they experienced in the preceding year. Total stress scores were obtained by multiplying each event the respondent reported experiencing by the corresponding weight from the SRRS (see Table 8.1). The SRE quickly became the predominant research tool for assessing stress (Holmes, 1979).

Research using the SRE and similar instruments confirmed the link between stress and both physical health and psychological adjustment. The occurrence of major stressful events has been associated with heart problems, cancer, depression, anxiety, isolation, suicide, paranoia, aggression, and a host of other difficulties (Byrne, & Whyte, 1980; B. S. Dohrenwend, 1973; Jacobs & Charles, 1980; Gersten, Langner, Eisenberg, & Orzeck, 1974; I. Sarason, Johnson, & Seigel, 1978; Theorell, 1974; Vinokur & Selzer, 1975; see also Kessler, 1997). The wealth of studies inspired by the SRE focused on the link between stress and maladjustment. Throughout the 1970s, the potential for growth as a result of stressful incidents was largely ignored.

STRESS, COPING, AND COMMUNITY PSYCHOLOGY

As community psychology began to take shape in the 1970s, researchers and practitioners were drawn to the concepts of stress and coping for

📄 Table 8.1   Social Readjustment Rating Scale

Life Event	Weight	Life Event	Weight
Death of spouse	100	Trouble with in-laws	29
Divorce	73	Outstanding personal achievement	28
Marital separation	65	Wife begin or stop work	26
Jail term	63	Begin or end school	26
Death of close family member	63	Change in living conditions	25
Personal injury or illness	53	Revision of personal habits	24
Marriage	50	Trouble with boss	23
Fired at work	47	Change in work hours or conditions	20
Marital reconciliation	45	Change in residence	20
Retirement	45	Change in schools	20
Change in health of family member	44	Change in recreation	19
Pregnancy	40	Change in church activities	19
Sex difficulties	39	Change in social activities	18
Gain of new family member	39	Mortgage or loan less than $10,000	17
Business readjustment	39	Change in sleeping habits	16
Change in financial state	38	Change in number of family get-togethers	15
Death of close friend	37	Change in eating habits	15
Change to a different line of work	36	Vacation	13
Change in number of arguments with spouse	35	Christmas	12
Mortgage over $10,000	31	Minor violations of the law	11
Foreclosure of mortgage or loan	30		
Change in responsibilities at work	29		
Son or daughter leaving home	29		

Reprinted from *Journal of Psychosomatic Research, 11,* Holmes, T. H., & Rahe, R. H., The social readjustment rating scale, 213–218, Copyright 1967, with permission from Elsevier Science.

several reasons. First, stress centers on the interface between the person and her or his context. An event happens in the environment, and the affected individual must find a way to respond. Thus, stress implicates *both* people and environments. In addition, community psychologists were drawn to the opportunities for intervention. If people could be helped to cope during the period of disequilibrium, maladjustment could be prevented. Third, community psychologists were attracted to the stress framework's departure from the deficit perspectives. Stressful events could pave the way for enhancement as well as impairment.

In 1978, Barbara Dohrenwend highlighted the appeal of a stress framework to community psychologists when she presented her model of psychosocial stress to Division 27 (see also Sandler, 1979). She noted the link between stress and psychopathology that research using the SRE demonstrated so persuasively and asserted that if community psychologists wanted to reduce the incidence of psychopathology, we needed to focus our attention on the stress process.

Figure 8.1 depicts the model of stress outlined by Dohrenwend in her presidential address. This influential model will help organize the information presented in the remainder of this chapter.

The boxes in bold represent the previously discussed relationship between stress and adjustment. After the stressful event takes place, an initial response occurs, which affects the individual's long-term adjustment. Long-term adjustment can reflect impairment, growth, or a return to the previous level of functioning. The boxes that are not bolded reflect the individual and environmental contributions to the stress process. The circles at the periphery of the diagram represent avenues for intervention. Let's begin exploring this model by looking at the three

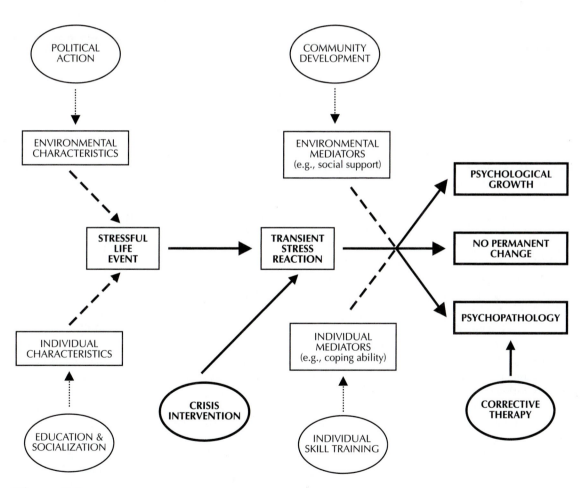

Figure 8.1
Dohrenwend's model of psychosocial stress. *Adapted from Dohrenwend, B. S. (1978). Social stress and community psychology.* American Journal of Community Psychology, 6, *1–14. Reprinted with permission.*

domains that affect adjustment to stress: the stress it-self, the individual, and the environment. Although these three components are discussed separately in the following sections, they are all interrelated—the role of each is defined in part by the other two.

⌘ Event Variables

What aspects of life events affect the degree to which they cause upset or enable growth? Many fea-tures of stressful events have been examined in the stress literature.

NUMBER OF EVENTS

One of the most important findings of early stress researchers was that life events exert a cumulative impact on mental and physical health. The more stress a person experiences within a limited time frame, the more that person's resources are taxed and the greater the risk for maladjustment. Michael Rutter (1979) examined how major stresses, including severe discord between parents, overcrowding, low socioeconomic status, and maternal psychiatric dis-order affected the likelihood of childhood psychi-atric disorder. He found that one isolated stress does not generally increase the risk of negative outcomes for children. Two stresses entail a fourfold increase, however, and the multiplicative effect is even more marked when four stresses co-occur. In a more recent study of 9,500 members of a large HMO, exposure to four or more adversities in childhood entailed a four- to twelve-fold increase in risk for alcoholism, drug abuse, depression, and suicide attempts in adulthood (Felitti, Anda, Nordenberg, Williamson, Spitz, Edwards, Koss, & Marks, 1998).

The multiplicative effects of stress would be less troublesome if stresses generally occurred in isola-tion, but stresses tend to co-occur. Look again at the events listed on the SRE (Table 8.1). Many of these events are interrelated. Trouble with one's boss may lead to a different line of work, financial troubles, and a loan. Divorce may lead to a change in resi-dence and social activities.

SEVERITY OF THE EVENT

In the earliest version of the still-popular SRE, total stress scores were derived by simply counting the number of events experienced (Hawkins, Davies, & Holmes, 1957). In the early era of stress research, in-vestigators focused on identifying generic stress re-actions (e.g., Selye's "general adaptation syndrome"). Thus, the commonalities among different types of stresses were emphasized. It soon became evident, however, that different events had different effects. A vacation, for example, would not take the same toll as the death of a spouse. This led Holmes and Rahe (1967) to develop their companion list of weights based on the severity of each event. Assessing the severity of events is not, however, as straightforward as one might initially think.

NORMATIVE AND INDIVIDUAL WEIGHTS

Holmes and Rahe (1967) established a weight for each event based on the amount of change or *social readjustment* it required. A group of 394 individuals assigned weights to each event based on an anchor value of 500 for marriage (later recalibrated to a weight of 50). Holmes and Rahe then averaged these ratings to obtain normative weights.

Subsequent researchers argued that a meaningful life-event scale must account for individual differ-ences in perceptions of life events. Knowledge of how events are perceived *on average* tells us little about how any individual views an event (e.g., Lazarus, 1991). The death of a parent may affect someone from a close, nurturing family very differ-ently than someone from a distant family in which the parent had been psychologically or physically absent. Researchers interested in accounting for subjective perceptions adopted methodologies that allowed respondents to assign self-determined weights to events (Byrne & Whyte, 1980; Sarason et al., 1978; Vinokur & Selzer, 1975).

Several studies have assessed which type of stress scores best predicts adjustment: simple counts of events, scores based on normative weights, or scores using individually determined ratings. Not all studies have found significant differences among techniques (Kale & Stenmark, 1983; Meuse, 1985;

Newcomb, Huba, & Bentler, 1981; Rahe & Arthur, 1978; Swearingen & Cohen, 1985a), but when differences are found, they generally favor individually determined weights (Chiriboga, 1978; Hurst, Jenkins, & Rose, 1978).

While the use of individual ratings avoids some of the problems encountered with normative weights, this methodology brings problems of its own, notably the possible confounding of subjective perceptions and adjustment. In other words, people who tend to rate events more negatively may be less well-adjusted to begin with. Thus, the stronger relationship between stress and adjustment obtained using individually determined weights is not really capturing the effect of events on later adjustment, but the effects of prior adjustment on perceptions of events (see Lazarus, DeLongis, Folkman, & Gruen, 1985; B. P. Dohrenwend & Shrout, 1985; Mueller, Edwards, & Yarvis, 1977; Rabkin & Struening, 1976).

MAJOR EVENTS AND EVERYDAY EVENTS

Most stress researchers have focused on major traumas. Richard Lazarus and Susan Folkman (1984) observed that traumatic events are fairly infrequent, yet most of us do not consider our lives to be stress free. They argued that everyday events, or **daily hassles** such as having concerns about one's weight or home maintenance concerns, constitute stresses that affect people's sense of well-being on an ongoing basis. Thus, Lazarus and his colleagues (Kanner, Coyne, Schaefer, & Lazarus, 1981) developed a measure of daily events.

Lazarus (1984) found that not only do hassles affect well-being, these daily irritants have a stronger relationship to well-being than exposure to life traumas. There are a number of possible explanations for this finding. It may be that daily hassles are manifestations of major events (e.g., Pillow, Zautra, & Sandler, 1996). Someone is more likely to gain unwanted weight when distressed about a failing marriage, for example. It is also possible that reports of daily hassles actually tap personality variables that are themselves related to health. Some suggest that minor hassles may be more subject to personal

interpretations than major events (see Hobfoll, Briggs, & Wells, 1995). A highly reactive and anxious person might experience traffic congestion as profoundly frustrating while easy-going drivers barely notice the delay. Regardless of the mechanism, research on daily hassles has encouraged stress researchers to rethink the literature's focus on large, infrequent events.

EVENT VALENCE

Holmes and Rahe derived event weights according to the amount of life change required *"regardless of the desirability of the event* (Holmes & Rahe, 1967, p. 213, italics in the original)." This strategy of ignoring event valence has been widely debated. Some researchers supported the view that the important dimension of a stressful event is the amount of readjustment required (e.g., B. S. Dohrenwend, 1973; Lloyd, Alexander, Rice, & Greenfield, 1980; Meuse, 1985; Rahe, 1974). Many others believed that the crucial component was the amount of *negative* change required or the event's *undesirability* (e.g., Gersten, et al., 1974; Gersten, Langner, Eisenberg, & Simcha-Fagan, 1977; Paykel, Prusoff, & Uhlenhuth, 1971; Ryff & Dunn, 1985; Sarason, et al., 1978; Swearingen & Cohen, 1985b; Vinokur & Selzer, 1975). Studies that compare the readjustment and undesirability views directly have generally found support for weights based on event undesirability rather than undifferentiated change (Chiriboga, 1978; Kale & Stenmark, 1983; Mueller, et al., 1977; Ross & Mirowsky, 1979).

What about desirable events? Holmes and Rahe (1967) included seemingly positive events on their list: marriage, vacation, gaining a new family member. Similarly, Lazarus and his colleagues assessed both daily hassles (as discussed previously) and daily uplifts (e.g., completing a task, visiting a friend). Do desirable events have an impact on adjustment? Research suggests that positive life events have little or no effect on physiological dysfunction or other indices of negative adjustment (e.g., Hirsch, Moos & Reischl, 1985; Mueller et al., 1977; Vinokur & Caplan, 1986). However, both desirable *and* undesirable events correlate with measures of positive adjustment (Block and Zautra, 1981; Ryff & Dunn, 1985; Vinokur & Caplan, 1986; Zautra & Reich, 1980; Zautra & Simons, 1979).

CONTROL, PREDICTABILITY, AND NORMATIVENESS

Another important event characteristic is the degree to which the event can be controlled. There are events in life we can control to a large degree (such as failing a test) and events that we cannot control at all (such as lightning strikes). Studies that differentiate controllable versus uncontrollable events find that events viewed as uncontrollable correlate much more highly with subsequent illnesses than controllable events (Stern, McCants, & Pettine, 1982; Suls & Mullen, 1981). This has led some stress researchers to develop measures in which events are classified as being within or beyond a person's control (e.g., B. S. Dohrenwend, Krasnoff, Askenasy, & B. P. Dohrenwend, 1978).

In general, people feel more control over events they can foresee. Sudden deaths, accidents, and illnesses, unexpected job losses, and natural disasters often occur with little or no warning. Thus, we cannot prepare for them emotionally or take proactive measures to mitigate their effects. Some events *can* be anticipated. One class of events that occurs on an expected timetable is **normative events**. Normative events are life experiences that generally occur during particular periods in the life span. Examples of normative events include puberty, high school graduation, and retirement. **Nonnormative events**, on the other hand, are not age-linked such as natural disasters or death of a close relative. Many researchers and theoreticians have noted the importance of distinguishing normative and nonnormative events, which have also been called *differentiated-maturational* versus *situational* crises (Aguilera & Messick, 1974), *accidental* versus *developmental* events (Morrice, 1976), and *idiosyncratic* versus *generic* crises (Jacobsen, Strickler, & Morley, 1968). Normative events differ from nonnormative events in two important respects: we can foresee them, and our peers experience them along with us. Thus,

normative events are particularly conducive to intervention. Researchers and practitioners can devise preventive efforts around these anticipated crises, such as programs to ease school transitions. Furthermore, we can simultaneously intervene with entire groups of people, such as an entering freshman class.

Research shows that normative events generate more stress when they occur out of their normal time frame—early retirement, for example, or the death of one's spouse at a young age (e.g., Borque & Back, 1977). We can hypothesize several reasons for this finding. Sense of control might come into play—if we have time to prepare for an event, we feel more in control. Off-time events also lack the sense of normalcy that exists when other people we know are going through the same experience. Research shows, for example, that being jobless at time of high unemployment is less detrimental to one's sense of well-being than joblessness at a time when rates of unemployment are low (Cohn, 1978). Experiencing a stress with others may also make it less threatening and confusing. Others can help us make sense of the event and provide models for how to cope.

CHRONIC VERSUS ACUTE STRESS

Life events, traumas, and daily hassles constitute stressful episodes in one's life. Some have argued that the stress literature has overemphasized episodic stresses and underemphasized enduring stressful conditions (e.g., Novaco & Vaux, 1985).

One source of chronic stress is the physical environment (Sigal, 1980; Stokols, 1978). For example, a naturalistic study of elementary school children in the flight path of Los Angeles International Airport found that children in high-noise schools suffered from signs of stress (Cohen, Evans, Stokols, & Krantz, 1986; see also Bronzaft & McCarthy, 1975). Some stress symptoms, such as high blood pressure, attenuated over time, but prolonged exposure continued to interfere with children's test performance. Chronic stress arises from the social

CLASSIC RESEARCH

Holmes and Rahe's Legacies
Influences on Studies Large and Small

Holmes and Rahe's (1967) simple, easy-to-use measure of stress, the SRE, revolutionized psychology and related fields. It had a broad impact on our knowledge of stress, coping, and adjustment, and also on our thinking about assessment techniques. Countless studies were inspired by their seminal work.

In the earliest version of the SRE, life events were simply counted to derive a stress score (Hawkins et al., 1957). The later versions used event weights that reflected the amount of social readjustment required, which was defined as "the intensity and length of time necessary to accommodate a life event *regardless of the desirability of the event*" (Holmes & Rahe, 1967, p. 213, italics in the original). Subsequent researchers found that undesirability was more important than change per se, and so events were then classified as either positive or negative. But does this dichotomy go far enough? Are events best classified as *either* negative *or* positive?

Some studies in the community psychology literature have attempted to tie Holmes and Rahe's research on life events to crisis theory. You will remember that crisis theory built on the belief that events have, at least potentially, positive as well as negative outcomes—they can lead to growth or maladjustment. The SRE's roots in the medical literature and goal of predicting illness led to an emphasis on pathological outcomes. In 1974, Norm Finkel switched attention to the growth-enhancing potential of events. He asked research respondents to report on their experiences with traumatic events and with events that he called *strens*. A stren was defined as the opposite of a trauma, that is, "an experience in an individual's life that builds strength into his [or her] personality" (Finkel, 1974, p. 266). One of the most interesting findings from Finkel's (1974, 1975) research was that individuals sometimes had difficulty deciding which category best described specific experiences in their lives. People described single events as *both* strens and traumas.

Finkel (1974) proposed the existence of three types of events: strens, traumas, and stren/traumas, which have elements of both. These stren/trauma events may be the same as those other researchers categorized as "ambiguous" (e.g., Kale & Stenmark, 1983) or "mixed" (Block & Zautra, 1981). Recognizing three types of events may be an advance over a negative–positive dichotomy, but it ignores the wisdom of one respondent in Finkel's (1994) study who wrote, "I cannot see how a stren experience if it is to have an influence on your life, can be devoid of trauma" (p. 268). Certainly seemingly positive events, such as the long-awaited birth of a child, inspire negative as well as positive life changes. Participation in the miracle of birth, feelings of overwhelming love, and the daily discoveries of childhood are among the unparalleled joys of parenting. And then there are the sleepless nights, worries about illnesses, lack of time for simple chores, and the continuously interrupted conversations with adult friends and relatives.

A stress study of my own grew from the conviction that *all* important life events contain, at least potentially, both positive (strenful) and negative (traumatic) elements. I assessed ninety-one events in a college student sample using a rating scheme that allowed respondents to rate each event twice, first based on how much negative change it caused and then on how much positive change it inspired. For some events the positive aspects predominated (e.g., success at an extracurricular activity), for some the negative aspects predominated (e.g., death of a close friend) and for others, the negative and positive aspects were comparable (e.g., remarriage of parents after a divorce). But *no event* was consistently viewed as purely negative or purely positive by the people who had experienced it (Kofkin & Reppucci, 1991).

I also compared my assessment technique (C below) with two parallel forms of the measure that corresponded to either Holmes and Rahe's social readjustment view (A below) or the undesirability view (form B). One third of the research participants received each version of the measure. I found that the assessment technique that allowed respondents to rate events as both negative and positive (form C) captured more of the variability in adjustment than the others (Kofkin, 1989).

A. *Social Readjustment Scale:*	Change of residence	0 1 2 3 4 5 6
B. *Desirability/Undesirability Scale:*	Change of residence	-3 -2 -1 0 +1 +2 +3
C. *Two-Dimension Scale:* (each event rated twice)	Change of residence	0 -1 -2 -3 0 +1 +2 +3

Holmes and Rahe's innovative research technique has influenced many people's thinking about stress and research. It has inspired countless studies of the impact of stress, both large and small, including one of my own.

as well as physical environment. For example, work environments can be stressful if bosses behave in arbitrary and coercive ways, if intense time pressures exist, or if tasks are extremely repetitive (see Novaco & Vaux, 1985).

Social position variables, such as minority status, have also been framed as chronic stresses (e.g., Moritsugu & Sue, 1983). Of course, it is not minority status per se that generates stress, but the conditions that surround it. Ethnic minority status may correlate with problems of adjustment because of its association with context-shaping events and conditions, many of which are outside individual control. People of color are more likely to be poor, live in violent neighborhoods, experience the challenges of migration and acculturation, and encounter racism and discrimination (GarcíaColl, Lamberty, Jenkins, McAdoo, Crnic, Wasik, & Vásquez García, 1996; Gonzales & Kim, 1997; see also Clark, Anderson, Clark, & Williams, 1999; McLoyd, 1990).

Some research suggests that chronic stress is more deleterious to health and well-being than acute stress (e.g., McGonagle & Kessler, 1990). A number of mechanisms might account for this finding. Chronic stress does not end, and so there is no

relief for the psychological and physical taxation it causes. To use Seyle's (1956) language, people under chronic stress enter the exhaustion phase. Not all researchers agree that chronic stress exerts a larger toll, however. Stevan Hobfoll's (1998) Conservation of Resource (COR) theory suggests that the most critical aspect of a stress experience is the loss of resources (Hobfoll, et al., 1995). People strive to obtain, retain, and protect their resources, which include homes, health, and jobs. Stress occurs when resources are threatened, lost, or not gained when gains were expected. Acute stress, which is associated with an identifiable loss, might therefore be perceived as more stressful than chronic stress.

Although COR theory posits a direct relationship between acute events and stress, chronic conditions such as poverty enter into the stress process through two avenues. First, they increase the chances that acute stresses occur (see Ennis, Hobfoll, & Schröder, 2000). A lack of access to reliable transportation and daycare can lead to job loss. Poorly heated homes and unsanitary living conditions increase health risks. A lack of resources also increases the stressfulness associated with acute stresses.

For example, money shortages increase the difficulty of coping with such events as a family health crisis, job loss, and even such minor hassles as a parking ticket.

RECENCY OF THE EVENT

Early researchers recognized that people pass through different stages as they cope with stress. Selye (1956) outlined an adaptational process that involved alarm, resistance, and exhaustion. Lindemann (1944) proposed three stages of mourning: shock and disbelief, awareness, and resolution of the loss. Other prominent researchers and theoreticians have outlined stages in adaptation. John Bowlby (1961) hypothesized that the loss of a loved one is followed by shock, yearning for the lost person (accompanied by anger), giving up the hope of seeing the person (accompanied by depression), and recovery and reintegration. These stages are similar to the five stages outlined by Elizabeth Kübler-Ross (1969) in her classic work on death and dying: denial, anger, bargaining, depression, and acceptance.

The stage view of stress and coping suggests that reactions to crises follow an expected pattern. Initially crisis theorists believed that these stages followed one another quite quickly. They proposed that the psychological issues associated with the occurrence of any stressful event would be resolved, either positively or negatively, within about eight weeks (Bloom, 1963; Caplan, 1961; Caplan, 1964; Darbonne, 1967). Subsequent research showed that the adjustment process often lasts much longer. One study found that the effects of undergoing surgery for cancer endured for up to 28 weeks (Lewis, Gottesman, & Gutstein, 1979). The Buffalo Creek flood in West Virginia had a persistent influence on a subgroup of survivors fourteen years after its occurrence (Green, 1995). The Holocaust continues to affect survivors more than half a century later and reverberates in the lives of survivors' children as well (Lomranz, 1995).

The disequilibrium and stress of major events do appear to be most marked in the earlier stages of adjustment, and stress measures that weight events differentially according to their remoteness in time can improve the researcher's ability to predict outcomes (e.g., Kale & Stenmark, 1983). Nevertheless, events in the distant past may continue to have a significant impact later in life. Major life events are best construed as influences that alter one's life course rather than episodic events that impact our lives only during a discrete period of adjustment (Felner, Farber, & Primavera, 1983; Hetherington, 1979).

⌘ Individual Factors

A number of event qualities influence the stress experience, including their number, severity, valence, controllability, predictability, and recency. Event characteristics alone do not determine event impact, however. We saw, for example, that individual circumstances affect the perceived severity of an event, with the death of a parent exacting a larger toll on someone from a close family. Stress represents an intersection between event characteristics, characteristics of the individual experiencing the event, and characteristics of that individual's surrounding environment. Let's look now at individual characteristics that affect the stress process.

Dohrenwend's model (Figure 8.1) shows that individual factors affect the stress-adjustment relationship in two ways. First, individual characteristics affect the occurrence of events (box on the lower left). In addition, individual mediators affect the way stress is resolved once it occurs (box in the lower middle of the diagram). These two avenues of influence are examined below.

INDIVIDUAL CHARACTERISTICS AND THE OCCURRENCE OF EVENTS

Different groups of people experience different life events (see Hurst et al., 1978; Kilmer, Cowen, Wyman, Work, & Magnus, 1998; Pine, Padilla, & Madonado, 1985). As described above, social position affects the likelihood of a variety of stressful events. For example people in lower socioeconomic classes and African Americans more often occupy high-stress and unstable jobs and live in violent and conflictual environments (e.g., Taylor, Repetti, & Seeman, 1997).

Consider again the events that appear on the SRE (Table 8.1). Although the SRE has been used with a variety of populations, the events are most relevant to a particular group—young adult Christian men. Many of these events focus on the workplace, and so this list would not be applicable to children in school or older people who have retired. A list of events for children might include not being picked for a sports team, while a list for seniors might include no longer being able to drive. The relative lack of family-related events on the SRE suggests the inappropriateness of the SRE for women. Research shows that women are more aware of and more affected by events that occur to important others, a child's illness for example (B. S. Dohrenwend, 1977; Kessler & McLeod, 1984; Lowenthal, Thurnher, Chiriboga, Beeson, Gigy, Lurie, Pierce, Spence, & Weise, 1975; Thomae & Lehr, 1986). The inclusion of Christmas on the SRE suggests a religious bias.

In addition to differences based on group membership, individual differences also affect what events occur. One source of individual differences that has received considerable attention in recent years is genetic make-up. Studies show that the occurrence of life events in the second half of the life span is largely determined by genetic factors (Plomin, Pederson, Lichtenstein, McClearn, & Nesselrode, 1990). How might genetic factors, which are decided before birth, influence the occurrence of events in later life?

It may be that genetically linked characteristics affect the likelihood that people experience certain events. For example, genetics help determine IQ, and people who score higher on intelligence tests are more likely to work in lucrative professions, as doctors, lawyers or engineers. Thus, they may be less likely to experience stresses stemming from economic crises. Genetics also influence personality characteristics, such as risk taking. People who take more risks may be more likely to experience personal accidents and injuries as a result, for example, of driving too fast in the rain or snowboarding on

treacherous slopes. Genetic components of diseases, such as alcoholism and schizophrenia, may also increase the likelihood of experiencing some life events, such as divorce or job loss.

INDIVIDUAL MEDIATORS: COPING STYLES

Individual factors affect which events occur. They also influence the impact stresses have once they happen. Barbara Dohrenwend used the term "mediator" to refer to qualities of people and situations that define the context of stress and influence adjustment (this differs somewhat from the current usage of the term, see Baron & Kenny, 1986).

In the 1970s and 1980s, stress research and theory focused on the direct link between stress and adjustment. The finding that stress scores could explain only about 10% of the variability in adjustment led researchers to search for better ways of measuring stress. Researchers devised assessment techniques that accounted for event characteristics such as severity, valence, and controllability. Some of these innovations led to improvements in predicting adjustment, but the improvements were usually small.

The modest relationship between stress and adjustment may be due not to imprecision in measuring stress, but to the fact that a variety of individual and environmental characteristics affect the impact of stress on adjustment. Since the 1970s, individual and environmental mediators of the stress–adjustment relationship have been studied. A vast literature has developed around one particular individual mediator: coping style (Holahan, Moos, & Schaefer, 1996).

Coping has been defined as "constantly changing cognitive and behavioral efforts to manage specific external and/or internal demands that are appraised as taxing or exceeding the resources of the person" (Lazarus & Folkman, 1984, p. 141). Simply put, coping is an attempt to reduce the negative impact of stress.

TYPES OF COPING

Several researchers have described different coping styles. Susan Folkman and Richard Lazarus (1988;

Lazarus, 1966) distinguished **problem-focused coping** and **emotion-focused coping**. Problem-focused coping directs attention to the stressful situation. This often involves evaluating possible responses and deciding on the best course of action. If one is fired from a job, is it best to try to appease the boss in order to get rehired, appeal the decision to a higher authority, or decide to look for another job? Emotion-focused coping directs attention not to the situation, but to the subjective experience of stress. Emotion-focused coping efforts that improve adjustment include positive reappraisal, in which the person focuses on the potential benefits of the events, and emotional expression, which involves talking about the event in order to come to terms with it. Escapism, denial, and wish-fulfilling fantasy are examples of emotion-focused coping efforts that may not be helpful as they seek to avoid the reality of the situation.

Which brings us to a second distinction between coping strategies: **approach** versus **avoidance coping**. Approach coping involves facing the stress and dealing with it directly (e.g., Holahan, et al., 1996). Avoidance coping involves distancing oneself from the stress by trying to forget the whole thing, occupying oneself with other activities, or seeking escape in alcohol and drugs. Avoidance coping has been associated with poorer psychological adjustment (e.g., Felton & Revenson, 1984).

People can respond to stress in a variety of ways. They can try to prevent the stress, alter the stressful situation, change the psychological meaning of the stress, or manage the symptoms of stress (Pearlin & Aneshensel, 1986). The appropriateness of different coping strategies depends, in part, on the nature of the stressful situation (e.g., Pearlin & Schooler, 1978). Strategies useful in resolving problems with one's boss would not necessarily be helpful in dealing with a diagnosis of cancer. Lazarus and Folkman (1984) found that while work-related events elicited more problem-focused coping, health-related events elicited more emotion-focused coping. This may be because concrete actions can alter work situations, whereas health conditions may be less amenable to change through action. An accurate appraisal of what can realistically be done in a stressful situation allows the stressed person to choose the most appropriate coping strategy.

COPING AND PERSONALITY

Individuals may find that different coping strategies are useful in different situations. In addition, individual characteristics affect the likelihood of engaging in particular coping efforts. A variety of personality characteristics have been studied in relation to coping, including anxiety, reactivity, and introversion versus extroversion (e.g., Costa, Somerfield, & McCrae, 1996; Strelau, 1995). One of the most researched aspects of personality as it relates to coping is negative versus positive thinking.

Many problems of adjustment stem from negative thinking about the events in our lives (e.g., Ellis, 1969). For example, some people catastrophize events so that disappointments, hassles, and setbacks are blown to gigantic proportions. Some people perseverate about events and prevent their resolution. Prolonged brooding can increase the detrimental effects of an event (Novaco & Vaux, 1985). Ideas about the causes of events also affect negative and positive thinking.

Chapter Seven examined attribution theory as a way of understanding how people think about an event's cause. People explain events with reference to either internal (dispositional) factors or external (situational) factors. Martin Seligman and his colleagues (e.g., Abramson, Seligman, & Teasdale, 1978) saw this distinction as one important aspect of people's *explanatory styles*. There are two additional components. People vary in their perceptions of the duration of the event's cause. Events can be seen as resulting from stable, long-lasting factors or unstable, short-lived factors. Finally, people differ in their perceptions of the generalizability of the event's cause. The cause can be seen as local and specific to the particular situation, or global and likely to occur in a variety of contexts. If a person makes internal, stable, and global attributions for negative events, then **learned helplessness** may result (Abramson, et al., 1978). When learned helplessness occurs, people believe themselves incapable of altering their fate, even if they can, and so do not cope well with adversity.

Consider, for example, students seeking to explain a bad test grade. One student might attribute the bad grade to having gone to a party the night before instead of studying. This is a dispositional attribution, but it is neither stable nor global. Thus, a decision to stay home and study before subsequent tests can lead to improvements in one's grade. A second student might attribute the bad grade to a lack of intelligence. Such explanations are internal (the student's cognitive abilities are innately inferior), stable (intelligence does not change from day-to-day), and global (intelligence affects performance in a variety of domains). The student sees bad grades as inevitable, and the belief in her or his incompetence dooms this student to failure.

Martin Seligman and his colleagues initially focused on the pathway from negative explanatory styles to depression. More recent research has looked at how positive explanatory styles facilitate healthy adjustment. People who explain events in optimistic ways cope more effectively with events (e.g., Holahan, et al., 1996; Peterson & Seligman, 1984; Peterson, Seligman, & Vaillant, 1988; Scheier & Carver, 1985; Scheier, Weintraub, & Carver, 1986; Schwarzer & Jerusalem, 1995). For example, Michael Scheier and his colleagues (1989) found that optimists as compared to pessimists recovered more quickly from heart surgery and had better long-term prognoses.

Another related personality construct that affects coping responses is sense of control (Cohen & Edwards, 1986; Rotter, 1966). People with an **internal locus of control** believe that their actions affect the occurrence and course of events. People who believe that their lives are controlled by outside forces have an **external locus of control.** An internal as opposed to external locus of control is associated with more positive outcomes following stress (Johnson & Sarason, 1978). For example, women diagnosed with cancer may actually lived longer if they believe they can control their cancer (Taylor, 1989).

OTHER INDIVIDUAL MEDIATORS

Research suggests that individual coping styles affect how people adjust to stress. It is not, however, the only important individual-level determinant of adjustment in the face of stress. Let's consider a few more.

Health behavior also affects the stress-adjustment relationship. One study showed that stress has a less deleterious effect on people who are physically fit (Brown, 1991), exercise (Kobasa & Maddi, 1985), and play sports (Danish, 1983; Reppucci, 1987). In addition to physical activity, relaxation techniques (e.g., meditation, hypnosis, biofeedback, and music therapy) affect the stress-adjustment relationship (Lehrer & Woolfolk, 1993).

Previous exposure to stress is another individual-level variable that helps determine adjustment. People who have already experienced similar stresses may have had a chance to find meaning in and adapt to the event; thus they may be less vulnerable to future stresses. Alternatively, previous exposure to stress may deplete resources so that the experience of one stress can increase vulnerability to future stresses. We do not yet know precisely what determines whether stress inoculates against or sensitizes to future stress (e.g., Block & Zautra, 1981; Hobfoll et al., 1995). The spacing of the stresses and their relative severity are probably relevant factors.

Yet another individual-level factor that affects the stress-adjustment relationship is religious involvement. A growing literature finds a positive relationship between involvement in religion and adjustment to stress (Pargament, Ensing, Falgout, Olsen, Reilly, Van Haitsma, & Warren, 1990; see also Levin, 1994; Levin & Chatter, 1998; McIntosh, Silver, & Wortman, 1993; Pargament & Maton, 2000; Smith, Pargament, Brant, & Oliver, 2000; Thorson, 1998). As described in Chapter Three, religious involvement encourages healthy living and positive thinking, promotes self-actualization, and addresses the human need to comprehend suffering and injustice. The rituals of religion also facilitate adjustment. They provide structure, stability, and a coherent meaning system during times of crisis (Vernberg & Vogel, 1993). Rituals and common beliefs also unite people and sustain connections among them. As we will see in the section on environmental mediators of stress, connections among people play an important role in buffering the effects of adversity.

PERSON–ENVIRONMENT FIT

As community psychologists know, we cannot understand stress and coping by studying individuals apart from their context. In considering individual factors that affect the stress–adjustment relationship, one must also consider the person–environment fit.

Suzanne Kobasa (1979) introduced into the stress literature, the construct of **hardiness**. People vary with regard to their ability to thrive in the face of stress. In an attempt to find out why some people handle stress better than others, Kobasa studied executives who experienced high levels of stress but did not suffer from stress-related illnesses. She identified a personality type that she labeled "hardy." Hardy individuals have a clear sense of direction, a sense of personal control, commitment to self and to work, and a tendency to see change as challenging rather than threatening. It seems, however, that hardiness may not only be a personality variable, but also an indication of person–environment fit. A sensation-seeking person who enjoys being tested by challenging situations would likely fare better in stimulating and demanding work environments (e.g., Smith, Johnson, & Sarason, 1978).

Consider, for example, air traffic controllers. Air traffic controllers continually make decisions about the flow of traffic that could have potentially disastrous consequences. This is a stressful job. Compared to pilots, air traffic controllers suffer from hypertension at six times the rate, develop diabetes at three times the rate, and experience peptic ulcers at twice the rate (Cobb & Rose, 1973, cited in Novaco & Vaux, 1985). Although most people would find controlling air traffic stressful, some people are better able to thrive under these work conditions than others. Imagine Sean Connery as an air traffic controller. Now think of Woody Allen.

⌘ Environmental Factors

The environment is the third and final player in Dohrenwend's (1978) model. Environmental factors, like individual factors, affect the stress-adjustment relationship in two ways. First, environmental characteristics affect the occurrence of events (box on the upper left in Figure 8.1). Second, environmental mediators affect the way stress is resolved once it occurs (box in the upper middle of the diagram).

ENVIRONMENTAL CHARACTERISTICS AND THE OCCURRENCE OF EVENTS

It is within our social environments that most stresses occur. Membership in families opens the door to the possibility of family conflict, the death of a relative, divorce, domestic violence, and a variety of other important events. The workplace is the source of firings, pay cuts and raises, and troubles with the boss. It is within our neighborhoods that we may be exposed to crime, gang activity, overcrowding, and physical hazards, such as noise, air, and water pollution (Taylor et al., 1997; Wandersman & Nation, 1998).

While unhealthy environments are associated with the occurrence of stressful events, healthy environments can help people to avoid stress. Families can provide the support needed to avoid school failure, resist substance abuse, and refrain from other problem behaviors that increase the likelihood of encountering stress. Consider again the events listed on the SRE (Table 8.1). There are numerous ways friends and families could help prevent many of negative events from occurring. Families and friends can discourage driving during a rainstorm and provide a safe harbor until the storm clears, thereby averting serious injuries. They can support marital relationship, thereby preventing a divorce. They can lend money that forestalls foreclosure on a loan. They can help troubleshoot about work experiences *before* difficulties develop that lead to being fired or provide emergency daycare that allows attendance at an important meeting.

Other microsystems can also help people to avoid stress. The workplace can help employees gain valuable skills, solve work-related problems, and enable them to remain employed and well paid. Religious settings can encourage healthy lifestyles and support family life (e.g., by offering marital counseling and child care). Neighborhoods provide infrastructures through which residents can satisfy their basic needs. For example, residents health and security can be fostered by the presence of food banks and crime watches (Sandler, 2001).

In understanding how environments affect the occurrence of stress, we also need to look beyond the proximal environment to larger systemic forces that exert their influences through microsystems. For example, a family's ability to meet basic needs increases in the context of robust economies and high employment rates (Long & Vaillant, 1984).

ENVIRONMENTAL MEDIATORS: SOCIAL SUPPORT

Just as the research on individual-level mediators of the stress-adjustment relationship has centered on one factor (coping styles), so too has research on environmental mediators focused on a single construct—**social support.** Although social support is a broad concept with varying definitions, it is generally viewed as interpersonal connections and exchanges that are perceived as helpful by the provider and/or the recipient. Research has clearly demonstrated a relationship between social support and health, both mental and physical (Caplan, 1974; Cassel, 1974; Cobb, 1976; Cohen & Syme, 1985). Indeed, social support plays an important role in sustaining life itself. Major studies in the United States, Scandinavia, and Japan find that socially disconnected people are two to five times more likely to die from all causes (Berkman & Glass, 2000).

The presence of supportive others during crises increases the chances that people will adjust well (e.g., Cohen & Wills, 1985; Cohen, Underwood, & Gottlieb, 2000; Kessler, Price, & Wortman, 1985). Social support cushions the impact of a variety of harmful stresses for people of all descriptions. One persuasive experiment assigned women with advanced breast cancer to either a social support condition or a no-support control condition (Spiegel, Bloom, Kraemer, & Gottheil, 1989). Women in the social support condition met weekly with other

patients and with doctors to discuss their concerns. They felt better than women in the control group and lived an average of eighteen months longer. Let's launch our exploration of social support by considering why it is helpful, then move on to an examination of who provides support, and end with a consideration of negative aspects of social support.

WHY SOCIAL SUPPORT HELPS

Support people can help in a number of ways, both directly and indirectly. The distinction between perceived and enacted support demonstrates that regardless of whether a stressed person actually receives social support, simply belonging to a web of human relationships can facilitate adjustment.

Perceived and Enacted Support. Some definitions of social support focus on enacted support, the actual exchange of resources between people. In times of stress, people call on friends and family members to lend an ear or a hand. Supportive transactions are not, however, the only way social support buffers stress. Some definitions of social support focus on perceived support—the belief that one is loved and valued (e.g., Cobb, 1976).

People have generalized ideas about the supportiveness of their social environment and the availability of support. People also have expectations about specific people in their social environments and their willingness to help. These feelings and expectations constitute perceived support (e.g., Pierce, Sarason, & Sarason, 1996). Interestingly, perceived support and enacted support do not necessarily coincide (see Lakey & Lutz, 1996). In one study, people who had been classified as either high or low in perceived support were observed interacting with friends following exposure to a stress. The individual's perceived support status was unrelated to the actual support provided by friends (Heller & Lakey, 1985).

Some researchers argue that perceived support affects adjustment to stress more than enacted support (e.g., Barrera, 1986, Cohen & Wills, 1985). If people believe that others are available to them in a crisis, the event takes less of a toll, regardless of whether support people are actually called upon or volunteer to help. This has led to the notion that social support may not be an environmental variable at all and that perceptions of support actually reflect personality variables, such as interpersonal sensitivity or the desire for intimacy (e.g., Gottlieb, 1983; Pierce et al., 1996). Personality likely plays a role in social support as well as in coping styles. For example, personality characteristics that promote positive coping (e.g., optimism, a sense of control) can also attract supportive social relationships. Social support is likely rooted both in the environment *and* in individual personalities (Lakey & Lutz, 1996). As described earlier, the characteristics of events, individuals, and environments work together to determine adjustment to stress.

Types of Support. In the section on individual mediators, coping responses were described as focusing either on managing the emotions generated by stress or addressing the stressful situation itself. Similarly, social support can help people cope with their emotional responses to stress or help ameliorate the actual effects of the stress.

Emotional Support. Social support fulfills a variety of emotional needs. First and foremost, it provides a sense of companionship (e.g., Mitchell & Trickett, 1980; Shumaker & Brownell, 1985). Companionship offers opportunities to engage in enjoyable activities and diversions that can be rejuvenating during times of stress. Perhaps more importantly, during periods of stress we benefit simply from feeling accompanied. I am reminded of the joke about the patient who advised his well-meaning therapist, "Don't just do something, stand there."

Social support also provides opportunities for stressed people to receive reassurance and encouragement. Stressed people benefit from the sense of being understood, respected, trusted, and valued (Gottlieb & Todd, 1985). Emotional support that bolsters self-esteem and self-confidence may be particularly important under conditions of stress when the stressed person's sense of control, and even their sense of worth, may be threatened (e.g., Cohen & Wills, 1985; Gottlieb, 1983; Holahan et al., 1996;

Sandler, Wolchik, MacKinnon, Ayers, & Roosa, 1997; Shumaker & Brownell, 1984). If social support enhances the stressed person's sense of mastery and efficacy, he or she may also cope more effectively with the demands presented by the stress.

In addition, supportive people provide opportunities for the stressed person to talk. Research shows that expressing feelings about a traumatic experience has therapeutic value (Pennebaker 1990; Pennebaker, Colder, & Sharp, 1990). For example, college students who wrote repeatedly about traumatic events found the writing to be upsetting in the short term but were less likely to visit the student health center and reported fewer illnesses in the six months that followed (Pennebaker & Beale, 1986). In another study, Holocaust survivors who disclosed the most about their experiences during World War II showed the greatest improvements in health over subsequent months (Pennebaker, Barger, & Tiebout, 1989). Self-expression may release the physical strain of holding back negative thoughts, allow the sufferer to gain perspective on the event, and foster close relationships with others.

Tangible Support. The emotional sustenance of social support is vitally important (e.g., House & Kahn, 1985), but it is not the only valuable aspect. Supportive others may also offer direct assistance. This may come in the form of material support (e.g., Cohen & Wills, 1985; Mitchell & Trickett, 1980). If someone is suddenly fired from a job, support people can supply food baskets to help tide the person over or even pay the next month's bills. If someone needs to spend time at the bedside of an ill family member, support people can babysit, mow the lawn, or walk the dog. Food, transportation, shelter, home repair—there are numerous types of tangible support that can help see people through stressful times.

Supportive others can also direct stressed people to relevant information and resources that enable them to cope (Gottlieb & Todd, 1985; Mitchell & Trickett, 1980; Sandler et al., 1997). They might, for example, refer a person who was fired to a local employment agency, a web-based job bank, or a recent magazine article on employment trends. Social support people can also help the stressed person assess the threat and gain a clearer and more complete understanding of the event's meaning and ramifications (Gottlieb, 1983; Gottlieb & Todd, 1985; Holahan, et al., 1996; Mitchell & Trickett, 1980; Shumaker & Brownell, 1985). They can, for example, help the person determine if the firing occurred because of individual factors ("You *did* always show up late."), characteristics of the work setting ("Your boss was such a tyrant."), or because of larger environmental factors ("Small businesses are closing all over the city."). They can then assist in planning a course of action and offer direct instruction on how to cope (Holahan, et al., 1996; Shumaker & Brownell, 1985), or serve as models of effective (or ineffective) coping (Gottlieb, 1983; Gottlieb & Todd, 1985; Sandler et al., 1997).

A third way in which support people can act as a resource is in using their skills or networks to intervene in the environment. A supportive co-worker might talk the boss into giving you another chance. A supportive neighbor might convince his aunt to interview you for another job.

Beyond Dyadic Interactions. Some researchers have focused on the functions of social support, in particular the ability of support people to provide emotional succor or tangible assistance. While the functional view of support centers on the level of the dyad, a structural analysis helps us to look at the larger support system.

How many people could you turn to in times of stress? Would these people also turn to you? How often do you see these people? How many of these people know each other? Are these people similar to you in terms of sex, age, ethnicity, profession? These questions tap structural aspects of social support networks.

Researchers focusing on social support networks assess such characteristics as the number of support people, the degree of reciprocity, the frequency of contact, social network density (interrelatedness of members), and the demographic homogeneity of network members. For example, some people have small, dense networks in which everyone knows each other. Other people have large diffuse networks

that correspond to segmented life domains (e.g., work friends don't know neighborhood friends, who don't know friends from the synagogue, and no one has ever met your family). Robert Putnam (2000) posited that a tightly knit community characterized by dense networks fosters honesty and trust. Reputations matter because network members are likely to encounter each other in the future and hear about one another through the grapevine. At the same time, dense communities exert pressure for homogeneity among members and tend to be distrustful of outsiders.

Different types of support may be required at different times. As an example, people in the early stages of grieving benefit from emotional support but at later stages need support that aids reintegration into normal social life (Shinn, Lehman, & Wong, 1984). When a spouse first dies, a small, close network of people can step in and sit by your bedside. Later on, when trying to adopt a new social identity as single person, a wider, less structured network can help introduce you around and involve you in a variety of activities (Walker, MacBride, & Vachon, 1977). This suggests the importance of broad social networks that have areas of density and also more dispersed network members. Putnam (2000) characterized the strengths of dense versus diffuse networks in this way: "Strong ties with intimate friends may ensure chicken soup when you are sick, but weak ties with distant acquaintances are more likely to produce leads for a new job" (p. 363).

WHO PROVIDES SUPPORT

Thus far, we have examined why social support helps without attention to the sources of support. Does it matter who does the helping?

Many people facing stressful situations turn to family members. Indeed, Gerald Caplan (1976) used the "ideal family" as a prototype for understanding social support more generally. An ideal family collects and disseminates information about the world, offers feedback and guidance, and grounds actions in value systems and codes of behavior. It mediates difficult situations—sharing in the problems and providing assistance in solving them. Families also furnish material aid—financial help, shelter, and so on. Ideal families are havens—a place to go when one is tired, hurt, or in need of nurture. When you knock, ideal families always take you in.

For many people, family members constitute the first line of defense against adversity. Based on her work with elderly populations, Marjorie Cantor (1979) proposed that the choice of support provider proceeds according to the primacy of relationships. For adults, spouses are the preferred source of assistance, and in their absence, support seekers turn to other relatives, and then to friends or neighbors. Formal organizations constitute a last option. For children, parents rather than spouse are the most important sources of support (see Garmezy & Rutter, 1983; Haggerty, Sherrod, Garmezy, & Rutter, 1994; Hetherington & Blechman, 1996; Wolchik & Sandler, 1997). Thus, developmental age affects where one turns for support.

Culture also play a role. Cultural norms about who should provide support to whom under what circumstances have a substantial impact on the shape of social support (e.g., Dilwoth-Anderson & Marshall, 1996; Dunkel-Shetter, Sagrestano, Feldman, & Killingsworth, 1996; Maton, Teti, Corns,

Vieira-Baker, Lavine, Gouze, & Keating, 1996; Sinha & Verma, 1994). A number of researchers have noted the crucial importance of family, including extended family, in the lives of ethnic minority group members. The impact of culture on social support is not simple, however. For example, respect of elders and strict gender hierarchies influences the flow of support between spouses and between generations in many Asian families (Dilsworth-Anderson & Marshall, 1996). As another example, despite the importance of family embodied in the cultural concept of *familism*, some research finds that Latinos are actually reluctant to seek support from family members (Kaniasty & Norris, 2000). Cultural norms affect the dynamics of support in numerous ways. As additional examples, some cultural traditions encourage emotional expression, and some do not; some foster interdependence and reliance on others, and some do not.

In the U.S. and many other countries women engage in more social support activities than men (e.g., Dwyer & Coward, 1991). Shelley Taylor and her colleagues (2000) have recently contrasted the commonly known "fight-or-flight" response to stress with the less-known "tend-and-befriend" response that characterizes women's reactions (see also Hobfoll, Dunahoo, Ben-Porath, & Monnier,

Calvin and Hobbes   by Bill Watterson

When you knock, ideal families let you in. Sometimes they even come to you. CALVIN AND HOBBES © Watterson. Reprinted with permission of UNIVERSAL PRESS SYNDICATE. All rights reserved.

1994). Women's inclination to care for others leads us to nurture and protect people in times of stress, while the propensity to befriend leads us to create and maintain supportive networks. Women's concern about relationships comes with benefits and costs; women are likely to have intimate relationships that can provide support but also have a greater number of people expecting help in times of stress (Belle, 1982; Hobfoll, 1986). The burdens of support fall disproportionately on the shoulders of women who are, for example, more likely to become the caretakers of disabled children and aging parents.

The nature of the support seekers' stress also affects who is approached (Litwak, 1985). Exceptions to the stereotype notwithstanding, women may be called upon for emotional support (a shoulder to cry on after the break up of a relationship, for example) while men might be called upon to help provide tangible assistance (help with home repairs, for example). Some challenges (e.g., the birth of triplets) require ongoing assistance from people in close proximity. Other problems (e.g., a cash flow problem) might require help from multiple friends across the miles (see Messeri, Silverstein, & Litwak, 1993).

One reason we approach different people to help with different stresses is that different people tend to offer different sorts of support. Remember the study by Emory Cowen (1982), that examined natural help-givers reported in Chapter Two. Cowen found that hairdressers and bartenders listened, offered sympathy, and tried to be light-hearted, while lawyers asked questions, gave advice, and pointed out the consequences of bad ideas. Other research shows that professionals, such as lawyers and doctors, tend to talk more and provide more information (Toro, 1986). Not only do different categories of people offer different types of support, but our willingness to listen also varies by category. In one study, cancer patients found offers of advice helpful if they came from professionals, but not from friends or family members (Dunkel-Shetter, 1984).

Given the different types of support that people offer, and our different ideas about the utility of this support depending on such variables as the source and the timing, it would make sense that people benefit from having a variety of support givers. For example, one study found that although family members are important sources of support, women adjusted more poorly to divorce if their support networks consisted *primarily* of family members (Wilcox, 1981). Is there a place for professional helpers in one's support network?

One of the most important findings of the 1961 report of the Joint Commission of Mental Health was that the vast majority of the population did *not* seek out professionals for help with mental health problems. Instead, they turned to family members, friends, neighbors, physicians, and religious leaders (see also Howard & Orlinsky, 1972). A more recent figure that points to the same conclusion is that only 1% to 5% of bereaved people seek professional help (Jacobs, 1993). Lindemann (1944) and others (e.g., Albee, 1959) have warned that there could never be enough professional helpers to meet the needs of all grieving and stressed people. Perhaps these scholars need not have worried about such shortages as the public has hardly been beating a path to our office doors.

There are many reasons why people do not approach professional helpers when faced with a crisis including the cost, the stigma of using professional services, and the lack of congruence between one's own background and that of most therapists (therapists are primarily White, middle class, and highly educated). Professional helpers may be most helpful when people have taxed their support networks or are dealing with crises that friends and family are ill-prepared to handle. Professional helpers are over represented, for example, in the support networks of people with major mental illnesses. Friends, neighbors, and acquaintances cannot always supply the quantity and quality of support that people suffering from depression or schizophrenia need (e.g., Schoenfeld, Halvey, Heemley-van der Velden, & Ruhf, 1986).

NEGATIVE ASPECTS OF SOCIAL SUPPORT

Although people most often turn to those closest to us in times of stress, these friends and relatives are not always the people most able to support us effectively. Camille Wortman and her colleagues (1995) found that bereaved people benefit from sharing their feelings of loss, but members of support networks may discourage this, saying, for example, that crying does no good. Support people may minimize the loss or promote a too-quick recovery, encouraging grieving people to date before they are ready, for example. They might also dispense inappropriate advice, perhaps telling someone to move to a new house without all the memories or to get a pet as a companion. Unhelpful exchanges can cause stressed people to withdraw from social relationships at a time when they need them most.

Well-intentioned members of a support network may also criticize grieving people for coping improperly—expressing too little or too much emotion, grieving for too long or not long enough (Coyne, Wortman, & Lehman, 1988; Shinn et al., 1984). Popular misconceptions about the universality of stages in grieving may lead people to believe they are being helpful when they are not. A review of five longitudinal studies, found that a substantial number of people who lost a spouse or child (as many as 78%) did not show what is believed to be the "typical" pattern of coping—intense upset in the initial weeks or months following the loss, and decreasing distress over time. Furthermore, some people never reach the resolution stage (Wortman & Silver, 1990). In a study of the loss of a child or spouse in a car accident, most bereaved people still reported painful thoughts and a lack of a sense of meaning many years after the loss (Lehman, Wortman, & Williams, 1987).

In additions to misconceptions about stages of adjustment, belief in a just world can also interfere with a support person's ability to be helpful. When we respond to misfortune by blaming the victim (see Chapter Seven) we do not help them cope. For example, a study of young women who had been raped found that unsupportive responses from others (e.g., criticisms for not being careful enough) far outweighed helping attempts that were perceived as supportive (Davis, Brickman, & Baker, 1991).

And the list of ways in which support network members impede positive adjustment goes on.

Indeed, psychological health sometimes is served by reconfiguring one's support network (e.g., Humphreys & Noke, 1997). Social networks can encourage unhealthy coping responses—encouraging people to deny problem or abuse substances. Support people also prevent positive adjustment if they foster emotional or material dependence. People have a basic need for relatedness and also a basic need to feel volitional and self-determined. The term *autonomy support* has been coined to describe the importance of encouraging of a strong self within the context of interpersonal relationships (R. Ryan & Solky, 1996).

Unhelpful comments and unsupportive reactions may stem from the strain suffering places on those closest to the stressed person. Support network strain may result from members of the support network also being affected by the stress. When a family matriarch dies, for example, the grief experienced by the matriarch's children might prevent them from being present for their own children who are simultaneously grieving the loss of their grandparent. In addition, providing support can be emotionally, physically, and financially exhausting. Caregiving can become a stress in itself (see Schulz, Visintainer, & Williamson, 1990). A study of homelessness found that people struggling financially often live with friends and relatives for extended periods of time and only become homeless after wearing out their welcome with supportive others (Shinn, 1992). Stressful experiences change the availability and quality of social support (e.g., Coyne et al., 1988). An interactive spiral often exists such that illnesses and other major stresses increase the need for, but decrease the availability, of helpful social support (e.g., Lane & Hobfoll, 1992).

⌘ Interventions

Now that we have discussed characteristics of events, individuals, and environments that affect adjustment to stress, let's discuss the implications of these characteristics for interventions. Consider once again the stress process outlined by Barbara Dohrenwend (1978; see Figure 8.1). In the first part of this chapter, we discussed the bolded boxes and the arrows connecting them. A stressful event occurs, which leads to a transient stress reaction and eventually a regained equilibrium that reflects growth, impairment, or no permanent change. We have discussed the three factors that affect this process: the stressful event or condition, the person, and the environment.

Now that we have looked at all the boxes in Dohrenwend's figure, let's begin to examine the circles on the periphery of the diagram. The circles represent means of intervention. Dohrenwend identified six. Only two of the six circles, however, impact the stress process directly: crisis intervention and corrective therapy. I have depicted this by connecting these two circles to the stress process with solid arrows. The next two sections of this chapter will focus on these two types of interventions. The interventions depicted in the remaining four circles exert their effects indirectly, through their effects on individuals and environments. The remaining circles will be discussed in Chapter Nine.

The interventions Dohrenwend labeled "corrective therapy" come into play during the last stage of the stress process, after the stressful event has run its course. Community psychologists today would no longer use the term Dohrenwend chose in 1978. Our goal is not to "correct" what is wrong with people, nor do we rely on "therapy" as a means of helping. We do, however, still attempt to assist people who have experienced problems as a result of adversity. In the ensuing discussion we will examine mutual help groups as an important context for gaining mastery over the ill effects of stress.

Crisis intervention also occurs immediately after the event happens, while the person (or group) is still in the midst of adjusting. Dohrenwend's term *crisis intervention* also hints of medical models and one-on-one helping exchanges, such as suicide prevention telephone hotlines (McGee, 1980). In recent years, community psychologists' interest in crisis intervention has extended beyond the individual level. We study, for example, how entire communities respond to crises that affect all community members. The literature on disaster responses will serve as an example of crisis intervention.

INTERVENING AFTER THE EVENT: MUTUAL HELP GROUPS

In the 1960s, researchers and practitioners became increasingly aware that most people experiencing stress did not seek professional help. They tended to rely on informal support networks instead: friends, family, clergy, or even hairdressers and bartenders. Sometimes people experiencing problems join together to offer each other support in **mutual help groups (MHGs)**[2].

Mutual help groups (MHGs) are established when ordinary people who share a common concern come together in settings they control to discuss their problems and learn from one another how to cope (Lieberman & Snowden, 1993; Salem, Reischl, Gallacher, & Randall, 2000). Mutual help groups are generally voluntary, democratic, nonprofessional, no-cost, and often spiritually based (Kingree & Thompson, 2000). MHGs are of great interest to community psychologists. They embody a view of people as capable of transforming their own lives and creating social change by joining together in community.

The most familiar mutual help group, Alcoholics Anonymous, began seven decades ago, and now claims two million members in the United States alone (Alcoholics Anonymous, 2000a, 2000b; see the Community Intervention box in Chapter Three). Alcoholics Anonymous has served as a model for countless other groups formed by overeaters, gamblers, and others struggling to cope. Alcoholism, like other problems of living, may be seen as a maladaptive effort to cope with stress. In addition, substance abuse inspires additional stresses. Thus, Alcoholics Anonymous and similar groups may constitute as a sort of "corrective therapy," whereby people help each other to improve their

---

[2]The term *mutual help group* is used in lieu of the term *self-help group* to emphasize that participants both give and receive help.

mental and physical health and devise better ways of coping with future stresses.[3]

Mutual help groups have become increasingly popular in recent years (e.g., Putnam, 2000). Across the country, people gather together in church basements, office buildings, living rooms, hospitals, and even shopping malls to improve their ability to function in a challenging world. In the United States, estimates suggest that 3% to 4% of the population participates in mutual help groups in a given year, and approximately 25 million people are likely to participate at some point in their lives (Kessler, Mickelson, & Zhao, 1997; Lieberman & Snowden, 1993).

Despite the popular view that MHGs are run by members, some, perhaps as many as 60%, are professionally led (Lieberman & Snowden, 1993). Thus, the boundaries between mutual help and therapy may blur. Nevertheless, the reach of mutual help groups extends further into the community than traditional psychotherapy. While psychotherapy is most attractive to young, verbal, intelligent, and financially successful people, MHGs appeal to the more "typical" American (Kessler et al., 1997; Lieberman & Snowden, 1993). This is not to say that all citizens use MHGs in equal numbers. Mutual help groups are most popular among women, Caucasians, and singles or divorcees as compared to married people (Katz & Bender, 1976; Kessler et al., 1997; Lieberman & Snowden, 1993).

Participation rates also vary by problem area. The most common focus of support groups is, by far, alcoholism. In research on support groups in four cities, AA groups constituted 87% of the 12,596 groups studied (Davison, Pennebaker, & Dickerson, 2000). Support groups most often form around problems viewed as stigmatizing or embarrassing (e.g., alcoholism, breast cancer, and prostate cancer more than heart disease, ulcers, or chronic pain). AIDS patients were 250 times more likely to participate in support groups than hypertension patients.

Given the finding that participation in MHGs is highest for people dealing with stigma, it is not surprising that these groups are an important source of support for people coping with marginalized social identities (e.g., Kingree & Thompson, 2000; Wuthrow, 1994). Exposure to people with the same identity who are coping well reduces self-stigma and allows insight into the public dimensions of private troubles (Gottlieb, 1983; Kingree & Thompson, 2000). As a result, adjustment to stress may improve (e.g., rates of depression and substance abuse may decline, see Kingree & Thompson, 2000). In addition, social change efforts may be launched as group members join forces to combat the environmental factors that make membership in a stigmatized group stressful.

Mutual help groups fulfill many of the functions of social support described earlier. They provide opportunities for emotional expression, companionship, insight, problem solving, a sense of belonging, and the exchange of resources (e.g., Humphreys, Finney, & Moos, 1994). Members both receive and provide knowledgeable support, advice, and information that can increase people's ability to cope actively and productively (Humphreys et al., 1994; Salem et al., 2000). Research suggests that providing help may be more beneficial to members than receiving help (Roberts, Salem, Rappaport, Toro, Luke, & Seidman, 1999).

Not all the news about mutual help groups is positive however. Some research suggests that they are not as helpful as many of us believe (e.g., Hinrichsen, Revenson, & Shinn, 1988; see also Levy, 2000). In addition, MHGs may not strengthen the larger social fabric. Robert Putnam (2000) suggested that support groups serve as a substitute for the intimate family and community ties that have weakened over time in our increasingly fragmented society. He observed that most forms of social participation co-occur. People who vote also join clubs and engage in community service. Of the twenty-two types of voluntary associations he studied, only mutual help groups were *not* associated with group affiliations in other realms. Putnam quoted Robert Wuthrow's (1994) statement that, some "small groups may not be fostering community

---

[3]Mutual help groups can also serve as a kind of crisis intervention in which people experiencing a stress seek help from similar others while they are still in the midst of responding to that stress.

as effectively as many of their proponents would like. Some small groups merely provide occasions for individuals to focus on themselves in the presence of others" (p. 152). As Judith Jordan (1992) observed, psychological perspectives that center on people's need to *receive* support may fail to acknowledge the broader need for mutuality and involvement in concerns that transcend narrow self interest.

INTERVENING WHEN THE EVENT OCCURS: DISASTER RELIEF

Crises are time-limited and anxiety-producing occasions that inspire feelings of uncertainty and highlight the inadequacies of existing personal and social resources (e.g., Miller & Iscoe, 1963). Immediately following a crisis, the affected person (or community) actively copes with the event by trying to determine its meaning and decide how best to respond. During the "transient stress reaction" (to use Dohrenwend's term) people demonstrate a heightened willingness to examine their situations and make changes (e.g., McGee, 1980). For example, a study of a stress management intervention found that people who had recently experienced significant negative events were most responsive to the new ideas and techniques presented in the intervention (Jason, 1998).

Crises are turning points that require those affected to do something new. Therefore, interventions occurring at this time have the potential not only to forestall pathology, but also to enhance competence (e.g., Rahe & Arthur, 1968; B. S. Dohrenwend, 1978). Many community psychologists recognize that in the immediate aftermath of a crisis, interventions can have profound effects.

Crisis intervention has its roots in the community mental health movement of the 1960s (McGee, 1980), and it experienced a revival of sorts in the 1980's, after post-traumatic stress disorder (PTSD) became an official diagnostic category (van der Kolk, van der Hart, & Burbridge, 1995). PTSD describes individual-level pattern of responses to life threatening experiences and extreme stress that includes: re-experiencing the trauma (e.g., intrusive thoughts, recurring dreams); persistent avoidance and numbing (e.g., feelings of detachment, avoidance of activities); and arousal (e.g., sleep disturbance, anger outbursts). The reinvigoration of the concept of trauma inspired by the entry of PTSD into the *Diagnostic and Statistical Manual* (DSM) also augmented an interest in community-wide traumas such as such as floods, hurricanes, and nuclear disasters (Ginexi, Weihs, & Simmens, 2000; Green, 1995; Kaniasty & Norris, 1995, 2000).

A plethora of new acronyms emerged to describe crisis intervention with distressed communities. People involved in Disaster Mental Health Services (DMHS) coordinated responses to community disasters by organizing community response teams (CRTs). Critical incident stress debriefing (CISD) was developed to assist emergency medical personnel, search and rescue workers, law enforcement agents, and other response team members cope with their exposure to stress. Richard Gist and his colleagues (1999) commented that, "[r]ecent large-scale disasters have found communities literally besieged by counselors and would-be counselors clamoring to serve anyone even tangentially connected to the circumstances of the event" (p. 3). In some cases, the rescue workers descending on a stressed community may outnumber the affected residents. Gist and his colleagues coined the term "trauma tourism" to refer to the influx of professional outsiders to stricken communities where they offer expert knowledge and charge themselves with fixing the problems people experience.

The infusion of outside help immediately following a community disaster may prevent communities from mobilizing their own resources. **Overhelping** refers to highly visible attempts to assist stressed people who would have succeeded in overcoming their challenges without that assistance (Gilbert & Silvera, 1996). At the individual level, overhelping interferes with a person's sense of self-efficacy. It sabotages autonomy and fosters dependency. Similar processes occur at the community level. Accumulating evidence suggests that professional-led community disaster relief efforts may actually worsen outcomes (e.g., Gist et al., 1999; Foa & Meadows, 1997).

When disasters occur, community members rally. The high level of community helping that follows a visible and devastating event has been labeled "the altruistic community" or "postdisaster utopia" (Jerusalem, Kaniasty, Lehman, Ritter, & Turnbull, 1995; Kaniasty & Norris, 1999). When community leaders attempt to marshal community resources, they may be surprised to find blood donation lines that extend for blocks or traffic jams consisting of people bringing flashlights to rescue workers. Disasters can bring diverse people together. Distinctions in social status may matter little when wealthy landowners line up with migrant farm workers to receive food rations. The need for cooperation and the sense of shared trauma may transcend superficial differences when community disasters occur (Bravo, Rubio-Stipec, Canino, Woodbury, & Ribera, 1990; Yates, Axsom, Bickman, & Howe, 1989).

At the same time, disasters do not have equivalent effects on everyone. Research suggests that members of dominant ethnic groups and citizens with more economic resources receive more support following a disaster (Jerusalem et al., 1995; Kaniasty & Norris, 1999). Indeed, some disasters that affect *only* marginalized subcommunities may not even be acknowledged as disasters at all. An event that threatens the homeless poor may receive minimal response at the larger community level (Jerusalem et al., 1995). Governmental responses to the AIDS crisis occurred only after the disease became a rampant epidemic that affected upstanding citizens like Rock Hudson.

Given the current state of our knowledge about disaster relief, how best can community psychologists help? We might assist in identifying common goals around which diverse segments of stricken communities could mobilize, and encourage the equitable distribution of resources (e.g., Hobfoll et al., 1995). It should be noted, however, that attempts to promote egalitarian distribution patterns may be seen as attempts by outsiders to interfere with the traditional social order (Kaniasty & Norris, 1999; see also O'Neill, 1999 for a discussion of conflicting interests and other ethical challenges in disaster relief).

Shortly after a killer tornado hit Tupelo, Mississippi, the disaster relief center filled with donations from community members. *AP/WIDE WORLD PHOTOS*

Despite community psychology's emphasis on prevention and early intervention, we might also resist the temptation to help too much too soon. Postdisaster utopias are usually short-lived. Conflict, competition, increased politicization and fragmentation may replace the mutual help and interdependence that immediately follow community traumas (Bolin & Stanford, 1990; Kaniasty & Norris, 1999). Some residents' need for support outlives the initial period of altruism. For example, four weeks after the Loma Prieta earthquake, t-shirts appeared on the streets proclaiming, "Thank you for not sharing your earthquake experience" (Pennebraker & Harber, 1993). Over time individual and community resources are drained, energies are redirected to other pressing needs, and people still suffering the ill effects of the disaster may find themselves without listening ears and shoulders to lean on.

The number of people in need of intensive support services is likely to be relatively small, however.

A wealth of research suggests that even the severe psychological suffering associated with major community traumas resolves over time (Gist et al., 1999). A review of longitudinal studies on stress responses showed that the overwhelming majority of disaster victims recover quickly—sometimes within days or weeks (Salzer & Bickman, 1999). Certainly the scale of the disaster bears on the time needed for recovery, but disaster responses too often operate from an *abnormalcy bias* in which the pathological consequences of disasters are assumed (van den Eynde & Veno, 1999). This might actually create self-fulfilling prophesies in which people who are coping normally learn to label their responses as pathological.

Converging research and theory argue for intervention efforts that help stricken communities build their resources and so become more competent (Bravo et al., 1990; Ginexi et al., 2000). Indeed, a working group of twelve internationally recognized experts in community stress from the United States, the Netherlands, Greece, and Italy emphasized the importance of building community capacities following a disaster (Figley, Giel, Borgo, Briggs, & Haritos-Fatouros, 1995). They advised reliance on local resources and held that survivors should do as much as possible for themselves. Community psychologists and others may best help by quietly supporting the community's own efforts to provide for the needs of its residents and to use the crisis as an opportunity to find unforeseen reservoirs of strength within the community.

⌘ The Promise of Community Psychology: Community-Level Frameworks

In proposing stress and coping as an orienting concept for community psychology, Betty Kalis (1970) recommended that we adopt a community-level perspective. She observed that most investigators limited their analyses to "the individual and his immediate life space, or to a family and its interactions." She recommended focusing instead "on interlocking crises in various community ecologies" (p. 86). Although the work on mutual help groups and community disasters hint at ways in which stress and coping has importance beyond the individual level, the potential of this reconceptualization has not yet been fully realized.

An individual-level perspective permeates most of the thousands of stress studies conducted thus far. Stress is not an individual-level phenomenon, however. Stresses generally affect multiple system members simultaneously, however. Look again at the SRE (Table 8.1). Which of these events occur to individuals in isolation? Gaining a family member, changing work hours, vacation—virtually all of the listed events affect entire systems. Brian Thompson and Alan Vaux (1986) posited that events vary in "bandwidth," that is, the number of people affected by the event. Some events (e.g., failing a college exam) have small bandwiths while others (e.g., a school shooting) have large ones.

Even events with small bandwiths reverberate throughout systems. Members of systems are interdependent, and so events that affect one member affect all others. This effect can be direct, as when an event impacts multiple system members simultaneously, or indirect, through the effect of an individual's coping efforts on other system members. If I react to a poor grade on a test by determining to study an extra six hours every day, people with whom I share a household might object to my absence from dinner or shirking of daily chores. Research suggests that the coping efforts of one system member can contribute to the stress experienced by others (Cronkite & Moos, 1984).

The concept of social support, too, would benefit from a systems-level perspective. Social support does not consist solely of one-to-one exchanges between specific relatives and friends. Even social network methodologies, which try to account for the multiple sources of support available to individuals, tend to view social support as various disconnected links to a target person rather than a system of interrelationships (Felton & Shinn, 1992). An appreciation of support *systems* would lead to different methodologies. For example, in assessing support networks we might allow research participants to

COMMUNITY INTERVENTION:

The Library at Columbine High School
Rituals of Recovery

In the 1990s one community after another confronted the trauma of school shootings. In many cities newscasters issued emergency reports from behind police barricades as paramedics wheeled gurneys to and from school buildings. Shocked students and teachers gave their accounts of gunfire reverberating through hallways. One after another, small towns and cities across the country became the center of national attention: Pearl, Mississippi; West Paducah, Kentucky; Jonesboro, Arkansas; Edinboro, Pennsylvania; Springfield, Oregon; Santee, California.

The deadliest of these tragic shootings took place on April 20, 1999. Two high school students opened fire on their teachers and classmates at Columbine High School in Littleton, Colorado. In a matter of minutes, thirteen students and teachers were killed and twenty-one were wounded (Jefferson County Sheriff's Office Report, 2000).

In the immediate aftermath of the shooting, diverse communities seemed to pull together. Before long, however, fractures were in evidence. Some divisions stemmed from efforts to lay blame. Did the police respond quickly enough or in the right way? Should school personnel have identified problems between the two young men and their classmates before they reached such tragic proportions? Should the parents of the killers be held accountable for their sons' actions? Were the killers victims as well? One early debate centered on whether a spontaneous memorial erected near the school should include 15 crosses—one for each person who died—or only 13 crosses—one for each of the murdered people but none for the killers who committed suicide.

The need for memorials was clear, however. Countless people from around the world sent flowers, stuffed animals, cards, and other tokens of sympathy that became an expansive altar on the school grounds. Those affected by the tragedy wandered through the spontaneous memorial, making their own contributions and witnessing the offerings of others.

Not long after the tragedy, the families of the murdered students and teachers formed a group called HOPE (Healing of People Everywhere) with the goal of establishing a permanent memorial. Most of the killings occurred in the school library, and HOPE organized to raise funds to tear down the existing library and replace it with a new library and atrium. The school board approved this initiative in a 4–1 vote. Others joined the dissent expressed by the lone school board member who voted no. The estimated cost of the project was close to $3 million. A Columbine graduate and witness to the rampage wrote a letter to a local newspaper arguing that the money should be spent on counseling, intervention, and increased security in school buildings, not new buildings (Kohler, 2000).

The question of how best to promote community healing is an important one. Formal memorials, in their attempt to meet the needs of diverse victims, can be controversial. The documentary, *Maya Lin: A Strong Clear Vision* is a compelling case study of contention arising from the building of the Vietnam Memorial in Washington, D.C. (Sanders, Norton, & Mock, 1994). Despite initial resistance, this memorial now receives praise from people around the world, including those who originally stood in opposition. The process of memorial-making might be a topic of interest to community psychologists dedicated to finding innovative ways of helping communities heal from crises. Disaster scholars and community psychologists have recognized the need for symbols of survival that solidify the historical and cultural significance of community tragedies (e.g., Contos, 2000; van der Kolk, van der Hart, & Burbridge, 1995). Might there be a role for community psychologists in developing and carrying out rituals of recovery, such as the design and construction of memorials?

It took only six months for HOPE to raise more than $3.1 million from thousands of families, children, schools, libraries, businesses, and individuals throughout the country (HOPE Columbine, 2001). In the summer of 2001, the library was completed.

nominate support groups (e.g., religious organizations, bridge clubs, and bowling leagues) as well as individuals (Felton & Shinn, 1992). Neighborhoods, schools, churches, and clubs help people adjust to stress by reinforcing individual skills, modeling positive values, bringing individuals into contact with supportive adults, assisting families in raising their children, and providing opportunities for people to realize their strengths.

Stress, coping, and social support are systems-level phenomena. Not only do these phenomena occur within microsystems, they are also shaped by larger macrosystemic forces. Shelley Taylor and her colleagues (1997) stated that individual and family characteristics must be considered in relation to the larger systems in which these behaviors are learned and expressed. For example, a sense of control over events is not simply an individual-level personality variable (e.g., locus of control). The degree to which control is possible for a person in a given situation varies, and marginalized groups often have fewer options available to them. Thus, the use of emotion-focused versus problem-focused coping may reflect, at least in part, the relative lack of control some groups (e.g., women) have over the social world (Jordan, 1992). Under the threat of AIDS, for example, women may be less able than men to cope actively by negotiating safer sexual practices (Ortiz-Torres, Serrano-García & Torres-Burgos, 2000).

By framing orienting concepts in ways that allow us to explore phenomena at a community level, we may find new pathways for understanding and intervention. With regard to stress-and-coping frameworks, a heightened awareness of the microsystems and macrosystems in which stress, coping, and social support take place may enable us, as individuals and communities, to turn crises into turning points that lead to new growth, better health, and a greater sense of well-being.

Action Agenda

Community Events in Your Community

What important community stresses have occurred in your community? You might want to learn more about these community events by reading articles in local news-papers papers and talking to community leaders. What were the coping responses of people at different levels: residents, community and professional groups, government? How has this event affected community health? Are there ways that the event strengthened the community? Are there ways in which community health was compromised? As a community psychologist, what might you have done (might you do) to facilitate coping with this event?

"Community Hassles and Uplifts"

Richard Lazarus and his colleagues (Kanner, et al., 1981; Lazarus, 1984) proposed that major stressful events exert their influence through daily hassles and uplifts. This notion has been explored at the individual level but not at the community level. What sorts of events would make up a community hassles scale? What about community uplifts? As a class, develop these lists. How do you think community hassles and uplifts affect well-being at both the individual and the community level? Does your list of community hassles and uplifts suggest ways of intervening to make your community a better place? Who, other than community psychologists, might be able to use information about community hassles and uplifts?

Assessing Social Support

Social support can be assessed in a variety of ways. Here are two. Try each of them.

1. Consider the following four life events: a) failing an important exam; b) car engine trouble in the middle of the night; c) learning of a close friend's diagnosis with cancer; d) a water main break that leaves everyone within a mile radius without water for a week. List each of these events in a column on the left hand side of a page. For each event, list the first person you would call first after the event occurred. Now list all the other people you might consider contacting in the event's aftermath. Who are these people—family, friends, co-workers, neighbors? How do they differ in terms of age, physical distance from you, and other potentially important variables? What kind of support might you expect from each (e.g., emotional, material, informational, problem-solving, direct intervention)? Do you think each of these people would call on you if they had been the one experiencing the stress? Why or why not? Are there people you did not list who would consider you part of their network? Does your thinking about stress and support change if you also consider *groups* you might contact in the aftermath of the event (e.g., church groups, book clubs, sports teams)? What conclusions would you draw about your social network from this exercise?
2. Draw a large circle on a piece of paper. Put a dot in the middle to represent yourself. Next, think about how many settings contain people who give you support and divide the circle into that many sections (like slicing a pie). Fill each section with dots that represent people within each of those settings who are part of your support network. You may want to put initials next to the dots to keep track. Now draw lines between pairs of people who know each other. After completing this diagram, think about the number of people in your network, network density (degree of interconnectedness among members), segmentation between life sectors, and the existence of boundary spanners—people in different segments who know each other. What conclusions would you draw about your social network from this diagram?

What are the strengths and weaknesses of each of these approaches? Do you have ideas on how to capture the phenomenon of social support more completely? You might work in small groups to devise new measures, perhaps three-dimensional representations that use colored materials.

Key Terms

approach coping

avoidance coping

coping

crisis theory

daily hassles

emotion-focused coping

external locus of control

general adaptation syndrome (GAS)

hardiness

internal locus of control

learned helplessness

mutual-help groups (MHGs)

nonnormative events

normative events

operationalization

overhelping

problem-focused coping

Schedule of Recent Events (SRE)

social support

stress

Chapter 9

Prevention

··

⌘ Introduction

Champions of prevention often tell some variation on the following story. One beautiful day you decide to picnic by the side of a river. You find a nice spot, shake out the checkered blanket, and arrange all your gear—lawn chair, sunscreen, paperback, sunglasses, and of course your lunch. Just as you reach into the picnic basket, you hear a call for help and see someone struggling in the water. You run to an overhanging branch, reach out your hand, and pull the person out of the river. After making sure that all is okay, you return to your picnic. You shake your head, take some deep breaths, and try to get back into the relaxing mood of a day in the park. You unwrap a sandwich, bring it to your mouth and . . . uh-oh, another cry for help! Wait, now there are *two* people struggling in the water. You rush again to the river, pull

243

off your shoes, jump into the water, and manage another rescue, this time dragging two people to shore. Eventually you make your way back to the blanket, and lie down to let the sun dry your clothes. Not the restful day you had anticipated! All that rescuing has made you *really* hungry. You reach into the picnic basket for your long-awaited lunch and . . . yup—more cries for help. How many people this time? There are *three* people in the water.

Depending on the storyteller's penchant for long tales, your uneaten lunch may continue to languish in the late afternoon sun as your picnic is interrupted by cries from groups of four, then five, then six people struggling in the water. At some point, you can no longer keep up with the demands for help and reluctantly allow a struggling swimmer to slip by. More follow. Finally, the story ends with a question: How long do you keep pulling people out of the river before deciding to go upstream and see who, or what, is pushing them in?

Prevention efforts are based in the belief that actions taken now can avert more serious problems in the future. Prevention has existed as an orienting concept in community psychology from the very beginning. Even at Swampscott prevention served as "an orientation, philosophy, and set of activities central to the identity of community psychology" (Elias, 1987, p. 540).

The orienting concepts of stress and coping and of prevention both emerged early in community

psychology's history, and each has informed the development of the other. Nevertheless, I began the chronology of the field's orienting concepts with stress and coping because this concept exploded more quickly in the literature. It also faded more quickly. Although the stress-and-coping framework continues to inform the work of many community psychologists, it no longer guides the field. Stress-and-coping research peaked in the late 1970s to early 1980s. Interest in prevention, however, has continued to grow. In 1999, Sheppard Kellam and his colleagues wrote, "There are periods in scientific development that arouse intense excitement and a sense of optimism that things are on the right track. This is such a time in prevention research" (p. 479).

⌘ Brief History

Interest in prevention is rooted in the public health movement of the nineteenth century (Bloom, 1979). During that time, modern scientific innovations allowed doctors and scientists to control or eradicate the major infectious ailments that plagued human society. Researchers found that the spread of physical diseases could be prevented by measures aimed at individuals (e.g., vaccinations for small pox and measles) and at the environment (e.g., improved sanitation to prevent cholera and dysentery). During the first half of the twentieth century, mental health researchers and practitioners began to explore the applicability of the prevention paradigm to mental disorders. Erich Lindemann (1944), whom we encountered in the previous chapter, was among the first. By the 1960s, many researchers and practitioners touted prevention as the best means of combating mental as well as physical health problems.

By the time clinical psychologists convened in Swampscott to establish the new field of community psychology, prevention had taken hold as an important mental health concept. The Zeitgeist of the

---

Better guide well the young
than reclaim them when old,

For the voice of true wisdom is calling.

"To rescue the fallen is good, but 'tis best
To prevent other people from falling."

Better close up the source
of temptation and crime

Than deliver from dungeons or galley;

Better put a strong fence 'round
the top of the cliff

Than an ambulance down in the valley

—*Joseph Malins (1895)*
Excerpt from "A Fence or an Ambulance"

1960s fueled interest in prevention. As seen in Chapter One, the Joint Commission on Mental Health (1961) recommended a preventive approach to reducing mental disorders, and John F. Kennedy sang praises to prevention in his landmark address to Congress two years later. In 1965 the rhetoric of prevention was put into practice with the establishment of Head Start, one of the most popular and widespread prevention programs of all times.

Interest in prevention can be traced to a number of trends in society. During the 1960s, aspects of the environment, especially social inequality and injustice, were seen as important contributors to the development of mental illness. This view corresponded with prevention's emphasis on the environmental causes of disease. Interest in prevention was reinforced by the awareness that mental health professionals could never be trained in sufficient numbers to meet the mental health needs of the populace (Lindemann, 1944; Albee, 1959, 1982). Prevention programs held the promise of reaching far more people than one-on-one therapy. Many hoped that prevention programs would be more effective and ethical as well as more far-reaching. In the 1960s, questions arose about whether psychological and psychiatric treatment had delivered on its promises of cure (e.g., Eysenck, 1961) and whether the diagnosis of mental illness was anything more than a myth designed to keep marginalized people on the margins (e.g., Szasz, 1961). Prevention held the promise of promoting new and better paradigms for mental health intervention.

By the mid-1970s, talk of prevention occurred around many tables. Several influential bodies, including The President's Commission on Mental Health, the Mental Health Association, and the National Institute of Mental Health, began to take prevention seriously (Lamb & Zusman, 1979). Researchers, practitioners, legislators, and others jumped onto what Emory Cowen (1996) called the "glitzy bandwagon" of prevention (p. 239). Everything from legalized abortion to Sesame Street to yogurt appeared under prevention's shimmering banner. As a result, prevention's proponents (e.g., Cowen, 1977) and critics (e.g., Lamb & Zusman, 1979) alike bemoaned the fuzziness of the concept and the lack of empirical support for programming.

While proponents called for the sharpening of definitions and a rigorous research agenda, critics recommended abandoning the concept completely.

In a frequently cited treatise against prevention, Richard Lamb and Jack Zusman (1979) maintained that although prevention programs sought to reduce the number of seriously ill, hospitalized, and disabled people, they did little more than help a few individuals lead happier lives. They questioned whether programs that simply prevented general emotional distress merited scarce funding. The authors also objected to the social change agenda of many preventionists, asserting that no proof existed that difficult life circumstances led to mental illness. They admitted a relationship between mental illness and "social disintegration" (e.g., crime, poverty, broken homes), but claimed that a *causal* link had not been established. And even if the link *was* causal, they argued, there was no proof that prevention programs could have a significant enough impact on the social environment to prevent mental illness. Lamb and Zusman claimed that intraindividual factors (e.g., genetics and biochemistry) probably caused major mental illnesses, and prevention programs might modify but could never prevent these causes.

George Albee (1982) spoke for many community psychologists when he disputed each of these objections. In particular, Albee justified prevention's focus on the environment and its social change agenda. He argued against the medical model of mental disorder in which illness was attributed to personal defects. According to Albee, psychiatrists and other defenders of the status quo promoted such models in the hope of avoiding the widespread, expensive, and tumultuous social reform required to eradicate racism, poverty, and other social conditions that sabotaged mental health.

Despite the criticisms of a few detractors, the concept of prevention gained favor throughout the 1970s and 1980s (Cowen, 1983; Elias, 1987). Two journals on the topic appeared, *Journal of Primary Prevention* and *Prevention in Human Services*. Influential books described effective prevention programs, notably *14 Ounces of Prevention: A Casebook for Practitioners* (Price, Cowen, Lorion, & Ramos-McKay, 1988). Conferences, conventions, and policy groups were organized to explore the potential of prevention. Definitions became more precise and research more sophisticated. Indeed, half of all outcome studies that used control groups, an ingredient many see as crucial to rigorous prevention research, occurred after 1980 (Durlak & Wells, 1997a).

By the 1990s, prevention had become a respectable area of inquiry. Several comprehensive reviews of the literature documented the efficacy of preventive interventions. Notably, Joseph Durlak and Anne Wells (1997a, 1998) conducted two **meta-analyses** that assessed research on more than 300 preventive interventions. A meta-analysis is a research technique that collapses data across many studies in order to obtain an overview of the magnitude of effects. Durlak and Wells' (1997a) first study focused on prevention programs geared to people who did not yet show any signs of disorder. They found that participants in these programs usually surpassed the performance of 59% to 82% of the people in the control groups. Such improvements were striking because the program participants functioned in the normal range to begin with, and so dramatic changes in behavior would not be expected. In their second study, Durlak and Wells (1998) analyzed prevention programs that targeted people who showed initial signs of maladjustment but did not yet suffer from full-blown problems. In this study, the average program participant outperformed 70% of the people in control group. In sum, Durlak and Wells found that most preventive interventions significantly reduced problems and were at least as effective as the more well-established treatment-oriented interventions.

The studies of Durlak and Wells appeared in community psychology journals, but favorable reviews of prevention programs also occurred in broader realms. In the 1990s, the federal government issued two influential reports summarizing the state of prevention. The NIMH Prevention Research Steering Committee (1993) published *Prevention of Mental Disorders: A National Research Agenda*. Many of the points made in this document were echoed in an even more exhaustive review of federally-sponsored research in prevention. A 1990 mandate by the U.S. Congress led the Institute of Medicine (IOM) to conducted a review that resulted in the 605-page **IOM Report**. This report concluded

that prevention programs were effective and merited additional federal funding and support (Mrazek & Haggerty, 1994; summarized in Muñoz, Mrazek, & Haggerty, 1996). In the 1990s, prevention research came of age and was embraced as legitimate governmental policy (Reppucci, Woolard, & Fried, 1999).

Researchers, practitioners, politicians, and the general public have embraced prevention for a number of reasons. It promises proactive efforts that reduce the total suffering of the population. It is potentially cost effective, in that people who might have drawn on collective resources through public assistance, hospitalization, or incarceration become contributing members of society instead. Even among prevention proponents, however, disagreement remains as to what makes prevention effective.

Despite the common goal of assessing the efficacy of extant prevention efforts and their conclusions about the merits of preventive approaches, the meta-analyses of Durlak and Wells and the IOM Report differed substantially (Cowen, 1997a). The two reports were based on a different set of studies—there existed only a 7% overlap between the 209 core citations in the Durlak and Wells meta-analysis and the 233 core citations in the IOM Report (Cowen, 1997a), and as we will see throughout this chapter these reviews resulted in very different ideas about how best to pursue a prevention agenda.

⌘ Typologies of Prevention

Over the years, there have been numerous attempts to clarify the definition of prevention, and several taxonomies have resulted. A review of these taxonomies illustrates the ways in which thinking about prevention has evolved over the past few decades.

PRIMARY, SECONDARY, AND TERTIARY PREVENTION

Because prevention has its roots in public health, public health terminology shaped the early thinking of mental health scholars. Public health distinguishes between the **incidence** and the **prevalence** of a disorder. The incidence is the number of new cases that arise in a population during a specified period of time, usually one year. The prevalence of a disorder is the total number of cases in a population at a given time. It reflects both the incidence and the duration of the disorder. Common colds only last a few days, and so the incidence over a year is much higher than the prevalence at a given time. Schizophrenia, on the other hand, generally affects individuals throughout their lives. Thus in a given year, the incidence of new cases is for lower than the total number of people who have schizophrenia (i.e., the prevalence). The distinction between incidence and prevalence differentiates the three types of prevention programs outlined in an early and still popular prevention taxonomy.

You may remember from the previous chapter that Gerald Caplan helped develop crisis theory. He also figured prominently in the early work on prevention. In 1964, Caplan introduced the distinction between tertiary prevention, secondary prevention, and primary prevention into the mental health literature. These three types of prevention programs have different effects on prevalence and incidence rates.

Tertiary prevention occurs after the disorder has developed. It seeks to alleviate the harmful, long-term effects of the problem. Tertiary prevention programs reduce the severity, discomfort, or disability associated with a disorder. George Fairweather's lodge societies, which helped people with mental illnesses live within the community, exemplify tertiary prevention (see the Community Intervention box in Chapter Two). Lodge residents continued to suffer from mental illnesses but became better able to live productively in spite of them.

Caplan (1964) originally applied the term tertiary prevention to large-scale community interventions rather than individual rehabilitation. Nevertheless, tertiary prevention reflects the traditional treatment approach of most mental (and physical) health professionals. It targets people's existing deficits (Rappaport, 1977). Tertiary prevention reduces neither the incidence nor the prevalence of a problem. Indeed, tertiary prevention programs may actually increase the prevalence because improvements in the lives of individuals with disorders may help them to live longer (Bloom, 1979).

While tertiary prevention corresponds to treatment, **secondary prevention** consists of early intervention. Secondary prevention decreases the prevalence of a disorder by reducing its duration through early case finding and prompt intervention. It does not, however, reduce the incidence. Problems still occur at the same rate, they are simply "nipped in the bud." Emory Cowen's efforts to assist natural helpers, such as hairdressers and bartenders, may be seen as an example of secondary prevention (see the Classic Research box in Chapter Two). Clients still experience the same problems, but natural helpers were taught to offer support more effectively so that the problems could be resolved more quickly.

Primary prevention differs from the other two types of prevention in that it targets people who do not show signs of disorder. The goal of primary prevention is to keep healthy people healthy. Primary prevention reduces the incidence of a disorder—new cases that would have occurred without the intervention do not develop. For example, the goal of Healthy Communities initiatives (see the Community Intervention box in Chapter Seven) is to develop a community's economic, political, and social capacities, thereby reducing the likelihood of various problems. Although these initiatives may form in response to a community problem, the goal is to create healthy contexts in which the incidence of crime, educational failure, housing shortages, and other problems declines.

Although the distinction between primary, secondary, and tertiary prevention served mental health practitioners for many years, problems with this taxonomy emerged. Boundaries among prevention types often blur. Tertiary prevention for one disorder may constitute primary prevention for another. Mutual help groups for postmastectomy patients, for example, may constitute tertiary prevention with regard to breast cancer but may be primary prevention with regard to depression or other emotional disorders that could result from the cancer diagnosis and treatment (Bloom, 1979). The distinction between primary and secondary prevention also blurs. When should "at-risk" populations be considered healthy (and so targets for primary prevention) and when do we see them as evidencing early indicators of a problem (and so requiring secondary prevention)? Is Head Start a primary or secondary prevention program?

The prevention activities of psychologists and other helping professionals do not fall neatly into the categories adopted from public health. Thus, the IOM Report promoted a new taxonomy of prevention activities for mental health (Mrazek & Haggerty, 1994).

INDICATED, SELECTIVE, AND UNIVERSAL PREVENTION

The IOM taxonomy, like the public health taxonomy, identifies three different types of prevention that fall along an intervention continuum (see Figure 9.1).

In the IOM taxonomy, tertiary prevention no longer qualifies as prevention. The IOM Report echoed Emory Cowen's (1983) sentiment that although the goals of reducing the adverse consequences of disorder "are neither unworthy nor unneeded, they are simply *not* prevention" (Cowen, 1983, p. 11).

A second innovation of the IOM taxonomy is the division of secondary prevention into two types. **Indicated prevention** targets people who have detectable signs of maladjustment that foreshadow more significant mental disorders or who have biological markers that are linked to disorder. **Selective prevention** targets people who are at high risk for

the development of a disorder (as evidenced by biological, psychological, and/or social risk factors) but do not yet show any indication of disorder.

The final type of prevention, **universal prevention**, corresponds to primary prevention. It targets all the people in a given population (e.g., school, neighborhood, country). Universal prevention programs generally reach large numbers of people, few of whom are at imminent risk for the problem of interest. Because of its wide net, universal prevention programs ideally cost little per individual, are of demonstrated effectiveness, are acceptable to the general population, and entail little risk of negative outcomes (Mrazek & Haggerty, 1994). In order to better understand the IOM taxonomy, let's consider an example of each type of prevention.

INDICATED PREVENTION EXAMPLE

One of the best-known and best-researched indicated prevention programs is the Primary Mental Health Project (PMHP) begun in 1957 by Emory Cowen and his associates in Rochester, New York (Cowen, 1997b; Cowen & Hightower, 1989; Cowen, Izzo, Miles, Telschow, Trost, & Zax, 1963; Cowen, Pederson, Babigian, Izzo, & Trost, 1973; Cowen, Trost, Izzo, Lorion, Dorr, & Isaacson, 1975; Cowen, Zax, Izzo, & Trost, 1966). After forty years in operation, PMHPs had been established in 2000 schools across 700 districts (Cowen, 1996).

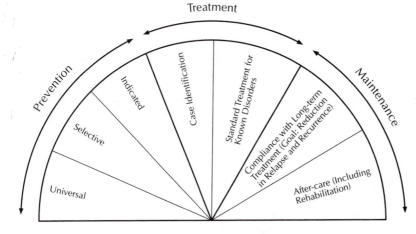

Figure 9.1
The Mental Health Intervention Spectrum for Mental Disorders.

Reprinted with permission from Reducing risks for mental disorder: Frontiers for preventive intervention research. *Copyright 1994 by the National Academy of Sciences. Courtesy of the National Academy Press, Washington, D.C.*

The idea for PMHPs grew from Cowen's observation that many older children with behavioral problems had experienced difficulties in school when they were much younger. He reasoned that intervention efforts directed at primary-aged children with school difficulties might prevent the development of more serious behavioral problems in later life. Based on classroom observations, interviews with parents, and psychological tests, children in a Rochester elementary school were classified as either at risk or not at risk for psychological problems. Because the PMHP targeted children who were already showing beginning signs of disorder, this was an indicated prevention program (despite its title *Primary* Mental Health Project).

The program originally consisted of informal conferences and education for the parents, and after-school groups for the children. The outcomes for children in the targeted school were then compared to outcomes for children in two similar schools where no intervention had occurred. Although PMHP professionals succeeded in identifying children at risk for problems, they did not successfully prevent the onset of disorder (Cowen, et al., 1963). Thus, the intervention program was revised. A staff consisting of homemakers, college students, and other nonprofessionals was carefully selected and trained to provide one-to-one and small group support for at-risk children. This support took place under the supervision of mental health professionals. In addition, school mental health counselors were encouraged to reduce their direct services to children and engage in prevention-oriented activities. Subsequent evaluations showed that the children in schools where PMHP was implemented fared better than children in control schools, as indicated by teacher ratings and school achievement (Cowen et al., 1966).

SELECTIVE PREVENTION EXAMPLE

An example of a selective intervention program is the School Transitional Environment Project (STEP), developed by Robert Felner and his colleagues (Felner & Adan, 1988; Felner, Farber & Primavera, 1983). As described in the previous chapter, some stressful life events (e.g., puberty, retirement) are predictable—they occur at particular stages of development. Because these normative events, or life transitions, represent important turning points that cohorts of people experience simultaneously, they present a promising opportunity for preventive intervention. The STEP program targeted the normative transition from middle school to high school. Research shows that this transition coincides with increased absenteeism, lower academic performance, and declines in well-being. These outcomes in turn, are, associated with more serious problems, such as school dropout, academic failure, and emotional dysfunction. These more serious problems may have lifelong consequences, including disenfranchisement from society, unemployment, and poor mental health (see Felner & Adan, 1988; Reyes, Gillock, Kobus, & Sanchez, 2000 for reviews).

STEP was a selective intervention program because the people targeted were at increased risk for the development of problems but did not yet evidence any signs of disorder. Program participants were at risk not only because they were about to undergo a school transition, but also because they attended large, urban schools predominantly serving students of low socioeconomic status. These schools tend to have higher rates of school dropout, as well as absenteeism, school failure, and a number of the other problems cited above.

For the STEP intervention, students entering high school were randomly assigned to an experimental or a control group. The intervention experienced by students in the experimental group consisted of two parts. First, the social system of the students was reorganized. Schedules were simplified and groups of new students took their core classes together in rooms located near to each other. Thus, students did not have to establish new peer relationships in each class or face threats and intimidation by older students when walking through the hallways to distant classrooms. They had more opportunities for informal interactions with classmates, and perceived the school as more stable, organized, and understandable than students in the control group.

The second aspect of the intervention involved restructuring the homeroom. STEP students were assigned to the same homeroom, and the homeroom teachers' role was modified to include administrative and counseling functions previously performed by other school personnel. For example, STEP homeroom teachers contacted family members to follow up on absences, helped students decide on elective classes, and provided information about educational and other resources. In order to fulfill these expanded roles, STEP teachers received training in such topics as academic and socioemotional counseling, listening skills, identification of emerging problems, referral processes, adolescent development, and college preparation. They also participated in team-building activities to enhance communication with other STEP teachers and personnel.

After one year, students who had been randomly assigned to the STEP program had higher grades, better attendance records, and more stable self-concepts than youth in the control group. While control group students saw teachers as less supportive as the year progressed, STEP students did not. A long-term follow-up showed that the dropout rate for STEP participants was less than half the rate of the students in the control group (21% versus 43%).

The STEP program appeals to community psychologists for numerous reasons. First and foremost, it focused on environmental rather than individual change. In addition, it cost little to implement—the intervention consisted of reorganizing existing resources, rather than obtaining new ones. The community psychology literature has described numerous school transition studies and programs that elaborate on the success of STEP (e.g., Compas, Wagner, Slavin, & Vannatta, 1986; Elias, Gara, Schuyler, Branden-Muller, & Sayette, 1991; Elias, Gara, Ubriaco, Rothbaum, Clabby, & Schuyler, 1986; Jason, Weine, Johnson, Danner, Kurasaki, & Warren-Sohlberg, 1993; Reyes et al., 2000; Seidman, Aber, Allen, & French, 1996; Weinstein, Soule, Colins, Cone, Mehlhorn, & Simontacchi, 1991).

UNIVERSAL PREVENTION EXAMPLE

While community psychologists designed and tested the Primary Mental Health Project (PMHP) and the School Transitional Environment Project (STEP), academic researchers do not spearhead all prevention programs. As an example, consider Project Venture, a program identified by the Western Regional Center for the Application of Prevention Technologies as a "best practice" intervention. Best practice interventions are strategies and programs that scientists at influential organizations (e.g., National Institute for Drug Abuse, Center for Substance Abuse and Prevention, and Centers for Disease Control and Prevention) deem promising based on the results of high-quality research (see *http://www.open.org/~westcapt/bestprac.htm*).

Project Venture was developed by the National Indian Youth Leadership Development Project specifically for American Indian youth in Pueblo and Navajo communities (Hall, Levis-Pilz, Pilz, & DeJong, No date). Although Project Venture was designed to reduce substance abuse, it did not feature explicit antidrug messages or target youth at highest risk. The program stressed personal and group wellness and emphasized leadership skills, confidence, problem-solving abilities, teamwork, and community commitment for all youth. The program consisted of a five- to ten-day summer camp and follow-up intergenerational activities. While at the camp, youth engaged in experiential adventures, such as hiking, mountain biking, canoeing, rappeling, and rock climbing. They also participated in a service component, designing and implementing community projects, such as the establishment of a community greenhouse.

Project Venture was designed to be culturally appropriate for Indian youth. It included intertribal activities, appropriate spiritual content, and an ethic of service to Indian communities. Youth were encouraged to forge connections with supportive elders and to invest themselves in their cultural heritage. Graduation from the camp program was marked by a rite of passage that built on traditional coming-of-age ceremonies.

In order to assess the impact of this intervention, the American Drug and Alcohol Survey (ADAS) was administered to 850 program participants and to a control group over a three year period. Overall, program participants were less likely than control youth to abuse alcohol, tobacco, and other drugs.

PRIMARY PREVENTION AND PROMOTION

To review, early mental health preventionists distinguished three types of prevention: primary, secondary, and tertiary. A more recent typology classified tertiary prevention as treatment rather than prevention, and refined the meaning of secondary prevention which now included indicated and selective prevention. In these two typologies, the meaning of primary prevention remained relatively consistent: efforts to reduce problems by preventing their occurrence. There is however, some debate about what activities should be included under the rubric of primary prevention, a debate highlighted by the contrasting conclusions drawn by Durlak and Wells in their meta-analyses and the IOM in their report.

DEBATE ABOUT PROMOTION

Some scholars, including many community psychologists, identify two different approaches to primary prevention (Albee, 1982; Bloom, 1979; Cowen, 1977, 1996, 1997a; Durlak & Wells, 1997a; Ford, 1985). The first approach, which virtually all preventionists embrace as primary prevention, attempts to reduce the likelihood of disorder. A second avenue for primary prevention is the enhancement of health. Health promotion programs seek to build resistance to a variety of disorders. They are based in the belief that interventions can reduce risk levels by helping people to develop skills and competencies.[1]

Relatively early in the history of community psychology, Bernard Bloom (1979) observed that there was "a substantial body of research from a variety of domains that appears to converge on competence building as perhaps the single most persuasive preventive strategy for dealing with individual and social issues in most communities" (p. 184). Many subsequent community psychologists concurred that prevention goals could be achieved through

the promotion of competence (e.g., Albee, 1982, 1996; Cowen, 1977, 1991, 1996; Seidman, 1987). Other scholars have been less positive. At the same time Bloom lauded competency-based prevention efforts, Lamb and Zusman (1979) argued against health promotion as a form of prevention, stating that "there is no evidence that it is possible to strengthen 'mental health' and thereby increase resistance to mental illness by general preventive activities" (p. 13).

This criticism may seem to carry little weight in that Lamb and Zusman discounted *all* forms of prevention. The NIMH (NIMH Prevention Research Steering House, 1993) and IOM Reports (Mrazek & Haggerty, 1994), though positive toward the concept of prevention in general, also argued against the utility of health promotion. They advocated for interventions aimed at the prevention of the specific mental disorders identified in the *Diagnostic and Statistical Manual* (DSM). Community psychologists have continued to challenge a "risk driven" view of prevention in which the most important criterion for acceptable prevention activities is the extent to which diagnosable psychiatric illnesses can be reduced (Cowen, 1996; see Albee, 1996; Durlak & Wells, 1997a). A number of programs have been cited in support of health-based prevention efforts.

PROMOTION EXAMPLE

In their meta-analysis of primary prevention programs, Durlak and Wells (1997a) identified training in interpersonal problem solving as an important competence-building approach to prevention. Interpersonal problem-solving interventions are based on the groundbreaking work of George Spivack and Myrna Shure (Shure, 1997; Shure & Spivack, 1988; Spivack & Shure, 1974).

Spivack and Shure noted that some inner-city preschool children act impatiently and are overly emotional, aggressive, or shy, behaviors that contributed to a number of problems. Further, Spivack and Shure found that children who evidenced these behaviors often lacked certain problem-solving skills. Thus, they developed a competence building intervention called Interpersonal Cognitive Problem Solving (ICPS), which the children called "I Can

---

[1]One can conceive of indicated and selective interventions based on a health-promotion model of prevention, but promotion models are usually associated with primary prevention efforts

Problem Solve." Instead of targeting aggression, shyness, or other problem behaviors, ICPS programs teach children useful skills, such as:

- *Alternative thinking:* The ability to generate different solutions to interpersonal problems
- *Consequential thinking:* The ability to foresee the results of one's actions
- *Causal thinking:* The ability to see events as the causes of other events
- *Sensitivity:* The awareness of the interpersonal nature of problems
- *Means/ends thinking:* The ability to conceptualize the steps necessary to reach a goal

ICPS programs build these skills through the use of fun activities conducted by teachers or parents. The goal is to teach children *how* to think, rather than what to think. Evaluation research showed that children who received this intervention gained in the relevant problem-solving skills. After two years, they were rated as better adjusted than children in a control group.

DOHRENWEND'S MODEL REVISITED

In considering the meaning of prevention, we have thus far examined two prevention typologies and the debate about prevention versus promotion. Before moving from conceptual maps to an examination of the issues involved in doing prevention work, let's consider one more way of thinking about prevention.

The stress-and-coping framework and the prevention framework both emerged as important orienting concepts when community psychology was founded. Several scholars, including Erich Lindemann and Gerald Caplan, helped develop both concepts. Given this close association, it is not surprising that Barbara Dohrenwend's (1978) stress model, described in Chapter Eight (see Figure 8.1) had important ramifications for prevention. Indeed her model could serve as yet another typology for organizing prevention research and practice.

Dohrenwend identified six types of interventions (the circles on the periphery of Figure 8.1). In Chapter Eight, we considered two of these circles. Mutual help groups were examined as an example of corrective therapy. Corrective therapies take place after a stressful event has run its course, and adjustment to the event, positive, negative, or unchanged, has occurred. In this way, corrective therapies exemplify tertiary prevention, or treatment.[2] Second, we examined disaster relief as a form of crisis intervention. Crisis intervention takes place soon after a stressful event occurs and before long-term adjustment to the event is achieved. Thus, crisis intervention constitutes a form of secondary prevention (usually selective, but also indicated).

Corrective therapy and crisis intervention target the stress process directly. The remaining four types of interventions in Dohrenwend's model do not depend on the occurrence of stress. They affect the context of stress, either at the individual or environmental level (see Table 9.1). These interventions can either prevent the occurrence of stress or facilitate the capacity to adjust after stresses occur. Let's look briefly at each.

The first type of individual-level intervention is skill training. In this chapter, we just discussed one example—the ICPS program. These programs build an individual's ability to adjust to interpersonal stresses by teaching interpersonal problem solving. As another example, Sharlene Wolchick and her colleagues (1993) developed an intervention aimed at facilitating adjustment to divorce. It sought to improve mothers' communication skills and help them to develop positive routines and enriching family activities. This program resulted in improvements in mother–child interactions and the quality of the home environment.

The second type of individual-level intervention identified by Dohrenwend was education and socialization. Although these interventions target individuals, they hold the potential to actually prevent stresses from occurring, as opposed to preventing

---

[2]It should be noted that mutual support groups, examined here in the context of corrective therapies, have also been conceptualized as primary and secondary prevention (e.g., Levy, 2000).

📄 Table 9.1	Four Interventions that Occur outside of the Stress Process	
Level of Intervention	**Facilitate Adjustment** (Target Stress Mediators)	**Prevent Stress** (Target Enduring Characteristics)
Individual	Skill training	Education and socialization
Environmental	Community organization and development	Political action

Based on Dohrenwend, B.S. (1978). Social stress and community psychology. *American Journal of Community Psychology, 6,* 1–14.

the problems that result from stress. Mental health education aims to help people gain the knowledge, attitudes, and behaviors that support psychological well-being. People might learn how to protect themselves from sexually transmitted diseases or how to talk to their children about resisting peer pressure to use drugs. One important vehicle for education and socialization is the media (see the Community Intervention box).

The remaining two circles in Dohrenwend's model target the environment rather than the individual. Just as individuals can be helped to develop skills, so too can communities. Community organization and development may be seen as skill building at the community level. Every community has untapped resources that can be developed to help the community meet the needs of its residents (e.g., Kretzmann & McKnight, 1993). Emory Cowen's (1982) workshops to strengthen the skills of informal helpers is an example of a small-scale community development intervention that builds the community's capacity to meet the needs of stressed residents.

The final intervention outlined by Dohrenwend is perhaps the most controversial: political action. If one believes that such factors as economic inequality and discrimination account for the occurrence of many stresses, than these stresses can best be prevented through social change efforts. Support for this type of prevention has not grown over the decades. In the 1960s and 1970s, prevention

researchers were clearly concerned about the mental health consequences of social ills such as poverty, racism, and sexism. As the sociopolitical Zeitgeist changed, the revolutionary zeal of early preventionists dissipated (Albee, 1996). Change efforts through sociopolitical action do occur, but not as often as they once did. In 1996, George Albee lamented the loss of interest in social change over the past few decades. He contended that the civil rights movement should be considered one of this country's most effective prevention programs.

⌘ Targeting Prevention Efforts

Now that we have considered some different ways of thinking about prevention programs, let's explore ways of maximizing the chances that these programs actually have a preventive effect. Which type of prevention works best, and how can we maximize program efficacy?

IS PRIMARY PREVENTION BEST?

Community psychologists sometimes hail primary (or universal) prevention as a particularly desirable form of prevention (e.g., Bloom, 1979; Cowen, 1977, 1980; Felner, Felner, & Silverman, 2000;

COMMUNITY INTERVENTION:

The Stanford Heart Disease Prevention Program
Media as a Means to Prevention

In the 1960s, half of all deaths in the United States could be attributed to coronary heart disease. Moreover, the victims of heart disease were often relatively young. Research evidence suggested that heart disease in people under the age of 60 resulted from three risk factors: smoking, high serum cholesterol, and hypertension. John Farquhar and his colleagues at the Stanford Medical School designed an intervention to reduce heart disease by improving diet and reducing smoking (Maccoby & Alexander, 1979; Farquhar, 1991).

The researchers decided to launch a media campaign targeting all community members between the ages of 35 and 59. Because random assignment of individuals to intervention and control groups is not possible in a community-wide intervention, they used a quasi experimental design. Similar Northern California communities received either a media intervention alone, a media intervention combined with an intensive interpersonal instruction program (ten group sessions for high-risk people and their spouses) or no intervention at all.

The Three-Community Study began in 1972 with a baseline survey. The intervention began in 1973, and follow-up surveys were administered on a yearly basis for three years. Researchers used both self-report and physiological data to assess such variables as knowledge of risk factors, smoking rates, and eating habits.

The researchers knew that previous attempts to modify behaviors through the media had been disappointing. Based on extant research, they decided to deliver risk reduction messages through a variety of means: television and radio spots, direct mail, print advertisements, newspaper articles, and bus placards. Other innovations incorporated into their media campaign, which continued for 18 months, included:

- Establishing specific objectives before the start of the campaign
- Targeting a circumscribed segment of the population
- Constructing clear and useful messages that related to clear objectives

- Utilizing creative scheduling (not relying on free television or radio spots during hours when few people were awake)
- Making the message salient to the individual in order to create motivation for change
- Attempting to stimulate interpersonal communication among community members
- Regularly assessing the effectiveness of the campaign through process evaluation
- Obtaining long-term commitments for the support of the campaign (Maccoby & Alexander, 1979)

Researchers also tailored messages to community subgroups. Between 10% and 15% of the targeted communities were Spanish speaking, and the researchers found that the risk factors in this population differed from the Anglo population. For example, Spanish speakers smoked less but were more overweight often. Thus, a second campaign was designed that differed not only in language, but also with regard to message content and message delivery. Media-use patterns revealed that radio would be the most effective means of reaching the Spanish-speaking population of interest, and three local stations with Spanish programming were used in the campaign. The Spanish campaign engaged bilingual English and Spanish speakers not merely in translating the messages, but in transforming them in ways that would increase their appropriateness to the Spanish-speaking communities.

Research showed that the risk of coronary disease was reduced by 17% to 18% in the treatment communities, while the risk level in the control community increased 6% during the same time period. Knowledge about coronary risk, attitudes toward risk behaviors, and actual behaviors also changed in the intervention communities. Furthermore, the positive changes were maintained and sometimes increased during the second year of the study. Although the effects in people receiving mass media plus high-risk group intervention occurred more quickly, the two intervention communities

Rappaport, 1977; Seidman, 1987). Primary prevention programs reach everyone while stigmatizing no

one, emphasize health rather illness, and generally target groups as opposed to individuals. The does showed comparable results after two years. After three years, however, results in the media-only community appeared to have faded more. After the three-year fol-low-up, risk-reduction materials were made available to the community that had served as the no-intervention control. The success of this program led Stanford re-searchers to continue to use media as a means of pre-venting coronary disease, and it served as a model for other media campaigns aimed at preventing mental and physical health problems (e.g., Jason, 1998).

not mean that primary prevention is the preferred approach in all situations, however. The nature of the problem of interest and the preventionist's goals may call for secondary (indicated or selective) and even tertiary prevention (e.g., Winnett, 1991).

In primary prevention, resources are not targeted. Everyone receives the intervention, whether they are at risk or not. A primary preventionist might argue that the behaviors promoted by these interventions are good for everyone. *Any* person can benefit from eating healthier, exercising more, abstaining from to-bacco, or becoming a better parent or friend. On the other hand, might people with high cholesterol ben-efit *more* from adopting low-fat diets? Isn't informa-tion on effective parenting best directed to people who are socially isolated or have other risk factors for child abuse and neglect?

Some scholars assert that people at highest risk for a problem should be targeted for preven-tion programs (e.g., Coie, Watt, West, Hawkins, Asarnow, Markman, Ramey, Shure, & Long, 1993). In order to be affordable, a population-wide inter-vention program may not be intense enough to benefit the people who need it most. By opting for primary prevention rather than selective or indicat-ed prevention, practitioners sometimes trade scope for intensity. The danger is that far-reaching pro-grams will become so diluted as to have no mean-ingful effect. N. Dickon Reppucci, Preston Britner, and Jennifer Woolard (1997) found that child abuse prevention programs in the form of parent education were only effective if they consisted of at least six sessions. A one-shot program geared to all parents might reach everyone but help no one. In-terestingly, more long-term programs may have better effects even if the content does not expand. One study found that the same 10.5 hours of pro-gramming relating to the prevention of sexual risk-taking had greater effects on adolescents if spread over seven sessions rather than compacted into three sessions (Rotherman-Borus, Gwadz, Fernan-dez, & Srinivasan, 1998).

In addition to the issue of intensity and program length, base rates also bear on decisions about the preferred type of prevention. Primary prevention programs for low frequency disorders need to cast an extremely wide net in order to reach even a few of the people who might be at risk. Even secondary prevention programs that target high-risk people may serve many people who would have turned out fine without the program. If a widespread program helps only a few people, can it be justified?

Sometimes the answer is yes. One reason for the appeal of early education programs such as Head Start is their promise of long-term payoffs for short-term investments. The Perry Preschool Project fol-lowed 123 low-IQ children who had lived in low-income African American families from the age of three or four to age twenty-seven. Program partic-ipants as compared to people in the control group scored higher on achievement tests, graduated from high school more often, pursued post-graduate edu-cation at higher rates, were arrested less often, had reduced rates of teenage pregnancy, earned more money as adults, and less often received welfare. These effects resulted in substantial savings—a seven-dollar return on every dollar spent on the pro-gram (Barnett, 2000). Not every preschooler had a "successful" outcome: some participants were arrest-ed for crimes or became teen parents. In addition, some of the children in the control group thrived without the intervention. Still, the benefits of this secondary prevention program justified its expense.

Leonard Jason (1998) demonstrated that a primary-prevention program that reached only a small number of high-risk people could be cost ef-fective. He reasoned that an antismoking media campaign broadcast to 450,000 people might reach only 150,000 smokers. Even if only 10% of these smokers achieved long-term abstinence, the lifetime savings in health care costs for these 15,000 people would approach $600,000,000.

In some cases, preventionists do not choose from among prevention approaches, but combine the best of different approaches. They might, for example, launch a large-scale primary prevention program in conjunction with a smaller-scale indicated or selective prevention effort. This was the approach taken in one of the communities in the Stanford Three Community Study (see the Community Intervention box). A primary prevention media campaign was supplemented by support groups targeting high-risk people. Leonard Jason (1998) also combined primary and targeted programming in his multilevel smoking cessation interventions. One intervention involved a televised self-help component to mass audiences, self-help manuals for all interested audience members, and a support group that specifically targeted smokers. At the end of the three-week program, 21% of the smokers who received the manuals and watched the television broadcast quit smoking, but 41% of those who participated in the support group meetings as well, were able to quit.

ASSESSING RISK

Our ability to implement effective programs requires consideration of the benefits of different prevention approaches. In some cases, limited funds, specificity of program content and other factors may lead preventionists to opt for indicated or selective (secondary) rather than primary prevention. The question then becomes how do we decide whom to target for intervention?

In the public health paradigm, specific disorders developed from single causes. A solitary virus or bacteria or contaminant led to a particular disease. Thus, the preventionists' task was straightforward: remove the pathogen from the environment or build resistance to it in the individual. If swamp-dwelling mosquitoes carry malaria, drain the swamps or develop antimalaria drugs. Mental health preventionists face different challenges. The problems of interest to us (from schizophrenia to delinquency to homelessness), cannot be traced to a single pathogen. They result from complex interactions of multiple factors, both individual and environmental. Because there is no one-to-one correspondence between problem and cause, we must instead talk about *risk* for problem development.

RISK FACTORS

Selective and indicated prevention programs require knowledge of what leads to disorder (or strengthens health) under what circumstances. At present, few or no signs or symptoms predict the onset of mental health and behavioral problems with certainty. Instead, researchers have rounded up a group of usual suspects—**risk factors** associated with a higher likelihood for the onset of a problem, and greater severity and longer duration of the problem once it occurs (see Table 9.2).

Risk factors can reside primarily within individuals (e.g., neurochemical imbalances, social incompetence) or in the environment (e.g., family disorganization, social isolation). Various individual and environmental risk factors act together as accomplices of sorts. There may be a ringleader, but rarely does one factor operate alone. A person with poor work skills is more likely to live in a low-income, disorganized neighborhood. A child with neurochemical imbalances may suffer more in a disorganized family.

In addition to risk factors, the development of disorder is also affected by **protective factors**—variables that improve people's resistance to risk factors and disorder. Protective factors can modify the disorder directly or influence the disorder by affecting risk factors—either preventing their occurrence or buffering their effects (Coie et al., 1993). Prevention efforts tend to focus on risk factors more than protective factors because preventionists (outside the realm of community psychology) tend to focus on disorder rather than health. Protective factors are more often studied by scholars interested in promoting competence, and will be examined in greater detail in Chapter Eleven.

Table 9.2 Generic Risk Factors

Family Circumstances
  Low social class
  Family conflict
  Mental illness in family
  Large family size
  Poor bonding to parents
  Family disorganization
  Communication deviance

Emotional Difficulties
  Child abuse
  Apathy/emotional blunting
  Emotional immaturity
  Stressful life events
  Low self-esteem
  Emotional dyscontrol

School Problems
  Academic failure
  Scholastic demoralization

Ecological context
  Neighborhood disorganization
  Racial injustice
  Unemployment
  Extreme poverty

Constitutional Handicaps
  Perinatal complications
  Sensory disabilities
  Organic handicaps
  Neurochemical imbalance

Interpersonal Problems
  Peer rejection
  Alienation and isolation

Skill Development Delays
  Subnormal intelligence
  Social incompetence
  Attentional deficits
  Reading disabilities
  Poor work skills and habits

Coie, J. D., Watt, N. F., West, S. G., Hawkins, J. D., Asarnow, J. R., Markman, H. J., Ramey, C., Shure, M. B., & Long, B. (1993). The science of prevention: A conceptual framework and some directions for a national research program. *American Psychologist, 48*, 1013–1023. Copyright © 1993 by the American Psychological Association. Reprinted with permission.

STRESS AND RISK: PRECIPITATING AND PREDISPOSING FACTORS

Many risk factors are long-standing characteristics of a person's make-up or environment. Thus, they correspond to what have been called **predisposing factors.** These longstanding characteristics may be individual traits that likely have a genetic component (e.g., neurochemical imbalances or subnormal intelligence) or personal background factors relating to social position (e.g., socioeconomic status) or family history factors (e.g., childhood abuse). While predisposing factors increase vulnerability, the onset of disorder often requires a **precipitating factor**. Precipitating factors are stressful occurrences that trigger the disorder. (In Table 9.2, Coie and his colleagues included stressful events under "Emotional Difficulties," subscribing to the notion that stresses are often seen as individual-level phenomena.)

The interaction between predisposing and precipitating factors reflects a conjoining of prevention and stress-and-coping frameworks and is evident in the prevention equation presented by George Albee in 1982.

$$\text{Incidence of Psychological Disorder} = \frac{\text{Stress} + \text{Physical Vulnerability}}{\text{Coping Skills} + \text{Social Support} + \text{Self-Esteem}}$$

This equation influenced people's thinking about prevention for many years. The numerator reflects the joint operation of intra-individual predisposing factors and a precipitating event. The denominator includes the two mediators of the stress-adjustment relationship discussed in Chapter Eight.

Five years after Albee's article, Maurice Elias (1987) reformulated the equation to deemphasize the individual-level and highlight environmental contributions to disorder. Elias included only environmental-level predisposing factors in his numerator, along with the occurrence of a precipitating event. He also emphasized system-level dynamics and structures in his denominator.

$$\text{Likelihood of Disorder in Population} = \frac{\text{Stress} + \text{Risk Factors in Environment}}{\text{Socialization Practices} + \text{Social Support Resources} + \text{Opportunities for Connectedness}}$$

Today, most preventionists agree that an understanding of the development of disorder requires consideration of individual and environmental factors, both longstanding and episodic. For example, a parent lacking in social competence (individual factor) living in a low-income and violent neighborhood (environmental factor) might be at particularly high risk for child abuse. She or he may, however, actually harm her or his child only in the presence of a precipitating stressful event—after being fired from a job, for example, or ending a romantic relationship.

ATTRIBUTABLE RISK

Theoretically, one can calculate the amount of risk associated with a given factor. Consider tobacco use. Smoking is an important risk factor for lung cancer. People who smoke cigarettes develop lung cancer at higher rates than nonsmokers. But even if interventionists completely eradicated smoking—not a single cigarette ever puffed again—some people would still fall victim to lung cancer. Other risk factors remain, such as genetic makeup and exposure to pollutants. **Attributable risk** is the proportion of new cases of a disorder (lung cancer in this example) that would be prevented if an intervention completely eliminated a risk factor (in this case, smoking) (Muñoz, Mrazek, & Haggerty, 1996). Assessments of attributable risk can help interventionists target programs by identifying which factors lead most directly to a problem.

The inability to eliminate a problem by removing known risk factors illustrates the limited effectiveness of interventions, no matter how powerful. Given the fact that social and behavioral problems are multiply determined, even the total eradication of a major risk factor will not reduce the incidence of the targeted problem to zero. The multiplicity of risk factors comes with good news, too. Just as one disorder is affected by multiple risk factors, a single risk factor can lead to a variety of disorders. Thus, reducing a single risk factor has a beneficial effect on many problems. If no one ever smoked again, not only would the incidence of lung cancer decrease, but the incidence of emphysema and throat cancer would decrease, as well. There would be fewer injuries, deaths, and property loss from accidental fires set by careless smokers. And the overall health and fitness of millions of people would improve. As Bernard Bloom (1979) observed two decades ago, prevention programs can have specific and nonspecific effects; smoking cessation has a specific effect with regard to lung cancer, as well as nonspecific effects with regard to general health.

Some risk factors play a role in only a few social and behavioral problems, and others are implicated in many. Poverty, for example, plays a role in virtually every problem that psychologists study: domestic violence, school failure, criminal behavior, mental illness, substance abuse. It is the "greatest risk factor of all" (Schorr, 1988, p. xxii). If preventionists could engineer a significant reduction in poverty, imagine the radiating effects throughout society.

READINESS TO CHANGE

One way to target prevention efforts is to direct them to high-risk people or environments. A second approach is to target the people and environments most likely to be receptive to change efforts. Some research suggests that a relatively small segment of any population (about 10% to 20%) is ready to change key behaviors at a given point in time (Winett, 1991). If we could reach those people, our chances of success would improve.

I once worked in a program for homeless people with a man who had previously been homeless himself. When asked how he turned his life around after years of substance abuse and a marginal existence on the streets, he explained that he finally got sick and tired of being sick and tired. At that point, he was ready to try something different. Waiting until people have exhausted their resources and hit rock bottom hardly represents a preventive approach, however.

There are ways of assessing the likelihood of benefiting from programs that are more in keeping with a preventive approach. For example, preventive interventions are best directed to people who are likely to develop the problem of interest or people already experiencing beginning stages of the problem who are ready to change. So, for example, interventions designed to prevent the health problems associated with smoking need not direct antismoking messages to nonsmokers who have no intention of smoking or to smokers who have no intention of quitting.

Some interventions further quantify readiness to change (e.g., the seriousness of intentions to quit smoking) utilizing the *stages of change* approach developed by James Prochaska and Carlo DiClemente (Prochaska & DiClemente, 1992; Prochaska, DiClemente, & Norcross, 1992). These authors identified five stages of change:

- *Precontemplation:* People are not thinking seriously about changing and are not interested in any kind of intervention.
- *Contemplation:* People are thinking seriously about changing but not anytime soon.

- *Preparation:* People are preparing to change in the near future.
- *Action:* People are actively changing or have recently changed their behavior.
- *Maintenance:* People have made changes and have successfully avoided temptations to return to the problematic behavior

One smoking cessation program using this stages of change model did find that readiness to change predicted program effectiveness (Turner, Morera, Johnson, Crittendon, Freels, Parsons, Flay, & Warnecke, 2001). Consideration of people's readiness to change also suggests that interventions can have two positive outcomes. They can either reduce the problem behavior or increase people's readiness to reduce that behavior in the future—a readiness that other interventions can build upon. Research suggests that people cycle through the various stages of change several times before terminating the problematic behavior (Prochaska et al., 1992).

Another approach to targeting people most likely to benefit from intervention is to focus on people who are experiencing a crisis. People in crisis may be receptive to significant and potentially life-enhancing changes they might not have embraced otherwise. For example, Leonard Jason (1998) found that people who had recently experienced significant negative events were most responsive to the new ideas and techniques presented in a stress management program. Yet another approach is to try to foster receptivity as a part of the program. For example, meditation or other relaxation techniques might increase openness to messages about change.

Readiness to change is not simply an individual-level phenomenon. In recent years the concept of **community readiness** has emerged (e.g., Edwards, Jumper-Thurman, Plested, Oetting, & Swanson, 2000; Kumpfer, Whiteside, Wandersman, & Cardenas, 1997; Pentz, Rothspan, Turner, Skara, & Voskanian, 1999). Communities go through different stages with regard to their willingness to embrace prevention programming. In general, the continuum of community readiness proceeds from a lack of awareness of the target problem to problem recognition and finally to action. E. R. Oetting and colleagues (1995) identified nine stages of community readiness. Using this framework, the National Institute of Drug Abuse (1997) described strategies to enhance community readiness at each stage. The nine stages and related strategies appear in Table 9.3.

Within any individual or community, readiness to change varies with respect to each problem. Someone might be ready to find alternatives to violence in a close relationship but be unwilling to stop smoking. At the community level, as well, the willingness to confront one problem, such as smoking, might surpass the willingness to confront another, such as violence.

In 1965 smoking prevalence in the U.S. was about 52% for men and 34% for women. By 1996, the rates had dropped to about 28% for men and 23% for women. This contrasts with the trend for violent crime. During roughly the same period, violent

Table 9.3   Community Readiness: Stages and Strategies

Stage	Characteristics	Strategies
Stage 1: Community Tolerance/ No Knowledge	Community (or subcommunity) norms either tolerate or encourage the problem behavior.	Small group and one-on-one discussions with community leaders about the problem, its costs (health, psychological, social), and the norms that support it.
Stage 2: Denial	Recognition that the behavior can be problematic but no perceived need to tackle it locally.	Education and outreach programs to community leaders and groups that might sponsor programs. Use of local incidents to illustrate harmfulness in one-to-one discussions and educational outreach programs
Stage 3: Vague Awareness	General sense that the problem exists and should be tackled locally but understanding is vague and stereotyped, and the motivation to act is low. No identifiable leadership.	Educational outreach programs on the problem's national and state prevalence rates, and rates in similar communities. Use of local incidents to illustrate harmfulness. Local media campaigns to illustrate consequences of the problem.
Stage 4: Preplanning	Clear recognition of problem and general knowledge but vague or stereotyped ideas about etiology and risk factors. Leaders are identifiable but no intervention plans have been developed.	Educational programs that identify prevalence rates, correlates, and causes of the problem for community leaders and sponsorship groups. Educational outreach to introduce concept of prevention and describe programs in similar communities. Local media campaigns on consequences of the problem and the promise of prevention.

Stage	Characteristics	Strategies
Stage 5: Preparation	Planning exists and focuses on practical details. Programs may have begun on a trial basis but are not grounded in formal data collection. Leadership is active and funding may be sought or has been obtained.	Educational outreach programs to general public on specific prevention programs. Educational outreach to community leaders and sponsorship groups that describes the prevention programs and their startup needs. Media campaigns on consequences of the problem and the promise of prevention.
Stage 6: Initiation	Trial program is up and running. Staff is in training or has just finished. Enthusiasm is high as limitations and problems have not yet occurred. Knowledge of risk factors remains stereotyped.	Inservice training for program staff on problem consequences, correlates, and causes. Publicity efforts to kickoff program. Meetings to update and inform community leaders and sponsorship groups.
Stage 7: Institutionalization/ Stabilization	One or two programs are running and accepted as valuable routine activity. Limitations of programs known but little perceived need to change or expand.	Inservice training on evaluation process, new trends associated with the problem, and new prevention initiatives. Periodic review meetings and recognition events for program supporters, with local publicity.
Stage 8: Confirmation/ Expansion	Standard programs are viewed as valuable, and new initiatives are being planned. Expansion funds are sought, data are obtained regularly on extent of local problem, and efforts are underway to assess risk factors and etiology.	Inservice programs on local need. Periodic review meetings and recognition events for program supporters. Results of research and evaluation of programs presented to public though local media and/or public meetings.
Stage 9: Professionalization	Detailed and sophisticated knowledge of risk factors and etiology exists. Staff is trained, authorities are supportive, and community involvement is high. Effective evaluation is used to test and modify programs.	Continued inservice training, assessment of the problem, and program evaluation. Continued updating of community leaders and public through local media and/or public meetings.

Adapted from National Institute of Drug Abuse (1997). *Community readiness for drug abuse prevention: Issues, tips, and tools.* (publication # PB#97-209605). Washington, D.C.: National Institute of Drug Abuse. Available at: *http://www.open.org/~westcapt/crstages.htm*.

crimes such as murder, rape, and assault increased by approximately 550% (Biglan & Taylor, 2000). Anthony Biglan and Ted Taylor (2000) argued that the readiness to tackle violent crime has lagged behind readiness to reduce smoking for several reasons. First, consensus exists about what causes smoking and how to reduce it, while problem definitions and intervention approaches with regard to violence are more varied. In addition, formal and informal antismoking organizations work together at all system levels, while there are fewer antiviolence organizations, especially nongovernmental organizations at the national level, and coordination among these organizations is less likely. Biglan and Taylor recommended that behavioral scientists interested in increasing community readiness for violence prevention articulate the progress that has been made in this domain and advocate for empirically supported violence prevention programs.

⌘ Assessing Effects

Prevention science has made great strides in the past decades. We have better typologies to guide our work and increased knowledge about how to target our efforts wisely. Let's turn now to important considerations in assessing the effects of preventive interventions.

THE BASICS OF PREVENTION RESEARCH

The IOM Report delineated a **preventive intervention research cycle** (Mrazek & Haggerty, 1994). It held that research is an ongoing cycle in which theories and methods are put into practice, tested, and revised based on their documented effects. This exemplifies Lewin's action research model described in Chapter Two (see section entitled *Research and the Guiding Principles*).

The research cycle proposed in the IOM Report has undergone some modifications, but its essential elements remain the same (Kellam, Koretz &

Moscicki, 1999; Valente & Dodge, 1997). The cycle requires a theoretical and empirical basis, ongoing testing, and dissemination. These requirements are met through five central tasks. First, identify the problem or mental health outcome, its prevalence, and its course over the life span. Second, review relevant research (across disciplines) on risk factors and protective factors with regard to the problem of interest. Third, develop and implement innovative pilot interventions and test the efficacy of those interventions. Fourth, design, implement, and analyze the effectiveness of promising interventions in large-scale field trials with different populations and in different settings. Fifth, implement and continually evaluate prevention programs in the community, and disseminate these findings.

In carrying out this research agenda, preventionists are likely to encounter a number of challenges. Emory Cowen (1983) delineated some of the "research-weakening vicissitudes" of community-based prevention efforts (p. 21). They include difficulties in finding appropriate control groups, antagonism between researcher and community needs, attrition of participants (i.e., participants leave the study before it is over), and changes during the course of the intervention that are not attributable to the program. Additional challenges identified in the IOM Report include difficulties in maintaining strict randomization in assigning people to intervention versus control groups and insufficient long-term follow up (Muñoz et al., 1996).

Considerable progress has been made in meeting these research challenges over the past few decades. In their meta-analysis, Durlak and Wells (1997a) found that most of the 177 primary prevention interventions they studied had little subject attrition (10% or less in 80% of the studies), relied on multiple outcome measures (90%), and used random assignment to experimental and control groups (61%).

The use of control groups is particularly notable. Change occurs over time, and events unrelated to the intervention can influence the behaviors of interest. For example, between 1981 and 1993, people reduced the number of cigarettes smoked by about 108 per person each year. In the mid-1990s, however, the yearly declines slowed to about 12 cigarettes. These changes in cigarette consumption reflected fluctuations in the cost of cigarettes. Thus, antismoking interventions implemented during periods when cigarette costs changed would need to factor in the effects of cost changes on smoking rates (Levine, 1998). Similarly, AIDS prevention interventions have been affected by a variety of historical events—Magic Johnson's announcement that he was HIV positive, for example (Hobfoll, 1998). Such historical events are one reason why control groups are helpful. If experimental groups and control groups consist of similar people who are tested in similar contexts at similar times, better outcomes for people in the experimental group can be attributed to the intervention rather than to other nonprogram factors, such as historical events.

THE CHALLENGE OF FOLLOW-UP

Intervention effects, even when documented in studies using a control group, do not necessarily mean that the program worked. The possibility remains that the intervention simply postponed rather than prevented the problem of interest. When can researchers say with confidence that a problem was actually *prevented?* Based on their meta-analysis, Durlak and Wells (1997a) concluded that research projects rarely continue long enough to ensure that a targeted problem was truly prevented and not merely delayed. Although the studies included in their meta-analysis evidenced methodological sophistication in several domains, they lacked long-term follow-up. A substantial minority of the studies (25%) collected *no* follow-up data. Studies that did follow participants rarely assessed outcomes more than one year after the intervention.

Long-term follow-up is not always easy. The academic institutions where many prevention researchers work reward multiple, short-term studies and continual publications. Funders and politicians want to see quick results that justify continued support of programs. How can preventionists meet the demands of their employers and funders while conducting methodologically sound research? In particular, how long must researchers follow program participants before concluding that the problem of interest was truly prevented? Researchers have responded to these questions in two different ways: by assessing short-term outcomes that are expected to lead to the long-term results of interest and by studying the development of the disorder over the life course in order to pinpoint when follow-up should occur. These two approaches are described below.

PROXIMAL AND DISTAL OUTCOMES

One way in which prevention researchers have tried to limit the length of time necessary for follow-up is to assess **proximal outcomes** rather than **distal outcomes**. Program effectiveness is established by showing that the intervention reduces the risk behaviors that lead to the problem of interest (proximal outcomes) rather than preventing the problem itself (distal outcome). For example, researchers developing a substance abuse prevention program for first graders might assess post-intervention levels of poor achievement, aggression, or other precursors of substance use. Thus, assessments of program efficacy can occur when children are still in primary school, and researchers need not wait until middle school or high school to see if actual substance abuse rates were lowered (e.g., Ialongo, Werthamer, Kellam, Brown, Wang, & Lin, 1999).

A number of the interventions described earlier have relied on proximal outcomes. For example, implementers of high school transition programs have assessed academic achievement at the end of the year, rather than drop out rates three years later or unemployment in adulthood. Sometimes proximal outcomes are assessed in the interim between intervention and long-term follow-up. More often, proximal outcomes are assessed in lieu of long-term follow-up.

The relatively small number of intervention programs that do evaluate long-term outcomes speak to the dangers of relying only on proximal outcome data. Consider again Emory Cowen's well-researched

Primary Mental Health Project (PMHP). You will remember that PMHP targeted young children and was designed to prevent serious problems of adjustment in later life. In a long-term follow-up study, Cowen and his colleagues (1973) found that although the PMHP did reduce proximal outcomes, it did not succeed in preventing the problem of primary interest: serious maladjustment as indicated by treatment for psychological disorders at local clinics thirteen years after children's involvement in the program. Thus, the assessment of proximal outcomes can suggest that a program is promising but cannot replace long-term follow-up as a means of ensuring the program did indeed prevent the problem of central interest.

LIFE SPAN DEVELOPMENT AND PROBLEM DEVELOPMENT

Although long-term follow-up is necessary, knowledge about problem development can streamline research efforts by pinpointing exactly when long-term assessments should occur. An understanding of how problems develop over time and across the life span can help prevention researchers accomplish three important tasks: 1) identify the appropriate risk behaviors to target at particular ages and stages in problem development, 2) identify the most effective time to intervene, and 3) determine when long-term assessments will be most informative.

Julian Rappaport (1977) noted that early intervention takes two forms. It can either occur early in the life cycle, which generally means targeting infants or children, or it can occur early in the disease process. Intervening early in the disease process does not always mean intervening early in the life cycle. Researchers interested in the prevention of Alzheimer's disease, for example, would not necessarily target preschoolers. Both developmental knowledge and knowledge of **etiology** (i.e., how a condition or disorder develops over time) can help researchers decide whom to target, what outcomes to assess, and when to assess them.

Consider the importance of developmental knowledge. Preventionists need to understand the form disorders take at different ages in order to

target interventions appropriately. Different behaviors mark risk at different developmental periods. It is developmentally normative for five- and six-year old boys to establish social dominance using physical aggression, but most children have developed more mature methods of interpersonal influence by the time they reach the age of eight or nine (Coie et al., 1993). Thus, physical aggression in six-year olds would not indicate a likelihood of later problems, but the same behavior in older children might signal risk.

Etiology also matters. Consider the interrelated factors of interpersonal communication, marital satisfaction, divorce, and domestic violence. How are these factors interrelated? Where should one intervene? Does marital distress disrupt communication patterns, or does poor communication lead to marital distress? Howard Markman (1991, cited in Coie et al., 1993) compared couples who received communication training with couples who did not and found that the trained couples interacted more positively and had a 50% lower divorce rate seven years later. Program participants also evidenced lower rates of marital violence. This suggests that marital communication is a cause of divorce and violence rather than the result of marital distress.

We need to know which behaviors occur first in a chain of problematic behaviors in order to intervene proactively. Knowledge of the timeline of the development of disorders also provides valuable information about when to assess outcomes.

Consider the different etiologies of depression and antisocial personality disorder presented by Ricardo Muñoz and his colleagues (1996). Fifty percent of people who develop depressive disorders have their first symptom by 25.8 years, and 50% meet the criteria for diagnosis by 38.8 years of age. In comparison to depressive disorders, antisocial disorders tend to appear at relatively early ages. Fifty percent of people who develop antisocial disorders evidence their first symptoms by 14.7 years of age and 50% are diagnosed by 25.0 years. Thus, an indicated preventive intervention might succeed in identifying people at risk for antisocial disorder during adolescence. Unlike those who develop antisocial disorders, most people prone to depression have not yet evidenced any symptoms by age fifteen. Thus, indicated prevention programs for depression could not identify people at risk until they reached adulthood. When could we best assess the efficacy of prevention programs? We might have some idea of a program's efficacy in preventing antisocial disorders by the time participants reach the age of 25, but at that age we would not yet know if a program prevented depression. To assess the efficacy of a depression prevention program, we would need to wait until participants passed the age of 38.

IATROGENESIS

Not only do researchers need to know when to assess outcomes, they also need to consider which outcomes to assess. As described earlier, risk factors can lead to a variety of problem behaviors, and so program efficacy might best be assessed by considering a number of outcomes associated with the risk factor(s) targeted. In addition, although the goal of prevention research is to document reductions in the prevalence and incidence of disorders, in some cases prevention programs may cause or exacerbate problems. Even well-meaning interventions can have negative repercussions. Raymond Lorion (1983) warned that assuming that interventions based in good intentions can have only positive or at worst neutral effects is both naïve and irresponsible. Thus researchers must assess negative as well as positive outcomes that could be associated with the intervention. The occurrence of unintended but deleterious effects is termed **iatrogenesis**.

LABELING, OVERREACTING, AND NET WIDENING

There are numerous sources of iatrogenesis. Perhaps the most frequently cited cause in prevention programming is labeling. In both selective and indicated prevention programs, program participants are often marked to themselves and to others as "in need of help." As labeling theory suggests (see Chapter Seven), placing a person already evidencing vulnerability into a special program that defines them as at risk may create self-fulfilling prophesies.

In addition, the perception that a problem needs immediate, aggressive, and large-scale intervention can inspire reactionary programs and policies that do not help and potentially hurt. When people feel a compelling need to take action, the effects of these actions are not always considered carefully. Consider responses to the rash of school shootings in one community after another at the end of the twentieth century. These events were well covered in the media and led to the popular perception that school violence was epidemic. In fact, juveniles were three times as likely to be killed by an adult as by another juvenile, and during the same time period, lightning strikes killed twice as many children as gun violence in schools (Donohue, Schiraldi, & Zeidenberg, 1998). Nevertheless, the perceived need to act decisively led hundreds of schools nationwide to adopt zero tolerance policies in which *any* sign of violent intent was met by strict disciplinary action, often expulsion from school (e.g., Donohue, et al., 1998; Razzano, 2001). Zero tolerance led to the suspension of one eleven-year old for wielding a Tweety Bird key chain. In a New Jersey district, no children were suspended in the year prior to the zero-tolerance policy, while 50 children, mostly in kindergarten through third grade, were suspended in the two-weeks following the policy's adoption (Zernike, 2001). Such extreme policies often do more harm than good. In addition to problems associated with laebling, suspending and expelling youth increases their opportunities to engage in negative behaviors.

Another source of iatrogenesis is the **widening of the net**. When programs become available, more people may be identified as in need of services, whether they really need them or not. This increases dependence on service systems. Fear of net widening led Julian Rappaport and his colleagues (1985) to develop an intervention for juvenile offenders that targeted *only* those youth most likely to become repeat offenders (as described in the Classic Research box in Chapter Six). Minimal involvement in criminal behaviors is a normative part of adolescent development. Thus, programming for adolescents who committed only minor offenses brought youth who presented little or no risk for committing future crimes into the correctional system. Furthermore, involvement in correctional systems holds the risk of actually increasing the likelihood of future crime by bringing youth into contact with career criminals who could pass on crime techniques, provide criminal contacts, and reinforce antisocial values (Rappaport et al., 1985; Biglan & Taylor, 2000).

INSENSITIVITY TO CONTEXT

Inattention to context, including cultural context and marginalized status, may also interfere with program effectiveness and open the door to iatrogenesis. Preventionists might focus on problems that are not of primary concern to participants and therefore craft irrelevant programs. One intervention program offering prizes to Mexican American parents and children for improvements in school attendance failed because it did not understand the real reasons for absence—the need for youth to help support their families by working. Given the reality

of their lives, two-cent candies and star stickers on a classroom chart did not constitute an adequate reinforcement for sustained behavior change (King, Cotler, & Patterson, 1975).

As Stevan Hobfoll (1998) put it, "male prostitutes do not risk their economic livelihoods to preserve self-esteem" (p. 139). One woman in a battered woman's shelter observed, "the staff come in here smelling of perfume and wanting me to talk about my feelings when I don't have a place to live with my kids" (Riger, 2001, p. 71).

Interventions that are insensitive to context not only risk irrelevance, they can cause harm as well. Is articulation of feelings the best priority with victims of domestic abuse? A relatively powerless person in an abusive relationship might suffer from a lack of voice, but interventions that succeed in helping people speak out without first ensuring that speech is safe can do more harm than good.

As yet another example, interventions that promote behavior changes in disenfranchised groups

"Thank God! A panel of experts!"

The Panel of Experts: Always ready to shed light on your problem. © The New Yorker Collection 1978 Brian Savage from cartoonbank.com. All Rights Reserved.

can leave program recipients marginal in two cultures (Dumas, Rollock, Prinz, Hops, & Blechman, 1999). If AIDS prevention programs convince individual program participants to practice safer sex, they may become alienated from their lovers, friends, family members, and their larger community if these important others do not affirm the importance of safer sex (Hobfoll, 1998). The resulting increase in isolation is not likely to improve the life circumstances of people at risk for AIDS, who may already suffer from social marginality. Interventions may increase the likelihood of succeeding and decrease the likelihood of alienating people from their sociocultural environment if they target people *within* their social systems.

Cultures define what is normal, socially acceptable, and valued (Dumas et al., 1999). Preventive interventions may seek to create behavior change by altering what behaviors are deemed acceptable by the social environment (e.g., Levine, 1998). This can be achieved by changing the social norms that prevail in the surrounding context or by relocating at risk people to new contexts where "better" norms prevail. Let's look at each of these approaches.

Attempts to change cultural norms are inherently risky and value laden. As discussed in Chapter Three, decisions about "good" and "bad" norms and values are problematic. One might hope to bypass this inherently value-laden area by deciding simply to support those cultural norms that aid prevention efforts and counter norms that exacerbate the problem of interest. Such an overly simplistic approach may open the door to iatrogenesis, even as the program achieves its goals.

Blanca Ortiz-Torres, Irma Serrano-García, and Nélida Torres-Burgos (2000) described cultural norms relevant to HIV/AIDS prevention efforts with Puerto Rican and Dominican women. The researchers identified several norms that hindered the practice of safe sex, including the following beliefs: women should not speak about sexuality; reproduction-linked sexual practices are more moral than other practices; pleasurable and complete sexual relations require penetration; and women need to please their male sexual partners. The researchers also found norms that facilitated the practice of safer sex, such as the beliefs that abstinence and virginity are moral choices, women should not be promiscuous, and women need to care for themselves in order to care for others.

The authors noted that decisions to reinforce risk-protective norms and discourage risk-promoting norms are complicated by two factors. First, norms are contradictory. Women cannot retain their virginity *and* please their partners sexually. Second and perhaps more importantly, these norms have meaning within a larger value system that community psychologists may not endorse. Is it ethical for researchers and practitioners who believe in the equality of all people to frame interventions within value systems that promote such double standards as the belief that only women should be virgins and that the man's sexual pleasure matters more than the woman's?

Changing the goals that prevail within a social system can be ethically questionable and also very difficult. A second approach to changing prevailing norms is to remove at risk people from high-risk environments. Thus, the severing of social ties is the explicit goal. As a recent example, problematic adolescents may be removed from their family and peer groups and sent to "camps" or wilderness survival schools where an entirely different code of conduct is required. Such "shock" strategies may enjoy political and popular support but do not have demonstrated effectiveness (e.g., Portwood, 2001). Even if they lead to improvements in behavior within the new setting, these improvements are not often maintained after the program ends and participants return to environments that support the prior set of norms.

Furthermore, social values taint our visions of which settings promote "better" norms. In the latter half of the nineteenth century, the federal government of the United States adopted the view that Indians could best be incorporated into White society by removing Indian children from their families and communities and teaching them in off-reservation boarding schools hundreds or thousands of miles away. This form of "child-saving" was believed to be in the best interest of the Indian children because the weaker Indian society was seen as doomed to extinction. Attempts to "civilize" Indian children, which is to say to inculcate them into Western

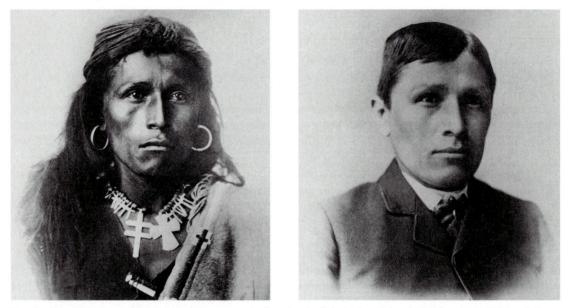

Tom Torlino (Navajo) as he appeared 1) upon arrival to the Carlisle Indian School October 21, 1882, and 2) three years later. *Photo courtesy of the Cumberland County Historical Society, Carlisle, PA.*

norms, often brought them into the homes of White families. Army Officer Richard Pratt, a key proponent of off-reservations schools wrote

> "I believe if we took one of those Indians—a little papoose from his mother's back, always looking backward—into our families, face it the other way, and keep it under our care and training until grown, it would then be Anglo-Saxon in spirit and American in all its qualities" (quoted in DeJong, 1993, p. 110).

This is yet another example of how planned behavior changes in disenfranchised groups can leave people marginal in two cultures (Dumas et al., 1999).

ENSURING PROGRAM INTEGRITY

Prevention is an inherently value-laden endeavor because it requires assessments of what constitutes desirable behaviors and how best to promote such behaviors. Unintended negative consequences often occur. One important mechanisms for ensuring both the efficacy and integrity of prevention programming is the use of rigorous evaluations.

THE IMPERATIVE OF EVALUATION

The meta-analyses conducted by Durlak and Wells (1997a, 1998) found little evidence of iatrogenesis. Only 9 of 177 primary prevention programs and 7 of 130 secondary prevention programs yielded negative effects. Furthermore, the magnitude of these effects was small. Although the lack of evidence of iatrogenesis could mean that prevention programs do little harm, it could also mean that study authors do not always look for evidence of iatrogenesis as thoroughly as they mght. The McCord Study (see the Classic Research box) makes clear that the possibility of negative consequences must be taken seriously by all preventionists.

ETHICAL GUIDELINES

Prevention scholars have identified several ethical responsibilities for preventionists, which are summarized in the following list.

1. The first ethical responsibility accounts for the possibility of iatrogenesis. In accordance

CLASSIC RESEARCH

The McCord Study
The Need for Evaluation

No study has highlighted the importance of program evaluation more clearly than the McCord study. In the late 1930s, an imaginative and exciting prevention program was designed to reduce the incidence of juvenile delinquency in young boys. It was a large-scale, comprehensive, and carefully designed intervention (McCord,1978; McCord & McCord, 1969; Powers & Witmer, 1972). Schools, welfare agencies, churches, and the police recommended "difficult" and "average" youngsters between the ages of 5 and 13 to take part in the program. These children were randomly assigned to either a control or intervention group. Participants in the intervention group were visited by counselors twice each month and were offered a variety of services. Some youth obtained academic tutoring, some received medical and psychiatric attention, some participated in summer camps, and some enrolled in community programs, such as the Boy Scouts.

In a 30-year follow-up, almost all of the original participants were located, and the majority agreed to participate in the study. Results showed that most of the men who had taken part in the program—about two-thirds—reported feeling favorably about their participation, and many recounted fond memories of their counselors. Respondents wrote of being diverted from a life of crime and "put on the right road" (McCord, 1978, p. 287) Such was the self-report data. But the evaluators did not rely solely on what participants said. They sought additional evidence of the program's effectiveness by examining official records, such as those kept by the Crime Prevention Bureau.

Here's where the plot thickens. Men who had been in the program were compared to similar men who had not been in the program along 57 dimensions. Seven of these comparisons showed significant differences between the two groups of men and *every comparison favored the men who had* **not** *been part of the program*. Men who had taken part in the intervention were more likely to:

- commit two or more crimes;
- abuse alcohol;
- become seriously mentally ill;
- die at an earlier age;
- suffer from stress-related illnesses;
- work in less prestigious occupations; and
- find their work unsatisfying.

The probability that all seven significant comparisons would favor the control group by chance is less than 1 in 10,000! (McCord, 1978).

These results are certainly disturbing. Well-intentioned people used the best knowledge available at the time to design and implement a thoughtful and comprehensive prevention program. Not only was the program ineffective, it seems to have had quite serious unintended negative effects.

What can one conclude from the McCord study? One conclusion is that researchers must not rely solely on self-report data. The data obtained from official records stand in stark contrast to the picture that would have emerged had the evaluators relied only on participants' subjective assessments of the program. Self-report data, especially data on client satisfaction, may be the easiest and most obvious way of evaluating interventions, but it does not tell the whole story. A second conclusion to be drawn from the McCord study is that preventionists must adhere to the ethical imperative of carefully evaluating program effects—both negative and positive.

with the Hippocratic oath, preventionists must do no harm. Even well-intentioned and well-designed prevention programs can have negative consequences, and it is incumbent on researchers to account for this possibility in their evaluations. As an additional safeguard, preventionists should intrude as little as possible into those aspects of the program recipients' lives that are not problematic.

2. Program should not be designed for the preventionist's gain. The primary purpose of preventive intervention is to improve the lives of others. The preventionist's own career advancement matters, but threats to pet theories, a reduced chance of publishing, possible loss of funding, and other potential difficulties cannot stand in the way of careful program development, rigorous evaluation, and proper dissemination of results.

3. Prevention programs should be piloted in small-scale studies to ensure their effectiveness before expanding. Pilot testing allows researchers to assess the efficacy of the program, address unforeseen problems, determine whether iatrogenesis has occurred, and estimate program costs.

4. Program participants should be treated with respect and should be active participants in planning, implementing, and evaluating the prevention effort. This means program participants should help define the problem to be prevented, identify program goals, agree on the means for achieving those goals, and assist in gathering and interpreting information on the program. Ownership on the part of program participants and stakeholders is not only an ethical responsibility, it also promotes the development of context-sensitive and effective interventions, and aids in the adoption of these programs.

5. Program planners, participants, and other involved people are entitled to professional courtesies. In particular, confidentiality must be maintained. This is essential if the program is to be developed, run, and evaluated honestly.

6. Informed consent should be obtained before implementation of the program. Informed consent is not always feasible, especially in large-scale efforts. Few of us were consulted about the fluoride in our water or antismoking billboards on our commuting routes. Nevertheless, it is incumbent on the researcher to acknowledge the importance of informed consent and live up to this ethical requirement to the greatest extent possible.

7. The prevention program should promote equity and justice. Programs require sensitivity to cultural differences and the dynamics of oppression. A long-term vision will help program planners to assess the degree to which the program contributes to positive and fundamental social change.

8. The preventionist is accountable for the impact of the program and must resolve any problems that result, intended or not.

Evaluation research is critical. It helps preventionists to identify any unintended consequences of the program. As described in the next section, it also provides evidence of which programs work with whom and under what circumstances.

PROGRAM POPULARITY AND EFFICACY

More than a decade ago, N. Dickon Reppucci and Jeffrey Haugaard (1989) emphasized the importance of evaluating the school-based sexual abuse prevention programs that were popular at the time. They feared that these programs did little good and might inflict harm, such as undue fear and worry in young children and negative influences on their trusting relationships with adults. Furthermore, a sense of accomplishment accompanies the establishment of *any* intervention, which reduces the perceived need to act. If the programs had no impact (or a negative impact), the perception that the problem was being addressed when it was not would mean a reduced likelihood of improving the situation for abused children (Reppucci & Haugaard, 1989; Reppucci et al., 1999).

Popular and political support for prevention programs do not depend on evidence of efficacy. Boot camps for juveniles, zero-tolerance school violence policies, and school-based sexual abuse programs have all enjoyed widespread support without evidence of program efficacy. The lack of relationship between popularity and efficacy is nowhere more apparent than in the example of DARE (Drug Abuse Resistance Education). DARE is a prevention program begun by the Los Angeles Police Department in 1983. Children in late elementary school receive 17 one-hour sessions designed to keep them from using drugs, tobacco and alcohol (Ennett, Tobler, Ringwalt, Flewelling, 1994). The DARE curriculum is presented by uniformed police officers who have undergone 80 hours of specialized training at a cost of more than $2,000 per officer (Wysong, Aniskiewicz, & Wright, 1994).

DARE's popularity skyrocketed after President Reagan declared his "War on Drugs" in 1986. In 1990 DARE programs were in place in more than 3,000 communities in all 50 states and reached an estimated 20 million students (Wysong et al., 1994). As of February 1994, DARE existed in at least half the public schools in the U.S. (Ennett et al., 1994), and the nationwide expenditures for DARE reached approximately $700 million per year (Wysong et al., 1994).

This price-tag has not seemed prohibitive, however; an interrelated network of organizational ties link DARE programs to local, state, and federal funding sources, as well as to private corporations. Police departments, law enforcement agencies, and politicians at every level of government have lobbied in support of the program. Congressional proposals have been crafted to earmark government funds for DARE, and corporate sponsors emerged—small local businesses and huge conglomerates such as McDonald's, Kentucky Fried Chicken, and Security Pacific National Bank. The extent of support for DARE became clear on September 10, 1992, the day U.S. Congress and former President George S. Bush designated as National DARE Day (Wysong et al., 1994).

It was into this context that reports of DARE's ineffectiveness emerged. In the early 1990s, numerous research studies and meta-analyses concluded that DARE had, at best, only a very small and very short-term effect on drug use (Ennett et al., 1994; Lynam, Milich, Zimmerman, Novak, Logan, Martin, Leukefeld, Clayton, 1999; Wysong et al., 1994). Other drug prevention programs existed that were more cost-effective and yielded better results.

Program evaluation often occurs in a political atmosphere. In Chapter One, I discussed the ongoing debate about the efficacy of Head Start programs. Since the 1960s, the federal government has slashed funding for most social programs but not Head Start, and so program evaluators face the challenge of providing accurate (and sometimes unfavorable) evaluation information without challenging the congressional faith and support that make early education programs possible (Hauser-Cram, Warfield, Upshur, & Weisner, 2000).

After about a decade of debate about the merits of studies that showed DARE to be ineffective (which DARE discounted) and about the worthiness of DARE as an intervention strategy (which evaluators questioned), common ground emerged. The widespread support and far-reaching influence of DARE constituted an important foundation for prevention programming, a foundation on which researchers and scientists could help to build an effective program. DARE, in turn, has heeded calls to base programming on sound research and evaluate program efficacy. In the twenty-first century, DARE. They have developed several principles of effectiveness, such as:

- Grounds activities in a thorough review of available data on drug and violence problems in the local community;
- Establishes local or regional advisory councils, on which community representatives serve, to set program goals and determine activities necessary to meet those goals;
- Designs activities based on research into the effectiveness of the strategies used in preventing or reducing drug use, violence, or disruptive behavior
- Conducts periodic program evaluations to determine success in meeting goals and to improve program efficacy. (DARE, No date)

⌘ Creating Long-Lasting and Widespread Change: From Demonstration to Adoption

The ultimate goal of prevention programs is to reduce problems and enhance wellness. Although prevention science has made great strides in the past few decades with regard to conceptualizing prevention, targeting efforts, and assessing outcomes, these strides have not translated into substantial improvements in health. Rates of mental disorders, substance abuse, violence, poverty, and other indicators of individual and community maladjustment remain high (e.g., Fleming, 1996; Weissberg, Gullotta, Hampton, Ryan, & Adams, 1997). One reason why innovative and effective prevention programs have not led to widespread improvements in health is that preventionists have not ensured that successful trial programs continue and are adopted in other settings (e.g., Schorr, 1997).

Many prevention programs begin as **demonstration projects.** A demonstration project is an intervention designed, implemented, and researched in the hope of developing an effective program that can be maintained in the original setting and replicated in other locales. In order to extend the reach of successful demonstration projects, researchers must understand the characteristics of programs, people, and organization that lead to program adoption. There are numerous challenges that must be surmounted in "scaling up" from small successes (Schorr, 1997, p.xiv).

As seen in Chapter Six (the Community Intervention box), George Fairweather was one of the first researchers dedicated to identifying the factors that promote the adoption of innovative programs. His active efforts contrast with the more common "publish and hope" approach (Stolz, 1984) in which prevention researchers seek to disseminate programs by describing their successes in esoteric journals that community-based professionals rarely read (Elias, 1997). Prevention programs will have a better chance of improving people's lives if researchers attend to the numerous factors that affect the adoption of prevention programs within communities and then use these findings to encourage program adoption.

ATTENDING TO CONTEXT

A review of the literature on social support interventions concluded that few interventions document any success, and successes that do occur are generally short-lived (Lakey & Lutz, 1996). The reviewers observed that most interventions train staff and volunteers to provide support to individuals, which may help people during a crisis, but this approach does not translate into enduring changes in participants' social support networks. They argued that improvements would not continue beyond the lifetime of the program unless changes transpired in the natural environment of program participants. Maurice Elias (1997) echoed this concern in calling for preventionists to challenge the prevailing view of people-as-program-recipients, and work to create enduring changes in both people *and* their natural settings.

Prevention programs often target individuals without attending to their social context. Reppucci and his colleagues (1999) warned that prevention programs disappoint if they fail to consider the surrounding community (see also Weissberg, Caplan, & Harwood, 1991). As an example, they cited research showing that smoking cessation programs for adolescents are more effective when they target the environmental context; cigarette-seller behavior, for example, or tobacco industry advertising, rather than the teens themselves.

Attention to natural settings also means tailoring interventions to fit the microsystems in which they occur: families, schools, workplaces, neighborhoods. This was evident in a study of successful program implementation within high-risk (i.e., low-income) schools. The researchers found several important preconditions for program adoption. Prevention programs that took hold were consistent with the goals and missions of the school and became part of the culture of the school as evidenced by incorporation of prevention activities into the schools ongoing practices (Gager & Elias, 1997).

OVERCOMING RESISTANCE TO CHANGE

Issues involved in moving from program demonstration to adoption have been studied under the terms "diffusion of innovation" (e.g., Rogers, 1983) or "dissemination of innovation" (e.g., Mayer & Davidson, 2000). These terms emphasize the notion that new programs represent changes in the status quo, and as we saw in Chapter Six, change inspires resistance. Resistance is more likely when individuals affected by the change do not have enough information about what is entailed, experience a lack of control, fear losing influence over or status within the setting, do not see personal benefits in changing, already feel overloaded by existing demands, perceive the change as a criticism of their previous efforts, fear being unable to handle the new responsibilities, or expect the change will disrupt their routines (K. Ryan, 1993). Certainly prevention programmers can work to counter these individual-level sources of resistance. In addition, they can try to make the context more conducive to change.

The settings in which people work shape individual responses to change. Some organizational forms support innovation. "Organic" organizations, which have flexible structures and decentralized decision-making processes, may adopt new programs and strategies more easily than "mechanistic" organizations, which are formal and hierarchical (Mayer & Davidson, 2000).

In addition, organizational support for specific changes also matters. This was well illustrated in a recent study by Pennie Foster-Fishman and her colleagues (1999). They surveyed 186 personnel in 32 human service agencies with regard to two reform movements: the increasing push toward interagency cooperation and the growing emphasis on strength-based service delivery (Foster-Fishman,

Salem, Allen, & Fahrbach, 1999). The providers' receptivity to change depended on support for reforms in their host agency (e.g., perceptions of the director's agenda), as well as the larger social context (e.g., interagency views on the reform movements, funder mandates). Receptivity to change at any level of analysis depends on perceptions of support for that change at other levels. The proliferation of DARE programs can be attributed, in large part, to the cooperation of community leaders, politicians, corporate sponsors, and governmental agencies from the local to federal levels.

Preventionists can increase the likelihood of adoption by ensuring (or building) community support before implementation. For example, Robert Slavin has widely disseminated his school-based *Success for All* program. This program operates on the principles that 1) learning problems can be prevented by using the best available classroom strategies with the support of parents (primary prevention) and 2) by implementing immediate and intensive corrective interventions when learning problems appear (secondary prevention). Slavin only implements this program when 80% of a school faculty agrees to invite it into the school (reported in Schorr, 1997). The more broad-based the support, the better the chances of program adoption.

Diplomacy is needed in promoting change efforts. People and systems resist new programs if they are seen as requiring fundamental change. Maurice Elias (1997) warned that innovative agendas are not best advanced through social change rhetoric. He proposed that the language of preventionists in the 1960s and 1970s, which emphasized ending social ills by disrupting the existing social order, might work against the adoption of innovation in more recent times. Preventionists might promote new programs as efforts to help settings become more effective rather than attempts to subvert the status quo. Most people and systems strive to adapt incoming information to fit within existing structures (**assimilation**) rather than using that information as an impetus to change the structures (**accommodation**).

The likelihood of program adoption increases when preventionists package programs in appealing ways. Innovations are more accepted when potential adopters clearly see the relative advantages of the new program, view the intervention as easy to implement, appreciate the cost savings, easily observe the key features of the intervention, and can easily understand the program and describe it to others (Mayer & Davidson, 2000).

MANIFEST VERSUS TRUE ADOPTION

Convincing service systems to adopt programs is only part of the challenge. Equally important is ensuring that the programs remain true to the demonstration project. Julian Rappaport, Edward Seidman, and William Davidson (1985) distinguished **manifest** and **true program adoption**. They developed an indicated prevention program targeting adolescents on the brink of involvement with the legal system (see the Classic Research box in Chapter Six). Their program was adopted by the setting and continued after the demonstration ended, but the program was not adopted as intended. It soon began to serve adolescents who were only superficially involved in criminal activities—a population purposely *not* targeted in the program as initially conceived and evaluated. Thus, true adoption did not occur.

Preventionists need to help program adopters understand and embrace the key tenets of programs. Some correspondence among critical features of the program across sites is necessary to maintain the integrity of the program and to ensure the relevance of the evaluation data. This is not to say that prevention programs should be identical across settings. Programs are more effective and their adoption more likely if participants and service deliverers have ownership of the project and adapt the program to the local culture. Consequently, researchers must clearly identify **core features** of the program, that is to say crucial and defining program elements, and **adaptive features**, program characteristics that may be altered to meet the needs of the local culture (Elias, 1997; Schorr, 1997; Valente & Dodge, 1997)

ACCOUNTING FOR "OPERATOR DEPENDENCE"

Even when settings agree to adopt a program, understand the core features, and work to fit the program into the local culture, success is not guaranteed. Peter Rossi (1978) argued that model programs often do not become enduring programs because researchers fail to consider the extent to which programs are "operator-dependent."

Researchers who implement demonstration programs differ from the community-based professionals who adopt and sustain programs in important ways (Kendall & Southam-Gerow, 1995). Areas of difference include theoretical perspectives, training, rewards for prevention work, and demands on time. A researcher implementing a demonstration project has generally received special funds for materials, training, consultation, and ongoing evaluation—luxuries that service delivery settings cannot always afford (Elias, 1997). In addition, demonstration programs benefit from the excitement of novelty that may occur when a new program is developed (see S. Sarason, 1972). For these reasons, the context of demonstration often differs substantially from the context of adoption.

Another important aspect of operator dependence that cannot be programmed is leadership. Not all sites have inspiring leaders who are willing and able to ensure program success by networking with diverse people and groups, fostering cooperation, building coalitions, and mobilizing varied resources (Elias, 1997; Reppucci et al., 1999; Schorr, 1997; see also S. Sarason, 1972 for discussion of the dynamics of leadership). Individuals with unique qualities carry out interventions within particular organizational settings.

I recently had lunch with a colleague from Great Britain who told me that in England, the word "program" does not exist as it does in the United States. The notion that one can export a prepackaged, presumably universal set of operating instructions from one setting to another setting that has a completely different history, set of values, staff, and community niche would make little sense. Prevention programs today less often rely on one-size-fits-all implementation "kits" (RMC Research Corporation, 1995), but they continue to be conceived as discrete packages that exist apart from a social context. A more holistic view of prevention programs as a process rather than a package might foster the dissemination of innovation and ultimately lead to more widespread and long-lasting improvements in individual and community health.

⌘ The Promise of Community Psychology: Planning for Synergy

The NIMH and IOM Reports signaled the growing acceptance of prevention as a legitimate research and intervention activity whose potential has not yet been realized. These reports both cited the need to attend to program setting, but neither report centered on the dynamics of community context. In these reports, as in most prevention studies, ecological perspectives help explain findings, but they are not the basis for developing programs, do not shape research methodologies, and do not inform evaluations (e.g., Hobfoll, 1998). Community psychologists may contribute to the larger field of prevention by underscoring the importance of attending to social context at *all* phases of intervention.

Consider, for example, the issue of random assignment. Prevention researchers frequently cite the need for strict randomization (e.g., Cowen, 1983; Mrazek & Haggerty, 1994). Often this means that a pool of potential program recipients is identified, and individuals are randomly assigned into treatment and control conditions. Preventive interventions may have a greater chance of success, however, if they target entire cohorts of people and the settings in which they reside, rather than individuals in isolation. Murray Levine (1998) observed that an experimental approach that requires "random assignment of individuals within a cohort to treatment conditions may dilute if not destroy the impact of the intervention" (p. 192).

The interactions among program participants can lead to synergistic effects that enhance prevention agendas. **Synergism** means that when discrete agents act in cooperation, the effects are not simply additive, but multiplicative—the whole is greater than the sum of its parts. A number of preventive interventions described in this chapter try to capitalize on this synergism. Researchers in the Stanford Heart Disease Prevention Program (see the Community Intervention box) crafted media messages with the explicit goal of stimulating conversations among community members. They also invited high-risk participants to attend group workshops with their spouses. These efforts support the view that when interventions target people within their social contexts, synergism becomes possible. Similarly, one likely reason for the success of the STEP program described earlier is that it targeted an entire cohort of youth and teachers, that is to say the social system of the youth (Barrera & Prelow, 2000). Thus, group norms could emerge that reinforced the goals of the program. Indeed, the synergistic effects of community not only shape the behavior of community members, they also can have radiating effects on people outside that system. Research suggests that women whose social network promotes safer sex not only get tested for AIDS more often, but their male partners are also more likely to use condoms (Ortiz-Torres, Serrano-García, & Torres-Burgos, 2000).

Preventive approaches that capitalize on synergism are more the exception than the rule. Indeed, popular conceptualizations of prevention frame synergy as an impediment to methodological rigor. Ernest Valente and Kenneth Dodge (1997) conveyed this perspective when they characterized interventions in the context of existing classrooms and school as entailing a "major problem." They held that "[r]andom assignment of children within a classroom (or school) to intervention versus control conditions could lead to contamination of the control group children, because they might indirectly benefit from intervention with the teacher or peers" (pp. 201–202). From a community perspective, synergism is not seen as a "problem," but a gift to preventionists. If community synergy "contaminates" our research, we need to find new ways to do research.

Not only do we fail to account for the synergistic potential of communities in designing programs, we also fail to account for it when documenting program impact. Edison Trickett (1997) observed that the ecological impact of prevention programs is rarely assessed as outcomes are almost exclusively measured at the individual level. In response to this criticism, Durak and Wells (1997b) noted that 10% of the interventions they assessed in their meta-analysis of primary prevention programs did include indices of ecological impact that *could have* been evaluated. Among these indices were changes in parent and teacher attitudes, changes in parent and teacher interactions with children, and effects of the intervention on the social climate of the school.

The recognition that prevention effects radiate through social systems shifts our thinking about how to measure program effectiveness. A program that convinces each participant to reduce his or her use of illegal substances may be effective, but a program that does this and also inspires the individuals to confront the social norms that promote substance abuse in their microsystems may be more effective. And a program that does all this, and helps program participants (and all their friends) recognize and confront the larger social conditions that impact substance abuse (e.g., community poverty, drug laws) could be a really powerful prevention program.

Synergism occurs not only among people in face-to-face interaction, but also across different levels of analysis. This led Ed Seidman (1987) to advocate mesosystem-level preventive interventions—interventions aimed at connections among systems. The recent interest in community coalitions as a base for prevention activities offers an opportunity to study synergistic effects across systems. In community coalitions, groups of individuals from diverse organizations and community constituencies work together toward a common goal (Feighery & Rogers, 1989). Community coalitions generally target factors at multiple levels and across multiple groups (e.g., Butterfoss, Goodman, & Wandersman, 1996,

Mitchell, Stevenson, & Florin, 1996). The Healthy Communities movement (see the Community Intervention box in Chapter Seven) is one example.

As another example, consider the ecologically oriented prevention initiatives supported by the National Center on Child Abuse and Neglect (reported by Earls, McGuire, & Shay, 1994). Although goal of the initiatives was to prevent child abuse and neglect, it did not focus on parents or families in isolation, but on system relationships within the broader community. Intervention efforts concentrated on building caring communities for families by providing families with a network of services, such as food pantries, home health visitors, literacy training, respite care, and mutual-help opportunities. Interventions directed to entire communities require assessment methods that do not rely solely on individual-level outcomes. New methods must become more complex to account for changes at multiple levels of analysis (Goodman, Wandersman, Chinman, Imm, & Morrissey, 1996).

Long-term multipronged interventions that converge around important goals can have a broad social impact (Levine, 1998). Leonard Jason (1998) incorporated the lessons learned in the Stanford Heart Disease Prevention Program (Maccoby & Alexander, 1979; Farqhar, 1991) into new media-based interventions. The creative multilevel interventions he devised used various voluntary associations, community groups, and for-profit agencies, as well as the media. One such program sought to reduce the incidence of smoking among African-American adolescents in Chicago. The Board of Education supplied an antismoking curriculum to 472 elementary schools. At the same time, a local newspaper with a large African American readership agreed to publish an antismoking series in their weekly children's page. A radio station popular among African American listeners ran a series of smoking prevention public service messages and aired a call-in talk show to help parents discuss smoking with their children. The radio station also played the five winning entries of a smoking prevention rap contest, and the overall winner appeared as a guest DJ. The owners of several local billboards agreed to display the winners of a smoking prevention poster contest. The contest winners also received a certificate and prizes for their schools at a special assembly. This multifaceted intervention, which targeted individuals-within-contexts, led to a decrease in student use of tobacco *and* in family use of cigarettes, alcohol, and marijuana.

Jason's interventions, like the Stanford heart disease interventions, drew on the notion of synergy (see also Schooler, Flora, & Farquhar, 1993). As Nathan Maccoby and Janet Alexander (1979) stated early in the development of the Stanford Heart Disease Prevention Program, "We tentatively attribute much of the success of the community education campaigns to the synergistic interaction of multiple educational inputs and to interpersonal communication stimulated by application of these inputs in a community setting" (p. 81). When interventions target entire groups of individuals and the systems where they reside, synergistic effects can ensure that the intervention as a whole is more than the sum of its parts.

Action Agenda

Community Readiness for Prevention

Assess your community's readiness to tackle a problem of interest to you. Clip newspaper articles. Talk to community leaders. Assess the quantity and quality of existing programs. You can use Table 9.3 as a starting point, or you might ask knowledgeable community leaders to complete the Community Key Leader Survey, devised by Robert Goodman and Abraham Wandersman, that appears on the website of the Western Region Center for Application of Preventive Technologies (*http://www.open.org/~westcapt/survey.html*) (see also Goodman et al., 1996). Additional tools are available at the Center for Substance Abuse Prevention web page (*http://www.preventiondss.org/*).

After deciding where on the scale of community readiness your community lies with regard to a particular problem, devise an intervention that you believe would increase community readiness. What would be a first step in implementing your intervention?

Taking the McCord Study Seriously

One understandable reaction to the McCord study is an attempt to attribute the findings of iatrogenesis to methodological problems—their control group was not well chosen, the outcomes assessed were not appropriate, and so on. The ethical principle of doing no harm requires, however, that preventionists take seriously the possibility that an intervention may well have unintended negative side effects. Choose a prevention study (perhaps one from *14 Ounces of Prevention*, Price et al., 1988) and list, individually or in groups, all the possible negative outcomes that *might* result. How would you assess these possible effects? What actions do you think you would be ethically obligated to take should these negative outcomes occur?

Norms, Values, and Prevention

Consider a problem that exists in a context with which you are familiar (e.g., smoking in your high school peer group, ethnic group tensions at your college, high employee turnover at your workplace). What norms that exist within these contexts help perpetuate the problem? Are there also norms that have, or potentially could have, a preventive effect? Can you think of interventions that would address the relevant norms (either changing norms that perpetuate the problem or strengthening norms that prevent it)? If you decided to implement such an intervention, what would be a first step, and what would be the ethical implications of that step?

 **Key Terms**

adaptive features

attributable risk

community readiness

core features

demonstration project

distal outcomes

etiology

iatrogenesis

incidence

indicated, selective

IOM report

manifest program adoption

meta-analysis

precipitating factors

predisposing factors

prevalence

preventive intervention research cycle

primary prevention

protective factors

proximal outcomes

risk factors

secondary prevention

synergism

tertiary prevention

true program adoption

universal prevention

widening of the net

Chapter 10

Empowerment

⌘ Introduction

The Dudley Street neighborhood lies just two miles from downtown Boston. In the early 1980s, a downtown high-rise overlooking the neighborhood would have glimpsed a landscape of urban blight. Dudley Street was a patchwork of vacant lots, burned-out office building, and abandoned houses. Rusting cars and litter dotted the pothole-ridden streets. Decades of disinvestment, redlining,[1] abandonment, and arson-for-profit had turned a thriving commercial and residential district into a virtual wasteland (Medoff & Sklar, 1994; Negri, 2000). The diverse denizens of Dudley Street, African Americans, Latinos and Latinas, Cape Verdeans, and Euro-Americans, were united primarily in their despair.

[1]Redlining is the discriminatory practice, once popular among financial institutions, of identifying the borders of low-income minority communities and refusing to do business with residents in those areas.

279

Such was the view of Dudley Street in the early 1980s. In 1984 residents formed the Dudley Street Neighborhood Initiative (DSNI) and determined to turn the dilapidated neighborhood into the community of their dreams. Members worked together to create a shared neighborhood vision that coalesced around the image of an urban village. A village is a wellspring fed by the communal energy of the villagers, and the villagers, in turn, draw sustenance from the well. A village provides food, goods and services, employment, opportunities for socialization, and recreational activities (DSNI, No Date a). The residents' shared vision of an urban village guided community organizing and development on Dudley Street.

Less than twenty years later, DSNI accomplishments inspire awe. About 13% of the community's 24,000 residents belong to this vibrant voluntary organization, and countless resident-driven plans have been realized in cooperation with local businesses, banks, nonprofit organizations, and religious groups, with supplemental assistance from government agencies and foundations (notably the Riley Foundation, which catalyzed the neighborhood revitalization). Since 1984, 600 of the 1300 vacant lots have been converted to affordable homes and common spaces, including community gardens, greenhouses, parks, playgrounds, and a town commons. Three hundred new homes have been built, and another 300 renovated. Dudley Street has cleaned up its streets, closed hazardous and illegal trash transfer centers, rehabilitated parks, established low-income and cooperative housing, restored rail service, formed daycare networks, founded a high school, begun youth recreation programs, opened a community center, and organized multicultural festivals (DSNI, No Date b).

The list of accomplishments only begins to give a sense of the urban village. Let's look at life on Dudley Street more closely. It is an innovation-embracing neighborhood that pursues community self-sufficiency and resident inter-reliance. Imagine a three-acre farm in the heart of an urban neighborhood! The fruit and vegetable farm, community gardens, and a local fish farm provide fresh food year round. This food is sold in small grocery stores that are walking distance from every home. No one needs a car on Dudley Street because almost everything is within walking distance. Residents stroll to drug stores, newsstands, tailors, dentists, beauty parlors, coffee shops, hardware stores, parks, concerts, and the authentic ethnic restaurants that enjoy widespread popularity—requests for Gladys' Splendid Sofritos have come from as far away as Puerto Rico. Dudley Street continues to look forward. The most recently built homes are solar powered and superinsulated (as well as affordable), virtually eliminating the need for gas, oil, and electric heat. Residents are currently assessing the feasibility of a stand-alone wastewater treatment system that would use aquatic plants and animals to treat sewage at a fraction of the cost of traditional systems (DSNI, No Date a).

The transformation of Dudley Street exemplifies empowerment. Demoralized residents of a devastated and largely abandoned neighborhood came together to create an urban village so vital and attractive that it now counts as one of Boston's major tourist attractions (DSNI, No Date a). People from around the world come to enjoy Dudley Street's culturally diverse food, specialty shops, music, theater, and festivals. How did this happen? Can it happen anywhere? How do the experiences on Dudley Street inform the theory, research, and practice of community psychology? Can community psychologists help bring similar transformations to other neighborhoods? Can the lessons and insights of Dudley Street guide change efforts on an even larger scale? These are some of the questions addressed in this chapter.

⌘ Brief History

The concept of empowerment has its roots in the 1960s. Empowerment was the goal of freedom fighters who turned their shared sense of identity and common understanding of the sociopolitical roots of their oppression into mandates for social change (Prilleltensky, 1998; Trickett, 1994). The ideology of empowerment figured prominently in the influential writings of Saul Alinsky (1971) and Paulo Freire (1970/1992). These two activists described how change agents (community organizers and educators, respectively) could join forces with members of disenfranchised communities to transform social relationships and redistribute social power (e.g., Shefner-Rogers, Rao, Rogers, & Wayangankar, 1998; Strawn, 1994). The term "empowerment" was not used to describe such activities until the mid-1970s, however.

Barbara Bryant Solomon (1976) was one of the first to articulate a theory of empowerment. She contended that the "devaluation" of African Americans in U.S. society resulted in widespread feelings of powerlessness among Black people in Black communities. She proposed empowerment as an antidote to the negative valuation—a way for social workers to engage African American clients and communities in efforts to reconstitute their lives. At about the same time, Peter Berger and Richard Neuhaus (1977) also used this new term and proposed that people become empowered through **mediating structures**—the systems that stand between the large impersonal institutions of public life and the private lives of individuals. Berger and Neuhaus posited that mediating structures, especially neighborhoods, families, churches, and voluntary associations play a vital role in a democratic society. They are expressions of people's collective needs and values and the means to citizen empowerment. Consequently, Berger and Neuhaus argued that public policy should actively support mediating structures, not undercut them, and utilize these structures to realize social goals.

A few years after this early work on empowerment in social work and public policy, Julian Rappaport (1981) outlined the relevance of the concept to community psychology. He noted that empowerment focuses on people's inherent strengths and directs attention to social change. Rappaport (1981, 1987; Wiley & Rappaport, 2000) asserted that community psychology's current orienting concept (prevention) failed to promote either of these central values of the field.

According to Rappaport, *prevention* evoked all the wrong symbols, images, and meta-messages.

Prevention highlights dysfunction—it targets at-risk people in order to save them from themselves. It focuses on what is currently going or soon will go wrong rather than on what is going right. It reinforces traditional models of unidimensional helping in which experts develop, package, operate, disseminate, and generally control interventions. Furthermore, despite its debt to public health, prevention seeks to improve *individual* mental health and pays insufficient attention to social contexts.

Empowerment, Rappaport argued, emphasizes strengths. It attempts to build competencies rather than correct deficiencies. It also suggests new paradigms of helping. Professionals are not distant experts but collaborators who work side by side with community members in efforts to change their social worlds. Rappaport asserted that empowerment promoted a new image of people as citizens with rights and choices that balanced the dominant images of people as needy. Members of helping professions too often viewed poor, physically disabled, mentally ill, retarded, elderly, and other marginalized people as child-like and dependent on professionals for socialization, training, and skill development. He warned that such a perspective blinded us to more productive ways of helping.

Several years after his initial treatise, Rapport (1987) clarified that his endorsement of empowerment was not a condemnation of prevention. Prevention could be seen as a strategy through which empowerment goals might be realized. Nevertheless, Rappaport asserted that community psychology could best remain faithful to its fundamental values by adopting empowerment as its primary orienting concept.

Rappaport's seminal articles placed him at the forefront of a groundswell of interest in empowerment. In the late 1980s and 1990s, talk of empowerment exploded. A search of Psycinfo, a psychological literature database that encompasses journal articles and books, revealed only twenty-two references to the root word *empower* between 1958 and 1980. The same search conducted for 1981 through 1995 revealed an incredible 4280 instances of the same word (search conducted October, 2001). Databases for education and sociology experienced similar explosions. The term also became ubiquitous in political parlance. The root word *empower* appeared in 360 different press releases between 1992 and 1994, and over 7000 state bills from 1991 to 1994 (Perkins, 1995; Perkins & Zimmerman, 1995). This is not to say that the multitude of articles, chapters, press releases and bills agreed on the meaning of the newly popular term. As we will later see, the term has taken on very different, even diametrically opposed, meanings by different factions. Let's begin our discussion by looking more closely at what community psychologists mean by empowerment.

⌘ Definitions

Definitions of emerging terms require time to consolidate. The lack of clarity in definition that hindered early prevention work also characterized early work on empowerment. Edison Trickett (1994) proposed that the evolution of any new concept not only requires, but benefits from, ambiguities in definitions. The initial ambiguity allows a concept to generate novel perspectives on what we need to do and how to do it.

Nevertheless, definitions need to solidify over time. Shortly after hailing empowerment as an orienting concept, Rappaport (1984c) voiced concern that if different people continued to use the term to advance different agendas, "empowerment" would become simply a new dressing for old ways of doing things. A decade later, community psychologists continued to call for care and precision in defining the construct, fearing that the term would otherwise "forever remain a warm and fuzzy, one-size-fits-all, concept with no clear or consistent meaning" (Perkins & Zimmerman, 1995, p. 572).

Numerous community psychologists have heeded these calls and elaborated the concept of empowerment with thought and insight. Rappaport's simple and concise definition provided a solid base. He defined empowerment as "a process, the mechanism by which people, organizations, and communities gain mastery over their affairs" (1987, p. 122). The Cornell Empowerment Group (1989)

expounded on Rappaport's initial work and developed one of the most widely used definitions:

> Empowerment is an intentional, ongoing process centered in the local community, involving mutual respect, critical reflection, caring, and group participation, through which people lacking an equal share of valued resources gain greater access to and control over those resources. (p. 2)

Community psychologists generally agree on these conceptual definitions, but as we will see, the operationalization of the term varies considerably. Empowerment may be exemplified by residents of blighted neighborhoods building vibrant villages, female dairy farmers in India gaining control over milk production or Native Americans resisting the construction of a dam on their land. Despite the diverse operationalizations of the term, defining features of empowerment can be identified.

MARC ZIMMERMAN'S KEY COMPONENTS

Marc Zimmerman, one of the most active scholars of empowerment (and a former student of Julian Rappaport), identified three key components of empowerment. They are: 1) efforts to gain access to resources; 2) participation with others to achieve goals; and 3) a critical understanding of the sociopolitical context (Perkins & Zimmerman, 1995; Zimmerman, 2000; see also Keiffer, 1984). Let's look at each of these components.

ACCESS TO RESOURCES

Basic to the concept of empowerment is the notion that resources are not distributed equally across segments of society and change is required to right this injustice. Thus, how we understand empowerment depends in large part on how we understand resources.

In general, **resources** are the elements available for the satisfaction of human needs and desires. Many community psychologists have made more fine-grained distinctions among types of resources.

Irma Serrano-García (1994) distinguished two types; **instrumental resources** actually fulfill human needs and aspirations, while **infraresources** facilitate access to instrumental resources. Stevan Hobfoll (1988, 1989) distinguished four types of resources that exist at individual and community levels (see Table 10.1). Serrano-García's infraresources correspond to what Hobfoll called *energies*—resources that help people obtain and protect other resources. Disenfranchisement coincides with a lack of resources of all descriptions—food, housing, health care, job opportunities, transportation, recreational activities, and so on.

Resources are often a battleground for power. Efforts to control resources lie at the root of struggles on small scales and large, from toddlers engaged in a tug-of-war over a coveted toy to the mutual destruction of Israelis and Palestinians battling over a homeland.

Struggles over resources often proceed on the assumption that for one person or group to gain control of a resource, another must lose control. In his groundbreaking work on empowerment, Richard Katz (1984) explored an alternative to this zero-sum approach. He proposed that competition over resources exists when **scarcity paradigms** prevail, as they do in Western society. Scarcity paradigms view resources as limited. Other societies operate from an alternative **synergy paradigm**, in which valued resources are viewed as renewable and expandable. To show how synergy paradigms operate, Katz described the distribution of the resource of healing in two synergistic communities: the !Kung of the Kalahari Desert and the rural indigenous people of the Fiji islands.

Among the !Kung, the central healing tradition is the all-night healing dance which occurs up to four times each month. The goal of the dance is for community healers to generate healing energy, called *n/um*. As the healers dance they experience *!kia*, a form of enhanced consciousness. *!Kia* allows the healer to experience the sickness of the community members and negotiate with spirits on behalf of those who suffer. Although only the community healers generate *n/um*, everyone in this egalitarian society shares in it. In addition, almost everyone is encouraged to become a healer, and all young boys and most girls try. Only about half of the men and 10% of the women succeed, however. Healers must have strength and resolve as *n/um* is a painful, mysterious, and feared energy.

The indigenous people of the Fiji islands are more hierarchically organized than the !Kung, and healing in their culture is more specialized. Nevertheless, the synergy paradigm operates. Healing is available to anyone in the community who needs it.

📄 Table 10.1   Types of Resources

Type of Resource	Examples at Individual Level	Examples at Community Level
Objects	Home, clothing	Roads, emergency equipment
Conditions	Secure work, good health	Employment opportunities, emergency services
Personal characteristics	Self-esteem, job skills	Sense of community, community competence
Energies (to obtain and protect resources)	Food, money	Government financing, fuel reserves

Based on Hobfoll S. E., (1988). *The ecology of stress.* New York: Hemisphere Publishing Corp. and Hobfoll, S. E. (1989). Conservation of resources: A new attempt of conceptualizing stress. *American Psychologist, 44,* 513-524.

Any person in need can present the yagona plant to a healer, and spiritual power called *mana,* is released as soon as the healer accepts this ritual offering. Again, healing requires strength and is seen as a responsibility more than a privilege. The healer's character makes healing possible, and the healer must follow a righteous path that includes living the truth, love for all, humility, respect for tradition, single-mindedness, and service to others. All healers in the Fijian community know each other and even though they have different ideas about the causes of illnesses and pathways to cure, they regularly refer clients to each other. Thus, power is shared and community members can make use of each healer's area of expertise. Katz observed that this contrasts with the U.S. approach, in which healing paradigms are often seen as mutually exclusive. Psychoanalysts, members of mutual help groups, and proponents of Eastern-based meditation practices generally do not refer clients to each other on a regular basis.

Katz's work on empowerment encourages creative thinking about resources. The following principles derive from his understanding of the !Kung.

- Valued community resources (such as healing) may be expanding and renewable.
- Valued resources are released by the community.
- Valued resources can be distributed equitably and made accessible to everyone in community.

The Fijian approach to empowerment provides two additional principles.

- Community members can more effectively use resources if they have extensive information about the variety of resources available.
- Extensive collaboration among the custodians of resources and the seekers of resources promotes the flexible and varied (i.e., empowered) use of resources.

Although the approaches of the !Kung and Fijian people seem appealing, Katz warned that they could not take hold in U.S. society without a radical paradigm shift. Synergistic communities see the embeddedness of self in community as highly desirable and the pursuit of individual gain as objectionable, two perspectives that oppose the dominant Western worldview.

PARTICIPATION WITH OTHERS

The first key feature of empowerment identified by Marc Zimmerman is that it requires equal access to resources. The second key feature is that the pursuit of a more equitable distribution of resources requires the coming together of disenfranchised people (see also Speer & Hughey, 1995). For empowerment to occur, disenfranchised people must create common cause. Initially, they may unite around their shared experience of stress and the desire to exchange social support in order to face challenges. Eventually, they may come to see the stress as resulting from a lack of resources and the lack of resources as resulting from inequities in society. This paves the ways for transformation in the group members' sense of self—no longer are they unfortunate people coping individually with their lot in life, but members of an oppressed group who can work together to create social change.

As described in Chapter Six, when individuals come together, change becomes possible (see the sections entitled *Awakening to Injustice* and *Creating Common Cause*). Dialogue and the exchange of information enhance people's understanding of their environment and can lead to transformative changes in society (Friere, 1970/1992). Although some authors conceive of empowerment as individual advancement through personal skill development (e.g., Fine, 1999; Caroselli, 1998), that is not the conceptualization consistent with community psychology (e.g., Watts, Griffith, & Abdul-Adil, 1999). For community psychologists, skill building relates to empowerment only to the extent that it inspires a confrontation with the existing sociopolitical context, and this confrontation requires joining forces with others.

UNDERSTANDING THE SOCIOPOLITICAL CONTEXT

When marginalized people come together to discuss their shared concerns, they become aware of shaping forces that exist beyond the individual level.

They identify with similar others, cease to blame themselves for problems stemming from social injustice, and assume responsibility for making changes (Gutiérrez, 1994). Thus, participation with others is inextricably linked to Zimmerman's third essential component of empowerment: an understanding of the sociopolitical context.

The development of sociopolitical understanding occurs in stages (Ander-Egg, 1980; Serrano-García, 1994; Watts & Abdul-Adil, 1994; Watts et al., 1999). In the *acritical* or *submissive stage*, social asymmetries remain unquestioned. If they are noticed at all, they are seen as part of the natural order. In the second, *adaptive stage*, power asymmetries are acknowledged but seen as immutable. Consequently, the task for oppressed people is to find ways of adapting to the status quo. In the next stage, called the *precritical stage*, awareness of asymmetries grows, as does dissatisfaction with the status quo. In the fourth stage, the *critical* or *critical-integrative stage*, the social and historical roots of asymmetries are understood, which generally leads to the conclusion that power asymmetries are unjust and should be changed. In the final stage, the *liberation stage*, oppressed people reject the status quo and demand social transformation.

WHAT ABOUT POWER?

In summary, Zimmerman proposed that the three key features of empowerment are access to resources, participation with others, and understanding of the sociopolitical context. These three components hint at, but do not explicitly grapple with the issue of power. Power is, however, the root of the term em*power*ment. A consideration of power adds to our understanding of empowerment. In this section we consider different ways of thinking about power, and then tackle a central

---

Self-empowerment is the most deeply political work there is, and the most difficult.

—Audre Lorde (1984, p. 170)

---

question in community psychology: Do we (does anyone) have the power to empower anyone else?

WHAT IS POWER?

Power is complex and value-laden term. Let's examine the concept of power from three perspectives: the distinction between perceived and actual power, *power over* versus *power to*, and the different sources of power.

PERCEPTION OF POWER VERSUS ACTUAL POWER

Zimmerman (1995) characterized actual power or control over resources as "not necessary for empowerment because in some contexts and for some populations real control or power may not be the desired goal" (p. 593). Perhaps this is one reason why Zimmerman identified the importance of *understanding* the sociopolitical context, but not necessarily *influencing* it.

Some scholars of empowerment have criticized conceptualizations of empowerment that ignore actual power (e.g. Gruber & Trickett, 1987; Riger, 1993; Serrano-García, 1994; Speer & Hughey, 1995; Swift & Levin, 1987). In an influential article entitled, *What's Wrong with Empowerment?* Stephanie Riger (1993) asserted that people may *feel* empowered while remaining quite powerless. For example, Judith Gruber and Edison Trickett (1987) described a failed empowerment effort in which a school policy council was formed to involve teachers, parents and students in decision-making (this case study is examined in more detail later in the chapter). According to Gruber and Trickett, the council failed because the teachers retained control over decisions. The parents and students generally *felt* empowered, but power was not redistributed. "It is still *not* enough for the transformation of society, this *feeling* of being free" (emphasis in original, Shor & Freire, 1987, p. 109–110; also cited in Strawn, 1994).

"Power Over" versus "Power To". Resistance to embracing the importance of actual power may stem from a view of power as requiring hierarchy or dominance. This seems antithetical to the goal of establishing equity. Stephanie Riger (1993) stressed the importance of distinguishing "power over," which implies dominance, and "power to," which consists of the opportunity to act more freely.

An emphasis on "power over" may reflect a traditionally masculine view of power. It views power as an *object* that can be possessed by an individual or group, and transferred willingly or unwillingly to other people or groups (Serrano-García, 1994). "Power to" (or "power with") may be seen as a more feminist way of thinking about power (Deutchman, 1991; Miller, 1986; Surrey, 1991; Watts, 1997).

Feminists often frame power as *receptive* rather than *active*. Power may come from openness (Rosenwasser, 1992b) or even vulnerability (Jordan, 1992). The activist Flor Fernandez conceptualized power as "*allowing* rather than controlling" (Rosenwasser, 1992c). To her, assuming a position of power meant being "in synchronicity with the energies around us" in order to "make a decision based on choices rather than on the need to control other people..." (p. 130). Katz (1984) also referred to receptive power, noting that when !Kung healers entered *!kia*, they reported feeling as if they were "opening up" or "bursting open" like a ripe pod (Katz, p. 210). This conception of power may be more in keeping with empowerment ideologies.

SOURCES OF POWER

A consideration of the sources of power also has implications for our understanding of empowerment. Katherine Klein and her colleagues (2000) explored ideas about power sources developed in the organizational literature. Of particular interest was French and Raven's (1960) enumeration of five sources of workplace power.

The first type, *legitimate power*, stems from an individual's position in the organization. Subordinates obey legitimate power because of the authority bestowed by position. Placement within the organizational hierarchy is the sole determinant of legitimate power. *Reward power* is based on the individual's ability to bestow rewards such as praise, recognition, or pay. Reward power is offered in return for compliance and depends on the other's desire for

the reward. *Coercive power* is the inverse of reward power. One person obeys another out of fear of reprimand or other punishment. People higher in the organization's hierarchy have more authority to bestow rewards or punishments, but they may also inspire people to seek their praise or avoid their reprimands for personal reasons. A subordinate may simply like the more powerful person and want to gain her or his respect. Thus, reward power and coercive power blend positional and personal power. Two additional types of power stem from personal characteristics alone. *Referent power* is based on the individual's personality, attractiveness, or charm. *Expert power* refers to the special skills or knowledge the individual possesses, and is obeyed because the expert's directives are likely to be informed and helpful. Organizations can confer neither referent nor expert power.

This analysis of power from the workplace literature has important implications for the construct of empowerment more generally (Klein et al., 2000). Positional power may derive not only from one's position in the workplace, but from one's position in society as well. Members of disenfranchised groups do not have authority bestowed by social position, and so personal power (i.e., referent power and expert power) may be more critical in their efforts to access and control resources. The importance of referent power may be one reason why social movements often look toward charismatic leaders, such as Martin Luther King, Jr., to advance their cause. Personal charm is not easily acquired, however, and so interventions crafted by community psychologists (and others) often focus on helping disenfranchised people develop expert power as an instrument of empowerment. Many empowerment-oriented interventions seek to teach skills, such as leadership skills, problem solving skills, and also skills in analyzing the sociopolitical environments.

Participatory research is one vehicle for the cultivation of expert power. An example often cited in the community psychology literature occurred in a town called Love Canal where Lois Gibbs lived as a homemaker and mother in the 1970s (Biklen, 1983; Center for Health and Environmental Justice, 2000a; Berkowitz, 1987; Gibbs, 1982). Love Canal had been built on a toxic waste site, and when chemical leakage began to make residents sick, Gibbs and others were dismayed to find that those with positional power (i.e., government officials) were in no hurry to help them out. The Love Canal Homeowners Association, with the 27-year old Gibbs as founder and president, launched a comprehensive and systematic study that yielded some startling statistics: 25% of pregnancies in the affected areas ended in miscarriage, and 56% of the children born in the area had birth defects. Moreover, homes with ill family members clustered along pathways of underground drainage ditches where several hundred tons of dangerous chemicals had been dumped during World War II. The townspeople took it upon themselves to collect data that clearly showed the compromised health of residents and traced it to toxic wastes. They became more informed than anyone else about the local situation and used their expert power to leverage change.

THE POWER TO EMPOWER

Although an analysis of power suggests strategies of potential use to community psychologists, a more basic question remains. Can community psychologists, or anyone else, bring about empowerment? I referred earlier to Judith Gruber and Edison Trickett's (1987) case study of an alternative public school interested in new models of governance. Their analysis of this failed empowerment effort led them to recognize a "fundamental paradox in the idea of people empowering others because the very institutional structure that puts one group in a position to empower also works to undermine the act of empowerment" (p. 353). Let's look at Gruber and Trickett's work more closely.

The social experiment in empowerment occurred in the early 1970s in an inner-city public high school in New Haven, Connecticut. Shortly after the school was founded, personnel established a governing council with an equal representation of parents, students, and teachers. Gruber and Trickett studied verbatim notes of the council meetings and conducted yearly interviews with all council members. They also interviewed every teacher in the

school on their perceptions of the council. As a result of this research, Gruber and Trickett sought to find out if the council succeeded in its empowerment goals, that is to say, if the council actually wielded significant decision-making power and so controlled resources within the school.

The context of this school was ripe for empowerment efforts. It sought to decentralize power in numerous ways. The school encouraged self-directed learning among students. Teachers paid personal visits to parents during which they emphasized the importance of parental involvement and input. Indeed, the school itself had been established without a principal, and teachers took responsibility for decision making through consensus rather than voting.

Teachers embraced the idea of a governing council as another way of eliminating traditional authority. The council was comprised of five parents, five students, and five teachers, each with one vote in all policy decisions. During its first year, the council played an active role in developing school policy. For example, the council decided not to admit ninth graders, a decision that went against the wishes of the teachers. Over time, however, the influence of the council diminished. The issues discussed became more trivial, and the faculty dominated discussions more. A new pattern emerged: faculty members made decisions on their own and then presented them to the council for feedback. Eventually, the council came to be seen as irrelevant. Interviews conducted four years after the council formed revealed that teachers did not trust parents to make good decisions, and neither parents nor teachers trusted the students' maturity of judgment. Attendance at the meetings decreased, as did the frequency of the meetings. Gruber and Trickett identified two constraints that limited the influence of the council. First, important *inequalities in power* existed among the council subgroups. The egalitarian group structure, as epitomized by equal voting power among the three constituencies, did not eliminate the pre-existing power differences among these groups. The teachers had founded the school, oversaw day-to-day operations, responded to district administrators, sought outside funding, and were generally more committed to the success of the school. Teachers knew more about and were more responsible for the school and also had greater familiarity with larger educational issues. For the council to function effectively, teachers would have had to equalize these imbalances by bringing relevant issues to the attention of the council, facilitating the informed participation of all group members and putting council decisions into effect. This did not occur. Parents and students often felt the need to defer to teachers with regard to important decisions, such as hiring personnel and allocating budgets. On the rare occasions when parents and students joined forces and outvoted the teachers, the teachers ultimately controlled the implementation of council decisions and so could effectively undo them.

The *organizational dynamics* contributed further to the failure of the empowerment effort. Paradoxically, the school's commitment to egalitarianism contributed to the demise of the council. By eschewing formal group structures (e.g., clear leadership, differentiated roles for council members), a **tyranny of structurelessness** resulted. Incessant group time and energy was spent on the group's internal process. No one was in charge. Grievances and suggestions were lost, resolutions were abandoned as quickly as they were formed, and promised reports were never delivered. To the extent that the group was led at all, leadership was informal. Informal leaders, no matter how ineffective, cannot be voted out. The structurelessness of the council precluded proactive efforts to minimize existing power differences among the three constituencies, and so the status quo of faculty power remained unchallenged.

The inability of the council to succeed led Gruber and Trickett to some pessimistic conclusions about empowerment. They suggested that if empowerment could occur anywhere, it should have occurred at that school. The school was committed in ideology and practice to egalitarian goals and to the empowerment of students and parents. In addition, the council began when the school was still a new organization. Entrenched power structures did not yet exist and standard operating procedures had not yet emerged. The idea for the council took

shape organically—it was not an intervention imposed by outside forces but an idea formulated by the stakeholders themselves. Despite all of these conditions that would seem to support empowerment, the council failed. Gruber and Trickett (1987) saw this failure as indicative of the fundamental obstacles in the empowerment process. They wrote, "Virtually all empowerment efforts involve a grant of power by a favored group to others in the organization. Unless the favored group changes the very circumstances that have given it power in the first place, the grant of power is always partial" (p. 370). As we will see throughout this chapter, this fundamental paradox of empowerment presents on ongoing challenge to those seeking to equalize imbalances in social power.

⌘ Levels of Analysis

Thus, far we have considered definitional issues in empowerment. We examined the three components Marc Zimmerman identified as crucial, as well as the often-overlooked construct of power. These conceptual issues create backdrop for a fuller discussion of empowerment theory, research, and practice.

Since the term *empowerment* first emerged in the social science literature in the mid-1970s, it has been used to describe a wealth of research, theory, and practice. In order to examine this vast literature, let's consider empowerment at three levels of analysis: the individual, the microsystem, and beyond the microsystem.

INDIVIDUAL LEVEL

Marc Zimmerman's work on empowerment centers on the individual. He recognized, however, the importance of considering the individual-in-context and proposed a distinction between individual empowerment, and **psychological empowerment** (Zimmerman, 1990). Individual empowerment remains at the level of the person. Empowerment is seen as an individual trait. Psychological empowerment, on the other hand, considers the person–environment interaction. Zimmerman identified three aspects of psychological empowerment: intrapersonal, interactional, and behavioral (Zimmerman, 1995; 2000).

THE INTRAPERSONAL ASPECT

The intrapersonal aspect of empowerment focuses on intrapsychic dynamics. A number of constructs in the psychological literature overlap with intrapersonal empowerment. That is to say, the concept of intrapersonal empowerment casts a wide **nomological net**. The nomological net is the universe of concepts related to a target construct that can inform our understanding of that construct. Many of the concepts caught in the nomological net of intrapersonal empowerment have long histories and rich traditions in psychology (Price, 1990).

Self-esteem, or assessment of personal worth, is one concept that relates to empowerment. If a marginalized person does not feel worthy of the good things in life, she or he will not seek change. Roderick Watts (1997) noted that the construct of *internalized oppression* puts self-esteem into a sociopolitical context. Members of oppressed groups may come to believe society's negative images of that group, leaving them with feelings of low self-worth. If they feel that they deserve inferior treatment, they will not seek empowerment.

Sense of control is another long-standing psychological concept that bears on the construct of empowerment. In particular, *locus of control* refers to one's beliefs about the causes of life experiences. People with an internal locus of control believe that they can affect the events that occur in their lives, while someone with an external locus of control views their life experiences as determined by outside forces (Rotter, 1966). People who feel a sense of control tend to enjoy better mental and physical health.

Of course, a sense of control does not develop independent of the context in which one lives. Disenfranchised people may have a more external sense of control because they actually *have* less control. Julian Rappaport (1981) observed that

empowerment confronts the paradox that even the people who seem most incompetent, in need, and unable to function benefit from more rather than less control over their lives. Consider the work of the social psychologists Ellen Langer and Judith Rodin (1976).

Some institutions, such as nursing homes and hospitals, contain people who have been placed there against their will. Moreover, the institutions control many aspects of the residents' life—what they eat, whom they see, and when they see them. Langer and Rodin (1976) reasoned that residents of such total institutions would benefit from an increased sense of control. They designed a simple intervention in which residents of a nursing home in Connecticut were placed in one of two groups. The director of the home called the first group of residents together and told them that they needed to make more decisions about their lives. In the future, they would be allowed to arrange their rooms as they saw fit, have input into the choice of movies, and generally make more decisions. The director gave each resident the gift of a houseplant to symbolize their control over the future—they could nurture the plant or allow it to die. A comparison group heard a speech that did not emphasize control over decisions, and although they too received houseplants, they were told that nurses would take care of them. Residents in the first group became happier, healthier, and lived longer than residents in the second group (Rodin & Langer, 1977). A follow-up study found that twice as many people in the group without control had died. Interestingly, additional research suggests that if conditions changed so that control was gained and then lost, residents who suffered the loss were worse off than those who never gained control in the first place (Schulz & Hanusa, 1978).

The related concept of *self-efficacy* also overlaps with empowerment. Self-efficacy refers to our judgments about the degree to which our behaviors can affect desired outcomes (Bandura, 1997). If people feel that they *can* control events through individual effort, they are more likely to take action. Researchers interested in linking notions of self-efficacy with the larger social context have coined an additional term: **political efficacy**. Political efficacy reflects a person's perceived ability to participate in and influence the political process. In studying the formation of a union for homeless people, Susan Yeich and Ralph Levine (1994) proposed that political efficacy includes three components: 1) feeling capable of entering into political arenas; 2) knowing how to get the system to respond to demands; and 3) recognizing collective action as the appropriate vehicle for change.

The willingness to work toward change derives from one's expectations. Repeated experiences of failure can reinforce a belief that efforts are futile, leading to *learned helplessness* (Abramson, Seligman, & Teasdale, 1978). Marc Zimmerman (1990) proposed *learned hopefulness* as an alternative to the deficit side of the expectation–effort relationship. He argued that when individuals gain control and mastery over their lives, they feel hopeful and become empowered. Where there is hope, there is the possibility of change.

At an individual level, hope (as well as fear) is evident in our beliefs about our future. Hazel Markus and Paula Nurius (1986) coined the term **possible selves** to describe what people believe they can become. Possible selves embody both ideals and fears. Hoped-for selves might include the happy self, the athletic self, the parent self, the doctor self, and the admired self. Feared selves might include the alone self, the depressed self, the unemployed self, the overweight self, and the smoker self.

The selves we see as possible do not emerge and take shape in isolation. Theoretically, a person could create any number of possible selves for herself or himself. The *actual* universe of any person's possible selves is bounded by that person's sociocultural and historical setting. Our ideas about who we might become depend on the models, images, and symbols invoked by our context, notably the people with whom we interact and the media that surrounds us. Stereotypes, false assumptions, and labeling can constrain our sense of personal potential. In his original treatise on empowerment, Rappaport (1981) wrote

> it makes a great difference if you are viewed as a child or as a citizen, since if you believe it you are quite likely to act the part, and if those in power believe it they are likely to develop programs, plans, and structures that will help you to believe it. (p. 11, embedded references deleted)

While negative possible selves can imprison us and stifle empowerment, positive possible selves can liberate and offer the hope of a better future. Role models and support people can foster the development of positive possible selves. It is easier today than it was fifty years ago for little girls to see themselves as astronauts and African American youths to believe they can be elected to high office. At the individual level, empowerment-based interventions may be seen as inspiring new possible selves.

Many of the concepts that fall within the nomological net of intrapersonal empowerment have higher level analogs that merit increased examination. For example, Albert Bandura (1997) devoted a chapter of his recent book on self-efficacy to the concept of *collective efficacy*. Jennifer Crocker and colleagues (e.g., Crocker & Luhtanen, 1990) have examined the notion of *collective self-esteem*. We might also think about *possible communities* (ideal and feared), as well as possible selves.

As another example of higher level analogs, Irma Serrano-García (1984) noted that learned helplessness exists at a societal level in the form of *colonialism*. In her country of Puerto Rico, colonialism means that the U.S. functions as the parent state, exercising control over Puerto Rican affairs such as foreign trade, citizenship, immigration, military service, transportation, currency, and postal services. Colonialism leads to self-debasement, alienation, loss of cultural identity, dependency, and internally directed hostility. Perhaps we need to coin a term for community-level learned hopefulness, as well.

THE INTERACTIONAL ASPECT

The intrapersonal aspect of empowerment includes such psychological factors as self-esteem, locus of control, sense of efficacy, and hope. The interactional component pertains to how people understand and seek to influence their social environment

(Zimmerman, 1995, 2000). Intrapersonal and interactional empowerment do not always co-occur. Disenfranchised people may feel in control, worthy of respect, and hopeful without understanding how to bring about needed changes, or they may know what is needed to create change but feel personally unwilling or unable to act on that understanding (Speer, 2000).

The interpersonal skills required for empowerment fall into two categories: skills needed to work in coalition with others and skills needed to obtain control from powers that be. The first category of skills may be seen as internal to the group (or groups) seeking change. Whether participation entails working within coalitions, community development initiatives, environmental action groups, neighborhood associations, or mutual help groups

(Perkins, 1995; Speer & Hughey, 1995), members must know how to function effectively as a group. After a thorough literature review, Pennie Foster-Fishman and her colleagues (2001) devised an exhaustive list of core skills needed to work in partnership with others. They include conflict-resolution skills, knowledge about the norms and perspectives of other members, propensity to share power, valuing of diversity, and willingness and ability to forge links with others. To maintain participation, individuals must also know how to recruit, train, organize, motivate, utilize, and retain group members (e.g., Wandersman & Florin, 2000).

The second type of interactional skill is externally focused and pertains to the relationship between members of the change-seeking group and those who control the desired resources. Effective groups

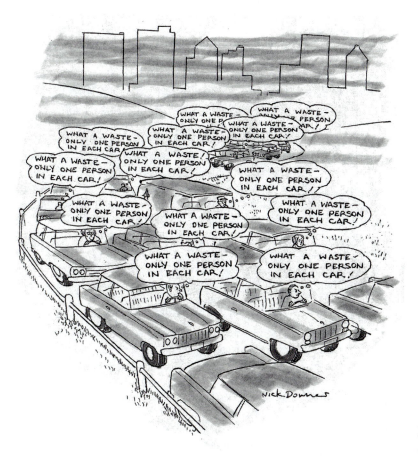

Individual insight may mean little without collective action. Copyright © 2002 by Nick Downes.

must know how best to use their resources to create change and what barriers to change exist or can be erected at different levels to block them (Zimmerman, 1995). Empowerment-oriented interventions may focus on increasing the interactional skills of people in change-seeking groups by promoting problem-solving around critical questions, such as Who ultimately controls the resources? How do the controlling people and groups operate? and What points of leverage can be used in order to gain influence? (e.g., Shefner-Rogers et al., 1998).

THE BEHAVIORAL ASPECT

Personal characteristics and interpersonal skills set the background for psychological empowerment, but empowerment hinges on a third component: taking action in an effort to access and control resources. Although the psychological literature has focused on the intrapsychic aspect of psychological empowerment (perhaps because of its relatedness to familiar constructs), some have argued that the behavioral component should be of central interest. Empowerment behaviors can be more reliably and directly measured than the intrapsychic dimensions (e.g., Perkins, 1995). In addition, to the extent that one is interested in actual as opposed to perceived control, empowerment behavior is of primary importance.

In the nomological net of empowerment, the construct that corresponds most closely to the behavioral aspect of empowerment is citizen participation. **Citizen participation** has been defined as "a process in which individuals take part in decision making in the institutions, programs, and environments that affect them" (Heller, Price, Reinharz, Riger, & Wandersman, 1984, p. 339). Like empowerment, citizen participation can be seen as a vehicle for improving people's lives. It increases people's feelings of control over their lives and enhances a sense of belonging (e.g., Wandersman & Florin, 2000; Zimmerman, 1990). Citizen participation also enables people to create environments that better meet their needs. Citizen participation is both a cause and an effect of empowerment (Perkins, Brown, & Taylor, 1996). That is to say, citizen

participation leads people to empowerment: citizen participants gain an understanding of the sociopolitical context and seek the redistribution of resources in participation with others. At the same time, empowered people are more likely to become citizen participants and so work for changes in the environments that affect them. In the next sections, we will examine the process by which people become citizen participants and the reasons why people do or do not become involved.

The Life Paths of Citizen Participants. The notion that empowerment both leads to and results from citizen participation suggests that empowerment evolves over time. It is a process rather than an end state, and one does not necessarily *achieve* empowerment (e.g., Gutiérrez, 1994).

Charles Keiffer (1984) adopted a life span developmental perspective in his study of how individual empowerment develops over time. Keiffer interviewed fifteen committed grassroots activists and identified four stages of development. Prior to their journey toward activism, the people he interviewed had a strong sense of pride and determination and felt rooted to their community. In the first stage of their journey, the *era of entry*, individuals experienced some direct threat to their own or their family's self-interest that provoked outrage. Keiffer noted that mobilization did not grow from an intellectual analysis of a problem or an outside intervention, but from an immediate and physical violation of the future activists' sense of integrity. This threat provided an impetus to confront authorities, which Keiffer saw as the hallmark of activism. According to Keiffer, people learned to speak with confidence in their own voice only after the symbolic (i.e., positional) power of authority was demystified.

In the next stage, the *era of advancement*, the budding activists became more connected with others who were engaged in similar struggles. During this stage, mentors, supportive peers, and collective organizational structures fostered a critical understanding of the social and political realities that underlay the threat the activists had experienced. In the next stage, the *era of incorporation*, self-concept, strategic abilities, and critical comprehension became mature. Finally, in the *era of commitment*, the transformation from uninvolved community member to social change activist was complete. The individual had become competent in identifying and transforming power relationships. Keiffer found that this journey generally required at least four years.

A failure to consider empowerment as a developmental process can impede interventions and lead to iatrogenesis (i.e., unintended negative consequences). For example, Irma Serrano-García (1984) wondered if it was appropriate to foster consciousness raising before citizens had the skills necessary to act upon their newly discovered reality. Similarly, Douglas Perkins and Marc Zimmerman (1995) observed that efforts to exert control can create more problems than they solve. People must have the skills to consider various strategies towards change and assess the risks and benefits associated with each. They offered the example of an urban teenager interested in reclaiming his neighborhood from gangs. Ill-considered strategies could well result in retaliation from gang members. Thus, at earlier stages of empowerment, people may need assistance in developing skills. At later stages, they might benefit more from help in managing the stress and strain that result from social change responsibilities (Keiffer, 1984).

People who do find pathways to empowerment report benefits from their participation in community action. Lois Gibbs was not the only resident of Love Canal who became an activist as a result of the threat hazardous wastes posed to the community. One study of 39 Love Canal residents, 24 of whom became activists and 15 of whom remained relatively uninvolved, found benefits to activism (Stone & Levine, 1985). Activists felt better about themselves and reported greater belief in their political efficacy. Although activists had lost some friends, presumably as a result of their social change efforts, they had gained new friends as well. This research cannot rule out the possibility that people who ultimately became activists were willing to get involved because they *already* enjoyed a sense of well-being and felt efficacious. The strong possibility remains, however, that involvement in the citizen movement led to improvements in their sense of self.

Why Individuals Do and Don't Participate.
The literature on citizen participation consistently finds a relationship between involvement in community action and feelings of personal and political efficacy and well-being (e.g., Stone & Levine, 1985; Wandersman & Florin, 2000; Zimmerman, 1990; Zimmerman & Rappaport, 1988). This led Abraham Wandersman and Paul Florin (2000) to ask, "If citizen participation is so beneficial, why don't more people get involved?" Certainly some of the variables discussed earlier come into play. People with low self-esteem, an external locus of control, little desire or hope for change, and a lack of appreciation of the social causes of personal problems will not become activists. A costs–benefits perspective also bears on this question. People get involved when they stand to gain more (e.g., in terms of neighborhood safety) than they stand to lose (e.g., in terms of lost time with family) (Prestsby, Wandersman, Florin, Rich, & Chavis, 1990). "Suprapersonal" factors also play a role—altruism, a sense of civic responsibility, and community-mindedness promote citizen participation (Perkins, et al., 1996; Stewart & Weinstein, 1997). (See also the section entitled *Social Change: Some Components* in Chapter Six.)

The existence of an external trigger is also a factor. Charles Kieffer (1984) found that citizen participants became interested in social change after encountering a threat they could not ignore. Similarly, David Chavis and Abraham Wandersman (1990) found that voluntary organizations tend to form in response to a precipitating event. These events often come from the physical environment—discovery of a hazardous waste site, the experience of a shocking crime, or an unwanted development project. External triggers do not always come from environmental events, however. Outside agents did not lead to activism for any of the fifteen people Keiffer studied, but the seminal works of Alinsky (1971) and Freire (1970/1992) are based on the notion that community organizers and educators can bring people to social action. A study of community organizing with women dairy farmers in India also showed that outside agents can inspire citizen participation (see the Community Intervention box).

COMMUNITY INTERVENTION:

Empowering Women Dairy Farmers in India
Community Organizing for Empowerment

In Latin America, Africa, and Asia, countless activists are working to increase women's awareness of their disadvantaged social position in order to effect change. They seek to help women gain access to education, employment, and health care, and to free them from physical, sexual, and emotional abuse. Corinne Shefner-Rogers and her colleagues (1998) described how community organizers in India have instigated the empowerment of female dairy farmers in rural villages.

Although women comprise 85% of the seven million dairy farmers in India, they are excluded from the male-dominated milk marketing industry and often do not reap the rewards of their hard work. In an attempt to rectify the existing inequities, the National Dairy Development Board devised a Cooperative Development (CD) program that reaches about 250,000 women in 4,000 Indian villages each year, making it one of the largest scale empowerment efforts in the world.

Here is how the CD program works. A five-member CD team approaches a village and conducts a survey to assess local needs. They present the survey results to the dairy cooperative leaders, who are almost always men and ask permission to conduct the CD program. Team members educate the men about advantages that would accrue from women's empowerment, notably an increase in family financial and social strength. With their husbands' permission, women can attend CD sessions without fear of being beaten upon their return home. CD team members then visit the homes of the women, often accompanied by village leaders, such as midwives, and invite them to attend a two-day education program. The program consists of group discussion and question–answer sessions. The women learn important skills, such as farm hygiene and how to artificially inseminate milk animals. They are also made aware of their inferior social position. "Who goes to bed last in your house?" they are asked. The reply: "We do."

"Who gets up first in your house?"

"We do." The questions and replies continue. Who works hardest, who hands over the milk to their husbands to sell? We do, we do. The final question: "Who are fools?"

"We are!" (Shefner-Rogers et al., 1998, p. 329).

The CD program attendees learn that women on dairy farms contribute 70% of the work hours, earn 10% of the national income, and own 1% of the land, milk animals, and other resources. They then discuss pathways to empowerment: ways for women to gain control of milk production and distribution and to become members in dairy cooperatives. Meetings conclude with group sings and inspirational sayings.

After the training, the CD team helps organize women's clubs, or support groups, to sustain conscientization and encourage income-generating activities. In these clubs women have taught each other how to make and sell detergents, how to start saving plans, and how to run antiliquor campaigns (many of the village men spend money from the women's work on alcohol). Although men may feel a loss of power as a result of the women's empowerment, marked improvements in the family's economic situation usually compensate for the perceived loss.

Shefner-Rogers and her colleagues (1998) conducted a study to assess the efficacy of the CD program. They interviewed ninety-six women in four villages that received CD training and 88 women in four villages that did not. They found that average scores on eleven of their twelve indicators of empowerment were higher among villagers who had received CD training. These items include:

The female respondent . . .

1. owns the milk animals.
2. belongs to the dairy cooperative.
3. gets the money made from milk sales.
4. controls the milk animals' reproduction.
5. determines if animals are vaccinated or not.
6. decides how to spend income generated from the milk animals.
7. believes that women should have the final say in how many children they bear.
8. believes in equity in formal education for boys and girls.

9. believes that girls should decide when they will be married.
10. has a bank account for saving money.
11. determines which animals to buy when.
12. has joined the dairy cooperative's board of directors.

The researchers corroborated these self-report data with measures of actual change. In the four villages where the CD training occurred, the dairy cooperatives experienced a greater increase in the number of women members, greater attendance of women at annual meetings, and greater increases in overall cattle-feed sales and milk production. Men as well as women benefited from the empowerment activities. When the women became empowered, their families and their villages also prospered.

While threats, community organizers, or other catalysts may be necessary to spur citizen involvement, supporting social conditions may be required to sustain it. Douglas Perkins and his colleagues (1996) found that more citizens participated in block associations if they lived on blocks high in neighboring behaviors. Another study found that while individuals with strong beliefs in their own efficacy may initiate actions designed to improve collective situations, they are often encouraged by "less confident" neighbors on whom they depend for moral support and tangible aid (Saegert & Winkel, 1996).

Citizen participation can be promoted not only by the support of friends and neighbors, but also by organizational structures. A study of resident participation in three cities (Baltimore, New York, and Salt Lake City) found that the variables that most consistently predicted citizen involvement were informal neighboring and involvement in religious and other community organizations (Perkins et al., 1996). People who participate in social organizations more often participate in change efforts. Indeed, the formation of organizations that support social involvement can provide needed outlets for budding citizen participants. Susan Yeich and Ralph Levine (1994) found that unions for homeless persons provided a needed forum for citizen action.

In considering citizen participation thus far, we have moved from a consideration of individual factors to a recognition of the importance of microsystem supports (e.g., neighborhood social networks and voluntary associations, such as religious organizations and unions). Larger macrosystem forces also come into play. Robert Putnam (2000) painstakingly

documented the powerful trend toward ever-deeper engagement in community life that swept the nation during the first two-thirds of the twentieth century and the dramatic reversal of this trend beginning in the 1980s. In the 1980s, citizens became less and less likely to participate in virtually all voluntary organizations, including neighborhood groups, religious fellowships, and workplace associations. Putnam examined a number of possible causes beyond the individual and microsystem levels that might account for this reversal in citizen's willingness to become participants.

Putnam found that busyness, mobility, suburbanization, and the growth of two-career families were not very important factors. From the 1960s to 1990s, civic participation diminished almost equally for men and women, married and single people, the financially stressed and the comfortably well off, workers and non workers, residents of cities and denizens of rural communities. He found that television viewing and other forms of electronic entertainment had a somewhat more powerful effect. People spent more of their discretionary time watching television and surfing the net in lieu of interacting with other community members and building consensus for action. In addition, television presented endless images of suffering in the guise of entertainment that dulled people's sense of outrage and perceived need to act (Pilisuk, McAllister, & Rothman, 1996). Of the variables Putnam studied, however, generational change played the largest role. As earlier generations of highly involved people died off, they were replaced by new generations of disconnected and uninvolved citizens (see Figure 10.1).

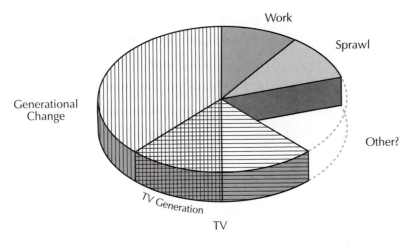

Work

Sprawl

Generational
Change

Other?

TV Generation

TV

Figure 10.1

Guesstimated explanation for civic disengagement, 1965–2000. *Reprinted with the permission of Simon & Schuster Adult Publishing Group from BOWLING ALONE: The Collapse and Revival of American Community by Robert D. Putnam. Copyright © 2000 by Robert D. Putnam.*

MICROSYSTEM LEVEL

Although the majority of empowerment research and theory elaborates individual-level dynamics, most scholars agree that all levels of analysis must be considered in a comprehensive model of empowerment. As described above, the understanding of psychological empowerment eventually takes us through the microsystem and to the realm of macrosystemic forces that affect an individual's willingness to engage in empowerment activities. One cannot truly understand empowerment at one level without also considering other levels. Let's now consider how our understanding of empowerment is enhanced if we *begin* our analyses at the microsystem level.

In their seminal work on empowerment, Peter Berger and Richard Neuhaus (1977) posited that microsystems drive empowerment efforts as they link individuals with higher-level systems. They analyzed four microsystems: families, churches, voluntary associations, and neighborhoods. Bill Berkowitz and Thomas Wolff (1996) proposed that neighborhoods warrant much more attention as a structure for empowerment. First, neighborhoods are close to home—in fact, they *are* home. They provide a basis of commonality on which interpersonal relationships can build (even if the starting point is merely an exchange of "hellos" on the street). In addition, the payoff of neighborhood vitalization is great in terms of both psychological and environmental well-being (e.g., a deeper sense of community, safer

streets, more beautiful settings). The Classic Research box describes one notable effort to promote empowerment by improving the capacity of neighborhood associations.

In addition to neighborhood associations, some community psychologists have identified mutual help groups as an important locus of empowerment work (e.g., Reissman & Bay, 1992; Rappaport, Reischl, & Zimmerman, 1992). Others have studied empowerment in the workplace (e.g., Bond, 1999; Klein et al., 2000; Spreitzer, 1995), schools (e.g., Gruber & Trickett, 1987), or religious institutions (e.g., Maton & Rappaport, 1984). Many of these interventions are described in this and other chapters. For now, let's look at a conceptual issue that emerges across these setting types, and then consider setting characteristics that are associated with empowerment.

MICROSYSTEMS AS AN EXPRESSION OF INDIVIDUALS

As seen throughout this text, behavior is a function of individuals and environments. Thus, the shape empowerment takes depends on the interaction of individual characteristics and setting properties. In one study, Marc Zimmerman (1995) compared and contrasted the concerns of people in two different microsystems: voluntary service organizations and mutual help groups. Voluntary service associations tend to advocate community change, and so setting

CLASSIC RESEARCH

The Block Boosters Project
Sustaining Voluntary Associations

The Block Boosters Project was an action research effort that began in the mid-1980s and continued for two and a half years. The study involved over 1000 residents of 48 blocks in three culturally and ethnically different New York City neighborhoods. The Project attempted to assess the organizational characteristics of vital and active block associations and build these characteristics into other associations (Florin, Chavis, Wandersman, & Rich, 1992; Wandersman & Florin, 2000).

As the researchers began their longitudinal analyses, they quickly learned how difficult it is to keep block associations active. Data were collected on 28 active associations in February through May of 1985, and by May of 1986, almost one-third of these associations had lapsed into inactivity. When compared to associations that folded, associations that survived were found to have:

1. Maximized incentives to participate and minimized the costs of participation;
2. Mobilized a greater proportion of residents to join and moved nominal members into active membership more often;
3. Offered a greater number of activities that provided varied opportunities for participation;
4. Had more officers, more committees, and more formalized rules of operation;
5. Performed more outreach activities, which included direct and proactive approaches to recruiting new members, diverse methods of communicating with existing members (newsletters, personal contacts, phone calls), active preparation of new leaders, and delegation of responsibilities to a greater proportion of membership (i.e., decentralization);
6. Fostered ties and so could receive help from a variety of external organizations (Wandersman & Florin, 2000).

After obtaining information on characteristics related to association viability, the Block Boosters Project field tested a "Block Booster Process." Randomly chosen block associations received a capacity-building intervention. Scientist-practitioner teams evaluated each association and prepared an individual profile delineating the organization's strengths and weaknesses as they related to the characteristics found to enhance association viability. The association leaders received the profile along with a handbook containing suggestions on how to improve organizational functioning. Leaders also participated in neighborhood workshops to discuss how to use the information they had received. Follow-up studies showed participation in the intervention increased the likelihood that the association remained active ten months later. Half as many block associations that received the "boost" became inactive during that period (22% as compared to 44% of the control organizations).

Douglas Perkins and his colleagues (1996) revisited the Block Booster Project seven years later. In 1992, they interviewed current and former block leaders and residents on forty-four blocks that had been involved in the original research. Interestingly, the factors that enhanced organizational viability in the short-run did not seem to increase long-term survival. Over time, demographic variables became more important. For example, viable associations more often occurred on blocks with long-term residents. Perkins and his colleagues also looked at the results of the New York City block association research in comparison to findings from similar studies in Salt Lake City and Baltimore. Across all three studies, the predictors of sustained citizen action varied greatly, depending on both the time frame and the local conditions. The variables that most consistently predicted citizen involvement were informal neighboring and participation in religious and other community organizations. Thus face-to-face interactions among individual residents, and involvement in a network of community structures can help sustain citizen participation in neighborhood associations.

members assumed an outward orientation. Mutual help groups, on the other hand, are internally oriented. Thus, different microsystems foster different types of psychological empowerment. Voluntary associations might foster a sense of political efficacy (intrapersonal development), an awareness of barriers to change (interactional development), and lobbying capabilities (behavioral development). Mutual help groups might promote self-efficacy rather than political efficacy, positive relationships within the group as opposed to awareness of outside forces that control resources, and outreach to current or potential members as opposed to member activism.

In another study of person–environment transactions in the context of empowerment, Eric Stewart and Rhona Weinstein (1997) identified three types of AIDS organizations in the San Francisco Bay Area: social change associations, information/referral settings, and individual support agencies. Different organizations attracted different people and engaged them in different activities. The social change setting was comprised mostly of gay and bisexual men and focused on halting the spread of HIV through community and political involvement. The information/referral setting contained more heterosexuals and women and sought to slow the spread of HIV/AIDS through the dissemination of frank information about safer sex practices and referrals to HIV-related programs and resources. The individual support setting, which had a mixed membership, provided emotional and tangible support to people living with HIV or AIDS.

The authors of both of these studies concluded that each setting was empowering in its own way. Others might disagree. Does a setting that maintains an exclusively internal focus (such as many support groups) really promote empowerment?

EMPOWERING AND EMPOWERED MICROSYSTEMS

Marc Zimmerman (1995; 2000) argued that organizational empowerment can be conceptualized in two ways: the extent to which the organization empowers its members, and the extent to which the

organization itself works toward empowerment. An **empowering organization** offers opportunities for members to gain control over their lives. Members have the chance to develop skills, such as leadership and resource management, and they might enjoy a boost in self-esteem. **Empowered organizations**, on the other hand, engage in change efforts. They may, for example, mobilize community resources, influence policy decisions, or establish alternative systems of service delivery.

Some organizations are both empowered and empowering. The Black church, for example, is one of the few organizations built, financed, and controlled by African Americans. It has fostered the empowerment of its members, providing them with leadership opportunities, a psychological sense of community, and a positive sense collective identity and efficacy. The church has also served as a hub from social change efforts, most notably during the civil rights movements of the 1960s and 1970s (Brashears & Roberts, 1996).

Empowered organizations are not always empowering, however. For example, many large lobbying organizations (such as the American Association of Retired People and the National Rifle Association) have long membership lists and may frequently request donations but do not enhance the psychological empowerment of their members. Similarly, organizations that foster the psychological empowerment of members may not work to alter the status quo (Zimmerman, 1995; 2000). Alcoholics Anonymous (AA), for example, encourages personal growth and mutual support but is avowedly apolitical (Reissman & Bay, 1992). Robert Putnam (2000), in his cogent analysis of the decrease in civic participation, suggested that there has been an increase in the number of organizations that encourage personal growth in the presence of others but do not foster the social responsibilities on which communities depend. He also documented an increase in organizations that allow citizens to express demands in ways that demand less of them. Organizations' mailing lists grow, but member involvement does not. As Putnam (2000) put it, we "kibitz, but we don't play" (p. 183). Although Putnam did not use the terms "empowering" and empowered" organizations, I think he would agree that the main problem of the turn of this century is that people participate in fewer organizations that are *both* empowering and empowered.

ELEMENTS OF ORGANIZATIONAL SUCCESS

There are a number of organizations that have managed to swim against the tide described by Putnam (2000). Some microsystems bring people together to create change in themselves *and* the world around them. For the sake of convenience, let's call them *empowerful* organizations. What can we learn from these organizations? Insights in this section are gleaned from a number of studies described earlier, and three additional sources. Kenneth Maton and Deborah Salem (1995) identified common elements of success across three community contexts for empowerment—a religious fellowship, a mutual help group for people with serious mental illness, and an educational program for African American college students. Greg Watson (1999) drew ten lessons about organizational success from his tenure as executive director of the Dudley Street Neighborhood Initiative (DSNI), described in the opening of this chapter. The activist Thomas Wolff identified several guiding principles for creating competent community coalitions (Berkowitz & Wolff, 1996). Elements of success that converge across various analyses are described below.

Inspiring Belief System. One of the key characteristics of empowerful organizations identified by Maton and Salem (1995) is a belief system that inspires growth, emphasizes strengths, and encourages considerations that extend beyond the self. Settings can bring out the best in people by calling on them to answer to a higher cause. For some settings, this means incorporating a spiritual dimension into empowerment work, but the higher goal need not be overtly religious or spiritual. The guiding vision of an urban village developed by residents of Dudley Street constituted a strength-based, growth-inspiring belief system that transcended the self-interest of the individual residents involved.

Watson (1999) noted the importance of organizations investing whatever it takes up front in terms

of time and effort to develop a shared vision. Visioning is not always easy. Lisbeth Schorr (1997) described the difficulties of a group charged with visioning health goals for a community development project in Baltimore. They aimed no higher than shortening the wait in emergency rooms from all day to a few hours. The harsh realities of life for disenfranchised people can make it difficult to "dream big," and service providers' ability to dream may be similarly constrained by the context of their lives—ongoing encounters with budget constraints, bureaucratic barriers, and political mandates.

Opportunities for Involvement. Maton and Salem (1995) also cited the importance of opportunities for organization members to assume multiple and meaningful roles. Indeed, one of the groups they studied purposely created underpopulated settings to encourage the involvement of ever-larger numbers of people (Zimmerman, Reischl, Seidman, Rappaport, Toro & Salem, 1991).

According to Julian Rappaport (1987) one goal of empowerment is the creation of formal roles and responsibilities for every member of the setting, regardless of the person's level of functioning, Empowerful organizations find a niche for anyone who wants to belong. Thomas Wolff (Berkowitz & Wolff, 1996) held that successful coalitions operate on the assumption that everyone in the community has a role to play, and it is only a matter of time before they are brought into the collaborative. On Dudley Street, local residents are seen as a reservoir of community wealth. Watson (1999) described the collective wisdom of *all* residents as an invaluable and expandable resource that must be continually tapped. DSNI has formed numerous committees to utilize resident wisdom (DSNI, No Date c). Similarly, the Block Booster Project (see the Classic Research box) confirmed the importance of opportunities for involvement. Block associations that stood the test of time had more officers, twice the number of committees, and sponsored more activities as compared to those that ceased operations. (Florin, et al., 1992; Wandersman & Florin, 2000).

In considering the importance of creating opportunities for involvement, attention should be paid to

Calvin and Hobbes   by Bill Watterson

Successful organizations offer multiple opportunities for involvement. CALVIN AND HOBBES © Watterson. Reprinted with permission of UNIVERSAL PRESS SYNDICATE. All rights reserved.

ensuring that disenfranchised people have a voice. This includes youth. Watson (1999) argued that youth involvement keeps a community's vision alive because young people are the most valuable renewable resource.

Leadership. A paradox of organizational empowerment is that strong leadership enhances the full participation of setting members. Research shows that group members prefer leaders who actively direct the group and enforce rules (Wandersman & Florin, 2000). Leaders must, however, lead with flair. Organization members do not simply want to be told what to do. Empowerful leaders provide direction, but also inspire community participation. The civil rights activist Dianne Nash noted that, "Charismatic leadership has not freed us and it never will, because freedom is, by definition, people realizing that they are their own leaders" (Ingram, 1990; pp. 221–222). DSNI has established a Leadership Development Committee devoted to cultivating leadership skills in residents (DSNI, No Date c).

Maton and Salem (1985) found that empowerful organizations relied on the shared, visionary leadership of interpersonally and organizationally talented people who were committed to the growth of members and the setting as a whole. This characterization of leaders coincides with the notion of *collaborative*

leadership (Chrislip & Larson, 1994). Collaborative leaders inspire a commitment to action, lead as peer problem solvers, foster broad-based involvement, and sustain hope.

Leadership may be particularly important when power differentials exist among setting subgroups. In their study of the failed policy council in an alternative school, Judith Gruber and Edison Trickett (1987) hypothesized that formal leaders could have minimized the pre-existing power differentials among members that contributed to the council's downfall. Checks on leadership are also important. DSNI established a Board Development Committee to ensure that the leadership operates as intended and that residents ultimately make decisions about policies that have neighborhood implications.

Organizational Structure. Gruber and Trickett (1987) found that resistance to formal structures (including elected leaders) led to a "tyranny of structurelessness." Research strongly suggests that setting members prefer formal as opposed to informal group structure (Wandersman & Florin, 2000). Formal structure is associated with greater member involvement and increased satisfaction with the group. Structure reduces ambiguities. Clear roles, tasks, responsibilities, and operating procedures allow group members to work together to achieve their goals.

Organizational structures, like visionary leadership, can also balance pre-existing power differences among setting subgroups. Meg Bond and Chris Keys (Bond, 1999; Bond & Keys, 1993) described the tensions between parents and nonparents on a community board seeking responsive and appropriate services for children with developmental disabilities. Tensions stemmed, in part, from the parents' subordinate social position. Parent board members came from predominantly working class backgrounds, while nonparents were almost exclusively middle class. Two formal group structures were instituted to reduce tensions and promote parent empowerment. First, group composition was changed so that parent status and socioeconomic status no longer intertwined. Board members who spanned the two categories (i.e., middle class parents and working class nonparents) enabled each subgroup to hear the other more willingly. Second, power differentials were balanced by the creation of bylaws that dictated a majority representation by parents at all times. DSNI has similar bylaws to ensure that all the diverse voices of the neighborhood have a say in the neighborhood organization (DSNI, No Date d).

Innovation. As described in the chapter opening, Dudley Street embraces innovation. Watson (1999) noted the importance of challenging conventional wisdom. It was business as usual that allowed disempowerment to occur in the first place, and so new paradigms are needed to promote empowerment. As the poet–activist Audre Lorde (1984) put it, "the master's tools will never dismantle the master's house" (p. 110).

For example, Dudley Street residents recognized that traditional urban planning is inherently flawed and biased. It focuses on functional urban designs without consideration of human values and the local community. Watson (1999) recounted that the plans for rebuilding Dudley Street crafted by planning professionals called for hotels, office towers and historical parks that would gentrify the area, displace current residents, and obliterate local culture. Watson noted that the willingness to explore new ways of doing things allowed DSNI to become

the first community-based nonprofit organization to be granted power of eminent domain. Dudley Street activists convinced the Boston city government to take the unprecedented step of allowing the community to acquire empty lots and use them for affordable housing and other development projects as the residents saw fit. On Dudley Street, the community ultimately decides what gets built. The importance of this power becomes clear to me when I think of the local coffee shops, hardware stores, and other businesses in my own neighborhood that have closed in the past three years as yet another Starbucks, Home Depot, and SuperTarget opened nearby.

Celebration of Identity. In reviewing the literature on effective community organizations, Abraham Wandersman and Paul Florin (2000) found that members appreciate team spirit and camaraderie. Similarly, Maton and Salem (1995) found that empowerful organizations have peer-based support systems that foster a shared sense of identity. The possibilities for empowerment increase when group members feel connected to each other, and when this connection constitutes a reason to rejoice. Thomas Wolff (Berkowtiz & Wolff, 1996) noted the importance of celebrating hope, having fun, and affirming the strengths of the community. On Dudley Street, the multicultural festival was one of the first organizing efforts of DSNI and continues to be a popular, community-building event.

BEYOND THE MICROSYSTEM

Empowerment links individuals, local settings, and the larger social structure (e.g., Chavis & Wandersman, 1990; Florin et al., 1992; Wandersman & Florin, 2000). It provides opportunities for individuals to join groups where they can develop new competencies, grow in confidence, gain a sense of control, decrease feelings of social alienation, and become hopeful about the future. People working in coalition can improve their neighborhoods—reclaim vacant lots, combat crime, ensure a better education for their children. Ideally, individual and organizational empowerment also lead to changes in the larger structures that shape our lives.

Change at the macrosystem level is difficult to effect, however. Thomas Wolff (Berkowtiz & Wolff, 1996) acknowledged that the community coalitions with which he has worked have succeeded in creating local changes but not larger-scale social and economic transformations. At the same time, Stephanie Riger (1993) questioned whether a view of empowerment as a lower-level phenomenon can ever address the all-important systemic causes of disenfranchisement that necessitate empowerment in the first place.

INFLUENCE OF THE MACROSYSTEM ON LOWER-LEVEL CHANGE EFFORTS

Can interventions that enhance perceived or even actual control of resources solely at the individual level, or even at the microsystem level, be considered empowerment? Let's look briefly at examples of "empowerment" interventions at the individual level and microsystem level and then consider two in-depth examples of how well-conceived empowerment efforts can be undone by higher-level processes.

As an individual-level example, Emily Ozer and Albert Bandura (1990) described an intervention they labeled as empowerment that targeted forty-three women, many of whom had previously been assaulted. These women were taught self-defense skills, including physical strategies (eye strokes, biting, kicking), verbal defense techniques, and ways of projecting a confident demeanor that might protect them from attack. The researchers found that women who participated in the intervention reported an enhanced perception of self-efficacy and an improved quality of life. As testimony to the effectiveness of the intervention, the researchers quoted a participant who recounted, " 'I feel freer and more capable now than ever. I now make choices about what I will or won't do based on whether or not I want to, not whether or not it's frightening me' " (Ozer & Bandura, 1990, p. 484). Can this intervention be considered an example of empowerment if the psychological transformation of individual

women did not coincide with a reduction in violence against women through improved social conditions? Even if program participants learned to stave off attacks, is the program successful if would-be assailants simply go off in search of easier targets?

At a microsystem level, consider an example from the workplace literature. Meg Bond (1999) observed that "worker empowerment" reached the status of buzzword near the end of the twentieth century. In the 1980s and 1990s, *quality circles* were an extremely popular means of "worker empowerment," used by 80% of Fortune 1000 companies (Klein et al., 2000). Quality circles consisted of groups of workers, usually numbering between six and twelve, who met regularly to address work-related problems. Although workers were authorized to make suggestions, they generally did not make final decisions. Thus, they did not have actual power. Managerial commitment to quality circles was often limited, and their adoption often stemmed from a desire to boost employee morale (and improve organizational performance!) rather than a true interest in redistributing organizational power. Can workplace programs be considered empowering if they support or even promote worker exploitation?

Questions remain as to whether individual-level or microsystem-level interventions that do not target injustices in the larger social system can be considered empowerment. In addition, even enlightened empowerment interventions that consider the sociopolitical context can be undone by higher-level processes. As Gruber and Trickett (1987) observed, the creation of an egalitarian structure does not ensure the equal distribution of power because these structures exists as part of larger systems in which the distribution of resources is not equal. In reading the following two examples, consider with the wisdom of hindsight what program planners *might* have done to increase the likelihood of true empowerment.

TWO EXAMPLES

Let's now look at two examples of how larger systems can undo empowerment-oriented interventions, one in the United States and one in Puerto Rico.

The Perinatal Outreach Program. Clare Strawn (1994) described the Perinatal Outreach Program (PNO), an outreach and education program designed to improve the perinatal care of low-income women in several ethnic communities in California. Using participant observation, analysis of program documents (e.g., grant proposals, evaluation reports, case files) and ethnographic interviews, Strawn showed that although the crafters of PNO articulated a philosophy of empowerment, the actual intervention did not match their objectives and philosophy.

The PNO goals implicitly and explicitly endorsed an empowerment approach. The program founders sought to provide outreach, case management, and support services in a nonjudgmental, culturally appropriate, respectful, and supportive manner to pregnant women and new mothers. They sought to assist women within their natural social support systems and aimed to encourage clients' self-determination and participation in decision-making and problem-solving. They explicitly sought to "facilitate the empowerment and autonomy of the client" (Strawn, 1994, p. 164).

Gradually, program features that would foster client empowerment disappeared. The idea of creating mutual support groups among women was one of the first ideas to go. It was eliminated from the final contract as it did not coincide with the priorities of the funding agency (the California Health Department). Information on the clients' natural support systems was gathered as intended, but these networks were not integrated into the interventions as the program developers originally planned. Caseworkers used these networks only to spread the word of the program After establishing contact with clients, the caseworkers adopted traditional models of helping that fostered dependency. PNO staff positioned themselves as the primary support givers. Their resources—cars, driving ability, knowledge of English, and direct connections to organizations of power—were on loan to the women, temporarily expanding their access to services. The women remained isolated from each other, however, and had no opportunity to develop their personal and communal resources.

The ethnic diversity and disenfranchisement of the clients received attention by PNO staff. The directors hired bilingual and sometimes bicultural caseworkers. No one attended, however, to the political, economic, and social context of disenfranchisement. An individualized notion of empowerment placed responsibility for the problem of poor prenatal care on the shoulders of the mothers-to-be and ignored such social conditions as the fragmentation of services, inadequate transportation, shortage of childcare and lack of employment opportunities.

Strawn showed that during this intervention, opportunities for real change occurred. An individual-level ideology enveloped the program, however, and opportunities for collective empowerment were not seized. For example, at one PNO meeting, a staff person asked residents what they most needed. Transportation emerged as the most pressing concern, but caseworkers dismissed it as a low priority because the original grant proposal did not address transportation issues. On another occasion, a group of Southeast Asian women requested a PNO class on birth control. Once again, PNO workers did not follow through. The expression of the felt needs of the community for transportation and birth control created openings for dialogue in which outside agents could have supported the clients as agents of the changes they viewed as necessary.

As yet another example, a Russian caseworker working with Russian clients in PNO learned that her community contained no medical practitioners. This shortage was traced to policies that prevented health care providers trained in Russia from practicing in the U.S. The caseworker devised an individual-level rather than system-changing solution to this problem—she decided to enroll in nursing school. Contrast this decision with the social change solution developed by immigrants from Cambodia in Lowell, Massachusetts, when faced with a similar situation (Silka & Tip, 1994). As a result of immigration, the local school system was in dire need of Khmer-speaking teachers, but potentially eligible teachers had lost their documentation in the Cambodian civil war. Local university representatives and members of the Cambodian American community worked together to develop an alternative teacher certification procedure so that immigrant teachers could teach in U.S. classrooms.

In the PNO intervention, workers did not incorporate community resident perspectives and resources into their intervention. Professionals predetermined the relevant problems and strategies in their grant proposal, which was expressly written to attract funding from a government organization that had a social agenda of its own. Despite the intentions of the program founders to design an empowerment intervention, clients gained no real access to resources. Strawn (1994) concluded, "the social organization of disempowerment was embedded in the macro-environment and filtered down to the interpersonal interactions between well-intentioned helpers and communities" (p. 172).

Proyecto Esfuerzo. Irma Serrano-García's (1984) description of Proyecto Esfuerzo also demonstrated how higher-level factors can sabotage empowerment interventions. Esfuerzo is a rural community of 1400 poor families in Puerto Rico. Residents' meager income derives mostly from welfare and other governmental programs. In 1980, a Community Mental Health Center in collaboration with University of Puerto Rico faculty and students launched Proyecto Esfuerzo to assist this impoverished community.

The project began with a familiarization stage during which personnel learned all they could about Esfuerzo as unobtrusively as possible (e.g., reading newspaper articles, visiting the community informally). The next stage consisted of a formal assessment of community needs, resources, and expectations. The most pressing community need was for relocation; residents believed that their land was in imminent danger of flooding. Other community problems included disastrous road conditions, erratic garbage collection, lack of telephone service, and a shortage of recreational activities. Resources included ideas about desirable activities and a willingness to work together to solve problems.

Community leaders and residents were then helped to organize into task forces to meet identified needs. Proyecto staff confirmed the seriousness of the threat posed by flooding, but decided not to address this long-standing and politically charged issue because other groups were spearheading relocation efforts. Instead task forces were formed to meet the social and recreational needs of the community and to share information gleaned from Proyecto interviews with the entire community. Residents were helped to develop the skills necessary to accomplish these tasks.

In assessing this intervention, Serrano-García noted some successes and some failures. The project succeeded in developing resident skills. Task force members increasingly took over group functions and expressed awareness of their learning. Community members also identified community resources and developed an internal sense of self-sufficiency. The project might even have succeeded in combating some components of colonialist ideology, such as a rigid value stance and an intolerance of dissidence. The larger social, economic, and political systems that kept residents in poverty and in danger of decimation by flooding remained unchallenged, however. Serrano-García concluded that the intervention created an *illusion* of empowerment. Residents felt more control over their lives but did not confront the colonial context that determined their lives and, in many ways, their thoughts.

Serrano-García became convinced that the project's small successes were possible only because the low-status residents were not recognized as a threat by people who controlled resources and because the project did not choose to deal with problems that led to direct confrontations with governmental institutions and other power brokers. Serrano-García reasoned that disenfranchised people are permitted to gain control only until they become threatening to dominant groups. Change efforts that hold the promise of redistributing societal power inspire counterforces that maintain the status quo.

Larger systems can limit empowerment efforts originating at lower levels, or they can support them. Serrano-García (1984) posited that Proyecto Esfuerzo might have grown into a powerful social change effort if there had been larger community or national organizations ready to build on the intervention's successes.

The examples of the Perinatal Outreach Program and Proyecto Esfuerzo demonstrate that interventions aimed at a particular level (individual, microsystem, or community) need to consider ever-higher levels of analysis in their quest for empowerment. Empowerment may be seen as a reiterative process. Individual empowerment and group empowerment are mutually enhancing and lead to increased engagement with civic life and concern for higher levels of influence (e.g., Saegert & Winkel, 1996). Empowerment efforts may be most complete when they connect proximal conditions and distal events in society and when actions are increasingly directed at less and less local conditions.

⌘ Empowerment and Community Psychology's Guiding Principles

Empowerment, as an orienting concept, has direct implications for each of community psychology's guiding principles (see Perkins & Zimmerman, 1995). We have already touched on how empowerment embodies several of these principles, but let's examine each more closely.

EMPOWERMENT AND CONTEXT

The preceding discussion of levels of analysis has already examined empowerment beyond the level of the individual, and so this section will be relatively brief. As described above, empowerment links individual well-being with larger social and political processes (see also Kroeker, 1995). A consideration of empowerment as a multilevel construct also highlights the need to view empowerment is a dynamic, context-dependent construct that varies across individuals (e.g., Keiffer, 1984) and across settings (e.g., Stewart & Weinstein, 1997).

Empowerment cannot be reduced to a single universal definition or set of rules (Zimmerman, 1995; 2000). Because the empowerment process is tied to context, its meaning varies across individuals,

settings, and cultures (Rappaport, 1987). Empowerment is indeed, as Edison Trickett (1994) proclaimed, "ecological in spirit" (p. 587). Precise definitions cannot be preordained by researchers, politicians, or any other outside force. Those of us dedicated to empowerment must take James Kelly's (1971) notion of an eco-identity (see Chapter Two) to heart. Without "a grounding in local conditions, the concept runs the risk of becoming either a slogan lacking in substance or an imperialist activity once again done to people rather than with them" (Trickett, 1994, p. 591).

Consider, for example, the meaning of empowerment among the women dairy farmers described in the Community Intervention box (Shefner-Rogers et al., 1998). Researchers developed an empowerment scale that included such items as whether or not the woman made decisions about vaccinating milk animals or belonged to the dairy cooperative. Obviously community organizers working with youth in urban Detroit would need to devise a very different measure of empowerment that reflected the resources, barriers, and mechanisms for change relevant to that group.

EMPOWERMENT AND SOCIAL CHANGE

Some community psychologists have described Julian Rappaport's (1981, 1987) call for empowerment as a rallying cry for social change (Price, 1990; Zimmerman, 2000). Empowerment rests on the belief that people must work together to address the unequal distribution of and access to resources that is at the root of many problems in society. This conception of empowerment is not universal, however.

LIBERAL AND CONSERVATIVE PERSPECTIVES

In politics, the term empowerment enjoys bipartisan support. Members of both liberal and conservative parties advocate an empowerment agenda, although not the *same* agenda. More conservative individuals view empowerment as consistent with self-reliance, private voluntarism, and the reduction of big government. More liberal people, including many community psychologists concerned about righting inequities, watch with dismay as the rhetoric of empowerment is used to individualize responsibility for social problems. The theme of self-sufficiency seems empowering, but it is often used to relieve governmental institutions of their obligation to provide care and to justify the withdrawal of federal funds that previously supported empowerment initiatives (Silka & Tip, 1994; Strawn, 1994; Zimmerman, 2000). In his seminal address twenty years ago, Julian Rappaport (1981) anticipated this misuse of the term. Along with his hopes for empowerment as a unifying concept, he expressed his fear that a position of benign neglect would be cloaked as deep respect for individual freedoms. Empowerment would then be misconstrued as a rationale for doing nothing to change the status quo.

More recently Rappaport (1995) has suggested that community psychologists not be so quick to dismiss conservative viewpoints. Although he confessed his willingness to join other progressives in disapproving of the ideologies and actions of many groups claiming an interest in empowerment, he also admitted to finding the debate more useful than not. Ultimately, he advised, we must engage in dialogue not with only like-minded colleagues, but with all interested citizens. Conservative perspectives can push liberals past the borders of political correctness into more meaningful territory (see also Redding, 2001). Polarization of the two political camps only limits thinking. Liberals may resist attempts to relieve government of responsibility for promoting equality, arguing that disenfranchised groups require basic resources and technical assistance in order to level the playing field. There are, however, significant areas of overlap in the conservative and liberal meanings of the term on which to build. We might agree, for example, about the importance of mediating structures in driving empowerment efforts.

SOCIAL CHANGE AND COMMUNITY PSYCHOLOGISTS' HABITS OF THOUGHT

Despite the popularity of the term, widespread social transformation has not resulted from the plethora of empowerment initiatives implemented over the past decades. Community psychologists cannot simply blame conservative co-optation of the term for this state affairs. Our own habits of thoughts also interfere with social change agendas. Three shifts in perspective might increase the likelihood that empowerment-oriented interventions lead to social change.

The first, discussed above, is the need to attend to evermore remote levels of analysis. The second is a consideration of both the *process* and the *outcomes* of empowerment efforts (e.g., Perkins & Zimmerman, 1995; Swift & Levin, 1987). Influential definitions encourage a view of empowerment as a process (e.g., Cornell Empowerment Group, 1989; Rappaport 1984c), but Stephanie Riger (1993) questioned community psychology's willingness to equate empowerment with participation in the political process, as if changes in procedure automatically led to changes in the distribution of resources. Organizations can have quality circles (Klein et al., 2000) and schools can have policy councils (Gruber & Trickett, 1987), but these "decision-making bodies" may actually wield very little power. As Arthur Himmelman suggests (Himmelman, Johnson, Kaye, Salzman, & Wolff, 2001), token participation can actually reinforce the status quo. The true test of an empowerment effort is whether a real redistribution of valued resources actually occurs.

A third potentially useful shift in perspective is a recognition of the ways that marginalized groups, *not* people in power, control the social change process. Empowerment theory simultaneously sees disenfranchised groups as marginalized and lacking in social power, but also strong and capable agents of social transformation (see Riger, 2001). Some argue that ultimate control of the power relationship lies with the target group members. Paulo Freire (1970/1992) posited that the oppressor has neither the insight nor the motivation to create change, and so oppressed people must unite to transform unjust systems in ways that ultimately liberate the oppressed and oppressor alike.

Irma Serrano-García (1994) identified two ways in which target groups have the power to define the terms of power struggles. First, they can disrupt existing power relationships by altering the importance of the resource in question. They might, for example, obtain the resource elsewhere or perhaps find ways to generate it themselves. On Dudley Street, residents grow much of their own food, lessening their dependence on factory farms and large supermarket chains. Alternatively, target group members can redefine the importance of the resource. A community's consideration of the meaning of wealth may lead to the conclusion that collective wisdom of community residents and youth energy are important resources to nurture, thereby de-emphasizing traditional indicators of wealth, such as the average square footage of the homes or per capita income.

EMPOWERMENT AND DIVERSITY

The majority of work on empowerment with diverse groups has focused on one population at a time. Also important is a consideration of how empowerment can take shape in a multicultural system where different groups seek control over resources. Such expanded notions of empowerment might benefit from a cross-cultural analysis of the very concept of empowerment.

POPULATION-SPECIFIC EMPOWERMENT

In 1994 the *American Journal of Community Psychology* devoted a special issue to the empowerment of marginalized groups. Articles examined the implications of empowerment to people with disabilities, gay and lesbian people, Southeast Asians, Latinas and Latinos, and Black women. Each article identified relevant issues for the group in question. The article on people with disabilities discussed the barriers imposed by the environment (Fawcett, White, Balcazar, Suarez-Balcazar, Mathews, Paine, Seekins, & Smith, 1994). The article on lesbian and gay people highlighted the challenges of creating community for a group whose members are exceedingly diverse, invisible to each other, and have no intergenerational continuity (Garnets and D'Augelli, 1994; see also Kofkin & Schwartz, 1995). A different set of issues pertains to Southeast Asians, who face challenges arising from immigration, language barriers, and other factors (Silka & Tip, 1994).

Population-specific examinations of disenfranchised groups demonstrate how empowerment interfaces with a particular local culture. In addition, some general challenges exist. As one example, each marginalized group struggles with attempts from outsiders to "help" them adapt to society (see Silka & Tip, 1994). These efforts may be labeled empowering, but encouraging minority group members to conform to the dominant culture actually supports the status quo and reinforces their marginalization. The editors of the special issue also noted several empowerment strategies that cut across group boundaries (Serrano-García & Bond, 1994). Diverse groups all experienced the need to generate new or strengthen existing social networks in order to maximize resources. All groups sought to develop political participation through grassroots movements and attempted to strengthen group identity as a means of achieving broad social goals.

COEMPOWERMENT

A new set of concerns emerges when we go beyond population-specific analyses of empowerment and consider the difficulties inherent in honoring diversity in a multicultural society where various disenfranchised groups with different agendas seek to create change. Stephanie Riger (1993) framed the question as follows, "If the empowerment of the disenfranchised group is the primary value, then what is to hold together societies made up of different groups?" (p. 290). Let's look at some ways of tackling Riger's question.

First we must question conceptualizations of empowerment in which one group's gain is another's loss. If the empowerment of one person or group requires the oppression of another, then the more things change, the more they remain the same (Moss, 1991). A system of inequity is a system of inequity regardless of which particular group manages to climb its way to the "top." We need to think of empowerment as something other than a shift in the balance of power that enables a new group to gain power over others. Empowerment cannot be a zero-sum game. Julian Rappaport (1987) proposed that empowerment itself may be seen not as a scarce resource, but as an ideology that once adopted can expand.

Meg Bond and Chris Keys (1993) explored the possibility that different groups with different values and different priorities can be simultaneously empowered. They conducted a case study of a community board working to improve services for children with developmental disabilities. Members of this board included parents and nonparents of different socioeconomic levels. They coined the term **coempowerment** to refer to the goal of shared authority over agenda setting, discussion, and decision making. It overlaps with the notion of "collaborative empowerment," (Fawcett, Paine-Andrews, Francisco, Schultz, Richter, Lewis, Williams, Harris, Berkley, Fisher, & Lopez., 1995; Himmelman, 2001; see also van Uchelen's [2000] notion of "field control"). When coempowerment occurs, multiple groups with divergent perspectives jointly influence the direction of a setting. Although the influence of any particular group ebbs and flows, a sense of mutuality exists (Bond, 1999). Coempowerment exemplifies synergy: different groups connect and strengthen the total system in ways no one could alone (Bond & Keys, 1993).

When culturally different groups come together, they bring with them different motivations, perspectives, investments, class and cultural backgrounds, and approaches to collaboration. These differences often cause bickering, entrenchment in opposing camps, and a variety of other "power struggles" (Bond & Keys, 1993). Sometimes the coalition is co-opted by the strongest subgroup (Gruber & Trickett, 1987), and sometimes one or more subgroups leave the coalition. However, differences do not inevitably lead to alienation, apathy, insurmountable conflict, irreversible organizational upheaval, or the disintegration of a setting.

Bond and Keys identified several aspects of a system's culture that promote the coempowerment of subgroups. First, mutual empowerment increases if the system culture supports each group's meaningful inclusion. This means recognizing both the differences and similarities among group members. As described earlier, boundary-spanning people and structures also facilitate inter-group understanding.

The community board Bond and Keys studied initially included parents who were of low socioeconomic status and nonparents who were middle class. When the setting expanded to include boundary-spanning people (i.e., parents from middle class backgrounds and nonparents from working class backgrounds), functioning of the board improved, in part because the boundary spanners could facilitate inter-group understanding. Finally, Bond and Keys recognized the importance of an organizational system that appreciated the interdependence of subgroups. This is reminiscent the findings of Muzafer Sherif and colleagues (1961) in their work with boys in Robber's Cave (see Chapter Five's Classic Research box). The reduction of negative inter-group attitudes and interactions required contexts of mutual interdependence and collaboration towards a common goal. Shared visions can bring people together across differences.

The Dudley Street Neighborhood Initiative provides another example of coempowerment. On Dudley Street, neighborhood diversity is honored. The uniqueness of different cultures is celebrated in restaurants, theaters, and festivals. The need for diverse groups to work together is also appreciated. The DSNI board composition reflects the neighborhood's diversity, with designated seats for different groups. The board is able to function as a whole because the common vision of an urban village serves as a superordinate goal that unites the diverse membership.

Another example involves a small tribe of Indians who live just north of Phoenix on the Fort McDowell reservation (O'Sullivan, Tausig, & Lindsey, 1984). In 1961, the reservation became the focus of government attention as it lay near the confluence of the Salt and Verde Rivers—the site of a proposed dam. Most people believed that the dam would solve two pressing problems in the area. It would alleviate water shortages in this desert state and also reduce the threat of flooding in heavily populated areas. Plans for the dam enjoyed tremendous support from the business, agricultural, and political leaders of Arizona. The Yavapai Indians, who now faced the prospect of their third forced relocation, did not share in the enthusiasm.

The tribe seemed to have little power to resist. They were small in number, poor, and inexperienced in political maneuvering. The government offered the Yavapai monetary compensation for the land and income from the recreational facilities that the new reservoir would make possible. Business leaders characterized the dam as "the best thing that could happen to the Indians" (O'Sullivan et al., 1984, p. 79).

Plans proceeded slowly, and the Yavapai united in their opposition. A few others, including environmentalists, pro-Indian supporters, antigovernment advocates, and river recreationists joined the resistance. In 1977 they convinced President Carter to refuse funding for the dam project. In 1978 however, the first of three major floods hit the Phoenix area and the ban on the dam project was lifted. The Yavapai realized that through legal and political wrangling, they could tie up the project for the foreseeable future. In order to move beyond this impasse, a four-year study was launched to explore flood control options. The study was to include a highly visible public participation program. In addition, the governor of Arizona, Bruce Babbitt, appointed a Governor's Advisory Committee comprised of twenty-nine representatives from cities, organizations, and interest groups that had a stake in the outcome. Babbitt purposely put representatives of significant competing interests on this committee and charged them with making one consensual recommendation to him at the completion of the study. This provided an opportunity for coempowerment (or disaster!).

The Yavapai gradually convinced other stakeholders of the unfairness of the dam project. They launched media campaigns and made entreaties that were both logical and spiritual. Religious organizations were among the first to become convinced. Eventually, all major religious groups came out in opposition to relocation and held prayer services on behalf of the Indians. The Yavapai appealed to their opponents' consciences by stressing the impact of being torn from a sacred land to which they had historical, emotional, cultural, and spiritual ties. The commissioned study of the flood control options recognized the psychological impact of compulsory relocation. Researchers warned that if forced relocation occurred, the Yavapai would suffer from a lost sense of control and destroyed cultural identity, conditions that would seriously compromise their physical and psychological health.

On October 2, 1981, the Governor's Advisory Committee opposed the dam and recommended an alternative plan with a vote of 19 to 1 (one environmentalist cast a vote for "no action"). It seems that one reason this committee of diverse and conflicting parties was able to reach consensus was because the research study provided a forum for the public participation of all stakeholders. Thus, every viewpoint was heard. In addition, the information generated during the research study was available to all. A reciprocal process where all parties became aware of and responsive to the needs of others resulted in a decision in which everyone had a say, and with which everyone could live.

LEARNING FROM THE MARGINS

Coempowerment is only one innovative response to Riger's question of how we can hold together diverse groups of empowered people. There are others. Every group, because of its unique position, will have a slightly different view of empowerment. If empowerment scholars can draw out alternative visions of what is meant by empowerment, we will gain new insight and build more complete models.

As described earlier, feminist perspectives on power suggest a model of empowerment based on receptivity rather than agency (e.g., Rosenwasser, 1992b; 1992c). African American perspectives suggest that a place exists for spiritual perspectives; virtually every African American empowerment effort has had God at its center (Watts, 1997).

People with disabilities might have important lessons to share on how to think about *control* (Fine & Asch, 1988). Empowerment is often framed as an effort to gain control. People in modern societies seek to gain more and more control over life. Indeed, cloning and genetic engineering are two examples of our efforts to control life itself. People with disabilities remind us that we *cannot* control everything. As human beings with physical existences, we are sometimes in control and sometime not. As members of social groups, we are sometimes in control, and sometimes not. What *kind* of control is important to well-being? And what benefits accrue from relinquishing control? There are important paradoxes to uncover. I am reminded, for example, that one step in twelve-step programs is to recognize that we as people do not ultimately have control, which paradoxically allows us to assume more control.

EMPOWERMENT AND VALUES

Values enter into discussions of empowerment from several directions. This section examines three. First, values underlie the very construct of empowerment. Second values affect the actions of both the interventionist interested in empowerment and the disenfranchised groups with whom interventionist works. Finally, values may themselves be a resource relevant to empowerment efforts.

THE VALUES OF EMPOWERMENT

A few scholars have discussed the values underlying the construct of empowerment. Julian Rappaport (1981) highlighted empowerment's emphasis on citizen's rights as compared to prevention's focus on people's needs. Isaac Prilleltensky (1998) examined the value base of empowerment in relation to the values he identified as important to psychologists (see the section entitled *Liberatory Ethics* in Chapter Three). He noted that empowerment challenges the status quo in its attention to *distributive justice,* but aligns with traditional psychological approaches in its valuing of *self-determination.* He argued that popular models of empowerment, which focus on obtaining resources for oneself and one's group, fail to disengage from *individualism* and so undermine the important values of *collaboration* and *caring compassion.*

Empowerment efforts that augment the mastery or control of one individual or group may actually work against a larger sense of community (Perkins, 1995; Speer, 2000). Stephanie Riger (1993) identified a primary task for community psychologists as articulating

the relationship between empowerment and community. Riger warned that a view of empowerment that emphasized individuation, mastery, and control overlooked the connectedness of human life. Empowerment research, theory, and practice can do a better job of balancing the existing attention to agency with an increased commitment to communion (Rappaport, 1995).

There exists a dialectical relationship between self and community in all societies. The question is to what degree each is emphasized. The strongly egalitarian !Kung society uses collaborative, community-based approaches to the distribution of both plentiful resources (e.g., building materials for their shelters) and scarce resources (e.g., water) (Katz, 1984). On the other hand, the strongly individualized society of the U.S. tends to adopt individualistic approaches to resource distribution no matter how plentiful the resource. Empowerment scholars can help balance the current focus in the U.S. on individuation by stressing the potential for empowerment to foster community.

THE VALUES OF EMPOWERMENT SEEKERS

Research and practice that promote empowerment (like all research and practice) are based in the interventionist's own values. These values may or may not conform to the values of the groups with which he or she works. In this section we will first examine the importance of a value match between interventionists and the targeted group, and then examine the implications of decisions to reveal or not reveal our values.

The Value Match. Several community psychologists have asked whether we really want to empower *all* disenfranchised groups (e.g., Price, 1990; Riger, 1993). Should we seek, for example, to empower neo-Nazis? Although many would have no problem responding to that question in the negative, not all value conflicts are as straightforward.

Value dilemmas revolve around not only who deserves to be empowered, but also what we want to empower people to do. A community psychologist may collaborate with a group deemed worthy of empowerment only to find that the group's empowerment agenda conflicts with her or his deeply held values. What should nonviolent interventionists who believe that children are a disempowered group do when efforts to honor the voices of powerless parents in school council meetings result in parental demands for the corporal punishment of children (Trickett, 1994)?

A more complete understanding of the local context can increase interventionists' sensitivity to different empowerment agendas. Still, community psychologists must grapple with the fact that empowerment does *not* mean helping people to do only what *we* think they should do.

The Veiling of Values. Because scientists enjoy a position of power in this society, the way in which our values affect our work requires careful consideration. The implications of expressing our values also merit attention.

Numerous community psychologists have argued for the importance of revealing our values whenever possible (see Chapter Three section entitled *The Cloak of Respectability*). In some instances, however, we may not have the freedom to do so. Irma Serrano-García's (1984) report on Proyecto Esfuerzo made clear that the project leaders operated from a particular value stance. They favored the independence of Puerto Rico from colonial rule. This belief put them in the minority; most Puerto Ricans favor either gaining statehood (Puerto Rico would become the fifty-first state of the United States) or remaining a commonwealth. When Proyecto Esfuerzo was launched, community members questioned the project staff about their political persuasions. The staff dodged these questions with reference to the nonpartisan position of their employer, the University of Puerto Rico. As employees of this purportedly apolitical organization, project staff did not have the freedom to express their pro-independence stance.

Serrano-García recognized the possibility that had the staff expressed their ideological views, the community would have rejected their involvement. Value differences may have created an insurmountable barrier. On the other hand, the staff's supposed neutrality hindered their consciousness-raising efforts by forcing the avoidance of pressing partisan issues. Had they not been shackled by university policy, project staff may well have decided to take the risk of unveiling their values. True, they may then have lost the opportunity to work with the disempowered community. They would not have ended up, however, in the morally compromised position of supporting the development of a community group that did not challenge and may even have supported a political ideology that the staff believed caused the community's problems in the first place.

VALUES AS A RESOURCE

Ten years after recounting her perceived failures with Proyecto Esfuerzo, Irma Serrano-García (1994) published a groundbreaking article on power. In this article she proposed that morality should be considered a resource. It can be an instrumental resource in that two parties may engage in conflict over whose vision of morality should prevail (that is, which value system is most valuable). It can also be an infraresource—a resource that facilitates access to instrumental resources.

The success of the Yavapai Indians in defeating the proposed dam stemmed, in large part, from their ability to use morality as an infraresource. When their plight became understood, people in power could not in good conscience build a dam that would force the Yavapai to leave their homeland for the third time. Nonviolent protesters in the civil rights movements also gained empowerment through appeals to morality. Perhaps moral power should be added to the list of power sources begun by French and Raven (1960). While legitimate power accrues only to people in positions of organizational or societal power, moral authority is conferred by a higher source.

You will remember that Serrano-García (1994) delineated different strategies disenfranchised people can use to disrupt power relationships. They can gain control of a resource, alter its importance by meeting their needs in other ways, or redefine the importance of the resource. Mahatma Gandhi, Martin Luther King, Jr., and other visionary leaders redefined the importance of *all* resources relative to morality. Their actions conveyed the conviction that morality was more important than job security, more important than food, more important than physical safety, and ultimately, more important than life itself. When disenfranchised people redefine the terms of power struggles and expose the moral emptiness of policies that enforce inequities, then "the power of morality will prevail over the morality of the powerful" (Serrano-García, 1994, p. 17).

EMPOWERMENT AND STRENGTHS

Empowerment directs attention toward health and competence. It promotes images of people as powerful, worthy, and capable. Individuals join forces to exercise their rights instead of passively waiting to have their needs fulfilled by others. In order for empowerment to occur, help providers need to relinquish their sense of omnipotence and omniscience and cease to defend professional territories and prerogatives (Katz, 1984).

Although empowerment efforts have a place for expertise (e.g., the building of *expert power*) there is no room for expert-helper models of helping.

Katz (1984) asserted that helpers must offer themselves and their knowledge under the same conditions as the people they seek to help. This includes being vulnerable to the same risks they face. Similarly, Serrano-García (1984) held that consciousness raising requires horizontal relationships between the change agent and participants. In the context of nonhierarchical relationships, genuine dialogue, respectful attention, and optimism about the possibility of change can lead to social transformation. As Ram Dass and Paul Gorman (1985) put it, "Our aim is to awaken together and see what follows, not to manipulate one another into this action or that" (p. 163).

For empowerment to occur, a change in roles must take place where client–expert relationships are replaced by relationships built on collaboration and co-participation. Lessons can be learned from a comparison of models of helping in mutual help groups as compared to professional helping relationships (Biklen, 1983). Mutual help groups:

1. Make professional information available to all and subject to questioning;
2. Value personal experience as a way of knowing;
3. Dispense with hierarchy and build a community where all members have equal status;
4. Operate via membership control;
5. Encourage active involvement of members;
6. Utilize problem definitions and solutions developed by the members;
7. Embrace a holistic orientation in which personal difficulties are seen as embedded in a developmental and social context;
8. Prefer flexibility in responding to individuals rather than bureaucratic routines.

In empowerment models, professionals develop, implement, and evaluate interventions in collaboration with community members. This requires the formation of an eco-identity—professionals must become members of the community in which they work, at least temporarily. We create opportunities for community members to learn our skills and so reduce their dependence on outsiders, thereby planning our own obsolescence.

⌘ The Promise of Community Psychology: Telling Stories

Julian Rappaport maintained his commitment to the concept of empowerment in the two decades that followed his seminal article. In his more recent writings, he has wedded the concept of empowerment to the notion of narrative.

Narratives can be understood as resources, and like most resources they are distributed unevenly throughout society. Stories about disenfranchised people are written by more powerful people, who present the others in a negative light (Rappaport, 1995). When people lack power, they are objects rather than subjects. They do not act in the world, rather their environments act upon them (Keiffer, 1984). One goal of empowerment is to establish the self as subject—to assist people who lack social, economic, and political power in becoming the authors of their own life stories. Thus, it is important to consider which stories are legitimated by whom and who has the right to tell whose story (Rappaport, 1995).

Supportive others can help disenfranchised and voiceless people become the authors of their own stories. When story-making happens in the context of community, the results can be profound. One of the functions of mutual help groups is that they provide a forum for people to reformulate and share personal stories. As people talk together about their experiences, they discover new ways to think about themselves (Rappaport, 1993). Sharing stories can also lead to social change. Ram Dass and Paul Gorman (1985) contended that "[t]he most effective political action often grows out of telling one another our stories" (p. 164). In the 1960s, stories shared by countless women gathered around kitchen tables and coffee tables gave shape and energy to a renewed women's movement. When people share stories, they gain insights about who they are, where they came from, what they believe, and perhaps most importantly, what they can become (Rappaport, 1995). This happens not only at the individual level, but the group level as well. Just as individuals have stories about their lives, so too do groups develop **community narratives**. Indeed, Rappaport (2000a) proposed that a community cannot be a community without shared stories. Similarly, David McMillan (1996) posited that a sense of community requires a shared *emotional connection* that results from shared stories about the community's history, traditions, and accomplishments.

Stories are not always spoken. Local arts projects of all types (theater, dance, music) provide a means for silenced groups to uncover, create, interpret, and control their narratives and therefore their identities (Thomas & Rappaport, 1996). Art also brings diverse people together. In outlining a change agenda to reverse the breakdown of community, Robert Putnam (2000) noted the importance of participation in cultural activities, from community theater to rap festivals. He encouraged activists to discover new ways of using art to build social capital.

The arts have always played an important role in empowerment efforts. As one of many examples, consider community mural making (Cockcroft, Weber, & Cockcroft, 1977/1998). Murals are community narratives in which disenfranchised people represent their history and their current lives on a heroic scale. Murals challenge existing stories written by others and present new interpretations of the community's reality. Neighborhood beautification comes second to meaning making, and so murals stir controversy. They involve community members who might never think to enter a museum in public discourse about art, identity, and politics. Every man, woman, and child can form an opinion about a mural that exists on the walls of their building, overlooking the streets on which they walk. No matter who actually painted it, the mural belongs to the community.

One role of the community psychologist is to find ways to give voice to stories that challenge dominant cultural narratives (Thomas & Rappaport, 1996). Some stories and narratives are terrifying, based in fear and oppression and shaped by the voices of others. Community psychologists can "use our tools (methods, critical observation and analysis, scholarship and social influence) to assist others in turning tales of terror into tales of joy" (Rappaport, 2000a, p. 7). As researchers and practitioners, we can aid empowerment efforts by creating settings where people participate in the discovery, creation, and enhancement of personal stories and community narratives (Rappaport, 1995).

This new role requires new approaches to intervention and research. Some innovative projects offer us direction. Charles Keiffer (1984) gathered information on the life courses of activists using what he called "dialogic retrospection." Researcher and activist engaged in a process of joint inquiry, and follow-up interviews were used to extend, correct, and clarify earlier conversations. Thus, the research participants validated and elaborated on the researcher's emerging interpretations of the activists' words. More recently, Lynne Bond and her colleagues (2000) established a group called "The Listening Partners Program," where rural mothers who felt unheard and powerless took turns telling their life stories to each other and found strength in their voices as a result. Autophotography might be a way for people to tell their stories without words (e.g., Ziller, 1990; Wang, 1999). In the process of developing new techniques for community psychology's research and practice, we have much to learn from other disciplines: anthropology, communications, the arts.

The payoff may be substantial. New research and intervention strategies will allow us to gain insights into the worlds of others that could never be gained through more traditional and constrained approaches. In addition, these strategies convey an important meta-message. Being listened to with respect is itself a transforming experience. (Rappaport, 1995).

Action Agenda

Power Animal Shield

Flor Fernandez is one of the women featured in *Visionary Voices: Women on Power* (Rosenwasser, 1992b). Fernandez is a psychologist, shaman, and psychic healer who works with abused women and children. In her work she has developed an activity drawn from ancient traditions. She asks people to draw or paint on shields their "power animals"; their personal symbols of empowerment. In Native American cultures, images used to decorate shields represents the spirit, the self, and one's journey through the lifetime. Fernandez recounted, "When you paint your symbols on the shield, you're actually using symbols that will remind you of your own personal power" (p. 126). In Native American traditions, the power animal connects the person to the earth and serves as a reminder that no one is alone in the universe; other kingdoms offer protection and support.

Think about your power animal. To what animal do you feel a special connection or affinity? What characteristics of that animal are attractive? Is it the graceful speed of a gazelle? The night vision of an owl? The good-natured cleverness of a fox? My power animal is a rhinoceros. I resonate to its solidity, its earth-boundedness, and I look to it for lessons about developing a tougher skin!

Make some sketches of your power animal (or several possible animals and see to which you most resonate). You may want to base your sketches on pictures from photography books or perhaps take a trip to the zoo or to an animal preserve to connect with that animal's essence. Your final drawing is not intended to be a realistic representation, however. It is *your* representation, and so it cannot be wrong. What colors do you associate with your animal? Is it a purple lion with a green mane? A red buffalo? When you think of your power animal, how is does it appear? Is it standing on a windblown cliff? Is it relaxing in the jungle sun? When you have a clear vision of your power animal, find or create a shield (a cardboard cutout would suffice) and draw or paint your power animal on it. Perhaps you will want to share your shields with classmates and tell each other the stories of your power animals.

Identification of Resources

Irma Serrano-García (1994) noted that most people interested in social change are unaware of the many resources available to them. She proposed that the ability to identify resources is a resource in and of itself.

Choose one of the empowerment efforts described in this chapter and consider the resources relevant to that effort. Think about the resources the group seeking power actually had, as well as the resources they sought (or could have/should have sought). For example, what resources were of interest to Dudley Street residents when the Neighborhood Initiative was formed? What resources did the residents of Dudley Street possess that enabled them to build their urban village? What resources were desired by the women dairy farmers in India, and on what resources did the community organizers build? You might consider resources at different levels.

Also consider the resources a community psychologist might bring to the empowerment initiative. For example, in Proyecto Esfuerzo, the intervention team brought to the community the results of the needs assessments, expertise on research methods, and access to information about governmental agencies (Serrano-García, 1994). The status and respect mental health professionals enjoy can also be a resource, providing a sort of power by proxy. Professionals can serve as advocates with inside knowledge about social institutions and an ability to speak the language of the powerful (e.g., Paradis, 2000). After brainstorming about resources, consider the strategies you might have adopted if you were a part of the intervention. Also consider the extent to which you believe the resources you identified are limited or expandable. How would the expandable versus limited nature of the resources affect the strategies you would attempt? After considering resources in the text examples, you might choose an intervention or social change effort in your community and conduct a similar analysis. Does this exercise suggest any next steps to create change in your community?

Shapes of Empowerment

Zimmerman (2000) suggested that measures of empowerment need to be developed in each setting of interest. Think about the settings that matter to you—your classroom, a religious fellowship, your neighborhood. What would empowerment look like in those settings? If you were developing a measure to assess empowerment, as Connie Shefner-Rogers and her colleagues (1998) did (see the Community Intervention box), what items would you include?

Key Terms

citizen participation

coempowerment

community narratives

empowered organizations

empowering organizations

infraresources

instrumental resources

mediating structures

nomological net

political efficacy

possible selves

psychological empowerment

resources

scarcity paradigm

synergy paradigm

tyranny of structurelessness

Chapter 11

Resilience

....

⌘ Introduction

In the early 1990s, two sisters, Sadie and Bessie Delany, wrote a bestselling book entitled *Having Our Say*. When the book was published, Sadie was 104 years old, and Bessie was 112. *Having Our Say*, which later served as the basis for a Broadway play, tells the story of these two sisters who lived together for most of their long lives, each having chosen careers over marriage in an era that required such choices. Bessie became a dentist and Sadie became a high school teacher who helped integrate the New York City school system. The book is not only a recounting of their two lives, but the story of a highly successful African American family. The father, who had been born into slavery, became the first elected Black bishop of the Episcopal Church of the United States, and all of his ten children were college-educated professionals at a time when few people, Black or White, continued their education beyond high school.

When slavery ended for the Delany's father, he began life as a free man with many resources. Members of his family were smart and also lucky. They could read, had not been abused, and had somehow managed to remain together as a family. The Delany's mother had also fared better than most, in part because her family included many White relatives and so her people enjoyed the advantages of light-colored skin. The Delany parents knew that they had been fortunate and felt committed to helping their fellow African Americans survive and thrive. The sisters recounted that Papa bypassed the

317

nearby A & P supermarket and dragged the family to Jones' grocery store because the Jones' needed the money more. "We are buying our economic freedom," Papa told the family (Delany, Delany, & Hearth, 1993, p. 97).

The Delany children grew up in a household filled with love. The sisters recalled that their parents were the two busiest people on earth, but they always had time for the children—to talk, to provide comfort after an encounter with racism, or just to watch a sunset together. The Delanys had a family creed that could be recounted by all: education as a means of advancement, public service, a strong moral code, and a willingness to help anyone at anytime. Many family rituals reinforced this creed—they prepared Thanksgiving baskets to give away each year, and each night Papa would read a Bible story to the children. Before going to sleep, any children who had argued during the day would make up. No one in the Delany household could go to bed with conflicts unresolved.

Although the parents surrounded their children with love, they were also strict disciplinarians. Sadie's first memory was of sitting on her mother's lap in front of a fire eating candy. Her mother told her to give some to her brother. When Sadie refused she watched the candy box fly into the flames. Next time, her mother counseled, it would be better to share. Mama lived out her ethic of generosity, and no one who ever knocked on the Delany door went away hungry. Papa also held the children to high standards. He lined them up for inspection every day to be sure that they had polished shoes, clean ears, and presented a dignified image to the world. Sadie and Bessie saw this as evidence of their father's pride in his children. The one and only time the sisters reported being whipped was when they had wandered further than they were allowed and their father feared for their safety. The parents kept a close eye on the Delany children, perhaps a little too close, as the children blossomed into adulthood.

Although Mama and Papa tried to shelter their children (not allowing them to read newspapers, for example), encounters with a hostile environment inevitably occurred. The Delany parents helped their children learn how to deal with racism: to remain proud, strong, and confident of their own

Sadie and Bessie Delany looking at a family album in their Mount Vernon home. *Reprinted by permission of Kodansha America, Inc.*

abilities and worth in the face of hatred, ignorance, and discrimination. Sweet Sadie, who believed people should live and let live, learned to manipulate the system by smiling and playing dumb. Bold Bessie, who would rather die than back down, confronted injustice everywhere, regardless of the cost.

Sadie and Bessie had many supporters in life, White and Black, who nurtured them as children and aided them as adults. The community ties went both ways. Bessie and Sadie tried to give to others as best they could and took on the task of writing their book as a way of feeling useful and passing on lessons learned to the next generation. The two sisters had both joined helping professions and served their community both professionally and personally. When she was an old woman, Bessie also assumed the fulltime job of looking out her window and watching over the neighborhood. "If it's going on in my neighborhood," she explained to her sister, "it's my business" (Delany, et al., 1993, p. 22). And the neighbors, in turn, watched over Bessie and Sadie. The sisters recounted how some of the people on the block paid the sisters a visit when they became convinced that the Delany house was haunted—so much noise and laughter coming from within their walls. It was just the two of them having fun together, the sisters recalled joyfully. The neighbors didn't think two old ladies could carry on like that at their age, but Sadie and Bessie explained that they did not sit around like sourpusses. In the end they were able to say, "We lived a clean life, but Lord, we had a good time" (Delany et al., 1993, p. 86).

Although the term *resilience* may conjure images of children, the Delany sisters' entire lives seem to me a testimony to the human spirit. This coincides with more recent views of resilience as a relevant construct across the life span. The Delany story also gives shape to notion of resilience-in-relationship or resilience-in-community. The family nurtured ties with the people around them, helping to create a sense of community for themselves and for others. Before we get to current thinking about resilience, however, let's look at how the construct emerged in the psychology and community psychology literature, keeping in mind the ways Sadie, Bessie, and their family manifest the insights gleaned from research.

⌘ The Emergence of Resilience as an Orienting Concept

The literature on resilience provides a welcome departure from psychology's traditional emphasis on what goes wrong in life. It encourages us to look instead at what goes right, how people, families, and communities can live and thrive in the midst of challenges and adversity. Numerous researchers and practitioners in developmental psychology, education, clinical psychology, social work, community psychology, and other fields resonate to the strengths-oriented approach to human behavior embodied in the concept of resilience.

EARLY ROOTS

Interest in resilience represents a convergence of several streams of research. Its earliest roots are in clinical research. Professionals who work with psychiatric populations have always sought to understand why some people become mentally ill and some do not. Traditionally, researchers have directed attention to those people who developed illness in an attempt to understand what goes wrong. Individuals who fared relatively well went unstudied. One of the earliest proponents of resilience, Norman Garmezy (1971; 1974; see also Rolf, 1999), broke with this tradition. In the 1940s and 1950s he noted the diverse backgrounds and prognoses for schizophrenic patients and became interested in why some patients actually functioned quite well. This interest eventually led Garmezy to study the "odds-defying" children who lived in ghettoes and faced extreme hardships from poverty, prejudice, and other stresses, but who became competent, well-adjusted citizens all the same.

Norman Garmezy, Ann Masten, and their colleagues (Garmezy, Masten, & Tellegen, 1984; Garmezy & Masten, 1986) conducted a longitudinal study entitled Project Competence to examine the factors that influenced the life courses of children at risk for the development of psychopathology. Around this time, others also began to take an interest in stressed children who fared well (e.g., Anthony, 1974; Rutter, 1979; Rutter, Cox, Tupling, Berger, & Yule, 1975). The development of competence under conditions of risk became a central interest of researchers in **developmental psychopathology**. Although this field ultimately seeks to understand the pathways to psychological disorders, it looks for clues in both normative and non-normative development.

Resilience also has roots in the overlapping literature on stress and coping. As described in Chapter Eight, psychologists have devoted considerable attention to the effects of stress on adjustment. For years, studies of people undergoing traumatic events and living under stressful circumstances ignored the relatively large percentage of individuals who did *not* develop disorders. Michael Rutter and David Quinton (1984) summarized decades of research and concluded that risk factors of all severities and in all combinations rarely gave rise to significant disorder or dysfunction in more than half of the children exposed.[1] As stress researchers

---

[1]Rutter (2001) later acknowledged that some environments (e.g., chronic combat) are so traumatic and corrosive that they exceed the coping abilities of most people.

turned attention to people who did not succumb to misfortune (e.g., in Suzanne Kobasa's 1979 work on hardiness), the notion of resilience began to permeate the literature.

A third literature that has contributed to interest in resilience is prevention. Knowledge of how people achieve positive outcomes despite significant adversity can suggest ways of helping people who are at risk to avoid maladaptation (Cowen & Work, 1988; Egeland, Jacobvitz, & Sroufe, 1993; Masten, 1999; Rolf & Johnson, 1999). The main difference between resilience and prevention frameworks is that resilience focuses on building competence, while prevention focuses on disease prevention (Luthar, Cicchetti, & Becker, 2000a). As we saw in Chapter Nine, some researchers, including many community psychologists, have argued that primary prevention should include a focus on promoting positive adjustment (e.g., Cowen, 1991; 1996; 2000b; Ford, 1985; Weissberg, Caplan, & Harwood, 1991). Mainstream conceptualizations of prevention have rejected such a focus, however (e.g., Mrazek & Haggerty, 1994; NIMH Prevention Research Steering Committee, 1993).

The popularity of resilience frameworks has exploded in recent years. Psychinfo, a database of psychological journals and chapters, listed 66 entries with the root resil–between 1958 and 1980, as compared to 2275 entries since 1980 (search conducted October 17, 2001). The recent embracing of the concept of resilience by federal governmental agencies is another sign of its growing acceptance. For example, a 1994 conference on resilience was cosponsored by the National Institute on Drug Abuse, National Institute on Alcohol Abuse and Alcoholism, National Institute of Mental Health, Center on Substance Abuse Prevention, Center for Mental Health Services, and the National Association for Children of Alcoholics (Luthar & Cicchetti, 2000).

RESILIENCE AND COMMUNITY PSYCHOLOGY

Seven years after Julian Rappaport (1981) made the case for empowerment as an orienting concept for community psychology, Emory Cowen and William Work (1988) reviewed existing research on resilience and highlighted the relevance of this concept for the field. They argued that not only does the study of resilience provide a welcome alternative to the prevailing emphasis on deficits, it was a natural extension of the stress and coping framework and had the potential to expand the vistas of primary prevention.

⌘ The First Generation of Resilience Research

Recent reviews of the concept of resilience have identified two generations of research (e.g., Masten & Coatsworth, 1998; Luthar & Cicchetti, 2000; Luthar, Cicchetti, & Becker, 2000b). The first generation was child focused and viewed resilience as a trait. The second generation is more developmental, ecological, and multicausal. Let's look first at the research questions that predominated in the 1970s and 1980s.

Resilience can be defined most simply as positive adaptation despite significant adversity. Thus, resilience has two components—the experience of adversity or stress, and healthy adjustment. Both of these components have been studied in numerous ways.

ADVERSITY

The first judgement a resilience researcher must make is what adversity to study. Adversity has been conceptualized in a variety ways (e.g., Luthar &

Adversity has the effect of eliciting talents, which in prosperous circumstances would have lain dormant.

—Horace

Cushing, 1999; Rolf, 1999). Some researchers have studied a significant historical event. For example Glen Elder (1974) examined how families in California coped with the economic crisis of the Great Depression (see also Long and Vaillant's [1984] research on the impact of the Great Depression on people in inner-city Boston). Other historical events of interest to resilience researchers include the Holocaust (e.g., Moskovitz, 1983), and school desegregation (e.g., Coles, 1967). Some resilience researchers have concentrated on more common events, such as divorce (Hetherington, 1989; Hetherington, Bridges, & Glendessa, 1998; Wallerstein & Kelly, 1980), or childhood illness and hospitalization (e.g., Wells & Schwebel, 1987). Adversity has also been operationalized in terms of chronic stresses such as poverty or parental mental illness (e.g., Garmezy, et al., 1984; Rutter, 1979, McLoyd, 1998). Often resilience researchers study people experiencing several challenges simultaneously. Emmy Werner and Ruth Smith's (1982) classic research on the children of Kauai looked at the life paths of children exposed to multiple stresses of different types, including poverty, perinatal distress, family discord, parental mental illness and parental alcoholism (see the Classic Research box). The list of adversities goes on: early childbearing, single parenthood, homelessness, natural disasters (see Cowen & Work, 1988; Masten & Coatsworth, 1998).

Researchers interested in resilience have had no shortage of adversities from which to choose. Recent statistics show that in the U.S. almost one-quarter of children (22%) live in poverty; 40% experience parental divorce before the age of 16; 19% have chronic illnesses or physical disabilities; 20% of females have been raped before the age of 18; as many as 5% of children suffer physical abuse, sexual abuse, or neglect each year; and more than 3% experience the death of a parent (Sandler, 2001; Wyman, Sandler, Wolchik, & Nelson, 2000).

Given the vast array of stresses studied in the first generation of resilience research, more recent scholars have attempted to specify the types of adversity necessary to conclude that resilience has occurred. Dante Cicchetti and Norman Garmezy (1993)

warned that resilience is not simply thriving in response to exposure to *any* stress—only to stress where it would be expected that most people would *not* thrive. Irwin Sandler (2001) provided further elaboration. He defined adversity as a relationship between the child and the environment that has at least one of two effects. First, it may threaten the person's ability to satisfy basic human needs and goals. These basic needs include physical safety, a sense of self-worth, belief in one's efficacy, and the maintenance of a supportive social network. The issue of safety has emerged as particularly important in resilience research (e.g., Garbarino, Dubrow, Kostelny & Pardo, 1998; Ozer, Weinstein, & Schotland, 2001). A strikingly large number of children experience assault and witness violence in their homes and in their neighborhoods (Sandler, 2001). If children do not feel safe, they will not be able to satisfy their other basic needs.

The second type of child–environment relationship Sandler qualified as adversity is one that impedes the child's ability to accomplish developmental tasks. Even conditions not perceived as stressful may qualify as adversity if they prevent children from developing the role competencies that allow them to meet their basic needs and goals in later life. As an example, young people may not be overly concerned with their lack of school achievement; however academic failure can lead to low self-esteem (resulting, for example, from teacher criticisms and negative comparisons with peers) and to later limitations in terms of employment opportunities, work satisfaction, and economic security.

ADJUSTMENT

In order for a determination of resilience to be made, people must first experience adversity. The second essential judgement is that successful adjustment has occurred nonetheless. The specific outcomes resilience researchers have used to assess positive adaptation have varied almost as much as the indicators used to assess adversity. There are many different ways to think about adjustment (Luthar et al., 2000b; Luthar & Cushing, 1999; Staudinger, Marsiske, & Baltes, 1993).

CLASSIC RESEARCH

The Children of Kauai
A Classic Study with Continuing Influence

In 1955 health professionals and researchers launched a prospective study of all 698 babies born on the Hawaiian island of Kauai (Werner, 1993; Werner & Smith, 1982; Werner & Smith, 1993). These babies were from Hawaiian, Chinese, Korean, Japanese, Anglo, and Filipino descent. Families were assessed before the children were born, and assessments of the study participants have continued into adulthood. Because of the low mobility of island residents and the provision of needed services by research personnel, contact has been maintained with almost all of the families for more than three decades.

The study initially focused on developmental outcomes for children exposed to serious risk factors. Over half of the sample (54%) grew up in poverty, and about a third of the sample experienced significant other risks as well, such as perinatal distress, family discord, parental mental illness and/or parental alcoholism. Two-thirds of the children who experienced four or more risk factors by the age of two developed serious learning and behavior problems by the age of 10. Most of these children went on to evidence difficulties (e.g., delinquency, teenage pregnancy, mental health problems) in their teenage years.

One third of the high-risk children, however, fared quite well. They did not evidence serious problems in childhood or adolescence and appeared to succeed in their schools, homes, and communities. Emmy Werner and Ruth Smith launched a research program to find out what distinguished these individuals, whom they called "vulnerable but invincible," from their less-fortunate peers.

At all ages, children who exhibited resilience were actively involved with their world and were connected to supportive people. In infancy they were described as active, affectionate, and good-natured. As toddlers they were alert, sought out novel experiences, had prosocial orientations, communicated well, and evidenced self-help skills. In elementary school, they got along with classmates, read well, and reasoned well. These children also had many interests and participated in various activities and hobbies. By the end of high school, the children who exhibited resilience were more nurturant, responsible, and achievement-oriented.

In addition to these dispositional differences, the high-risk children who did not evidence problems grew up in families with fewer children and a space of at least two years between them and their siblings. They had bonded with at least one caregiver and received a great deal of positive attention from others as well. Girls evidenced considerable autonomy and often took care of younger siblings. Boys were often firstborns and had positive male role models.

Children who evidenced resilience also enjoyed support from the broader community. They had at least one close friend, nurturing kin and neighbors, and favorite teachers. They participated in extracurricular activities that brought them into contact with supportive adults, and many found additional encouragement in church groups or other faith-based activities.

The research of Werner and Smith contributed enormously to early research on resilience and has continued to shape the field as the researchers have followed these children into adulthood (Werner & Smith, 1993). As adults, all but two of the children who evidenced resilience early in life exceeded their high-risk peers in terms of educational and work achievements. Indeed, their accomplishments matched the achievements of peers from affluent, secure, and stable environments. The children Werner and Smith had earlier labeled invincible demonstrated competence, enjoyed support from spouses, and relied on faith and prayer. In addition, many people previously classified as maladjusted showed considerable improvements in functioning in adulthood. Early adversity did take some toll, however, even on those who seemed most successful. For example, as adults, stressed children had to form new commitments to loved ones while loosening family ties with parents and siblings whose ongoing problems threatened to overwhelm them.

Overall, the long-term follow-up study of Werner and Smith highlighted the multiple pathways in and out of resilience. These dynamics have been of central interest to the second generation of resilience scholars.

One important consideration in determining positive adaptation is level of accomplishment. Some resilience researchers have attempted to show that individuals who encountered adversity are *free from impairment:* for example, uninvolved in delinquent activities or without diagnoses of mental illness. Other resilience researchers have defined adjustment as *unexpected achievements*. Is it enough to meet normal expectations, or must people excel in order for researchers to conclude that resilience has occurred? The current thinking is that a determination of resilience requires *better-than-expected* outcomes, but not extraordinary excellence (Luthar et al., 2000b). High school graduates need not be valedictorians, and individuals who avoid criminal activity need not be candidates for canonization.

A second issue is the number of domains in which positive adjustment must be documented. Some researchers have assessed adjustment in one domain; antisocial behavior *or* school achievement *or* psychological functioning. In the first generation of resilience research, many operated under the assumption that resilient children would evidence resilience everywhere at all times. This suggests that one could choose virtually *any* outcome measure, and if the person was resilient, he or she would inevitably show positive adjustment.

Resilience researchers who examined adjustment in more than one domain, however, found that the same person sometimes exhibited competence in one context but not in another. For example, a study of maltreated children found that two-thirds evidenced success in academic domains, but less then one quarter succeeded in social domains (Kauffman, Cook, Arny, Jones, & Pittinsky, 1994). Another study of highly stressed inner-city children found that 85% of the participants who exhibited competence in at least one domain at the first

assessment had significant difficulties when performance was examined in more than one domain across a six-month period (Luthar, Doernberger & Zigler, 1993). Differences in outcomes also occur when one considers external versus internal indices of adjustment. Based on external criteria, such as academic achievement or peer relationships, some individuals may appear to be succeeding in life. At the same time, they may manifest enough subjective misery on measures of well-being or distress to warrant a psychological diagnosis (Luthar, 1991; Luthar et al., 1993; Masten & Curtis, 2000).

As the second generation of resilience research began in the late 1980s, questions arose as to which domain (or domains) of adjustment should be assessed. Emmy Werner (1987) proposed that resilience entailed the ability to work, play, love, and hope. Given the strong ties to developmental psychology, others have suggested that adaptation be defined in terms of success in accomplishing appropriate developmental tasks. In particular, people exhibiting resilience might be expected to successfully accomplish two hallmarks of early development: the formation of healthy attachment systems (i.e., secure relationships with caring adults) and the ability to self-regulate enough to act in socially appropriate ways and perform well in school (Masten & Coatsworth, 1998).

Variability in adjustment has been seen by some as reason to question the utility of the very concept of resilience (e.g., Tolan, 1996). Do people need to exhibit competence across domains in order to conclude that resilience has occurred? Recent researchers have questioned such a requirement, noting that uniformity in development across domains is not expected for normally developing children, so why would we anticipate consistency of performance in studies of resilience (Luthar et al.,

2000b)? Indeed, recent research has shown that "success" in one domain might actually work against "success" in another. For example, among inner-city youth, competence in conventionally valued domains, such as academia, may actually interfere with social competence as assessed by peer acceptance (e.g., Luthar, 1995; Seidman, Aber, Allen, & French, 1996).

Suniya Luthar and her colleagues (2000b) argued that the domains in which researchers assess adjustment should be theoretically linked to the adversity under consideration. So, for example, if a risk factor is expected to disrupt social relationships (e.g., parental maltreatment) it would make sense to assess social competence (e.g., attachment behaviors or peer relationships) rather than competence in academic or other domains. Resilience, like competence, may best be viewed not as an absolute, unitary concept, but as domain-specific (Luthar, 1993; Luthar et al., 2000b). Researchers and practitioners have identified various domains of competence, including physical, academic, psychological, and social competence (see Durlak, 1997). Just as we qualify competence, so might we use terms such as "educational resilience" (e.g., Wang, Haertel, Walberg, 1999) or "relational resilience" (Jordan, 1992) to specify particular domains of unexpected achievement in the face of adversity.

In summary, questions of how to define adjustment have occurred alongside questions of how to define adversity. Recent researchers have argued that our definitions of each need to be refined. Adversity is currently seen as unfavorable conditions under which most people would *not* thrive, and adjustment is seen as better than expected (but not necessarily spectacular) adjustment in domains that the adversity would be expected to jeopardize.

PROTECTIVE FACTORS

Although resilience requires the documentation of adversity and of adjustment, these components are simply the conditions that allow us to say resilience exists. Once researchers have determined that resilience has occurred, we can tackle the question of central interest: What factors enable some people to thrive under conditions of adversity?

The main accomplishment of the first generation of resilience research was to develop a list of **protective factors** that help people achieve adaptation despite adversity. Protective factors are enduring characteristics of individuals, microsystems, and larger environments that modify the stress-adjustment relationship in a positive direction. Protective factors enable stressed people to adapt positively by preventing, counteracting, or ameliorating the effects of adversity (Coie, Watt, West, Hawkins, Asarnow, Markman, Ramey, Shure, & Long, 1993; Masten, 2001; Masten & Coatsworth, 1998; Rutter, 2000; 2001; Sandler, 2001).

As described in Chapter Nine (see section on *Risk Factors*), prevention research emphasizes risk factors while resilience research emphasizes protective factors. Risk factors are aspects of people and environments that either cause or increase the likelihood of maladjustment. In most cases, protective factors and risk factors are two sides of the same coin. For example, the quality of parenting may be the important factor, while the nature of the parenting reflects its two sides. Negative parenting generally increases risk while positive parenting generally increases protection (Masten, 2001; Stouthamer-Loeber, Loeber, Farrington, Zhang, van Kammen, & Maguin, 1993).

Despite incredibly diverse conceptions and measures of both adversity and adjustment, the first generation of research studies were remarkably consistent in pointing to three aspects of people and their environments that enable resilience (Masten & Coatsworth, 1998; Kumpfer, 1999; Masten & Garmezy, 1985; Luthar et al., 2000b). The well-documented triad of protective factors consists of:

1. Aspects of the *individual's disposition* that elicit positive responses from the environment, such as physical robustness, easygoing temperament, good intellectual functioning, communication skills, self-confidence, faith, and a special talent that is valued by society;
2. Features of the *family* that bring out the best in children, such as a close relationship with at least one competent caretaker (e.g., parent,

grandparent, older sibling), few and/or widely spaced siblings, and parenting characterized by warmth, structure, and high expectations;

3. *Support systems outside the family* (e.g., neighborhoods, schools, churches, clubs) that reinforce individual skills, model positive values, bring individuals into contact with supportive adults, assist families in raising their children, and provide opportunities for people to realize their strengths.

This triad of protective factors has emerged in research using different conceptions of adversity and adjustment and also studies employing a variety of methodologies. Large-scale studies relying on positivist techniques have been most influential, but research using case studies (e.g., Radke-Yarrow & Sherman, 1990) and other less conventional methods provide converging evidence.

As one example, Daniel Challener (1997) conducted a narrative analysis of five autobiographies of people who grew up amidst poverty, divorce, absent parents, abuse (sexual, physical, and verbal), alcoholism, and discrimination based on race, gender, and language. Many of us are familiar with the books he reviewed: Maya Angelou's *I Know Why the Caged Bird Sings*; Tobias Wolff's *This Boy's Life*; Maxine Hong Kingston's *The Woman Warrior*; Richard Rodriguez's *Hunger of Memory*; and John Edgar Wideman's *Brothers and Keepers*. Challener found that the five autobiographies offered compelling support for the triad of protective factors. As children, the authors of these autobiographies had high energy, above-average cognitive skills, and keen interpersonal sensitivity. They usually lived in warm cohesive families or had at least one caring adult who assured them of their worth. In addition, they generally attended schools and lived in communities that provided additional support.

Just as multiple adversities exponentially increase the likelihood of maladjustment (see Chapter Eight section on *Number of Events*), so too do multiple protective factors work together to improve adjustment (e.g., Fergusson & Lynskey, 1999; Furstenberg, Cook, Eccles, Elder, & Sameroff, 1999; Jessor, Turbin, & Costa, 1998; Masten & Coatsworth,

1998; Wyman et al., 2000). Ideally, resilience-promoting interventions seek to reduce multiple risk factors and support multiple protective factors.

RESILIENCE AS AN ABSOLUTE TRAIT

The triad of protective factors points to the importance of the family and the larger environment in fostering resilience. Nevertheless, early resilience research promoted a person-centered view. Resilience was conceptualized as a trait—a characteristic that some individuals possessed and others did not. Children who beat the odds were described as "superkids" (Kauffman, Grunebaum, Cohler, & Gamer, 1979), who were "invulnerable" (Anthony, 1987) or "invincible" (Werner & Smith, 1982).

A trait view of resilience is problematic for a variety of reasons. On the surface, a focus on people's inherent strengths seems to be an advance over psychology's traditional deficit orientation. However, praise is the reverse side of blame. To congratulate those who overcome adversity, thereby assigning them responsibility for their success, is to hold those who succumb to adversity responsible for their failure. A celebration of people who beat the odds can promote the belief that *anyone* can succeed on their own if they really want to, thereby justifying the limited protection of children growing up in unfavorable environments (Luthar & Cicchetti, 2000). An individual analysis paves the way for victim blaming.

In addition, an individual focus constrains our ability to intervene effectively. The peer group literature provides an excellent example. The predominant social-skill deficit perspective holds that unpopular children are unpopular because they interact poorly with their peers. The solution is, therefore, to provide interpersonal skill training for socially incompetent children. Some research shows, however, that unpopularity may result from biases held by classmates (e.g., Putallaz & Wasserman, 1990). If unpopular children are perceived negatively regardless of how they behave (perhaps because the child behaved poorly in the past or because of classmate prejudices), social-skill training will have limited results. A more effective intervention might involve intervening at the level of the classroom, or even sending the unpopular child to another school where she or he has no "reputational bias" (Hymel, 1986; Hymel, Wagner, & Butler, 1990).

In the first generation of research, resilience was seen not only as an individual trait, but as an *immutable* trait. Many embraced the "myth of invulnerability" in which resilient children were believed to be resilient in all situations and for all time (see Felsman & Vaillant, 1987). Resilient children were likened to steel dolls. Unlike glass or plastic dolls, steel dolls were so sound that adversity of any severity could have no lasting effect (Anthony, 1974).

Marian Radke-Yarrow and Tracy Sherman (1990) warned against the tendency to view resilience as absolute. The "resilient" children they studied all showed evidence of suffering despite their manifest competence. They concluded that just as early researchers "failed to acknowledge and follow the group of children who survived, so, too, there is risk in the study of resilient or invulnerable children of failing to attend to the costs that these children are paying for their 'successful' survival" (pp. 99–100).

A truer perspective might recognize that all people living under adversity, even the most maladjusted, exhibit some evidence of competence, and that stress takes its toll even on those who appear to be adjusting well. Indeed, stress reactions may be seen as *healthy* for individuals experiencing extreme disadvantage. Failure to be affected by severe stress may indicate *mal*adjustment. For example, one study found that people most immune to stress had a "sociopathic" personality, and another found that elderly people undergoing crises who survived best were most aggressive, narcissistic and demanding (Hinkle, 1974 and Lieberman, 1975, reported in Rutter, 1983). Camille Wortman and her colleagues (1995) documented enormous variability in how people responded to major losses and wondered if individuals who experienced a significant loss without showing signs of stress should be considered resilient or pathological (see also Flach, 1988)

As the first generation of resilience research came to a close in the 1980s, resilience was increasingly viewed as a reciprocal process involving relationships between people and their environments over time (Rutter, 1985; Sameroff & Chandler, 1975; Sameroff & Seifer, 1983; Werner, 1986). Many resilience researchers united in a call to reject the trait perspective (Cicchetti & Garmezy, 1993; Felsman & Vaillant, 1987; Luthar & Cicchetti, 2000; Luthar et al., 2000b; Masten, Best, & Garmezy, 1990). Toward this goal, two changes in terminology have been advocated: the use of the term "resilience" as opposed to "resiliency," in the belief that the latter carries connotations of personality characteristics rather than person-environment transactions; and the avoidance of the adjective "resilient" to describe people (Luthar & Cicchetti, 2000).

⌘ The Second Generation of Resilience Research

The second generation of resilience research moved away from a trait view and studied resilience as a process (Luthar et al., 2000b). Instead of seeking to catalogue protective and vulnerability factors ("what" questions) it has described mechanisms that underlie positive adjustment under stress ("how" questions) (Cowen, Wyman, Work, Kim, Fagen, & Magnus, 1997). In the second generation of research, resilience was no longer seen as absolute, global, and internal to the individual, but as relative, circumscribed, and based on the person's ongoing interactions with environments (Luthar et al., 2000b).

In 1988, Emory Cowen and William Work proposed that resilience, like empowerment, should be an orienting concept for community psychologists, with two key distinctions. First, empowerment focuses on alienated adults, while resilience focuses on children. Second, empowerment reflects a system-centered level of analysis while resilience is person-centered. The conceptualization of resilience promoted by Cowen and Work reflected the Zeitgeist of resilience research in the 1980s, but not necessarily the most productive view of resilience, nor the view most in keeping with the unifying themes and mandates of community psychology.

In one of the last publications before his death, Emory Cowen (2000a; see also Cowen, 1991; 1994) called for community psychologists to adopt the related orienting concept of **wellness,** and many have heeded this call. Peter Wyman, Irwin Sandler, Sharlene Wolchik, and Kathleen Nelson (2000) posited that the wellness framework provides a welcome alternative to psychology's emphasis on maladaptation and has direct implications for intervention. Isaac Prilleltensky and Geoffrey Nelson (2000) have also written in support of wellness as a guiding framework for community psychology. James Kelly (2000) embraced wellness as an "ecological enterprise" (p. 103).

Wellness, like resilience, is concerned with people's recuperability under stress. In addition, Cowen described wellness as relative, not absolute, changing across the life span, and affected by multiple cross-setting interactions. This differs substantially from his earlier support of resilience as a primarily child-centered and individual-level concept. His formulation of wellness parallels the concept of resilience as conceived in the second generation.

Resilience researchers no longer assume consistency across either time or context. Let's consider how second-generation resilience researchers think about the role of time and then consider the role of context.

THE ROLE OF TIME

An understanding of resilience requires the study of processes over time; the continual interplay between individual and context. Even markers of resilience viewed as dispositional, such as sense of optimism or internal locus of control, are not immutable characteristics residing in children (Luthar & Cicchetti, 2000). They reflect the person's ongoing experiences with his or her environments.

EVENT CHAINS

Michael Rutter (1994; 2001), in reviewing decades of research on stress, commented that few life events are random occurrences. Later experiences result from earlier experiences. As resilience researchers

have begun to consider how protective and risk factors exert their effects, it has become increasingly clear that important influences on the life course are connected in positive and negative **event chains**.

Consider, for example, parental divorce. This event has a significant impact on children's lives not because it has fixed effects, but because it sets into motion a chain of events, and each link of the chain brings with it new vulnerabilities (as well as new opportunities). The "single" event of divorce may lead to relocation, which may mean a disruption of the child's friendship networks. Parental divorce may also result in economic difficulties, which might make extracurricular activities unaffordable. Separation from friends and loss of recreational outlets can further stress children of divorce, who might look to their parents for support. The stress of divorce leads to less adept parenting, however, which may make children even less able to cope with divorce-related events. As children require more assistance, parental stress increases, which results in even more inept parenting, which makes children even more needy, and so on (Forgatch, Patterson, & Ray, 1996). Thus divorce can set into motion a variety of challenges. Remember, too, that the divorce is itself an outcome. Divorce occurs more often among people with histories of problems, such as low incomes, criminal offenses, substance abuse, or prior family transitions (Wyman et al., 2000). All of the factors that contribute to the divorce can also exacerbate the multitude of events caused by the divorce.

Problematic behaviors are both outcomes of past challenges and causes of future challenges. As another example, high levels of aggression in childhood may provide evidence that earlier problems, such as poor parenting or family discord, have taken a toll. At the same time, childhood aggression impedes future development by disrupting peer relationships or leading to encounters with the criminal system (Windle, 1999). The good news is that just as problem behaviors are both outcomes of past difficulties and causes of later problems, so too do positive behaviors link together in positive event chains. Secure attachment to a caregiver may indicate that a young child has adjusted well to past difficulties (i.e., is evidencing resilience) and also increases the likelihood that she will thrive amidst future challenges—forming supportive relationships with peers and teachers, for example (e.g., Rubin, Coplan, Nelson, & Cheah, 1999).

The events we experience are not independent influences; they are linked together in a process of mutual causation (Compas, Hinden, & Gerhardt, 1995; Wyman et al., 2000). One negative event can set a negative event chain in motion by increasing the likelihood that other negative events will occur. Thus positive adjustment becomes increasingly difficult. In 1975, Byron Egeland and his colleagues launched a longitudinal study of children growing up in poverty (Egeland, Carlson, & Sroufe, 1993). A sample of 267 women was recruited during the last trimester of pregnancy, and their children were assessed regularly for eighteen years. The researchers confirmed that poverty confers risk, and that this risk is cumulative. At birth, *most* of the babies were robust and healthy. At twelve months, only about *two-thirds* of the children evidenced secure attachments, and by the time they reached preschool, only *one third* displayed social competence with their peers.

Egeland and colleagues found that child neglect and maltreatment constituted particularly strong links in negative event chains. Of the nineteen neglected children (children with unresponsive or passively rejecting caretakers), 46% were securely attached at twelve months, but by eighteen months, every toddler was classified as anxiously attached. Likewise, not one of the forty-four maltreated children in their sample was functioning competently by preschool age. For neglected and maltreated children, periodic improvements occurred when their quality of care improved (e.g., placement in a supportive foster home or increased contact with caring adults), but adaptation over time continued to be poor.

It is interesting to note that in some contexts (e.g. abusive families) events that would generally seem negative (e.g., removal from the family) may actually serve to interrupt a negative event chain and so have beneficial effects. Consider parental divorce. One study obtained the surprising finding that parental divorce had the *most* negative effect on

children with the *fewest* emotional and behavior problems (Chase-Lansdale, Cherlin, & Kiernan, 1995). A possible explanation is that the children with few emotional problems came from the most functional families. Thus, the divorce disrupted what the children experienced as a supportive home environment. For children in more dysfunctional families, divorce may have reduced family conflict or removed an uncaring adult from the household, and so improved their home environment. For these children, divorce was a positive development. Thus a seemingly negative experience, such as divorce, may actually have protective effects if it interrupts negative event chains (Rutter, 2000).

A number of longitudinal studies of resilience show the power of interrupting negative event chains and setting positive event chains in motion (e.g., Elder, 1974; Werner, 1993). David Olds and his colleagues (Olds, Eckenrode, Henderson, Kitzman, Powers, Cole, Sidora, Morris, Pettitt, & Luckey, 1997; Olds, Henderson, Chamberlin, & Tatelbaum, 1986; Olds, Henderson, Eckenrode, Kitzman, Luckey, Pettitt, Sidora, Morris, & Powers, 1998; Olds, Pettitt, Robinson, Henderson, Eckenrode, Kitzman, Cole, & Powers, 1998) have shown that early interventions with at-risk mothers continue to have a dramatic impact on the lives of both mothers and their children fifteen years later (see the Community Intervention box).

LIFE-SPAN DEVELOPMENTAL PERSPECTIVE

Event chains show that early experiences reverberate in later life. One important reason why experiences that occur early in life, or even before birth, have longlasting effects, is because they set event chains in motion. This does not mean that fate is sealed in childhood. Although the lion's share of resilience research has focused on children, several scholars have emphasized the importance of considering resilience across the life span (e.g., Cicchetti & Garmezy, 1993; Luthar et al., 2000b). In this section we examine continuities and discontinuities in resilience over time and then consider how an understanding of shifts in resilience status might suggest ways of intervening in later life.

COMMUNITY INTERVENTION:

David Olds
Setting Positive Chains in Motion

David Olds and his colleagues (Olds, Eckenrode, Henderson, Kitzman, Powers, Cole, Sidora, Morris, Pettitt, & Luckey, 1997; Olds, Henderson, Chamberlin, & Tatelbaum, 1986; Olds, Henderson, Eckenrode, Kitzman, Luckey, Pettitt, Sidora, Morris, & Powers, 1998; Olds, Pettitt, Robinson, Henderson, Eckenrode, Kitzman, Cole, & Powers, 1998) developed a home visitation program that led to greatly improved outcomes for mothers under stress and their children. The program targeted mothers who were considered high risk: first-time mothers who were single, lived in poverty, and/or had become pregnant at a very young age. Community health nurses began their visits when the women were still pregnant and continued to visit for up to two years. The nurses' visits had two goals: improve the mother's knowledge and practice of behaviors that promote healthy infant and child development and encourage the mother's use of formal and informal support networks.

In his research, Peter Wyman and colleagues (2000) identified two main avenues to protection, both of which were evident in Olds' home visitation program. First, the intervention supported factors that could protect people from adversity (the *stress-protective function of resources*). The home visitation program decreased the chances that existing risk factors (e.g., poverty or the young mother's developmental immaturity or poor coping strategies) would set negative risk chains into action. For example, the mothers engaged in fewer unhealthy behaviors during pregnancy (e.g., smoking), which resulted in fewer birth complications and fewer low-birth-weight children. Thus, their children entered the world without perinatal risk factors that would have increased their vulnerability to stress. The intervention program also reduced the likelihood that mothers would have multiple closely spaced children. Four years after delivery of the first child, the rate of subsequent pregnancies was 43% lower among mothers who received the intervention. Thus, mothers did not have added stresses that

result from trying to rear many young children at the same time.

The intervention program also enhanced the mothers' ability to facilitate their children's mastery of developmental challenges. This corresponds to what Wyman and colleagues called the *development-enhancing function of resources*. After birth, mothers provided more appropriate stimulation, were more involved with their children, and used more consistent discipline that was not overly harsh. Thus, children grew up in warmer, more enjoyable, and more predictable environments.

Within a few years, the benefits of this intervention were clearly in evidence. Families in the program had fewer state-verified cases of child maltreatment and fewer health care encounters for children's injuries. (Another home-visit program, the "Healthy Start" program in Hawaii, reduced the incidence of abuse and neglect in 241 mothers at-risk for child maltreatment to an unexpected zero [reported in Schorr, 1997]). Children were less often the targets of abuse and received more appropriate stimulation. The outcomes for mothers who received visits for close to two years also improved markedly. Four years after the intervention, mothers' participation in the workforce was 84% higher for mothers who had received the home visits.

Furthermore, benefits of the intervention were still in evidence fifteen years later; mothers continued to evidence self-sufficiency and were less dependent on government subsidies. Adolescents who had been born to women in the program as compared to control adolescents were less likely to run away from home, get arrested and convicted, or violate parole if they were convicted. They had fewer lifetime sexual partners and fewer substance-abuse problems. Thus, long-term follow-up research shows that efforts to interrupt negative chains and put positive chains into place early in life reap rewards years, even decades later.

Although resilience is not an immutable trait, many studies find that resilience classifications are stable. The Rochester Child Resilience Project is but one example (see also Egeland et al., 1993; Werner

& Smith, 1993). For this project, Emory Cowen and his colleagues (1997) identified urban families who had experienced at least four major stresses, such as family violence, death, illness, divorce, or poverty. Two cohorts of children, second to third graders and fourth to sixth graders, were classified as either stress-resistant (SR) or stress-affected (SA) based on adjustment ratings by parents, current teachers, and past teachers. One-and-a-half to two years later, participants were retested to assess the stability of the findings. The group distinctions were even more marked at the second testing. For example, parents of SR children evidenced even stronger parenting efficacy, more positive expectations for their children, and greater personal well-being in the second testing. These findings may reflect the power of positive event chains.

Even studies that find a high degree of consistency in classifications across time detect some people for whom resilience status changes, however. One study of adolescents in families where a parent experienced depressive illness classified eighteen research participants as evidencing resilience. Only thirty months later, one in six of these adolescents had developed *serious* mental illnesses (Beardslee & Podorefsky, 1988). Emmy Werner (1989) followed seventy-two individuals who had evidenced resilience at age eighteen to the age of thirty, and found that three of these people considered themselves unhappy or dissatisfied with their life, two had sought professional mental health services, and three had substance abuse problems. Perhaps more importantly for this discussion, the inverse was also true. Some people who did not evidence resilience at age eighteen were functioning quite well by the time they were thirty. This shift toward positive adaptation was most marked among study participants who were juvenile delinquents or teenaged mothers.

Initial expectations for stability in classifications of resilience stemmed from a framing of resilience as an immutable trait and also from the belief that early experiences determine future adjustment. Development may be seen, however, as a lifelong process. Consider for example the fate of infants and young children who spent their formative years under conditions of extreme deprivation and neglect in Romanian orphanages. Studies of these children after adoption showed that many made spectacular gains in physical and cognitive domains when normative child-rearing environments were restored (Rutter & the English and Romanian Adoptees Study Team, 1998).

A growing number of scholars recognize the need to improve our understanding of what pulls people toward or away from risk at different ages (Cicchetti & Toth, 1992; Kellam, Koretz, & Moscicki, 1999; Mrazek & Haggerty, 1994; NIMH Prevention Research Steering Committee, 1993; Sroufe & Rutter, 1984). Developmental processes interact with contextual factors to affect risk and resilience across the life span, and the balance of vulnerability and strength shifts as people proceed through different life stages and life experiences.

One important factor that affects the continuity of adjustment or maladjustment under stress is the manner in which challenges are handled. Irwin Sandler (2001) noted that stressed people's attempts to satisfy their basic needs can result in better or worse developmental outcomes. An adolescent from an unsupportive family who meets his needs for affiliation through membership in a gang increases his chances of encountering violence and substance abuse. Thus, an attempt to resolve a negative experience (poor familial support) actually forges a new link in a negative event chain.

There are numerous instances where behaviors that allow individuals to adapt to their environments at one point in time lead to problems later on. Multiple personality disorder may be seen as a creative (even *healthy*) way for very young children who are totally dependent on caregivers to survive serious physical or sexual abuse (Ross, 1995). In later life, however, multiple personality disorder interferes with personal, family, and work success. As Alan Sroufe and Michael Rutter (1984) observed

> an adaptation that may be serviceable at one point in development (e.g., avoiding an abusing caregiver, blunting emotional experiences, etc.) may later compromise the child's ability to maximally draw upon the environment in the service of more flexible adaptation . . . (p. 23)

As a final example, consider social control. Children growing up under stressful conditions, such as extreme poverty, appear to have a particularly strong need for structure and control, perhaps due in part to the dangerous environments in which they live. One study found that some families in low-income urban settings try to protect their children by restricting them from playing outside or by teaching them to avoid dangerous areas (Black & Krishnakumar, 1998). Another study showed that mothers who perceived their community as unsafe were less likely to encourage independence in their children (Taylor, Jacobson, Rodriguez, Dominguez, Cantic, Doney, Boccuti, Alejandro, & Tobon, 2000). It may be, however, that while children subject to extreme parental control do well in childhood, they are deprived of opportunities to develop flexible, independent perspectives and behaviors that would assist them in later life (Barocas, Seifer, & Sameroff, 1985). Parental vigilance is a double-edged sword. Authors of the two studies cited above found that parental control prevented the children from getting into trouble but imperiled the children's development by limiting their opportunities to establish autonomy and self-reliance. The restrictions also undermined the children's sense of community and reduced the likelihood that they would come into contact with supportive adults, role models, and other positive influences in their neighborhoods (Black & Krishnakumar, 1998; Taylor et al, 2000).

The ongoing need for structure and control may be one reason why people exposed to adversity in childhood benefit from military service in adulthood (Elder & Runck, 1979; Werner, 1993; Rutter, 2001) The armed forces can provide a sense of structure and control that enlistees find helpful. This finding hints at ways in which interventions in adulthood might be informed by studying resilience beyond childhood.

The focus on children in the resilience literature may be due, in part, to the original purpose of the research: to identify childhood antecedents of disorder. In addition to this historical emphasis, many scholars influenced by prevention frameworks argue for the efficacy of promoting resilience as early as possible rather than attempting to repair existing disorders (Cowen, 1991; 1994; Luthar et al., 2000b). Emory Cowen (1996) spoke for many when he asserted that the earlier the primary prevention

intervention occurs, the more likely it is to succeed. Nevertheless, experiences in infancy and early childhood do not have irreversible consequences. As Jerome Kagan (1976) put it, "[t]he first messages written on the *tabula rasa* may not necessarily be the most difficult to erase" (p. 121).

One of the key tenets of the life-span developmental perspective is that **plasticity** characterizes human development. That is to say, the potential to change and adapt positively exists at all ages (Baltes, 1987; Luthar & Cicchetti, 2000; Staudinger et al., 1993). In the current view of resilience, specific early experiences do not determine the course of development. Continuity across development results in large part from ongoing negative and positive event chains. Negative chains may be set into motion early in life and gain power over the years, but it is possible to disrupt them or initiate positive chains in later life.

Consider for example, the teen mothers who showed improvements in adjustment as adults (Werner, 1989). Teen pregnancy is often a link in a negative event chain. It may be seen as an unsuccessful outcome, and it can also contribute to future problems—school drop out, divorce, employment instability, welfare dependence, health problems (e.g., Coley & Chase-Lansdale, 1998). If, however, the teen mother completes high school, restricts further childbearing, and has a stable marriage, she will likely experience economic success and subsequently enjoy a variety of opportunities in life (Furstenberg, Brooks-Gunn, & Morgan, 1987).

Entering into a stable marriage can also interrupt negative event chains and set positive event chains in motion. Michael Rutter and David Quinton (1984) found that all aspects of psychosocial functioning for women raised in institutions improved in adulthood after marriage to a supportive spouse. Indeed, marriage to a supportive spouse not only set positive event chains in motion for the two partners, it also set the stage for the next generation.

In the study by Rutter and Quinton (1984), the childhood adversity of women raised in institutions deprived them of normal parenting. Institutional rearing had an effect on the women's own parenting only *indirectly*, however, through the effect of institutional rearing on choice of spouse. If the women married supportive partners, their institutional rearing did not compromise their own parenting. This findings is consistent with more recent findings that abused children are less likely to become abusive parents themselves if they have emotionally supportive relationships with others. This can take the form of support from another adult in childhood or a nonabusive and supportive spouse in adulthood, or even a sensitive therapist (Egeland, et al., 1988). Close relationships with others, be they family members, friends, spouses, or therapists, can improve life trajectories in children *and* in adults (Furstenberg et al., 1987; Rutter, 2001; Werner, 1993) and help pave the way for success in future generations.

We have thus far identified several factors that may promote resilience in later life: restricted childbearing at an early age, military service, and close relationships with supportive others. School completion is also important because education can provide new opportunities for growth and stability and ultimately widen one's horizons and broaden one's choices (e.g., of marriage partners, careers) (Rutter, 1979, 2001). There are other factors, as well. Involvement in church activities and religious communities may serve as another route out of poverty and despair (Werner, 1993).

Negative event chains may be interrupted and positive event chains initiated at any point in the life span. It may be wise to intervene early in life before too many links in negative event chains have been forged. Still, the possibility of change remains as people grow older. People may be uniquely receptive to change during life transitions (see also Chapter Eight). This may help account for the success of David Olds' home visitation program for pregnant women (see the Community Intervention box). Targeting people at high-risk during times of transition (e.g., marriage, pregnancy) may be a particularly promising avenue for intervention.

THE ROLE OF CONTEXT

In this section, we will examine three ways in which context matters in studies of resilience. First, an understanding of resilience requires an understanding

of the systems in which people live. Second, not only do different systems affect the development of resilience, resilience itself can be conceptualized at a system level. Finally, we will consider culture as an especially important aspect of the social context.

FAMILIES, SCHOOLS, NEIGHBORHOODS, AND BEYOND

The first generation of resilience research conceptualized resilience as most applicable to children and also person-centered. This is paradoxical in that childen's adjustment to adversity is integrally related to their caregiving system. Longitudinal studies repeatedly show that virtually all prenatal and perinatal risk factors lead to later physical and psychological difficulties *only* if the child develops under poor environmental conditions, such as familial instability or chronic poverty (Kopp & Krakow, 1983; Sameroff & Chandler, 1975; Sameroff & Seifer, 1983; Werner & Smith, 1982; Wilson, 1985). The resolution of stress that occurs in childhood also depends on their caregiving system. Gerald Patterson (1983) went as far as to say that external stresses affect children *only* to the extent that they disrupt microsocial family processes: "It is not the child who is vulnerable or invulnerable; it is, rather, the system in which he or she resides that determines eventual adjustment" (p. 260; see also Elder, Caspi, & Downey, 1985; Rutter, 1983).

A study of children during wartime offers a compelling illustration of this point (reported by Garmezy, 1983). Researchers found that 25–50% of children removed from areas under air attack, and consequently from their families, showed neurotic symptoms. These symptoms appeared in only 4% of children who remained under attack, but with their families. Similarly, in a study of the Ash Wednesday fires of 1983 in South Australia, mothers' responses to the fire predicted children's adjustment better than the children's own exposure to the fires (McFarlane, Policansky, & Irwin, 1987).

Families can protect children from stress. They can satisfy basic needs and keep adverse events from occurring. They can promote the development of age-appropriate competencies and help children interpret and cope with events that do occur (Sandler, 2001; see also Compas, 1987; Garmezy & Rutter, 1993; Swearingen & Cohen, 1985a). At the same time, families are an important source of risk. It is in the home environment that children encounter abuse, neglect, and other adverse experiences that either set in motion or exacerbate negative event chains.

Resilience researchers have long understood the role of families in fostering risk and resilience. Some have studied resilience in other systems as well. Michael Rutter (1979; 1989) has found that the adjustment of stressed youth improves when they attend schools that provide high expectations for achievement, meaningful responsibilities, useful feedback, praise, admired teachers, a comfortable environment, and appropriate control (see also Henderson & Milstein, 1996). Other researchers have emphasized the importance of school environments that offer order and structure and foster feelings of involvement in and belonging to the school rather than disengagement and alienation from it (see Wang et al., 1999 for a review). In terms of mechanisms that underlie resilience, Rutter found that the improved outcomes for children placed in better schools related to their increased ability to choose rewarding careers and select supportive life partners. He has long noted the importance of planning ability to resilience (e.g., Quinton, Rutter, & Liddle, 1984).

Researchers have become increasingly interested in how neighborhoods affect risk and resilience. Abraham Wandersman and Maury Nation (1998) argued that the majority of ecological effects actually occur at the neighborhood level. As an example, they cited the finding that poverty at the neighborhood level is the best predictor of child maltreatment (Garbarino & Sherman, 1980; see also Melton, 1992). Other studies also report that neighborhood variables may be more important than family variables in some instances (e.g., Luthar & Cushing, 1999). For example, children have higher cognitive scores, higher rates of school completion, and lower rates of teenage births if they live in affluent as opposed to low-income neighborhoods *regardless* of the socioeconomic

status of their own families (Brooks-Gunn, Duncan, Klebanov, & Sealand, 1993).

Neighborhoods, like families, are the source of both risks and resources. Neighborhoods can promote resilience in a number of ways (Cook, 1999; Wandersman & Nation, 1998; Sampson, 1999; Sampson, Raudenbush, & Earls, 1997; Sandler, 2001). Integrated and available services can help people receive the resources they need when they need them—respite care when the demands of caregiving become overwhelming, emergency housing in times of crisis, psychological counseling when emotional needs are great, appropriate medical care in the event of an accident. The health of a community can be assessed, at least in part, by its ability to meet the challenges of its residents (Cottrell, 1976; Duhl, 1995; Iscoe, 1974). In addition to help during crises, neighborhood institutions provide infrastructures through which residents' can satisfy their basic needs and develop competencies. Supportive individuals and role models from schools, religious institutions, community centers, and other settings can offer encouragement and motivation for achievement. Parks, clubs, and sports teams offer opportunities for socialization and recreation.

The availability of support services varies greatly from community to community. One study of four cities found significant differences in the number of mutual help groups (Davison, Pennebaker, & Dickerson, 2000). Dallas had the lowest level of support, with only 140 groups per million residents, while Chicago had more than five times as many (755 groups per million). Los Angeles and New York fell in between. Income level also is an important determinant of resource level. Residents of well-to-do communities have more access to high-quality housing, diverse shops, banks, health-care services and transportation (Troutt, 1993). Communities differ greatly in the number and diversity of resources they have to offer (and the degree to which available resources are tapped).

Life in some neighborhoods entails frequent encounters with risk: active gangs, high levels of crime, rampant substance abuse. Within neighborhoods, people can feel isolated, unsafe, and hopeless. Families play an important role in negating the effects of neighborhoods that are detrimental to development (Jarrett, 1995). The family strategies associated with resilience for urban families in toxic environments include:

- Establishing supportive relationships between children and adults within and outside of the family;
- Limiting children's interactions with people and places that do not support the family's values;
- Careful monitoring of where and with whom youth spend time;
- Facilitating interactions with institutions and organizations that promote growth such as schools and clubs;
- Fostering skills and competencies that enable children and adolescents to avoid the pressures of urban life, such as negotiation skills to combat the advances of drug dealers or gang leaders.

A variety of systems, including families, schools, and neighborhoods interact to promote risk or resilience. Resilience results from a confluence of different levels of experience, including genetic, biological, psychological, neighborhood, and also cultural, and sociopolitical (Egeland et al., 1993; Jessor, 1993). In seeking to understand resilience, we need to look beyond the individual and beyond proximal environments to the larger systemic forces that exert their influences through microsystems. For example, a family's ability to provide needed resources increases as broader social and economic conditions improve. Robust economies and high employment rates have beneficial effects on individual resilience (Long & Vaillant, 1984).

To highlight the importance of system factors beyond the immediate environment, consider the "greatest risk factor of all": poverty (Schorr, 1997, p. xxii). In different historical eras and in different locales, the risks afforded by poverty vary substantially. For example, the low-income families in the study by Byron Egeland and his colleagues (1993) fared poorly as compared to the low-income families in the Great Depression studied by Glen Elder (1974) or the children growing up in poverty on Kauai (Werner & Smith, 1982; 1993). On Kauai,

one-half of the sample grew up in poverty; nevertheless, by adulthood 97% had graduated from high school, and only about 17% of marriages ended in divorce. In the sample studied by Egeland and his colleagues, outcomes were decidedly less positive. There was a large number of single-parent households, many very young mothers, drug- and alcohol-abusing parents, and considerable family violence. Poverty may be different now than in 1930 to 1950s, and different in mainland U.S. cities as compared to Kauai (Egeland et al., 1993).

SYSTEMS PERSPECTIVE

In resilience research, portraits of families (or schools or neighborhoods) are painted with very broad brushstrokes. As a result, the system dynamics remain blurry. Consider the research of Marian Radke-Yarrow and Tracy Sherman (1990). They conducted case studies of four children who had been identified as evidencing resilience in a larger study of children raised by affectively ill parents. They found that the resilience of these four children contrasted sharply with the poor outcomes of their siblings. This suggested that the families were not positive overall, as general family strengths would have benefited the siblings as well.

Radke-Yarrow and Sherman found that the children who evidenced resilience played particular roles in their family system that afforded them advantages over their siblings. The four children had a sense that there was something good about them, and this "good" quality stemmed from a *match* between a psychological or physical characteristic of the child and a core need of one or both parents. For example, one child who manifested resilience was the only boy in a family that valued males. Another was the only healthy child in a family where the mother viewed her children's health as testament to her mothering skills. Because of the match, children who evidenced resilience received virtually *all* of the limited love and positive regard their stressed families could muster.

An awareness of system dynamics can help elucidate the varying pathways toward and away from resilience. It may also yield new insights on old findings. Resilience researchers have found caring for younger siblings to be protective, especially for female children (Hetherington, 1989; Werner & Smith, 1982). This could be explained (as it usually is) on an individual level. By taking care of younger siblings, older children gain a sense of responsibility and purpose and develop problem-solving skills. The protective nature of caring for siblings may also be explained, however, on a systems level. The child caretaker may reduce the workload of the highly stressed mother, and thus increase her ability to contribute to the family as a whole.

A systems perspective alerts us to the possibility that intervening on behalf of one system member can cause additional hardships for other members. For example, the recommendation that a young boy targeted for parental hostility become involved in extracurricular activities outside the home may simply mean that another more available child will become the recipient of parental hostility. Interventions may need to target not individual members in isolation, but systems as wholes. The goal of interventions might be, for example, to foster resilience at the family level.

In the resilience literature, researchers have generally attempted to determine which aspects of families, schools, and neighborhoods enable some *individuals* who experience severe and sustained environmental assaults to thrive amidst adversity. We might also consider the possibility that the family, school, and community system *as a whole* may adapt positively or negatively to stress. System-level resilience has been recognized in the family literature, where Reuben Hill (1949) proposed a system-level analogue of the invincible individual. Half a century ago, he described the "crisis-proof" family. More recently, Hamilton McCubbin and his colleagues (1998) have discussed "family hardiness," and Isaac Prilleltensky and Geoffrey Nelson (2000) wrote of "family wellness."

A systems view of resilience requires consideration of each element of the system as well as the system as a whole. In their exploration of family resilience, Hamilton and Marilyn McCubbin (1988) noted that both the individual strengths of family members and family-level strengths protect families from breakdown under stress (of course resources outside the family also matter). Families that evi-

dence resilience are characterized by supportive and gratifying relationships among family members that promote both the personal development of each member, and the collective well-being of the family as a whole. Similarly, Prilleltensky and Nelson (2000) noted the importance of family members balancing individual aspirations with concern for other family members in order to achieve family wellness.

Most resilience research, like psychological research more generally, views mothers as the key to understanding individual resilience. System-level approaches implicate the importance of *all* family members. Fathers, both as individuals and as family members, have effects on children's resilience (e.g., Zimmerman, Salem, & Notaro, 2000). As an early example, Glen Elder and his colleagues (1986) found that the father represented the critical link between hardships stemming from the Great Depression and children's adjustment. Economic hardship led unstable fathers to become more punitive and arbitrary. Children had better outcomes when raised by resourceful fathers who stayed calm under stress. More recent research has also found a direct link between father behaviors and child outcomes under conditions of adversity. A study of resilience in African Americans found that involvement and support from fathers reduced the likelihood of problem behaviors in adolescents (Zimmerman, Schmeelk-Cone, & Caldwell, 2001).

Fathers are important in understanding resilience not only because of the direct link between their behavior and the adjustment of their children, but also because they contribute to the well-being of the family as a whole. The system-level resource of **adaptability** has received a great deal of theoretical and empirical support in the family literature (see McCubbin, Joy, Cauble, Comeau, Patterson, & Needle, 1980). System-level adaptability is characterized by the capacity for system members to change role relationships in response to crises (Olson, Sprenkle, & Russell, 1979; Pratt, 1976). The family may be seen as a semienclosed system of interrelated positions. As any one member changes her or his position, all members must adjust (Nock, 1982). A stress such as maternal hospitalization may be disruptive to the extent that it necessitates a shift in role relationships. A family may be viewed as resilient to the extent that fathers, older children, and extended family members can assume the mother's role of homemaker and/or breadwinner.

Required helpfulness is an example of adaptability. An older child who cares for younger siblings may have the opportunity to develop individual-level strengths while also contributing to the well-being of the family. Glen Elder found that when adolescent boys in families undergoing economic adversity assumed some responsibilities as breadwinner, they developed new skills and competencies while also contributing to the economic well-being of the family as a whole (see also Compas et al., 1995).

In the above examples, family members responded to stress in ways that benefited themselves and their families. Cases also exist where an individual's coping efforts produce additional stress in other system members (Walker, 1985). If an older child in an economically stressed family responds by spending as much time as possible hanging out with friends, he would not contribute to the family's ability to meet its responsibilities. Separation from a stressed system may, however, facilitate individual adjustment, and in some cases there may be little that one family member, especially a young child, can do to improve the family environment as a whole. The term *adaptive distancing* has been coined to refer to the personally advantageous strategy of children separating from abusive or neglectful families (Chess, 1989). This may help account for the finding that children's autonomy and independence are associated with resilience (see Cowen & Work, 1988).

An understanding of family-level resilience requires an understanding of how stresses affect families as systems. Hamilton McCubbin and his colleagues (1998) observed that stresses can require changes in the five domains of family functioning: family rules, family routines and traditions, coalitions within the family unit, the family's communication patterns, and the family's relationship to the community (McCubbin & McCubbin, 1988; McCubbin et al., 1998).

Just as individuals go through developmental stages that affect which stresses they encounter and the resources they bring to their coping efforts,

families, too, go through life stages that affect encounters with stress. As depicted in Table 11.1 on page 338–39, some family strengths, such as family rituals, remain important across life stages. Family rituals include celebrations, traditions, and routines that provide guideposts for what the family believes and how members should act. They encourage smoothness in family operation, reduce tension, and foster family cooperation in that they require deliberate planning. Rituals have a stabilizing effect during stress. They add to family members' sense of predictability, provide the family with a sense of meaning, and connect family members to something larger than themselves (McCubbin & McCubbin, 1988; Sameroff & Fiese, 2000). Family rituals can take an infinite number of forms. In the Delany family, described at the opening of this chapter, rituals included the preparation of Thanksgiving baskets for less fortunate community members, nightly reading of the Bible, time for quarreling members to make up before bed, and the daily inspections of the children's appearance (Delany et al., 1993). Family rituals are a source of family satisfaction and a manifestation of family pride.

While rituals matter throughout the family's life, other strengths are most important at particular stages. For example, financial management strategies are critical during early stages. At first, the couple's careers may not yet be secure, and the addition of children to the family increases financial burdens. According to Hamilton McCubbin and Marilyn McCubbin (1988), The most stressful time period in a family's life is when children become adolescents. At this time, family support networks are particularly valuable.

Family resilience has received some attention, but system-level resilience in other settings has not been as carefully examined. System-level conceptions of resilience are possible for daycare centers, schools, clubs, workplaces. Ira Iscoe's (1974) notion of the *competent community* points the way to a system-level exploration of resilience beyond the microsystem. More recent research on community assets and social capital also describe what might be considered community resilience (see, for example, the section in Chapter Seven entitled *Putting* the "Health" Back into Mental Health). Communities might manifest resilience when they provide structures that allow residents to realize their common values and goals (Sampson, 1999; Sampson, Raudenbush, & Earls, 1997). In order to realize common values, communities, like families, benefit from rules (e.g., intolerance of antisocial behaviors, shared commitment to monitoring children's play), resources (e.g., neighborhood social networks, community centers, libraries), and rituals (e.g., community festivals and parades).

RESILIENCE IN CULTURAL CONTEXT

Two vitally important aspects of context in the study of resilience are culture and social marginalization. We have elsewhere discussed the role of culture and social position in affecting the two key judgements in resilience research: adversity and adjustment. These aspects of context affect which stresses occur in life and how they are dealt with (see Chapter Eight). For example, people of minority racial status face stresses that result from racism and the resulting segregation (e.g., García Coll, Lamberty, Jenkins, McAdoo, Crnic, Wasik, & Vásquez García, 1996). We have also discussed the fact that social position and culture affect what constitutes healthy adjustment (see Chapters Three and Seven). Notions of what people need to be able to do in order to be considered well-adjusted depend on cultural contexts. (e.g., Kâgitçibasi, 1996; Masten & Coatsworth, 1998; Ogbu 1981). Culture and social position also affect the dynamics of protective factors, which are key to understanding the process of resilience.

Factors that protect people in one culture may not protect people in other cultures. One often-cited example is the finding that an easygoing temperament contributes to resilience in the U.S., but Masai infants who would be considered temperamentally difficult had better survival rates during drought in Africa (de Vries, 1984). As another example, consider parenting styles. Based on research with White, middle class families, Diana Baumrind developed a well-known parenting typology that

deemed **authoritative parenting** the most effective child-rearing strategy. Authoritative parents are high in acceptance and warmth and also high in control demands (Baumrind, 1971; Maccoby & Martin, 1983). Cross-cultural research shows that authoritative parenting is more common in White than in Black, Hispanic, or Asian families. In addition, for all ethnic groups authoritative parenting occurs more often in middle class than in working-class families (Steinberg, Mounts, Lamborn, & Dornbusch, 1991). Perhaps these differences reflect the different demands placed on people of color and low-income families, rather than the inferiority of their parenting techniques.

For low-income and ethnic minority people living under adverse conditions, the structure and control side of parenting may be more important than the warmth side. Research on children growing up in poor and stressful home environments has found that strict parental monitoring of children's activities plays a larger role in preventing delinquency than a warm family atmosphere (see Luthar, 1999). Indeed, parental monitoring may be helpful not only when limit setting is reasonable, but also when families impose limits that are intrusive and restrictive (Wilson, 1974). This may be due to the importance of close monitoring in dangerous environments (e.g., McLoyd, 1998) and also due to the possibility that more controlling child-rearing practices better prepare children to survive in adverse environments (Le Vine, 1974; see also the section in Chapter Four entitled Extensions of Bronfenbrenner's Work). Authoritative parenting may not be the most effective child-rearing strategy in all contexts.

Cynthia García Coll and her colleagues (1996) argued that an understanding of the development of resilience in minority children requires putting social position at the center rather than the periphery of our explanatory frameworks. They argued that resilience researchers need to understand how families and other systems help people cope with racism, segregation and other stresses (I might add violence to this list). They need to understand how families and other systems help people develop a positive sense of self and social group within a society that devalues their heritage and root culture.

📄 Table 11.1   Critical Family Strengths and Coping Skills over the Family Life Cycle

Family Strengths	Couple	Child Bearing and School Age	Teenage and Young Adult	Empty Nest and Retirement
ACCORD: Balanced interrelationships among family members that allow them to resolve conflicts and reduce chronic strain	X	X		
CELEBRATIONS: Acknowledging birthdays, religious occasions, and other special events	X	X	X	X
COMMUNICATIONS: Sharing beliefs and emotions. Emphasis on how family members exchange information and caring with each other	X	X		X
FINANCIAL MANAGEMENT: Sound decision-making for money management and satisfaction with economic status	X	X	X	
HARDINESS: Family members' sense of control over their lives, commitment to the family, confidence in the family's survival, and ability to grow, learn, and challenge each other	X	X	X	X
HEALTH: Physical and psychological well-being of family members, which can reduce stress and preserve a healthy home atmosphere	X			X
LEISURE ACTIVITIES: Similarities and differences in how family members like to spend free time (e.g., active or passive interests, social or personal activities)	X			
PERSONALITY: Acceptance of others' traits, behaviors, general outlook, and dependability	X		X	X
SUPPORT NETWORK: Positive aspects of relationships with in-laws, relative and friends		X	X	

Family Strengths	Couple	Child Bearing and School Age	Teenage and Young Adult	Empty Nest and Retirement
TIME AND ROUTINES: Family meals, chores, togetherness, and other ordinary routines	X	X	X	X
TRADITIONS: Honoring holidays and important family experiences across the generations	X	X	X	X

Adapted from McCubbin, H. I., & McCubbin, M. A. (1988). Typologies of resilient families: Emerging roles of class and ethnicity. *Family Relations, 37,* 247–254. (p. 248). Copyrighted 1998 by the National Council on Family Relations, 3959 Central Ave. NE, Suite 550, Minneapolis, MN 55421. Reprinted by permission.

Thus, for non-White families, effective ethnic and racial socialization may constitute a crucial protective factor (see also Gonzales & Kim, 1997; Sonn & Fisher, 1998).

Other resources that have also been identified as powerful protective factors for minority families, especially African American families. They include a belief in hard work and achievement, religion and spirituality, and family bonds (Black & Krishnakumar, 1998; Denby, 1996; García Coll et al., 1996; Hill, 1972; Hrabowski, Maton, & Grief, 1998; Jones, 2001; Maton, Hrabowski, Greene, 2001; Stack, 1974; Taylor & Roberts, 1995; Zimmerman & Maton, 1992). A wealth of research argues for the central importance of family in non-White cultures. For example, one study found that Puerto Rican adolescents' own distress was closely linked to maternal distress, ostensibly because a cultural belief in *familism* means that family problems are shared across family members (Taylor et al., 2000). Another study found that in White families, stress leads to family conflict, which then leads to adolescent problems. In Hispanic families, however, stress does not lead to fighting among family members, perhaps because traditional Hispanic values discourage family conflict (Barrera, Li, & Chassin, 1995).

Mainstream research has historically viewed members of marginalized groups through deficit-colored glasses. This has blinded us to the many strengths of ethnic minority families. For example reliance on extended family and "fictive kin" (friends who become as close as kin) offers numerous advantages under adverse circumstances (García Coll et al., 1996; Harrison, Wilson, Pine, Chan, & Buriel, 1990; Kissman & Allen, 1993; Manns, 1997; Tam & Detzner, 1998). Family and kin networks can encourage more positive parenting (Taylor & Roberts, 1995), protect children from economic hardships, and assist children in coping with social and psychological oppression (García Coll et al., 1996). The varied participation of extended and fictive kin bears on the notion of adaptability that emerged in the family literature on resilience. African Americans often have extremely elastic and adaptable households and family roles that buffer children from the negative effects of stresses (Black & Krishnakumar, 1998). Despite this evidence, extended families have sometimes been pathologized (e.g., viewed as socially disorganized) or simply ignored. Many ethnic minority research participants who are categorized as single mothers may actually enjoy more support than mothers in "intact" nuclear families whose partners work for long hours and whose extended family lives far away.

Cultural values, beliefs, and goals can be a source of strength and protection for minority families. Culture is a human invention that imposes coherence on our otherwise chaotic existence. It helps us to feel in control rather than overwhelmed by life's realities (Jones & Jones, 2001). As Terry Cross (1998) said of resilience from a Native American perspective: "The richness of our histories and heritages provides an anchor that holds us to who we are" (p. 151). Such anchors are particularly important in times of extreme stress. A strong belief in family is one such anchor. The importance of family may be a cultural belief that is reinforced under some social conditions. Poverty or marginalized status, for example, may intensify reliance on family members, but the importance of family also has roots in longstanding cultural traditions (see Genovese, 1976; Griswold Del Castillo, 1984). Even during slavery, when devastating tribal and family separations occurred, African Americans gained a sense of themselves and their place in the world within the context of extended networks and kinship relationships (Jones, 2001).

Sensitivity to cultural context should not lead to a focus exclusively on differences among social groups. Processes that underlie resilience are not necessarily culture-specific. For example, in a study of urban African American and White children, similar variables differentiated stress-resistant and stress-affected children in both racial groups (Magnus, Cowen, Wyman, Fagen, & Work, 1999). Perceived competence, a positive view of self, empathy, and realistic attributions about control facilitated the adjustment of Black and White individuals alike.

In addition, it is important for researchers in dominant groups to recognize that risk is not a relevant construct *only* for marginalized people. Resilience research has focused on the stresses associated with poverty and minority group membership. This has deflected attention from the possibility that children in middle- and upper-class families may also suffer adversity and benefit from interventions. How do we explain the finding, for example, that affluent suburban teenagers abuse substances at higher rates than inner-city youth (Luthar & Cicchetti, 2000)? The rash of school shootings that swept the nation at the end of the twentieth century affected *White* teenagers in *middle-class* schools. Researchers and practitioners

need to consider risk and resilience in all families and not rely on preconceived and stereotypical notions about who is at risk and who is not (Luthar & Cicchetti, 2000).

SEX DIFFERENCES: THE INTERPLAY OF TIME AND CONTEXT

Ethnicity and class are not the only social position variables that affect the process of resilience. Gender also merits consideration. Numerous early studies of resilience reported sex differences in adjustment. This research consistently found that boys fared worse than girls. Male children appeared to be more adversely affected by marital conflict, divorce, physical stress, and other challenges (Emery, 1982; Hetherington, Cox, & Cox, 1979; Rutter, 1970; Zaslow & Hayes, 1985). Male sex seemed to constitute an important risk factor.

When researchers began to study resilience beyond childhood, however, the picture changed. Longitudinal and cross-sectional research on adolescents and young adults found a shift in vulnerability. In adolescence girls appear to be at greater risk than boys. In Emmy Werner and Ruth Smith's (1982; 1993) study of the children of Kauai, the sex ratio of all disordered behaviors except delinquency shifted from a majority of boys in childhood to a majority of girls in adolescence. In adolescence, twice as many girls as boys developed severe mental health problems. By the age of eighteen, more boys than girls with serious learning and/or behavior problems improved, and more girls than boys developed these problems during the second decade. Girls who bore children as teenagers faced additional risks.

A similar shift in risk status was found by Glen Elder in his study of children of the Great Depression (e.g., Elder, 1974; Elder, Liker, & Cross, 1984; Elder et al., 1985; see the Classic Research box in Chapter Four). You may remember that Elder and his colleagues followed two cohorts of children. The Berkeley cohort consisted of children who were preadolescent at the time of the Great Depression, and the Oakland cohort consisted of children who were entering adolescence at that time. In the Berkeley cohort, outcomes were less favorable for boys as compared to girls. The opposite was true in the Oakland cohort. In fact, in this cohort, boys who suffered economic deprivation during adolescence fared better than boys who did *not* suffer deprivation.

Life-span developmental and system perspectives provide insights into this shift in risk status. Research suggests that under stressful circumstances, parents relate differently to sons and daughters. Parents comfort, help, and discuss problems more frequently with daughters than with sons (Fagot, 1978) and fight more frequently in front of sons (Hetherington et al., 1979). Even when parenting behavior is positive toward both sons and daughters, girls seem to benefit more than boys from supportive family environments. Under conditions of high stress, positive parenting reduces the likelihood of disruptive behavior in girls but not in boys (Garmezy & Masten, 1986; Masten, Garmezy, Tellegen, Pellegrini, Larkin, & Larsen, 1988).

Differential and seemingly preferential treatment of daughters under stressful circumstances does not necessarily mean that parents are predisposed against sons. A systems view recognizes the bidirectional nature of parent–child interaction. Aggression-eliciting behaviors tend to be more prominent in boys (Maccoby & Jacklin, 1974) and may become even more pronounced in times of stress due to boys' higher physiological reactivity and their socialization toward externalizing behavior (e.g., Moss, 1974; Zaslow & Hayes, 1985). Highly stressed girls tend to interact more positively with others. As one example, many girls but few boys evidenced extreme prosocial behavior in response to stress (Hetherington, 1989). Parental criticisms are more often directed to difficult children (Rutter, 1977) and so boys may become more likely targets for parental sanctions because they act out more.

During childhood, when girls and boys are both embedded in the family system, more positive relationships between female children and other family members may provide girls with greater protection from adversity. In adolescence, vulnerability status may shift due to boys' growing independence and separation from the family. Indeed, autonomy may offer some protection for boys during adolescence. A recent study found that parental attachment and monitoring improved the outcomes for adolescent girls but exacerbated problems for adolescent boys (Formoso, Gonzales, & Aiken, 2000). The finding that high-crime neighborhoods affect boys more than girls may be due to the tendency for boys to play further from home and in larger groups, thereby increasing the likelihood that they encounter negative influences outside the home (see Olds et al., 1997; see also Luthar & Cushing, 1999).

As they approach adolescence, boys begin to spend more time away from the family. Girls remain at home more often, and so if the family environment is conflictual or dysfunctional, girls may face greater exposure to stress (Elder et al., 1985; McLoyd, 1989). In addition, while higher expectations for independence and achievement in sons may create more background stress for boys early in life (Gove & Herb, 1974), independence becomes increasingly advantageous at later ages. In adolescence, when young people are expected to assume adult roles (Zaslow & Hayes, 1985), girls who are less practiced in autonomy may be less prepared to cope with the pressures of growing up.

Families' efforts to buffer young girls from stress may cause problems later if this buffering prevents girls from experiencing upset and developing appropriate responses. One study found that positive family climates actually exacerbated the negative effects of stress among adolescents. The researchers argued that

> when confronted with a high level of stress, young adolescents who are accustomed to a 'positive' family climate are at a disadvantage relative to those accustomed to a more 'negative' family climate; because the latter are familiar with disruptive life experiences, they are less 'stressed' by negative life events (Burt, Cohen, & Bjork, 1988, p. 119)

Perhaps girls experience greater exposure to these disadvantageous "positive" family climates. In line with this finding, it is interesting to note recent research reporting that adolescent girls mature faster in families characterized by conflict and distance with parents (Steinberg, 1988).

In addition to the family and neighborhood, macrosystem factors may also help explain the shift in risk status for males and females. The finding that girls become more depressed and self-critical and move into silence during adolescence has been attributed to the dominant culture's denigration of women and assault to their sense of self-worth and aliveness (e.g., Gilligan, Lyons, & Hammer, 1990). Thus, larger societal blueprints for gender-role behavior may also bear on our understanding of resilience.

Emmy Werner and Ruth Smith (1993; Werner, 1989) have now followed the children of Kauai into adulthood. Interesting gender differences continued to emerge in later life. For example, adult males as compared to females evidenced a greater reluctance to begin their own families or to remarry after divorce. These findings suggest a hesitancy or inability to connect with others. It may be that boys growing under adverse conditions were protected by autonomy and so have difficulty forming connections to others in later life. On the other hand, girls in adverse circumstances may find protection in close relationships. This view is consistent with research showing that social support from family members helps adult women adjust to stress, while men benefit from self-confidence (Holahan & Moos, 1985; Moos, 1984).

Werner and Smith also found a sex difference in child-rearing philosophies. More women than men expected high achievement from and fostered early independence in their children, while more men than women tolerated dependence and considered the "opportunity to care for others" as the most positive aspect of being a parent (Werner, 1989). Might this reflect the parental desire to shield children from the trials and tribulations of their own development? While women may have struggled with their lack of opportunity for autonomy in early life, men may have felt shortchanged by their lack of connectedness.

Additional insights into resilience will likely be gleaned from studying adults as they continue to age. For the more family-oriented females, do new challenges arise when their children leave home or when they become widows, as many undoubtedly will given the longer life expectancies of women? What challenges await the more autonomous male as he ages and needs to negotiate an increased reliance on others for financial, emotional, and physical support? The second generation of resilience research highlighted the importance of life-span developmental and system-level analyses. Such analyses yielded new ways of explaining existing findings (e.g., why required helpfulness is helpful and how gender confers protection). As we trace the dynamics of resilience into old age, life-span developmental and system perspectives may also allow us to glean new insights that might alter the way future researchers think about resilience.

⌘ A Third Generation of Resilience Research?

Following the first generation of resilience research, numerous scholars expressed doubt about the utility of the construct. Some early criticisms reflected the usual misgivings that arise whenever a new construct develops (see Cicchetti & Garmezy, 1993; Luthar, 1993). Concerns about the fuzziness of definitions and rigor of methodologies arose in the beginning stages of resilience research as they had when research on prevention and empowerment began in earnest.

Some concerns about the concept of resilience have not abated, however. A few scholars have argued that the notion of resilience does not add anything to our existing constructs of positive adjustment and competence (e.g., Tarter & Vanyukov, 1999). Howard Kaplan acknowledged that resilience research alerted us to the possibility that experiences of adversity do not necessarily lead to negative outcomes, and conversely that negative outcomes do not necessarily require adversity. Having served its purpose, this critic proposed that resilience now be "permitted to retire from the field gracefully and with honor" (Kaplan, 1999, p. 77;

see also Gordon & Wang, 1994). In this section we examine the current thinking of two important scholars in the second generation of resilience research, Suniya Luthar and Ann Masten, as they tackle the question: Is resilience a useful concept?

PATHWAYS TO COMPETENCE UNDER STRESS

Suniya Luthar and her colleagues (Luthar & Cicchetti, 2000; Luthar et al., 2000a) argued that resilience adds to the larger social science literature in three ways. First, as noted above, it compels a focus on positive outcomes. Second, it provides a basis for prevention efforts. Knowing how individuals and systems achieve resilience during times of stress can suggest ways of intervening in the lives of people and groups experiencing adversity. Finally, resilience explicitly examines processes that might account for healthy adjustment *in the presence of stress*, which are not necessarily the same processes that underlie healthy adjustment more generally.

This is a matter of some debate. Luthar and her colleagues have argued that healthy development under stressful conditions *differs* from development under more "normal" circumstances. They proposed that protective factors operate in a number of different ways, as depicted in Figure 11.1.

The first graph (A) shows the pattern of results we would expect if the same processes occurred in the presence or absence of stress. Protective factors increase competence in a similar fashion for people at both low risk and high risk. That is to say, people perform better when the protective factor exists whether they encounter adversity or not. In statistics, this is called a **main effect**. The effect of one variable of interest (in this case, the protective factor) on the outcome (in this case, adjustment or competence) is the same regardless of the level of another variable (in this case, adversity or risk). Suniya Luthar and her colleagues referred to this type of effect as simply *protective*.

Interaction effects, however, are at the heart of resilience research (Luthar et al., 2000a; Roosa, 2000). An interaction is in evidence when the effect of one variable of interest (the protective factor) on the outcome variable (competence) differs depending on the level of a third variable (adversity). In Figure 11.1, graphs B, C, and D depict interaction effects. (In line graphs, interactions are evident when the lines depicting the effects of variables at different levels are *not* parallel.)

Interaction effects describe the ways in which pathways to positive adjustment differ for people who are experiencing adversity as compared to non-stressed people. Some examples will make this clear. As we have seen, extreme environmental structure and control may have particularly beneficial effects for people experiencing severe stress (Black & Krishnakumar, 1998; Hetherington, 1989; Rutter, 1979; Taylor et al., 2000; Werner & Smith, 1982; Wilson, 1974). As another example, extracurricular activities appear to be most beneficial for young people living under the adverse conditions associated with poverty, presumably because youth in poverty-stricken areas encounter few environments that help them to feel good about themselves. Consequently, when they encounter the positive environments that characterize extracurricular activities, the benefits can be profound (Dubois, Felner, Meares, & Krier, 1994; Dubois, Felner, Brand, Adan, & Evans, 1992; see also Werner, 1993). For similar reasons, close relationships with caring adults exert an extremely positive effect on children with disturbed parent–child interactions (Cicchetti & Toth, 1995).

Most of these examples describe the protective effect depicted in graph B. The protective factor may have some positive effect for people under low stress, but under high stress, the factor affords a marked advantage. It allows people to perform competently despite increases in adversity. If the protective factor is not present, the experience of adversity can seriously compromise adjustment. Luthar and colleagues called this a *protective-stabilizing* effect.

Michael Rutter (1979; 2001) provided a classic example of a protective-stabilizing effect. He documented the importance of a good relationship with at least one parent for children living in quarrelsome and unhappy homes. Only about 25% of children in discordant homes fared well when they did *not* have a

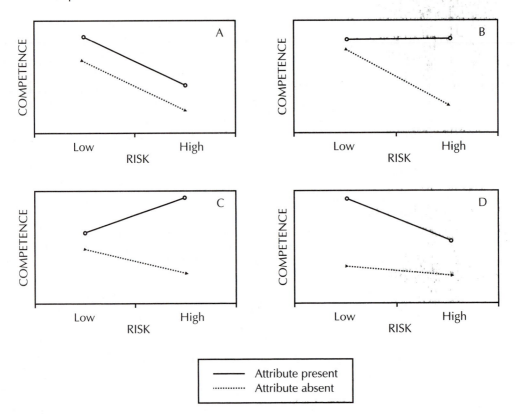

Figure 11.1

Protective effects of moderator variables in interaction with risk status in relation to competent outcomes. A) protective, B) protective-stabilizing, C) protective-enhancing, D) protective reactive. *Luthar, S. S., Cicchetti, D. Becker, B. (2000b). The construct of resilience: A critical evaluation and guidelines for future work. Child Development, 71, 543–562.*

good relationship. When a good relationship existed, however, about 75% of the children in discordant homes were free of conduct disorder. Thus, under stress a good relationship provided a great advantage. Indeed, if a good relationship existed, children living in adversity resembled children living without adversity. In harmonious homes, about 85% of children who had a good relationship with a parent were free of conduct disorder. This was only a small advantage over children without a good relationship, about 75% of whom were free of conduct disorder.

In graph C, the presence of the protective factor actually *increases* the competence of people under stress. Luthar and colleagues called this a *protective-enhancing* effect. We have already discussed an

example of this type of interaction. Glen Elder found that adolescent boys in families undergoing economic adversity during the Great Depression actually fared *better* than peers who did not experience adversity; presumably this occurred because the youth who needed to contribute to the family's economic well-being developed new skills and competencies.

The interaction depicted in graph D has been of less interest to resilience researchers. Briefly, it shows a protective factors that confers some advantage, but less so when stress levels are high. Luthar and colleagues called this a *protective-reactive* effect.

In summary, Luthar and her colleagues have argued that the pathways to competence are often similar for stressed and nonstressed people. Some protective factors, however, have a *more* positive effect on adjustment in the presence of stress and in some instances may even *enhance* adjustment so that stressed people can actually outperform non-stressed people. Thus, the study of resilience offers unique windows into the processes that underlie healthy adjustment.

RESILIENCE AS AN ORDINARY PROCESS

Unlike Luthar, Ann Masten and her colleagues (Masten, 2001; Masten & Coatsworth, 1998; Masten, Hubbard, Gest, Tellegen, Garmezy, & Ramirez, 1999) have emphasized the *common* pathways to competence among stressed and nonstressed people, and yet they too are enthusiastic about the concept of resilience.

Masten and her colleagues held that the same adaptive systems protect development under both favorable and unfavorable conditions. In support of this contention, they studied children who varied across two dimensions, adversity, and competence (Masten et al., 1999). Variations in these two dimensions resulted in four groups (see Table 11.2).

One group consisted of children who experienced low adversity and manifested high levels of competence. This might be considered the "normal" group. They did not suffer from extreme stresses, and they performed well. A second group experienced high adversity and high competence. This group exhibited

resilience. A third group also experienced high adversity, but manifested low competence. This might be considered the stress-affected group. Under conditions of adversity, they did not thrive. Finally, one group was low in adversity and low in competence. This group might be considered highly vulnerable as they fared poorly even in the absence of stress. Interestingly, there were very few highly vulnerable children. Children rarely exhibited low competence under conditions of low adversity.

The researchers found that children who exhibited high competence in three domains (academic, conduct, and social) showed extremely similar profiles regardless of their exposure to adversity. The well-adjusted children, both "normal" and "resilient," evidenced good intellectual functioning, positive self-concepts, and experienced positive parenting. The profiles of children who experienced adversity but did not adjust well ("stress-affected" children) were quite dissimilar. Thus, despite the fact that children exhibiting resilience were similar to stress-affected children in terms of life experiences, they closely resembled "normal" children in terms of resources and attributes. These results suggest that competence is a similar phenomenon for stressed and nonstressed people.

This research did not lead Masten and Coatsworth to conclude that resilience was therefore a useless and superfluous concept, however. Rather, they suggested that resilience research elucidated basic protective systems that operate in the lives of

🗎 Table 11.2   Possible Outcomes for Children

Level of Adversity	Level of Adjustment	
	Low	*High*
Low	Vulnerable	Normal
High	Stress-affected	Resilient

Based on Masten, A. S., Hubbard, J. J., Gest, S. D., Tellegen, A., Garmezy, N., & Ramirez, M. (1999). Competence in the context of adversity: Pathways to resilience and maladaptation from childhood to late adolescence. *Development and Psychopathology, 11*, 143–169.

all children. Protective systems offer enough redundancy to sustain reasonably good development even under adversity. Competence is compromised only when systems basic to human functioning are disrupted either prior to or as a result of adversity. These basic adaptational systems include cognitive systems (the ability to reason, for example), parenting systems (the presence of warm and responsive caregiving relationships), and also motivational systems (the ability to derive pleasure from acting effectively in the environment). (See White [1959] for an early description of the motivation system.)

According to Masten (2001), the "gloom-and-doom" approach (p. 235) that predominated in research before the concept of resilience emerged suggested that adversity inevitably led to maladjustment. In contrast, the "rosy resiliency" approach (2001, p. 235) of the first generation of resilience research suggested that resilience was an extraordinary process that allowed only a few superkids to survive crises. She held that the current view of resilience is more positive than either of these early attempts to understand development under adversity.

Although extraordinary talents, exceptional families, ideal communities and uncommon good fortune can have positive effects on adjustment, resilience most often results from the operation of ordinary human processes. Children require basic adapational systems to develop. If we can protect these basic systems when they exist and restore them when they are interrupted, then children can thrive. Resilience results from the "everyday magic of ordinary, normative human resources in the minds, brains, and bodies of children, in their families, and in their communities" (Masten, 2001, p. 235).

⌘ The Promise of Community Psychology: Nonshared Environments

In the second generation, resilience researchers less often viewed individuals who thrived despite adversity as possessing some global, absolute quality that conferred protection in all situations and for all time. Studies increasingly focused on the process of resilience, which directed attention to the systems in which resilience was manifested. Our understanding of systems processes is not, however, by any means complete.

As described earlier, Marian Radke-Yarrow and Tracy Sherman (1990) demonstrated that two siblings living in the same family environment can have very different outcomes. Daniel Challener (1997) recounted one dramatic example of this in his analysis of resilience narratives. In the narrative *Brother and Keepers*, John Edgar Wideman (1984) described the markedly contrasting life paths taken by him and his brother Robby. Both grew up in the same home and suffered together from various adversities, but John demonstrated high levels of academic, social, and athletic achievement in his early years and grew to become a college professor and prize-winning author. Robby was a rebellious child and militant adolescent who eventually received a life sentence for his role in committing a murder.

A better understanding of why children in the same family differ substantially from each other across numerous outcomes despite shared family environments—and shared genes—may enhance our understanding of system processes. Thus, some scholars have called for increased attention to **nonshared family environments** (e.g., Henderson, Hetherington, Mekos, & Reiss, 1996; Hetherington, Reiss & Plomin, 1994; Plomin & Daniels, 1987). Research into nonshared family environments has found that easily examined structural variables, such as birth order and sibling age difference, do not elucidate within-family differences. Thus, attention has turned to process variables, such as differential parenting, sibling interaction, peer relationships, and sibling deindividuation (i.e., siblings develop in different or opposite directions to defend against sibling rivalry) (Feinberg & Hetherington, 2000).

While numerous researchers study nonshared environments within families, the concept has not been extended to other systems. An understanding of how system processes differentially affect system members might also contribute to our understanding of schools, workplaces, communities, and other environments.

There are a number of community psychology concepts that suggest the importance of such an approach. The research of Radke-Yarrow and Sherman (1990) is an excellent demonstration of *person–environment fit*. When the characteristics of a sibling matched a need that characterized the caregiving system, resilience was more likely. This is consistent with the notion that some environments benefit some people more than others. Behaviors, including resilience, are a function of both the person and the environment.

Systems have differential effects on members not only due to individual personalities, but also people's social position and roles within the system. Roger Barker and Phil Schoggen (1973) used the term *habitant–inhabitant bias* to refer to the uneven distribution of people from different social groups across behavior settings. They found, for example, that African Americans of all ages and preschoolers of all races were not well-represented in the community settings that Barker's methods assessed.

This would suggest that different communities better support the participation of some subcommunities. It might be easier for older citizens to evidence resilience in communities that have senior centers, good public transportation, and responsive medical systems. It might be easier for preschoolers to thrive under adversity when their communities offer respite care to stressed parents; low-cost, high-quality childcare, pleasant parks where parents can share support while their children play, and so on.

The research of Radke-Yarrow and Sherman clearly demonstrated that family systems better serve some system members as compared to others. Similarly, communities may serve some subgroups better than others. An examination of nonshared environments at various levels can elucidate system dynamics and enhance our ability to provide the resources that allow people to live, play, and work well.

Action Agenda

Promoting System-Level Resilience

Ann Masten & J. Douglas Coatsworth (1998) identified three approaches to promoting resilience:

1. Eliminate risk (e.g., provide prenatal care to reduce the incidence of low-birthweight babies);
2. Add resources (e.g., provide Big Brothers and Big Sisters to stressed children); or
3. Target basic adaptational process (e.g., improve parenting skills of young mothers, ensure proper nutrition for early brain development)

How might each of these approaches be applied beyond the individual level, in families, schools, or communities? What risks might proponents of system-level resilience focus on eliminating? What resources would we try to build? How might we affect basic adaptational processes? Think not only about how systems influence the lives of individuals, but how phenomena exist at system levels as well. That is to say, what are examples of system-level risks, resources, and adapational systems that interventionists might target?

Community Competence Revisited

Review the section on community competence in this chapter (section entitled *Families, Schools, Neighborhoods, and Beyond*) and in Chapter Seven (section entitled *Putting the "Health" Back into Mental Health*). What might be gleaned from studying competent communities under stress (i.e., community resilience as compared to community competence)? What community-level stresses have your communities encountered in recent times? What evidence of resilience do you see in how the community as a whole or subgroups within your community have responded? What resources/protective factors do you think would assist your community in responding well to stress? How might you individually or as a class promote the development of important community resources? What would be a first step in this process?

Shapes of Orienting Concepts

Now that we have discussed the four orienting concepts of community psychology, think about how they do or do not succeed in giving shape to the guiding principles of the field. Working alone or in small groups, decide which of the five guiding principles you believe is most central to each concept. Then decide which principles each orienting concept captures least well. Each person or group can discuss all four orienting concepts in turn, or groups can choose to focus on one in particular.

Now refer back to the amoeba-like pictures in Chapter One that show how the principles of community psychology may have different emphases (Figure 1.2). Draw pictures of each orienting concept to illustrate the relative importance of each guiding principle. Use your assessments of the most and least well represented principles as anchors for the drawings.

Put all the pictures on the wall, grouped by orienting concept. Do the pictures describing each concept clearly resemble each other and differ from the pictures of other concepts? Where are the points of agreement and disagreement? Discuss why the agreements and disagreements occurred. Can disagreements be resolved?

 **Key Terms**

adaptability (system level)

authoritative parenting

developmental psychopathology

event chains

interaction effect

main effect

nonshared family environments

plasticity

protective factors

resilience

wellness

Chapter 12

Community Psychology in the Twenty-First Century

....

⌘ Introduction

The preceding chapters have described community psychology since its birth in 1965. This final chapter briefly reviews some of the material presented in the text with an eye toward the future. How will community psychology take shape in and help shape the twenty-first century?

Prognostication is a risky business. Those who have tried it have met with mixed success, from the twentieth-century author George Orwell, to the sixteenth-century prophet Nostradamus, to the ancient priests of Israel who divined messages of the future from the configurations of animal entrails, birds in flight, and oil poured on water (Orwell, 1949; Roberts, 1994; Johnson, 1962; Lindblom, 1967).

Still, a lack of concern for the world to come is dooming. Future generations will inherit the problems that we either cause or fail to solve, from global warming to deep-seated cultural conflicts that threaten to destroy us all in a nuclear age. American Indian cultures speak of the importance of acting with an awareness of people who will walk the earth in seven generations. The span of even one generation stretches the imagination of many in the U.S., where policy-makers rarely look beyond the horizons of the two- or four-year terms of elected office.

To paraphrase from the poet Kahlil Gibran's (1946) work *The Prophet*, our children's souls dwell in the house of tomorrow, which we cannot visit, even in our dreams. We are vastly ill-equipped for the task of preparing for (or preparing others for) the future. We have at our disposal only lessons from the past. Nevertheless, I hope readers will join me in the important and impossible assignment of looking ahead. As I draw a few broad lessons from the first decades of community psychology, you might fill in some details. What lessons speak most loudly to you? What challenges will likely arise in the future for you as an individual, in your microsystems, and in the larger world? Are there ways in which the perspectives of community psychology might help formulate responses to these challenges?

In this chapter we will first revisit some fundamental and recurring paradoxes that have underlain community psychology's unique way of thinking and then try to glean lessons for future orienting

349

concepts by analyzing the four that have emerged this far. Finally, we will consider challenges that future orienting concepts will likely encounter.

⌘ Praising Paradox

Community psychology is an inherently paradoxical field, beginning with its name. The question I most often hear when I identify myself as a community psychologists is, " 'Community psychology' —isn't that an oxymoron?" The willingness to embrace and even seek out paradox is one of community psychology's greatest strengths. In our increasingly complex, technologically advanced, global, and multicultural world, this strength will likely serve us well. If we can search out paradox, tolerate ambiguity, and enfold the multiple realities of human existence, we will grow as a field and help our communities to grow as a result.

The paradoxes of community psychology are everywhere apparent in this text. Even the organizational structure reflects a paradox. Community psychology, if it is to be a coherent field, needs to define itself as a circumscribed and stable entity. At the same time, if it is to remain relevant in a changing world, it must continually respond to evolving knowledge and shifting Zeitgeists. We must remain anchored to our fundamental values and open to paradigm-shaking perspectives. I have tried to capture this tension by dividing the book into two sections: the guiding principles, which remain constant, and the orienting concepts, which change with the times.

In calling for community psychologists to embrace paradox, Julian Rappaport (1981) described the notion of the **dialectic**. "The point is simply that much of what underlies the substance of our field requires us to recognize that we are being pulled in two ways at once and that we often need to pay attention to two different and apparently opposed poles of thought" (p. 3). One of the functions of community psychology has been to direct attention to poles of thought neglected in more mainstream psychology. We do this not in an attempt to

supplant existing mindscapes but in an effort to right the balance—awareness of *both* poles of dialectics enhances the work of psychology.

In Chapter One, we examined the dialectic between the past and the future. Past and future are apparent opposites, but they function as a whole. We saw, for example, that our understanding of human history depends on the perspectives of our historians, whose vantage points shift as the world they live in changes. Community psychology cannot, like chemistry, biology, astronomy, and other "hard" sciences, see current knowledge as "rendering past scientific knowledge obsolete, [and so view] its past as more interesting than it was usable" (Sarason, 1978, p. 372). Community psychology is about human experience. As the poet Nikki Giovanni (1994) observed, "Life is not a problem similar to science or mathematics where solutions can be discerned and tested" (p. 40). In other words, objective facts and cumulative knowledge do not advance the social sciences as they do physical sciences. As Seymour Sarason (1978) pointed out, problems of society are seldom really solved but must be resolved over and over again as new circumstances dictate the shape of society at any given time.

Thus, lessons drawn from history allow us to navigate the future. Sarason (1986) observed that a community psychology without grounding in history "lacks not only scholarship, but direction" (p. 407). I began this text with a consideration of community psychology's before-the-beginning not solely out of academic interest but because the context that gave birth to this field continues to shape it. We can trace community psychology's interests in questioning the status quo and exploring better social arrangements to our 1960s roots, but these interests remain central today. This means that ours is, by its history, a forward-looking field—one reason why this final chapter gazes into the future.

A key dialectic underlying Chapter Two was the tension between reflection and action. Although some community psychologists (our "practitioners") may be said to operate primarily from an action orientation and others (our "academics") from a reflection orientation, this dichotomy is false. As Dick Reppucci (1999) noted, the field places equal value on "seeking knowledge for the sake of understanding and using that knowledge for the sake of action" (p. 308).

All community psychologists seek to understand the world around us (reflect) and also use that understanding to make the world a better place (act). As Kurt Lewin described in his action-research model, there exists a continual interplay between our efforts to gather information and to make changes based on that information. Although community psychologists credit Lewin with integrating the action and research dichotomy, such efforts have a long history in human inquiry. Indeed, Aristotle described the existence of knowledge-generating cycles that begin and end in practice (Newbrough, 1992).

In the twentieth century, psychology and other sciences tipped the balance of thought in the direction of reflection. Research became the sine qua non of knowledge. Community psychology offers a reminder that research gains meaning through action. This places community psychologists in the precarious position of being at the same time scientists and activists. We struggle to balance our responsibilities as trained professionals with expert knowledge and our responsibilities as citizens who are affected by the contexts we seek to understand and influence (see Berkowitz, 2000; Chavis, Stucky, & Wanderman, 1983; Elias, 1994; Walsh-Bowers, 1993; Watts, 1993b; Wicker & Sommer, 1993).

The chapters on guiding principles also revolve around tensions that are fundamental to human experience and inquiry. Chapter Three focused on the dialectic between science and values. Major eras of human history correspond to shifts in the pole of influence that places science on one end and values on the other. For hundreds of years, the pendulum of popular thought has shifted from one pole to the other, science in the Age of Reason, values during Romanticism.

In modern times, psychology, like other sciences, has swung in the direction of science. Throughout the twentieth century, psychological expertise was based more and more on objectivity and rationality. Community psychology again has directed attention to the neglected pole, offering reminders that

values shape science. They determine the questions we ask, the methods we use to explore our questions, and the meaning we take from the answers we obtain. The importance placed on rationality may lead scientists to cloak our values, but they are no less ubiquitous when unacknowledged. Many community psychologists advocate unveiling our values. Indeed, the delineation of community psychology's guiding principles is at heart an attempt to articulate the fundamental values of the field.

Chapter Four examined tensions between self and community. No paradox has a longer human history than the **paradox of the one and the many** (see Newbrough, 1992). The tension between self and community is a precondition of human life. We each, as unique individuals, strive to develop, grow, and meet our own needs, and yet we are at the most basic level social animals who require relationships with others in order to survive and thrive. The tension between the one and the many was well described by the French philosopher Alexis de Toqueville early in U.S. history (Toqueville, 1835/1969). Upon visiting the U.S. in the 1830s, he observed that Euro-Americans were intimately connected to others through family, religious traditions, and local politics, but that a pull toward individualism threatened to isolate us from each other.

United States culture in general, and psychology in particular, have succumbed to the pull toward "the one." The importance of our social environments has been vastly underemphasized. Community psychology attempts to shift focus to the neglected pole of "the many"—the multileveled contexts in which individual behaviors occur and gain meaning. Community psychologists offer reminders that people do not exist as independent actors but as members of social systems.

Thematic tensions were detailed in the subsequent chapters on guiding principles as well. In Chapter Five we saw that an appreciation of diversity requires a consideration of how our similarities are different—the way individuals and groups are both alike and unique. Chapter Six examined stability and change as two sides of the same coin and proposed ways of confronting the paradoxical finding that the more things change, the more they remain the same. In Chapter Seven we saw that people have both strengths and weaknesses, and we can create contexts which pull for either one or the other. Community psychology attempts to reverse dominant thinking by drawing out assets rather than compensating for deficits. Against the backdrop of these thematic tensions, numerous smaller paradoxes emerged: balancing patience and zeal, connecting through disruption, reconciling optimism and realism.

Orienting concepts also rest on paradox. They develop precisely because the quality of reflection and action is compromised by overemphasis of one pole over another. New orienting concepts force attention to neglected poles of dialectics. Rappaport (1981) wrote his influential article *In Praise of Paradox* out of the belief that the orienting concept of prevention upheld the traditional view of people as having needs. He proposed empowerment as an orienting concept that provided a corrective to this imbalance by emphasizing rights over needs. *Exclusive* attention to needs had forced one-sided approaches and solutions. Undue attention to rights could ultimately have the same effect. Rappaport (1981) wrote, "Should empowerment become dominant as a way of thinking I have no doubt that it too will force one-sided solutions" (p. 21).

⌘ Shaping Orienting Concepts

Are there ways in which empowerment has indeed become one-sided? Let's glean some lessons from orienting concepts past as a way of informing an analysis of orienting concepts yet to come.

LESSONS FROM CONCEPTS PAST

An analysis of previous orienting concepts suggests some predictions. First, we can expect that new concepts will initially be criticized as "buzzwords" that lack clear definition. The popularity of the concept will outpace its empirical verification, and burgeoning attention will be paralleled by a growing concern over the quality of theory and research (e.g., Luthar, Cicchetti, & Becker, 2000b). Proponents of the concept will call for a sharpening of definitions and increased methodological rigor, while critics will question whether the concept merits attention at all. Several scholars have noted that the definitional and methodological ambiguities of this early period are useful in that they provoke innovative ways of thinking (e.g., Trickett, 1994; Luthar et al., 2000b). If we can meet new orienting concepts with open minds, a tolerance for ambiguity, and receptivity to the voices of denunciation (which likely foresee challenges the term will encounter down the road), we will be well positioned to use these concepts to their fullest potential.

A second conclusion to be drawn from the chapters on orienting concepts past is that they easily become new labels for old ways of doing things. The initial appeal of the concept derives from a recognition that it supplies a needed corrective to dominant thinking. At the same time (and paradoxically), the concept's popularity increases the likelihood that the term will be co-opted by prevailing mindscapes. Assimilation is always easier than accommodation.

The mindscape that has presented the greatest challenge to the orienting concepts of community psychology is the tendency to conceive all phenomena at the level of the individual. In recognition of this challenge, Rappaport (2000b) warned that orienting concepts must powerfully convey a nonindividual focus to compensate for pulls in psychology and U.S. society toward the pole of "the one." When Emory Cowen (1991; 1994; 2000a) proposed *the pursuit of wellness* as a fifth orienting concept, Julian Rappaport (1987; 2000b) objected to this candidate for "phenomenon of interest" on the grounds that wellness brought to mind an image of the personal body, rather than the body politic. Thus, it remained mired at the individual level. Although empowerment may offer more resistance to the pull toward "the one," it too can succumb. Person-centered views have co-opted the concept of empowerment as well (e.g., Riger, 1993).

Orienting concepts might more successfully resist the pull toward "the one" if they emphasize *processes*. Promoters of orienting concepts generally understand this imperative. In presenting her model of stress and coping, Barbara Dohrenwend (1978) asserted that community psychology would benefit from focusing more attention on the stress *process*. Marc Zimmerman (1995) advised that the concept of empowerment risks compromise when it is "inappropriately conceptualized as a static personality trait instead of a more dynamic contextually driven construct" (p. 596). Resilience scholars in the second generation attempted to move from a trait view toward an understanding of *how* risk and protective factors contributed to positive outcomes. In proposing the orienting concept of wellness, Emory Cowen (1991) framed his discussion in terms of *the pursuit of wellness,* recognizing, perhaps, the need to emphasize process. A focus on processes should not imply that outcomes are irrelevant. For example, I noted in Chapter Ten that the test of empowerment is not whether people participate in their environments (the process of empowerment), but whether a shift in the balance of power actually occurs (an outcome of empowerment). Still, a lack of attention to processes, which signal the existence of dynamic systems, increases the risk that concepts will be conceived as traits that reside within individuals.

This may help explain the great staying power of prevention. Prevention emerged as a potential orienting concept at Swampscott and remains popular today. In a search of all program entries for the 2001 SCRA conference, the root word *prevent* appeared 354 times, more than *stress* (104), *crisis* (6), *empower* (86), and *resil-* and *wellness* combined (25). Perhaps one reason for prevention's appeal is that it cannot be construed as an individual trait. We can talk about people as stressed, empowered, resilient, or well, but we cannot turn prevention into an adjective that describes an individual. Although prevention has faced its own challenges in trying to look beyond the individual level (see the *Promise of Psychology* section in Chapter Nine), it succeeds in focusing attention on processes.

RETURNING TO COMMUNITY (AGAIN)

Let's try now to foresee possible orienting concepts yet to come and consider how they might fare given these lessons from the past. One way to generate candidates for future orienting concepts is to consider what poles of dialectics psychological research and practice currently ignore to the detriment of the field.

Empowerment sought to balance psychology's emphasis on individual needs with a commensurate focus on people's rights. Although the helping professions have not always approached patients/clients/consumers with an eye toward their rights, the rights of individuals more generally have hardly been neglected in U.S. culture. Our country was founded on the notion that people have basic inalienable rights. Debates in the U.S. have centered on questions of who has which rights under what circumstances, but the fact of individual rights has never been in question.

In the early 1990s, numerous social critics argued that the emphasis on individual rights in the U.S. had reached new heights and needed to be balanced by attention to social responsibilities (e.g., Etzioni, 1993; Glendon, 1991). This argument emerged most articulately in the movement called **communitarianism**. Communitarians advocated a shift in balance toward the pole of "the many." They challenged the prevailing view of the individual as a disembodied self, with no ties to value systems nor roots in community. They warned that an unchecked focus on individual rights would turn us into a collection of self-centered people in a normless and fragmented society. The solution was to acknowledge and assume the responsibilities of communal life, including compliance to a moral code (e.g., Etzioni, 1995; Selznick, 1992).

Communitarianism has not caught on as a widespread movement, but the notion that we need to balance concern for individual rights with attention to social responsibilities warrants consideration. As Robert Bellah and his colleagues (1985) compellingly described in their book *Habits of the Heart,* an emphasis on individual rights works against the bonds of attachment and cooperation that give meaning to life. Perhaps future orienting concepts for community psychology will promote attention to the neglected pole of "the many" by replacing the needs–rights dialectic with a trialectic that seeks to balance needs, rights, and also responsibilities.

COMMUNITY AND THE ZEITGEIST AT THE END OF THE TWENTIETH CENTURY

The movement for a return to community heralded by the communitarians in the early 1990s was in clear evidence by the turn of the twenty-first century. Many authors contributed to the sense that U.S. society suffered from a loss of community. Notably, Robert Putnam (2000) reviewed a plethora of research studies and data sources and concluded that the movement toward engagement in community life that characterized U.S. society in the first two-thirds of the twentieth century reversed dramatically beginning in the 1980s. In the final two decades of the twentieth century, citizens became less and less likely to participate in virtually all voluntary organizations and associations. Across the country, churches, union halls, bowling alleys, and clubrooms emptied or closed, and fewer people gathered together around committee tables, dinner tables, and card tables.

In the 1990s, many private foundations and governmental agencies resonated to the notion that a loss of community accounted for the social ills of the day. Consensus grew that societal problems could not be addressed piecemeal—one new preschool program here, a delinquency diversion project there—and that a long-term, comprehensive *community*-wide approach was needed (e.g., Schorr, 1997). Numerous agencies and organizations chose community as an umbrella concept for their broad-based initiatives. *Community development corporations (CDCs)* were increasingly used to revitalize low-income neighborhoods (Connell & Kubisch, 2001; Sampson, 1999). In 1990 the Center for Substance Abuse Prevention launched its influential Community Partnership Program, which enabled

251 localities to support and coordinate existing substance abuse prevention efforts (Center for Substance Abuse Prevention, 1993). Widespread talk of *community partnerships* soon followed. In addition, *community coalitions* became omnipresent. As one activist observed, "Coalitions are the rage. Every community has one by now or one is most certainly coming to a community near you" (Kaye, 1990, p. 269). Efforts to develop the capacity of stressed neighborhoods became known as *comprehensive community initiatives*, or CCIs (see Connell & Kubisch, 2001). The *Healthy Communities* movement described in Chapter Seven became a global movement for tackling problems of living.

In 1999 the sociologist and community researcher Robert Sampson (1999) observed that "community seems to be the modern elixir for much of what ails American society" (p. 241). There has emerged, he asserted, a "widespread idea that something has been lost in American society and a return to community is in order" (p. 242).

COMMUNITY IN COMMUNITY PSYCHOLOGY

Numerous community psychologists have discussed the meaning of the community movement to our work (e.g., Foster-Fishman, Salem, Allen, & Fahrbach, 1999; Kaftarian & Hansen, 1994; Norris, 2001, Wolff, 2001a). The discussion of a movement to community in the 1990s was not, however, entirely new.

HISTORICAL PERSPECTIVE

Numerous scholars have highlighted the irony of a field called community psychology failing to adequately attend to the concept of community. A few years after the field's birth, James Kelly (1970) observed that few books, conferences, or professional meetings actually discussed the term "community." He hypothesized that this reflected the resistance of professionals to locate themselves within a locale and to identify with a particular community. Two decades later, Kenneth Heller (1989a) marveled that "almost a quarter of a century after the Swampscott conference, it is legitimate to ask: 'Where is the community in community psychology?' " (p. 1). Heller echoed some of Kelly's observations, commenting that in a time when few people really lived in their neighborhoods, professionals, including community psychologists, were among the most transient and least connected of all.

Periodic calls to return to community have punctuated the development of community psychology. In 1974, Seymour Sarason argued for the importance of studying what he called the *psychological sense of community*. Twelve years later, he lamented that his earlier call for community had gone unheeded and warned that neglect of this central concept had resulted in a field that "had no moral and/or conceptual center. It was, and still largely is, a hodge podge" (Sarason, 1986, p. 406). At that time, Sarason was heartened to see a revival of interest in a sense of community, as evidenced by a special issue of *Journal of Community Psychology* dedicated to the concept (see Chavis & Newbrough, 1986). Still, sense of community did not catch fire as an orienting concept. Only a few hundred articles using the term have been written to date, as compared to the many thousands written on stress, prevention, empowerment, and resilience. Sarason's hope that community psychology would begin studying the concept of community in earnest remained unrealized. Three years after Sarason's optimistic introduction to the special issue of the *Journal of Community Psychology,* Kenneth Heller (1989a) issued yet another call for community psychologists to "return to community."

Seymour Sarason wrote *The Psychological Sense of Community: Prospects for a Community Psychology* in 1974 because he saw the lack of a sense of community as increasingly frequent and enormously destructive to human life. It seems that his observation was, once again, ahead of its time. By the turn of the twentieth century, many researchers and practitioners from a variety of fields had come to agree with his analysis. Perhaps *now* the time is ripe for an orienting concept that returns community to community psychology.

A Community-Related Orienting Concept. If initial ambiguity in terminology is advantageous in breaking molds of thinking, then orienting concepts relating to community are well placed to make a difference. One scholar identified almost 100 definitions of community (Hillery, 1984). It has variously been described as linkages based in blood, personal ties, common interests, geographic proximity, cultural solidarity, national identity, and the experience of a common stressor (Jerusalem, Kaniasty, Lehman, Ritter, & Turnbull, 1995).

A similar ambiguity surrounds a specific candidate for future orienting concept that answers the call for community: *social capital*. As described in Chapter Four, social capital refers to interpersonal relationships but also informal associations, participation in social groups, and community norms that foster social connections, such as trust and reciprocity. The term currently has the characteristics of a buzzword. Robert Sampson (2001) observed that, "Unfortunately, the concept of social capital has come to mean so many things that it has lost much of its meaning" (p. 9). As described earlier, this is not necessarily a problem.

More problematic is the observation that social capital, like the term *community* more generally, does not evoke process. It has become something we *have* rather than something we *do*. As Sampson (1999) put it, "the term *social capital* is perhaps misleading in that it alludes to a commodity or thing rather than a process" (p. 256). This may help explain why James Coleman's (1990) original formulation of social capital as being based in social structures, not in individuals has begun to succumb to the pull to "the one." Social capital has frequently "been recast into individual-level terms" (Sampson, 2001, p. 9).

A focus on concepts as objects makes it difficult to keep processes at the forefront. Ours appears to be a culture of objects. As one example, nouns dominate the early phases of language acquisition for English speakers, while verbs play a larger role in the development of other languages, such as Mandarin Chinese and Korean (Bloom, 1993; Choi & Gopnik, 1995; Tardif, Gelman, & Xu, 1999). Several recent authors have attempted to subvert what may be a cultural drift toward nountalk by titling their books, *God is a Verb* (Cooper, 1997;

Zdenek, 1974), *Love is a Verb* (O'Hanlon & Hudson, 1995), and even *News is a Verb* (Hammill, 1998). If community psychology does respond to the current calls for community with a new orienting concept for the field, we would be well served by a concept that makes clear that community, too, is a verb.

AVERTING ONE-SIDEDNESS

If a return to community is at hand, two considerations may help researchers and practitioners avoid one-sidedness. First, a historical perspective can help put the current enthusiasm into context. Second, while we hail community as a modern elixir, we might also consider the downsides of an emphasis on community.

History, Again. The perceived need for a return to community is not without precedent. Communities have been "lost" and rediscovered many times, and it is important to resist the temptation to wax nostalgic for a mythical past or reinvent old solutions (Sampson, 1999). Many of the concerns and insights that seem new today hark back to ideas from previous decades and even previous centuries.

In 1887, the German sociologist Ferdinand Tönnies (1957) distinguished *gemeinschaft* from *gessellshaft*. According to Tönnies, there exist two forms of human will, one an essential and instinctive force, the other deliberative and purposive. These two types of will lead to the formation of two different social arrangements. The first type, *gemeinschaft*, which has been translated as *community*, is an organic collective based in essential will. Membership in this group is self-fulfilling. The second type, *gessellshaft*, often translated as *society*, is functional rather than instinctive. Membership is sustained as long as benefits accrue from group membership. Tönnies noted that industrialization was causing a transition from intimate community located in extended families and neighborhoods (*gemeinschaft*), to a more arbitrary and discordant society without deep social ties (*gessellshaft*).

The French sociologist Émile Durkheim (1897/ 1951, 1893/1964), also writing at the end of the nineteenth century, observed as Tönnies had that community was increasingly impersonal and formed around functional interests rather than shared values. Durkheim held that common values provided social cohesion and social order, and that the loss of such values was leading to social instability and individual disorientation. He believed that this accounted for the increase in suicide at that time. More than half a century later, Robert Nisbet (1953) echoed the ideas of these early sociologists in his book, *Quest for Community*. Nisbet asserted that the need for community was innate and that the loss of community greatly compromised modern society. Robert Bellah and his colleagues examined a similar thesis in their popular 1985 book, *Habits of the Heart*.

Thus, scholars from the 1880s through the 1990s observed that communal life was becoming instrumental rather than sentimental. To use Tönnies' distinction, in the new *societies*, people became motivated by the promise of rewards: "One hand washes the other." "You scratch my back, I'll scratch yours." In the old *communities*, members gave without worrying about what they would get in return. A key differences between these two social groups is that societies can exist without caring, but communities cannot. At the end of his 1995 book entitled *The Careless Society*, John McKnight (1995) concluded, "It is only in community that we can find care" (p. 172). Rewards come to members of communities, but they do not motivate communal life. Indeed, they come, paradoxically, when one is not looking to receive them. In communities, caring is an end, not a means to an end (Mayerhoff, 1971, cited in Dokecki, 1992).

While scholars in the nineteenth and early twentieth centuries attributed the erosion of traditional community to such factors as industrialization and the growth of centralized bureaucracies, the list of possible culprits expanded at the end of the twentieth century. Robert Putnam (1996; 2000) assessed the roles of a plethora of factors, such as: busyness, mobility, suburbanization, the growth of two-career families (none of which he found to be very important), television viewing and other forms of electronic entertainment (somewhat important), and generational change (very important). Sampson

(1999) added to Putnam's list the fear of crime and violence. Lisbeth Schorr (1997) also noted the importance of such fears in curtailing the public participation of two important groups. The elderly, who had been the backbone of many communities in earlier times, feared leaving their houses, and children, who represented the future of a community, were kept off the streets by protective parents.

Thus, the shape of the current "breakdown of community" may differ from the breakdowns observed in bygone eras, but alongside this observation of change is an awareness of continuity. Many scholars in earlier times, and perhaps for time immemorial, have recognized the human need for community and the difficulties in fulfilling this need. We are pulled, simultaneously in two directions. The paradox of "the one and the many" reflects a fundamental dialectic in human life.

What Community Supplies . . . and Denies. An historical perspective may provide one antidote to one-sidedness. A second important consideration is the downside of communal life. Supporters of a return to community emphasize "what community supplies" (Sampson, 1999) Numerous books and articles have specified the beneficial aspects of community. We have examined a number of them throughout this book. People who are connected to their communities feel better about themselves and their lives and are less lonely (Davidson & Cotter, 1991; Pretty, Andrews, & Collett, 1994; Prezza & Constantini, 1998). They are more likely to participate in block associations, vote, communicate with government officials, and work to solve community problems (Chavis & Wandersman, 1990; Davidson & Cotter, 1989, 1993; Florin & Wandersman, 1984). Community support systems reinforce individual skills, model positive values, bring individuals into contact with supportive adults, assist families in raising their children, and provide opportunities for people to realize their strengths (e.g., Luthar, et al., 2000b; Masten & Coatsworth, 1998).

In addition to asking what community supplies, however, we might also consider what community denies (Sampson, 1999). Despite popular conceptions of community as embodying all things good, if

community were purely positive, we probably would have clung to it tighter, and lost less of it as a result. The drawback of community most central to this discussion is the limits communal life places on individual rights.

Citizens of the U.S. have little tolerance for communal obligations and social contracts. We tend to experience social institutions of all types as threats to the basic freedoms on which this country was founded (Bellah, Madsen, Sullivan, Swidler & Tipton, 1991). Since revolutionary times, people have waved flags that depict a rattlesnake poised to strike and the slogan "Don't tread on me."

The idea that social systems threaten personal liberties was at the heart of 1960s protest movements and so at the heart of community psychology, as well. In the 1960s, "the system" was viewed as the root of social problems. Protesters rejected demands for conformity and celebrated personal liberation. Psychology joined in exalting individual freedom and each person's right to self actualize (i.e., in part by removing external constraints). This view was evident in an important psychological movement of the time, humanistic psychology (see section entitled *Clinical Psychology and Community Psychology* in Chapter One).

It is yet another paradox that community lies at the center of a field that traditionally positions itself left of center. Community movements have historically been associated with the political right. Nisbet's (1953) book *The Quest for Community* was essentially a conservative argument that "ultimately aided the Republican capture of the issues of local autonomy, church, family, and community" (Forcey, 1996). Similarly, the communitarians' call for a guiding moral voice aligned the movement with politically conservative perspectives. Perhaps some of community psychology's hesitancy to embrace community can be traced to its roots in the 1960s' celebration of individual rights.

FINDING THE BALANCE

An emphasis on community can lead to conformity and repression. The interdependent relationships of social life afford benefits, but require compromises.

In his article *Self-Determination: The Tyranny of Freedom*, Barry Schwartz (2000) suggested that because the balance had shifted so far toward the pole of "the one" in the twenty-first century, even the need to compromise has become a benefit.

Schwartz observed that from the late 1960s to the late 1990s individual rights expanded to a degree unimaginable in earlier generations. The material wealth of many Americans allowed unprecedented choices. As consumers, we could choose from a wide variety of goods and services, arrayed appealingly before us by advertisers in our market economy. Mobility combined with educational opportunities to offer enormous freedom with regard to career choices—not only what to do, but where to do it. In our personal lives, mate selection was no longer confined by religious, class, geographic, or even gender barriers. After selecting a mate, we could choose when, if, and for how long to be married; whether or not to have children; the mechanism for having children; and arrangements for their care once they arrived. According to Schwartz, freedom of choice expanded to the point where it became oppressive. He posited that the emphasis on individual autonomy at the end of the twentieth century accounted for the marked increase in depression and that the best remedy for such despair was a deep commitment and belonging to social groups.

Schwartz proposed that in the twenty-first century, limits on individual rights imposed by communal responsibilities would be welcomed by many. Moreover, such limits would actually increase our freedom. We have seen elsewhere in this book that constraints on behavior can, paradoxically, promote freedom (see, for example, the discussion of the "tyranny of structurelessness" in Chapter 10). Schwartz (2000) drew an analogy to language. The capacity to use language frees people from numerous constraints. We can say anything about any time and any place anywhere and anytime. We can even talk about things that have never existed to people we do not know and still make ourselves understood. This liberating feature of language occurs only because we *cannot* say anything; We must follow grammatical rules in order to enjoy the freedoms language provides. Linguistic constraint (e.g., syntax) makes linguistic freedom possible. Schwartz argued that psychology now needs to "figure out the 'grammar' of human life choices—the set of constraints that actually enables freedom rather than impeding it" (p. 87).

⌘ Community in the Twenty-First Century

Whatever orienting concepts emerge in the future, they will need to respond to a new Zeitgeist. Can we identify trends that will likely affect community psychology in years to come? Many far-reaching societal transformations are captured by the term **globalization**. In 1995, the International Monetary Fund defined globalization as the growing "interdependence of countries worldwide through increasing volume and variety of cross-border transactions in goods and services and of international capital flows, and also through the more rapid and widespread diffusion of technology (cited in Cattaui, 1998, pp. 167–168).

In recognition of the challenges globalization poses to psychology, the *American Psychologist* inaugurated a new journal section on globalization in 1996 (Mays, Rubin, Sabourin, & Walker, 1996; see also Pawlik, & d'Ydewalle, 1996). In a contribution to this *American Psychologist* initiative, Anthony Marsella (1998) outlined the need for a "global-community psychology," and listed twenty-five forces that entail worldwide interdependence. Marsella observed, for example, that people across the globe are linked by telecommunication and the media (e.g., email, television); transportation (e.g., bullet trains and Concorde jets); economics (e.g., multinational corporations, rapid transfer of capital); the environment (e.g., pollution, global warming); terrorism (with roots at home and abroad); bacteria and viruses (e.g., HIV, Ebola); high rates of migration and large numbers of refugees. Marsella argued that human survival and well-being are now tied to global economic, political, social, and environmental conditions. We are all in this world together, like it or not.

In their book *The Good Society*, Robert Bellah and his colleagues (1991) wrote that the old meaning of freedom consisted of the right to be left alone. "In an older America, where one could spend most of one's life on one's own homestead, that kind of notion had a certain plausibility. But in the great society of today, freedom cannot mean simply getting away from other people" (Bellah, et al., 1991, p. 9). Similarly, Edward Sampson (1989) argued that in the modern era, the functional social unit shifted from the household and community to the individual. Industrialization, technology, secularism, individualism, and democracy led to a view of the individual person as disembodied, unencumbered, self-contained, detached and self-defined. Such a view may have served both U.S. society and psychology in the past, but in the postmodern information-based and globally linked world system, a new understanding of the person is required. A view of the individual as a free-standing, independent actor has become untenable, if not outright dangerous.

Indeed a view of communities or cultures as free-standing and independent is equally false (Hermans & Kempen, 1998). Bernice Johnson Reagon (1992) warned that advances of the modern era eliminated the possibility of staying in independent and isolated villages. We may need to recreate that village on a temporary basis, retreating to what Reagon called "the barred room" to feel safe, gain strength, and have a sense of home. However, our survival depends on our ability to live outside the barred rooms. Robert Putnam (2000) provided one way of thinking about the resources needed to live both within and outside of barred rooms. He distinguished between the social capital that connects people within groups, which he termed **bonding social capital**, and social capital that links a group with the outside world, which he called **bridging social capital**.

Boundaries define community. Julian Rappaport (1977) posited that a community is "a subgroup within society, which is perceived or perceives itself as distinct in some respects from the larger society" (p. 3). Within the boundaries of a community, shared values, a unified worldview, common rituals, and mutual support foster well-being and health of the members (e.g., Levine, 1998). These features, however, do not necessarily contribute to the well-being of a global, multicultural, and multinational world. Strong boundaries, such as those drawn by fundamentalist leaders, will not promote a global society in which diverse people participate freely. While our similarities bond us within groups, the well-being of larger social systems depend on ties that link people across groups.

Globalization unites people across the world, but the connections that bind us are not the same as they once were. One difference is that community no longer occurs primarily in space. Community psychologists have often distinguished between *geographic communities* and *relational communities* (e.g., Aber & Nieto, 2000; Glynn 1986; Heller, 1989a; Kuo, Sullivan, Coley, & Brunson, 1998; McMillan & Chavis, 1986; Rivlin, 1987; Shumaker & Taylor, 1983). In geographic communities, people who live in a common place share life circumstances. In relational communities, people share norms and values, common goals, and feelings of identification and trust.

Throughout the twentieth century, scholars noted that community was based less and less in geographic space (e.g., Nisbet, 1953; McKnight, 1995). Neighborhood ceased to be the hub of activities it once was (Glynn, 1986), and neighbors no longer looked primarily to each other for psychological support, recreational activities, or cultural and religious nourishment.[1] While increases in industrialization and the growth of service economies loosened the ties between people and place, globalization has dispersed them irretrievably through space.

A sense of sadness for the loss of geographic community may be fueled by memories, real or imagined, of children bicycling through tree-lined streets with playing cards flapping in the spokes of

[1]This has important implications for community practitioners—as people's social ties spread beyond geographic space, interventions at the local community level become less likely to penetrate people's important life spaces (Sampson, 1999).

their wheels, young couples sharing ice cream sodas with two straws at the local malt shop, and old men in rocking chairs laughing and whittling on grocery store porches. Despite our nostalgia for a community that may or may not have ever been, there can be no return to the past. Perhaps we are better served by a view of community as neither lost nor saved, but as transformed (Sampson, 1999).

As with most transformation, the news is neither all good nor all bad. Nongeographic communities have decided advantages over geographic ones. One advantage is that citizens can base social ties on commonalities that are more meaningful that shared space. The term **community liberated** has been coined to refer to community beyond propinquity (Wellman, 1979).

Virtual communities represent the most extreme version of community liberated. In a virtual community, relationships are built through technologically mediated exchanges (e.g., computer bulletin boards.) Community exists in cyberspace only. Virtual communities still operate as communities; they have, for example, a social contract to guide interactions (e.g., "netiquette"), but the community develops in a decidedly different way. A common interest constitutes the starting point for virtual communities, and members may or may not ever meet. This is the opposite of the process for geographic communities, where people meet each other and may or may not find a common interest that unites them (Rheingold, 1998).

Perhaps the greatest potential of electronic communication is the enhanced capacity to span intergroup, spatial, temporal, perceptual, psychological, and social boundaries in the pursuit of social connection (Wittig & Schmitz, 1996). One important advantage of virtual communities is that they can form across barriers that prohibit assembly in space. Geographically isolated people can greatly expand their social worlds through virtual communities. Physically handicapped people who find it difficult to travel can meet in cyberspace. People with stigmatized identities (e.g., gay youth) can talk with others who share that identity while remaining anonymous. Individuals with a highly specific concern or interest—parents of children with

a rare illness for example or aficionados of an esoteric art form—can create community with the handful of others across the globe who share that concern or interest.

Virtual communities also fit more easily into rushed and fragmented lives. As much as we might like to chat with a neighbor, exchanges are cut short when meetings occur in driveways and both parties are rushing to work. More purposeful meetings require coordination and persistence. Weeks of telephone tag finally lead to in-person conversations during which an agreeable dinner date is scheduled months in advance. Arranging meetings of larger groups compound the difficulties. Virtual communities are more easily accessed at any time. One can retrieve and send messages in the middle of a sleepless night or in a spare five minutes while dinner cooks.

Participants in virtual communities usually do not see each other. This, too has some advantages. Most importantly, participants cannot filter communications through false expectations and prejudices based on race, sex, age, or other physically apparent aspect of social identity. In virtual communities, the identity of the communicator is known only if she or he chooses to disclose it (and is honest). There are disadvantages to this, as well: a community member can claim to be anyone; metacommunication through facial expressions, body language, and tone does not occur; and invisibility can be disinhibiting and lead to rude and negative messaging (i.e., "flaming") (Rheingold, 1998; Sypher & Collins, 2001). Still, the lack of identifying characteristics seems to provide some sort of leveling of the field. Community members can enter into discussions without prejudging each other based on social positions and social roles.

A final advantage is that virtual communities are, at least potentially, democratic. Computer-mediated communication is a "many-to-many" phenomenon (Rheingold, 1998). Newspapers, books, television, and radio are few-to-many media: a few authors, disc jockeys, or stations broadcast messages to large audiences. Virtual communities have the potential to be democratizing in that any one node in the network can be a printing press, broadcast station, or place of assembly (Rheingold, 1998). In order to realize this democratizing potential, however, we must find ways of overcoming the **digital divide**. Not everyone has equal access to computers, which cost money and require some level of technological skill. Electronic communication has the potential to further marginalize already marginalized populations.

One innovative attempt to bridge the digital divide and democratize computer-mediated communication began in Santa Monica, California, in 1989 (Wittig & Schmitz, 1996). The city established a public electronic network (PEN) and provided free access to the network so that everyone in the city could participate, city leaders and homeless people alike. The goals of the network were to foster awareness of city programs, facilitate service delivery, provide a means for residents to share information and resources with each other and with government officials, and build community through public discourse (Sypher & Collins, 2001). PEN services included email for all users, online registration to city services (job applications, recreational class registration, petty theft reports), community bulletin boards (e.g., library events, bus schedules), and online forums and conferences on such topics as homelessness, public art, and the environment (Sypher & Collins, 2001). Research suggests that PEN succeeded in fostering links among diverse people who might not otherwise have communicated (Wittig & Schmitz, 1996). (For descriptions of other projects geared toward community building through technology, see Harrison, Zappen, Stephen, Garfield, & Prell, 2001 and Francisco, Fawcett, Schultz, Berkowitz, Wolff, & Nagy 2001).

We do not yet know if virtual communities will or will not be the ultimate network (Putnam, 2000). Some scholars see great potential for community building through computer-mediated communication. Notably, Howard Rheingold (1993) wrote a groundbreaking book in which he hailed this new technology as a way for people across the world to feed their hunger for community. Virtual communities have been celebrated as the innovation needed to reinvigorate community life in the twenty-first century. At the other extreme, authors have warned that new technologies will further isolate people and fragment fragile social ties, destroying whatever hope exists that meaningful community can be regained (e.g., Lockard, 1997; Turkle, 1996). An influential study of 256 people in 93 families during their first two years of internet use found that greater participation in the internet was associated with decreased communication among family members, a shrinking social circle, and heightened depression and loneliness (Kraut, Patterson, Lundmark, Kiesler, Mukopadhyay, & Scherlis, 1998). A middle ground position is that virtual communities do not rebuild traditional communities but complement it with alternative forms of interaction that can fill gaps in people's social lives (e.g., Sypher & Collins, 2001).

The promises and perils associated with virtual communities seem symbolic of the problems and perils associated with globalization more generally. Surely changes await us that will present formidable challenges—crises, even. Great crises pave the way, however, for unanticipated opportunities as well as dangers.

Marsella (1998) advised that globalization requires the development of "premises, methods, and practices for psychology based on multicultural, multidisciplinary, multisectoral, and multinational foundations that are global in interest, scope, relevance, and applicability" (p. 1282). That is indeed a formidable challenge. The good news is that we have resources at our disposal that our predecessors could never have imagined. In this global world, we can learn from the creative solutions to the problems of living devised by cultures around the world. We have unprecedented opportunities to expand our horizons and connect with others across, spatial, temporal, perceptual, psychological, social, and cultural boundaries. We can discover, devise, and utilize countless ways of reflecting and acting in this world, drawing on the insights of both scientific and soulful inquiries. In the realm of science, technological advances allow investigators working in different places and using a variety of innovative techniques to analyze enormous amounts of data gathered from multisite, multimeasure, longitudinal research projects from around the world in a matter of seconds. With regard to the insights of the soul, we have available to us the wisdom of all the world religions and the perceptions of great poets, musicians, and artists from across the globe.

Discussions of globalization generally focuses on the perils—if we fail to attend to globalization we shall surely perish, if not from nuclear war, then from deadly bacteria or global warming. Such avoidance motivations do not serve us well. Avoidance motivations are associated with less persistence in goal seeking, less flexibility in problem-solving, less creativity in generating solutions, poorer outcomes, and lower subjective well-being (Schneider, 2001; see the section in Chapter Seven entitled *Putting the "Health" Back into Mental Health*). If we read the future as doomsayers, we will not capitalize on our unprecedented opportunities. Furthermore, we risk causing the very situation we most fear. As Leonard Duhl (1985) warned, "A human race that believes it is drifting fatally and inevitably toward the destruction of life will destroy life" (p. 8).

Surely there exists in the configurations of birds in flight, oil on water, or whatever other signpost of the future we manage to glimpse, reasons for hope as well as fear. Duhl suggested that if we believe in our destruction, we will destroy life. It would follow, then, that if we believe in the irrepressible, creative, and fundamentally life-affirming human spirit, we will not only survive in the world of tomorrow, we will thrive.

Action Agenda

Gifts Interview

For this final Action Agenda exercise, consider the appeal made by the poet–activist Audre Lorde (1984) in a talk given at Harvard University entitled *Learning from the 60s*:

> To refuse to participate in the shaping of our future is to give up. Do not be misled into passivity either by false security (they don't mean me) or by despair (there's nothing we can do). Each of us must find our work and do it. (p. 141)

In reporting on the progress of community assets assessments, John Kretzmann (1995) observed that some communities had developed a "gifts interview." The gifts interview seems a helpful way of responding to Lorde's plea.

Either on your own or in dialogue with classmates, consider the gifts you have to bring to this world. Reflect on three domains. What are your "gifts of the head?" For example, where does your knowledge lie? What are your "gifts of the hand?" What skills do you have? Finally, what are your "gifts of the heart?" Where do your spirit, your values, and your commitment lie? How might you imagine using these gifts in your communities? (Kretzmann, 1995)

 **Key Terms**

bonding social capital
bridging social capital
communitarianism
community liberated
dialectic

digital divide
globalization
paradox of the one and the many
virtual communities

References

Abdul-Adil, J. K., & Jason, L. A. (1991). Community psychology and Al-Islam: A religious framework for social change. *Community Psychologist, 25 (1)*, 28–30.

Aber, M. S., & Nieto, M. (2000). Suggestions for the investigation of psychological wellness in the neighborhood context:. In D. Cicchetti, J. Rappaport, I. Sandler, & R. P. Weissberg (Eds.), *The promotion of wellness in children and adolescents* (pp. 185–219). Washington, D.C.: CWLA Press.

Abramson, L. Y., Seligman, M. E. P., & Teasdale, J. D. (1978). Learned helplessness in humans: Critique and reformulation. *Journal of Abnormal Psychology, 87*, 49–74.

ACT UP (1990). ACT UP/New York 1990. Retrieved September 6, 2000 from ***http://www.actupny.org/documents/cron-90.html***.

ACT UP (No Date). (Mission). Retrieved September 6, 2000 from ***http://www.actupny.org***.

Adams, P., & Nelson, K. (1995). (Eds.). *Reinventing human services: Community and family centered practice*. New York: Aldine de Gruyter.

Adelson, D., & Kalis, B. L. (1970). Introduction—The emergence of community psychology: A question of models. In D. Adelson & B. L. Kalis (Eds.), *Community psychology and mental health: Perspectives and challenges* (pp. 1–4). Scranton, PA: Chandler Publishing Co.

Administration for Children and Families (ACF) (2000, Dec. 6). New statistics show only small percentage of eligible families receive child care help. *HHS News*. Retrieved April 12, 2001 from ***http://www.acf.hhs.gov/news/news_bk/press/2000/ccstudy.htm***.

Agosín, M. (1996). *Tapestries of hope, threads of love: The arpillera movement in Chile, 1974–1994*. Albuquerque: University of New Mexico Press.

Aguilera, D.C., & Messick, J. M. (1974). *Crisis intervention: Theory and methodology*. New York: Mosby.

Ahlquist, R. (1992). Manifestations of inequality: Overcoming resistance in a multicultural foundations course. In C. A. Grant (Ed.), *Research and multicultural education: From the margins to the mainstream* (pp. 89–106). London: The Falmer Press.

Ainsworth, M. D., & Bell, S. M. (1974). Mother–infant interaction and the development of competence. In K. Connelly & J. Bruner (Eds.), *The growth of competence* (pp. 97–118). New York: Academic Press.

Albee, G. W. (1959). *Mental health manpower trends*. New York: Basic Books.

Albee, G. W. (1980). A competency model to replace the defect model. In M. S. Gibbs, J. R. Lachenmeyer, & J. Sigal (Eds.), *Community psychology: Theoretical and empirical approaches* (pp. 213–238). New York: Gardner Press, Inc.

Albee, G. W. (1981). Politics, power, prevention, and social change. In J. M. Joffe & G. W. Albee (Eds.), *Prevention through political action and social change* (pp. 3–24). Hanover, NH: University Press of New England.

Albee, G. W. (1982). Preventing psychopathology and promoting human potential. *American Psychologist, 37*, 1043–1050.

Albee, G. W. (1986). Toward a just society: Lessons from observations on the primary prevention of psychopathology. *American Psychologist, 41*, 891–898.

Albee, G. W. (1996). Revolutions and counterrevolutons in prevention. *American Psychologist, 51*, 1130–1133.

Albee, G. W., & Gullotta, T. P. (Eds.) (1997). *Primary prevention works*. Thousand Oaks, CA: Sage.

Alcade, J., & Walsh-Bowers, R. (1996). Community psychology values and the culture of graduate training: A self study. *American Journal of Community Psychology, 24*, 389–411.

Alcoholics Anonymous (1999a). Membership. Retrieved August 7, 2000, from ***http://www.alcoholics-anonymous.org/english/E_FactFile/M-24_d4.html***.

Alcoholics Anonymous (1999b). The twelve steps of Alcoholics Anonymous. Retrieved August 7, 2000, from ***http://www.alcoholics-anonymous.org/english/E_FactFile/M-24_d6.html***.

Alcoholics Anonymous (1999c). The twelve traditions of Alcoholics Anonymous. Retrieved August 7, 2000, from ***http://www.alcoholics-anonymous.org/english/E_FactFile/M-24_d7.html***

Alcoholics Anonymous (2000a). Membership. Retrieved February 15, 2000, from ***http://www.alcoholics-anonymous.org/english/E_FactFile/M-24_d4.html***.

Alcoholics Anonymous (2000b). Historical data: The birth of AA and its growth in U.S./Canada. Retrieved February 15, 2000, from ***http://www.alcoholics-anonymous.org/english/E_FactFile/M-24_d14.html***.

Alinsky, S. D. (1971). *Rules for radicals*. New York: Vintage.

Allen, J. P., Hauser, S. T., Bell, K. L., & O'Connor, T. G. (1994). Longitudinal assessment of autonomy and relatedness in adolescent–family interactions as predictors of adolescent ego development and self-esteem. *Child Development, 65*, 179–194.

Alloy, L. B., & Abramson, L. Y. (1979). Judgment of contingency in depressed and nondepressed students: Sadder but wiser. *Journal of Experimental Psychology: General, 108,* 441–485.

Allport, G. W. (1954). *The nature of prejudice.* Reading, MA: Addison-Wesley.

Allport, G. W. (1950). *The individual and his religion: A psychological interpretation.* New York: MacMillan.

Allport, G. W., & Ross, J. M. (1967). Personal religious orientation and prejudice. *Journal of Personality and Social Psychology, 5,* 432–443.

Altman, I., & Wandersman, A. (1987) (Eds.). *Neighborhood and community environments.* New York: Plenum Press.

American Psychological Association (1992). APA Ethical Principles of Psychologists and Code of Conduct. Retrieved September 15, 1999, from ***http://www.apa.org/ethics/code.html.***

American Psychological Association (1994). *Publication manual of the American Psychological Association (4th ed.).* Washington, D.C.: American Psychological Association.

American Psychological Association (2000). APA's resources for the public: What you need to know about gay, lesbian, and bisexual issues. Retrieved August 24, 2000, from ***http://www.apa.org/psychnet/lgbc.html.***

American Psychological Association Research Office (1999). *Membership characteristics of APA members by race/ethnicity, 1999* (Table 5). Washington, D.C.: APA.

Amir, Y. (1969). Contact hypothesis in ethnic relations. *Psychological Bulletin, 71,* 319–342.

Ander-Egg, E. (1980). *Metodológica y práctica del desarrollo de comunidad.* Madrid: Ed. Universitaria Europea.

Anderson, K. B., Cooper, H., & Okamura, L. (1997). Individual differences and attitudes toward rape: A meta-analytic review. *Personality and Social Psychology Bulletin, 23,* 295–315.

Anderson, V. N. (1992). For whom is this world just? Sexual orientation and AIDS. *Journal of Applied Social Psychology, 22 (3),* 248–259.

Angelique, H. L. & Culley, M. R. (2000). Searching for feminism: An analysis of community psychology literature relevant to women's concerns. *American Journal of Community Psychology, 28,* 793–813.

Anthony, E. J. (1974). The syndrome of the psychologically invulnerable child. In E. J. Anthony & C. Koupernik (Eds.), *The child in his family: Children at psychiatric risk.* New York: Wiley.

Anthony, E. J. (1987). Risk, vulnerability, and resilience: An overview. In E. J. Anthony & B. J. Cohler (Eds.), *The invulnerable child.* New York: Guilford Press.

Archer, R. P., & Amuso, K. F. (1980). Comparisons of staff's and clients' perceptions of ward atmosphere. *Psychological Reports, 46,* 959–965.

Argyris, C., Putnam, R., & Smith, D. M. (1985). *Action science.* San Francisco: Jossey-Bass.

Aronson, E. (1978). *The jigsaw classroom.* Beverly Hills, CA: Sage.

Aronson, E., & Bridgeman, D. (1979). Jigsaw groups and the desegregated classroom: In pursuit of common goals. *Personality and Social Psychology Bulletin, 5,* 438–446.

Aronson, E., & Thibodeau, R. (1992). The jigsaw classroom: A cooperative strategy for reducing prejudice. In J. Lynch, C. Modgil, & S. Modgil (Eds.), *Cultural diversity in the schools.* London: Falmer Press.

Aronson, E., Wilson, T. D., & Akert, R. M. (1997). *Social psychology (2nd ed.).* New York: Longman.

Asch, S. E. (1951). Effects of group pressure upon the modification and distortion of judgment. In H. Guetzkow (Ed.), *Groups, leadership, and men.* Pittsburgh: Carnegie Press.

Asch, S. E. (1955). Opinions and social pressure. *Scientific American, 193,* 31–35.

Asch, S. E. (1956). Studies of independence and conformity: A minority of one against a unanimous majority. *Psychological Monographs No. 416, 70 (9).*

Austin, D. M. (2000). Greeting the second century: A forward look from a historical perspective. In J. G. Hopps & R. Morris (Eds.), *Social work at the millennium: Critical reflections on the future of the profession* (pp. 18–41). New York: Free Press.

Babock, M., & McKay, M. C. (Eds.). (1995). *Challenging codependency: Feminist critiques.* Toronto, ON, Canada: University of Toronto Press.

Bachman, J. G., & O'Malley, P. M. (1984). Yes-saying, nay-saying, and going to extremes: Black–white differences in response styles. *Public Opinion Quarterly, 48,* 491–509.

Bailey, J. (1991). The spirituality of 12-step programs. *St. Anthony's Messenger,* 23–27.

Balcazar, F. E. (1999). Lessons from liberation theology. *The Community Psychologist, 32 (3),* 19–23.

Baldwin, J. (1985). The Creative Process. In *The price of the ticket: Collected non-fiction, 1948–1985* (pp. 1–4). New York: St. Martin's Press.

Baltes, P. B. (1987). Theoretical propositions of life-span developmental psychology: On the dynamics between growth and decline. *Developmental Psychology, 23,* 611–626.

Bandura, A. (1997). *Self-efficacy: The exercise of control.* New York: W. H. Freeman and Company.

Bank, B. J., & Hall, P. M. (1997). *Gender, equity, and schooling: Policy and practice.* New York: Garland Publishing, Inc.

Barakat, M. (2000, July 4). Women continue to narrow pay gap. New York: Associated Press Retrieved August 16, 2000, from ***http://www.pioneerplanet.com/80/seven-days/7/business/docs/031696.htm.***

Barbour, I. (1974). *Myths, models, and paradigms.* New York: Harper and Row.

Barker, R. G. (1964). *Big school, small school; High school size and student behavior*. Stanford, CA: Stanford University Press.

Barker, R. G. (1965). Explorations in ecological psychology. *American Psychologist, 20*, 1–14.

Barker, R. G. (1968). *Ecological psychology*. Stanford, CA: Stanford University Press.

Barker, R. G., & Schoggen, P. (1973). Qualities of community life: *Methods of measuring environment and behavior applied to an American and an English town*. San Francisco: Jossey-Bass.

Barnett, S. W. (2000). Economics of early childhood intervention. In J. P. Shonkoff & S. J. Meisels (Eds.), *Handbook of early childhood intervention* (pp. 589–610). New York: Cambridge University Press.

Barocas, R., Seifer, R., & Sameroff, A. J. (1985). Defining environmental risk: Multiple dimensions of psychological vulnerability. *American Journal of Community Psychology, 13 (4)*, 433–447.

Baron, R. M., & Kenny, D. A. (1986). The moderator–mediator variable distinction in social psychological research: Conceptual, strategic, and statistical considerations. *Journal of Personality and Social Psychology, 51*, 1173–1182.

Barreca, R. (1991). *They used to call me Snow White but I drifted: Women's strategic use of humor*. New York: Viking.

Barrera, M. Jr., & Prelow, H. (2000). Inteventions to promote social support in children and adolescents. In D. Cicchetti, J. Rappaport, I. Sandler, & R. P. Weissberg (Eds.), *The promotion of wellness in children and adolescents* (pp. 309–340). Washington, D.C.: CWLA Press.

Barrera, M. Jr., Li, S. A., & Chassin, L. (1995). Effects of parental alcoholism and life stress on Hispanic and non-Hispanic Caucasian adolescents: A prospective study. *American Journal of Community Psychology, 23*, 479–507.

Barrera, M., Jr. (1986). Distinctions between social support concepts, measures, and models. *American Journal of Community Psychology, 14*, 413–445.

Barrett, M. B. (1990). *Invisible lives: The truth about millions of women-loving women*. New York: Harper and Row.

Bateson, G. (1972). *Steps to an ecology of the mind*. New York: Ballantine.

Baumeister, R. F., Stillwell, A., & Wotman, S. R. (1990). Victim and perpetrator accounts of interpersonal conflict: Autobiographical narratives about anger. *Journal of Personality and Social Psychology, 59*, 994–1005.

Baumrind, D. (1971). Current patterns of parental authority. *Developmental Psychology Monograph, 4, (1, Part 2)*.

Bazelon, D. L. (1982). Veils, values, and social responsibility. *American Psychologist, 37*, 115–121.

Beardslee, W. R., & Podorefsky, D. (1988). Resilient adolescents whose parents have serious affective disorders: Importance of self-understanding and relationships. *American Journal of Psychiatry, 145 (1)*, 63–69.

Becker, C. (Ed.). (1994). *The subversive imagination: Artists, society, and social responsibility*. New York: Routledge.

Becker, H. S. (1963). *Outsiders*. New York: Free Press.

Belenky, M. F., Clinchy, B., Goldberger, N. R., & Tarule, J. M. (1986). *Women's ways of knowing: The development of self, voice, and mind*. New York: Basic Books.

Bellah, R. N., Madsen, R., Sullivan, W. M., Swidler, A., & Tipton, S. M. (1985). *Habits of the heart: Individualism and commitment in American life*. New York: Harper and Row.

Bellah, R. N., Madsen, R., Sullivan, W. M., Swidler, A., & Tipton, S. M. (1991). *The good society*. New York: Alfred A. Knopf.

Belle, D. (1982). The stress of caring: Women as providers of support. In L. Goldberger & S. Breznitz (Eds.), *Handbook of stress: Theoretical and clinical aspects* (pp. 496–505). New York: Free Press.

Belsky, J. (1980). Child maltreatment: An ecological integration. *American Psychologist, 35*, 320–335.

Belsky, J. (1995). Expanding the ecology of human development: An evolutionary perspective. In P. Moen, G. H. Elder, & K. Lüscher (Eds.), *Examining lives in context: Perspectives on the ecology of human development*. Washington, D.C.: American Psychological Association.

Bem, S. L. (1975). Sex role adaptability: One consequence of psychological androgyny. *Journal of Personality and Social Psychology, 31*, 634–643.

Ben and Jerry's (2000). Statement of mission. Retrieved December 15, 2000, from ***http://www.benjerry.com/ mission.html***.

Bennett, C. C., Anderson, L. S., Cooper, S., Hassol, L., Klein, D.C., & Rosenblum, G. (1966). *Community psychology: A report of the Boston Conference on the Education of Psychologists for Community Mental Health*. Boston: Boston University.

Berger, P. J., & Neuhaus, R. J. (1977). *To empower people: The role of mediating structures in public policy*. Washington, D.C.: American Enterprise Institute for Public Policy Research.

Bergin, A. E., & Jensen, J. (1990). Religiosity of psychotherapists: A national survey. *Psychotherapy, 27*, 3–7.

Bergin, A. E., Payne, I. R., & Richards, P. S. (1996). Values in psychotherapy. In E. P. Shafranske (Ed.), *Religion and the clinical practice of psychology* (pp. 297–325). Washington, D.C.: APA.

Berkman, L. F., & Glass T. (2000). Social integration, social networks, social support, and health. In L. F. Berkman & I. Kawachi (Eds.), *Social epidemiology* (pp. 137–174). New York: Oxford University Press.

Berkowitz, B. (1987). (Ed.). Lois Gibbs: Citizen's Clearinghouse for Hazardous Wastes. *Local heroes* (pp. 109–122). Lexington, MA: Lexington Books.

Berkowitz, B. (1996). Personal and community sustainability. *American Journal of Community Psychology, 24,* 441–460.

Berkowitz, B. (2000a). The community psychologist as citizen. In. J. Rappaport & E. Seidman (Eds.), *Handbook of community psychology* (pp. 764–767). New York: Kluwer Academic/Plenum Publishers.

Berkowitz, B. (2000b). Community and neighborhood organization. In J. Rappaport & E. Seidman (Eds.), *Handbook of community psychology* (pp. 331–357). New York: Kluwer Academic/Plenum Publishers.

Berkowitz, B. (2001). Studying the outcomes of community-based coalitions. *American Journal of Community Psychology, 29,* 213–227.

Berkowitz, B., & Wolff, T. (1996). Rethinking social action and community empowerment: A dialogue. In M. B. Lykes, A. Banuazizi, R. Liem, & M. Morris (Eds.), *Myths about the powerless: Contesting social inequalities* (pp. 296–316). Philadelphia: Temple University Press.

Bernal, G., & Enchautegui-de-Jesus, N. (1994). Latinos and latinas in community psychology: A review of the literature. *American Journal of Community Psychology, 22,* 531–557.

Bernard, J. A. (1998). Cultural competence plans: A strategy for the creation of a culturally competent system of care. In M. Hernandez & M. R. Isaacs (Eds.), *Promoting cultural competence in children's mental health services* (pp. 29–46). Baltimore: Paul H. Brookes Publishing Co.

Berry, J. W., & Kim, U. (1993). The way ahead: From indigenous psychologies to a universal psychology. In U. Kim & J. W. Berry (Eds.), *Indigenous psychologies: Research and experience in cultural context.* (pp. 277–280). Newbury Park, CA: Sage.

Berscheid, E. (1992). A glance back at a quarter of a century of social psychology. *Journal of Personality and Social Psychology, 63,* 525–533.

Betancourt, H., & Lopez, S. R. (1993). The study of culture, ethnicity, and race in American psychology. *American Psychologist, 48,* 629–637.

Biglan, A., & Taylor, T. K. (2000). Why have we been more successful in reducing tobacco use than violent crime? *American Journal of Community Psychology. 28,* 269–302.

Biklen, D. P. (1983). *Community organizing: Theory and practice.* Englewood Cliffs, NJ: Prentice Hall.

Biko, S. (1978). *Steve Biko: Black consciousness in South Africa.* M. Arnold (Ed.). New York: Random House.

Billingsley, A. (1968). *Black families in white America.* Englewood Cliffs, NJ: Prentice Hall.

Billingsley, A. (1999). *Mighty like a river: The Black church and social reform.* New York: Oxford University Press, 1999.

Birman, D. (1994). Acculturation and human diversity in multicultural society. In E. J. Trickett, R. J. Watts, & D. Birman (Eds.), *Human diversity: Perspectives on people in context* (pp. 261–284). San Francisco: Jossey-Bass.

Black, M. M., & Krishnakumar, A. (1998). Children in low-income, urban settings. *American Psychologist, 53,* 635–646.

Blau, P. M. (1964). *Exchange and power in social life.* New York: Wiley.

Block, M., & Zautra, A. (1981). Satisfaction and distress in a community: A test of the effects of life events. *American Journal of Community Psychology, 9,* 165–180.

Bloom, B. L. (1963). Definitional aspects of the crisis concept. *Journal of Consulting Psychology, 27,* 498–502.

Bloom, B. L. (1979). Prevention of mental disorder: Recent advances in theory and practice. *Community Mental Health Journal, 15,* 179–191.

Bloom, L. (1993). *The transition from infancy to language: Acquiring the power of expression.* Cambridge: Cambridge University Press.

Bloom, M. (1993). Toward a code of ethics for primary prevention. *Journal of Primary Prevention 13*(3), 173–182.

Bohan, J. S. (1995). *Re-placing women in psychology: Readings toward a more inclusive history (2nd edition).* Dubuque, IA: Kendall/Hunt.

Bok, M. (1992). *Civil rights and the social programs of the 1960s.* Westport, CT: Praeger.

Bolin, R. (1993). Natural and technological disasters: Evidence of psychopathology. In A-M. Ghadirian & H. E. Lehmann (Eds.), *Environment and psychopathology* (pp. 121–140). New York: Springer.

Bolin, R., & Stanford, L. (1990). Shelter and housing issues in Santa Cruz County. In R. Bolin (Ed.), *The Loma Prieta Earthquake: Studies of short-term impacts.* (pp. 99–108). Boulder, CO: University of Colorado.

Bond, L. A., Belenky, M. F., & Weinstock, J. S. (2000). The Listening Partners Program: An initiative toward feminist community psychology in action. *American Journal of Community Psychology, 28,* 697–730.

Bond, L., & Compas, B. (Eds.) (1989). Primary prevention and promotion in the schools. Newbury Park, CA: Sage.

Bond, M. A. (1990). Defining the research relationship: Maximizing participation in an unequal world. In P. Tolan, C. Keys, F. Chertok, & L. Jason (Eds.), *Researching community psychology: Issues of theory and methods* (pp. 183–186). Washington, D.C.: American Psychological Association.

Bond, M. A. (1999). Gender, race, and class in organizational contexts. *American Journal of Community Psychology, 27,* 327–355.

Bond, M. A., & Keys, C. B. (1993). Empowerment, diversity, and collaboration: Promoting synergy on community boards. *American Journal of Community Psychology, 23,* 37–57.

Bond, M. A., & Pyle, J. L. (1998). Diversity dilemmas at work. *Journal of Management Inquiry, 7* (3), 252–269.

Bond, M. A., Hill, J., Mulvey, A., & Terenzio, M. (2000). (Eds). Special issue: Feminism and community psychology. *American Journal of Community Pyschology, 28,* 759–909.

Booth, J., & Martin, J. E. (1998). Spiritual and religious factors in substance use, dependence, and recovery. In H. G. Koenig (Ed.), *Handbook of religion and mental health* (pp. 175–200). San Diego: Academic Press.

BootsMiller, B. J., Davidson, W. S., Luke, D. A., Mowbray, C. T., Ribisl, K. M., & Herman, S. E. (1997). Social climate differences in a large psychiatric hospital: Staff and client observations. *Journal of Community Psychology, 25,* 325–336.

Borque, L. B., & Back, K. W. (1977). Life graphs and life events. *Journal of Gerontology, 32,* 669–674.

Boskin, J. (1997). African-American humor: Resistance and retaliation. In J. Boskin (Ed.), *The humor prism in 20th century America* (pp. 145–158). Detroit: Wayne State University Press.

Bowlby, J. (1961). Process of mourning. *The International journal of Psychoanalysis, 42,* 317–340.

Bowlby, J. (1969). *Attachment and loss (Vol. 1, Attachment).* New York: Basic Books.

Boyer, E. L. (1990). *Scholarship reconsidered: Priorities of the professorate.* Princeton: Carnegie Foundation for the Advancement of Teaching.

Boykin, A. W., & Toms, F. (1985). Black child socialization: A conceptual framework. In H. McAdoo & J. McAdoo (Eds.), *Black children: Social, educational, and parental environments* (pp. 33–52). Newbury Park, CA: Sage.

Brashears, F., & Roberts, M. (1996). The Black church as a resource for change. In S. L. Logan (Ed.), *The Black family: Strengths, self-help, and positive change* (pp. 181–192). Boulder, CO: Westview Press.

Bravo, M., Rubio-Stipec, M., Canino, G. J., Woodbury, M. A., & Ribera J. C. (1990). The psychological sequelae of disaster stress prospectively and retrospectively evaluated. *American Journal of Community Psychology, 18,* 661–680.

Brennan, B. (2000). National. Moving to opportunity research. Retrieved August 29, 2001, from ***http://www.wws.princeton.edu/~kling/mto/national.htm***.

Brewer, M. B. (1979). In-group bias in the minimal intergroup situation: A cognitive-motivational analysis. *Psychological Bulletin, 86,* 307–324.

Brewer, M. B. (1999). The psychology of prejudice: Ingroup love or outgroup hate? *Journal of Social Issues, 55,* 429–444.

Brickman, P., Rabinowitz, V. C., Karuza, J., Coates, D., Cohn, E., & Kidder, L. (1982). Models of helping and coping. *American Psychologist, 37,* 368–384.

Brody, J. G. (1986). Community psychology in the eighties: A celebration of survival. *American Journal of Community Psychology, 14 (2),* 139–145.

Bronfenbrenner, U., & Ceci, S. J. (1994). Nature–nurture reconceptualized in developmental perspective: A bioecological model. *Psychological Review, 101,* 568–586.

Bronfenbrenner, U. (1977). Toward an experimental ecology of human development. *American Psychologist, 32,* 513–531.

Bronfenbrenner, U. (1979). *The ecology of human development: Experiments by nature and design.* Cambridge, MA: Harvard University Press.

Bronzaft, A. L., & McCarthy, D. P. (1975). The effects of elevated train noise on reading ability. *Environment and Behavior, 7,* 517–527.

Brookins, C. C. (1996). Promoting ethnic identity development in African American youth: The role of rites of passage. *Journal of Black Psychology, 22 (3),* 388–417.

Brookins, C. C., & Robinson, T. L. (1995). Rites-of-passage as resistance to oppression. *The Western Journal of Black Studies, 19 (3),* 172–181.

Brooks, D., & Goble, F. G. (1997). The case for character education: The role of the school in teaching values and virtues. Northridge, CA: Studio 4 Productions.

Brooks-Gunn, J., Duncan, G. J., Klebanov, P. K., & Sealand, N. (1993). Do neighborhoods influence child and adolescent behavior? *American Journal of Sociology, 99,* 353–395.

Broverman, I. K., Broverman, D. M., Clarkson, F. E., Rosenkrantz, P. S., & Vogel, S. R. (1970). Sex-role stereotypes and clinical judgments of mental health. *Journal of Consulting and Clinical Psychology, 34,* 1–7.

Brown, D. G. (1957). Masculinity–femininity development in children. *Journal of Counseling and Consulting Psychology, 21,* 197–202.

Brown, H. P., & Peterson, J. H. (1991). Assessing spirituality in addition to treatment and follow-up: Development of the Brown-Peterson Recovery Progress Inventory (B-PRI). *Alcoholism Treatment Quarterly, 8,* 21–50.

Brown, J. D. (1991). Staying fit and staying well: Physical fitness as a moderator of life stress. *Journal of Personality and Social Psychology, 60,* 555–561.

Brown, L. S. (1994). *Subversive dialogue: Theory in feminist therapy.* New York: Basic Books.

Brown, L. S. (1997). Ethics in psychology: Cui bono? In D. Fox & I. Prilleltensky (Eds.), *Critical psychology: An introduction.* (pp. 51–67). London: Sage.

Brown, L., & Tandon, R. (1983). Ideology and political economy in inquiry: Action research and participatory research. *Journal of Applied Behavioral Science, 19,* 277–294.

Brown, P. (1995). The role of the evaluator in comprehensive community initiatives. In J. P. Connell, A. C. Kubisch, L. B. Schorr, & C. H. Weiss (Eds.), *New approaches to Evaluating community initiatives, Vol. 1: Concepts, methods, and contexts.* Washington, D.C.: The

Aspen Institute. Retrieved August 28, 2001, from *http://www.aspenroundtable.org/vol1/brown.htm*.

Brown, R. (1986). *Social psychology, 2nd edition*. New York: The Free Press.

Brownmiller, S. (1975). *Against our will: Men, women, and rape*. New York: Simon & Schuster.

Buber, M. (1958). *I and Thou*. Translated by R. G. Smith. Edinburgh: T and T Clark.

Buhrke, R., Ben-Ezra, L., Hurley, M., & Ruprecht, L. (1992). Content analysis and methodological critique of articles concerning lesbian and gay male issues in counseling journals. *Journal of Counseling Psychology, 39*, 91–99.

Bunkers, S. L. (1997). Why are these women laughing? The power and politics of women's humor. In J. Boskin (Ed.), *The humor prism in 20th century America* (pp. 159–171). Detroit: Wayne State University Press.

Burger, J. M. (1981). Motivational biases in the attribution of responsibility for an accident: Meta-analysis of the defensive-attribution hypothesis. *Psychological Bulletin, 90*, 462–512.

Burgess, L. (1990). A block association president's perspective on citizen participation and research. *American Journal of Community Psychology, 18*, 159–162.

Burnette, E. (1997). Learning about behavior by studying the environment. *APA Monitor*, July 2, 1997.

Burt, C. E., Cohen, L. C., & Bjork, J. P. (1988). Perceived family environment as a moderator of young adolescents' life stress adjustment. *American Journal of Community Psychology, 16 (1)*, 101–122.

Butterfoss, F. D., Goodman, R. M., & Wandersman, A. (1996). Community coalitions for prevention and health promotion: Factors predicting satisfaction, participation, and panning. *Health Education Quarterly, 23*, 65–79.

Buxton, M. E., Smith, D. E., & Seymour, R. B. (1987). Spirituality and other points of resistance to the 12-step recovery process. *Journal of Psychoactive Drugs, 19*, 275–286.

Byrne, D. G., & Whyte, H. M. (1980). Life events and myocardial infraction revisited: The role of measures of individual impact. *Psychosomatic Medicine, 42*, 1–10.

Cairns, E., & Darby, J. (1998). The conflict in Northern Ireland: Causes, consequences, and controls. *American Psychologist, 53*, 754–760.

Cairns, R. B., Gariepy, J. L., & Hood, K. E. (1990). Development, microevolution, and social behavior. *Psychological Review, 97*, 49–65.

Caldwell, C. H., Jackson, J. S., Tucker, M. B., & Bowman, P. J. (1999). Culturally-competent research methods. In R. L. Jones (Ed.), *Advances in African American psychology* (pp. 101–126). Hampton, VA: Cobb and Henry Publishers.

Campbell, R., Angelique, H., BootsMiller, B. J., & Davidson, W. S., III (2000). Practicing what we preach: Integrating community psychology into the job search process. In C. R. O'Donnell & J. R. Ferrari (Eds.), *Employment in community psychology: The diversity of opportunity* (pp. 33–43). Binghamton, NY: Haworth Press.

Campbell, R., Baker, C. K., Mazurek, T. L. (1998). Remaining radical? Organizational predictors of rape crisis centers' social change initiatives. *American Journal of Community Psychology, 26*, 457–483.

Campbell, R., Sefl, T., Barnes, H. E., Ahrens, C. E., Wasco, S. M., & Zaragoza-Diesfeld, Y. (1999). Community services for rape survivors: Enhancing psychological well-being or increasing trauma? *Journal of Consulting and Clinical Psychology, 67*, 847–858.

Cantor, M. H. (1979). Neighbors and friends: An overlooked resource in the informal support system. *Research on Aging, 1*, 434–463.

Caplan, G. (1961). *An approach to community mental health*. New York: Grune and Stratton.

Caplan, G. (1964). *Principles of preventive psychiatry*. New York: Basic Books.

Caplan, G. (1970). *The theory and practice of mental health consultation*. New York: Basic Books.

Caplan, G. (1974). *Support systems and community mental health*. New York: Behavioral Publications.

Caplan, G. (1976). The family as a support system. In G. Caplan & M. Killilea (Eds.), *Support systems and mutual help*. New York: Grune and Stratton.

Caplan, N., & Nelson, S. D. (1973). On being useful: The nature and consequences of psychological research on social problems. *American Psychologist, 28*, 199–211.

Capra, F. (1982). *The turning point: Science, society, and rising culture*. New York: Simon & Schuster.

Champagne, A., & Nagel, S. S. (1983). Law and social change. In E. Seidman (Ed.), *Handbook of social intervention* (pp. 187–211). Beverly Hills: Sage.

Caroselli, M. (1998). *Empower yourself!* New York: AMACOM.

Cassel, J. (1974). Psychosocial processes and "stress": Theoretical formulations. *International Journal of Health Services, 4*, 471–482.

Cattaui, M. L. (1998). Opportunities in the global economy. In F. Hesselbein, M. Goldsmith, R. Beckhard, & R. F. Schubert (Eds.), *The community of the future* (pp. 167–174). San Francisco: Jossey-Bass.

Cauce, A. M. (1990). A cautionary note about adventuresome research: Musings of a junior researcher. In P. Tolan, C. Keys, F. Chertok, & L. Jason (Eds.), *Researching community psychology: Issues of theory and methods* (pp. 205–209). Washington, D.C.: American Psychological Association.

Cauce, A. M., Coronado, N., & Watson, J. (1998). Conceptual, methodological, and statistical issues in culturally competent research. In M. Hernandez & M. R. Isaacs (Eds.), *Promoting cultural competence in children's mental health services* (pp. 305–329). Baltimore: Paul H. Brookes Publishing Co.

Center for Health and Environmental Justice (2000a). A history of the Love Canal. Retrieved June 10, 2000, from *http://www.chej.org/lcsum.html*.

Center for Health and Environmental Justice (2000b). Who we are. Retrieved June 10, 2000, from *http://www.chej.org/cchwinf.html*.

Center for Substance Abuse Prevention (CSAP). (1993). *National evaluation of the Community Partnership Demonstration Grant Program: Third annual report.* Rockville, MD: Substance Abuse and Mental Health Services Administration, U.S. Department of Health and Human Services.

Challener, D. D. (1997). *Stories of resilience in childhood: The narratives of Maya Angelou, Maxine Hong Kingston, Richard Rodriguez, John Edgar Wideman, and Tobias Wolff.* New York: Graland.

Chalmers, D. M. (1996). *And the crooked places made straight: The struggle for social change in the 1960s (2nd ed.).* Baltimore: The Johns Hopkins University Press.

Chase-Lansdale, P. L., Cherlin, A. J., & Kiernan, K. E. (1995). The long-term effects of parental divorce on the mental health of young adults: A developmental perspective. *Child Development, 66,* 1614–1634.

Chavis, D. M. (1993). A future for community psychology practice. *American Journal of Community Psychology, 21,* 171–181.

Chavis, D. M. (2000). Community development and the community psychologist. In J. Rappaport & E. Seidman (Eds.), *Handbook of community psychology* (pp. 767–771). New York: Kluwer Academic/Plenum Publishers.

Chavis, D. M. (2001).The paradoxes and promise of community coalitions. *American Journal of Community Psychology, 29,* 309–320.

Chavis, D. M., & Newbrough, J. R. (1986). The meaning of "community" in community psychology. *Journal of Community Psychology, 14,* 335–340.

Chavis, D. M., Stucky, P., & Wandersman, A. (1983). Returning basic research to the community: A relationship between scientists and citizens. *American Psychologist, 38,* 424–434.

Chavis, D. M., & Wandersman, A. (1990). Sense of community in the urban environment: A catalyst for participation and community development. *American Journal of Community Psychology, 18,* 55–81.

Chemers, M., Oskamp, S., & Constanzo, M. (1995). *Diversity in organizations: New perspectives for changing workplace.* Thousand Oaks, CA: Sage.

Cherniss, C. (1980). *Professional burnout in human service organizations.* New York: Praeger.

Cherniss, C., & Deegan, G. (2000). The creation of alternative settings. In J. Rappaport & E. Seidman (Eds.), *Handbook of community psychology* (pp. 359–377). New York: Kluwer Academic/Plenum Publishers.

Chesler, P. (1972/1989). *Women and madness.* San Diego: Harcourt Brace Jovanovich.

Chess, S. (1989). Defying the voice of doom. In T. Dugan & R. Coles (Eds.), *The child in our times* (pp. 179–199). New York: Brunner/Mazel.

Children's Defense Fund (2000). Key facts about child poverty. Retrieved September 4, 2001, from *http://childrensdefensefund.org/fairstart-faqs.htm*.

Chiriboga, D. A. (1978). Life event weighting systems: A comparative analysis. *Journal of Psychosomatic Research, 21,* 415–422.

Choi, S., & Gopnick, A. (1995). Early acquisition of verbs in Korean: A cross-linguistic study. *Journal of Child Language, 22 (3),* 497–529.

Chrislip, D., & Larson, C. (1994). *Collaborative leadership.* San Francisco: Jossey Bass.

Christensen, A., & Jacobson, N. S. (1994). Who (or what) can do psychotherapy: The status and challenge of nonprofessional therapies. *Psychological Science, 5 (1),* 8–14.

Cicchetti, D., & Garmezy, N. (1993). Editorial: Prospects and promises in the study of resilience. *Development and Psychopathology, 5,* 497–501.

Cicchetti, D., & Toth, S. L. (1992). The role of developmental theory in prevention and intervention. *Development and Psychopathology, 4,* 489–493.

Cicchetti, D., & Toth, S. L. (1995). Developmental psychopathology and disorders of affect. In D. Cicchetti & D. J. Cohen (Eds.), *Developmental psychopathology: Risk, disorder, and adaptation, Vol. 2* (pp. 369–420). New York: Wiley.

Cicchetti, D., & Toth, S. L. (1998). The development of depression in children and adolescents. *American Psychologist, 53,* 221–241.

Claassen, W. (2000). *Alone in community: Journeys into monastic life around the world.* Leavenworth, KS: Forest of Peace Books.

Clark, K. B., & Clark, M. P. (1939). The development of consciousness of self and the emergence of racial identity in Negro preschool children. *Journal of Social Psychology, 10,* 591–599.

Clark, K. B., & Clark, M. P. (1947). Racial identification and preference in Negro children. In T. M. Newcomb & E. L. Hartley (Eds.), *Readings in social psychology,* (pp. 169–178). New York: Holt.

Clark, R., Anderson, N. B., Clark, V. R., & Williams, D. R. (1999). Racism as a stressor for African Americans: A biopsychosocial model. *American Psychologist, 54,* 805–816.

Cloward, R. D. (1967). Studies in tutoring. *Journal of Experimental Education, 36,* 14–25.

Coakes, S. J., & Bishop, B. J. (1996). The experience of moral community in a rural context. *Journal of Clinical Child Psychology, 24,* 108–117.

Coates, D., Wortman, C. B., & Abbey, A. (1979). Reactions to victims. In I. H. Frieze, D. Bar-Tal, & J. S.

Carrol (Eds.), *New approaches to social problems*. San Francisco: Jossey-Bass.

Cobb, S. (1976). Social support as a moderator of life stress. *Psychosomatic Medicine, 38*, 300–314.

Cockcroft, E. S., & Barnet-Sánchez, H. (1993). Signs from the heart: California Chicano murals: Venice, CA: Social and Public Art Resource Center: Albuquerque: University of New Mexico Press.

Cockcroft, E. S., Weber, J. P., & Cockcroft, J. (1977/1998). *Toward a people's art: The contemporary mural movement*. Albuquerque: University of New Mexico Press.

Cohen, R., & Lavach, C. (1995). Strengthening partnerships between families and service providers. In P. Adams & K. Nelson (Eds.), *Reinventing human services: Community and family-centered practice* (pp. 109–125). New York: Aldine de Gruyter.

Cohen, S., & Edwards, J. R. (1986). Personality characteristics as moderators of the relationship between stress and disorder. In R. J. Newfield (Ed.), *Advances in the investigation of stress* (pp. 235–283). New York: Wiley.

Cohen, S., & Syme, S. L. (Eds.). (1985). *Social support and health*. Orlando, FL: Academic Press.

Cohen, S., & Wills, T. A. (1985). Stress, social support and the buffering hypothesis. *Psychological Bulletin, 98*, 310–357.

Cohen, S., Evans, G. W., Stokols, D., & Krantz, D. (1986). *Behavior, health, and environmental stress*. New York: Plenum.

Cohen, S., Underwood, L. G., & Gottlieb, B. H. (2000) (Eds.). *Social support measurement and intervention: A guide for health and social scientists*. New York: Oxford University Press.

Cohn, R. M. (1978). The effect of unemployment status change on self-attitudes. *Social Psychology, 41*, 81–93.

Coie, J. D., Watt, N. F., West, S. G., Hawkins, J. D., Asarnow, J. R., Markman, H. J., Ramey, C., Shure, M. B., & Long, B. (1993). The science of prevention: A conceptual framework and some directions for a national research program. *American Psychologist, 48*, 1013–1023.

Colapinto, J. (2000). *As nature made him: The boy who was raised as a girl*. New York: HarperCollins.

Colby, A., Kohlberg, L., Gibbs, J., & Lieberman, M. (1983). A longitudinal study of moral judgment. *Monographs of the study of child development, 48* (1–2, Serial No. 200).

Coleman, J. S. (1988). Social capital in the creation of human capital. *American Sociological Review, 44*, 588–608.

Coleman, J. S. (1990). *Foundations of social theory*. Cambridge, MA: Harvard University Press.

Coles, R. (1967). *Children of crisis: A study of courage and fear (Children of Crisis, Vol. 1)*. Boston: Little, Brown, and Co.

Coles, R. (1977). *Privileged ones: The well-off and rich in America, (Children of Crisis, Vol. 5)*. Boston: Little, Brown and Co.

Coley, R. L., & Case-Lansdale, P. L. (1998). Adolescent pregnancy and parenthood. *American Psychologist, 53*, 152–166.

Collier, P., & Horowitz, D. (1984). *The Kennedys: An American drama*. New York: Summit Books.

Collins, A. (1991). Shared views and parent-adolescent relationships. *New Directions for Child Development, 51*, 103–110.

Collins, B. G. (1993). Reconstruing codependency using self-in-relation theory: A feminist perspective. *Social Work, 38*, 470–476.

Compas, B. E, Hinden, B. R., & Gerhardt, C. A. (1995). Pathways and processes of risk and reslience. *Annual Review of Psychology, 46*, 265–293.

Compas, B. E. (1987). Coping with stress during childhood and adolescence. *Psychological Bulletin, 101* (3), 393–403.

Compas, B. E., Wagner, B. M., Slavin, S. L., & Vannatta, K. (1986). A prospective study of life events, social support, and symptomatology during the transition from high school to college. *American Journal of Community Psychology, 14*, 241–258.

Cone, J. H. (1991). *Martin and Malcolm and America: A dream or a nightmare*. Maryknoll, NY: Orbis Books.

Connell, J. P., & Kubisch, A. C. (2001). Community approaches to improving outcomes for urban children, youth, and families: Current trends and future directions. *Does it take a village? Community effects on children, adolescents, and families* (pp. 177–201). Mahwah, NJ: Erlbaum.

Connolly, M., & Noumair, D. A. (1997). The white girl in me, the colored girl in you, and the lesbian in us: Crossing boundaries. In M. Fine, L. Weis, L. C. Powell, & L. M. Wong (Eds.), *Off White: Readings on race, power and society* (pp. 322–332). New York: Routledge.

Connors, J. L., & Donnellan, A. M. (1998). Walk in beauty: Western perspectives on disability and Navajo family/cultural resilience. In H. I. McCubbin, E. A. Thompson, A. I. Thompson, & J. E. Fromer (Eds.), *Resiliency in Native American and immigrant families* (pp. 159–182). Thousand Oaks, CA: Sage.

Contos, N. (2000). The Pinjarra Massacre Site Project: From doctoral student to community consultant. In C. R. O'Donnell & J. R. Ferrari (Eds.) *Employment in community psychology: The diversity of opportunity* (pp. 13–19). Binghamton, NY: Haworth Press.

Cook, T. D. (1999). How do neighborhoods matter? In F. Furstenburg Jr., T. D. Cook, J. Eccles, G. H. Elder, & A. Semeroff (Eds.). *Managing to make it: Urban families and adolescent success*. Chicago: University of Chicago Press.

Coontz, S. (1992). *The way we never were: American families and the nostalgia trap*. New York: Basic Books.

Cooper, C. R., & Denner, J. (1998). Theories linking culture and psychology: Universal and community-specific processes. *Annual Review of Psychology, 49*, 559–584.

Cooper, D. A. (1997). *God is a verb: Kabbalah and the practice of mystical Judaism*. New York: Riverhead Books.

Cornell Empowerment Group (1989). Empowerment and family support. *Networking Bulletin, 1* (2). 1–23.

Costa, P. T., Somerfield, M. R., & McCrae, R. R. (1996). Personality and coping: A reconceptualization. In M. Zeidner & N. S. Endler (Eds.), *Handbook of coping: Theory, research, and applications* (pp. 44–61). New York: John Wiley & Sons, Inc.

Cottrell, L. S. (1964). *Social planning, the competent community and mental health*. New York: Group for the Advancement of Psychiatry.

Cottrell, L. S. (1976). The competent community. In B. H. Kaplan, R. H. Wilson, & A. H. Leighton (Eds.), *Further explorations in social psychiatry*. New York: Basic Books.

Coughlin, P. J., Janecek, F. J., Jr., & Milberg, Weiss, Bershad, Hynes and Lerach (1998). A Review of R. J. Reynolds' Internal Documents Produced in *Mangini vs. R. J. Reynolds Tobacco Company*, Civil Number 939359—The Case that Rid California and the American Landscape of "Joe Camel" 2000. Retrieved December 15, 1999, from ***http://www.library.ucsf.edu/tobacco/mangini/report***.

Covey, S. R. (1989). *The seven habits of highly effective people*. New York: Simon & Schuster.

Cowen, E. L. (1973). Social and community interventions. *Annual Review of Psychology, 24*, 423–472.

Cowen, E. L. (1977). Baby steps toward primary prevention. *American Journal of Community Psychology, 5*, 1–22.

Cowen, E. L. (1980). The wooing of primary prevention. *American Journal of Community Psychology, 8*, 258–284.

Cowen, E. L. (1982). Help is where you find it: Four informal helping groups. *American Psychologist, 37*, 385–395.

Cowen, E. L. (1983). Primary prevention in mental health: Past, present, and future. In R. D. Felner, L. A. Jason, J. N. Moritsugu, & S. S. Farber (Eds.), *Preventive psychology: Theory, research, and practice*. (pp. 11–25). New York: Pergamon.

Cowen, E. L. (1991). In pursuit of wellness. *American Psychologist, 46*, 404–408.

Cowen, E. L. (1994). The enhancement of psychological wellness: Challenges and opportunities. *American Journal of Community Psychology, 22*, 149–179.

Cowen, E. L. (1996). The ontogenesis of primary prevention: Lengthy strides and stubbed toes. *American Journal of Community Psychology, 24*, 235–249.

Cowen, E. L. (1997a). On the semantics of primary prevention and wellness enhancement (Or will the real primary prevention please stand up). *American Journal of Community Psychology, 25*, 245–255.

Cowen, E. L. (1997b). Schools and the enhancement of children's wellness: Some opportunities and some limiting factors. In R. P. Weissberg, T. P. Gulotta, R. L. Hampton, B. A. Ryan, & G. R. Adams (Eds.), *Establishing preventive services* (pp. 97–123). Thousand Oaks, CA: Sage.

Cowen, E. L. (2000a). Community psychology and routes to psychological wellness. In J. Rappaport & E. Seidman (Eds.), *Handbook of community psychology* (pp. 79–99). New York: Kluwer Academic/Plenum Press.

Cowen, E. L. (2000b). Now that we all know that primary prevention in mental health is great, what is it? *Journal of Community Psychology, 28*, 5–16.

Cowen, E. L., & Hightower, A. D. (1989). The Primary Mental Health Project: Thirty years later. *Prevention in Human Services, 6*, 225–257.

Cowen, E. L., & Work, W. C. (1988). Resilient children, psychological wellness, and primary prevention. *American Journal of Community Psychology, 16*, 591–607.

Cowen, E. L., Izzo, L. D., Miles, H., Telschow, E. F., Trost, M. A., & Zax, M. (1963). A mental health program in the school setting: A description and evaluation. *Journal of Psychology, 56*, 307–356.

Cowen, E. L., Pederson, A., Babigian, H., Izzo, L. D., & Trost, M. A. (1973). Long-term follow-up of early detected vulnerable children. *Journal of Consulting and Clinical Psychology, 41*, 438–446.

Cowen, E. L., Trost, M. A., Izzo, L. D., Lorion, R. P., Dorr, D., & Isaacson, R. V. (1975). *New ways in school mental health*. New York: Human Science Press.

Cowen, E. L., Wyman, P. A., Work, W. C., Kim, J. Y., Fagen, D. B., & Magnus, K. B. (1997). Follow-up of young stress-affected and stress-resilient urban children. *Development and Psychopathology. 9*, 565–577.

Cowen, E. L., Zax, M., Izzo, L. D., & Trost, M. A. (1966). Prevention of emotional disorders in the school setting: A further investigation. *Journal of Consulting Psychology, 30*, 381–387.

Coyne, J. C., Wortman, C. B., & Lehman, D. R. (1988). The other side of support: Emotional overinvolvement and miscarried helping. In B. H. Gottlieb (Ed.), *Marshalling social support* (pp. 305–330). Newbury Park, CA: Sage.

Crocker, J., & Luhtanen, R. (1990). Collective self-esteem and ingroup bias. *Journal of Personality and Social Psychology, 58*, 60–67.

Crocker, J., & Lutsky, N. (1986). Stigma and the dynamics of social cognition. In S. C. Ainlay, G. Becker, & L. M. Coleman (Eds.), *The dilemma of difference: A multidisciplinary view of stigma* (pp. 95–121). New York: Plenum.

Cronkite, R. C., & Moos, R. H. (1984). The role of predisposing and moderating factors in the stress-illness relationship. *Journal of Health and Social Behavior, 25,* 372–393.

Crosby, D., & Bender, D. (2000). *Stand and be counted: Making music, making history: The dramatic story of artists and events that changed America.* San Francisco: HarperSanFrancisco.

Cross, T. L. (1998). Understanding family resiliency from a relational world view. In H. I. McCubbin, E. A. Thompson, A. I. Thompson, & J. E. Fromer (Eds.), *Resiliency in Native American and immigrant families* (pp. 143–157). Thousand Oaks, CA: Sage.

Cross, T. L., Bazron, B. J., Dennis, K. W., & Isaacs M. R. (Eds.). (1989). *Towards a culturally competent system of care, Vol. I. A monograph on effective services for minority children who are severely emotionally disturbed.* Washington, D.C.: Child Development Center, Child and Adolescent Services Program, Technical Assistance Center.

Cross, W. E., Jr. (1985). Black identity: Rediscovering the distinction between personal identity and reference group orientation. In M. B. Spencer, G. K. Brokins, & W. A. Allen (Eds.) *Beginnings: The social and affective development of black children* (pp. 155–172). Hillsdale, NJ: Erlbaum.

Cross, W. E., Jr. (1971). The Negro-to-Black conversion experience. *Black World, 20,* 13–27.

Cross, W. E., Jr. (1978). The Thomas and Cross models of psychological nigrescence: A review. *Journal of Black Psychology, 5,* 13–31.

Cross, W. E., Jr. (1995). The psychology of nigrescence: Revising the Cross model. In J. G. Ponterotto, J. M. Casa, L. A. Suzuki, & C. M. Alexander (Eds.), *Handbook of multicultural counseling* (pp. 93–122). Thousand Oaks, CA: Sage.

Cunningham, M. (1982). If you're queer and you're not angry in 1982, you're not paying attention; If you're straight it may be hard to figure out what all the shouting's about. *Mother Jones, 17,* 60–68.

Cushman, P. (1990). Why the self is empty: Toward a historically situated psychology. *American Psychologist, 45,* 599–611.

D'Augelli, A. R. (1994). Identity development and sexual orientation: Toward a model of lesbian, gay, and bisexual development. In E. J. Trickett, R. J. Watts, & D. Birman (Eds.), *Human diversity: Perspectives on people in context* (pp. 312–333). San Francisco: Jossey-Bass.

Dahlberg, G., Moss, P., & Pence, A. (1999). *Beyond quality in early childhood education and care: Postmodern perspectives.* Philadelphia: Falmer Press.

Dalton, J. H., Elias, M. J., & Howe, G. W. (1985). Studying the research community in community psychology. In E. Susskind & D. Klein (Eds.), *Research in community psychology.* New York: Plenum Press.

D'Andrade, R. (1996). Culture. In *Social Science Encyclopedia, 2nd Ed.* (pp. 161–163). London: Routledge.

Danish, S. J. (1983). Musings about personal competence: The contributions of sport, health, and fitness. *American Journal of Community Psychology, 11,* 221–240.

Danziger, K. (1990). Constructing the subject: Historical origins of psychological research. Cambridge, England: Cambridge University Press.

Darbonne, A. (1967). Crisis: Review of theory, practice, and research. *Psychotherapy: Theory, Research, and Practice, 4,* 184–189.

DARE (No Date). Suggested response to principles of effectiveness. Retrieved October 5, 2001, from ***http://www.dare-america.com/index2.htm.***

Dass, R., & Gorman, P. (1985). *How can I help? Stories and reflections on service.* New York: A. A. Knopf.

Datta, L. (1979). Another spring and other hopes. In E. Zigler & J. Valentine (Eds.), *Project Head Start: A legacy of the War on Poverty* (pp. 405–432). New York: Free Press.

Davidson, W. B., & Cotter, P. R. (1989). Sense of community and political participation. *Journal of Community Psychology, 21,* 119–128.

Davidson, W. B., & Cotter, P. R. (1991). The relationship between sense of community and subjective well-being: A first look. *American Journal of Community Psychology, 19,* 246–253.

Davidson, W. B., & Cotter, P. R. (1993). Psychological sense of community and support for public school taxes. *American Journal of Community Psychology, 21,* 59–66.

Davidson, W. S. (1989). Ethical and moral dilemmas in community psychology: Tarnishing the angels' halo. *American Journal of Community Psychology, 17,* 385–389.

Davis, A. F. (1994). *Spearheads for reform: The social settlements and the progressive movement, 1890–1914.* New Brunswick, NJ: Rutgers University Press.

Davis, R. C., Brickman, E., & Baker, T. (1991). Supportive and unsupportive responses of others to rape victims: Effects on concurrent victim adjustment. *American Journal of Community Psychology, 19,* 443–451.

Davison, K. P., Pennebaker, J. W., & Dickerson, S. S. (2000). Who talks? The social psychology of illness support groups. *American Psychologist, 55,* 205–217.

DeJong, D. H. (1993). *Promises of the past: A history of Indian education in the United States.* Golden, CO: North American Press.

Delany, S. L., Delany, E., & Hearth, A. H. (1993). *Having our say: The Delany sisters' first 100 years.* New York: Dell Publishing.

Delgado, M., & Humme-Delgado, D. (1992). Natural support systems: Source of strength in Hispanic communities. *Social Work, 1,* 83–88.

Deloria, V. (1992). Indian humor. In M. L. Anderson & P. H. Collins (Eds.), *Race, class, and gender: An anthology* (341–346). Belmont, CA: Wadsworth.

DeLoria, V. (1997). Alcatraz, activism, and accommodation. In T. Johnson, J. Nagel, & D. Champagne (Eds.), *American Indian activism: Alcatraz to the Longest Walk.* (pp. 45–51). Urbana, IL: University of Illinois Press.

Denby, R. W. (1996). Resiliency and the African American family: A model of family preservation. In S. L. Logan (Ed.), *The Black family: Strengths, self-help, and positive change* (pp. 144–163). Boulder, CO: Westview Press.

Denzin, N. K., & Lincoln, Y. S. (2000) (Eds.). *Handbook of qualitative research, Second edition.* Thousand Oaks, CA: Sage.

Department of Health and Human Services (No Date). Head Start 1998 fact sheet. Retrieved July 10, 2000, from *http://www.acf.dhhs.gov/programs/opa/hsfacts98. htm*.

DeRenzo, E. G. (1996). A bioethicist's perspective. In K. Hoagwood, P. S. Jensen, & C. B. Fisher (Eds.), *Ethical issues in mental health research with children and adolescents* (pp. 269–286). Mahwah, NJ: Lawrence Erlbaum Associates.

Derman-Sparks, L. (1989). *Anti-bias curriculum: Tools for empowering young children.* Washington, D.C.: National Association for the Education of Young Children.

Deutchman, I. (1991). The politics of empowerment. *Women and Politics, 11* (2), 1–18.

Devine, P. G. (1989). Stereotyping and prejudice: Their automatic and controlled components. *Journal of Personality and Social Psychology, 56*, 5–18.

Devlin, B., Fienberg, S. E., Resnick, D. P., & Roeder, K. (1997). *Intelligence, genes, and success: Scientists respond to the bell curve.* New York: Springer.

Devor, H. (1989). *Gender blending: Confronting the limits of duality.* Bloomington: Indiana University Press.

Dewey, J. (1899). Psychology and social practice. In J. Boydston (Ed.), *The middle works of John Dewey, 1899–1924 (Vol. 1)* (131–150). Carbondale: Southern Illinois University Press.

Dewey, J. (1931). Social science and social control. In J. Boydston (Ed.), *The later works of John Dewey, 1925–1953 (Vol. 6)* (pp. 64–68). Carbondale: Southern Illinois University Press.

Dewey, J. (1946). *Problems of men.* New York: Philosophical Library.

Dilworth-Anderson, P., & Marshall, S. (1996). Social support in its cultural context. In G. R. Pierce, B. R. Sarason, & I. G. Sarason (Eds.), *Handbook of social support and the family* (pp. 67–79). New York: Plenum Press.

Ditton, P. M. (1999). Bureau of Justice Statistics special report: Mental health and treatment of inmates and probationers. Retrieved July 27, 2001, from *http://www. ojp.usdoj.gov:80/bjs/pub/pdf/mhtip.pdf*.

Dohrenwend, B. P., & Shrout, P. E. (1985). "Hassles" in the conceptualization and measurement of life stress variables. *American Psychologist, 40*, 780–785.

Dohrenwend, B. S. (1973). Life events as stressors: A methodological inquiry. *Journal of Health and Social Behavior, 14*, 167–175.

Dohrenwend, B. S. (1977). Anticipation and control of stressful life events: An exploratory analysis. In J. S. Strauss, H. M. Babigian, & M. Rolf (Eds.), *The origins and course of psychopathology.* New York: Plenum.

Dohrenwend, B. S. (1978). Social stress and community psychology. *American Journal of Community Psychology, 6*, 1–14.

Dohrenwend, B. S., Krasnoff, L., Askenasy, A. R., & Dohrenwend, B. P. (1978). Exemplification of a method for scaling life events: The PERI life events scale. *Journal of Health and Social Behavior, 19*, 205–229.

Dokecki, P. (1982). Liberation: Movement in theology, theme in community psychology. *Journal of Community Psychology, 10*, 185–196.

Dokecki, P. (1992). On knowing the community of caring persons: A methodological basis for the reflective-generative practice of community psychology, *Journal of Community Psychology, 20*, 26–35.

Dokecki, P. (1996). *The tragi-comic professional: Basic considerations for ethical reflective-generative practice.* Pittsburgh: Duquesne University Press.

Donahue, M. J., & Benson, P. L. (1995). Religion and the well-being of adolescents. *Journal of Social Issues, 51*, 145–160.

Donohue, E., Schiraldi, V., Zeidenberg, J. (1998). School house hype: The school shootings, and the real risk kids face in America. Washington, D.C.: The Justice Policy Institute. Retrieved March 27, 2001, from *http://www.cjcj.org/jpi/schoolhouse.html*.

"Don't Be Too Serious" (1999). SCRA Community News. *Community Psychologist, Summer 1999, Volume 32, (3)*, pp. 38–39.

Dougherty, A. M. (1990). *Consultation: Practice and perspectives.* Belmont, CA: Brooks/Cole.

Dougherty, A. M. (2000). *Psychological consultation and collaboration in school and community settings, 3rd ed.* Belmont, CA: Brooks/Cole.

Dressel, P., Carter, V., & Balachandran, A. (1995). Second-order victim blaming. *Journal of Sociology and Social Welfare, 22* (2), 107–123.

DSNI (No Date a). Welcome to Dudley Village. Retrieved April 25, 2001 from *http://www.dsni.org/dudley_ village.htm*.

DSNI (No Date b). Timeline. Retrieved April 25, 2001, from *http://www.dsni.org/Comunity%20Information/ timeline.htm*.

DSNI (No Date c). DSNI committees. Retrieved April 25, 2001, from *http://www.dsni.org/board_information/ committees.htm*.

DSNI (No Date d). Who we are. Retrieved April 25, 2001, from *http://www.dsni.org/Comunity%20Information/ who_we_are.htm*.

Dubois, B., & Krogsrud, K. (1996). *Social work: An empowering profession, 2nd ed.* Boston: Allyn & Bacon.

Dubois, D. L., Felner, R. D., Brand, S., Adan, A. M., & Evans, E. G. (1992). A prospective study of life stress, social support, and adaptation in early adolescent adjustment. *Child Development, 63,* 542–557.

Dubois, D. L., Felner, R. D., Meares, G., & Krier, M. (1994). Prospective investigation of the effects of socioeconomic disadvantage, life stress, and social support on early adolescent adjustment. *Journal of Abnormal Psychology, 103,* 511–522.

Duhl, L. (1995). *The social entrepreneurship of change.* Lanham, MD: Pace University Press, 1995.

Dumas, J. E. Rollock, D., Prinz, R. J., Hops, H., & Blechman, E. (1999). Cultural sensitivity: Problems and solutions in applied and preventive interventions. *Applied and Preventive Psychology, 8,* 175–196.

Dunkel-Shetter, C. (1984). Social support and cancer: Findings based on patient interviews and their implications. *American Journal of Community Psychology, 40,* 77–98.

Dunkel-Shetter, C., Sagrestano, L., Feldman, P., & Killingsworth, C. (1996). Social support and pregnancy: A comprehensive review focusing on ethnicity and culture. In G. Pierce, B. Sarason, & I. Sarason (Eds.), *Handbook of social support and the family* (pp. 375–412). New York: Plenum.

Durkheim, E. (1893/1964). *The division of labor in society.* New York: Free Press.

Durkheim, E. (1897/1951). *Suicide: a study in sociology* (J. A. Spaulding, Trans., G. Simpson, Ed.). Glencoe, IL: Free Press.

Durlak, J. (1979). Comparative effectiveness of professional and paraprofessional helpers. *Psychological Bulletin, 86,* 80–92.

Durlak, J. A. (1995). School-based prevention programs for children and adolescents. Thousand Oaks, CA: Sage.

Durlak, J. A. (1997). *Successful prevention programs for children and adolescents.* New York: Plenum.

Durlak, J. A., & Wells, A. M. (1997a). Primary prevention mental heath programs for children and adolescents: A meta-analytic review. *American Journal of Community Psychology, 25,* 115–152.

Durlak, J. A., & Wells, A. M. (1997b). Primary prevention mental health programs: The future is exciting. *American Journal of Community Psychology, 25,* 233–243.

Durlak, J. A., & Wells, A. M. (1998). Evaluation of indicated preventive intervention (secondary prevention) mental health programs for children and adolescents. *American Journal of Community Psychology, 26,* 775–802.

Dwyer, J. W., & Coward, R. T. (1991). A multivariate comparison of the involvement of adult sons versus daughters in the care of impaired parents. *Journal of Gerontology: Psychological Sciences, 56,* S259–269.

Earls, F., McGuire, J., Shay, S. (1994). Evaluating a community intervention to reduce the risk of child abuse: Methodological strategies in conducting neighborhood surveys. *Child Abuse and Neglect, 18,* 473–485.

Edelman, M. (1995). *From art to politics: How artistic creations shape political conceptions.* Chicago: University of Chicago Press.

Edelman, M. W. (1992). *The measure of our success: A letter to my children and yours.* Boston: Beacon Press.

Edelwich, J., & Brodsky, A. (1980). *Burn-out: Stages of disillusionment in the helping professions.* New York: Human Sciences Press.

Edwards, K. L. (1999). African American definitions of self and psychological health. In R. L. Jones (Ed.), *Advances in African American psychology* (pp. 287–311). Hampton, VA: Cobb and Henry.

Edwards, R. W., Jumper-Thurman, P., Plested, B. A., Oetting, E. R., & Swanson, L. (2000). Community readiness: Research to practice. *Journal of Community Psychology, 28,* 291–307.

Edwards, S. D. (1998). A community psychology narrative with special reference to Zululand, South Africa. *Journal of Psychology in Africa; South of the Sahara, the Caribbean, and Afro-Latin America, 2,* 101–122.

Egeland, B., Carlson, E., & Sroufe, A. (1993). Resilience as process. *Development and Psychopathology, 5,* 517–528.

Egeland, B., Jacobvitz, D., & Sroufe, L. A. (1988). Breaking the cycle of abuse. *Child Development, 59,* 1080–1088.

Elder, G. H. (1974). *Children of the Great Depression.* Chicago: University of Chicago Press.

Elder, G. H. (1998). The life course as developmental theory. *Child Development, 69,* 1–12.

Elder, G. H., & Runck, B. (1979). Families in hard times: A legacy. In E. Corfman (Ed.), *Families Today, Vol. 1.* NIMH Monograph: U.S. Department of Health, Education and Welfare.

Elder, G. H., Caspi, A., & Downey, G. (1985). Problem behavior and family relationships: Life course and intergenerational themes. In A. B. Sorensen, F. E. Weinert, & L. R. Sherrod (Eds.), *Human development and the life course: Multidisciplinary perspectives.* Hillsdale, NJ: Erlbaum.

Elder, G. H., Caspi, A., & van Nguyen, T. (1986). Resourceful and vulnerable children: Family influence in hard times. In R. K. Silbereisen, K. Eyferth, & G. Rudkinger (Eds.), *Development as action context* (pp. 167–186). Berlin: Springer-Verlag.

Elder, G. H., Liker, J. K., & Cross, C. E. (1984). Parent–child behavior in the Great Depression: Life course and intergenerational influences. *Lifespan Development and Behavior, Vol. 6,* 109–158.

Elias, M. J. (1987). Establishing enduring prevention programs: Advancing the legacy of Swampscott. *American Journal of Community Psychology, 15*, 539–553.

Elias, M. J. (1994). Capturing excellence in applied settings: A participant conceptualizer and praxis explicator role for community psychologists. *American Journal of Community Psychology, 22*, 293–318.

Elias, M. J. (1997). Reinterpreting dissemination of prevention programs as widespread implementation with effectiveness and fidelity. In R. P. Weissberg, T. P. Gulotta, R. L. Hampton, B. A. Ryan, & G. R. Adams (Eds.), *Establishing preventive services* (pp. 253–289). Thousand Oaks, CA: Sage.

Elias, M. J., Dalton, J. H., Franco, R., & Howe, G. W. (1984). Academic and nonacademic community psychologists: An analysis of divergence in settings, roles, and values. *American Journal of Community Psychology, 12*, 281–302.

Elias, M. J., Gara, M., Schuyler, T. F., Branden-Muller, L. R., & Sayette, A. M. (1991). The promotion of social competence: A longitudinal study of a preventive school-based program. *American Journal of Orthopsychiatry, 61*, 409–417.

Elias, M. J., Gara, M., Ubriaco, M., Rothbaum, P. A., Clabby, J. F., & Schuyler, T. (1986). Impact of a preventive social problem solving intervention children's coping with middle school stressors. *American Journal of Community Psychology, 14*, 259–275.

Elliot, J. (1970). *The eye of the storm* (videorecording). Mount Kisco, NY: Center for the Humanities.

Ellis, A. (1969). *The essence of rational psychotherapy: A comprehensive approach to treatment*. New York: Institute for Rational Living.

Ellison, R. (1947). *Invisible man*. New York: Vintage Books.

Ellsworth, E. (1997). Double binds and whiteness. In M. Fine, L. Weis, L. C. Powell, & L. M. Wong (Eds.), *Off White: Readings on race, power and society* (pp. 259–269). New York: Routledge.

Ellsworth, J. (1998). Inspiring delusions: Reflections on Head Start's enduring popularity. In J. Ellsworth & L. J. Ames (Eds.), *Critical perspectives on Project Head Start* (pp. 318–333). Albany: State University of New York Press.

Ellsworth, J., & Ames, L. J. (1998a). Introduction. In J. Ellsworth & L. J. Ames (Eds.), *Critical perspectives on Project Head Start* (pp. vii–xvii). Albany: State University of New York Press.

Ellsworth, J., & Ames, L. J. (1998b). Concluding thoughts: Hope and challenge: Head Start past, present, and future. In J. Ellsworth & L. J. Ames (Eds.), *Critical perspectives on Project Head Start.* (pp. 334–341). Albany: State University of New York Press.

Emery, R. E. (1982). Interparental conflict and the children of discord and divorce. *Psychological Bulletin, 86* (3), 574–595.

Ennett, S. T., Tobler, N. S., Ringwalt, C. L., & Flewelling, R. L. (1994). How effective is Drug Abuse Resistance Education? A meta-analysis of Project DARE outcome evaluations. *The American Journal of Public Health, 84* (9), 1394–1402.

Ennis, N. E, Hobfoll, S. E., & Schröder, E. E. (2000). Money doesn't talk, it swears: How economic stress and resistance resources impact inner-city women's depressive mood. *American Journal of Community Psychology, 28*, 149–173.

Erikson, E. (1950/1963). *Childhood and society*. New York: W. W. Norton.

Etzioni, A. (1993). *The Spirit of Community: The Reinvention of American Society*. New York: Touchstone.

Etzioni, A. (1995). *Rights and the common good: The communitarian perspective*. New York: St. Martin's Press, 1995.

Ewald, W. (2000). *Secret games: Collaborative works with children 1969–1999*. New York: Scalo.

Eysenck, H. J., (1961). The effects of psychotherapy. In H. J. Eysenck (Ed.), *Handbook of abnormal psychology* (pp. 697–725). New York: Basic Books.

Fagot, B. I. (1978). The influence of sex of child on parental reactions to toddler children. *Child Development, 49*, 459–465.

Fairchild, H. H., & Cozens, J. A. (1981). Chicano, Hispanic, or Mexican American: What's in a name? *Hispanic Journal of Behavioral Sciences, 3* (2), 191–198.

Fairweather, G. W. (1979). Experimental development and dissemination of an alternative to psychiatric hospitalization: Scientific methods for social change. In R. F. Munoz, L. R. Snowden, & J. G. Kelly (Eds.), *Social and psychological research in community settings* (305–326). San Francisco: Jossey-Bass.

Fairweather, G. W., Sanders, D. H., Maynard, H., & Cressler, D. L. (1969). *Community life for the mentally ill*. Chicago: Aldine.

Farquhar, J. W., (1991). The Stanford cardiovascular disease prevention programs. *Annals of the New York Academy of Sciences, 623*, 327–331.

Farwell, L., & Weiner, B. (2000). Bleeding hearts and the heartless: Popular perceptions of liberal and conservative ideologies. *Personality and Social Psychology Bulletin, 26*, 845–852.

Faver, C. A. (2001). Rights, responsibility, and relationship: Motivations for women's social activism. *Affilia: Journal of Women and Social Work, 16* (3), 314–336.

Fawcett, S. B. (1991). Some values guiding community research and action. *Journal of Applied Behavior Analysis, 24*, 621–636.

Fawcett, S. B., Paine-Andrews. A., Francisco, V. T., Schultz, J. A., Richter, K. P., Lewis, R. K., Williams, E. L., Harris, K. J., Berkley, J. Y., Fisher, J. L., & Lopez, C. M. (1995). Using empowerment theory in collaborative partnerships for community health and development. *American Journal of Community Psychology, 23*, 677–698.

Fawcett, S. B., White, G. W., Balcazar, F. E., Suarez-Balcazar, Y., Mathews, R. M., Paine, A. L., Seekins, T., & Smith, J. F. (1994). A contextual-behavioral model of empowerment: Case studies involving people with physical disabilities. *American Journal of Community Psychology, 22,* 471–486.

Feighery, E., & Rogers, T. (1989). *Building and maintaining effective coalitions* (No. 12 in *How-to guides on community health promotion).* Palo Alto, CA: Stanford Health Promotion Resource Center.

Fein, S., & Spencer, S. J. (1997). Prejudice as self-image maintenance: Affirming the self through derogating others. *Journal of Personality and Social Psychology, 73,* 31–45.

Feinberg, L. (1998). *Trans liberation: Beyond pink or blue.* Boston: Beacon Press.

Feinberg, M. E., & Hetherington, E. M. (2000). Sibling differentiation in adolescence: Implications for behavioral genetic theory. *Child Development, 71,* 1512–1524.

Feis, C. L., Mavis, B. E., Weth, M. E., & Davidson, W. S. (1990). Graduate training and employment experiences of community psychologists. *Professional Psychology, 21,* 94–98.

Felitti, V. J., Anda, R. R., Nordenberg, D. Williamson, D. F., Spitz, A. M., Edwards, V., Koss, M. P., & Marks, J. S. (1998). Relationship of childhood abuse and household dysfunction to many of the leading causes of death in adults: The Adverse Childhood Experiences Study. *American Journal of Preventive Medicine, 14,* 245–258.

Felner, R. D., & Adan, A. M. (1988).The School Transitional Environment Project: An ecological intervention and evaluation. In R. H. Price, E. L. Cowen, R. P. Lorion, & J. Ramos-McKay (Eds.), *14 ounces of prevention: A casebook for practitioners* (pp. 111–122). Washington, D.C.: American Psychological Association.

Felner, R. D., Farber, S. S., & Primavera, J. (1983). Transitions and stressful life events: A model for primary prevention. In R. D. Felner, L. A. Jason, J. N. Moritsugu, & S. S. Farber (Eds.), *Preventive Psychology: Theory, research and practice* (pp. 199–215). New York: Pergamon Press.

Felner, R. D., Felner, T. Y., & Silverman, M. M. (2000). Prevention in mental health and social intervention. In J. Rappaport & E. Seidman (Eds.), *Handbook of community psychology* (pp. 9–42). New York: Kluwer Academic/Plenum Publishers.

Felshin, N. (Ed.). (1995). *But is it art? The spirit of art as activism.* Seattle: Bay Press.

Felsman, J. K., & Vaillant, G. E. (1987). Resilient children as adults: A 40-year study. In J. A. Anthony & B. J. Cohler (Eds.), *The invulnerable child.* New York: Guilford Press.

Felton, B. J., & Revenson, T. A. (1984). Coping with chronic illness: A study of illness controllability and the influence of coping strategies on psychological adjustment. *Journal of Consulting and Clinical Psychology, 52,* 343–353.

Felton, B. J., & Shinn, M. (1992). Social integration and social support: Moving social support beyond the individual level. *Journal of Community Psychology, 20,* 103–115.

Fennema, E., & Peterson, P. (1985). Autonomous learning behavior: A possible explanation for gender-related differences in mathematics. In L. C. Wilkinson & C. B. Marrett (Eds.), *Gender influences in classroom interaction* (pp. 17–35). Orlando, FL: Academic Press.

Fergusson, D. M., & Lynskey, M. T. (1999). Adolescent resiliency in family adversity. *Journal of Child Psychology and Psychiatry, 37,* 281–292.

Festinger, L. A. (1954). A theory of social comparison processes. *Human Relations, 7,* 117–140.

Festinger, L., Schachter, S., & Back, K. (1950). *Social pressures in formal groups.* New York: Holt Rinehart and Winston.

Fetterman, D. M. (1998). *Ethnography: Step by step.* Thousand Oaks, CA: Sage.

Fetterman, D. M., Kaftarian, S. J., & Wandersman, A. (Eds.). (1996). *Empowerment evaluation: Knowledge and tools for self-assessment and accountability.* Thousand Oaks, CA: Sage.

Fields, G. S. (1980). *Poverty, inequality, and development.* New York: Cambridge University Press.

Figley, C., Giel, R., Borgo, S., Briggs, S., & Haritos-Fatouros, M. (1995). Prevention and treatment of community stress: How to be a mental health expert at the time of disaster. In S. E. Hobfoll & M. W. de Vries (Eds.). (1995). *Extreme stress and communities: Impact and intervention* (pp. 489–497). Boston: Kluwer Academic Publishers.

Fine, A. R., (1999). *Empower your self: A framework for personal success.* Minneapolis: Sunrise Press.

Fine, M., & Asch, A. (1988). Disability beyond stigma: Social interaction, discrimination, and activism. *Journal of Social Issues, 44,* 3–21.

Finkel, N. J. (1974). Strens and traumas. *American Journal of Community Psychology, 2,* 265–273.

Finkel, N. J. (1975). Strens, traumas, and trauma resolution. *American Journal of Community Psychology, 3,* 173–178.

Finkelstein, N. W., & Haskins, R. (1983). Kindergarten children prefer same-color peers. *Child Development, 54,* 502–508.

Fisher, A. (1992). Community psychology in Australia. *The Community Psychologist, 25,* 19–20.

Fiske, S. T., & Taylor, S. E. (1984). *Social cognition.* Reading, MA: Addison-Wesley.

Fiske, S. T., Bersoff, D. N., Borgida, E., Deaux, K., & Heilman, M. E. (1991). Social science research on trial: The use of sex stereotyping research in *Price Waterhouse vs. Hopkins. American Psychologist, 46,* 1058–1069.

Fiske, S. T., Xu, J., Cuddy, A. C., & Glick, P. (1999). (Dis)respecting versus (dis)liking: Status and interdependence predict ambivalent stereotypes of competence and warmth. *Journal of Social Issues, 55,* 473–489.

Flach, F. (1988, May). The resilience hypothesis. *The Psychiatric Times,* 5–6.

Flanagan, C. A., & Eccles, J. (1993). Changes in parents' work status and adolescents' adjustment at school. *Child Development, 64,* 246–257.

Fleming, M. (1996). *Healthy youth 2000: A mid-decade review.* Chicago: American Medical Association, Department of Adolescent Health.

Florin, P., & Wandersman, A. (1984). Cognitive social learning and participation in community development. *American Journal of Community Psychology, 12,* 689–708.

Florin, P., Chavis, D., Wandersman, A., & Rich, R. (1992). A systems approach to understanding and enhancing grassroots organizations: The Block Booster Project. In R. Levine & H. Fitzgerald (Eds.), *Analysis of dynamic psychological systems, Vol. 2: Methods and applications* (pp. 215–243). New York: Plenum.

Flower, J. (1993). Building healthy cities: Excerpts from a conversation with Leonard J. Duhl, M. D. *Healthcare Forum Journal, 36, 3.* Retrieved September 27, 2001, from ***http://www.well.com/user/bbear/duhl.html***.

Foa, E. B., & Meadows, E. A. (1997). Psychological treatments to posttraumatic stress disorder: A critical review. *Annual Review of Psychology, 48,* 449–480.

Folkman, S., & Lazarus, R. S. (1998). Coping as a mediator of emotion. *Journal of Personality and Social Psychology, 54,* 466–475.

Forcey, C. B. (1996). From the quest for community to the quest for authority: Robert A. Nisbet and the traditionalist response to the sixties. Retrieved October 26, 2001, from ***http://www.columbia.edu/~cf27/pubs/nisbet60.html***.

Ford, M. E. (1985). Primary prevention: Key issues and a competence perspective. *Journal of Primary Prevention, 5,* 264–266.

Fordham, S., & Ogbu, J. U. (1986). Black students' school success: Coping with the "burden of 'acting white.'" *The Urban Review, 18,* 176–206.

Forgatch, M. S., Patterson, G. R., & Ray, J. A. (1996). Divorce and boys' adjustment problems: Two paths with a single model. In E. M. Hetherington & E. A. Blechman (Eds.), *Stress, coping, and resiliency in children and families* (pp. 67–105). Mahwah, NJ: Lawrence Erlbaum.

Formoso, D., Gonzales, N. A., & Aiken, L. S. (2000). Family conflict and children's internalizing and externalizing behaviors: Protective factors. *American Journal of Community Psychology, 28,* 175–199.

Foster-Fishman, P. G., Berkowitz, S. L., Lounsbury, D. W., Jacobson, S., & Allen, N. A. (2001). Building collaborative capacity in community coalitions: A review and integrative framework. *American Journal of Community Psychology, 29,* 241–261.

Foster-Fishman, P. G., Salem, D. A., Allen, N. E., & Fahrbach, K. (1999). Ecological factors impacting provider attitudes toward human service delivery reform. *American Journal of Community Psychology, 27,* 785–816.

Fowers, B. J., & Richardson, F. C. (1996). Why is multiculturalism good? *American Psychologist, 51,* 609–621.

Fox, D. R. (1993). Psychological jurisprudence and radical social change. *American Psychologist, 48,* 234–241.

Frable, D. E. S. (1997). Gender, racial, ethnic, sexual, and class identities. *Annual Review of Psychology, 48,* 139–162.

Francisco, V. T., Fawcett, S. B., Schultz, J. A., Berkowitz, B., Wolff, T. J., & Nagy, G. (2001). Using internet-based resources to build community capacity: The Community Toolbox [http://ctb.ukans.edu]. *American Journal of Community Psychology, 29,* 293–300.

Frankenberg, R. (1993). *White women race matters: The social construction of whiteness.* Minneapolis, MN: University of Minnesota Press.

Fraser, S. (1995). (Ed.). *The bell curve wars: Race, intelligence, and the future of America.* New York: BasicBooks.

Freire, P. (1970/1992). *Pedagogy of the oppressed.* New York: Continuum.

Freire, P. (1975). Cultural action for freedom. *Harvard Educational Review, Monograph 1.*

Freitas, M. (2000). Voices from the south: The construction of Brazilian community psychology. *Journal of Community and Applied Social Psychology, 10 (4),* 315–326.

French, J., & Raven, B. (1960). The bases of social power. In D. Cartwright & A. Zanier (Eds.), *Group dynamics: Research and theory* (pp. 607–623). New York: Row, Peterson.

Freud, S. (1907/1963). Obsessive acts and religious practice. In P. Reiff (Ed., Trans.), *Character and culture* (pp. 17–26). New York: MacMillan.

Frey, D., & Gaertner, S. L. (1986). Helping and the avoidance of inappropriate interracial behavior: A strategy that can perpetuate a non-prejudiced self-image. *Journal of Personality and Social Psychology, 50,* 1083–1090.

Frontline (1998). Inside the tobacco deal. Retrieved December 6, 2000, from ***http://www.pbs.org/wgbh/pages/frontline/shows/settlement***.

Frye, M. (1983). *The politics of reality.* Freedom, CA: Crossing Press.

Fullan, M. (1999). *Change forces: The sequel.* Philadelphia: Falmer Press.

Furman, W., & Buhrmester, D. (1992). Age and sex differences in perceptions of networks and personal relationships. *Child Development, 63,* 103–115.

Furstenberg, F. F., Brooks-Gunn, J., & Morgan, S. P. (1987). *Adolescent mothers in later life.* Cambridge: Cambridge University Press.

Furstenberg, F. F., Cook, T. D., Eccles, J., Elder, G. H., & Sameroff, A. (1999). *Managing to make it: Urban families and adolescent success.* Chicago: University of Chicago Press.

Gaertner, S. L., & Dovidio, J. F. (1986). The aversive form of racism. In J. F. Dovidio & S. L. Gaertner (Eds.), *Prejudice, discrimination, and racism* (pp. 61–90). Orlando, FL: Academic Press.

Gaertner, S. L., Dovidio, J. F., Anastasio, P. A., Bachman, B. A., & Rust, M. C. (1993). The common in-group identity model: Recategorization and the reduction of intergroup bias. In W. Stroebe & M. Hewstone (Eds.), *European review of social psychology, Vol IV* (pp. 1–26). London: Wiley.

Gager, P. J., & Elias, M. J. (1997). Implementing prevention programs in high-risk environments: Applications of the resiliency paradigm. *American Journal of Orthopsychiatry, 67 (3),* 363–373.

Galano, J. (1996). Academic on a mission: Run and run and run. (community psychology practice). *American Journal of Community Psychology, 24,* 681–696.

Gallup, G. H. (1993). *Religion in America: 1992–1993.* Princeton, NJ: Gallup Organization.

Gallup, G. H., & Lindsay, D. M. (2000). *Surveying the religious landscape: Trends in U.S. Beliefs:* Harrisburg, PA: Morehouse Publishing.

Gamson, J. (1989). Silence, death, and the invisible enemy: AIDS activism and social movement "newness." *Social Problems, 36,* 351–367.

Garbarino, J., & Sherman, D. (1980). High-risk neighborhoods and high-risk families: The human ecology of child maltreatment. *Child Development, 51,* 188–198.

Garbarino, J. (1999). *Lost boys: Why our sons turn violent and how we can save them.* New York: Free Press.

Garbarino, J., Dubrow, N., Kostelny, K., & Pardo, C. (1998). *Children in danger: Coping with the consequences of community violence.* San Francisco: Jossey-Bass.

García Coll, C. T., Lamberty, G., Jenkins, R., McAdoo, H. P., Crnic, K., Wasik, B. H., & Vásquez García, H. (1996). An integrative model for the study of developmental competencies in minority children. *Child Development, 67,* 1891–1914.

García, I., Giuliani, F., & Wiesenfeld, E. (1999). Community and sense of community: The case of an urban barrio in Caracas. *Journal of Community Psychology, 27,* 727–740.

García-Preto, N. (1982). Puerto Rican families. In M. McGoldrick, J. K. Pearce, & J. Giordano (Eds.), *Ethnicity and family therapy* (pp. 164–186). New York: Guilford Press.

Garmezy, N., & Masten, A. S. (1986). Stress, competence, and resilience: Common frontiers for therapist and psychopathologist. *Behavior Therapy, 17,* 500–521.

Garmezy, N. (1971). Vulnerability research and the issue of primary prevention. *American Journal of Orthopsychiatry, 41,* 101–116.

Garmezy, N. (1974). The study of competence in children at risk for severe psychopathology. In E. J. Anthony & C. Koupernik (Eds.), *The child in his family, Vol. 3. Children at psychiatric risk* (pp. 77–97). New York: Wiley.

Garmezy, N. (1983). Stressors of childhood. In N. Garmezy & M. Rutter (Eds.), *Stress, coping and development in children.* New York: McGraw-Hill.

Garmezy, N., & Rutter, M. (Eds.). (1983). *Stress, coping, and development in children.* New York: McGraw-Hill.

Garmezy, N., Masten, A. S., & Tellegen, A. (1984). The study of stress and competence in children: A building block for developmental psychopathology. *Child Development, 55,* 97–111.

Garnets, L. D., & D'Augelli, A. R. (1994). Empowering lesbian and gay communities: A call for collaboration with community psychology. *American Journal of Community Psychology, 22,* 447–470.

Gartner, A., & Reissman, F. (1977). *Self-help in the human services.* San Francisco: Jossey-Bass.

Gartner, J. (1996). Religious commitment, mental health, and prosocial behavior: A review of the empirical literature. In E. P. Shafranske (Ed.), *Religion and the clinical practice of psychology* (pp. 187–214). Washington, D.C.: APA.

Gates, H. L., Jr. (1993, May 17). Blacklash? (African Americans object to gay rights-civil rights analogy). *New Yorker, 69 (13),* 42–45.

Gaventa, J. (1993). The powerful, the powerless, and the experts: Knowledge struggles in an information age. In P. Park, M. Brydon-Miller, B. Hall, & T. Jackson (Eds.), *Voices of change: participatory research in the United States and Canada.* (pp. 21–40). Westport, CT.

Genovese, E. D. (1976). *Roll, Jordan, roll.* New York: Random House.

George, J. M., & Brief, A. P. (1992). Feeling good-doing good: A conceptual analysis of the mood at work-organizational spontaneity relationship. *Psychological Bulletin, 112,* 310–329.

Gerard, H., & Miller, N. (1975). *School desegregation.* New York: Plenum Press.

Gergen, K. J., Gulerce, A., Lock, A., & Misra, G. (1996). Psychological science in cultural context. *American Psychologist, 51,* 496–503.

Gersten, J., Langner, T. S., Eisenberg, J. G., & Orzeck, L. (1974). Child behavior and life events: Undesirable change or change per se? In B. S. Dohrenwend & B. P. Dohrenwend (Eds.), *Stressful life events: Their nature and effects.* New York: John Wiley.

Gersten, J., Langner, T. S., Eisenberg, J. G., & Simcha-Fagan, O. (1977). An evaluation of the etiologic role of stressful life-change events in psychological disorders. *Journal of Health and Social Behavior, 18,* 228–244.

Ghee, K. L. (1990). The psychological importance of self definition and labeling: Black versus African American. *Journal of Black Psychology, 17 (1)*, 75–93.

Gibbs, J. T. (1980). The interpersonal orientation in mental health consultation: Toward a model of ethnic variations in consultation. *Journal of Community Psychology, 8*, 195–207.

Gibbs, J. T., & Fuery D. (1994). Mental health and well-being of Black women: Toward strategies of empowerment. *American Journal of Community Psychology, 22*, 559–582.

Gibbs, L. M. (1982). *Love Canal: My story* (as told to Murray Levine). Albany: State University of New York Press.

Gibran, K. (1946). *The prophet*. New York: Knopf.

Gilbert, D. T., & Silvera, D. H. (1996). Overhelping. *Journal of Personality and Social Psychology, 70*, 678–690.

Gilbert, K. (2001). (Ed.). *The emotional nature of qualitative research*. Boca Raton, FL: CRC Press.

Gilbert, K. R. (1988). The dynamics of inaction: Psychological factors inhibiting arms control activism. *American Psychologist, 43*, 755–764.

Gilligan, C. (1982). *In a different voice: Psychological theory and women's development*. Cambridge: Harvard University Press.

Gilligan, C., & Attanucci, J. (1988). Two moral orientations. In C. Gilligan, J. V. Ward, J. M. Taylor, & B. Bardige (Eds.), *Mapping the moral domain*. (pp. 73–86). Cambridge, MA: Harvard University Press.

Gilligan, C., Lyons, N., & Hammer, T. (1990). *Making connections: The relational worlds of adolescent girls at Emma Willard School*. Troy, NY: Emma Willard School.

Ginexi, E. M., Weihs, K., & Simmens, S. J. (2000). Natural disaster and depression: A prospective investigation of reactions to the 1993 Midwest Floods. *American Journal of Community Psychology, 28*, 495–518.

Giovanni, N. (1994). The sixties. In *Racism 101*. New York: William Morrow and Company, Inc.

Gist, R. M., Lubin, B., & Redburn, B. G. (1999). Psychosocial, ecological, and community perspectives on disaster response. In R. M. Gist & B. Lubin (Eds.), *Response to disaster: Psychosocial, community, and ecological approaches* (1–20). London: Taylor and Francis.

Gittell, R., & Vidal, A. (1998). *Community organizing: Building social capital as a development strategy*. Thousand Oaks, CA: Sage.

Glendon, M. (1991). *Rights Talk: The impoverishment of political discourse*. New York: Free Press.

Glick, P., & Fiske, S. T. (2001). An ambivalent alliance: Hostile and benevolent sexism as complementary justifications for gender inequality. *American Psychologist, 56*, 109–118.

Glover, P. (No Date). Creating economic democracy with local currency. Retrieved August 16, 2000, from **http://www.ratical.com/many_worlds/cc/CED.html**.

Glynn, T. J. (1981). Psychological sense of community: Measurement and application. *Human Relations, 34*, 780–818.

Glynn, T. J. (1986). Neighborhood and sense of community. *Journal of Community Psychology, 14*, 341–352).

Goeppinger, J., & Baglioni, A. J. (1985). Community competence: A positive approach to needs assessment. *American Journal of Community Psychology, 13*, 507–523.

Goffman, E. (1961). *Essays on the social situation of mental patients and other inmates*. Garden City, NJ: Doubleday.

Golan, N. (1978). *Treatment in crisis situations*. New York: Free Press.

Goldenberg, I. I. (1971). *Build me a mountain: Youth, poverty, and the creation of new settings*. Cambridge, MA: MIT Press.

Goldenberg, I. I. (1978). *Oppression and social intervention*. Chicago: Nelson-Hall.

Goldman, A. L. (1991, April 10). Portrait of religion in U.S. holds dozens of surprises. *The New York Times*, pp. A1, A11.

Goldstein, M. S. (1979). The sociology of mental health and illness. *Annual Review of Sociology, 5*, 381–409.

Gonzales, N. A., & Kim, L. S., (1997). Stress and coping in an ethnic minority context: Children's cultural ecologies. In In S. A Wolchik & I. N. Sandler (Eds.), *Handbook of children's coping: Linking theory and intervention* (pp. 481–511). New York: Plenum Press.

Goode, E. (2000, August 8). How culture molds habits of thought. *The New York Times*, Section 6, pp. 1, 4.

Goodman, R. M., Wandersman, A., Chinman, M., Imm, P., & Morrissey, E. (1996). An ecological assessment of community-based interventions for prevention and health promotion: approaches to measuring community coalitions. *American Journal of Community Psychology, 24*, 33–62.

Goodstein, L. D., & Sandler, I. (1978). Using psychology to promote human welfare: A conceptual analysis of the role of community psychology. *American Psychologist, 33*, 882–892.

Goodwin, D. K. (1987). *The Fitzgeralds and the Kennedys*. New York: Simon & Schuster.

Gordon, E. W., & Wang, M. C. (1994). Epilogue: Educational resilience—Challenges and prospects. In M. C. Wang & E. W. Gordon (Eds.), *Educational resilience in inner-city America: Challenges and prospects* (pp. 191–194). Hillsdale, NJ: Erlbaum.

Gorsuch, R. L (1988). Psychology of religion. *Annual Review of Psychology, 39*, 201–221.

Gorsuch, R. L. (1995). Religious aspects of substance abuse and recovery. *Journal of Social Issues, 51 (2)*, 65–83.

Gottlieb, B. H. (1983). Social support as a focus for integrative research in psychology. *American Psychologist, 38*, 279–287.

Gottlieb, B. H., & Todd, D. M. (1985). Characterizing and promoting social support in natural settings. In R. F. Munoz, L. R. Snowden, J. G. Kelly, & Associates (Eds.),

Social and psychological research in community settings, 3rd edition (pp. 182–242). San Francisco: Jossey-Bass.

Gould, J. (1992). Ontogeny and phylogeny revisited and reunited. *Bioessays, 14,* 275–279.

Gove, W. R. (Ed.). (1980). *The labelling of deviance, 2nd edition.* Beverly Hills, CA: Sage.

Gove, W. R., & Herb, T. R. (1974). Stress and mental illness among the young: A comparison of the sexes. *Social Forces, 53,* 256–265.

Graham, S. (1992). "Most subjects were White and middle class": Trends in published research on African Americans in selected journals, 1970–1989. *American Psychologist, 47,* 629–639.

Granello, D. H., & Beamish, P. M. (1998). Reconceptualizing co-dependency in women: A sense of connectedness, not pathology. *Journal of Mental Health Counseling, 20 (4),* 344–358.

Gray, P., Froh, R., & Diamond, R. (1992). *A national study of research universities: On the balance between research and undergraduate teaching.* New York: Syracuse University Center for Instructional Development.

Green, B. L. (1995). Long-term consequences of disasters. In S. E. Hobfoll & M. W. de Vries (Eds.). (1995). *Extreme stress and communities: Impact and intervention* (pp. 307–324). Boston: Kluwer Academic Publishers.

Greenberger, E. (1983). A researcher in the policy arena: The case of child labor. *American Psychologist, 38,* 104–111.

Greenburg, I. (1986). Introduction: Righteous rescuers. In C. Rittner & S. Myers (Eds.), *The courage to care: Rescuers of Jews during the Holocaust* (pp. 3–15). New York: New York University Press.

Greenwald, A. G. (1980). The totalitarian ego: Fabrication and revision of personal history. *American Psychologist, 35,* 603–618.

Griswold Del Castillo, R. (1984). *La familia: Chicano families in the urban southwest, 1848 to the present.* Notre Dame, IN: University of Notre Dame Press.

Groce, N. (1985). *Everyone here spoke sign language: Hereditary deafness on Martha's Vineyard.* Cambridge, MA: Harvard University Press.

Grotevant, H. D., & Cooper, C. R. (1985). Patterns of interaction in family relationships and the development of identity exploration in adolescence. *Child Development, 56,* 415–428.

Gruber, J., & Trickett, E. J. (1987). Can we empower others? The paradox of empowerment in the governing of an alternative public school. *American Journal of Community Psychology, 15,* 353–371.

Guba, E. G., & Lincoln, Y. S. (1994). Competing paradigms in qualitative research. In N. K. Denzin & Y. S. Lincoln (Eds.), *Handbook of qualitative research* (pp. 105–117). Thousand Oaks, CA: Sage.

Guisinger, S., & Blatt, S. J. (1994). Individuality and relatedness: Evolution of a fundamental dialectic. *American Psychologist, 49,* 104–111.

Guthrie, R. V. (1998). *Even the rat was white: A historical view of psychology* (2nd ed.). Boston: Allyn Bacon Press.

Gutierrez, L. (1994). Beyond coping: An empowerment perspective on stressful life events. *Journal of Sociology and Social Welfare, 21(3).* 201–220.

Gutiérrez-Mayka, M., & Contreras-Neira, R. (1998). A culturally receptive approach to community participation in system reform. In M. Hernandez & M. R. Isaacs (Eds.), *Promoting cultural competence in children's mental health services* (pp. 133–148). Baltimore: Paul H. Brookes Publishing Co.

Haberman, M. (1971). Twenty-three reasons universities can't educate teachers. *The Journal of Teacher Education, 22,* 133–140.

Haggerty, R., Sherrod, L., Garmezy, N., & Rutter, M. (Eds.). (1994). *Stress, risk, and resilience in children and adolescents: Processes, mechanisms, and interventions.* New York: Cambridge University Press.

Hall, B. (1993). Introduction. In P. Park, M. Brydon-Miller, B. Hall, & T. Jackson (Eds.), *Voices of change: participatory research in the United States and Canada.* (pp. xiii–xxii). Westport, CT.

Hall, C. C. I. (1997). Cultural malpractice: The growing obsolescence of psychology with the changing U.S. population. *American Psychologist, 52,* 642–651.

Hall, M., Levis-Pilz, G., Pilz, A., & DeJong, J. (No Date). Project Venture: An Outdoor Adventure/Service-Leadership Approach to Prevention. Retrieved March 11, 2001, from ***http://www.niylp.org/main/pvart.html***.

Hallie, P. P. (1979). *Lest innocent blood be shed: The story of the village of Le Chambon and how goodness happened there.* New York: Harper and Row.

Halpern, R. (2000). Early childhood intervention for low-income children and families. In J. P. Shonkoff & S. J. Meisels (Eds.), *Handbook of early childhood intervention* (pp. 361–386). New York: Cambridge University Press.

Hammill, P. (1998). News is a verb: Journalism at the end of the 20th century. New York: Ballantine Pub. Group.

Haney, C. (1993). Psychology and legal change: The impact of a decade. *Law and Human Behavior, 17,* 371–396.

Haney, C., Banks, C., & Zimbardo, P. (1973). Interpersonal dynamics in a simulated prison. *International Journal of Criminology and Penology, 1,* 69–97.

Hanley, G. L., O'Donohue, W. T., & Krasner, L. (1984). Community psychologies and values: The importance of being urnless. *Journal of Community Psychology, 12,* 217–221.

Harrell, S. P. (Ed.), & Potts, R. (Guest Ed.). (1999). Special feature section: The spirit of community psychology: Spirituality, religion, and social action. *The Community Psychologist, 32 (3).*

Harris, J. R. (1998). *The nurture assumption: Why children turn out the way they do.* New York: Free Press.

Harrison, A. O., Wilson, M. N., Pine, C. J., Chan, S. Q., & Buriel, R. (1990). Family ecologies of ethnic minority children. *Child Development, 61,* 347–362.

Harrison, T. M., Zappen, J. P., Stephen, T., Garfield, P., & Prell, C. (2001). Building an electronic community: A town-gown collaboration. In G. J. Shepherd & E. W. Rothenbuhler (Eds.), *Communication and community* (pp. 201–216). Mahwah, NJ: Lawrence Erlbaum.

Hauser-Cram, P., Warfield, M. E., Upshur, C. C., & Weisner, T. S. (2000). An expanded view of program evaluation in early childhood intervention. In J. P. Shonkoff & S. J. Meisels (Eds.), *Handbook of early childhood intervention* (pp. 487–509). New York: Cambridge University Press.

Havel, V. (1990). *Disturbing the peace: A conversation with Karel Hvízdala*. New York: Knopf.

Hawkins, N. G., Davies, R., & Holmes, T. H. (1957). Evidence of psychosocial factors in the development of pulmonary tuberculosis. *American Review of Tuberculosis and Pulmonary Disorders, 75*, 768–780.

Heller, K. (1989a). Ethical dilemmas in community intervention, *American Journal of Community Psychology, 17*, 367–378.

Heller, K. (1989b). Return to community. *American Journal of Community Psychology, 17*, 1–15.

Heller, K., & Lakey, B. (1985). Perceived support and social interaction among friends and confidants. In G. Sarason & B. R. Sarason (Eds.), *Social support: Theory, research and applications* (pp. 287–300). The Hague: Martinus Nijhoff.

Heller, K., Price, R. H., Reinharz, S., Riger, S., Wandersman, A., & D'Aunno, T. A. (1984). *Psychology and community change: Challenges of the future*. Homewood, IL: The Dorsey Press.

Helms, J. E. (1994). The conceptualization of racial identity and other "racial" constructs. In E. J. Trickett, R. J. Watts, & D. Birman (Eds.), *Human diversity: Perspectives on people in context* (pp. 285–311). San Francisco: Jossey-Bass.

Henderson, N., & Milstein, M. M. (1996). *Resiliency in schools: Making it happen for students and educators*. Thousand Oaks, CA: Corwin Press/Sage.

Henderson, S. H., Hetherington, E. M., Mekos, D., & Reiss, D. (1996). Stress, parenting, and adolescent pathology in nondivorced and step families: A within-family perspective. In E. M. Hetherington & E. A. Blechman (Eds.), *Stress, coping, and resiliency in children and families* (pp. 39–66). Mahwah, NJ: Lawrence Erlbaum.

Hermans, H. J. M., & Kempen, H. J. G. (1998). Moving cultures: The perilous problems of cultural dichomtomies in a globalizing society. *American Psychologist, 53*, 1111–1120.

Hernandez, M., Isaacs, M. R., Nesman, T., & Burns, D. (1998). Perspectives on culturally competent systems of care. In M. Hernandez & M. R. Isaacs (Eds.), *Promoting cultural competence in children's mental health services* (pp. 1–28). Baltimore: Paul H. Brookes Publishing Co.

Herrnstein, R. J., & Murray, C. (1994). *The bell curve: Intelligence and class structure in American life*. New York: Free Press.

Hetherington, E. M. (1979). Divorce: A child's perspective. *American Psychologist, 34*, 851–858.

Hetherington, E. M. (1989). Coping with family transitions: Winners, losers, and survivors. *Child Development, 60*, 1–14.

Hetherington, E. M., & Blechman, E. A. (Eds.). (1996). *Stress, coping and resiliency in children and families*. Mahwah, NJ: Erlbaum.

Hetherington, E. M., Bridges, M., & Glendessa, M. I. (1998). What matters? What does not? Five perspectives on the association between marital transitions and children's adjustment. *American Psychologist, 53*, 167–184.

Hetherington, E. M., Cox, M., & Cox, R. (1979). Play and social interaction in children following divorce. *Journal of Social Issues, 35*, 26–49.

Hetherington, E. M., Reiss D., & Plomin R. (1994). (Eds.). *Separate social worlds of siblings: Importance of nonshared environment on development*. Hillsdale, NJ: Erlbaum.

Hewstone, M. (1990). The "ultimate attribution error"? A review of the literature on intergroup causal attribution. *European Journal of Social Psychology, 20* (4), 311–335.

Hewstone, M., & Brown, R. (1986). Contact is not enough: An intergroup perspective on the "contact hypothesis". In M. Hewstone & R. Brown (Eds.), *Contact and conflict in intergroup encounters* (pp. 1–44). Oxford: Basic Blackwell, Inc.

Hill, J. (2000). A rationale for the integration of spirituality into community psychology. *Journal of Community Psychology, 28*, 139–149.

Hill, J. P., & Holmbeck, G. N. (1986). Attachment and autonomy during adolescence. *Annals of Child Development, 3*, 145–189.

Hill, R. (1949). *Families under stress: Adjustment to the crises of war separation and reunions*. New York: Pergamon Press.

Hill, R. (1972). *The strengths of Black families*. New York: Emerson Hall.

Hillery, G. A. (1984). Definitions of community: Areas of agreement. *Rural Sociology, 20*, 111–123.

Hilliard, T. O. (1972). Personality characteristics of Black student activists and non-activists. In R. Jones (Ed.), *Black psychology* (p.136–144). New York: Harper and Row.

Himmelman, A. T., Johnson, D., Kaye, G., Salzman, P., & Wolff, T. (2001). Roundtable discussion and final comments [on successful coalitions]. *American Journal of Community Psychology, 29*, 205–211.

Hinkle, L. E. (1974). The effect of exposure to culture change, social change, and changes in interpersonal relationships on health. In B. S. Dohrenwend & B. P.

Dohrenwend (Eds.), *Stressful life events: Their nature and effects.* New York: John Wiley.

Hinrichsen, G. A., Revenson, T. A., & Shinn, M. (1988). Does self-help help? An empirical investigation of scoliosis peer support groups. *Journal of Social Issues, 41,* 65–87.

Hirsch, B. J., Moos, R. H., & Reischl, T. M. (1985). Psychological adjustment of children of a depressed, arthritic or normal parent. *Journal of Abnormal Psychology, 94 (2),* 154–164.

Hoagwood, K., Jensen, P. S., & Fisher, C. B. (1996). Toward a science of scientific ethics in research on child and adolescent mental disorders. In K. Hoagwood, P. S. Jensen, & C. B. Fisher (Eds.), *Ethical issues in mental health research with children and adolescents* (pp. 3–14). Mahwah, NJ: Lawrence Erlbaum Associates.

Hobfoll, S. E. (1988). *The ecology of stress.* New York: Hemisphere Publising Corp.

Hobfoll, S. E. (1989). Conservation of resources: A new attempt of conceptualizing stress. *American Psychologist. 44,* 513–524.

Hobfoll, S. E. (1986). The ecology of stress and social support among women. In S. E. Hobfoll (Ed.), *Stress, social support and women* (pp. 3–14). Washington, D.C.: Hemisphere Publications.

Hobfoll, S. E. (1998). Ecology, community, and AIDS prevention. *American Journal of Community Psychology, 26,* 133–144.

Hobfoll, S. E. (1998). *Stress, culture, and community: The psychology and philosophy of stress.* New York: Plenum Press.

Hobfoll, S. E., Briggs, S., & Wells, J. (1995). Community stress and resources: Actions and reactions. In S. E. Hobfoll & M. W. de Vries (Eds.). (1995). *Extreme stress and communities: Impact and intervention* (pp. 137–158). Boston: Kluwer Academic Publishers.

Hobfoll, S. E., Dunahoo, C. L., Ben-Porath, Y., & Monnier, J. (1994). Gender and coping: The dual-axis model of coping. *American Journal of Community Psychology, 22,* 49–82.

Hodge, J. L, Struckman, D. K., & Trost, L. D. (1975). *Cultural bases of racism and group oppression: An examination of traditional "Western" concepts, values, and institutional structures which support racism, sexism, and elitism.* Berkeley, CA: Two Riders Press.

Hoffman, R. (1981). Is altruism part of human nature? *Journal of Personality and Social Behavior, 40,* 121–137.

Hohmann, A. A., & Larson, D. B. (1993). Psychiatric factors predicting use of clergy. In E. L. Worthington Jr. (Ed.), *Psychotherapy and religious values* (pp. 71–84). Grand Rapids, MI: Baker Book House.

Holahan, C. J., & Moos, R. H. (1985). Life stress and health: Personality, coping, and family support in stress resistance. *Journal of Personality and Social Psychology, 49 (3),* 739–747.

Holahan, C. J., Moos, R. H., & Schaefer, J. A. (1996). Coping, stress resistance, and growth: Conceptualizing adaptive functioning. In M. Zeidner & N. S. Endler (Eds.), *Handbook of coping: Theory, research, and applications* (pp. 24–43). New York: John Wiley & Sons, Inc.

Holleb, G., & Abrams, W. (1975). *Alternatives in community mental health.* Boston: Beacon Press.

Hollingshead, A. B., & Redlich, F. C. (1958). *Social class and mental illness.* New York: Wiley.

Holmes, T. H. (1979). Development and quantification of a quantitative measure of life change magnitude. In J. E. Barrett (Ed.), *Stress and mental disorder.* New York: Raven Press.

Holmes, T. H., & Rahe, R. H. (1967). The social readjustment rating scale. *Journal of Psychosomatic Research, 11,* 213–218.

Hooker, E. (1957). The adjustment of the male overt homosexual. *Journal of Projective Techniques, 21,* 18–31.

HOPE Columbine (2000). Retrieved February 15, 2001, from ***http://www.hopecolumbine.org/.***

Hopson, R. E. (1996). The 12-step program. In E.P. Shafranske (Ed.), *Religion and the clinical practice of psychology* (pp. 533–558). Washington, D.C.: APA.

House, J. S., & Kahn, R. L. (1985). Measures and concepts of social support. In S. Cohen & S. L. Syme (Eds.), *Social support and health* (pp. 83–108). Orlando, FL: Academic.

Howard, G. S. (1985). The role of values in the science of psychology. *American Psychologist, 40,* 255–265.

Howard, K. I., & Orlinsky, D. E. (1972). Psychotherapeutic processes. *Annual Review of Psychology, 23,* 615–668.

Hrabowski, F. A. III, Maton, K. I., & Grief, G. L. (1998). *Beating the odds: Raising academically successful African American males.* New York: Oxford University Press.

Hughes, D., Seidman, E., & Williams, N. (1993). Cultural phenomena and the research enterprise: Toward a culturally anchored methodology. *American Journal of Community Psychology, 21,* 687–703.

Hui, C. H., & Triandis, H. C. (1989). Effects of culture and response format on extreme response style. *Journal of Cross-Cultural Psychology, 20 (3),* 296–309.

Humphreys, K., & Noke, J. M. (1997). The influence of post-treatment mutual help group participation on the friendship networks of substance abuse patients. *American Journal of Community Psychology, 25,* 1–16.

Humphreys, K., & Rappaport, J. (1993). From the community mental health movement to the war on drugs: A study in the definition of social problems. *American Psychologist, 48,* 892–901.

Humphreys, K., Finney, J. W., & Moos, R. H. (1994). Applying a stress and coping framework to research on mutual help organizations. *Journal of Community Psychology, 22,* 312–327.

Hunsberger, B. (1995). Religion and prejudice: The role of religious fundamentalism, quest, and right-wing authoritarianism. *Journal of Social Issues, 51* (2), 113–129.

Hurst, M. W., Jenkins, C. D., & Rose, R. M. (1978). The assessment of life change: A comparative and methodological inquiry. *Psychosomatic Medicine, 40*(2), 126–140.

Hymel, S. (1986). Interpretations of peer behavior: Affective bias in childhood and adolescence. *Child Development, 57,* 431–445.

Hymel, S., Wagner, E., & Butler, L. (1990). Reputational bias: View from the peer group. In S. Asher & J. Coie (Eds.), *Peer rejection in childhood.* (pp. 156–186). New York: Cambridge University Press.

Ialongo, N., Werthamer, L., Kellam, S. G., Brown, C. H., Wang, S., & Lin, Y. (1999). Proximal impact of two first-grade preventive interventions on the early risk behaviors for later substance abuse, depression, and antisocial behavior. *American Journal of Community Psychology, 27,* 599–641.

Inglehart, R. (1985). Aggregate stability and individual-level flux in mass belief systems: The level of analysis paradox. *American Political Science Review, 79,* 97–116.

Ingram, C. (1990). David Steindl-Rast [Interview]. *In the footsteps of Gandhi: Conversations with spiritual social activists* (pp. 249–271). Berkeley: Parallax Press.

Ingram, C. (1990). Diane Nash [Interview]. *In the footsteps of Gandhi: Conversations with spiritual social activists* (pp. 201–222). Berkeley: Parallax Press.

Institute for Intercultural Studies (November 11, 2001). "Frequently asked questions" in *Margaret Mead 1901–1978.* Retrieved July 15, 2001, from ***http://www. mead2001.org/faq_page.html***.

Iscoe, I. (1974). Community psychology and the competent community. *American Psychologist, 29,* 607–613.

Iscoe, I. (1997). Reaching out: Community psychologists. In R. J. Sternberg (Ed.), *Career paths in psychology: Where your degree can take you* (pp. 117–132). Washington, D.C.: American Psychological Association.

Iscoe, I., & Spielberger, C. D. (1977). Community psychology: Historical context. In I. Iscoe, B. L. Bloom, & C. D. Spielberger (Eds.), *Community psychology in transition: Proceedings of the national conference on training in community psychology* (pp. 3–16). New York: John Wiley & Sons.

Iscoe, I., Bloom, B. L., & Spielberger, C. D. (1977). (Eds.). *Community psychology in transition: Proceedings of the national conference on training in community psychology.* New York: John Wiley & Sons.

Isen, A. M., & Levin, P. A. (1972). Effects of feeling good on helping: Cookies and kindness. *Journal of Personality and Social Psychology, 21,* 384–388.

Jackson, P. B., Thoits, P. A., & Taylor, H. F. (1995). Composition of the workplace and psychological well-being: The effects of tokenism on America's Black elite. *Social Forces, 74,* 543–557.

Jacobs, S. (1993). *Pathological grief: Maladaptation to loss.* Washington, D.C.: American Psychiatric Press.

Jacobs, T. J., & Charles, E. (1980). Life events and the occurrence of cancer in children. *Psychosomatic Medicine, 42,* 11–24.

Jacobsen, G. F., Strickler, M., & Morley, W. E. (1968). Generic and individual approaches to crisis intervention. *American Journal of Public Health, 58* (2), 338–343.

Jaffe, E. D. (1988). Ethnic preferences of pre-school children. *Early Child Development and Care, 39,* 83–94.

Jahoda, M. (1958). *Current concepts of positive mental health.* New York: Basic Books.

James, W. (1902/1961). *The varieties of religious experience.* New York: Collier.

Janoff-Bulman, R. (1979). Characterological versus behavioral self-blame: Inquiries into depression and rape. *Journal of Personality and Social Psychology, 37,* 1798–1809.

Janoff-Bulman, R., Timko, C., & Carli, L. L. (1985). Cognitive biases in blaming the victim. *Journal of Experimental Social Psychology, 21,* 161–177.

Jarrett, R. L. (1995). Growing up poor: The family experiences of socially mobile youth in low-income African-American neighborhoods. *Journal of Adolescent Research, 10,* 111–135.

Jason, L. A. (1991). Participating in social change: A fundamental value for our discipline. *American Journal of Community Psychology, 19,* 1–16.

Jason, L. A. (1997). Community building: Values for a sustainable future. Westport, CT: Praeger.

Jason, L. A. (1998). Tobacco, drug, and HIV preventive media interventions. *American Journal of Community Psychology, 26,* 151–173.

Jason, L. A. (1999). Testifying at a Congressional hearing on the tobacco settlements. *Professional Psychology, Research and Practice, 30* 372–378.

Jason, L. A., Berk, M., Schnopp-Wyatt, D. L., & Talbot, B. (1999). Effects of enforcement of youth access laws on smoking prevalence. *American Journal of Community Psychology, 27,* 143–160.

Jason, L. A., Pokorny, S., & Katz, R. (2001). Passive versus active consent: A case study in school settings. *Journal of Community Psychology, 29,* 53–68.

Jason, L. A., Weine, A. M., Johnson, J. H., Danner, K. E., Kurasaki, K. S., & Warren-Sohlberg, L. (1993). The School Transitions Project: A comprehensive preventive intervention. *Journal of Emotional and Behavioral Disorders, 1,* 65–70.

Jefferson County Sheriff's Office Report (2000). Foreword. Retrieved May 15, 2000, from ***http://info.jefferson. lib.co.us/columbine-cd/Columbine%20REPORT/ Pages/FORWARD.htm***.

Jencks, C. (1994). *The homeless.* Cambridge: Harvard University Press.

Jennings, P., & Brewster, T. (1998). *The century*. New York: Doubleday.

Jensen, A. R. (1969). How much can we boost IQ and scholastic achievement? *Harvard Educational Review, 39*, 1–123.

Jensen, P. S., & Hoagwood, K. (1997). The book of names: DSM-IV in context. *Development and Psychopathology, 9 (2)*, 231–249.

Jerusalem, M., Kaniasty, K., Lehman, D. R., Ritter, C., & Turnbull, G. J. (1995). Individual and community stress: Integration of approaches at different levels. In S. E. Hobfoll & M. W. de Vries (Eds.). (1995). *Extreme stress and communities: Impact and intervention* (pp. 105–129). Boston: Kluwer Academic Publishers.

Jessor, R. (1993). Successful adolescent development among youth in high-risk settings. *American Psychologist, 48*, 117–126.

Jessor, R., Turbin, M. S., & Costa, F. M. (1998). Risk and protection in successful outcomes among disadvantaged adolescents. *Applied Developmental Science, 2*, 194–208.

Ji, L., Peng, K., & Nisbett, R. E. (2000). Culture, control, and perception of relationships in the environment. *Journal of Personality and Social Psychology, 78*, 943–955.

Johnson, A. R. (1962). *The cultic prophet in ancient Israel*. Cardiff, England: University of Wales Press.

Johnson, D. W., & Johnson, R. T. (1992). Positive interdependence: Key to effective cooperation. In R. Hertz-Lazarowitz & N. Miller (Eds.), *Interaction in cooperative groups: The theoretical anatomy of group learning* (pp. 174–199). Cambridge, MA: Cambridge University Press.

Johnson, J. S., & Sarason, I. G. (1978). Life stress, depression, and anxiety: Internal–external locus of control as a moderator variable. *Journal of Psychosomatic Research, 22*, 205–208.

Joint Commission on Mental Illness and Health (1961). *Action for mental health*. New York: Basic Books.

Jones, A. C. (1985). Psychological functioning in Black Americans: A conceptual guide for use in psychotherapy. *Psychotherapy, 22*, 363–369.

Jones, A. C. (1993). *Wade in the water: The wisdom of the spirituals*. Maryknoll, NY: Orbis Books.

Jones, A. C. (2001). Upon this rock: The foundational influence of the spirituals. In F. Jones & A. C. Jones (Eds.). *The triumph of the soul: Cultural and psychological aspects of African American music* (pp. 3–34). Westport, CT: Praeger.

Jones, C. (2000). *Stitching a revolution: How the quilt put a human face on AIDS and brought healing to America* (with Jeff Dawson). San Francisco: HarperSanFrancisco.

Jones, E. E., & Nisbett, R. E. (1972). The actor and the observer: Divergent perception of the causes of behavior. In E. E. Jones, D. E. Kanouse, H. H. Kelley, R. E. Nisbett, S. Valins, & B. Weiner (Eds.), *Attribution:*

Perceiving the causes of behavior (pp. 79–94). Morristown, NJ: General Learning Press.

Jones, F., & Jones, A. C. (2001). Introduction. In F. Jones & A. C. Jones (Eds.), *The triumph of the soul: Cultural and psychological aspects of African American music* (pp. xiii–xviii). Westport, CT: Praeger.

Jones, J. M. (1993). Racism and civil rights: Right problem. Wrong solution. Invited address to Society for the Psychological Study of Social Issues, 101st Annual Convention, American Psychological Association. Toronto.

Jones, J. M. (1994). Our similarities are different: Toward a psychology of affirmative diversity. In E. J. Trickett, R. J. Watts, & D. Birman (Eds.), *Human diversity: Perspectives on people in context* (pp. 27–45). San Francisco: Jossey-Bass.

Jones, J. M. (1997). *Prejudice and racism, 2nd edition*. New York: The McGraw-Hill Companies, Inc.

Jones, S. L. (1996). A constructive relationship for religion with the science and profession of psychology: Perhaps the boldest model yet. In E. P. Shafranske (Ed.), *Religion and the clinical practice of psychology* (pp. 113–147). Washington, D.C.: APA.

Jordan, J. V. (1992). Relational resilience. Paper presented at the Stone Center Colloquium Series, Wellesley, MA.

Jordan, J. V., Kaplan, A. G., Miller, J. B., Stiver, I. P., & Surrey, J. L. (1991). *Women's growth in connection: Writings from the Stone Center*. New York: The Guilford Press.

Jung, C, G, (1933). *Modern man in search of a soul*. New York: Harcourt, Brace, and World, Inc.

Jung, C. G. (1938). *Psychology and religion*. New Haven, CT: Yale University Press.

Jung, C. G. (1951/1983). Aion: Researches in to the phenomenology of the self (excerpts). In A. Storr (Ed.), *The essential Jung*. Princeton, NJ: Princeton University Press.

Kaftarian, S., & Hansen, W. (1994). (Eds.), Community program, Center for Substance Abuse Prevention (Special Issue). *Journal of Community Psychology, 22*.

Kagan, J. (1976). Resilience and continuity in psychological development. In A. M. Clarke & A. D. Clarke (Eds.), *Early experience: Myth and evidence* (pp. 97–121). New York: Free Press.

Kâgitçibasi, C. (1987). Individual and group loyalties. In C. Kâgitçibasi (Ed.), *Growth and progress in cross-cultural psychology* (pp. 94–103). Lisse: Swets and Zeitlinger.

Kâgitçibasi, C. (1996). *Family and human development across cultures: A view from the other side*. Mahwah, NJ: Lawrence Erlbaum Associates.

Kale, W. L., & Stenmark, D. E. (1983). A comparison of four life event scales. *American Journal of Community Psychology, 11*, 441–458.

Kalis, B. L. (1970). Crisis theory: Its relevance for community psychology and directions for development. In D. Adelson & B. L. Kalis (Eds.), *Community psychology* and mental health: Perspectives and challenges (pp. 69–88). Scranton, PA: Chandler Publishing Co.

Kane, R. (1998). Dimensions of value and the aims of social inquiry. *American Behavioral Scientist, 41*, 578–597.

Kaniasty, K., & Norris, F. H. (1995). In search of altruistic community: Patterns of social support mobilization following Hurricane Hugo. *American Journal of Community Psychology, 23*, 447–477.

Kaniasty, K., & Norris, F. H. (1999). The experience of disaster: Individuals and communities sharing trauma. In R. Gist & B. Lubin (Eds.), *Response to disaster: Psychosocial, community, and ecological approaches* (pp. 25–61). Philadelphia, PA: Brunner/Mazel.

Kaniasty, K., & Norris, F. H. (2000). Help-seeking comfort and receiving social support: The role of ethnicity and context of need. *American Journal of Community Psychology, 28*, 545–581.

Kanner, A. D., Coyne, J. C., Schaefer, C., & Lazarus, R. S. (1981). Comparison of two modes of stress measurement: Daily hassles and uplifts versus major life events. *Journal of Behavioral Medicine, 4*, 1–29.

Kaplan, A. (1964). *The conduct of inquiry.* San Francisco: Chandler.

Kaplan, H. B. (1999). Toward an understanding of resilience: A critical review of definitions and models. In M. D. Glantz & J. L. Johnson (Eds.), *Resilience and development: Positive life adaptations* (pp. 17–83). New York: Kluwer Academic/Plenum.

Katz, A. H., & Bender, E. I. (Eds.). (1976). *The strength in us: Self-help groups in the modern world.* New York: Franklin Watts.

Katz, D., & Braly, K. W. (1935). Racial prejudice and racial stereotypes. *Journal of Abnormal and Social Psychology, 30*, 174–193.

Katz, P. (1994). *The new urbanism: Toward an architecture of community.* New York: McGraw-Hill.

Katz, P. A., & Katz, M. (1997). *The Feminist Dollar: The Wise Woman's Buying Guide.* New York: Plenum Press.

Katz, P. A., & Kofkin, J. A. (1997). Race, gender, and young children. In S. S. Luthar, J. A. Burack, D. Cicchetti, & J. R. Weisz (Eds.), *Developmental psychopathology: Perspectives on adjustment, risk, and disorder* (pp. 51–74). Cambridge, UK: Cambridge University Press.

Katz, R. (1984). Empowerment and synergy: Expanding the community's healing resources. *Prevention in Human Services, 3*, 201–226.

Kauffman, C., Grunebaum, H., Cohler, B., & Gamer, R. (1979). Superkids: Competent children of psychotic mothers. *American Journal of Psychiatry, 136 (11)*, 1398–1402.

Kauffman, J., Cook, A., Arny, L., Jones, B., & Pittinsky, T. (1994). Problems defining resiliency: Illustrations from the study of maltreated children. *Development and Psychopathology, 6*, 215–229.

Kawasaki, G., Rickbaugh, Q., Bolles, R. N., & Livingston, J. (1994). *Hindsights: The wisdom and breakthroughs of remarkable people.* Hillsboro, OR: Beyond Words.

Kaye, G. (1990). A community organizer's perspective on citizen participation research and the researcher-practitioner partnership. *American Journal of Community Psychology, 18*, 151–158.

Keefe, S. E. (1984). Real and ideal familism among Mexican Americans and Anglo Americans: On the meaning of "close" family ties. *Human Organization, 43*, 65–70.

Keiffer, C. H. (1984). Citizen empowerment: A developmental perspective. In J. Rappaport, C. Swift, & R. Hess (Eds.), *Studies in empowerment: Steps toward understanding and action* (pp. 9–36). New York: Haworth Press.

Kellam, S., Koretz, D., & Moscicki (1999). Core elements of developmental epidemiologically based prevention research. *American Journal of Community Psychology, 27*, 463–482.

Kellert, S. R., & Wilson, E. O. (1993). (Eds.). *The biophilia hypothesis.* Washington, D.C.: Island Press.

Kelly, J. G. (1966). Ecological constraints on mental health services. *American Psychologist, 21*, 535–539.

Kelly, J. G. (1968). Toward an ecological conception of preventive interventions. In J. Carter (Ed.), *Research contributions from psychology to community mental health* (pp. 75–99). New York: Behavioral Publications.

Kelly, J. G. (1970). Antidote for arrogance: Training for community psychology. *American Psychologist, 25*, 524–531.

Kelly, J. G. (1971). Qualities for the community psychologist. *American Psychologist, 26*, 897–903.

Kelly, J. G. (1979) (Ed.). *Adolescent boys in high school: A psychological study of coping and adaptation.* Hillsdale, NJ: Erlbaum.

Kelly, J. G. (2000). Wellness as an ecological enterprise. In D. Cicchetti, J. Rappaport, I. Sandler, & R. P. Weissberg (Eds.), *The promotion of wellness in children and adolescents* (pp. 101–131). Washington, D.C.: Child Welfare League of American Press.

Kelly, J. G. (2001, June 9). Oral histories and quantitative analyses of interviews with community leaders. Presentation to the Biennial Conference on Community Research and Action, Atlanta, GA.

Kelly, J. G., Azelton, S., Burzette, R. G., & Mock, L. O. (1994). Creating social settings for diversity: An ecological thesis. In E. J. Trickett, R. J. Watts, & D. Birman (Eds.), *Human diversity: Perspectives on people in context* (pp. 424–451). San Francisco: Jossey-Bass.

Kelly, J. G., Ryan, A., Altman, B. E., & Stelzner, S. P. (2000). Understanding and changing social systems: An ecological view. In J. Rappaport & E. Seidman (Eds.), *Handbook of community psychology* (pp. 133–159). New York: Kluwer Academic/Plenum Publishers.

Kendall, P. C., & Southam-Gerow, M. A. (1995). Issues in the transportability of treatment: The case of anxiety disorders in youths. Special section: Efficacy and effectiveness in studies of child and adolescent psychotherapy. *Journal of Consulting and Clinical Psychology, 63*, 702–708.

Kendler, H. H. (1999). The role of value in the world of psychology. *American Psychologist, 54*, 828–835.

Kennedy, J. F. (1956). *Profiles in courage*. New York: Harper.

Kerr, S. (1983). On the folly of rewarding A while hoping for B. In B. M. Staw (Ed.), *Psychological foundation of organizational behavior, 2nd edition*. Glenview, IL: Scott Foresman Co.

Kerwin, C., & Ponterotto, J. G. (1995). Biracial identity development: Theory and research. In J. G. Ponterotto & J. M. Casas (Eds.), *Handbook of multicultural counseling* (pp. 199–217). Thousand Oaks, CA: Sage Publications, Inc.

Kesey, K. (1962). *One flew over the cuckoo's nest*. New York: Viking.

Kessler, R. C. (1997). The effects of stressful life events on depression. *Annual Review of Psychology, 48*, 191–214.

Kessler, R. C., & McLeod, J. D. (1984). Sex differences in vulnerability to undesirable life events. *American Sociological Review, 49*, 620–631.

Kessler, R. C., Mickelson, K. D., & Zhao, S. (1997). Patterns and correlates of self-help group membership in the United States. *Social Policy, 27*, 27–46.

Kessler, R. C., Price, R. H., & Wortman, C. (1985). Social factors in psychopathology: Stress, social support, and coping processes. *Annual Review of Psychology, 36*, 531–572.

Kiesler, C. A. (1982). Mental hospitals and alternative care: Noninstitutionalization as potential public policy for mental patients. *American Psychologist, 37*, 349–360.

Kilby, R. W. (1993). *The study of human values*. Lanham, MD: University of America

Kilmer, R. P., Cowen, E. L., Wyman, P. A., Work, W. C., & Magnus, K. B. (1998). Differences in stressors experienced by urban African American, White, and Hispanic children. *Journal of Community Psychology, 26*, 415–428.

Kim, U., & Berry, J. W. (1993). Introduction. In U. Kim & J. W. Berry (Eds.), *Indigenous Psychologies: Research and experience in cultural context.* (pp. 1–29). Newbury Park, CA: Sage.

Kim, U., & Berry, J. W. (1993). *Indigenous psychologies: Research and experience in cultural context*. Newbury Park, CA: Sage.

Kincheloe, J. J., Steinberg, S. R., & Gresson, A. (1996). *Measured lies: The bell curve examined*. New York: St. Martin's Press.

Kinder, D. R., & Sears, D. O. (1981). Prejudice and politics: Symbolic racism versus racial threats to the good life. *Journal of Personality and Social Psychology, 40*, 414–431.

King, L. W., Cotler, S. B., Patterson, K, (1975). Behavior modification in a Mexican-American school: A case study. *American Journal of Community Psychology, 3*, 229–235.

King, M. L., Jr. (1968). The role of the behavioral scientist in the Civil Rights Movement. *Journal of Social Issues, 24*, 1–12.

Kingree, J. B., & Thompson, M. (2000). Mutual help groups, perceived status benefits, and well-being: A test with adult children of alcoholics with personal substance abuse problems. *American Journal of Community Psychology, 28*, 325–342.

Kirk, S. A., & Kutchins, H. (1992). The selling of DSM: The rhetoric of science in psychiatry. Hawthorne, NY: Aldine de Gruyter.

Kissman, K., & Allen, J. (1993). *Single-parent families*. Newbury Park, CA: Sage.

Kivel, P. (1995). *Uprooting racism: How white people can work for racial justice*. Philadelphia: New Society Publishers.

Klein, K. J., Ralls, R. S., Smith-Major, V., & Douglas, C. (2000). Power and participation in the workplace: Implications for empowerment theory, research, and practice. In J. Rappaport & E. Seidman (Eds.), *Handbook of community psychology* (pp. 273–295). New York: Kluwer Academic/Plenum Publishers.

Kloos, B., & Moore, T. (2000a). The prospect and purpose of locating community research and action in religious settings. *Journal of Community Psychology, 28* (2), 119–138.

Kloos, B., & Moore, T., (Eds.). (2000b). Special issue: Religion and community psychology. *Journal of Community Psychology, 28* (2).

Kluckhorn, C. (1951). Values and value orientations in the theory of action: An exploration in definition and classification. In T. Parsons & E. Shils (Eds.), *Toward a general theory of action* (pp. 388–433). Cambridge, MA: Harvard University Press.

Kobasa, S. C. (1979). Stressful life events and health: An inquiry into hardiness. *Journal of Personality and Social Psychology, 37*, 1–11.

Kobasa, S. C., & Maddi, S. R. (1985). Effectiveness of hardiness, exercise and social support as resources against illness. *Journal of Psychosomatic Research 29*, 525–533.

Koch, S. (1959). *Psychology: A study of a science*. New York: McGraw-Hill.

Kochman, T. (1981). *Black and White styles in conflict*. Chicago: University of Chicago Press.

Kofkin, J. A., & Schwartz, C. (1995). Lesbian, gay, and bisexual youth: Search for community. Poster presented at Biennial Conference of Society for Community Research and Action, Chicago, June, 1995.

Kofkin, J. A. (1989). An alternative way of assessing life events. Poster presented at Annual Meeting of the American Psychological Association. New Orleans, LA.

Kofkin, J. A., & Reppucci, N. D. (1991). A reconceptualization of life events and its application to parental divorce. *American Journal of Community Psychology, 19*, 227–250.

Kofkin, J. A., Katz, P. A., & Downey, E. P. (1995, June). A longitudinal perspective on the roles of sex and race in playmate choices. Poster presented at Biennial Conference on Community Research and Action, Chicago, IL.

Kohlberg, L. (1976). Moral stages and moralization: The cognitive-developmental approach. In T. Lickona (Ed.), *Moral development and behavior: Theory, research, and social issues* (pp. 31–53). New York: Holt.

Kohlberg. L. (1964). Development of moral character and moral ideology. In M. L. Hoffman & L. W. Hoffman (Eds.), *Review of child development research (Vol. 1)* (pp. 283–332). New York: Russell Sage Foundation.

Kohler, J. (2000). 'Life will be better': Columbine school board votes to replace library with atrium. Associated Press. Retrieved January 21, 2001, from ***http:// abcnews.go.com/sections/us/DailyNews/ columbine_library000121.html***.

Kopp, C. B., & Krakow, J. B. (1983). The development and study of biological risk: A view of the past with an eye toward the future. *Child Development, 54*, 1086–1108.

Krause, N., & Shaw, B. A. (2000). Role-specific feelings of control and mortality. *Psychology and Aging, 15*, 617–626.

Kraut, R., Patterson, M., Lundmark, V., Kiesler, S., Mukopadhyay, T., & Scherlis, W. (1998). Internet paradox: A social technology that reduces social involvement and psychological well-being. *Amerocan Psychologist, 53*, 1017–1031.

Kress, J. S., & Elias, M. J. (2000). Infusing community psychology and religion: Themes from an action-research project in Jewish identity development. *Journal of Community Psychology, 28*, 187–198.

Kretzmann, J. P. (1992). *Community-based development and local schools: A promising partnership*. Chicago, IL: The Asset-Based Community Development Institute.

Kretzmann, J. P. (1995, September/October). Building communities from the inside out. *Shelterforce*, pp. 8–11.

Kretzmann, J. P., & McKnight, J. L. (1993). *Building communities from the inside out: A path toward finding and mobilizing a community's assets*. Evanston, IL: The Asset-based Community Development Institute for Policy Research.

Kroeker, C. J. (1995). Individual, organizational, and societal empowerment: A study of the processes in a Nicaraguan agricultural cooperative. *American Journal of Community Psychology, 23*, 749–765

Kübler-Ross, E. (1969). *On death and dying*. New York: Macmillan.

Kumpfer, K. L. (1999). Factors and processes contributing to resilience: The resilience framework. In M. D.

Glantz & J. L. Johnson (Eds.), *Resilience and development; Positive life adaptations* (pp. 179–224). New York: Kluwer Academic/Plenum.

Kumpfer, K., Whiteside, H. O., Wandersman, A. H., & Cardenas, E. (1997). *Community readiness for drug abuse prevention: Issues, tips, and tool*. Rockville, MD: National Institute for Drug Abuse (NIH Pub. No. 97–4110).

Kuntz, K. (1998). A lost legacy: Head Start's origins in community action. In J. Ellsworth & L. J. Ames (Eds.), *Critical perspectives on Project Head Start*. (pp. 1–48). Albany: State University of New York Press.

Kuo, F. E., Sullivan, W. C., Coley, R. L., & Brunson, L. (1998). Fertile ground for community: Inner-city neighborhood and common space. *American Journal of Community Psychology, 26*, 823–851.

Kushner, H. S. (1981). *When bad things happen to good people*. New York: Avon Books.

Lachenmeyer, J. R. (1992). Consultation. In M. S. Gibbs, J. R., Lachenmeyer, & J. Sigal (Eds.), *Community psychology and mental health* (pp. 101–113). New York: Gardner.

Lager, F. (1994). *Ben and Jerry's: The inside scoop: How two real guys built a business with a social conscience and a sense of humor*. New York: Crown Publishers, Inc.

Laing, R. D., & Esterson, A. (1970). *Sanity, madness, and the family*. New York: Pelican Books.

Lakey, B., & Lutz, C. J. (1996). Social support and preventive and therapeutic interventions. In G. R. Pierce, B. R. Sarason, & I. G. Sarason (Eds.), *Handbook of social support and the family* (pp. 435–465). New York: Plenum Press.

Lam, D. J., & Ho, D. Y. F. (1989). Community psychology in Hong Kong. *American Journal of Community Psychology, 17*, 83–97.

Lamb, H. R., & Zusman, J. (1979). Primary prevention in perspective. *American Journal of Psychiatry, 136*, 12–17.

Lambert, A. J., & Raichle, K. (2000). The role of political ideology in mediating judgments of blame in rape victims and their assailants: A test of the just world, personal responsibility, and legitimization hypotheses. *Personality and Social Psychology Bulletin, 26*, 853–863.

Lambert, W. E. (1992). Challenging established views on social issues: The power and limitations of research. *American Psychologist, 47*, 533–542.

Lambert, W. E., Tucker, G. R., D'Anglejan, A. (1973). Cognitive and attitudinal consequences of bilingual schooling: The St. Lambert project through grade five. *Journal of Educational Psychology, 65*, 141–159.

Lane, C., & Hobfoll, S. E. (1992). How loss affects anger and alienates potential supporters. *Journal of Consulting and Clinical Psychology, 60*, 935–942.

Langer, E. J., & Rodin, J. (1976). The effects of choice and enhanced personal responsibility for the aged: A field experiment. *Journal of Personality and Social Psychology, 34*, 191–198.

Laosa, L. M. (1977). Socialization, education, and continuity: The importance of the sociocultural context. *Young Children, 32*, 21–27.

Lawrence, J., Phillips, D., & Rundquist, P. S. (1993). "Mr. Chairman and Members of the Committee": The Congressional hearing process. In K. McCartney & D. Phillips (Eds.), *An insider's guide to providing expert testimony before Congress* (pp. 4–10). Chicago: Society for Research in Child Development.

Lazarus, R. S. (1966). Psychological stress and the coping process. New York: McGraw-Hill.

Lazarus, R. S. (1984). Puzzles in the study of daily hassles. *Journal of Behavioral Medicine, 7*, 375–389.

Lazarus, R. S. (1991). *Emotion and adaptation.* New York: Oxford University Press.

Lazarus, R. S., & Folkman, S. (1984). *Stress, appraisal, and coping.* New York: Springer-Verlag.

Lazarus, R. S., DeLongis, A., Folkman, S., & Gruen, R. (1985). Stress and adaptational outcomes: The problem of confounded measures. *American Psychologist, 40*, 770–779.

Lazarus, S., & Prinsloo, R. (1995). Community psychology in South Africa. *The Community Psychologist, 28*, 24–26.

Le Vine, R. A. (1974). Parental goals: A cross-cultural view. In H. J. Leichter (Ed.), *The family as educator* (pp. 52–65). New York: Teachers College Press.

Lee, M. Y., Campbell, A. R., & Mulford, C. L. (1999). Victim-blaming tendency toward people with AIDS among college students. *Journal of Social Psychology, 139* (3), 300–308.

Lehman, D. R., Wortman, C. B., & Williams, A. F. (1987). Long-term effects of losing a spouse or child in a motor vehicle crash. *Journal of Personality and Social Psychology, 52*, 218–231.

Lehrer, P. M., & Woolfolk, R. L. (Eds.). (1993). *Principles and practice of stress management.* New York: Guilford Press.

Lerner, H. G. (1985). *The dance of anger: A woman's guide to changing the patterns of intimate relationships.* New York: Harper & Row.

Lerner, M. J. (1970). The desire for justice and reactions to victims. In J. McCauley & L. Berkowitz (Eds.), *Altruism and helping behavior* (pp. 205–209). New York: Academic Press.

Lerner, M. J. (1980). *The belief in a just world: A fundamental delusion.* New York: Plenum Press.

Levant, R. F., & Pollack, W. S. (1997). (Eds.). *A new psychology of men.* New York: Basic Books.

Levin, Gloria <leving@csr.nih.gov>, "Re: Students, please come," June 6, 2001, <listserv://scra-l@lists.apa.org> (June 6, 2001).

Levin, J. S. (1994). Religion and health: Is there an association, is it valid, and is it causal? *Social Science and Medicine, 38*, 1475–1482.

Levin, J. S., & Chatters, L. M. (1998). Research on religion and mental health: An overview of empirical findings and theoretical issues. In H. G. Koenig (Ed.), *Handbook of religion and mental health* (pp. 33–50). San Diego: Academic Press.

Levine, M. (1981). *The history and politics of community mental health.* New York: Oxford University Press.

Levine, M. (1998). Prevention and community. *American Journal of Community Psychology, 26*, 189–206.

Levine, M., & Levine, A. (1970). *A social history of helping services: Clinic, court, school, and community.* New York: Appleton-Century-Crofts.

Levine, M., & Perkins, D. V. (1997). *Principles of community psychology: Perspectives and Application, 2nd Ed.* New York: Oxford University Press.

Levy, L. H. (2000). Self-help groups. In J. Rappaport & E. Seidman (Eds.), *Handbook of community psychology* (pp. 591–613). New York: Kluwer Academic/Plenum Publishers.

Lewin, K. (1948/1997). Action research and minority problems. In G. Lewin & D. Cartwright (Eds.), *Resolving social conflicts* and *Field theory in social science* (pp. 143–152). Washington, D.C.: American Psychological Association.

Lewin, K. (1951). *Field theory in social science.* New York: Harper and Row.

Lewin, T. (2000, June 25). Growing up, growing apart: Fast friends try to resist the pressure to divide by race. *New York Times*, pp. 1, 14–16.

Lewinsohn, P., Mischel, W., Chaplin, W., & Barton, R. (1980). Social competence and depression: The role of illusory self-perceptions. *Journal of Abnormal Psychology, 89*, 203–212.

Lewis, M. S., Gottesman, D., & Gutstein, S. (1979). The course and duration of crisis. *Journal of Consulting and Clinical Psychology, 47*, 128–134.

Li, D. (1989). The effect of role change on intellectual ability and on the ability self-concept in Chinese children. *American Journal of Community Psychology, 17*, 73–81.

Lichtenstein, E., Lopez, K., Glasgow, R. E., Gilbert-McRae, S., & Hall, R. (1996). Effectiveness of a consultation intervention to promote tobacco control policies in Northwest Indian tribes: integrating experimental evaluation and service delivery. *American Journal of Community Psychology, 24*, 639–656.

Lieberman, M. A. (1975). Adaptive processes in late life. In N. Datan, & L. H. Ginsberg (Eds.), *Lifespan developmental psychology: Normative life crises.* New York: Academic Press.

Lieberman, M. A., & Snowden, L. R. (1993). Problems in assessing prevalence and membership characteristics of self-help group participants. *Journal of Applied Behavioral Science, 29*, 166–180.

Liebkind, K., & Jasinskaja-Lahti, I. (2000). The influence of experiences of discrimination on psychological stress: A comparison of seven immigrant groups. *Journal of Community and Applied Social Psychology, 10,* 1–16.

Lindblom, C. E., & Cohen, D. K. (1979). *Useable knowledge: Social science and social problem solving.* New Haven, CT: Yale University Press.

Lindemann, E. (1944). Symptomatology and management of acute grief. *American Journal of Psychiatry, 101,* 141–148.

Lindblom, J. (1967). *Prophecy in ancient Israel.* Philadelphia: Fortress Press, 1967.

Linney, J. A. (1990). Community psychology into the 1990's: Capitalizing opportunity and promoting innovation. *American Journal of Community Psychology, 18,* 1–19.

Linney, J. A. (2000). Assessing ecological constructs and community context. In J. Rappaport & E. Seidman (Eds.), *Handbook of community psychology* (pp. 647–668). Kluwer Academic/Plenum Publishers.

Linville, P. W., Fischer, G. W., & Salovey, P. (1989). Perceived distributions of characteristics of in-group and out-group members: Empirical evidence and a computer simulation. *Journal of Personality and Social Psychology, 57,* 165–188.

Lippard, L. R. (1990). Mixed Blessings: New art in a mulitcultural America. New York: Pantheon.

Litwak, E. (1985). *Helping the elderly.* New York: Guilford.

Lloyd, C., Alexander, A. A., Rice, D. G., & Greenfield, N. S., (1980). Life events as predictors of academic performance. *Journal of Human Stress, 6,* 15–25.

Lockard, J. (1997). Progressive politics, electronic individualism and the myth of virtual community. In D. Porter (Ed.), *Internet culture* (pp. 55–71). New York: Routledge.

Loftus, E. F. (1991). Resolving legal questions with psychological data. *American Psychologist, 46,* 1046–1048.

Logan, S. L. (1996). *The Black family: Strengths, self-help, and positive change.* Boulder, CO: Westview Press.

Lomranz, J. (1995). Endurance and living: Long-term effects of the Holocaust. In S. E. Hobfoll & M. W. de Vries (Eds.). (1995). *Extreme stress and communities: Impact and intervention* (pp. 325–352). Boston: Kluwer Academic Publishers.

Long, J. V., & Vaillant, G. E. (1984). Natural history of male psychological health, XI: Escape from the underclass. *American Journal of Psychiatry, 141,* 341–346.

Longino, C. F., Jr. (1988). Who are the oldest Americans? *The Gerontologist, 28,* 515–523.

Longshore, D. (1979). Color connotations and racial attitudes. *Journal of Black Studies, 11,* 105–120.

Loo, C., Fong, K. T., & Iwamasa, G. (1988). Ethnicity and cultural diversity: An analysis of work published in community psychology journals, 1965–1985. *Journal of Community Psychology, 16,* 332–349.

Lorde, A. (1984). *Sister outsider.* Freedom, CA: The Crossing Press.

Lorion, R. P. (1983). Evaluating preventive interventions: Guidelines for the serious social change agent. In R. D. Felner, L. A. Jason, J. N. Moritsugu, & S. S. Farber (Eds.), *Preventive psychology: Theory, research, and practice.* New York: Pergamon.

Lounsbury, D., Skourtes, S., & Cantillon, D. (1999, Fall). 1999 survey of graduate training programs in community psychology [Electronic version]. *The Community Psychologist, 32 (4),* 10–33.

Lowenthal, M. F., Thurnher, M., Chiriboga, D., Beeson, D., Gigy, L., Lurie, E., Pierce, R., Spence, D., & Weise, L. (1975). *Four stages of life.* San Francisco: Jossey-Bass.

Luke, D. A., Rappaport, J., & Seidman, E. (1991). Setting phenotypes in a mutual help organization: Expanding behavior setting theory. *American Journal of Community Psychology, 19,* 147–167.

Luthar, S. S. (1991). Vulnerability and resilience: A study of high-risk adolescents. *Child Development, 62,* 600–616.

Luthar, S. S. (1993). Annotation: Methodological and conceptual issues in the study of resilience. *Journal of Child Psychology and Psychiatry, 34,* 441–453.

Luthar, S. S. (1995). Social competence in the school setting: Prospective cross-domain associations among inner-city teens. *Child Development, 66,* 416–429.

Luthar, S. S. (1999). *Poverty and children's adjustment.* Newbury Park, CA: Sage.

Luthar, S. S., & Cicchetti, D. (2000). The construct of resilience: Implications for interventions and social policies. *Development and Psychopathology. 12,* 857–885.

Luthar, S. S., & Cushing, G. (1999). Measurement issues in the empirical study of resilience: An overview. In M. D. Glantz & J. L. Johnson (Eds.), *Resilience and development; Positive life adaptations* (pp. 129–160). New York: Kluwer Academic/Plenum.

Luthar, S. S., Cicchetti, D., & Becker, B. (2000b). The construct of resilience: A critical evaluation and guidelines for future work. *Child Development, 71,* 543–562.

Luthar, S. S., Cicchetti, D., & Becker, B. (2000a). Research on resilience: Response to commentaries. *Child Development, 71,* 573–575.

Luthar, S. S., Doernberger, C. H., & Zigler, E. (1993). Resilience is not a unidimensional construct: Insights from a prospective study of inner-city adolescents. *Development and Psychopathology, 5,* 703–717.

Lynam, D. R., Milich, R., Zimmerman, R., Novak, S. P., Logan, T. K., Martin, C., Leukefeld, C., & Clayton, R. (1999). Project DARE: No effects at 10-year follow-up. *Journal of Consulting and Clinical Psychology, 67,* 590–594.

Maccoby, E. E., & Jacklin, C. N. (1974). *The psychology of sex differences.* Stanford: Stanford University Press.

Maccoby, E. E., & Martin, J. A. (1983). Socialization in the context of the family: Parent–child interaction. In E. M. Hetherington (Ed.), *Handbook of child psychology:*

Socialization, personality, and social development (Vol. 4) (pp. 1–102). New York: Wiley.

Maccoby, N., & Alexander, J. (1979). Reducing heart disease risk using the mass media: Comparing the effects on three communities. In R. F. Muñoz, L. R. Snowden, J. G. Kelly, & Associates (Eds.), *Social and psychological research in community settings* (pp. 69–100). San Francisco: Jossey-Bass.

MacCoun, R. J. (1998). Biases in the interpretation and use of research results. *Annual Review of Psychology, 49*, 259–287.

Mack, M. (1994). Understanding spirituality in counseling psychology: Consideration for research, training, and practice. *Counseling and Values, 39*, 15–31.

Madigan, L., & Gamble, N. (1991). *The second rape: Society's continued betrayal of the victim.* New York: Lexington Books.

Madigan, R., Johnson, S., & Linton, P. (1995). The language of psychology: APA style as epistemology. *American Psychologist, 50*, 428–436.

Madsen, W. (1969). Mexican Americans and Anglo Americans: A comparative study of mental health in Texas. In S. C. Plog & R. B. Edgerton (Eds.), *Changing perspectives in mental illness* (pp. 217–247). New York: Holt, Rinehart, and Winston.

Madsen, W. (2001, June 9). Making the workplace a better place: Towards a collaborative, inclusive culture. Presentation to the Biennial Conference on Community Research and Action, Atlanta, GA.

Maeder, T. (1989). *Children of psychiatrists and other psychotherapists.* New York: Harper and Row.

Magnus, K. B., Cowen, E. L., Wyman, P. A., Fagen, D. B., & Work, W. C. (1999). Correlates of resilient outcomes among highly stressed African American and White urban children. *Journal of Community Psychology, 27*, 473–488.

Maher, B. (1988). Abnormal and clinical psychology. In E. R. Hilgard (Ed.), *Fifty years of psychology: Essays in honor of Floyd Ruch.* (pp. 153–168). Glenview, IL: Scott, Foresman and Co.

Mannino, F. V., & Shore, M. F. (1972), Research in mental health consultation. In S. E. Golann & C. Eisdorfer (Eds.), *Handbook of community mental health* (pp. 755–777). New York: Appleton-Century-Croft.

Manns, W. (1997). Supportive roles of significant others in African American families. In H. P. McAdoo (Ed.), *Black families, 3rd ed.* (pp. 198–213). Thousand Oaks, CA: Sage.

Marcus, E. (1992a). The Drag Queen [Interview with Rey "Sylvia Lee" Rivera]. *Making history: The struggle for gay and lesbian equal rights, 1945–1990* (pp. 187–196). New York: HarperCollins.

Marcus, E. (1992b). The Psychologist [Interview with Evelyn Hooker]. *Making history: The struggle for gay and lesbian equal rights, 1945–1990* (pp. 16–25). New York: HarperCollins.

Marcus, E. (1992c). *Making history: The struggle for gay and lesbian equal rights 1945–1990: An oral history.* New York: HarperCollins.

Marín, B.V., Tschann, J. M., Gomez, C. A., & Gregorich, S. (1998). Self-efficacy to use condoms in unmarried Latino adults. *American Journal of Community Psychology, 26*, 53–71.

Marín, G. (1993). Defining culturally appropriate community interventions: Hispanics as a case study. *Journal of Community Psychology, 21*, 149–161.

Marín, G., Gamba, R. J., & Marín, B. V. (1992). Extreme response style and acquiescence among Hispanics: The role of acculturation and education. *Journal of Cross-Cultural Psychology, 23 (4)*, 498–509.

Marin, M. V. (1991). *Social protest in an urban barrio: A study of the Chicano movement, 1966–1974.* Lanham, MD: University Press of America.

Markus, H. R., & Kitayama, S. (1991). Culture and the self: Implications for cognition, emotion, and motivation. *Psychological Review, 98*, 224–253.

Markus, H., & Nurius, P. (1986). Possible selves. *American Psychologist, 41*, 954–969.

Marotta, T. (1981). *The politics of homosexuality.* Boston: Houghton Mifflin Co.

Marsella, A. J. (1998). Toward a "global-community psychology": Meeting the needs of a changing world. *American Psychologist, 53*, 1282–1291.

Marsella, A. J., Oliveira, J. M., Plummer, C. M., & Crabbe, K. M. (1998). Native Hawaiian culture, mind, and well-being. In H. I. McCubbin, E. A. Thompson, A. I. Thompson, & J. E. Fromer (Eds.), *Resiliency in Native American and immigrant families* (pp. 93–113). Thousand Oaks, CA: Sage.

Martineau, W. H. (1972). A model of the social functions of humor. In J. H. Goldstein & P. E. McGhee (Eds.), *The psychology of humor: Theoretical perspectives and empirical issues.* New York: Academic Press.

Maruyama, M. (1983). Cross-cultural perspectives on social and community change. In E. Seidman (Ed.), *Handbook of social intervention* (33–47). Beverly Hills: Sage.

Maslow, A. H. (1970). *Religions, values, and peak experiences.* New York: Viking.

Masten, A. S (2001). Ordinary magic: Resilience processes in development. *American Psychologist, 56*, 227–238.

Masten, A. S, Coatsworth, J. D. (1998). The development of competence in favorable and unfavorable environments: Lessons from research on successful children. *American Psychologist. 53*, 205–220.

Masten, A. S. (1999). Commentary: The promise and perils of resilience research as a guide to preventive interventions. In M. D. Glantz & J. L. Johnson (Eds.), *Resilience and development: Positive life adaptations* (pp. 251–257). New York: Kluwer Academic/Plenum.

Masten, A. S., & Curtis, W. (2000). Integrating competence and psychopathology: Pathways toward a comprehensive science of adaptation in development. *Development and Psychopathology. 12*, 529–550.

Masten, A. S., & Garmezy, N. (1985). Risk, vulnerability, and protective factors in development. In B. B. Lahey & A. E. Kazdin (Eds.), *Advances in clinical child psychology: Vol. 8*. New York: Plenum.

Masten, A. S., & Garmezy, N., Tellegen, A., Pellegrini, D. S., Larkin, K., & Larsen, A. (1988). Competence and stress in school children: The moderating effects of individual and family qualities. *Journal of Child Psychiatry, 29*, 745–764.

Masten, A. S., Best, K., & Garmezy, N. (1990). Resilience and development: Contributions from the study of children who overcome adversity. *Development and Psychopathology, 2*, 425–444.

Masten, A. S., Hubbard, J. J., Gest, S. D., Tellegen, A., Garmezy, N., & Ramirez, M. (1999). Competence in the context of adversity: Pathways to resilience and maladaptation from childhood to late adolescence. *Development and Psychopathology, 11*, 143–169.

Maton, K. I. (1987). Patterns and psychological correlates of material support within a religious setting: The bidirectional support hypothesis. *American Journal of Community Psychology, 15*, 185–207.

Maton, K. I. (1989). Community settings as buffers of life stress? Highly supportive churches, mutual help groups, and senior centers. *American Journal of Community Psychology, 17*, 203–232.

Maton, K. I. (1999). SCRA moving forward: Multidisciplinary minority-pipeline initiative, diversity within SCRA, and member dues increase (President's column). *The Community Psychologist, 32 (1)*, 4–7.

Maton, K. I. (2000). Making a difference: The social ecology of social transformation. *American Journal of Community Psychology, 28*, 25–57.

Maton, K. I., & Rappaport, J. (1984). Empowerment in a religious setting: A multivariate investigation. *Prevention in Human Services, 3*, 37–70.

Maton, K. I., & Salem, D. A. (1995). Organizational characteristics of empowering community settings: A multiple case study approach. *American Journal of Community Psychology, 23*, 631–656.

Maton, K. I., & Wells, E. A. (1995). Religion as a community resource for well-being: Prevention, healing, and empowerment pathways. *Journal of Social Issues, 51*, 177–193.

Maton, K. I., Hrabowski, F. A. III, & Greene, M. L. (2001). Overcoming the odds: Raising academically successful African American young women. Poster presented at the 8th Biennial Conference of the Society for Community Research and Action. Atlanta, GA, June, 2001.

Maton, K. I., Teti, D. M., Corns, K. M., & Vieira-Baker, C. C. (1996). Cultural specificity of support sources, correlates and contexts: Three studies of African-American and Caucasian youth. *American Journal of Community Psychology, 24*, 551–587.

Mayer, J. P., & Davidson, W. S., II (2000). Dissemination of innovation as social change. In J. Rappaport & E. Seidman (Eds.), *Handbook of community psychology* (pp. 421–438). New York: Kluwer Academic/Plenum Publishers.

Mayerhoff, M. (1971). *On caring*. New York: Harper and Row.

Mays, V. M., & Cochran, S. D. (1990). Methodological issues in the assessment and prediction of AIDS related behaviors among Black Americans. In B. Voeller, J. M. Reinsch, & M. Gottlieb (Eds.), *AIDS and sex: An integrated and biobehavioral approach* (pp. 97–120). New York: Oxford University Press.

Mays, V. M., Rubin, J., Sabourin, M., & Walker, L. (1996). Moving toward a global psychology: Changing theories and practice to meet the needs of a changing world. *American Psychologist, 51*, 485–487.

McAdoo, H. P. (1988). *Black families, 2nd edition*. Newbury Park, CA: Sage Publications.

McArthur, L. Z. (1981). What grabs you? The role of attention in impression formation and causal attribution. In E. T. Higgins, C. P. Herman, & M. P. Zanna (Eds.), *Social cognition: The Ontario Symposium, Vol. 1* (pp. 201–246). Hillsdale, NJ: Erlbaum.

McConahay, J. B. (1986). Modern racism, ambivalence, and the Modern Racism Scale. In J. F. Dovidio & S. L. Gaertner (Eds.), *Prejudice, discrimination, and racism: Theory and research* (pp. 91–125). New York: Academic Press.

McCord, J. (1978). A thirty-year follow-up of treatment effects. *American Psychologist, 33*, 284–289.

McCord, W., & McCord, J. (1969). *Origins of crime: A new evaluation of the Cambridge-Somerville Youth Study*. Montclair, NJ: Patterson Smith.

McCubbin, H. I, Joy, C.B., Cauble, A. E., Comeau, J. K., Patterson, J. M., & Needle, R. H. (1980). Family stress and coping: A decade review. *Journal of Marriage and the Family, 42*, 855–871.

McCubbin, H. I., & McCubbin, M. A. (1988). Typologies of resilient families: Emerging roles of class and ethnicity. *Family Relations, 37*, 247–254.

McCubbin, H. I., & McCubbin, M. A. Thompson, A. I., & Thompson, E. A. (1998). Resiliency in ethnic families: A conceptual model for predicting family adjustment and adaptation. In H. I. McCubbin, E. A. Thompson, A. I. Thompson, & J. E. Fromer (Eds.), *Resiliency in Native American and immigrant families* (pp. 3–48). Thousand Oaks, CA: Sage.

McFadden, S. H. (1995). Religion and well-being in aging persons in an aging society. *Journal of Social Issues, 51*, 161–175.

McFarlane, A. C., Policansky, S., & Irwin, C. (1987). A longitudinal study of the psychological morbidity in children due to a natural disaster. *Psychological Medicine, 17,* 727–738.

McGee, T. F. (1980). Crisis intervention. In M. S. Gibbs, J. R. Lachenmeyer, & J. Sigal (Eds), *Community psychology: Theoretical and empirical approaches* (pp. 239–266). New York: Gardner Press, Inc.

McGonagle, K. A., & Kessler, R. C. (1990). Chronic stress, acute stress, and depressive symptoms. *American Journal of Community Psychology, 18,* 681–706.

McHugh, M. C., Koeske, R., & Frieze, I. (1986). Issues to consider in conducting nonsexist psychological research: A guide for researchers. *American Psychologist, 41,* 879–890.

McIntosh, D. N., Silver, R. C., & Wortman, C. B. (1993). Religion's role in adjustment to a negative life event: Coping with the loss of a child. *Journal of Personality and Social Psychology, 65,* 812–821.

McIntosh, P. (1989). White privilege: Unpacking the invisible knapsack. *Peace and Freedom (July/August),* 10–12.

McIntosh, P. (1992). White privilege and male privilege: A personal account of coming to see correspondences through work in women's studies. In M. L. Anderson & P. H. Collins (Eds.), *Race, class, and gender: An anthology* (pp. 70–81). Belmont, CA: Wadsworth.

McKnight, J. (1995). *The careless society: Community and its counterfeits.* New York: BasicBooks.

McLeod, D. L., & Meyer, H. J. (1967). A study of the values of social workers. In E. J. Thomas (Ed.), *Behavioral science for social* workers (p. 401–416). New York: Free Press.

McLoyd, V. C. (1989). Socialization and development in a changing economy. *American Psychologist, 44 (2),* 293–302.

McLoyd, V. C. (1990). The impact of economic hardship on Black families and children: Psychological distress, parenting, and socioemotional development. *Child Development, 61,* 311–346.

McLoyd, V. C. (1998). Socioeconomic disadvantage and child development. *American Psychologist, 53,* 185–204.

McLoyd, V., & Randolph, S. (1985). Secular trends in the study of Afro-American children: A review of *Child Development,* 1936–1980. *Monographs of the Society for Research in Child Development, 50,* 78–92.

McMillan, D. W. (1996). Sense of community. *Journal of Community Psychology, 24,* 315–325.

McMillan, D. W. (2001, June 8). [Comments distributed for] Panel on empirical advances in sense of community: Current issues and applications. Biennial Conference on Community Research and Action. Atlanta, GA.

McMillan, D. W., & Chavis, D. M. (1986). Sense of community: A definition and theory. *Journal of Community Psychology, 14,* 6–23.

Medoff, P., & Sklar, H. (1994). *Streets of hope: The fall and rise of an urban neighborhood.* Boston: South End Press.

Melton, G. (1995). Bringing psychology to Capitol Hill: Briefings on child and family policy. *American Psychologist, 50,* 766–770.

Melton, G. B. (1992). It's time for neighborhood research and action. *Chid Abuse and Neglect, 16,* 909–913.

Melton, G. B. (2000). Community change, community stasis, and the law. In J. Rappaport & E. Seidman (Eds.), *Handbook of community psychology* (pp. 523–540). New York: Kluwer Academic/Plenum Publishers.

Merriam-Webster (1999). *WWWebster Dictionary.* Retrieved from ***http://www.m-w.com/dictionary.htm***

Merriam-Webster (2000). *WWWebster Dictionary.* Retrieved from ***http://www.m-w.com/dictionary.htm***

Messeri, P., Silverstein, M., & Litwak, E. (1993). Choosing optimal support group: A review and reformulation. *Journal of Health and Social Behavior, 34 (2),* 122–137.

Meuse, K. P. (1985). The life events stress-performance linkage: An exploratory study. *Journal of Human Stress, 11,* 111–117.

Meyer, D. S., & Tarrow, S. (1998). (Eds.). *The social movement society: Contentious politics for a new century.* Lanham, MD: Rowman & Littlefield.

Meyers, J. C. (2000). A community psychologist in the public policy arena. In J. Rappaport & E. Seidman (Eds.), *Handbook of community psychology* (pp. 761–764). New York: Kluwer Academic/Plenum Publishers.

Midgeley, J., & Livermore, M. (1998). Social capital and local economic development: Implications for community social work. *Journal of Community Practice, 5 (1/2),* 29–40.

Miles, M. B., & Huberman, A. M. (1984). *Qualitative data analysis: A sourcebook of new methods.* Newbury Park, CA: Sage.

Milgram, S. (1963). Behavioral study of obedience. *Journal of Abnormal and Social Psychology, 8,* 377–383.

Milgram, S. (1974). *Obedience to authority: An experimental view.* New York: Harper and Row.

Miller, D. T. (1999). The norm of self-interest. *American Psychologist, 54,* 1053–1060.

Miller, G. A. (1969). Psychology as a means of promoting human welfare. *American Psychologist, 24,* 1065–1075.

Miller, G. D., & Baldwin, D. C., Jr. (2000). Implications of the wounded healer paradigm for the use of self in therapy. In M. Baldwin (Ed.), *The use of self in therapy, 2nd edition* (pp. 243–261). New York: Haworth Press.

Miller, J. B. (1976). *Toward a new psychology of women.* Boston: Beacon Press.

Miller, J. B. (1986). *Toward a new psychology of women, 2nd edition.* Boston: Beacon Press.

Miller, J. B. (1991). The development of women's sense of self. In J. V. Jordan, A. G. Kaplan, J. B. Miller, I. P. Stiver, & J. L. Surrey (Eds.), *Women's growth in connection:*

Writings from the Stone Center (pp.11–26). New York: The Guilford Press.

Miller, J. G. (1984). Culture and the development of everyday social explanation. *Journal of Personality and Social Psychology, 46,* 961–978.

Miller, J. G., Bersoff, D. M., & Harwood, R. L. (1990). Perceptions of social responsibilities in India and the United States: Moral imperatives or personal decisions. *Journal of Personality and Social Psychology, 58,* 33–47.

Miller, K. E., & Banyard, V. L. (Eds.). (1998). Qualitative research in community psychology (Special Issue). *American Journal of Community Psychology, 26 (4).*

Miller, K. S., & Iscoe, I. (1963). The concept of crisis. *Human Organization, 22* (3), 195–201.

Mills, C. W. (1959). *The sociological imagination.* New York: Oxford University Press.

Mindess, H. (1971). *Laughter and liberation.* Los Angeles: Nash.

Misra, G., & Agarwal, R. (1985). The meaning of achievement: Implications for a cross-cultural theory of achievement motivation. In I. R. Lagunes & Y. H. Poortinga (Eds.), *From a different perspective: Studies of behaviors across cultures* (pp. 250–266). Lisse: Swets and Zeitlinger.

Mitchell, R. E., & Trickett, E. J. (1980). Task force agent: Social networks as mediators of social support. *Community Mental Health Journal, 16,* 27–44.

Mitchell, R. E., Stevenson, J. F., & Florin, P. (1996). A typology of prevention activities: Applications to community coalitions. *Journal of Primary Prevention, 16 (4),* 413–436.

Mitford, J. (1973). *Kind and usual punishment: The prison business.* New York: Knopf.

Moffit, T. E. (1993). Adolescence-limited and life-course-persistent antisocial behavior: A developmental taxonomy. *Psychological Review, 100,* 674–701.

Moghaddam, F. M. (1990). Modulative and generative orientations in psychology: Implications for psychology in the three worlds. *Journal of Social Issues, 46,* 21–41.

Moghaddam, F. M., & Studer, C. (1997). Cross-cultural psychology: The frustrated gadfly's promises, potentials, and failures. In D. Fox & I. Prilleltensky (Eds.), *Critical psychology: An introduction* (pp. 185–201). Thousand Oaks, CA: Sage.

Moke, P., & Bohan, J. S. (1992). Reconstructing curriculum: Psychology's paradigm and the virtue of iconoclasm. *Women's Studies Quarterly, 16,* 7–27.

Molock, S. D., & Douglas, K. B. (1999). Suicidality in the Black community: A collaborative response from a womanist theologian and a community psychologist. *The Community Psychologist, 32* (3), 32–35.

Montero, M. (1996). Parallel lives: Community psychology in Latin America and the United States. *American Journal of Community Psychology, 24,* 589–606.

Moore, T. (1992). The African American church: A source of empowerment, mutual help, and social change. In K. I. Pargament, K. I. Maton, & R. E. Hess (Eds.), *Religion and prevention in mental health: Research, vision, and action.* Binghamton, NY: Haworth Press.

Moos, R. H. (1973a). Conceptualizations of human environments. *American Psychologist, 28,* 652–665.

Moos, R. H. (1973b). Changing the social milieus of psychiatric treatment settings. *Journal of Applied Behavioral Science, 9,* 575–593.

Moos, R. H. (1974a). *The social climate scales: An overview.* Palo Alto, CA: Consulting Psychologists Press, Inc.

Moos, R. H. (1974b). *Community oriented programs environment scale manual.* Palo Alto, CA: Consulting Psychologists Press, Inc.

Moos, R. H. (1976). *The human context: Environmental determinants of behavior.* New York: Wiley.

Moos, R. H. (1984). Context and coping: Toward a unifying conceptual framework. *American Journal of Community Psychology, 12 (1),* 5–36.

Moos, R. H., (1979). Social climate measurement and feedback. In R. Munoz, L. Snowden, & J. Kelly (Eds.), *Social and psychological research in community settings* (pp. 145–182). San Francisco: Jossey-Bass.

Morgan, J. R. (2000). Applied community psychology: A ten-year field trial. In J. Rappaport & E. Seidman (Eds.), *Handbook of community psychology* (pp. 745–748). New York: Kluwer Academic/Plenum Publishers.

Morison, S. J., Ames, E. W., & Chisholm, K. (1995). The development of children adopted from Romanian orphanages. *Merrill-Palmer Quarterly, 41,* 411–430.

Moritsugu, J., & Sue, S. (1983). Minority status as a stressor. In R. D. Felner, L. A. Jason, J. N. Moritsugu, & S. S. Farber (Eds.), *Preventive Psychology: Theory, research, and practice* (pp. 162–174). New York: Pergamon Press.

Morrice, J. (1976). *Crisis intervention: Studies in community care.* New York: Pergamon.

Morris, M. W., & Peng, K. (1994). Culture and cause: American and Chinese attributions for social and physical events. *Journal of Personality and Social Psychology, 67,* 949–971.

Morris, M., & Frisman, L. K. (1987). The competent community revisited: A case study of networking in policy implementation. *Journal of Community Psychology, 15,* 29–34.

Moskovitz, S. (1983). *Love despite hate: Child survivors of the holocaust and their adult lives.* New York: Schocken Books.

Moss, H. A. (1974). Early sex differences and mother–infant interaction. In R. M. Richart & R. L. Eile (Eds.), *Sex differences in behavior.* New York: Wiley.

Moss, J. (1991). Hurling oppression: Overcoming anomie and self-hatred. In B. Bowser (Ed.), *Black male* adolescents: Parenting and education in community context. Lanham, MD: University Presses of America.

Mrazek, P. J., & Haggerty, R. J. (Eds). (1994). *Reducing risks for mental disorder: Frontiers for preventive intervention research.* Washington, D.C.: National Academy Press.

Mueller, D. P., Edwards, D. W., & Yarvis, R. M. (1977). Stressful life events and psychiatric symptomatology: Change or undesirability? *Journal of Health and Social Behavior, 18*, 307–317.

Mulvey, A. (1988). Community psychology and feminism: Tensions and commonalities. *Journal of Community Psychology, 16*, 70–83.

Mulvey, A., Terenzio, M., Hill, J., Bond, M. A., Huygens, I., Hamerton, H. R., & Cahill, S. (2000). Stories of relative privilege: Power and social change in feminist community psychology, *American Journal of Community Psychology, 28*, 883–911.

Mulvey, E. P., & Hicks, A. (1982). The paradoxical effects of a juvenile code change in Virginia. *American Journal of Community Psychology, 10*, 705–721.

Muñoz, R. F., Mrazek, P. J., & Haggerty, R. J. (1996). Institute of Medicine report on prevention of mental disorders: Summary and commentary. *American Psychologist, 51*, 1116–1122.

Murphy, D. E. (2001, March 7). Queens Library moves past 'shh' (and books). *The New York Times*, Metropolitan Desk (p. A1)

Murray, D. (1988). *A history of Western psychology, 2nd ed.* Englewood Cliffs, NJ: Prentice Hall.

Murray, H. (1938). *Exploration in personality.* New York: Oxford University Press.

Myers, J. K., & Shaffer, L. (1954). Social stratification and psychiatric practice: A study of an out-patient clinic. In E. Gartly Jaco (Ed.), *Patients, physicians, and illness* (pp. 501–506). Glencoe, IL: The Free Press.

Myers, L. J. (1999). Transforming psychology: An African American perspective. In R. L. Jones (Ed.), *Advances in African American psychology* (pp. 9–25). Hampton, VA: Cobb and Henry.

Nagel, S. (1970). Overview of law and social change. In S. Nagel (Ed.), *Law and social change.* Beverly Hills: Sage.

National Civic League (1998, November 14). Healthy Communities pioneers honored: Conference cites work of Leonard Duhl, Trevor Hancock and Judith Kurland (Press Release). Denver, CO. Retrieved September 27, 2001, from *http://www.ncl.org/ncl/press18.htm.*

National Institute of Drug Abuse (1997). *Community readiness for drug abuse prevention: Issues, tips, and tools.* (publication # PB#97–209605). Washington, D.C.: National Institute of Drug Abuse. Retrieved May 2, 2001, from *http://www.open.org/~westcapt/crstages.htm.*

Negri, G. (2000, Nov. 26). A sense of renewal stirs in Roxbury: John Barros, head of Dudley Street, is seen as catalyst. *Boston Sunday Globe*, C1. Retrieved April 25, 2001, from *http://www.dsni.org/News%20articles/In%20the%20News/globe_nov_26_2000.htm.*

Neitzsche, F. W. (1997). *Twilight of the idols, or, how to philosophize with the hammer* (R. Polt, trans.). Indianapolis, IN: Hackett.

Nelson, G., Ochocka, J., Griffin, K., & Lord, J. (1998). "Nothing about me without me": Participatory action research with self-help/mutual aid organizations for psychiatric consumer/survivors. *American Journal of Community Psychology, 26*, 881–912.

Nelson. K. (1981). Social cognition in a script framework. In J. H. Flavell & L. Ross (Eds.), *Social cognition.* Cambridge: Cambridge University Press.

Nemec, K., Hungerford, R., Hutchings, L., & Huygens, I. (2000). Community psychology graduate employment in Aotearoa, New Zealand. In C. R. O'Donnell & J. R. Ferrari (Eds.), *Employment in community psychology: The diversity of opportunity* (pp. 45–52). Binghamton, NY: Haworth Press.

Nemeth, C. J., & Kwan, J. (1987). Minority influence, divergent thinking, and detection of correct solutions. *Journal of Applied Social Psychology, 17*, 788–799.

New York City Coalition to End Lead Poisoning (2001). Brief of amicus curiae in support of plaintiffs' motion for leave to appeal to the court of appeals: Clarissa Stover v. James O'Connor. Retrieved June 20, 2001, from *http://www.nmic.org/nyccelp/documents/Stover-amicus-brief-in-support-of—leave-to-appeal.PDF.*

Newbrough, J. R. (1970). Community psychology: A new specialty. In D. Adelson & B. L. Kalis (Eds.), *Community psychology and mental health.* (pp. 36–51). Scranton, PA: Chandler Publishing Co.

Newbrough, J. R. (1992). Community psychology in the postmodern world. *Journal of Community Psychology, 20*, 10–25.

Newcomb, M. D., Huba, G. J., & Bentler, P. M. (1981). A multidimensional assessment of stressful life events among adolescents: Deviations and correlates. *Journal of Health and Social Behavior, 22*, 400–415.

Newman, M. A., Liss, M. B., & Sherman, F. (1983). Ethnic awareness in children: Not a unitary concept. *The Journal of Genetic Psychology, 143*, 103–112.

Nicholson, I. A. M. (1998). Ethics, objectivity, and personal authority. *American Psychologist, 53*, 321–322.

NIMH Prevention Research Steering Committee (1993). *The prevention of mental disorders: A national research agenda.* Bethesda, MD: NIMH.

Nisbet, R. (1953). *The quest for community.* New York: Oxford Press.

Nisbett, R. E. (1998). Race, genetics, and IQ. In C. Jencks & M. Phillips (Eds), *The Black-White test score gap* (pp. 86–102). Washington, D.C.: Brookings Institution.

Nobuo, A. (1989). Community psychology in Japan: A historical review. *Applied Psychology: An International Review, 38*, 397–408.

Nock, S. L. (1982). The life-cycle approach to family analysis. In B. B. Wolman (Ed.), *Handbook of Developmental Psychology*. Englewood Cliffs, NJ: Prentice Hall.

Noddings, N. (1984). *Caring: A feminine approach to ethics and moral education*. Berkeley: University of California Press.

Noelle-Newman, E. (1984). *The spiral of silence: Public opinion—our social skin*. Chicago: University of Chicago Press.

Norenzayan, A., Choi, I., & Nisbett, R. E. (1999). Eastern and Western perceptions of causality for social behavior: Lay theories about personalities and situations. In D. A Prentice, D. T. Miller, et al. (Eds.), *Cultural divides: Understanding and overcoming group conflict* (pp. 239–272). New York: Russell Sage Foundation.

Norris, T. (2001). America's community movement: Investing in the civic landscape. *American Journal of Community Psychology, 29*, 301–307.

Norris-Baker, C. (1999). Aging on the old frontier and the new: A behavior setting approach to the declining small towns of the Midwest. *Environment and Behavior, 31*, 240–258.

Novaco, R. W., & Monahan, J. (1980). Research in community psychology: An analysis of work published in the first six years of the American Journal of Community Psychology. *American Journal of Community Psychology, 8*, 131–145.

Novaco, R. W., & Vaux, A. (1985). Human stress: A theoretical model for the community-oriented investigator. In E. C. Susskind & D. C. Klein (Eds.), *Community research: Methods, paradigms, and applications*. New York: Praeger.

Nowak, A., Szamrej, J., & Latane, B. (1990). From private attitude to public opinion: A dynamic theory of social impact. *Psychological Review, 97*, 362–376.

Nucci, L. (1996). Morality and the personal sphere of actions. In E. Reed, E. Turiel, & T. Brown (Eds.), *Values and knowledge* (pp. 41–60). Hillsdale, NJ: Erlbaum.

O'Donnell, C. R., & Ferrari, J. R. (2000). Diversity of opportunity, consensus of experience. In C. R. O'Donnell & J. R. Ferrari (Eds.), *Employment in community psychology: The diversity of opportunity* (pp. 129–131). Binghamton, NY: Haworth Press.

O'Donohue, W. T., Hanley, G. L., & Krasner, L. (1984). Toward the explication of the value contexts of the community psychologies. *Journal of Community Psychology, 12*. 199–205.

O'Hanlon, B., & Hudson, P. (1995). *Love is a verb: How to stop analyzing your relationship and start making it great!* New York: W. W. Norton.

O'Neill, P., & Trickett, E. J. (1982). *Community consultation*. San Francisco: Jossey-Bass.

O'Neill, P. (1989). Responsible to whom? Responsible for what? Some ethical issues in community intervention. *American Journal of Community Psychology, 17*, 323–341.

O'Neill, P. (1999). Ethical issues in working with communities in crisis. In R. M. Gist & B. Lubin (Eds.), *Response to disaster: Psychosocial, community, and ecological approaches* (241–267). London: Taylor and Francis.

O'Sullivan, M. J., Tausig, M., & Lindsey, M. L. (1984). The Fort McDowell Yavapai: From pawns to powerbrokers. *Prevention in Human Services, 3*, 73–97.

Oetting, E. R., Donnermeyer, J. J., Plested, B. A., Edwards, R. W., Kelly, & Beauvais, F. (1995). Assessing community readiness for prevention. *International Journal of Addictions, 30*, 659–683.

Ogbu, J. U. (1981). Origins of human competence: A cultural-ecological perspective. *Child Development, 52*, 413–429.

Ogbu, J. U. (1988). Minority coping responses and school experience. *Journal of Psychohistory, 18*, 433–456.

Okagaki, L., & Sternberg, R. J. (1993). Parental beliefs and children's school performance. *Child Development, 64*, 36–56.

Okin, R. L., Borus, J., Baer, L., & Jones, A. L. (1995). Long-term outcome of state hospital patients discharged into structural community residential settings. *Psychiatric Services, 46*, 73–78.

Olds, D., Eckenrode, J., Henderson, C. R. Jr., Kitzman, H., Powers, J., Cole, R., Sidora, K., Morris, P., Pettitt, L. M., & Luckey, D. (1997). Long-term effects of home visitation on maternal life course and child abuse and neglect: 15 year follow-up of a randomized trial. *Journal of the American Medical Association, 278*, 637–643.

Olds, D., Henderson, C. R. Jr., Eckenrode, J., Kitzman, H., Luckey, D., Pettitt, L. M., Sidora, K., Morris, P., & Powers, J. (1998). Long-term effects of nurse home visitation on children's criminal and antisocial behavior: 15 year follow-up of a randomized controlled trial. *Journal of the American Medical Association, 20 (14)*, 1238–1244.

Olds, D., Henderson, C. R., Jr., Chamberlin, R., & Tatelbaum, R. (1986). Preventing child abuse and neglect: A randomized trial of nurse home visitation. *Pediatrics, 78*, 65–78.

Olds, D., Pettitt, L. M., Robinson, J., Henderson, C. R., Jr., Eckenrode, J., Kitzman, H., Cole, B., & Powers, J., (1998). Reducing risks for antisocial behavior with a program of prenatal and early childhood home visitation. *Journal of Community Psychology, 26*, 65–83.

Oliver, W. (1989). Black males and social problems. *Journal of Black Studies, 20 (1)*, 15–39.

Olson, D. H., Sprenkle, D. H., & Russell, C. S. (1979). Circumplex model of marital and family types, and clinical applications. *Family Process, 18*, 3–28.

Omprakash, S. (1989). Toward a synergism of rural development and community psychology. *American Journal of Community Psychology, 17*, 109–119.

Ortiz-Torres, B., Serrano-García, I., & Torres-Burgos, N. (2000). Subverting culture: Promoting HIV/AIDS prevention among Puerto Rican and Dominican women. *American Journal of Community Psychology, 28,* 859–881.

Orwell, G. (1949). *Nineteen eighty-four: A novel.* New York, Harcourt, Brace and company.

Oxley, D. (2000). The school reform movement. Opportunities for community psychology. In J. Rappaport & E. Seidman (Eds.), *Handbook of community psychology* (pp. 565–590). New York: Kluwer Academic/Plenum Publishers.

Ozer, E., & Bandura, A. (1990). Mechanisms governing empowerment effects: A self-efficacy analysis. *Journal of Personality and Social Psychology. Vol 58*(3) 472–486.

Ozer, E., Weinstein, R., & Schotland, M. (2001). Violence and adaptation among urban middle school students. Paper presented at the 8th Biennial Conference of the Society for Community Research and Action. Atlanta, GA, June, 2001.

Palmer, P. J. (1998). *The courage to teach.* San Francisco: Jossey-Bass.

Pancer, S. M. (1997). Social psychology: The crisis continues. In D. Fox & I. Prilleltensky (Eds.). *Critical psychology: An introduction* (pp. 150–165). Thousand Oaks, CA: Sage.

Paradis, E. K. (2000). Feminist and community psychology ehtics in research with homeless women. *American Journal of Community Psychology, 28,* 839–858.

Pargament, K. I., & Maton, K. I. (2000). Religion in American life: A community psychology perspective. In J. Rappaport & E. Seidman (Eds.), *Handbook of community psychology* (pp. 495–522). New York: Kluwer Academic/Plenum Publishers.

Pargament, K. I., & Park, C. L. (1995). Merely a defense? The variety of religious means and ends. *Journal of Social Issues, 51,* 13–32.

Pargament, K. I., Ensing, D. D., Falgout, K., Olsen, H., Reilly, B., Van Haitsma, K., & Warren, R. (1990). God help me: Religious coping efforts as predictors of the outcomes to significant life events. *American Journal of Community Psychology, 18,* 793–825.

Pargament, K. I., Smith, B. W., Koenig, H. G., & Perez, L. (1998). Patterns of positive and negative religious coping with major life stressors. *Journal for the Scientific Study of Religion, 37,* 710–724.

Park, P. (1993). What is participatory research? A theoretical and methodological perspective. In P. Park, M. Brydon-Miller, B. Hall, & T. Jackson (Eds.), *Voices of change: participatory research in the United States and Canada.* (pp. 1–19). Westport, CT.

Parkes, C. M. (1971). Psycho-social transitions: A field of study. *Social Science and Medicine. 5,* 101–115.

Patterson, G. R. (1983). Stress: A change agent for family process. In N. Garmezy & M. Rutter (Eds.), *Stress, coping, and development in children.* New York: McGraw-Hill.

Patton, M. Q. (1987). *How to use qualitative methods in evaluation.* Newbury Park, CA: Sage.

Pawlik, K., & d'Ydewalle, G. (1996). Psychology and the global commons: Perspectives on international psychology. *American Psychologist, 51,* 488–495.

Paykel, E. S., Prusoff, B. A., & Uhlenhuth, E. H. (1971). Scaling of life events. *Archives of General Psychiatry, 25,* 340–347.

Payne, I. R., Bergin, A. E., Bielema, K. A., & Jenkins, P. H. (1991). Review of religion and mental health: Prevention and the enhancement of psychosocial functioning. *Prevention in Human Services, 9* (2), 11–40.

Pearlin, L. I., & Aneshensel, C. (1986). Coping and social supports: Their functions and applications. In L. Aikin & D. Mechanic (Eds.), *Application of social science to clinical medicine and health policy.* New Brunswick, NJ: Rutgers University Press.

Pearlin, L. I., & Schooler, C. (1978). The structure of coping. *Journal of Health and Social Behavior, 19,* 2–21.

Peavey, F. (1986). *Heart politics.* Philadelphia: New Society Publishers.

Peng, K., & Nisbett, R. E. (1999). Culture, dialectics, and reasoning about contradiction. *American Psychologist, 54,* 741–754.

Pennebaker, J. W., & Harber, K. (1993). A social stage model of collective coping: The Loma Prieta earthquake and the Persian Gulf War. *Journal of Social Issues, 49* (4), 125–145.

Pennebaker, J. W. (1990). *Opening up: The healing powers of confiding in others.* New York: William Morrow.

Pennebaker, J. W., Barger, S. D., & Tiebout, J. (1989). Disclosure of traumas and health among Holocaust survivors. *Psychosomatic Medicine, 51,* 577–589.

Pennebaker, J. W., & Beale, S. K. (1986). Confronting a traumatic event: Toward an understanding of inhibition and disease. *Journal of Abnormal Psychology, 95,* 274–281.

Pennebaker, J. W., Colder, M., & Sharp, K. L. (1990). Accelerating the coping process. *Journal of Personality and Social Psychology, 58,* 528–537.

Pentz, M. A., Rothspan, S., Turner, G., Skara, S., & Voskanian, S. (1999). Multi-ethnic considerations in community-based drug abuse prevention research. In S. B. Kar (Ed.), *Substance abuse prevention* (pp. 43–75). Amityville, NY: Baywood Publishing Co.

Perkins, D. D. (1988). The use of social science in public interest litigation: A role for community psychologists. *American Journal of Community Psychology, 16,* 465–485.

Perkins, D. D. (1995). Speaking truth to power: Empowerment ideology as social intervention and policy. *American Journal of Community Psychology, 23,* 765–794.

Perkins, D. D., & Zimmerman, M. A. (1995). Empowerment theory, research, and application. *American Journal of Community Psychology, 23,* 569–579.

Perkins, D. D., Brown, B. B., & Taylor, R. B. (1996). The ecology of empowerment: Predicting participation in community organizations. *Journal of Social Issues, 52 (1),* 85–110.

Perkins, D. V., Burns, T. F., Perry, J. C., & Nielsen, K. P. (1988). Behavior setting theory and community psychology: An analysis and critique. *American Journal of Community Psychology, 16,* 355–372.

Perkins, D. D., & Wandersman, A. (1990). "You'll have to work to overcome our suspicions." Benefits and pitfalls of research with community organizations. *Social Policy, 21,* 32–41.

Peterson, C., & Seligman, M. E. P. (1984). Causal explanations as a risk factor for depression: Theory and evidence. *Psychological Review, 91,* 347–374.

Peterson, C., Seligman, M. E. P., & Vaillant, G. E. (1988). Pessimistic explanatory style is a risk factor for physical illness: A thirty-five year longitudinal study. *Journal of Personality and Social Psychology, 55,* 23–27.

Pettifor, J. L. (1998). The Canadian Code of Ethics for psychologists: A moral context for ethical decision making in emerging areas of practice. *Canadian Psychology, 39,* 231–238.

Pettigrew, T. F. (1979). The ultimate attribution error: Extending Allport's cognitive analysis of prejudice. *Personality and Social Psychology Bulletin, 5,* 461–476.

Pharr, S. (1988). *Homophobia: A weapon of sexism.* Little Rock, AR: Chardon Press.

Phillips, D. A. (2000). Social policy and community psychology. In J. Rappaport & E. Seidman (Eds.), *Handbook of community psychology* (pp. 397–419). New York: Kluwer Academic/Plenum Publishers.

Phillips, D. A., Howes, C., & Whitebrook, M. (1992). The social policy context of child care: effects on quality. *American Journal of Community Psychology, 20,* 25–52.

Phinney, J. S. (1996). Understanding ethnic diversity. *American Behavioral Scientist, 40,* 143–152.

Pierce, G. R., Sarason, B. R., & Sarason, I. G. (Eds.) (1996). *Handbook of social support and the family.* New York: Plenum Press.

Pierce, G. R., Sarason, B. R., Sarason, I. G., Joseph, H. J., & Henderson, C. A. (1996). Conceptualizing and assessing social support in the context of the family. In G. R. Pierce, B. R. Sarason, & I. G. Sarason (Eds.), *Handbook of social support and the family* (pp. 3–23). New York: Plenum Press.

Pilisuk, M., McAllister, J., & Rothman, J. (1996). Coming together for action: The challenge of contemporary grassroots community organizing. *Journal of Social Issues, 52, 1,* 15–38.

Pillow, D. R., Zautra, A. J., & Sandler, I. (1996). Major life events and minor stressors: Identifying mediational links in the stress process. *Journal of Personality and Social Psychology, 70,* 381–394.

Pine, C. J., Padilla, A. M., & Madonado, J. (1985). Ethnicity and life event cognitive appraisals and experiences. *Journal of Clinical Psychology, 41(4),* 460–465.

Pittinsky, T. L., Shih, M., & Ambady, N. (1999). Identity adaptiveness: Affect across multiple identities. *Journal of Social Issues, 55,* 503–518.

Plante, T. G., & Pardini, D. A. (2000). Religious denomination affiliation and psychological health: Results from a substance abuse population. Presentation to the 108th Annual Conventions of the APA, Washington, D.C. (August 7, 2000. Full text of the presentation is available from the APA Public Affairs Office. Session 4013, 8:00–8:50 AM, August 7, 2000, Capital Hilton Hotel - Pan American Room).

Plas, J. M., & Lewis, S. E. (1996). Environmental factors and sense of community in a planned town. *American Journal of Community Psychology, 24,* 109–143.

Plomin, R., & Daniels, D. (1987). Why are children within the family so different from one another? *Behavioral and Brain Sciences, 10,* 1–16.

Plomin, R., & Rende, R. (1991). Human behavior genetics. *Annual Review of Psychology, 42,* 161–190.

Plomin, R., Pederson, N. L., Lichtenstein, P., McClearn, G. E., & Nesselrode, J. R. (1990). Genetic influence on life events during the last half of the life span. *Psychology and Aging, 5,* 25–30.

Plomin, R., Rende, R., & Rutter, M. (1991). Quantitative genetics and developmental psychopathology. In D. Cicchetti & S. L. Toth (Eds.), *Internalizing and externalizing expressions of dysfunction: Rochester symposium on developmental psychopathology* (pp. 155–202). Hillsdale, NJ: Erlbaum.

Pollack, W. (1998). *Real boys: Rescuing our sons from the myths of boyhood.* New York: Ransom House.

Ponterotto, J. G., & Pederson, P. B. (1993). *Preventing prejudice: A guide for counselors and educators.* Newbury Park, CA: Sage.

Pope, K. S. (1990). Identifying and implementing ethical standards for primary prevention. *Prevention in Human Services, 8,* 43–64.

Porter, C. P. (1991). Social reasons for skin tone preferences of Black school-age children. *American Journal of Orthopsychiatry, 61,* 149–154.

Portwood, S. (2001). (Chair). Popular but ineffective juvenile justice interventions: Empirical evidence doesn't matter. Symposium presented at the 8th Biennial Conference on Community Research and Action. June 8, Atlanta, GA.

Potts, R. (1999a, June 10). Values in partnerships with African American groups. In Symposium, Values in partnerships with community groups: Ideas to action-Action to ideas. Biennial Conference on Community Research and Action. New Haven, CT.

Potts, R. (1999b). The spirit of community psychology: Spirituality, religion, and community action. *The Community Psychologist, 32 (3)*, 17–18.

Powers, E., & Witmer, H. (1972). *An experiment in the prevention of delinquency: The Cambridge-Somerville Youth Study*. Montclair, NJ: Patterson Smith.

Pratt, L. (1976). *Family structure and effective health behavior: The energized family*. Boston: Houghton Mifflin Company.

Prelow, H. M., Tein, J., Roosa, M. W., & Wood, J. (2000). Do coping styles differ across sociocultural groups? The role of measurement equivalence in making this judgment. *American Journal of Community Psychology, 28*, 225–244.

Prestby, J. E., Wandersman, A., Florin, P., Rich, R. C., & Chavis, D. M. (1990). Benefits, costs, incentive management, and participation in voluntary organizations: A means to understanding and promoting empowerment. *American Journal of Community Psychology, 18*, 117–149.

Pretty, G. M. H., Andrews, L., & Collett, C. (1994). Exploring adolescents' sense of community and its relationship to loneliness. *American Journal of Community Psychology, 18*, 346–357.

Prelow, H. M., Tein, J., Roosa, M. W., & Wood, J. (2000). Do coping styles differ across sociocultural groups? The role of measurement equivalence in making this judgment. *American Journal of Community Psychology, 28*, 225–244.

Prezza, M., & Constantini, S. (1998). Sense of community and life satisfaction: Investigation in three different territorial contexts. *Journal of Community and Applied Social Psychology, 8*, 181–194.

Price, R. H. (1990). Wither participation and empowerment. *American Journal of Community Psychology, 18*, 163–167.

Price, R. H., & Cherniss, C. (1977). Training for a new profession: Research as social action. *Professional Psychology, 8 (2)*, 222–231.

Price, R. H., Cowen, E., Lorion, R., & Ramos-McKay, J. (Eds.). (1988). *Fourteen ounces of prevention: A casebook*. Washington, D. C.: APA.

Price, R. H., & Smith, S. S. (1983). Two decades of reform in the mental health system (1963–1983). In E. Seidman (Ed.), *Handbook of social intervention*. Beverly Hills, CA: Sage Publications.

Prilleltensky, I. (1989). Psychology and the status quo. *American Psychologist, 44*, 795–802.

Prilleltensky, I. (1997). Values, assumptions, and practices: Assessing the moral implications of psychological discourse and action. *American Psychologist, 52*, 517–535.

Prilleltensky, I. (1998). Values and assumptions about values and assumptions. *American Psychologist, 53*, 325–326.

Prilleltensky, I. (1999). Value-based praxis in community psychology: Moving towards social justice and social action. Paper presented at the Seventh Biennial Conference on Community Research and Action. New Haven, CT.

Prilleltensky, I., & Gonick, L. (1996). Polities change, oppression remains: On the psychology and politics of oppression. *Political Psychology, 17*, 127–148.

Prilleltensky, I., & Nelson, G. (2000). Promoting child and family wellness: Priorities for psychological and social interventions. *Journal of Community and Applied Social Psychology, 10*, 85–105.

Prochaska, J. O., & DiClemente, C. C. (1992). Stages of change in the modification of problem behaviors. In M. Hersen, R. M. Eisler, & P. M. Miller (Eds.), *Progress in behavior modification* (pp. 184–218). Sycamore, IL: Sycamore Press.

Prochaska, J. O., DiClemente, C. C., & Norcross, J. C. (1992). In search of how people change: Applications to addictive behaviors. *American Psychologist, 47*, 1102–1114.

Putallaz, M., & Wasserman, A. (1990). Children's entry behavior. In S. R. Asher & J. D. Coie (Eds.), *Peer rejection in childhood: Cambridge studies in social and emotional development* (pp. 60–89). New York: Cambridge University Press.

Putnam, R. D. (1993). The prosperous community: Social capital and public life [Electronic version]. *The American Prospect, 4 (13)*, 34–48.

Putnam, R. D. (1996). The strange disappearance of civic America. *American Prospect (Winter)*, 34–48.

Putnam, R. D. (2000). *Bowling alone: The collapse and revival of American community*. New York: Simon & Schuster.

Quinton, D., Rutter, M., & Liddle, C. (1984). Institutional rearing, parenting difficulties and marital support. *Psychological Medicine, 14*, 107–124.

Rabkin, J. G., & Struening, E. L. (1976). Life events, stress, and illness. *Science, 194*, 1013–1020.

Radke-Yarrow, M., & Sherman, T. (1990). Hard growing: Children who survive. In J. Rolf, A. S. Masten, D. Cicchetti, K. H. Neuchterlein, & S. Weintraub (Eds.), *Risk and protective factors in the development of psychopathology* (pp. 97–119). New York: Cambridge University Press.

Rahe, H., & Arthur, R. J. (1968). Life change patterns surrounding illness experiences. *Journal of Psychosomatic Research, 15*, 19–24.

Rahe, R. H. (1974). The pathway between subjects' recent life changes and their near future illness reports: Representative results and methodological issues. In B. S. Dohrenwend & B. P. Dohrenwend (Eds.), *Stressful life events: Their nature and effects* (pp. 73–86). New York: Wiley.

Rahe, R. H., & Arthur, R. J. (1978). Life change and illness studies: Past history and future directions. *Journal of Human Stress, 4*, 3–15.

Rapkin, B. D., & Luke, D. A. (1993). Cluster analysis in community research: Epistemology and practice. *American Journal of Community Psychology, 21,* 247–277.

Rappaport, J. (1977a). *Community psychology: Values, research, and action.* New York: Holt, Rinehart, and Winston.

Rappaport, J. (1977b). From Noah to Babel: Relationships between conceptions, values, analysis levels, and social intervention strategies. In I. Iscoe, B. L. Bloom, & C. D. Spielberger (Eds.), *Community psychology in transition: Proceedings of the national conference on training in community psychology* (pp. 185–194). New York: John Wiley & Sons.

Rappaport, J. (1980). Labeling theory and the social psychology of experts and helpers. In M. S. Gibbs, J. R. Lachenmeyer, & J. Sigal (Eds.), *Community psychology: Theoretical and empirical approaches* (pp. 71–96). New York: Gardner Press, Inc.

Rappaport, J. (1981). In praise of paradox: A social policy of empowerment over prevention. *American Journal of Community Psychology, 9,* 1–25.

Rappaport, J. (1984a). Seeking justice in the real world: A further explication of value concepts. *Journal of Community Psychology, 12,* 208–221.

Rappaport, J. (1984b). Foreword. In S. Sue & T. Moore (Eds.), *The pluralistic society* (pp. 19–20). New York: Human Science Press.

Rappaport, J. (1984c). Empowerment as a guide to doing research. In E. J. Trickett, R. J. Watts, & D. Birman (Eds.), *Human diversity: Perspectives on people in context* (pp. 359–382). San Francisco: Jossey-Bass.

Rappaport, J. (1986). Comment and reaction to the special issue: Cultural relativity and diversity in the pursuit of science. *The Community Psychologist, 19* (2), 13–14.

Rappaport, J. (1987). Terms of empowerment/exemplars of prevention: Toward a theory of community psychology. *American Journal of Community Psychology, 15,* 121–148.

Rappaport, J. (1990). Research methods and the empowerment social agenda. In P. Tolan, C. Keys, F. Chertok, & L. Jason (Eds.), *Researching community psychology: Issues of theory and methods.* Washington, D.C.: American Psychological Association. 51–63.

Rappaport, J. (1993). Narrative studies, personal stories, and identity transformation in the mutual help context. *Journal of Applied Behavioral Science, 29* (2), 239–256.

Rappaport, J. (1995). Empowerment meets narrative: Listening to stories and creating settings. *American Journal of Community Psychology, 23,* 795–807.

Rappaport, J. (2000a). Community narratives: Tales of terror and joy (Seymour B. Sarason Award address). *American Journal of Community Psychology, 28,* 1–24.

Rappaport, J. (2000b). Commentaries on Prilleltensky and Nelson. *Journal of Community and Applied Social Psychology, 10,* 107–122.

Rappaport, J., Reischl, T. M., & Zimmerman, M. A. (1992). Mutual help mechanisms in the empowerment of former mental patients. In D. Saleebey (Ed.), *The strengths perspective in social work practice* (pp. 84–97). New York: Longman.

Rappaport, J., Seidman, E., & Davidson, W., II (1985). Demonstration research and manifest versus true adoption: The natural history of a research project to divert adolescents from the legal system. In R. F. Munoz, L. R. Snowden, & J. G. Kelly (Eds.), *Social and psychological research in community settings* (101–132). San Francisco: Jossey-Bass.

Razzano, D. (2001). *Have zero tolerance policies gone too far?* Retrieved March 27, 2001, from ***http://www.time2act.org/archives/032601.html***.

Reagon, B. J. (1991). *The songs are free* (videorecording). New York: Mystic Fire Video.

Reagon, B. J. (1981). *Ella's song.* Songtalk Publishing Co.

Reagon, B. J. (1992). Coalition politics: Turning the century. In M. L. Anderson & P. H. Collins (Eds.), *Race, class, and gender: An anthology.* Belmont, CA: Wadsworth.

Rector and Visitors of the University of Virginia (1998). Four radical groups. In *The Psychedelic 60s: Literary traditions and Social Change.* Charlottesville, VA: Special Collections Department of University of Virginia Library. Retrieved May 15, 2000, from ***http://www.lib.virginia.edu/speccol/exhibits/sixties/radical.html***.

Redding, R. E. (2001). Sociopolitical diversity in psychology: The case for pluralism. *American Psychologist, 56,* 205–215.

Reid, P. T. (1994). The real problem in the study of culture. *American Psychologist, 49,* 524–525.

Rein, M. (1983). *Social policy: Issues of choice and change.* Armonk, NY: M. E. Sharpe.

Reinharz, S. (1983). Consulting to the alternative work setting: A suggested strategy for community psychology. *Journal of Community Psychology, 11,* 199–212.

Reinharz, S. (1994). Toward an ethnography of "voice" and "silence." In E. J. Trickett, R. J. Watts, & D. Birman (Eds.), *Human diversity: Perspectives on people in context* (pp. 178–200). San Francisco: Jossey-Bass.

Reissman, F. (1965). The "helper-therapy" principle. *Social Work, 10,* 27–32.

Reissman, F., & Bay, T. (1992). The politics of self-help. *Social Policy, 23* (2), 28–38.

Reppucci, N. D. (1984). Psychology in the public interest. In A. M. Rogers & C. J. Scheirer (Eds.), *The G. Stanley Hall lecture series.* Washington, DC: American Psychological Association.

Reppucci, N. D. (1987). Prevention and ecology: Teenage pregnancy, child sexual abuse, and organized youth sports. *American Journal of Community Psychology,15*, 1–22.

Reppucci, N. D. (1999). Adolescent development and juvenile justice. *American Journal of Community Psychology, 27*, 307–326.

Reppucci, N. D., Britner, P. A., & Woolard J. L. (1997). *Preventing child abuse and neglect through parent education*. Baltimore, MD: Paul H. Brookes.

Reppucci, N. D., & Haugaard, J. J. (1989). Prevention of child sexual abuse: Myth or reality. *American Psychologist, 44*, 1266–1275.

Reppucci, N. D., Sarata, B. P. V., Saunders, J. T., McArthur, A. V., & Michlin, L. M. (1973). We bombed in Mountville: Lessons learned in consultation to a correctional facility for adolescent offenders. In I. I. Goldenberg (Ed.), *The helping professions in the world of action* (pp. 145–164). Lexington, MA: Lexington Books.

Reppucci, N. D., Woolard, J. L., & Fried, C. S. (1999). Social, community, and preventive interventions. *Annual Review of Psychology, 50*, 387–418.

Researching community psychology: Issues of theory and methods. (pp. 209–214). Washington, D.C.: American Psychological Association.

Reyes, O., Gillock, Kobus, K., & Sanchez, B. (2000). A longitudinal examination of the transition into senior high school for adolescents from urban, low-income status and predominantly minority backgrounds. *American Journal of Community Psychology, 28*, 519–544.

Reynolds, A. J., Walberg, H. J., & Weissberg, R. P. (1999). *Promoting positive outcomes*. Washington, D.C.: CWLA Press.

Rheingold, H. (1993). *The virtual community: Homesteading on the electronic frontier*. New York: Addison-Wesley.

Rheingold, H. (1998). Virtual communities. In F. Hesselbein, M. Goldsmith, R. Beckhard, & R. F. Schubert (Eds.), *The community of the future* (pp. 115–122). San Francisco: Jossey-Bass.

Ribisl, K. M. (2000). Employment as a community psychologist in a university-based research institute. In C. R. O'Donnell & J. R. Ferrari (Eds.), *Employment in community psychology: The diversity of opportunity* (pp. 93–100)). Binghamton, NY: Haworth Press.

Ricketts, W. (1995). Political funerals. *Bay Area Reporter*. Retrieved September 6, 2000, from ***http://www.actupny.org/diva/polfunreview.html***

Riger, S. (2001). Transforming community psychology. *American Journal of Community Psychology, 29*, 69–81.

Rivlin, L. G. (1987). The neighborhood, personal identity, and group affiliations. In I. Altman & A. Wandersman (Eds.), *Neighborhood and community environments* (pp. 1–34). New York: Plenum Press.

RMC Research Corporation. (1995). *National Diffusion Network schoolwide promising practices: Report of a pilot effort*. Portsmouth, NH: Author.

Robarchek, C. A., & Robarchek, C. J. (1992). Cultures of war and peace: A comparative study of Waorani and Semai. In J. Silverberg & J. P. Gray (Eds.), *Aggression and peacefulness in humans and other primates* (pp. 189–213). New York: Oxford University Press.

Roberts, H. C. (1994) (Trans., Ed.). *The complete prophecies of Nostradamus*. New York: Crown Publishers.

Roberts, L. J., Salem, D., Rappaport, J., Toro, P. A., Luke, D. A., & Seidman, E. (1999). Giving and receiving help: Interpersonal transactions in mutual-help meetings and psychosocial adjustment of members. *American Journal of Community Psychology, 27*, 841–868.

Roberts, S. (Moderator). (2000, July 16). Writing about race (and trying to talk about it): *Times* editors and writers discuss how race is lived in America. *New York Times Magazine, 16*, 18–20, 22.

Roccas, S., & Schwartz, S. H. (1997). Church-state relations and the association of religiosity with values: Study of Catholics in six countries. *Cross-Cultural Research: The Journal of Comparative Social Science, 31 (4)*, 356–375.

Rodin, J., & Langer, E. (1980). Aging labels: The decline of control and the fall of self esteem. *Journal of Social Issues, 36*, 12–29.

Rodin, J., & Langer, E. J. (1977). Long-term effects of a control relevant intervention with the institutional aged. *Journal of Personality and Social Psychology, 35*, 897–902.

Roesch, R. (1995). Creating change in the legal system: Contributions form community psychology. *Law and Human Behavior, 19*, 325–342.

Roesch, R., & Carr, G. (2000). Psychology in the international community. In J. Rappaport & E. Seidman (Eds.), *Handbook of community psychology* (pp. 811–831). New York: Kluwer Academic/Plenum Publishers.

Rogers, E. M (1983). *Diffusion of innovations, 3rd ed.* New York: Free Press.

Rogers, E. M. (1995). *Diffusion and innovations, 4th ed.* New York: Free Press.

Rogler, L. H. (1999). Methodological sources of cultural insensitivity in mental health research. *American Psychologist, 54*, 424–433.

Rokeach, M. (1973). *The nature of human values*. New York: Free Press.

Rokeach, M., & Ball-Rokeach, S. J. (1989). Stability and change in American value priorities. *American Psychologist, 44*, 775–784.

Rolf, J. E. (1999). Resilience: An interview with Norman Garmezy. In M. D. Glantz & J. L. Johnson (Eds.), *Resilience and development; Positive life adaptations* (pp. 5–14). New York: Kluwer Academic/Plenum.

Rolf, J. E., & Johnson, J. L. (1999). Opening doors to resilience intervention for prevention research. In M. D. Glantz & J. L. Johnson (Eds.), *Resilience and development; Positive life adaptations* (pp. 229–249). New York: Kluwer Academic/Plenum.

Roosa, M. W. (2000). Some thoughts about resilience versus positive development, main effects versus interactions, and the value of resilience. *Child Development, 71*, 567–569.

Root, M. P. (Ed.). (1996). *The multiracial experience: Racial borders as the new frontier.* Thousand Oaks, CA: Sage Publications, Inc.

Rosales, F. A. (1996). *Chicano!: The history of the Mexican American civil rights movement.* Houston: Arte Publico Press.

Rose, S., & Rose, H. (1980). The myth of the neutrality of science. In R. Arditti, P. Brenna, & S. Cavrak (Eds.), *Science and liberation* (pp. 17–32). Boston, MA: South End Press.

Rosenberg, A., Solarz, A. L., & Bailey, W. A. (1991). Psychology and homelessness: A public policy and advocacy agenda. *The American Psychologist, 46*, 1239–1245.

Rosenhan, D.L. (1973). On being sane in insane places. *Science, 179*, 250–258.

Rosenthal, R. (1991). Straighter from the source: Alternative methods of researching homelessness. *Urban Anthropolgy, 20* (2), 109–123.

Rosenthal, R., & Jacobson, L. F. (1968). Teacher expectations for the disadvantaged. *Scientific American, 218* (4), 3–7.

Rosenwasser, P. (1992a). Through the darkness [Interview with Deena Metzger]. *Visionary Voices: Women on power: Conversations with shamans, activists, teachers, artists, and healers* (pp. 102–113). San Francisco: Aunt Lute Books.

Rosenwasser, P. (1992b). From the heart [Interview with Fran Peavey]. *Visionary Voices: Women on power: Conversations with shamans, activists, teachers, artists, and healers* (pp. 175–193). San Francisco: Aunt Lute Books.

Rosenwasser, P. (1992c). Spirit healer [Interview with Fran Fernandez]. *Visionary Voices: Women on power: Conversations with shamans, activists, teachers, artists, and healers* (pp. 125–134). San Francisco: Aunt Lute Books.

Rosier, K. B., & Corsaro, W. A. (1993). Competent parents, complex lives: Managing parenthood in poverty. *Journal of Contemporary Ethnography, 22* (2), 171–204.

Ross, C. A. (1995). Current treatment for dissociative identity disorder. In L. M. Cohen, J. N. Berzoff, & M. R. Elin (Eds.), *Dissociative identity disorder: Theoretical and treatment controversies* (pp. 413–434). Northvale, NJ: Jason Aronson, Inc.

Ross, C. E., & Mirowsky, J. A. (1979). A comparison of life-event-weighting schemes: Change, undesirability, and effect proportional indices. *Journal of Health and Social Behavior, 20*, 166–177.

Ross, L. (1977). The intuitive psychologist and his shortcomings: Distortions in the attribution process. In L. Berkowitz (Ed.), *Advances in experimental social psychology, Vol. 10* (pp. 173–220). Orlando, FL: Academic Press.

Rossi, P. H. (1978). Issues in the evaluation of human service delivery. *Evaluation Quarterly, 2*, 573–599.

Rotherman-Borus, M. J., Gwadz, M., Fernandez, & M. I., Srinivasan, S. (1998). Timing of HIV interventions on reductions in sexual risk among adolescents. *American Journal of Community Psychology, 26*, 73–96.

Rothschild-Whitt, J. (1979). The collectivist organization: An alternative to rational-bureaucratic models. *American Sociological Review, 44*, 509–527.

Rotter, J. B. (1966). Generalized expectancies for internal versus external control of reinforcement. *Psychological Monographs No. 609, 80*, (1).

Rouhana, N. N., & Bar-Tal, D. (1998). Psychological dynamics of intractable ethnonational conflicts: The Israeli-Palestinian Case. *American Psychologist, 53*, 761–770.

Rubin, K. H., Coplan, R. J., Nelson, L. J., & Cheah, C. S. L. (1999). Peer relationships in childhood. In M. H. Bornstein & M. E. Lamb (Eds.), *Developmental psychology: An advanced textbook* (pp. 451–501). Mahwah, NJ: Lawrence Erlbaum.

Rubin, L. B. (1976). *Worlds of pain: Life in the working class family.* New York: Basic Books, Inc.

Rutter, M. (1970). Sex differences in children's response to family stress. In E.J. Anthony & C. Koupernick (Eds.), *The child in his family, Vol. 1.* New York: Wiley.

Rutter, M. (1977). Individual differences. In M. Rutter & L. Hersov (Eds.), *Child psychiatry: Modern approaches.* Oxford: Blackwell.

Rutter, M. (1979). Protective factors in children's response to stress and disadvantage. In M. W. Kent & J. E. Rolf (Eds.), *Primary prevention of psychopathology, Vol 3: Social competence in children* (pp. 49–74). Hanover, NH: University Press of New England.

Rutter, M. (1983). Stress, coping and development: Some issues and some questions. In N. Garmezy & M. Rutter (Eds.), *Stress, coping and development in children.* New York: McGraw-Hill.

Rutter, M. (1985). Resilience in the face of adversity: Protective factors and resistance to psychiatric disorder. *British Journal of Psychiatry, 147*, 598–611.

Rutter, M. (1989). Pathways from childhood to adult life. *Journal of Child Psychology and Psychiatry, 30*, 23–51.

Rutter, M. (1994). Stress research: Accomplishments and tasks ahead. In R. J. Haggerty, L. R. Sherrod, N. Garmezy, & M. Rutter (Eds.), *Stress, risk, and resilience in children and adolescents: Processes, mechanisms, and interventions* (pp. 354–385). New York: Cambridge University Press.

Rutter, M. (1997). Nature–nurture integration: The example of antisocial behavior. *American Psychologist, 52*, 390–398.

Rutter, M. (2000). Resilience reconsidered: Conceptual considerations, empirical findings, and policy implications. In J. P. Shonkoff & S. J. Miesels (Eds.), *Handbook of early childhood intervention, 2nd edition* (pp. 651–682). New York: Cambridge University Press.

Rutter, M. (2001). Psychosocial adversity: Risk resilience and recovery. In J. M. Richman & M. W. Fraser (Eds.), *The context of youth violence: Resilience, risk, and protection.* Westport, CT: Praeger.

Rutter, M., & Quinton, D. (1984). Long-term follow-up of women institutionalized in childhood: Factors promoting good functioning in adult life. *British Journal of Developmental Psychology, 2,* 191–204.

Rutter, M., & the English and Romanian Adoptees Study Team (1998). Developmental catch-up and deficit following adoption after severe global early privation. *Journal of Child Psychology and Psychiatry, 39,* 465–476.

Rutter, M., Cox, A., Tupling, C., Berger, M., & Yule, W. (1975). Attainment and adjustment in two geographical areas: The prevalence of psychiatric disorder. *British Journal of Psychiatry, 126,* 493–509.

Ryan, K. (1993). Resistance to change. In C. Vyrus (Ed.), *Experiencing race, class, and gender in the United States* (pp. 400–404). Mountain View, CA: Mayfield Publishing Co.

Ryan, R. M., & Solky, J. A. (1996). What is supportive about social support?: On the psychological needs for autonomy and relatedness. In G. R. Pierce, B. R. Sarason, & I. G. Sarason (Eds.), *Handbook of social support and the family* (pp. 249–267). New York: Plenum Press.

Ryan, W. (1971). *Blaming the victim.* New York: Vintage Books.

Ryan, W. (1994). Many cooks, brave men, apples and oranges: How people think about equality. *American Journal of Community Psychology, 22,* 25–35.

Ryff, C. D., & Dunn, D. D. (1985). A life-span developmental approach to the study of stressful events. *Journal of Applied Developmental Psychology, 6,* 113–127.

Saegert, S., & Winkel, G. H. (1990). Environmental psychology. *Annual Review of Psychology Annual, 41,* 441–478.

Saegert, S., & Winkel, G. H. (1996). Paths to community empowerment: Organizing at home. *American Journal of Community Psychology, 24,* 517–550.

Sagiv, L., & Schwartz, S. (2000). Value priorities and subjective well-being: Direct relations and congruity effects. *European Journal of Social Psychology, 30 (2),* 177–198.

de Saint Exupery, A. (1943, 1971). *The little prince.* San Diego, Harcourt Brace Jovanovich.

Salem, D. A., Reischl, T. M., Gallacher, F., & Randall, K. W. (2000). The role of referent and expert power in mutual help. *American Journal of Community Psychology, 28,* 303–324.

Saliers, E. (1990). Hammer and a nail. Godhap Music (BMI).

Salzer, M. S., & Bickman, L. (1999). The short- and long-term psychological impact of disasters: Implications for mental health interventions and policy. In R. M. Gist & B. Lubin (Eds.), *Response to disaster: Psychosocial, community, and ecological approaches* (63–82). London: Taylor and Francis.

Sameroff, A. J., & Chandler, M. J. (1975). Reproductive risk and the continuum of caretaking casualty. In F. D. Horowitz (Ed.), *Child development research, Vol. 4.* Chicago: University of Chicago Press.

Sameroff, A. J., & Fiese, B. H. (2000). Transactional regulation: The developmental ecology of early intervention. In J. P. Shonkoff & S. J. Miesels (Eds.), *Handbook of early childhood intervention, 2nd edition* (pp. 135–159). New York: Cambridge University Press.

Sameroff, A. J., & Seifer, R. (1983). Familial risk and child competence. *Child Development, 54,* 1254–1268.

Sampson, E. E. (1989). The challenge of social change for psychology: Globalization and psychology's theory of the person. *American Psychologist, 44,* 914–921.

Sampson, E. E. (2000). Reinterpreting individualism and collectivism: Their religious roots and monologic versus dialogic person-other relationships. *American Psychologist, 55,* 1425–1432.

Sampson, R. J. (1999). What "community" supplies. In R. F. Ferguson & W. T. Dickens (Eds.), *Urban problems and community development* (pp. 241–292). Washington, D.C.: Brookings Institution.

Sampson, R. J. (2001). How do communities undergird or undermine human development? Relevant contexts and social mechanisms. In A. Booth & A. C. Crouter (Eds.), *Does it take a village: Community effects on children, adolescents, and families* (pp. 3–30). Mahwah, NJ: Lawrence Erlbaum.

Sampson, R. J., Raudenbush, S., & Earls, F. (1997). Neighborhoods and violent crime: A multilevel study of collective efficacy. *Science, 277,* 918–924.

Sanders, T., Norton, E. H., & Mock, F. L. (1994). *Maya Lin: A strong clear vision* [videorecording]. Santa Monica, CA: Sanders and Mock Productions/American Film Foundation.

Sandler, I. N. (1979). Life stress and community psychology. In I. G. Sarason & C. D. Spielberger (Eds.), *Stress and anxiety, vol. 6* (pp. 213–232). New York: Wiley.

Sandler, I. N. (2001). Quality and ecology of adversity as common mechanisms of risk and resilience. *American Journal of Community Psychology, 29,* 19–55.

Sandler, I. N., Wolchik, S. A., MacKinnon, D., Ayers, T. S., & Roosa, M. W. (1997). Developing linkages between theory and intervention in stress and coping processes. In S. A. Wolchik & I. N. Sandler (Eds.), *Handbook of children's coping: Linking theory and intervention* (pp. 3–40). New York: Plenum Press.

Sarason, S. B. (1978). The nature of problem solving in social action. *American Psychologist, 33,* 370–380.

Sarason, I. G., Johnson, J. H., & Siegel, J. M. (1978). Assessing the impact of life changes: Development of the Life Experiences Survey. *Journal of Consulting and Clinical Psychology, 46*, 932–946.

Sarason, S. B. (1972). *The creation of settings and the future societies.* San Francisco: Jossey-Bass.

Sarason, S. B. (1974). *The psychological sense of community: Prospects for a community psychology.* San Francisco: Jossey-Bass.

Sarason, S. B. (1977). Community psychology, networks, and Mr. Everyman. In I. Iscoe, B. L. Bloom, & C. D. Spielberger (Eds.), *Community psychology in transition: Proceedings of the national conference on training in community psychology* (pp. 25–43). New York: John Wiley & Sons.

Sarason, S. B. (1978). The nature of problem solving in social action. *American Psychologist, 33*, 370–380.

Sarason, S. B. (1986). The emergence of a conceptual center. *Journal of Community Psychology, 14*, 405–407.

Sarason, S. B. (1993). American psychology and the needs for transcendence and community. *American Journal of Community Psychology, 21*, 185–202.

Sarbin, T. R. (1970). A role theory perspective for community psychology: The structure of social identity. In D. Adelson & B. L. Kalis (Eds.), *Community psychology and mental health: Perspectives and challenges* (pp. 89–113). Scranton, PA: Chandler Publishing Co.

Sauvage, P. (1990, videorecording). *Weapons of the spirit.* Los Angeles: Chambon Foundation (and Greenvalley Productions).

Scarr, S. (1988). Race and gender as psychological variables: Social and ethical issues. *American Psychologist, 43*, 56–59.

Scarr, S. (1998). American child care today. *American Psychologist, 53*, 95–108.

Schachter-Shalomi, Z. (1994, Winter). Saging - Not aging: "Are you saved yet?" *Context: A Quarterly of Humane Sustainable Culture.* Retrieved August 16, 2000, from **http://www.context.org/ICLIB/IC37/Shalomi.htm**.

Schanks, R. C. (1982). *Dynamic memory.* Cambridge, England: Cambridge University Press.

Scheff, T. J. (Ed.). (1975). *Labeling madness.* Englewood Cliffs, NJ: Prentice Hall.

Scheier, M. F., & Carver, C. S. (1985). Optimism, coping, and health: Assessment and implications of generalized outcome expectancies. *Health Psychology, 4*, 219–247.

Scheier, M. F., Matthews, K. A., Owens, J., Magovern, G. J., Sr., Lefebre, R. C., Abbott, R. A., & Carver, C. S. (1989). Dispositional optimism and recovery from coronary artery bypass surgery: The beneficial effects on physical and psychological well-being. *Journal of Personality and Social Psychology, 57*, 1024–1040.

Scheier, M. F., Weintraub, J. K., & Carver, C. S. (1986). Coping with stress: Divergent strategies of optimists and pessimists. *Journal of Personality and Social Psychology, 51*, 1257–1264.

Scheirer, M. A. (1994). Designing and using process evaluation. In J. S. Wholey, H. P. Hatry, & K. E. Newcomer (Eds.), *Handbook of practical program evaluation* (pp. 40–66). San Francisco: Jossey-Bass.

Schimel, J., Arndt, J., Pyszczynski, T., & Greenberg, J. (2001). Being accepted for who we are: evidence that social validation of the intrinsic self reduces general defensiveness. *Journal of Personality and Social Psychology, 80*, 35–52.

Schindler, F., Berren, M. R., Hannah, M. T., Beigel, A., & Santiago, J. M. (1987). How the public perceives psychiatrists, psychologists, nonpsychiatric physicians, and members of the clergy. *Professional Psychology: Research and Practice, 18*, 371–376.

Schneider, K. J. (1998). Toward a science of the heart: Romanticism and the revival of psychology. *American Psychologist, 53*, 277–289.

Schneider, S. L. (2001). In search of realistic optimism. *American Psychologist, 56*, 250–263.

Schneir, M. (1972). Sojourner Truth: Ain't I a woman? In *Feminism: The essential historical writings* (pp. 93–95). New York: Vintage Books.

Schoenfeld, P., Halvey, J., Heemley-van der Velden, E., & Ruhf, L. (1986). Long-term outcome of network therapy. *Hospital and Community Psychiatry, 37 (4)*, 373–386.

Schofield, J. W. (1978). School desegregation and intergroup relations. In D. Bar-Tal & L. Saxe (Eds.), *Social psychology of education: Theory and research.* Washington, D.C.: Hemisphere Press.

Schooler, C., Flora, J. A., & Farquhar, J. W. (1993). Moving toward synergy: Media supplementation in the Stanford Five-City Project. *Communication Research, 20*, 587–610.

Schorr, L. B. (1988). *Within our reach: Breaking the cycle of disadvantage.* New York: Anchor Press.

Schorr, L. B. (1997). *Common purpose: Strengthening families and neighborhoods to rebuild America.* New York: Anchor Books.

Schulman, S. (1994). *My American history: Lesbian and gay life during the Reagan/Bush years.* New York: Routledge.

Schulz, R., & Hanusa, B, H, (1978). Long-term effects of control and predictability-enhancing interventions: Findings and ethical issues. *Journal of Personality and Social Psychology, 36*, 1194–1201.

Schulz, R., Visintainer, P., & Williamson, G. M., (1990). Psychiatric and physical morbidity effects of caregiving. *Journal of Gerontology: Psychological Sciences, 45* 181–191.

Schwartz, B. (1990). The creation and destruction of value. *American Psychologist, 45*, 7–15.

Schwartz, B. (1997). Psychology, idea technology, and ideology. *Psychological Science, 8*, 21–27.

Schwartz, B. (2000). Self-determination: The tyranny of freedom. *American Psychologist, 55*, 79–88.

Schwartz, S. H. (1992). Universals in the content and structure of values: Theoretical advances and empirical tests in 20 countries. In M. Zanna (Ed.), *Advances in experimental social psychology* (Vol. 25, pp. 1–65). Orlando, FL: Academic.

Schwartz, S. H. (1994). Are there universal aspects in the structure and content of human values? *Journal of Social Issues, 50*, 19–45.

Schwartz, S. H., & Sagiv, G. (2000). Value consensus and importance. *Journal of Cross-Cultural Psychology, 31*, 465–497.

Schwarzer, R., & Jerusalem, M. (1995). Optimistic self-beliefs as a resource factor in coping with stress. In S. E. Hobfoll & M. W. de Vries (Eds.). (1995). *Extreme stress and communities: Impact and intervention* (pp. 159–177). Boston: Kluwer Academic Publishers.

SCRA (2001, Summer). Mission statement. *The Community Psychologist, 34* (3), 4.

Sears, D. O. (1986). College sophomores in the laboratory: Influences of a narrow data base on social psychology's view of human nature. *Journal of Personality and Social Psychology, 51*, 515–530.

Seekins, T., Mathews, M. R., & Fawcett, S. B. (1984). Enhancing leadership skills for community self-help organizations through behavioral instruction. *Journal of Community Psychology, 12*, 155–163.

Seekins, T., Maynard-Moody, S., & Fawcett, S. (1987). Understanding the policy process: Preventing and coping with community problems. In L. A. Jason, R. D. Felner, R. Hess, & J. N. Moritsugu (Eds.), *Communities: Contributions for allied disciplines* (pp. 65–89). New York: Haworth.

Segall, M. H., Lonner, W. J., & Berry, J. W. (1998). Cross-cultural psychology as a scholarly discipline: On the flowering of culture in behavioral research. *American Psychologist, 53*, 1101–1110.

Seidman, E. (1983). Unexamined premises of social problem solving. In E. Seidman (Ed.), *Handbook of social intervention* (48–67). Beverly Hills: Sage.

Seidman, E. (1984). The adolescent passage and entry into the juvenile justice system. In N. D. Reppucci (Ed.), *Children, mental health, and the law*. Beverly Hills : Sage Publications.

Seidman, E. (1987). Toward a framework for primary prevention research. In J. Steinberg & M. Silverman (Eds.), *Preventing mental disorders: A research perspective* (pp. 2–19). Washington, D.C.: U.S. Government Printing Office.

Seidman, E. (1988). Back to the future, community psychology: Unfolding a theory of social intervention. *American Journal of Community Psychology, 16*, 3–24.

Seidman, E., Aber, J. L., Allen, L., & French, S. E. (1996). The impact of the transition to high school on the self-system and perceived social context of poor urban youth. *American Journal of Community Psychology, 24*, 489–515.

Seligman, M. E. P., & Csikszentmihalyi, M. (Eds.). (2000). Positive psychology: An introduction. *American Psychologist, 55*, 5–14.

Seligman, M. E. P. (1990). *Learned optimism*. New York: A. A. Knopf.

Selye, H. (1956). *The stress of life*. New York: McGraw-Hill.

Selznick, P (1992). *The moral commonwealth: Social theory and the promise of community*. Berkeley, CA: University of California Press.

Senge, P. M. (1994). *The fifth discipline: The art and practice of the learning organization*. New York: Doubleday.

Sepúlveda, E. (Ed.). (1996). *We, Chile: Personal testimonies of the Chilean arpilleristas* (B. Morgan, Trans.). Falls Church, VA: Azul Editions.

Serrano-Garcia, I, & Lopez-Sanchez, G. (1991). Community interventions in Puerto Rico: The impact of social-community psychology. *Applied Psychology: An International Review, 40* (2), 201–218.

Serrano-García, I. (1984). The illusion of empowerment: Community development within a colonial context. *Prevention in Human Services, 3*, 173–200.

Serrano-García, I. (1990). Implementing research: Putting our values to work. In P. Tolan, C. Keys, F. Chertok, & L. Jason (Eds.), *Researching community psychology: Issues of theory and methods.* (pp. 171–182). Washington, D.C.: American Psychological Association.

Serrano-García, I. (1994). The ethics of the powerful and the power of ethics. *American Journal of Community Psychology, 22*, 1–20.

Serrano-García, I., & Bond, M. A. (1994). Empowering the silent ranks: Introduction. *American Journal of Community Psychology, 22*, 433–445.

Shadish, W. R. (1990). Defining excellence criteria in community research. In P. Tolan, C. Keys, F. Chertok, & L. Jason (Eds.), *Researching community psychology: Issues of theory and methods* (pp. 9–20). Washington, D.C.: American Psychological Association.

Shapiro, J. P. (1993). A hidden army for civil rights. In *No pity: People with disabilities forging a new civil rights movement* (pp. 105–142). New York: Random House.

Shaver, K. (1970). Defensive attributions: Effects of severity and relevance on the responsibility assigned for an accident. *Journal of Personality and Social Psychology, 14*, 101–113.

Shefner-Rogers, C. L., Rao, N., Rogers, E. M., & Wayangankar, A. (1998). The empowerment of women dairy farmers in India. *Journal of Applied Communication Research, 26*, 319–337.

Sherif, M., & Sherif, C. W. (1953). *An outline of social psychology*. New York: Harper and Row.

Sherif, M., Harvey, O. J., White, J. B., Hood, W. R., & Sherif, C. W. (1961). *Intergroup conflict and cooperation:*

The Robber's Cave experiment. Norman, OK: University of Oklahoma Book Exchange.

Sherman, A., Amey, C., Duffield, B., Ebb, N., & Weinstein, D. (1998). *Welfare to What? Early findings on family hardship and well-being.* Washington, D.C.: Children's Defense Fund and the National Coalition for the Homeless. Retrieved August 8, 2001, from *http://www.childrensdefense.org/pdf/wlfwhat.pdf.*

Shinn, M. (1987). Expanding community psychology's domain. *American Journal of Community Psychology, 15,* 555–574.

Shinn, M. (1990). Mixing and matching: Levels of conceptualization, measurement, and statistical analysis in community research. In P. Tolan, C. Keys, F. Chertok, & L. Jason (Eds.), *Researching community psychology: Issues of theory and methods.* (pp. 111–126). Washington, D.C.: American Psychological Association.

Shinn, M. (1992). Homelessness: What is a psychologist to do? *American Journal of Community Psychology, 20,* 1–24.

Shinn, M., Lehman, S., & Wong, N. W. (1984). Social interaction and social support. *Journal of Social Issues, 40,* 55–76.

Shor, I., & Freire, P. (1987). *A pedagogy for liberation: Dialogues on transforming education.* New York: Bergin & Garvey.

Shumaker, S. A., & Brownell, A. (1985). Introduction: Social support interventions. *Journal of Social Issues, 41,* 1–4.

Shumaker, S. A., & Taylor, R. B. (1983). Toward a clarification of people–place relationships: A model of attachment to place. In N. R. Feimer & E. S. Geller (Eds.), *Environmental psychology: Directions and perspectives* (pp. 219–251). New York: Prager.

Shure, M. B. (1997). Interpersonal cognitive problems solving: Primary prevention of early high-risk behaviors in the preschool and primary years. In G. W. Albee & T. P. Gulotta (Eds.), *Primary prevention works.* Thousand Oaks, CA: Sage.

Shure, M. B., & Spivack, G. (1988). Interpersonal cognitive problem solving. In R. H. Price, E. L. Cowen, R. P. Lorion, & J. Ramos-McKay (Eds.), *14 ounces of prevention: A casebook for practitioners* (pp. 69–82). Washington, D.C.: American Psychological Association.

Shweder, R. A., Mahapatra, M., & Miller, J. G. (1987). Culture and moral development. In J. Kagan & S. Lamb (Eds.), *The emergence of morality in young children* (pp. 1–82). Chicago: The University of Chicago Press.

Sigal, J. (1980). Physical environmental stressors. In M. S. Gibbs, J. R. Lachenmeyer, & J. Sigal (Eds), *Community psychology: Theoretical and empirical approaches* (pp. 145–171). New York: Gardner Press, Inc.

Silka, L., & Tip, J. (1994). Empowering the silent ranks: The Southeast Asian experience. *American Journal of Community Psychology, 22,* 497–529.

Silverstein, O., & Rashbaum, B. (1994). *The courage to raise good men.* New York: Viking.

Simonton, D. K. (1997). Foreign influence and national achievement: The impact of open milieus on Japanese civilization. *Journal of Personality and Social Psychology, 72,* 86–94.

Simonton, D. K. (2000). Creativity: Cognitive, personal, and social aspects. *American Psychologist, 55,* 151–158.

Sinha, D., & Holtzman, W. H. (Eds.). (1984). Special issue: The impact of psychology on Third World development. *International Journal of Psychology, 19 (1/2).*

Sinha, J., & Verma, J. (1994). Social support ad a moderator of the relationship between allocentrism and psychological well-being. In U. Kim, H. Triandis, C. Kagiticibasi, S. Choi, & G. Yoon (Eds.), *Individualism and collectivism: Theory, method, and applications* (pp. 267–275). Thousand Oaks, CA: Sage.

Skinner, B. F. (1948/1976). *Walden Two.* New York: MacMillan Publishing Co.

Skitka, L. J., & Tetlock, P. E. (1993). Providing public assistance: Cognitive and motivational processes underlying liberal and conservative policy preferences. *Journal of Personality and Social Psychology, 65,* 1205–1223.

Skjaeveland, O., Garling, T., & Maeland, T. G. (1996). A multidimensional measure of neighboring. *American Journal of Community Psychology, 24,* 413–436.

Smith, B. W., Pargament, K. I., Brant, C., & Oliver, J. M. (2000). Noah revisited: Religious coping by church members and the impact of the 1993 midwest flood. *Journal of Community Psychology, 28 (2),* 169–186.

Smith, D. N. (1998). The psychocultural roots of genocide: Legitimacy and crisis in Rwanda. *American Psychologist, 53,* 743–753.

Smith, E. R. (1993). Social identity and social emotions: Toward new conceptualizations of prejudice. In D. M. Mackie & D. L. Hamilton (Eds.), *Affect, cognition, and stereotyping: Interactive processes in group perceptions* (pp. 297–315). San Diego: Academic Press.

Smith, P. C., & Warrior, R. A. (1996). *Like a Hurricane: The Indian Movement from Alcatraz to Wounded Knee.* New York: The New Press.

Smith, R. E., Johnson, J. H., & Sarason, I. G. (1978). Life change, the sensation seeking motive, and psychological distress. *Journal of Consulting and Clinical Psychology, 46,* 348–349.

Smith, S. E. (1997). Deepening participatory action research. In S. E. Smith, D. G. Williams, & N. A. Johnson (Eds.), *Nurtured by knowledge: Learning to do participatory action-research* (pp. 173–263). New York: The Apex Press.

Snarey, J. R. (1985). Cross-cultural universality of social-moral development: A critical review of Kohlbergian research. *Psychological Bulletin, 97,* 202–232.

Snow, D. L., Grady, K., & Goyette-Ewing, M. (2000). A perspective on ethical issues in community psychology.

In J. Rappaport & E. Seidman (Eds.), *Handbook of community psychology* (pp. 897–917). New York: Kluwer Academic/Plenum Publishers.

Snowden, L. R., Martinez, M., & Morris A. (2000). Community psychology and ethnic minority populations. In J. Rappaport & E. Seidman (Eds.), *Handbook of community psychology* (pp. 833–855). New York: Kluwer Academic/Plenum Publishers.

Society for the Teaching of Psychology's Task Force on Defining Scholarship in Psychology (1998). Scholarship in psychology: A paradigm for the 21st century. *American Psychologist, 53,* 1292–1297.

Solarz, A. (2000). (Ed.). Special feature section: Community psychology and public policy. *Community Psychologist, 33 (1),* 27–36.

Sollod, R. N. (1998). Unexamined nonreligious assumptions. *American Psychologist, 53,* 324–325.

Solomon, B. (1976). *Black empowerment: Social work in oppressed communities.* New York: Columbia University Press.

Solomon, D., Watson, M., Battistich, V., Schaps, E., & Delucchi, K. (1996). Creating classrooms that kids experience as communities. *American Journal of Community Psychology, 24,* 719–748.

Solomon, M., Pistrang, N., & Barker, C. (2001). The benefits of mutual support groups for parents of children with disabilities. *American Journal of Community Psychology, 29,* 113–132.

Sonn, C. C., & Fisher, A. T. (1998). Sense of Community: Resilient responses to oppression and change. *Journal of Community Psychology, 26 (5),* 457–472.

Speer, P. W., & Hughey, J. (1995). Community organizing: An ecological route to empowerment and power. *American Journal of Community Psychology, 23,* 729–749.

Speer, P. W. (2000). Intrapersonal and interactional empowerment: Implications for theory. *Journal of Community Psychology, 28,* 51–61.

Speer, P. W., Dey, A., Griggs, P., Gibson, C., Lubin, B., & Hughey, J. (1992). In search of community: An analysis of community psychology research from 1984–1988. *American Journal of Community Psychology, 20,* 195–209.

Spencer, M. B. (1984). Black children's race awareness, racial attitudes, and self-concept: A reinterpretation. *Journal of Child Psychology and Psychiatry, 25,* 433–441.

Spencer, M. B. (1990). Development of minority children: An introduction. *Child Development, 61,* 267–269.

Spiegel, D., Bloom, J. R., Kraemer, H. C., & Gottheil, E. (1989). Psychological support for cancer patients. *Lancet, 2,* 1447.

Spielberger, C. D., & Iscoe, I. (1977). Community psychology in transition: Reflections on the Austin Conference. In I. Iscoe, B. L. Bloom, & C. D. Spielberger (Eds.), *Community psychology in transition: Proceedings of the national conference on training in community psychology* (pp. 315–327). New York: John Wiley & Sons.

Spilka, B. (1989). Functional and dysfunctional roles of religion: An attributional approach. *Journal of Psychology and Christianity, 8,* 5–15.

Spitz, R. A. (1945). Hospitalism: An inquiry into the genesis of psychiatric conditions in early childhood. In R. S. Eissler et al., *The psychoanalytic study of the child, Vol. 1* (pp. 53–74). New York: International Universities Press.

Spitz, R. A. (1946). Hospitalism: A follow-up report. In R. S. Eissler et al., *The psychoanalytic study of the child, Vol. 2* (pp. 113–117). New York: International Universities Press.

Spitzer, R. L. (1976). More on pseudoscience in science and the case of the psychiatric diagnosis: A critique of D. L. Rosenhan's "On being sane in insane places" and "The contextual nature of psychiatric diagnosis." *Archives of General Psychiatry, 33,* 459–470.

Spivak, G., & Shure, M. B. (1974). *Social adjustment of young children.* San Francisco: Jossey-Bass.

Spreitzer, G. M. (1995). An empirical test of a comprehensive model of intrapersonal empowerment in the workplace. *American Journal of Community Psychology, 23,* 601–629.

Sroufe, L. A., & Rutter, M. (1984). The domain of developmental psychopathology. *Child Development, 55,* 17–29.

Stack, C. (1974). *All our kin: Strategies for survival in a Black community.* New York: Harper and Row.

Staley, J. M., & Lapidus, L. B. (1997). Attributions of responsibility in father–daughter incest in relation to gender, socio-economic status, ethnicity, and experiential differences in participants. *Journal of Clinical Psychology, 53 (4),* 331–347.

Stark, L. (1986). Strangers in a strange land: The chronically mentally ill homeless. *Journal of Mental Health, 14,* 95–111.

Staudinger, U. M., Marsiske, M., & Baltes, P. B. (1993). Resilience and levels of reserve capacity in late adulthood: Perspectives from a life span theory. *Development and Psychopathology, 5,* 541–566.

Steele, C. M. (1997). A threat in the air: How stereotypes shape intellectual identity and performance. *American Psychologist, 52,* 613–629.

Steele, S. (1990). *The content of our character: A new vision of race in America.* New York: St. Martin Press.

Steinberg, L. (1988). Reciprocal relations between parent–child distance and pubertal maturation. *Developmental Psychology, 24,* 122–128.

Steinberg, L. (1990). Interdependence in the family: Autonomy, conflict, and harmony in the parent–adolescent relationship. In S. S. Feldman & G. R. Elliott (Eds.), *At the threshold: The developing adolescent* (pp. 255–276). Cambridge: Harvard University Press.

Steinberg, L., Mounts, N. S., Lamborn, S. D., & Dornbusch, S. D. (1991). Authoritative parenting and adolescent adjustment across varied ecological niches. *Journal of Research on Adolescence, 1*, 19–36.

Stephan, W., & Stephan, C. (1995). *Intergroup relations.* Dubuque, IA: Brown and Benchmark.

Stern, G. S., McCants, T. R., & Pettine, P. W. (1982). Stress and illness: Controllable and uncontrollable life events' relative contributions. *Personality and Social Psychology Bulletin, 8*, 140–145.

Stevenson, H. C. (1998). Raising safe villages: Cultural-ecological factors that influence the emotional adjustment of adolescents. *Journal of Black Psychology, 24*, 44–59.

Stewart, E. (2000). Thinking through others: Qualitative research and community psychology. In J. Rappaport & E. Seidman (Eds.), *Handbook of community psychology* (pp. 725–736). New York: Kluwer Academic/Plenum Publishers.

Stewart, E., & Weinstein, R. (1997). Volunteer participation in context: motivations and political efficacy within three AIDS organizations. *American Journal of Community Psychology, 25*, 809–838.

Stewart, L. P., Cooper, P. J., Stewart, A. D., & Friedley, S. A. (1998). *Communication and gender, 3rd edition.* Boston: Allyn & Bacon.

Stokols, D., & Altman, I. Introduction. In D. Stokols & I. Altman (Eds.), *Handbook of environmental psychology* (pp. 1–4). New York: Wiley.

Stokols, D. (1978). Environmental psychology. *Annual Review of Psychology, 29*, 253–295.

Stolz, S. B. (1984). Preventive models: Implications for a technology of practice. In M. Roberts & L. Peterson (Eds.), *Prevention of problems in childhood* (pp. 391–413). New York: John Wiley.

Stone, R. A., & Levine, A. G. (1985). Reactions to collective stress: Correlates of active citizen participation. *Prevention in Human Services, 4*, 153–177.

Stouthamer-Loeber, M., Loeber, R., Farrington, D. P., Zhang, Q., van Kammen, W., & Maguin, E. (1993). The double edge of protective and risk factors for delinquency: Interrelations and developmental patterns. *Development and Psychopathology, 5*, 683–701.

Strawn, C. (1994). Beyond the buzz word: Empowerment in community outreach and education. *Journal of Applied Behavioral Science, 30*, 159–174.

Strelau, J. (1995). Temperament risk factor: The contribution of temperament to the consequences of the state of stress. In S. E. Hobfoll & M. W. de Vries (Eds.). (1995). *Extreme stress and communities: Impact and intervention* (pp. 63–81). Boston: Kluwer Academic Publishers.

Strickland, B. R., & Janoff-Bulman, R. (1980). Expectancies and attributions: Implications for community mental health. In M. S. Gibbs, J. R. Lachenmeyer, & J. Sigal (Eds.), *Community psychology: Theoretical and empirical approaches* (pp. 97–119). New York: Gardner Press, Inc.

Suarez-Balcazar, Y., Durlak, J. A., & Smith, C. (1994). Multicultural training practices in community psychology programs. *American Journal of Community Psychology, 22*, 785–799.

Sue, D. W., Bingham, R. P., Porche-Burke, L., & Vasquez, M. (1999). The diversification of psychology: A multicultural revolution. *American Psychologist, 54*, 1061–1069.

Sue, S. (1999). Science, ethnicity, and bias: Where have we gone wrong? *American Psychologist, 54*, 1070–1077.

Sullivan, J. L., & Transue, J. E. (1999). The psychological underpinnings of democracy: A selective review of research on political tolerance, interpersonal trust, and social capital. *Annual Review of Psychology, 50*, 625–650.

Suls, J., & Mullen, B. (1981). Life events, perceived control, and illness: The role of uncertainty. *Journal of Human Stress, 7*, 30–34.

Surrey, J. L. (1991). Relationship and empowerment. In J. V. Jordan, A. G. Kaplan, J. B. Miller, I. P. Stiver, & J. L. Surrey (Eds.), *Women's growth in connection: Writings from the Stone Center* (pp. 162–180). New York: Guilford Press.

Swearingen, E. M., & Cohen, L. H. (1985a). Life events and psychological distress: A prospective study of young adolescents. *Developmental Psychology, 21*, 1045–1054.

Swearingen, E. M., & Cohen, L. H. (1985b). Measurement of adolescents' life events: The junior high life experiences survey. *American Journal of Community Psychology, 13*, 69–85.

Swift, C. F. (1990). Research as intervention. In P. Tolan, C. Keys, F. Chertok, & L. Jason. (Eds.), *Researching community psychology: Issues of theory and methods* (pp. 196–198). Washington, D.C.: American Psychological Association.

Swift, C. F., Bond, M. A., & Serrano-Garcia, I. (2000). Women's empowerment: A review of community psychology's first 25 years. In J. Rappaport & E. Seidman (Eds.), *Handbook of community psychology* (pp. 857–895). New York: Kluwer Academic/Plenum Publishers.

Swift, C. F., & Levin, G. (1987). Empowerment: An emerging mental health technology. *Journal of Primary Prevention, 8*, 71–94.

Sypher, H. E., & Collins, B. (2001). Virtual-online communities: How might new technologies be related to community? In G. J. Shepherd & E. W. Rothenbuhler (Eds.), *Communication and community* (pp. 191–200). Mahwah, NJ: Lawrence Erlbaum.

Szasz, T. (1961). *Myth of mental illness.* New York: Dell.

Tajfel, H. (1969). Cognitive aspects of prejudice. *Journal of Social Issues, 25*, 79–97.

Tajfel, H. (1982). *Social identity and intergroup relations.* Cambridge, England: Cambridge University Press.

Takano, Y., & Osaka, E. (1999). An unsupported common view: Comparing Japan and the U.S. on individualism and collectivism. *Asian Journal of Social Psychology, 2* (3), 311–341.

Talen, E. (1996). Sense of community and neighbourhood form: An assessment of the social doctrine of new urbanism. *Urban Studies, 36* (8), 1361–1379.

Tam, V. C., & D. F. Detzner (1998). Grandparents as a family resource in Chinese-American families: Perceptions of the middle generation. In H. I. McCubbin, E. A. Thompson, A. I. Thompson, & J. E. Fromer (Eds.), *Resiliency in Native American and immigrant families* (pp. 243–263). Thousand Oaks, CA: Sage.

Tapanya, S. (1989). Community psychology in Thailand. *American Journal of Community Psychology, 17,* 121–132.

Tardif, T., Gelman, S. A., & Xu, F. (1999). Putting the "noun bias" in context: A comparison of English and Mandarin. *Child Development, 70,* 620–635.

Tarrow, S. (1992). Mentalities, political cultures, and collective action frames: Constructing meaning through action. In A. D. Morris & C. M. Mueller (Eds.), *Frontiers in social movement theory* (pp. 174–202). New Haven, CT: Yale University Press.

Tarrow, S. (1994). *Power in Movement: Social Movements, Collective Action and Politics.* New York: Cambridge University Press.

Tarter, R. E., & Vanyukov, M. (1999). Re-visiting the validity of the construct of resilience. In M. D. Glantz & J. L. Johnson (Eds.), *Resilience and development; Positive life adaptations* (pp. 85–100). New York: Kluwer Academic/Plenum.

Tatum, B. D. (1992). Talking about race, learning about racism: The application of racial identity development theory in the classroom. *Harvard Educational Review, 62,* 1–24.

Tavris, C. (1989). *Anger: The misunderstood emotion, 2nd edition.* New York: Simon & Schuster.

Taylor, R. D., & Roberts, D. (1995). Kinship support and maternal and adolescent well-being in economically disadvantaged African-American families. *Child Development, 66,* 1585–1597.

Taylor, R. D., Jacobson, L., Rodriguez, A. U., Dominguez, A., Cantic, R., Doney, J., Boccuti, A., Alejandro, J., & Tobon, C. (2000). Stressful experiences and the psychological functioning of African-American and Puerto Rican families and adolescents. In R. D. Taylor & M. C. Wang (Eds.), *Resilience across contexts: Family, work, culture, and community* (pp. 35–53). Mahwah, NJ: Lawrence Erlbaum.

Taylor, R. J. (1986). Receipt of support from family among black Americans: Demographic and familial differences. *Journal of Marriage and the Family, 48,* 67–77.

Taylor, S. E. (1983). Adjustment to threatening events: A theory of cognitive adaptation. *American Psychologist, 38,* 1161–1173.

Taylor, S. E. (1989). *Positive illusions: Creating self-deception and the healthy mind.* New York: Basic Books.

Taylor, S. E., & Brown, J. D. (1988). Illusion and well-being: A social psychological perspective on mental health. *Psychological Bulletin, 103,* 193–210.

Taylor, S. E., Kemeny, M. E., Reed, G. M., Bower, J. E., & Gruenwald, T. L. (2000). Psychological resources, positive illusions, and health. *American Psychologist, 55,* 99–109.

Taylor, S. E., Klein, L. C., Lewis, B. P., Gruenewald, T. L., Gurung, R. A. R., & Updegraff, J. A. (2000). Biobehavioral responses to stress in females: Tend-and-befriend, not fight-or-flight. *Psychological Review, 107,* 411–429.

Taylor, S. E., Repetti, R. L., & Seeman, T. (1997). Health psychology: What is an unhealthy environment and how does it get under the skin? *Annual Review of Psychology,* 48, 411–448.

Temerlin, M. K. (1968). Suggestion effects in psychiatric diagnosis. *Journal of Nervous and Mental Disease, 147,* 349–353.

Theorell, T. (1974). Life events before and after the onset of myocardial infarction. In B. S. Dohrenwend & B. P. Dohrenwend (Eds.), *Stressful life events: Their nature and effects* (pp. 101–117). New York: John Wiley.

Thibaut, J. W., & Kelly, H. H. (1959). *The social psychology of groups.* New York: Wiley.

Thomae, H., & Lehr, U. (1986). Stages, crises, conflicts, and life-span development. In A. Sorensen, F. E. Weinert, L. R. Sherrod (Eds.), *Human development and the life course: Multidisciplinary perspectives.* Hillsdale, NJ: Lawrence Erlbaum Associates.

Thomas, R. E., & Rappaport, J. (1996). Art as community narrative: A resource for change. In M. B. Lykes, A. Banuazizi, R. Liem, & M. Morris (Eds.), *Myths about the powerless: Contesting social inequalities* (pp. 317–336). Philadelphia: Temple University Press.

Thompson, B., & Vaux, A. (1986). The importation, transmission, and moderation of stress in the family system. *American Journal of Community Psychology, 14,* 39–57.

Thompson, C. (1992). On being heterosexual in a homophobic world. In W. J. Blumenfeld (Ed.), *Homophobia: How we all pay the price* (pp. 235–248). Boston: Beacon Press.

Thompson, L. L., & Crocker, J. (1990). Downward social comparison in the minimal intergroup situation: a test of a self-enhancement interpretation. *Journal of Applied Social Psychology, 20,* 1166–1185.

Thornton, W. (1984). Defensive attribution of responsibility: Evidence for an arousal-based motivational bias. *Journal of Personality and Social Psychology, 46,* 721–734.

Thorson, J. A. (1998). Religion and anxiety: Which anxiety? Which religion? In H. G. Koenig (Ed.), *Handbook of religion and mental health* (pp. 147–160). San Diego: Academic Press.

Timeout. (No date). "Sting reassesses his roots." Retrieved July 17, 2002, from ***http://www.sting.com/newspress/ interviews/timeout/html***.

Tolan, P. T. (1996). How resilient is the concept of resilience? *The Community Psychologist, 29,* 12–15.

Tolan, P., Chertok, F., Keys, C., & Jason, L. (1990). Conversing about theories, methods, and community research. In P. Tolan, C. Keys, F. Chertok, & L. Jason. (Eds.), *Researching community psychology: Issues of theory and methods* (pp. 3–8). Washington, D.C.: American Psychological Association.

Tolan, P., Keys, C., Chertok, F., & Jason, L. (Eds.), (1990). *Researching community psychology: Issues of theory and methods*. Washington, D.C.: American Psychological Association.

Tönnies, F. (1957). *Community and society (Gemeinschaft and gessellschaft)*. East Lansing, MI: Michigan State University Press.

Toro, P. A. (1986). A comparison of natural and professional help. *American Journal of Community Psychology, 14,* 147–159.

Toro, P. A., Rappaport, J., & Seidman, E. (1987). Social climate comparison of mutual help and psychotherapy groups. *Journal of Consulting and Clinical Psychology, 55,* 430–431.

Torrey, E. F. (1997). *Out of the shadows: Confronting America's mental illness crisis*. New York: John Wiley & Sons.

de Toqueville, A. (1835/1969). *Democracy in America* (G. Lawrence, Trans.; J. P. Mayer, Ed.). New York: Doubleday.

Triandis, H. C. (1989). Cross-cultural studies of individualism and collectivism. *Nebraska Symposium on Motivation, 37,* 41–133.

Triandis, H. C. (1995). *Individualism and collectivism*. Boulder, CO: Westview Press.

Trickett, E. J, & Birman, D. (1989). Taking ecology seriously: A community development approach to individually-based interventions. In L. Bond & B. Compas (Eds.), *Primary prevention in the schools* (pp. 187–204). Hanover, NH: University Press of England.

Trickett, E. J. (1991). *Living an idea: Empowerment and the evolution of an alternative high school*. Boston: Brookline Books.

Trickett, E. J. (1994). Human diversity and community psychology: Where ecology and empowerment meet. *Journal of Community Psychology, 22,* 583–593.

Trickett, E. J. (1997). Ecology and primary prevention: Reflections on a meta-analysis. *American Journal of Community Psychology, 25,* 197–205.

Trickett, E. J., & Lustman, N. M. (1977). Research, knowledge, and professional growth. In I. Iscoe, B. L. Bloom, & C. D. Spielberger (Eds.), *Community psychology in transition: Proceedings of the national conference on training in community psychology* (pp. 185–194). New York: John Wiley & Sons.

Trickett, E. J., & Moos, R. H. (1974). Personal correlates of contrasting environments: Student satisfaction in high school classrooms. *American Journal of Community Psychology, 2,* 1–12.

Trickett, E. J., Barone, C., & Watts, R. (2000). Contextual influences in mental health consultation: Toward an ecological perspective on radiating change. In J. Rappaport & E. Seidman (Eds.), *Handbook of community psychology* (pp. 303–330). New York: Kluwer Academic/Plenum Publishers.

Trickett, E. J., Watts, R. J., & Birman, D. (1993). Human diversity and community psychology: Still hazy after all these years. *Journal of Community Psychology, 26,* 264–279.

Trickett, E. J., Watts, R. J., & Birman, D. (1994). Toward an overarching framework for diversity. In E. J. Trickett, R. J. Watts, & D. Birman (Eds.), *Human diversity: Perspectives on people in context* (pp. 7–26). San Francisco: Jossey-Bass.

Trickett, E., J. (1990). Partial paradigms and professional identity: Observations on the state of community psychology research. In P. Tolan, C. Keys, F. Chertok, & L. Jason (Eds.), *Researching community psychology:Issues of theory and methods.* (pp. 209–214). Washington, D.C.: American Psychological Association.

Trocmé, M. (1986). In C. Rittner & S. Myers (Eds.), *The courage to care: Rescuers of Jews during the Holocaust.* (pp. 100–107). New York: New York University Press.

Trolander, J. (1987). *Professionalism and social change: From the settlement house movement to neighborhood centers, 1886 to the present*. New York: Columbia University Press.

Troutt, D. D. (1993). *The thin red line: How the poor still pay more*. San Francisco: Consumers Union U.S. West Coast Office.

Turiel, E. (1998). The development of morality. In W. Damon & N. Eisenberg (Eds.), *Handbook of child psychology (5th ed.), Vol. 3: Social, emotional, and personality development* (pp. 863–932). New York: Wiley.

Turiel, E., Killen, M., & Helwig, C. C. (1987). Morality: Its structure, functions, and vagaries. In J. Kagan & S. Lamb (Eds.), *The emergence of morality* (pp. 155–243). Chicago: Chicago University Press.

Turkle, S. (1996, Winter). Virtuality and its discontents: Searching for community in cyberspace. *The American Prospect, 24,* 50–57.

Turner, L. R., Morera, O. F., Johnson, T. P., Crittendon, K. S., Freels, S., Parsons, J., Flay, B., & Warnecke, R. B. (2001). Examining the effectiveness of a community-based self-help program to increase women's readiness for smoking cessation (2001). *American Journal of Community Psychology, 29,* 465–491.

Tyler, F. B., Pargament, K. I., & Gatz, M. (1983). The resource collaborator role: A model for interactions involving psychologists. *American Psychologist, 38,* 388–398.

U.S. Bureau of the Census (1992). *Statistical abstract of the United States: The national data book (112th ed.).* Washington, D.C.: U.S. Government Printing Office.

U.S. Bureau of the Census (1998). Census, *Poverty in the United States: 1998,* P60–207, Table B-1. Retrieved September 3, 2001, from **http://www.ssc.wisc.edu/irp/ faqs/faq3dir/povtab98-two.htm**.

U.S. Bureau of the Census (2001, April 2). *Difference in population by race and Hispanic or Latino origin, for the United States: 1990 to 2000* (Table). Retrieved September 4, 2001, from **http://www.census.gov/population/ cen2000/phc-t1/tab04.pdf**.

U.S. Bureau of the Census (2001, March 12). Census 2000 shows American Diversity. *Commerce News.* Washington D.C. Retrieved September 4, 2001, from **http://www.census.gov/Press-Release/www/2001/ cbo1cn61.htm**.

U.S. Department of Justice (1999, December). *Juvenile Justice Bulletin: Minorities in the Juvenile Justice System.* Washington, D.C.: Office of Juvenile Justice and Delinquency Prevention, Office of Justice Programs.

U.S. Surgeon General (D. M. Satcher). (2001). *Mental Health: Culture, Race, Ethnicity Supplement to Mental Health: Report of the Surgeon General.* Washington, D.C.: Department of Health and Human Service, U.S. Public Health Service. Retrieved August 15, 2001, from **http://www.mentalhealth.org/cre/execsummary2. html**.

Unger, D. G., & Wanderman, A. (1982). Neighboring in an urban environment. *American Journal of Community Psychology, 10,* 493–509.

Unger, D. G., & Wanderman, A. (1985). The importance of neighbors: The social, affective, and cognitive components of neighboring. *American Journal of Community Psychology, 13,* 139–169.

Vaillant, G. (2000). Adaptive mental mechanisms: Their role in a positive psychology. *American Psychologist, 55,* 89–99.

Valente, E., Jr., & Dodge, K. A. (1997). Evaluation of prevention programs for children. In R. P. Weissberg, T. P. Gulotta, R. L. Hampton, B. A. Ryan, & G. R. Adams (Eds.), *Establishing preventive services* (pp. 183–218). Thousand Oaks, CA: Sage.

van den Eynde, J., & Veno, A. (1999). Coping with disastrous events: An empowerment model of community healing. In R. M. Gist & B. Lubin (Eds.), *Response to disaster: Psychosocial, community, and ecological approaches* (167–192). London: Taylor and Francis.

van der Kolk, B. A., van der Hart, O., & Burbridge, J. (1995). The treatment of post traumatic stress disorder. In S. E. Hobfoll & M. W. de Vries (Eds.). (1995). *Extreme stress and communities: Impact and intervention* (pp. 421–443). Boston: Kluwer Academic Publishers.

van Uchelen, C. (2000). Individualism, collectivism, and community psychology. In J. Rappaport & E. Seidman (Eds.), *Handbook of community psychology* (pp. 65–78). New York: Kluwer Academic/Plenum Publishers.

Vega, W. A. (1992). Theoretical and pragmatic implications of cultural diversity for community research. *American Journal of Community Psychology, 20,* 375–391.

Vega, W. A., & Kolody, B. (1985). The meaning of social support and the mediation of stress: across cultures. In W. A. Vega & M. R. Miranda (Eds.), *Stress and Hispanic mental health: Relating research to service delivery* (pp. 48–75). Rockville, MD: National Institute of Mental Health.

Ventis, W. L. (1995). The relationship between religion and mental health. *Journal of Social Issues, 51 (2),* 33–48.

Vernberg, E. M., & Vogel, J. M. (1993). Children's psychological responses to disaster. *Journal of Clinical Child Psychology, 22,* 464–484.

Vincent, T. A. (1990). A view from the Hill: The human element in policy making on Capitol Hill. *American Psychologist, 45,* 61–64.

Vinokur, A., & Caplan, R. D. (1986). Cognitive and affective components of life events: Their relations and effects on well-being. *American Journal of Community Psychology, 14,* 351–370.

Vinokur, A., & Selzer, M. L. (1975). Desirable vs. undesirable life events: Their relationship to stress and mental distress. *Journal of Personality and Social Psychology, 32,* 329–337.

de Vries, M. W. (1984). Temperament and infant mortality among the Masai of East Africa. *American Journal of Psychiatry, 141,* 1189–1194.

Vygotsky, L. S. (1978). *Mind in society: The development of higher psychological processes.* Cambridge, MA: Harvard University Press.

Wachter, R. M. (1991). *The fragile coalition: Scientists, activists and AIDS.* New York: St. Martin's Press.

Walker, A. J. (1985). Reconceptualizing family stress. *Journal of Marriage and the Family, 47,* 827–837.

Walker, K. N., MacBride, A., & Vachon, M. L. S. (1977). Social support networks and the crisis of bereavement. *Social Science and Medicine, 11,* 35–41.

Walker, L. J., de Vries, B., & Trevethan, S. D. (1987). Moral stages and moral orientations in real-life and hypothetical dilemmas. *Child Development, 58,* 842–858.

Walker, L. J., Pitts, R. C., Henning, K. H., & Matsuba, M. K. (1995). Reasoning about morality and real-life moral problems. In M. Keller & D. Hart (Eds.). *Morality in everyday life.* Cambridge: Developmental Perspectives.

Wallerstein, J. S., & Kelly, J. B. (1980). *Surviving the breakup: How children and parents cope with divorce.* New York: Basic Books.

Walsh, R. T. (1987). The evolution of the research relationship in community psychology. *American Journal of Community Psychology, 15,* 773–788.

Walsh, R. T. (1988). Current development in community psychology in Canada. *Journal of Community Psychology, 16*, 296–305.

Walsh-Bowers, R. (1993). The resident researcher in social ethical perspective. *American Journal of Community Psychology, 21*, 495–500.

Walsh-Bowers, R. (1998). Community psychology in the Canadian Psychological Family. *Canadian Psychology, 39*, 280–287.

Walsh-Bowers, R. (2000). A personal sojourn to spiritualize community psychology. *Journal of Community Psychology, 28*, 221–236.

Walster, E. (1966). Assignment of responsibility for an accident, *Journal of Personality and Social Psychology, 3*, 73–79.

Walters, K. L., & Simoni, J. M. (1993). Lesbian and gay male group identity attitudes and self-esteem: Implications for counseling. *Journal of Counseling Psychology, 40* (1), 94–99.

Wandersman, A., & Florin, P. (2000). Citizen participation and community organizations. In J. Rappaport & E. Seidman (Eds.), *Handbook of community psychology* (pp. 247–272). New York: Kluwer Academic/Plenum Publishers.

Wandersman, A., & Nation, M. (1998). Urban neighborhoods and mental health: Psychological contributions to understanding toxicity, resilience, and interventions. *American Psychologist, 53*, 647–656.

Wang, C. C. (1999) Photovoice: A participatory action research strategy applied to women's health. *Journal of Women's Health, 8(2)*, 185–192.

Wang, M. C., Haertel, G. D., & Walberg, H. J. (1999). Psychological and educational resilience. In A. J. Reynolds, H. J. Walberg, & R. P. Weissberg (Eds). *Promoting positive outcomes* (pp. 329–365). Washington, D.C.: CWLA Press.

Watson, G. (1999, May 26–29). Block by block: Ten lessons we've learned on Dudley Street [6 pages]. Presentation at 24th Annual Neighborhoods U.S.A Conference, Madison WI. Retrieved April 25, 2001, from ***http://www.dsni.org/Archives/ten_lessons.htm***.

Watts, R. J. (1997). Community psychology's action faction. In Symposium on Social Contexts for the SCRA, J. Kelly, Chair. APA, August 1997, Chicago, IL.

Watts, R. J. (1993a). Community action through manhood development: A look at concepts and concerns from the frontline. *American Journal of Community Psychology, 21*, 333–359.

Watts, R. J. (1993b). "Resident research" and community psychology. *American Journal of Community Psychology, 21*, 483–486.

Watts, R. J. (1994). Paradigms of diversity. In E. J. Trickett, R. J. Watts, & D. Birman (Eds.), *Human diversity: Perspectives on people in context* (pp. 49–80). San Francisco: Jossey-Bass.

Watts, R. J., & Abdul-Adil, J. (1994). Psychological aspects of oppression and sociopolitical development: Building young warriors. In R. Newby & T. Manley (Eds.), *The poverty of inclusion, innovation, and interventions: The dilemma of the African-American underclass* (pp. 1–13). Chicago: Red Feather Institute.

Watts, R. J., Griffith, D. M., & Abdul-Adil, J. (1999). Sociopolitical development as an antidote for oppression—Theory and action. *American Journal of Community Psychology, 27*, 255–271.

Watzlawick, P., Weakland, J. H., & Fisch, R. (1974). *Change; Principles of problem formation and problem resolution*. New York, Norton.

Weaver, A. J. (1998). Mental health professionals working with religious leaders. In H. G. Koenig (Ed.), *Handbook of religion and mental health* (pp. 349–364). San Diego: Academic Press.

Weaver, A. J., Kline, A. E., Samford, J. A., Lucas, L. A., Larson, D. B., & Gorsuch, R. I. (1998). Is religion taboo in psychology: A systematic analysis of research on religion in seven major American Psychological Association journals: 1991–1994. *Journal of Psychology and Christianity, 17* (3), 220–232.

Weick, K. E. (1984). Small wins: Redefining the scale of social problems. *American Psychologist, 39*, 40–49.

Weinstein, R. S. (1994). Pushing the frontiers of multicultural training in community psychology. *American Journal of Community Psychology, 22*, 811–819.

Weinstein, R. S., Soule, C. R., Colins, F., Cone, J., Mehlhorn, M., & Simontacchi, K. (1991). Expectations and high school change: Teacher–researcher collaboration to prevent school failure. *American Journal of Community Psychology, 19*, 333–363.

Weissberg, R. P., Caplan, M., & Harwood, R. L. (1991). Promoting competent young people in competence-enhancing environments: A systems-based perspective on primary prevention. *Journal of Consulting and Clinical Psychology, 59*, 830–841.

Weissberg, R. P., Gullotta, T. P., Hampton, R. L., Ryan, B. A., & Adams, G. R. (Eds.) (1997). *Enhancing children's wellness*. Thousand Oaks, CA: Sage.

Weissberg, R. P., Caplan, M., & Harwood, R. (1991). Promoting competent young people in competence-enhancing environments: A systems-based perspective on primary prevention. *Journal of Consulting and Clinical Psychology, 59*, 830–841.

Weithorn, L. A. (1987). Informed consent for prevention research involving children: Legal and ethical issues. In J. A. Steinberg & M. M. Silverman (Eds.), *Preventing mental disorders: A research perspective*. Rockville, MD: National Institute of Mental Health.

Wellman, B. (1979). The community question: The intimate networks of East Yorkers. *American Journal of Sociology, 84*, 1201–1231.

Wells, R. D., & Schwebel, A. I. (1987). Chronically ill children and their mothers: Predictors of resilience and vulnerability to hospitalization and surgical stress. *Journal of Developmental and Behavioral Pediatrics, 8 (2)*, 83–88.

Werner, E. E. (1986). The concept of risk from a developmental perspective. *Advances in Special Education, 5*, 1–23.

Werner, E. E. (1987). Vulnerability and resilience in children at risk for delinquency: A longitudinal study from birth to young adulthood. In J. D. Burchard & S. N. Burchard (Eds.), *Prevention of delinquent behavior* (pp. 16–43). Newbury Park, CA: Sage.

Werner, E. E. (1989). High-risk children in adulthood: A longitudinal study from birth to 32 years. *American Journal of Orthopsychiatry, 59*, 72–81.

Werner, E. E. (1993). Risk, resilience, and recovery: Perspectives from the Kauai Longitudinal Study. *Development and Psychopathology, 5*, 503–515.

Werner, E. E., & Smith, R. S. (1982). *Vulnerable but invincible: A study of resilient children*. New York: McGraw-Hill.

Werner, E. E., & Smith, R. S. (1993). *Overcoming the odds: High risk children from birth to adulthood*. Ithaca, NY: Cornell University Press.

West, C. (1982). Malcolm X and Black rage. In J. Wood (Ed.), Malcolm X in our own image (pp. 48–58). New York: St. Martin's Press.

West, G. (1990). Cooperation and conflict among women in the welfare rights movement. In L. Albrecht & R. M. Brewster (Eds.), *Bridges of power: Women's multicultural alliances* (pp. 149–171). Philadelphia: New Society Publishers.

White, R. W. (1959). Motivation reconsidered: The concept of competence. *Psychological Review, 66*, 297–333.

Wholey, J. S., Hatry, H. P., & Newcomer, K. E. (Eds.). (1994). *Handbook of practical program evaluation* (pp. 40–66). San Francisco: Jossey-Bass.

Whyte, W. H. (1980). *The social life of small urban spaces*. Washington, D.C.: The Conservation Foundation.

Wicker, A. W. (1979). Ecological psychology: Some recent and prospective developments. *American Psychologist, 34*, 755–765.

Wicker, A. W., & Sommer, R. (1993). The resident researcher: an alternative career model centered on community. *American Journal of Community Psychology, 21*, 469–483.

Wideman, J. E. (1984). *Brothers and keepers*. New York: Random House.

Wiesenfeld, E. (1998). Paradigms of community social psychology in six Latin American nations. *Journal of Community Psychology, 26*, 229–242.

Wilcox, B. C. (1981). Social support in adjusting to marital disruption: A network analysis. In B. H. Gottlieb (Ed.), *Social networks and social support*. Thousand Oaks, CA: Sage.

Wilcox, B. L. (2000). What a long strange trip it's been: The career path of a policy-oriented community psychologist. In C. R. O'Donnell & J. R. Ferrari (Eds.), *Employment in community psychology: The diversity of opportunity* (pp. 83–91). Binghamton, NY: Haworth Press.

Wiley, A., & Rappaport, J. (2000). Empowerment, wellness, and the politics of development. In D. Cicchetti, J. Rappaport, I. Sandler, & R. P. Weissberg (Eds.), *The promotion of wellness in children and adolescents* (pp. 59–100). Washington, D.C.: CWLA Press.

Williams, C. B. (1999). Claiming a biracial identity: Resisting social constructions of race and culture. *Journal of Counseling and Development, 77 (1)*, 32–35.

Williams, J. E. (1984). Secondary victimization: Confronting public attitudes about rape. *Victimology, 9*, 66–81.

Williams, R. M. (1979). Change and stability in values and value systems: A sociological perspective. In M. Rokeach (Ed.), *Understanding human values* (pp. 15–46). New York: Free Press.

Wills, T. A. (1981). Downward comparison principles in social psychology. *Psychological Bulletin, 90*, 245–271.

Wilson, H. (1974). Parenting in poverty. *British Journal of Social Work, 128*, 391–396.

Wilson, M. (Ed.). (1997). Women of color: Special challenges of dual minority status and competing community contexts [Special Issue]. *American Journal of Community Psychology, 25 (5)*.

Wilson, M. N. (1986). The Black extended family: An analytical consideration. *Developmental Psychology, 22*, 246–258.

Wilson, R. S. (1985). Risk and resilience in early mental development. *Developmental Psychology, 21 (5)*, 795–805.

Windle, M. (1999). Critical conceptual and measurement issues in the study of resilience. In M. D. Glantz & J. L. Johnson (Eds.), *Resilience and development; Positive life adaptations* (pp. 161–176). New York: Kluwer Academic/Plenum.

Winett, R. A. (1991). Caveats on values guiding community research and action. *Journal of Applied Behavior Analysis, 24*, 637–639.

Wingenfeld, S., & Newbrough, J. R. (2000). Community psychology in international perspective. In J. Rappaport & E. Seidman (Eds.), *Handbook of community psychology* (pp. 779–810). New York: Kluwer Academic/Plenum Press.

Winzelberg, A., & Humphreys, K. (1999). Should patients' religiosity influence clinicians' referral to 12-step self-help groups? Evidence from a study of 3,018 male substance abuse patients. *Journal of Consulting and Clinical Psychology, 67*, 790–794.

Wittig, M. A., & Schmitz, J. (1996). Electronic grassroots organizing. *Journal of Social Issues, 52*, 53–69.

Wolchick, S. A., West, S. G., Westover, S., Sandler, I. N., Martin, A., Lustig, J., Tein, J. Y., & Fisher, J. (1993). The children of divorce parenting intervention: Outcome evaluation of an empirically based program. *American Journal of Community Psychology, 21,* 293–331.

Wolchik, S. A., & Sandler, I. N. (Eds.). (1997). *Handbook of children's coping: Linking theory and intervention.* New York: Plenum Press.

Wolfe, E. N. (1996). *Top heavy: A study of the increasing inequality of wealth in America.* New York: The Twentieth Century Fund.

Wolff, T. (1987). Community psychology and empowerment: An activist's insights. *American Journal of Community Psychology, 15,* 151–166.

Wolff, T. (2000). Applied community psychology: On the road to social change. In J. Rappaport & E. Seidman (Eds.), *Handbook of community psychology* (pp. 771–777). New York: Kluwer Academic/Plenum Publishers.

Wolff, T. J. (2001a). Community coalition building—Contemporary practice and research: Introduction. *American Journal of Community Psychology, 29,* 165–172.

Wolff, T. J. (2001b). A practitioner's guide to successful coalitions. *American Journal of Community Psychology, 29,* 173–191.

Wolff, T. J. (2001c). (Ed.). Special section: Community Coalition building—Contemporary practice and research. *American Journal of Community Psychology, 29,* 163–329.

Woliver, L. R. (1996). Mobilizing and sustaining grassroots dissent. *Journal of Social Issues, 52,* 1, 139–152.

Wortman, C. B., & Lehman, D. R. (1985). Reactions to victim of life crises: Support attempts that fail. In I. G. Sarason & B. R. Sarason (Eds.), *Social support: Theory, research and applications.* Boston: Martinus Nijhoff Publishers.

Wortman, C. B., & Silver, R. C. (1990). Successful mastery of bereavement and widowhood: A life course perspective. In P. B. Baltes & M. M. Baltes (Eds.), *Successful aging: Perspectives from the behavioral sciences* (pp. 225–264). New York: Cambridge University Press.

Wortman, C. B., Carnelly, K. B., Lehman, D. R., Davis, C. G., & Exline, J. J. (1995). Coping with the loss of a family member: Implications for community-level research and intervention. In S. E. Hobfoll & M. W. de Vries (Eds.), *Extreme stress and communities: Impact and intervention* (pp. 83–103). Boston: Kluwer Academic Publishers.

Wright, S. C., Taylor, D. M., & Moghaddam, F. M. (1990). Responding to membership in a disadvantaged group: From acceptance to collective protest. *Journal of Personality and Social Psychology, 58,* 994–1003.

Wulff, D. M. (1996). The psychology of religion: An overview. In E. P. Shafranske (Ed.), *Religion and the clinical practice of psychology* (pp. 43–70). Washington, D.C.: American Psychological Association.

Wursten, A., & Sales, B. (1988). Community psychologists in state legislative decision-making. *American Journal of Community Psychology, 16,* 487–502.

Wuthrow, R. (1994). *Sharing the journey: Support groups and America's new quest for community.* New York: Free Press.

Wyman, P. A., Sandler, I., Wolchik, S., & Nelson, K. (2000). Resilience as cumulative competence promotion and stress protection: Theory and intervention. In D. Cicchetti, J. Rappaport, I. Sandler, & R. P. Weissberg (Eds.), *The promotion of wellness in children and adolescents* (pp. 133–184). Washington, D.C.: CWLA Press.

Wysong, E., Aniskiewicz, R., & Wright, D. (1994). Truth and DARE: Tracking drug education to graduation and as symbolic politics. *Social Problems, 41,* 448–473.

Yamada, M. (1983). Invisibility is an unnatural disaster: Reflections of an Asian American women. In C. Moraga & G. Anzaldúa (Eds.), *This bridge called my back: Writings by radical women of color* (pp. 35–40). New York: Kitchen Table: Women of Color Press.

Yang, K-S. (1986). Chinese personality and its change. In M. H. Bond (Ed.), *The psychology of the Chinese people* (pp. 106–170). New York: Oxford University Press.

Yates, S., Axsom, D., Bickman, L., & Howe, G. (1989). Factors influencing help seeking for mental health problems after disasters. In R. Gist & B. Lubin (Eds.), *Psychological aspects of disaster* (pp. 163–189). New York: Wiley.

Yeich, S. (1994). *The politics of ending homelessness.* Lanham, MD: University Press of America.

Yeich, S. (1996). Grassroots organizing with homeless people: A participatory research approach. *Journal of Social Issues, 52 (1),* 111–121.

Yeich, S., & Levine, R. (1994). Political efficacy: Enhancing the construct and its relationship to mobilization of people. *Journal of Community Psychology, 22,* 259–269.

Zaslow, M. J., & Hayes, C. D. (1985). Sex differences in children's responses to psychosocial stress: Toward a cross-context analysis. In M. Lamb, A. Brown, & B. Rogoff (Eds.), *Advances in developmental psychology, Vol. 4.* Hillsdale, NJ: Erlbaum Press.

Zautra, A., & Reich, J. (1980). Positive life events and reports of well-being: Some useful distinctions. *American Journal of Community Psychology, 8,* 657–670.

Zautra, A., & Simons, L. S. (1979). Some effects of positive life events on community mental health. *American Journal of Community Psychology, 7,* 441–451.

Zdenek, M. (1974). *God is a verb!* Waco, TX: Word Books.

Zeichner, K. (1983). Alternative paradigms of teacher education, *Journal of Teacher Education, 34 (3)*, 3–9.

Zernike, K. (2001, May 17). Crackdown on threats in school fails a test. *New York Times*, pp. A1, A21.

Zigler, E. F., & Muenchow, S. (1992). *Head Start: The inside story of America's most successful educational experiment*. New York: Basic Books.

Zigler, E., & Finn-Stevenson, M. (1999). *Schools of the 21st century: Linking child care and education*. Boulder, CO: Westview Press.

Ziller, R. C. (1990). Autophotography: Observations from the inside-out. Beverly Hills: Sage.

Zimbardo, P. G. (1988). Social psychology. In E. R. Hilgard (Ed.), *Fifty years of psychology: Essays in honor of Floyd Ruch*. (pp. 169–189). Glenview, IL: Scott, Foresman and Co.

Zimmerman, M. A., & Rappaport, J. (1988). Citizen participation, perceived control, and psychological empowerment. *American Journal of Community Psychology, 16*, 725–750.

Zimmerman, M. A. (1990). Toward a theory of learned hopefulness: A structural model analysis of participation and empowerment. *Journal of Research in Personality, 24*, 71–86.

Zimmerman, M. A. (1995). Psychological empowerment: Issues and illustrations. *American Journal of Community Psychology, 23*, 581–599.

Zimmerman, M. A. (2000). Empowerment theory. In J. Rappaport & E. Seidman (Eds.), *Handbook of community psychology* (pp. 43–63). New York: Kluwer Academic/Plenum Publishers.

Zimmerman, M. A., Reischl, T. M., Seidman, E., Rappaport, J., Toro, P. A., & Salem, D. (1991). Expansion strategies of a mutual help organization. *American Journal of Community Psychology, 19*, 251–278.

Zimmerman, M. A., & Maton, K. I., (1992). Life-style and substance use among male African-American urban adolescents: A cluster analytic approach. *American Journal of Community Psychology, 20*, 121–138.

Zimmerman, M. A., Salem, D. A., & Notaro, P. C. (2000). Make room for Daddy II: The positive effects of fathers role in adolescent development. In R. D. Taylor & M. C. Wang (Eds.), *Resilience across contexts: Family, work, culture, and community* (pp. 233–253). Mahwah, NJ: Lawrence Erlbaum.

Zimmerman, M. A., Schmeelk-Cone, K., & Caldwell, C. (2001). Adolescent resiliency: Examples from the Flint Adolescent Study. Poster presented at the 8th Biennial Conference of the Society for Community Research and Action. Atlanta, GA, June, 2001.

Zinnbauer, B. J., Pargament, K. I., Cole, B., Belavich, T. G., Hipp, K. M., Scott, A. B., & Kader, J. L. (1997). Religion and spirituality: Unfuzzying the fuzzy. *Journal for the Scientific Study of Religion, 36*, 548–564.

Zucker, G. S., & Weiner, B. (1993). Conservativism and perceptions of poverty: An attributional analysis. *Journal of Applied Social Psychology, 23*, 925–943.

Index

A

abuse. *See* child maltreatment, domestic violence
academic achievement. *See* school success/failure
accommodation of information, 273, 353
achieved status, 187
action research, 41-42, 94, 111, 168, 262, 297, 351
active consent, 79-80
actor/observer difference, 186
adaptability in families, 335-337, 339
adaptation in ecological analogy, 105, 168
adaptive features of programs, 274
adolescence, 94, 110, 264-265, 329, 340-342, 344
Adolescent Diversion Project, 169-170, 265-266, 274
affirmative diversity, 124, 147, 157, 204, 361-362
Africa, African, 14, 60-61, 93, 145, 152, 161, 198, 338
African American liberation, 3, 4, 45, 60, 109, 125, 130,
 154, 161, 162, 166, 170, 257, 298, 300, 311. *See*
 also racism, oppression
 terminology, 124-125
 in U.S. population, 121
agent group, 126
AIDS, HIV, 138, 142, 192, 193, 235, 237, 240, 263,
 267, 275, 358
 AIDS organizations, 51, 136, 166-167, 298
Albee, George, 10, 16, 44, 158, 180, 232, 245, 251, 253,
 257-258
Alcatraz, occupation of, 5-6
Alcoholics Anonymous, 12, 75, 234-235, 298
alcoholism. *See* substance abuse
Alinsky, Saul, 52, 53, 165, 166-167, 173, 281, 293
allies, 161
American Indian liberation, 5-6, 119
 oppression of, 2, 125, 127, 173-174, 267-268, 282,
 308-309
 in U.S. population, 120-121
 traditions, 152, 250, 314, 340, 349
 youth, 6, 250-251
anger, 141-142,153-154, 160, 173
annunciation, 177, 198, 299, 308
anonymity in research, 80. *See also* confidentiality
approach coping, 225
Aristotle, 29
arpilleras, 138, 139, 140-141

art, artists, 3, 6, 31, 138, 140,140-141, 157, 313-314,
 361
ascribed status, 187
Asian, 72, 93, 121, 136, 137, 152, 307, 338
assimilation of information, 273, 352
attachment, attachment theory, 91, 323, 327-328
attributable risk, 258
attribution theory, 185-186
Australia, 14, 198, 332
authoritative parenting, 338-339
aversive racism, 143
avoidance coping, 225
avoidance motivation, 197, 362

B

B = f (P, E), 94, 203, 296, 347
Barker, Roger, 95-98, 101, 104, 107, 347
basic and applied research, 41
before the beginning, 1, 24, 26
behavior settings, 95, 96, 98, 106-107
 minority status and, 97
 setting programs, 95
 time and, 97-98
behaviorism, 63
Bellah, Robert, 92, 353-354, 356, 357, 359
Berkowitz, Bill, 52, 53, 84, 296, 299, 301, 302, 351
bicultural, 146
Biennial Conference on Community Research and
 Action, 14, 37, 77, 103, 164, 353
bioecological model, 114-116
biracial, multiracial, 120, 129
block associations, 295
Block Boosters Project, 53, 297, 299
Bond, Meg, 35, 43, 44, 53, 67, 83, 134, 136, 144, 145,
 146, 148, 157, 161, 296, 301, 307, 308
bonding social capital, 359
boundary spanners, 146, 241, 301, 308
Bowlby, John, 223
bridging social capital, 359
Bronfenbrenner, Urie, 39, 106, 107-112, 114-116, 137
Broverman, Inge and colleagues, 7